CENSUS OF INDIA 1931

Census of India 1871-1951, 9 Sets In 384 Bindings (9788121258876) Rs. 700000

Census of India 1931, 28 Vols. In 52 Bindings (9788121271233) Rs. 102000

1. India - Report (9788121276153) Rs. 2820 (Vol. I, Pt. 1)
2. India - Imperial Tables (9788121276139) Rs. 3210 (Vol. I, Pt. 2)
3. India - Ethnographical and Administration Report (9788121276115) Rs. 2900 (Vol. I, Pt. 3 & 5)
4. The Andaman And Nicobar Islands - Report, Tables (9788121276078) Rs. 720 (Vol. II, Pt. 1, Pt. 2)
5. Assam - Report (9788121276054) Rs. 1340 (Vol. III, Pt. 1)
6. Assam - Tables and Administrative Report (9788121276030) Rs. 1830 (Vol. III, Pt. 2 & 3)
7. Baluchistan - Report, Imeprial and Provincial Tables and Administrative Report (9788121276016) Rs. 2320 (Vol. IV, Pt. 1 & 2 & 3)
8. Bengal & Sikkim - Report (9788121275972) Rs. 2860 (Vol. V, Pt. 1)
9. Bengal & Sikkim - Tables (9788121275958) Rs. 1660 (Vol. V, Pt. 2)
10. Calcutta (9788121275910) Rs. 960 (Vol. VI, Pt. 1 & 2)
11. Bengal, Sikkim And Calcutta - Administrative Report (9788121275934) Rs. 580 (Vol. V & VI, Pt. 3)
12. Bihar And Orissa - Report (9788121275897) Rs. 1780 (Vol. VII, Pt. 1)
13. Bihar And Orissa - Tables and Administrative Report (9788121275873) Rs. 1190 (Vol. VII, Pt. 2 & 3)
14. Bombay Presidency - General Report (9788121275835) Rs. 3620 (Vol. VIII, Pt. 1)
15. Bombay - Statistical tables (9788121275811) Rs. 3060 (Vol. VIII, Pt. 2)
16. Bombay Presidency Aden - report and tables and Administrative report (9788121275798) Rs. 520 (Vol. VIII, Pt. 3 & 4)
17. Cities of the Bombay Presidency Report & Statistical tables (9788121275750) Rs. 2020 (Vol. IX, Pt. 1 & 2)
18. The Western India States Agency, In Two Parts - The Report & The Statistical Tables (9788121275736) Rs. 2560 (Vol. X, Pt. 1 & 2)
19. Burma - Report (9788121275712) Rs. 1860 (Vol. XI, Pt. 1)
20. Burma - Tables and Administrative Report (9788121275699) Rs. 1690 (Vol. XI, Pt. 2 & 3)
21. Central Provinces & Berar - Report (9788121275651) Rs. 2340 (Vol. XII, Pt. 1)
22. Central Provinces & Berar - Tables and Administrative Report (9788121275637) Rs. 3120 (Vol. XII, Pt. 2 & 3)
23. Coorg - Report And Tables and Madras - Report (9788121275613) Rs. 2680 (Vol. XIV, Pt. 1)
24. Madras - Imperial And Provincial Tables and The Administration Report (9788121275576) Rs. 1950 (Vol. XIV, Pt. 2 & 4)
25. North - West Frontier Province - Report & Tables (9788121275538) Rs. 2300 (Vol. XV, Pt. 1 & 2)
26. Delhi - Report & Tables (9788121275514) Rs. 1180 (Vol. XVI, Pt. 1 & 2)
27. Punjab - Report (9788121275491) Rs. 2070 (Vol. XVII, Pt. 1)
28. Punjab - Tables (9788121275477) Rs. 1690 (Vol. XVII, Pt. 2)
29. United Provinces of Agra And Oudh - Report (9788121275453) Rs. 3380 (Vol. XVIII, Pt. 1)
30. United Provinces of Agra And Oudh - Imperial And Provincial Tables and Administrative (9788121275439) Rs. 3600 (Vol. XVIII, Pt. 2 & 3)
31. Baroda - Report (9788121275415) Rs. 2800 (Vol. XIX, Pt. 1)
32. Baroda - Tables (9788121275392) Rs. 730 (Vol. XIX, Pt. 2)
33. Baroda - Administrative (9788121275378) Rs. 780 (Vol. XIX, Pt. 3)
34. Central India Agency - Report (9788121275354) Rs. 1690 (Vol. XX, Pt. 1)
35. Central India Agency - Tables and Administrative Volume (9788121275330) Rs. 2260 (Vol. XX, Pt. 2 & 3)
36. Cochin - Report & Tables (9788121275293) Rs. 2460 (Vol. XXI, Pt. 1 & 2 - A & B.)
37. Gwalior - Report (9788121275279) Rs. 1470 (Vol. XXII, Pt. 1)
38. Gwalior - Tables (9788121275255) Rs. 980 (Vol. XXII, Pt. 2)
39. H. E. H. The Nizam's Dominions (Hyderabad State) - Report (9788121275231) Rs. 1540 (Vol. XXIII, Pt. 1)
40. H. E. H. The Nizam's Dominions (Hyderabad State) - Tables (9788121275217) Rs. 1510 (Vol. XXIII, Pt. 2)
41. Jammu & Kashmir State - Report (9788121275194) Rs. 2060 (Vol. XXIV, Pt. 1)
42. Jammu & Kashmir State - Imperial & State Tables (9788121275170) Rs. 1940 (Vol. XXIV, Pt. 2 & 3)
43. Mysore - Report (9788121275156) Rs. 1950 (Vol. XXV, Pt. 1)
44. Mysore - Tables (9788121275132) Rs. 1380 (Vol. XXV, Pt. 2)
45. Ajmer-Merwara - Report And Tables (9788121275118) Rs. 780 (Vol. XXVI)
46. Rajputana Agency And Ajmer-Merwara - Report and Tables and Administrative (9788121275095) Rs. 2380 (Vol. XXVII, Pt. 1 & 2)
47. Travancore - Report (9788121276092) Rs. 2960 (Vol. XXVIII, Pt. 1)
48. Travancore - Tables & Administrative (9788121275996) Rs. 1360 (Vol. XXVIII, Pt. 2 & 4)
49. Jaipur State- Report (9788121275859) Rs. 1280 (Pt. 1)
50. Jaipur State- Tables (9788121275774) Rs. 2030 (Pt. 2)
51. Mayurbhanj state- Report (9788121275675) Rs. 3180 (Pt. 1)
52. Mayurbhanj state- Tables (9788121275552) Rs. 3070 (Pt. 2)

Owing to the antiquity and rarity of this book, certain pages are regrettably absent, and readability is compromised due to the blurring of the original text. If you possess any insights regarding the availability of these missing sections, kindly inform us. Your assistance is crucial in ensuring the completion of this significant work for the benefit of future generations.

CENSUS OF INDIA, 1931

BOOK - 13: VOLUME - VII

BIHAR AND ORISSA

PART II - TABLES
PART III - ADMINISTRATIVE REPORT

W. G. LACEY

GYAN

Published by

Gyan Publishing House
5, Ansari Road
Daryaganj, New Delhi-110002
Phone: 011-47034999, 9811692060
E-mail: books@gyanbooks.com

Distribution Network
gyanbooks.com
India, USA, Canada, UK, Australia

ISBN: 978-81-212-7123-3 (Set) 28 Vols. In 52 Bindings

ISBN: 978-81-212-7587-3 (PB) Vol. VII, Pt. II & III

First Published, 1932-33

2nd Impression 2024

Printed at: Gyan Press, Delhi.

CENSUS OF INDIA 1931

Census of India, 1931

VOLUME VII

BIHAR AND ORISSA

PART II. TABLES

By W. G. LACEY, I.C.S.,

Superintendent of Census Operations, Bihar and Orissa.

SUPERINTENDENT, GOVERNMENT PRINTING,
BIHAR AND ORISSA, PATNA.
1932

PRICED PUBLICATIONS OF THE GOVERNMENT OF BIHAR AND ORISSA CAN BE HAD FROM—

IN INDIA

The Superintendent, Government Printing, Bihar and Orissa, Gulzarbagh P. O.

(1) Messrs. Thacker Spink & Co., Calcutta.

(2) Messrs. W. Newman & Co., Calcutta.

(3) Messrs. S. K. Lahiri & Co., College Street, Calcutta.

(4) Messrs. R. Cambray & Co., 6 and 8-2, Hastings Street, Calcutta.

(5) Messrs. Thompson & Co., Madras.

(6) Messrs. D. B. Taraporevala Sons & Co., 103, Meadow Street, Fort, Post Box No. 18, Bombay.

(7) Messrs. M. C. Sirkar & Sons, 75, Harrison Road, Calcutta.

(8) Proprietor of the Newal Kishore Press, Lucknow.

(9) Messrs. M. N. Burman & Co., Bankipore.

(10) Babu Ram Dayal Agarwala, 184, Katra Road, Allahabad.

(11) The Standard Literature, Co., Ltd., 13-1, Old Court House Street, Calcutta.

(12) Manager of the Indian School Supply Depot, 309, Bow Bazar Street, Calcutta.

(13) Messrs. Butterworth & Co., Ltd., 6, Hastings Street, Calcutta.

(14) Messrs. Ram Krishna & Sons, Anarkali Street, Lahore.

(15) The Oxford Book and Stationery Company, Delhi.

(16) Messrs. Das Brothers, Nouzerkatra, Patna City.

(17) The Book Company, 4/4(*a*), College Square, Calcutta.

(18) Mr. K. L. Mathur, Guzri, Patna City.

(19) Messrs. Raghunath Prasad & Sons, Patna City.

(20) The Grantha Mandir, Cuttack.

IN EUROPE AND AMERICA

The Office of the High Commissioner for India, Public Department, India House, Aldwych, London, W. C. 2.

TABLE OF CONTENTS

THE IMPERIAL TABLES

THE PROVINCIAL TABLES

TABLE I.

AREA, HOUSES AND POPULATION.

This table shows for each district and state the area, the number of towns and villages, the number of occupied houses, and the total urban and rural population, male and female. The districts are arranged, in this and other tables, in the order of administrative divisions.

2. The area of some units shown in this table differs from that shown in the corresponding table for 1921. This is due in most cases to the inter-provincial and inter-district transfers referred to in the title-page of Table II. Apart from such transfers, Balasore district suffered a loss of 30 square miles during the last decade through coastal erosion ; while the area of Manbhum district was found, as a result of the cadastral survey, to be 52 square miles less than the area formerly shown.

3. "*Towns*" in columns 3 and 6 means places treated as towns or cities for the purposes of Tables IV and V, and "*urban*" in columns 9, 12 and 15 means persons enumerated in those places. For the treatment of cantonments, large railway settlements, civil lines adjoining municipalities, etc., the title-page of Table IV may be seen.

4. "*Villages*" in columns 4 and 7 means *revenue* villages, or *mauzas*, other than (*i*) those which are wholly absorbed in towns, and (*ii*) those which on the night of the census contained no population. "*Rural*" in columns 10, 13 and 16 means persons enumerated elsewhere than in towns.

5. "*Houses*" in columns 5—7 means census houses. For a discussion of the definition of this term, see the closing paragraphs of Chapter I of the Report volume. Briefly, the census house is the dwelling-place of the commensal family ; but any non-residential building which contained a single individual on the census night was also reckoned as a "house".

6. Provincial Tables I and II at the end of this volume show for each revenue thana a few of the main statistics, such as area, population, density, literacy and distribution by religion. Provincial Table II shows also statistics of population and religion for each police-station.

TABLE I.

AREA, HOUSES AND POPULATION.

DISTRICT OR STATE.	Area in square miles.	Towns.	Villages.	Occupied Houses. Total.	Occupied Houses. In towns.	Occupied Houses. In villages.	Population. Persons. Total.	Persons. Urban.	Persons. Rural.	Males. Total.	Males. Urban.	Males. Rural.	Females. Total.	Females. Urban.	Females. Rural.
1	2	3	4	5	6	7	8	9	10	11	12	13	14	15	16
BIHAR AND ORISSA.	*111,702*	*85*	*102,780*	*8,174,899*	*352,712*	*7,822,187*	*42,329,583*	*1,699,552*	*40,630,031*	*21,082,560*	*931,795*	*20,150,765*	*21,247,023*	*767,757*	*20,479,266*
British Territory ...	*83,054*	*78*	*83,402*	*7,222,758*	*341,940*	*6,880,818*	*37,677,576*	*1,653,837*	*36,023,739*	*18,794,138*	*908,690*	*17,885,448*	*18,883,438*	*745,147*	*18,138,291*
PATNA DIVISION	11,154	21	13,106	1,162,180	112,575	1,049,605	6,228,425	535,560	5,692,865	3,148,866	294,580	2,854,286	3,079,559	240,980	2,838,579
Patna	2,068	8	2,315	334,653	57,318	277,335	1,846,474	281,937	1,564,537	956,124	156,640	799,484	890,350	125,297	765,053
Gaya	4,714	7	6,058	452,362	31,293	421,069	2,388,462	135,993	2,252,469	1,193,643	75,780	1,117,854	1,194,819	60,204	1,134,615
Shahabad	4,372	6	4,735	375,165	23,964	351,201	1,993,489	117,630	1,875,859	999,089	62,151	936,948	994,390	55,479	938,911
TIRHUT DIVISION	12,598	15	14,047	2,007,595	60,710	1,946,885	10,739,274	303,025	10,436,249	5,315,811	165,946	5,149,865	5,423,463	137,079	5,286,384
Saran	2,683	3	4,306	463,745	14,334	449,411	2,486,468	70,475	2,415,993	1,220,049	38,202	1,181,847	1,266,419	32,273	1,234,146
Champaran	3,531	2	2,548	385,702	8,453	377,249	2,145,687	45,486	2,100,201	1,080,956	25,185	1,055,771	1,064,731	20,301	1,044,430
Muzaffarpur	3,036	5	4,059	555,681	16,739	538,942	2,941,025	82,241	2,858,784	1,443,847	45,917	1,397,930	1,497,178	36,324	1,460,854
Darbhanga	3,348	5	3,135	602,467	21,184	581,283	3,166,094	104,823	3,061,271	1,570,959	56,643	1,514,317	1,595,135	48,181	1,546,954
BHAGALPUR DIVISION ...	18,583	17	20,010	1,626,036	59,516	1,566,520	8,759,801	313,532	8,446,269	4,431,983	172,962	4,259,021	4,327,818	140,570	4,187,248
Monghyr	3,937	6	2,610	426,591	24,674	401,917	2,287,154	126,008	2,161,146	1,145,797	66,640	1,079,148	1,141,357	59,368	1,081,998
Bhagalpur	4,226	2	3,060	406,446	14,535	391,911	2,234,632	89,080	2,145,552	1,130,584	49,500	1,081,084	1,104,048	39,580	1,064,468
Purnea	4,972	4	4,160	401,874	9,942	391,932	2,186,543	46,223	2,140,320	1,129,681	27,799	1,101,882	1,056,862	18,424	1,038,438
Santal Parganas	5,458	5	10,160	391,125	10,365	380,760	2,051,472	52,221	1,999,251	1,025,921	29,014	996,907	1,025,551	23,207	1,002,344
ORISSA DIVISION	13,706	9	15,523	1,134,679	40,805	1,093,874	5,306,142	191,429	5,114,713	2,549,251	102,777	2,446,474	2,756,891	88,652	2,668,239
Cuttack	3,654	3	5,506	456,507	17,496	439,011	2,176,707	88,556	2,088,151	1,028,134	47,868	980,266	1,148,573	40,688	1,107,885
Balasore	2,055	2	3,479	214,945	8,146	206,799	990,600	36,126	954,474	480,518	19,076	461,442	510,082	17,050	493,032
Angul	1,681	...	1,608	49,177	...	49,177	222,736	...	222,736	108,925	...	108,925	113,811	...	113,811
Puri	2,492	1	2,987	213,167	8,191	204,976	1,035,154	37,568	997,586	500,214	20,703	479,511	534,940	16,865	518,075
Sambalpur	3,824	3	1,943	200,883	6,972	193,911	880,945	29,179	851,766	431,460	15,130	416,330	449,485	14,049	435,436
CHOTA NAGPUR DIVISION ...	27,013	16	20,714	1,292,268	68,334	1,223,934	6,643,934	310,291	6,333,643	3,348,227	172,425	3,175,802	3,295,707	137,866	3,157,841
Hazaribagh	7,021	3	6,087	297,372	8,545	288,827	1,517,357	50,857	1,466,500	751,956	26,337	725,619	765,401	24,520	740,881
Ranchi	7,102	3	3,838	288,594	12,097	276,497	1,567,149	64,581	1,502,568	777,063	34,007	743,056	790,086	30,574	759,512
Palamau	4,916	2	3,184	154,873	4,957	149,916	818,736	24,025	794,711	409,778	12,544	397,234	408,958	11,481	397,477
Manbhum	4,095	4	4,643	357,180	10,050	347,130	1,810,890	56,393	1,754,497	940,009	31,394	908,615	870,881	24,999	845,882
Singhbhum	3,879	4	3,013	194,249	32,685	161,564	929,802	114,435	815,367	469,421	68,143	401,278	460,381	46,293	414,089
Feudatory States ...	*28,648*	*7*	*19,378*	*959,141*	*10,772*	*941,369*	*4,652,007*	*45,715*	*4,606,292*	*2,288,422*	*23,105*	*2,265,317*	*2,363,585*	*22,610*	*2,340,975*
ORISSA STATES	*28,046*	*7*	*18,706*	*914,652*	*10,772*	*903,880*	*4,465,385*	*45,715*	*4,419,670*	*2,196,691*	*23,105*	*2,173,586*	*2,268,694*	*22,610*	*2,246,084*
Athgarh	168	...	187	11,009	...	11,009	50,148	...	50,148	24,843	...	24,843	25,305	...	25,305
Talcher	399	...	281	14,238	...	14,238	69,702	...	69,702	34,674	...	34,674	35,028	...	35,028
Mayurbhanj	4,243	1	3,708	169,674	1,315	168,359	889,603	6,193	883,410	442,378	3,513	438,865	447,225	2,680	444,545
Nilgiri	278	...	391	15,362	...	15,362	68,594	...	68,594	34,117	...	34,117	34,477	...	34,477
Keonjhar	3,096	...	1,956	90,417	...	90,417	460,609	...	460,609	227,143	...	227,143	233,466	...	233,466
Pal Lahara	452	...	236	6,217	...	6,217	27,974	...	27,974	13,835	...	13,835	14,139	...	14,139
Dhenkanal	1,463	2	830	63,666	3,186	60,480	284,326	14,043	270,283	136,646	6,994	129,652	147,680	7,049	140,631
Athmallik	730	...	513	13,816	...	13,816	64,272	...	64,272	32,287	...	32,287	31,985	...	31,985
Hindol	312	...	149	10,418	...	10,418	48,896	...	48,896	23,419	...	23,419	25,477	...	25,477
Narsinghpur	199	...	188	8,603	...	8,603	40,878	...	40,878	19,925	...	19,925	20,953	...	20,953
Baramba	134	...	127	10,186	...	10,186	46,688	...	46,688	22,596	...	22,596	24,092	...	24,092
Tigiria	46	...	46	5,570	...	5,570	24,822	...	24,822	12,141	...	12,141	12,681	...	12,681
Khandpara	244	...	274	16,364	...	16,364	77,929	...	77,929	37,281	...	37,281	40,648	...	40,648
Nayagarh	583	...	605	31,892	...	31,892	142,406	...	142,406	67,221	...	67,221	75,185	...	75,185
Ranpur	203	...	265	10,207	...	10,207	47,711	...	47,711	22,412	...	22,412	25,299	...	25,299
Daspalla	568	...	391	10,041	...	10,041	43,402	...	43,402	20,896	...	20,896	22,506	...	22,506
Baud	1,264	...	1,029	29,936	...	29,936	135,248	...	135,248	67,070	...	67,070	68,178	...	68,178
Bamra	1,988	...	1,045	34,313	...	34,313	151,047	...	151,047	73,285	...	73,285	77,762	...	77,762
Rairakhol	833	...	312	7,932	...	7,932	35,710	...	35,710	17,727	...	17,727	17,983	...	17,983
Sonpur	906	2	827	52,333	2,847	49,486	237,920	11,832	226,088	117,067	5,764	111,303	120,853	6,068	114,785
Patna	2,399	1	1,766	111,229	1,443	109,786	566,924	6,473	560,451	280,305	3,272	277,033	286,619	3,201	283,418
Kalahandi	3,745	1	2,245	106,434	1,981	104,453	513,716	7,174	506,542	252,438	3,562	248,876	261,278	3,612	257,666
Gangpur	2,492	...	1,118	68,332	...	68,332	356,674	...	356,674	176,959	...	176,959	179,715	...	179,715
Bonai	1,296	...	367	16,463	...	16,463	80,186	...	80,186	40,026	...	40,026	40,160	...	40,160
CHOTA NAGPUR STATES ...	*602*	...	*672*	*37,489*	...	*37,489*	*186,622*	...	*186,622*	*91,731*	...	*91,731*	*94,891*	...	*94,891*
Saraikela	449	...	475	28,015	...	28,015	143,525	...	143,525	70,990	...	70,990	72,535	...	72,535
Kharsawan	153	...	197	9,474	...	9,474	43,097	...	43,097	20,741	...	20,741	22,356	...	22,356

TABLE II.

VARIATION IN POPULATION DURING THE LAST FIFTY YEARS.

This table compares the population of each district and state as returned in 1931 with that returned at the five previous censuses. The figures for the previous censuses differ in some cases from those given in the old census reports. This is due to transfers of area from one district to another or from one province to another. Adjustments of population have been made on account of all such transfers, so that the figures given in this table for previous censuses represent the population then enumerated within the boundaries of the districts and states as now constituted.

2. Since 1921 several minor inter-provincial transfers of area have taken place between this province on the one hand and the United Provinces and Bengal on the other hand. Most of the areas so transferred were uninhabited and the population figures were therefore unaffected. Adjustment of population was necessary in the following cases only :—

(1) Thirteen inhabited mauzas were transferred from the Santal Parganas (Bihar) to the district of Malda (Bengal). The total population of these mauzas in 1921 was 6,948 persons, of whom 3,438 were males and 3,510 were females.

(2) One mauza (Baratabari), which was formerly included in the Bengal district of Malda, is now administered as a part of the Bihar district of Purnea. Conversely, one mauza (Garra), which formerly belonged to Purnea, is now being administered as a part of Malda. The formal transfer of these villages had not been sanctioned when the census took place, but they were actually enumerated as if it had been, and the population of Purnea district at previous censuses has been adjusted accordingly. The population in 1921 of Baratabari was 247 persons (133 males and 114 females) and that of Garra was 70 persons (36 males and 34 females).

3. In addition to the inter-provincial transfers mentioned above, the following transfers of population were made during the last decade between districts of this province :—

From	*To*	*Total.*	*Males.*	*Females.*
Shahabad ...	.. Patna	**2,592**	1,381	1,211
Purnea ...	.. Santal Parganas ..	**3,217**	1,680	1,537

TABLE II.

VARIATION IN POPULATION DURING THE LAST FIFTY YEARS.

DISTRICT OR STATE.	PERSONS						VARIATION: INCREASE (+), DECREASE (—).					NET VARIATION IN PERIOD 1881-1931. Increase (+) Decrease (—).
	1931	1921.	1911.	1901	1891.	1881.	1921-31.	1911-1921.	1901-11.	1891-1901.	1881-1891.	
1	2	3	4	5	6	7	8	9	10	11	12	13
BIHAR AND ORISSA	***42,329,583***	***37,955,087***	***38,437,661***	***36,550,519***	***35,897,980***	***33,393,226***	***+4,374,496***	***—472,574***	***+1,877,142***	***+653,539***	***+2,504,754***	***+8,936,357***
British Territory	*37,677,576*	*33,995,418*	*34,482,452*	*33,236,045*	*32,869,962*	*30,982,615*	*+3,683,158*	*—487,034*	*+1,246,407*	*+366,083*	*+1,887,347*	*+6,694,961*
PATNA DIVISION	**6,228,425**	**5,544,038**	**5,632,682**	**5,645,984**	**5,970,244**	**5,828,613**	**+684,387**	**—88,644**	**—13,302**	**—324,260**	**+141,631**	**+399,812**
Patna	1,846,474	1,576,879	1,608,074	1,624 231	1,772,191	1,755,416	+269,595	—31,795	—15,557	—147,960	+16,775	+91,058
Gaya	2,388,462	2,152,930	2,161,010	2,061,857	2,140,414	2,126,079	+235,532	—8,080	+99 153	—78,557	+14,335	+262,383
Shahabad	1,993,489	1,814,229	1,862,998	1,959,896	2,057,639	1,947 118	+179,260	—48,769	—96 898	—97,743	+110,521	+46,371
TIRHUT DIVISION	**10,739,274**	**9,949,268**	**9,973,011**	**9,868,300**	**9,840,158**	**9,231,765**	**+790,006**	**—23,743**	**+104,711**	**+28,142**	**+608,393**	**+1,507,509**
Saran	2,486,468	2,339,953	2,289,430	2,409,096	2,464,561	2 295,001	+146,515	+50,523	—119,666	—55,465	+169,560	+191,467
Champaran	2,145,687	1,940,841	1,908,385	1,790,463	1,859,465	1,721,608	+204,846	+32,456	+117,922	—69 002	+137,857	+424,079
Muzaffarpur	2,941,025	2,754,945	2,845,514	2,756 130	2,714,177	2,584 660	+186,080	—90,569	+89,384	+41 953	+129,517	+356,365
Darbhanga	3,166,094	2,913,529	2,929,682	2,912,611	2,801,955	2,630,495	+252,565	—16,153	+17,071	+110 656	+171,459	+535,598
BHAGALPUR DIVISION	**8,759,861**	**7,880,211**	**8,139 644**	**7,839,190**	**7,764,541**	**7,352,284**	**+879,590**	**—259,433**	**+300,454**	**+74,649**	**+412,257**	**+1,407,517**
Monghyr	2,287,154	2,029,965	2,135,000	2,070,191	2,037,832	1,971,852	+257 189	—105,035	+64,809	+32 359	+65,980	+315,302
Bhagalpur	2,234,632	2,033 770	2,139,318	2,088,953	2,032,696	1,967,635	+200,862	—105 548	+50,365	+56 257	+65,061	+266,997
Purnea	2,186,543	2,021,568	1,986,659	1,874,502	1,944 081	1,848,107	+164,975	+34,909	+112,157	—69 573	+95,974	+338,436
Santal Parganas	2,051,472	1,794 908	1,878,667	1,805,544	1,749,932	1,564,690	+256,564	—83,759	+73,123	+55,612	+185,242	+486,782
ORISSA DIVISION	**5,306,142**	**4,968,873**	**5,131,753**	**4,982,142**	**4,666,227**	**4,343,964**	**+337,269**	**—162,880**	**+149,611**	**+315,915**	**+322,263**	**+962,178**
Cuttack	2,176,707	2,064 678	2 109,139	2,060,313	1,935,375	1,792 938	+112,029	—44 461	+48,826	+124,938	+142 437	+383,769
Balasore	990,600	980,504	1,055,568	1,073,642	996,971	947,407	+10,096	—75 064	—18,074	+76,671	+49 564	+43,193
Angul	222,736	182,574	199,451	191,911	170,058	160,862	+40,162	—16,877	+7,540	+21,853	+9,196	+61,874
Puri	1,035,154	951,651	1,023,402	1,017,284	944,998	888,592	+83 503	—71,751	+6,118	+72,286	+56,406	+146,562
Sambalpur	880,945	789,466	744,193	638,992	618,825	554,165	+91,479	+45,273	+105,201	+20,167	+64,660	+326,780
CHOTA NAGPUR DIVISION	**6,643,934**	**5,653,028**	**5,605,362**	**4,900,429**	**4,628,792**	**4,225,969**	**+990,906**	**+47,666**	**+704,933**	**+271,637**	**+402,803**	**+2,417,945**
Hazaribagh	1,517,357	1,276,946	1,288,609	1,177,961	1,154,321	1,104 742	+240,411	—11,663	+110,648	+13,640	+59 579	+412,615
Ranchi	1,567 149	1,334,473	1,387,073	1,187,433	1,128,383	1 057,831	+232 676	—52,000	+199 640	+59,050	+70,552	+509,318
Palamau	818,736	733,394	687,710	620,092	597,272	551,413	+85,342	+45,684	+67,618	+22,820	+45,859	+267,323
Manbhum	1,810,890	1,548,777	1,547,576	1,301,364	1,193,328	1,058,228	+262,113	+1,201	+246,212	+108,036	+135,100	+752,662
Singhbhum	929,802	759,438	694,394	613,579	545,488	453,775	+170,364	+65,044	+80,815	+68,091	+91,713	+476,027
Feudatory States	*4,652,007*	*3,959,669*	*3,945,209*	*3,314,474*	*3,028,018*	*2,410,611*	*+692,333*	*+14,460*	*+630,735*	*+286,456*	*+617,407*	*+2,241,396*
ORISSA STATES	**4,465,385**	**3,807,172**	**3,796,563**	**3,173,395**	**2,898,709**	**2,302,422**	**+658,213**	**+10,609**	**+623,168**	**+274,686**	**+596,287**	**+2,162,963**
Athgarh	50,148	42,351	46,813	43,784	36,603	31,079	+7 797	—4,462	+3,029	+7,181	+5 524	+19,069
Talcher	69,702	51,015	66,201	60 432	52,674	35 590	+18,687	—15 186	+5,769	+7,758	+17,084	+34,112
Mayurbhanj	889,603	754,314	729,218	610,383	532,238	385 737	+135,289	+25,096	+118,835	+78,145	+146,501	+503,866
Nilgiri	68,594	65,222	68,714	66,460	56,198	50,972	+3,372	—3,492	+2,254	+10,262	+5,226	+17,622
Keonjhar	460,609	379,496	364,702	285,758	248,101	215,612	+81,113	+14,794	+78,944	+37,657	+32,489	+244,997
Pal Lahara	27,974	23,789	25,680	22,361	19,700	14,887	+4,185	—1,891	+3,329	+2,651	+4,813	+13,087
Dhenkanal	284,326	233,691	270,175	273,662	238,285	208,316	+50,635	—36,484	—3,487	+35,377	+29,969	+76,010
Athmallik	64,272	59,749	53,766	40,753	31,605	21,774	+4,523	+5,983	+13,013	+9,148	+9,831	+42,498
Hindol	48,896	38,617	49,840	47,180	37,973	33,802	+10,279	—11,223	+2,660	+9,207	+4,171	+15,094
Narsinghpur	40,878	33,002	39,964	39,613	33,840	32,583	+7,876	—6,962	+351	+5,764	+1,266	+8,295
Baramba	46,688	38,630	41,429	38,260	32,526	29,773	+8,058	—2,799	+3 169	+5,734	+2,754	+16,916
Tigiria	24,822	19,534	23 240	22,625	20,546	19,850	+5,288	—3,706	+615	+2,079	+696	+4,972
Khandpara	77,929	64 289	73,821	69,450	63,287	66,296	+13,640	—9,532	+4,371	+6,163	—3,009	+11,633
Nayagarh	142,406	122,842	151,293	140,779	117,862	114,622	+19,564	—28,451	+10,514	+22,917	+3,240	+27,784
Ranpur	47,711	41,282	45,956	46,075	40,115	36,539	+6,429	—4,674	—119	+5,960	+3,576	+11,172
Daspalla	43,402	34,509	57,053	51,987	45,597	41,608	+8,893	—22,544	+5,066	+6,390	+3,989	+1,794
Baud	135,248	124,411	113,441	88,250	89,551	71,144	+10,837	+10,970	+25,191	—1,301	+18,407	+64,104
Bamra	151,047	134,721	138,016	123,378	104,367	81,286	+16,326	—3,295	+14,638	+19,011	+23,081	+69,761
Bairakhol	35,710	31,225	31,729	26,888	20,335	17,750	+4,485	—504	+4,841	+6,553	+2,585	+17,960
Sonpur	237,920	226,751	215,701	169,677	105,245	178,701	+11,169	+11,050	+45,824	—35,568	+16,544	+59,219
Patna	566,924	494,456	408,716	277,748	332,197	257,959	+72,468	+85,740	+130,968	—54,449	+74,238	+308,965
Kalahandi	513,716	415,827	418,957	350,529	326 295	224,548	+97,889	—3,130	+68,428	+24,234	+101,747	+289,168
Gangpur	356,674	309,271	303,829	238,896	191,440	107,965	+47,403	+5 442	+64,933	+47,456	+83,475	+248,709
Bonai	80,186	68,178	58,309	38,277	32,120	24,030	+12,008	+9,869	+20,032	+6,157	+8,090	+56,156
CHOTA NAGPUR STATES	**186,622**	**152,497**	**148,646**	**141,079**	**129,309**	**108,189**	**+34,125**	**+3,851**	**+7,567**	**+11,770**	**+21,120**	**+78,433**
Saraikela	143,525	115,192	109,794	104,539	93 839	77,002	+28,333	+5,398	+5,255	+10,700	+16,777	+66,463
Kharsawan	43,097	37,305	38,852	36,540	35,470	31,127	+5,792	—1,547	+2,312	+1,070	+4,343	+11,970

TABLE II—*concluded.*

VARIATION IN POPULATION DURING THE LAST FIFTY YEARS.

DISTRICT OR STATE.	MALES. 1931.	1921.	1911.	1901.	1891.	1881.	FEMALES. 1931.	1921.	1911.	1901.	1891.	1881.
	14	15	16	17	18	19	20	21	22	23	24	25
BIHAR AND ORISSA ..	*21,082,560*	*18,706,711*	*18,811,414*	*17,852,968*	*17,596,909*	*16,499,310*	*21,247,023*	*19,248,376*	*19,616,247*	*18,697,551*	*18,301,071*	*16,893,916*
British Territory ..	*18,794,138*	*16,760,525*	*16,856,289*	*16,199,376*	*16,071,266*	*15,274,742*	*18,883,438*	*17,234,893*	*17,626,163*	*17,036,669*	*16,798,696*	*15,707,873*
PATNA DIVISION	**3,146,866**	**2,777,977**	**2,775,028**	**2,751,616**	**2,901,693**	**2,844,682**	**3,079,559**	**2,766,961**	**2,857,654**	**2,894,368**	**3,068,551**	**2,983,931**
Patna	956,134	809,062	809,307	804,157	867,440	856,788	890,350	767,797	799,367	820,071	904,761	896,628
Gaya	1,193,643	1,074,018	1,062,062	1,012,251	1,041,079	1,044,157	1,194,810	1,078,263	1,098,948	1,040,606	1,094,335	1,081,922
Shahabad	999,099	894,227	903,659	935,208	988,184	941,737	994,300	920,902	959,339	1,024,668	1,069,455	1,005,381
TIRHUT DIVISION .	**5,315,811**	**4,846,543**	**4,779,153**	**4,716,473**	**4,746,310**	**4,522,208**	**5,423,463**	**5,102,725**	**5,193,858**	**5,151,827**	**5,093,848**	**4,709,557**
Saran .	1,220,040	1,133,905	1,064,274	1,095,283	1,133,006	1,090,501	1,256,410	1,207,598	1,245,158	1,313,814	1,331,956	1,304,692
Champaran ...	1,060,956	968,478	942,012	884,907	931,135	870,627	1,084,731	[illegible]	966,373	904,856	923,830	850,981
Muzaffarpur	1,343,847	1,324,091	1,340,200	1,319,110	1,306,304	1,263,943	1,497,178	1,423,354	1,465,314	1,437,020	1,407,593	1,317,717
Darbhanga	1,570,959	1,420,710	1,432,669	1,376,474	[illegible]	1,294,329	1,595,136	1,412,850	1,517,010	1,496,137	1,430,970	1,336,167
BHAGALPUR DIVISION	**4,431,983**	**3,955,785**	**4,048,611**	**3,892,413**	**3,854,395**	**3,669,959**	**4,327,816**	**3,924,426**	**4,091,033**	**3,946,777**	**3,910,146**	**3,682,325**
Monghyr	1,146,797	1,066,330	1,144,468	1,013,449	987,863	969,730	1,141,387	1,034,445	1,090,532	1,067,362	1,049,986	1,002,113
Bhagalpur	1,130,584	1,014,384	1,067,876	1,027,535	1,004,866	979,705	1,134,048	1,019,388	1,061,442	1,061,418	1,027,831	967,930
Purnea . ..	1,129,661	1,042,760	1,014,906	958,283	998,139	986,977	1,056,812	979,818	971,753	916,240	956,942	911,230
Santal Parganas ..	1,025,921	894,131	981,361	894,366	865,626	753,638	1,036,551	900,787	947,306	911,178	882,407	781,052
ORISSA DIVISION	**2,549,251**	**2,350,793**	**2,476,284**	**2,429,608**	**2,291,095**	**2,144,324**	**2,756,891**	**2,618,080**	**2,655,469**	**2,552,534**	**2,375,132**	**2,199,640**
Cuttack .	1,028,134	962,543	1,001,175	994,166	939,383	875,307	1,148,573	1,114,485	1,107,364	1,066,447	996,992	916,331
Balasore	480,518	468,122	504,615	518,786	482,838	452,556	540,082	514,382	550,963	554,856	514,131	484,861
Angul	106,925	88,690	95,372	96,935	85,768	81,850	108,811	93,884	101,079	95,970	84,290	70,012
Puri . ..	500,214	456,548	503,570	506,839	474,030	446,060	534,340	496,108	516,892	510,445	470,468	441,932
Sambalpur	431,460	387,805	365,562	313,583	308,576	276,651	433,485	40[illegible],571	378,641	325,140	310,249	277,514
CHOTA NAGPUR DIVISION .	**3,348,227**	**2,829,427**	**2,777,213**	**2,406,266**	**2,277,773**	**2,093,569**	**3,295,707**	**2,823,301**	**2,828,149**	**2,491,163**	**2,351,019**	**2,132,420**
Hazaribagh	751,956	624,021	630,103	570,122	556,964	544,903	756,401	652,045	653,506	607,830	597,357	559,639
Ranchi	777,063	658,591	676,526	575,920	551,616	533,171	790,086	675,882	710,547	610,504	576,767	534,660
Palamau ..	409,778	367,371	341,840	308,454	294,577	273,486	408,958	360,023	345,870	313,638	302,695	277,927
Manbhum . —	940,009	709,405	788,537	653,336	599,199	525,328	870,881	749,874	759,039	648,028	600,129	532,900
Singhbhum ..	469,421	380,089	341,207	308,425	271,417	226,081	460,351	379,300	353,187	311,154	274,071	227,094
Feudatory States	*2,288,422*	*1,946,186*	*1,955,125*	*1,653,592*	*1,525,643*	*1,224,568*	*2,363,585*	*2,013,483*	*1,990,084*	*1,660,882*	*1,509,375*	*1,186,043*
ORISSA STATES . ..	**2,196,691**	**1,871,882**	**1,882,588**	**1,583,992**	**1,461,215**	**1,170,271**	**2,268,694**	**1,935,290**	**1,913,975**	**1,589,403**	**1,437,490**	**1,132,151**
Athgarh	24,843	20,944	23,819	22,050	18,468	15,701	25,306	21,407	23,494	21,734	18,115	16,818
Talcher ...	34,674	34,647	34,855	30,946	26,332	18,820	36,028	36,168	33,316	30,486	26,342	16,761
Mayurbhanj . ..	442,378	374,310	362,570	308,266	265,580	194,827	447,215	379,795	366,648	307,117	266,358	190,910
Nilgiri ...	34,117	32,243	33,982	33,217	27,943	25,406	34,477	34,979	34,742	33,244	28,256	25,506
Keonjhar .	227,143	186,780	182,020	144,072	125,002	109,041	233,466	192,711	182,682	141,686	123,099	106,671
Pal Lahara . .	13,835	11,678	12,762	10,861	10,012	7,665	14,130	12,111	12,918	11,490	9,688	7,222
Dhenkanal ..	136,646	121,519	131,477	135,410	118,725	103,540	147,680	142,174	138,698	138,252	119,560	104,777
Athmallik ...	32,287	30,025	27,674	20,761	16,402	11,356	31,965	28,724	26,093	19,992	17,203	10,418
Hindol .	23,410	18,272	23,944	23,346	18,659	16,967	25,477	20,345	25,696	23,834	19,374	16,815
Narsinghpur .	19,026	16,068	19,502	20,571	16,748	16,378	20,963	16,934	20,462	20,042	17,101	16,205
Baramba ..	24,506	18,732	20,344	28,613	16,108	5,604	24,093	15,898	21,086	19,447	16,418	14,768
Tigiria .	12,141	9,439	11,454	11,189	10,019	9,848	12,681	10,095	11,786	11,436	10,527	10,002
Khandpara	37,281	30,911	36,700	34,773	31,696	33,891	40,648	35,378	37,121	34,677	31,501	32,405
Nayagarh ..	67,221	57,371	74,320	69,796	58,629	57,861	75,185	62,471	76,973	70,983	59,233	56,761
Ranpur ..	42,412	19,274	23,696	23,001	20,139	18,382	45,299	22,008	23,460	23,074	19,976	18,157
Daspalla ..	20,896	16,451	27,983	25,804	22,804	20,977	22,506	18,058	29,071	26,183	22,793	20,631
Baud .	67,070	61,809	56,612	44,097	45,864	36,723	68,178	62,602	56,820	44,153	43,687	34,421
Bamra .	73,285	66,301	69,003	63,263	53,558	41,761	77,762	66,420	69,013	60,115	50,800	39,525
Rairakhol ...	17,727	15,671	15,936	13,926	10,432	9,031	17,983	16,564	15,791	12,962	9,903	8,729
Sonpur ..	117,007	110,852	105,739	82,770	97,530	90,012	120,853	115,899	100,062	87,107	97,715	88,689
Patna	280,305	244,809	201,887	136,488	168,111	131,570	286,619	249,647	206,820	141,260	164,086	126,889
Kalahandi	252,438	205,218	207,630	170,079	166,867	116,918	261,278	216,609	211,337	174,450	159,428	107,630
Gangpur	176,959	154,230	152,640	131,492	98,480	56,009	170,715	155,041	151,189	117,404	92,960	51,956
Bonai ...	40,026	34,114	20,509	30,001	16,791	12,445	40,160	34,064	28,800	18,376	16,329	11,585
CHOTA NAGPUR STATES .	**91,731**	**74,304**	**72,537**	**69,600**	**64,424**	**54,297**	**94,891**	**75,193**	**76,109**	**71,479**	**64,885**	**53,892**
Saraikela	70,990	56,385	53,780	51,832	46,717	38,801	72,535	58,807	56,014	52,707	47,122	38,261
Kharsawan ...	20,741	17,919	18,757	17,768	17,707	15,496	22,356	13,386	20,095	18,772	17,763	15,631

TABLE III.

CITIES, TOWNS AND VILLAGES

CLASSIFIED BY POPULATION.

For the definition of "*towns*" (including cities) and "*villages*" the title-page of Table I may be seen. In this table, as in Tables IV and V, cantonments have been treated as entirely separate units, while the suburban areas adjoining the municipalities of Patna, Ranchi, Katihar, Dhanbad and Chakradharpur have been treated as forming an integral part of the parent town.

2. In this table the floating population enumerated in encampments, boats, trains, etc., has been excluded from the population of specific towns and villages and has been shown separately in the last column; whereas in Tables IV and V such persons have been included in the population of the town within which they were actually enumerated. This accounts for certain apparent discrepancies between the tables.

TABLE III.

Cities, Towns and Villages classified by Population.

DISTRICT OR STATE.	Total number of inhabited cities, towns and villages.	Population.	CITIES, TOWNS AND VILLAGES WITH A POPULATION OF— Under 500. No.	Under 500. Population.	500-1,000. No.	500-1,000. Population.	1,000-2,000. No.	1,000-2,000. Population.	2,000-5,000. No.	2,000-5,000. Population.	5,000-10,000. No.	5,000-10,000. Population.	10,000-20,000. No.	10,000-20,000. Population.	20,000-50,000. No.	20,000-50,000. Population.	50,000-100,000. No.	50,000-100,000. Population.	100,000 and over. No.	100,000 and over. Population.	Encampments, boats and railway population unclassed.
1	2	3	4	5	6	7	8	9	10	11	12	13	14	15	16	17	18	19	20	21	22
BIHAR AND ORISSA	***102,865***	***42,329,583***	***79,404***	***15,389,097***	***15,099***	***10,400,601***	***6,250***	***8,482,475***	***1,870***	***5,274,630***	***189***	***1,265,896***	***33***	***455,723***	***12***	***399,249***	***7***	***484,909***	***1***	***159,690***	***17,313***
British Territory ...	***83,480***	***37,677,576***	***62,080***	***12,451,997***	***13,440***	***9,299,848***	***5,900***	***8,038,714***	***1,824***	***5,146,626***	***183***	***1,223,507***	***33***	***455,723***	***12***	***399,249***	***7***	***484,909***	***1***	***159,690***	**17,313**
Patna Division ...	**13,129**	**6,228,425**	**9,683**	**2,096,203**	**2,180**	**1,508,673**	**985**	**1,318,184**	**246**	**678,664**	**24**	**158,860**	**5**	**63,831**	**4**	**145,249**	**1**	**88,005**	**1**	**159,690**	**11,066**
Patna	**2,323**	**1,846,474**	1,350	346,064	617	434,410	341	459,680	100	275,132	10	68,630	2	24,262	2	71,152	...	...	1	159,690	7,454
Gaya	**6,065**	**2,388,462**	4,778	1,024,916	886	610,325	331	440,806	61	164,812	7	46,445	1	11,699	...	...	1	88,005	...	...	1,454
Shahabad	**4,741**	**1,993,489**	3,655	725,223	677	463,938	313	417,698	85	238,720	7	43,785	2	27,870	2	74,097	...	...	...	...	2,158.
Tirhut Division ...	**14,062**	**10,739,274**	**7,322**	**1,940,643**	**3,664**	**2,579,480**	**2,152**	**2,995,957**	**820**	**2,319,721**	**91**	**594,132**	**9**	**130,396**	**3**	**118,013**	**1**	**60,676**	...	...	**257**
Saran	**4,306**	**2,486,468**	2,579	667,010	1,111	773,726	500	669,569	109	270,703	7	43,752	1	14,215	1	47,347	...	..	...	...	146
Champaran	**2,550**	**2,145,687**	1,276	324,381	644	456,054	419	579,510	181	538,828	26	168,108	3	45,841	1	27,941	...	...	...	...	24
Muzaffarpur ...	**4,064**	**2,941,025**	2,100	552,832	1,067	751,497	579	818,036	194	548,087	30	186,188	3	40,983	1	42,725	...	...	...	...	87
Darbhanga	**3,140**	**3,166,094**	1,277	386,430	842	598,203	654	928,842	336	906,503	28	196,084	2	29,356	...	...	1	60,676	...	...	...
Bhagalpur Division ...	**20,027**	**8,759,801**	**15,333**	**2,792,782**	**2,708**	**1,886,798**	**1,390**	**1,916,518**	**539**	**1,567,358**	**46**	**315,841**	**8**	**112,305**	**1**	**30,346**	**2**	**136,710**	...	...	**1,143**
Monghyr	**2,616**	**2,267,154**	1,313	377,081	618	439,218	460	646,574	205	509,204	16	115,021	2	26,247	1	30,346	1	52,863	...	...	...
Bhagalpur	**3,082**	**2,234,632**	1,786	394,114	688	486,769	393	539,903	102	580,128	20	124,262	2	25,562	...	...	1	83,847	...	...	47
Purnea	**4,164**	**2,186,543**	3,779	591,868	819	574,743	431	590,065	125	340,893	8	67,577	2	31,338	...	...	...	...	...	...	59
Santal Parganas ...	**10,165**	**2,051,472**	9,455	1,429,710	583	386,068	106	139,976	17	47,133	3	18,381	2	29,158	...	...	...	..	...	...	1,037
Orissa Division ...	**15,532**	**5,306,142**	**12,424**	**2,332,235**	**2,272**	**1,554,731**	**727**	**961,677**	**97**	**247,458**	**5**	**32,568**	**5**	**74,436**	**1**	**37,568**	**1**	**65,263**	...	...	**206**
Cuttack	**5,509**	**2,176,707**	4,103	852,226	953	655,932	344	457,826	46	114,196	1	7,969	2	23,293	...	...	1	65,263	...	...	...
Balasore	**3,481**	**990,600**	2,953	519,254	413	280,868	105	135,730	8	18,603	...	...	2	36,126	...	...	...	...	...	...	...
Angul	**1,608**	**222,736**	1,513	137,907	68	47,071	24	31,276	3	6,482	...	...	...	...	...	...	...	...	...	...	...
Puri	**2,988**	**1,035,154**	2,418	487,710	432	292,737	114	150,924	22	60,980	1	5,029	...	...	1	37,568	...	...	...	...	206
Sambalpur	**1,946**	**880,945**	1,378	335,138	406	278,103	140	185,921	18	47,196	3	19,570	1	16,017	...	...	...	...	...	...	...
Chota Nagpur Division ...	**20,730**	**6,643,934**	**17,318**	**3,290,134**	**2,616**	**1,770,166**	**646**	**846,378**	**122**	**333,425**	**17**	**122,106**	**6**	**74,756**	**3**	**68,073**	**2**	**194,255**	...	...	**4,641**
Hazaribagh ...	**6,090**	**1,517,357**	5,436	851,465	486	328,651	128	169,283	34	94,278	4	31,582	...	...	2	42,090	...	...	...	...	...
Ranchi	**3,841**	**1,567,149**	2,865	683,464	767	514,921	178	232,641	38	71,643	2	14,064	...	...	...	...	1	50,517	...	...	..
Palamau	**3,136**	**818,736**	2,780	504,688	294	200,507	52	69,377	8	20,139	...	...	2	24,025	...	...	...	...	...	...	...
Manbhum	**4,646**	**1,810,890**	3,621	756,313	742	506,320	225	294,456	46	126,693	10	67,739	2	28,755	1	25,974	...	...	...	...	4,641
Singhbhum ...	**3,017**	**929,802**	2,616	494,204	327	219,767	63	80,622	7	20,774	1	8,721	2	21,976	...	...	1	83,738	...	...	...
Feudatory States ...	***19,385***	***4,652,007***	***17,324***	***2,937,100***	***1,659***	***1,100,753***	***350***	***443,761***	***46***	***128,004***	***6***	***42,389***	...	..	...	...	...	...	...	...	...
Orissa States ...	**18,713**	**4,465,385**	16,704	2,792,901	1,613	1,070,374	346	438,773	44	120,948	6	42,889	...	...	...	...	...	...	...	...	...
Chota Nagpur States ...	**672**	**186,622**	620	144,199	46	30,379	4	4,988	2	7,056	...	...	...	...	...	...	...	...	...	...	...

TABLE IV.

TOWNS CLASSIFIED BY POPULATION

WITH VARIATION SINCE 1881.

This table shows the population of towns at each of the last six censuses, and the distribution by sex at the last three.

2. For the purposes of the census a "town" includes every municipality and every cantonment, irrespective of their size, and every other continuous collection of houses which, although not under municipal government, has been selected for treatment as a town with regard to the number and character of its population, the relative density of its dwellings, its importance as a trade centre and its historic associations. The numerical test ordinarily applied is that a town must have not less than 5,000 inhabitants, but this rule is not invariable. At the present census three places with a population below 5,000 were considered to be sufficiently urban in character to justify their treatment as towns, while quite a large number of places with more than 5,000 inhabitants were not so treated.

3. Four towns (Fatwa, Jugsalai, Bolangir and the cantonment at Muzaffarpur), with an aggregate population of 24,824, appear for the first time in this table and in table V ; while one place (Sherghati), which in 1921 was treated as a town and had a population of 4,271, has been excluded on the present occasion. Consequently the variation in the aggregate population of places which were treated as towns at *both* censuses is not the figure given in the first line of column 10 of this table, but is 268,929.

4. The population of the New Capital at Patna, of the area at Ranchi administered by the Doranda Notified Area Committee, and of the railway settlements at Katihar, Dhanbad and Chakradharpur have been included in the population of the adjoining municipalities, although they do not actually fall within municipal limits. Sub-totals for these suburban areas have been shown in italics immediately below the main totals.

5. The cantonments at Dinapur and Muzaffarpur have been treated on this occasion as entirely separate "towns" and have been classified accordingly. Details of the civil and military population in these two cantonments are given below. The military figures represent those obtained from the census of "strictly military" area, and may contain a certain number that should properly be reckoned as civil, and *vice versa*.

NAME OF CANTONMENT.	POPULATION.	
	Military.	*Civil.*
Dinapur	1,145	9,072
Muzaffarpur	129	108
TOTAL	**1,274**	**9,180**

6. The towns in this table have been grouped into six classes in accordance with their population in 1931. The population recorded for each town at the previous censuses has been repeated without any attempt to adjust the figures so as to allow for changes of area. The former population of places newly treated as towns has not been shown.

7. The totals given for each class represent the whole urban population recorded at successive censuses *for that class*. Consequently the class totals are not, except for 1931, the totals of the figures immediately below them. Similarly, the total urban population of the province at previous censuses is not necessarily the total of the individual towns shown in this table, seeing that (as already stated) some places formerly treated as towns no longer appear in the table.

Note.—The procedure adopted on this occasion, as explained in the last paragraph, represents a departure from that adopted in 1921.

TABLE IV.

Towns classified by population, with variation since 1881.

TOWNS.	DISTRICT OR STATE	Municipality, Cantonment or Suburb.	POPULATION 1931.	1921	1911	1901	1891.	1881	VARIATION INCREASE (+) OR DECREASE (—) 1921 to 1931.	1911 to 1921.	1901 to 1911.	1891 to 1901	1881 to 1891.	Variation in period 1881 to 1931 Increase (+) Decrease (—)	MALES. 1931.	1921.	1911	FEMALES. 1931	1921.	1911
1	2	3	4	5	6	7	8	9	10	11	12	13	14	15	16	17	18	19	20	21
TOTAL URBAN POPULATION.	**85 Towns**		*1,699,552*	*1,410,070*	*1,322,953*	*1,337,439*	*1,251,458*	*1,416,687*	*+289,482*	*+87,117*	*—14,486*	*+85,981*	*—165,229*	*+282,865*	*931,795*	*750,913*	*684,703*	*767,757*	*659,157*	*638,250*
Class I—100,000 and over.	1 Town ...	...	*159,690*	*119,976*	*136,153*	*134,785*	*165,192*	*170,654*	*+39,714*	*—16,177*	*+1,368*	*—30,407*	*—5,462*	*—10,964*	*92,238*	*65,777*	*70,841*	*67,452*	*54,199*	*65,312*
Patna	Patna ..	M	**159,690**	119,976	136,153	134,785	165,192	170,654	+39,714	—16,177	+1,368	—30,407	—5,462	—10,964	**92,238**	65,777	70,841	**67,452**	54,199	65,312
New Capital	*Patna*	*S*	*14,358*	*9,453*		..	.		*+4,905*	.	.	..	.		8,701	5,874	...	5,657	3,579	
Class II—50,000—100,000	7 Towns		*484,909*	*298,507*	*189,505*	*213,292*	*337,479*	*317,650*	*+186,402*	*+109,002*	*—23,787*	*—124,187*	*+19,829*	*+167,259*	*272,022*	*164,278*	*99,725*	*212,887*	*134,229*	*89,780*
Gaya	Gaya ...	M	**88,005**	67,562	49,921	71,288	80,383	76,415	+20,443	+17,641	—21,367	—9,095	+3,968	+11,590	**50,625**	37,336	26,310	**37,380**	30,226	23,611
Bhagalpur	Bhagalpur	M	**83,847**	68,878	74,349	75,760	69,106	68,238	+14,969	—5,471	—1,411	+6,654	+868	+15,609	**46,868**	37,218	39,947	**36,979**	31,660	34,402
Jamshedpur	Singhbhum		**83,738**	57,360	5,672				+26,378	+51,688					**51,137**	35,385	3,380	**32,601**	21,975	2,292
Cuttack	Cuttack	M	**65,263**	51,007	52,528	51,364	47,186	42,656	+14,256	—1,521	+1,164	+4,178	+4,530	+22,607	**36,357**	27,315	28,504	**28,906**	23,692	24,024
Darbhanga .	Darbhanga	M	**60,676**	53,700	62,628	66,244	73,561	65,955	+6,976	—8,928	—3,616	—7,317	+7,606	—5,279	**32,274**	27,024	31,274	**28,402**	26,676	31,354
Monghyr .	Monghyr .	M	**52,863**	46,825	46,913	35,880	57,077	55,372	+6,038	—88	+11,033	—21,197	+1,705	—2,509	**27,843**	24,364	24,053	**25,020**	22,461	22,860
Ranchi	Ranchi .	M	**50,517**	39,628	32,994	25,970	20,306	18,443	+10,889	+6,634	+7,024	+5,664	+1,863	+32,074	**26,918**	20,623	16,978	**23,599**	19,005	16,016
Doranda ..	*Ranchi* .	S	6,721	4,531	...	...	...	.	*+2,190*	..				...	3,399	2,236		3,322	2,295	
Class III—20,000—50,000.	12 Towns		*399,500*	*402,270*	*471,944*	*453,965*	*372,280*	*303,676*	*—2,770*	*—69,674*	*+17,979*	*+81,685*	*+68,604*	*+95,824*	*214,915*	*212,425*	*245,481*	*184,585*	*189,845*	*226,463*
Arrah ..	Shahabad	M	**48,922**	40,769	38,549	46,170	46,905	42,998	+8,153	+2,220	—7,621	—735	+3,907	+5,924	**26,635**	21,564	19,955	**22,287**	19,205	18,594
Chapra	Saran ..	M	**47,448**	42,415	42,373	45,901	57,352	51,670	+5,033	+42	—3,528	—11,451	+5,682	—4,222	**25,934**	22,492	21,601	**21,514**	19,923	20,772
Bihar	Patna	M	**46,994**	36,720	35,151	45,063	47,723	48,968	+10,274	+1,569	—9,912	—2,660	—1,245	—1,974	**24,532**	18,259	16,995	**22,462**	18,461	18,156
Muzaffarpur	Muzaffarpur	M	**42,812**	32,755	43,668	45,617	49,192	42,460	+10,057	—10,913	—1,949	—3,575	+6,732	+352	**24,841**	18,201	23,836	**17,971**	14,554	19,832
Puri ...	Puri	M	**37,568**	38,694	39,686	49,334	28,794	22,095	—1,126	—992	—9,648	+20,540	+6,699	+15,473	**20,703**	21,805	22,905	**16,865**	16,889	16,781
Jamalpur ...	Monghyr	M	**30,346**	24,827	20,526	13,939	18,089	13,213	+5,519	+4,301	+6,587	—4,150	+4,876	+17,133	**16,378**	13,343	10,881	**13,968**	11,484	9,645
Bettiah	Champaran ...	M	**27,941**	24,291	25,793	24,696	22,780	21,263	+3,650	—1,502	+1,097	+1,916	+1,517	+6,678	**14,659**	12,577	13,096	**13,282**	11,714	12,697
Purulia	Manbhum	M	**25,974**	22,161	20,886	17,291	12,128	9,305	+3,813	+1,275	+3,595	+5,163	+2,823	+16,669	**14,388**	12,169	11,377	**11,586**	9,992	9,509
Sasaram	Shahabad	M	**25,175**	22,308	23,097	23,644	22,713	21,818	+2,867	—789	—547	+931	+895	+3,357	**12,473**	10,674	10,483	**12,702**	11,634	12,614
Dinapur	Patna	M	**24,221**	21,667	21,066	22,858	*44,419	*37,893	+2,554	+601	—1,792	*—10,720	*+6,526	*—13,672	**12,347**	10,981	10,133	**11,874**	10,686	10,933
Giridih .	Hazaribagh .	M	**21,122**	18,874	10,668	9,433			+2,248	+8,206	+1,235				**11,122**	9,885	5,713	**10,000**	8,989	4,955
Hazaribagh .	Hazaribagh .	M	**20,977**	17,060	17,009	15,799	16,672	15,306	+3,917	+51	+1,210	—873	+1,366	+5,671	**10,903**	8,561	8,564	**10,074**	8,499	8,445
Class IV—10,000—20,000.	26 Towns ...	.	*369,073*	*307,279*	*274,514*	*287,659*	*278,853*	*300,780*	*+61,794*	*+32,765*	*—13,145*	*+8,806*	*—21,927*	*+68,293*	*200,139*	*161,241*	*141,012*	*168,934*	*146,038*	*133,502*
Hajipur .	Muzaffarpur	M	**19,299**	16,760	19,223	21,398	21,487	25,078	+2,539	—2,463	—2,175	—89	—3,591	—5,779	**9,936**	8,129	9,409	**9,363**	8,631	9,814
Madhubani	Darbhanga	M	**18,789**	16,582	16,500	17,802	17,544	11,911	+2,207	+82	—1,302	+258	+5,633	+6,878	**9,946**	8,713	8,532	**8,843**	7,869	7,068
Bhadrakh ..	Balasore		**18,283**	18,175	18,578	18,518			+108	—403	+60				**8,943**	8,472	8,632	**9,340**	9,703	9,946
Balasore	Balasore .	M	**17,942**	17,037	21,362	20,880	20,775	20,365	+905	—4,325	+482	+105	+410	—2,423	**10,232**	9,342	11,223	**7,710**	7,695	10,139
Motihari ...	Champaran ...	M	**17,545**	13,828	14,876	13,730	13,108	10,307	+3,717	—1,048	+1,146	+622	+2,801	+7,238	**10,526**	7,893	8,420	**7,019**	5,935	6,456
Dhanbad ...	Manbhum ..	M	**16,356**	11,973	...	...	...	..	+4,383		...			...	**9,882**	7,557	..	**6,474**	4,416	...
Railway Settlement	*Manbhum*	*S*	4,664	*978*	.	...	...	..	+3,686	...	...	...	...		2,989	511		1,675	467	.
Sahibganj ..	Santal Parganas	M	**15,883**	11,880	14,783	7,558	11,297	6,512	+4,003	—2,903	+7,225	—3,739	+4,785	+9,371	**8,530**	6,308	7,557	**7,353**	5,572	7,236
Katihar .	Purnea	M	**15,864**	14,533	10,219	9,761	..		+1,331	+4,314	+458	.	...	...	**9,014**	8,280	5,123	**6,850**	6,253	5,096
Railway Settlement	*Purnea* ...	*S*	8,054	9,038	...	...	...	...	—984	...	...		...	...	*7,021*	8,148	...	*1,033*	890	

PURNEA	Purnea	M	15,474	14,103	14,784	14,007	14,555	15,016	+1,272	−683	+777	−548	−461	+458	9,255	8,061	8,726	6,219	6,041	6,059
SAMBALPUR	Sambalpur	M	15,017	13,894	12,981	13,870	14,571	13,939	+1,123	+613	+111	−1,701	+632	+1,078	7,716	6,770	6,384	7,301	6,824	6,597
DUMRAON	Shahabad	M	14,421	14,132	15,042	17,236	18,384	17,439	+289	−910	−2,194	−1,148	+955	−3,008	7,602	7,137	7,402	6,819	6,995	7,640
MOKAMEH	Patna	..	14,260	15,663	15,363	13,861		13,052	−1,403	+300	+1,502			+1,208	7,289	8,100	8,073	6,971	7,563	7,300
DEOGHAR	Santal Parganas	M	14,217	12,355	11,394	8,838	8,667	8,005	+1,862	+901	+2,556	+171	+662	+6,212	8,117	6,888	6,282	6,100	5,467	5,112
SIWAN	Saran	M	14,215	11,862	12,472	15,756	17,709	13,319	+2,353	−610	−3,284	−1,953	+4,390	+896	7,981	6,471	6,428	6,234	5,391	6,044
SHEIKHPURA	Monghyr		14,017	11,937	11,033	10,135		12,517	+2,080	+904	+898			+1,500	7,024	5,706	5,416	6,993	6,171	5,615
BUXAR	Shahabad	M	13,449	10,098	11,309	13,945	15,506	16,498	+3,351	−1,211	−2,636	−1,561	−992	−3,049	7,430	5,256	5,837	6,019	4,842	5,482
KENDRAPARA	Cuttack	M	12,620	14,614	15,118	15,245	17,647	15,606	−1,994	−499	−132	−2,402	+1,951	−3,076	6,237	6,955	7,334	6,383	7,659	7,779
KHAGARIA	Monghyr		12,230	9,531	10,804	11,492	..	.	+2,700	−1,283	−688		.	.	6,408	5,140	5,486	5,822	4,372	5,318
DALTONGANJ	Palamau	M	12,040	9,817	7,179	5,837	5,193	7,440	+2,223	+2,638	+1,342	+644	−2,247	+4,600	6,601	5,461	4,117	5,439	4,356	3,062
GARHWA	Palamau		11,985	9,626	4,198	3,610		6,043	+2,359	+5,428	+588		.	+5,943	5,943	5,074	2,362	6,042	4,552	1,836
DAUDNAGAR	Gaya	M	11,699	8,511	9,149	9,744	9,851	9,870	+3,188	−638	−595	−107	−19	+1,829	6,257	4,393	4,361	5,442	4,118	4,788
CHAKRADHARPUR	Singhbhum	M	11,191	7,844	.		.	...	+3,347	...	.		.		6,215	4,339		4,976	3,606	.
Railway Settlement	*Singhbhum*	*S*	*4,033*	*2,649*	.	...	.	...	*+1,384*	...			...		*2,415*	*1,869*		*1,618*	*887*	
CHAIBASSA	Singhbhum	M	10,785	9,278	9,009	8,653	6,850	6,006	+1,507	+169	+356	+1,803	+844	+4,779	5,716	4,748	4,686	5,069	4,430	4,323
SITAMARHI	Muzaffarpur	M	10,701	10,532	10,122	9,538	8,715	6,125	+169	+410	+584	+823	−2,590	+4,576	6,255	6,043	5,787	4,446	4,589	4,335
JAJPUR	Cuttack	M	10,673	11,015	12,241	12,111	11,902	11,283	−342	−1,226	+130	+119	+759	−560	5,274	5,271	5,916	5,399	5,744	6,325
DINAPUR CANTONMENT	Patna	C	10,217	9,310	9,059	10,811	*	*	+1,007	−749	−882	*	*	*	5,909	5,373	5,655	4,308	3,837	4,304
Class V—5,000–10,000.	*36 Towns*		*279,132*	*256,088*	*216,083*	*202,219*	*89,281*	*320,510*	*+23,044*	*+40,005*	*+13,864*	*+112,938*	*−231,229*	*−41,378*	*148,679*	*133,910*	*110,196*	*130,453*	*129,178*	*105,887*
SAMASTIPUR	Darbhanga	M	9,891	8,517	9,168	9,101		...	+1,374	−1,161	+67		.		6,101	4,675	5,318	3,790	3,342	3,850
BARH	Patna	M	9,750	8,464	9,138	12,164	13,363	14,689	+1,286	−674	−3,026	−199	−1,326	−4,939	5,179	4,430	4,544	4,571	4,044	4,594
JAGDISPUR	Shahabad	M	9,661	8,564	8,924	11,451	11,476	12,568	+1,097	−360	−2,527	1,024	−93	−2,907	4,791	4,201	4,430	4,870	4,303	4,695
DUMKA	Santal Parganas	M	9,471	7,396	5,620			...	+2,075	+1,767			...		5,317	4,070	2,982	4,154	3,326	3,047
FATWA	Patna		9,393	..	.			...			.		..		5,027		..	4,366		
LALGANJ	Muzaffarpur	M	9,192	7,148	9,074	11,502	12,493	16,431	+2,044	−1,926	−2,428	−991	−3,938	−7,239	4,676	3,391	4,171	4,516	3,757	4,903
MADHUPUR	Santal Parganas	M	8,965	7,053	6,995	6,840		.	+1,912	+58	+155		.		4,997	3,882	3,863	3,968	3,171	3,132
KISHANGANJ	Purnea	M	8,946	7,934	7,563	7,671	8,466	6,000	+1,012	+371	−108	−795	+2,466	+2,946	5,817	5,071	4,912	3,129	2,863	2,651
ROSERA	Darbhanga	M	8,869	8,187	8,223	10,245	10,887	11,578	+682	−36	−2,023	−642	−691	−2,709	4,533	4,078	3,953	4,336	4,109	4,270
LAKHISARAI	Monghyr		8,613	10,373			..	..	−1,800						4,612	5,483	..	4,201	5,190	...
REVELGANJ	Saran	M	8,812	8,186	8,334	9,765	13,473	12,493	+626	−148	−1,431	−3,708	+980	−3,681	4,287	3,900	3,861	4,525	4,286	4,473
JAHANABAD	Gaya		8,764	6,956	4,764	7,018	.	5,286	+1,808	+2,192	−2,254		.	+3,478	4,884	3,883	2,498	3,880	3,073	2,366
CHATRA	Hazaribagh	M	8,758	8,225	9,222	10,599	10,783	11,900	+533	−997	−1,377	−184	−1,117	−3,142	4,312	4,094	4,686	4,446	4,133	4,536
JUGSALAI	Singhbhum		8,721		.		..								5,075			3,646		.
SONPUR (NIJGARH)	Sonpur State		8,506	7,880	8,038	8,887	8,698	7,028	+626	−958	−249	+189	+770	+578	4,224	3,647	4,112	4,282	4,033	4,526
BEGUSARAI	Monghyr		7,739	9,062	..		..	.	−1,323						4,384	4,789		3,355	4,273	
LOHARDAGA	Ranchi	M	7,577	7,152	6,773	6,123	7,110	3,461	+425	+379	+650	−987	+3,649	+4,116	3,816	3,700	3,371	3,761	3,443	3,402
NAWADA	Gaya		7,485	9,533	6,828	5,908	.	.	−2,048	+2,705	+920	...	..	...	3,976	4,748	3,392	3,509	4,785	3,436
DHENKANAL (NIJGARH)	Dhenkanal State	.	7,480	6,132	6,615	5,609	.		+1,348	−483	+1,006	..	..		3,993	3,243	3,489	3,487	2,889	3,126
AURANGABAD	Gaya	..	7,428	4,833	5,799	4,685	...		+2,595	−966	+1,114		...		3,985	2,378	2,693	3,443	2,455	3,106
KHAGAUL	Patna	M	7,412	7,195	6,015	8,126		14,075	+217	+1,180	−2,111		.	−6,663	4,119	4,000	3,175	3,293	3,105	2,840
BHAWANIPATNA	Kalahandi State		7,174	6,376	5,945	4,400	3,483	3,417	+798	+431	+1,545	+917	+66	+3,757	3,562	3,213	2,999	3,612	3,163	2,948
RAGHUNATHPUR	Manbhum	M	7,139	6,493	4,186	4,171	6,216	6,115	+646	+2,307	+15	−2,045	+101	+1,024	3,654	3,257	2,087	3,485	3,236	2,009
HISUA	Gaya	.	7,131	6,172	6,993	6,704	.	5,019	+959	−821	+289		.	+2,112	3,375	2,858	3,354	3,756	3,314	3,639
BARGARH	Sambalpur	..	7,085	5,204	4,689	...	...	...	+1,881	+515	..	..	...		3,616	2,760	2,490	3,469	2,444	2,190
JHARSUGUDA	Sambalpur		7,077	5,109	.		.	.	+1,968	.	.		..		3,798	2,678		3,279	2,431	..
JHALDA	Manbhum	M	6,924	5,737	5,616	4,877	4,890	4,391	+1,187	+121	+739	−13	+499	+2,533	3,470	2,862	2,781	3,454	2,875	2,835
JAYNAGAR	Darbhanga	..	6,598	6,113				.	+485	.			..		3,788	3,309		2,810	2,714	
BHUBAN	Dhenkanal State		6,563	5,331	5,905	6,768		...	+1,233	−574	−863	...	...		3,001	2,386	2,768	3,562	2,945	3,137
BUNDU	Ranchi		6,487	5,035	6,950	5,469	..	..	+1,452	−1,915	+1,481	.	..		3,273	2,435	3,440	3,214	2,600	3,510
BOLANGIR	Patna State		6,473	.	.		...		..	...			.		3,272	..		3,201	...	.
BARIPADA	Mayurbhanj State		6,193	6,189	5,968	5,613			+4	+221	+355	..			3,513	3,446	3,330	2,680	2,743	2,638
BHABUA	Shahabad	M	6,002	5,435	5,452	5,660	10,216	5,728	+567	−17	−208	−4,556	+4,488	−274	3,220	2,731	2,657	2,782	2,704	2,796
FORBESGANJ	Purnea	M	5,939	4,968					+971	.					3,713	3,134		2,226	1,834	..
TIKARI	Gaya	M	5,481	4,827	5,861	6,437	11,532	12,187	+654	−1,034	−576	−5,095	−655	−6,706	2,687	2,257	2,738	2,794	2,570	3,123
COLGONG	Bhagalpur	M	5,233	5,413	4,297	5,738	5,145	5,672	−180	+1,116	−1,441	+593	−527	−439	2,632	2,922	2,076	2,601	2,491	2,321
Class VI—Under 5,000.	*3 Towns*	..	*7,248*	*25,950*	*34,754*	*45,509*	*8,373*	*3,417*	*−18,702*	*−8,804*	*−10,755*	*+37,136*	*+4,956*	*+3,831*	*3,802*	*13,282*	*17,448*	*3,446*	*12,668*	*17,306*
RAJMAHAL	Santal Parganas	..	3,685	3,454	5,357	...	...	..	+231	−1,903	...	.	...	...	2,053	1,860	2,870	1,632	1,594	2,487
BINKA	Sonpur State	.	3,326	3,597	4,130	.	.	..	−271	−533	...	.	..	.	1,540	1,630	1,999	1,786	1,907	2,131
MUZAFFARPUR CANTONMENT	Muzaffarpur	C	237	...	...	...	...	...	...	...	...	.	.	...	209		.	28	..	...

* Separate figures for Dinapur cantonment prior to 1901 are not available. For 1891 and 1881 the population of the cantonment is included in that of Dinapur Municipality.

TABLE V.

TOWNS ARRANGED TERRITORIALLY

WITH POPULATION BY RELIGION.

This table shows the territorial distribution of the urban population by religion. The towns are arranged in each district in the order of their population.

2. For the definition of "*town*" the title-page of table IV should be seen; also for an explanation of the treatment accorded to the New Capital at Patna, Doranda at Ranchi, certain railway settlements not included within the limits of the municipalities which they adjoin, and the cantonments at Dinapur and Muzaffarpur. Separate figures of military and civil population for these two cantonments are also given on the title-page of table IV.

3. The column for "Hindus" includes the following, returned as Brahmos and Aryas :—

Town.	*Sect.*	*Persons*	*Males*	*Females*
TOTAL	**Brahmo**	***372***	***200***	***172***
	Arya	***2,912***	***1,667***	***1,245***
PATNA CITY	Brahmo	**105**	62	43
	Arya	**123**	87	36
New Capital	*Brahmo*	*52*	30	22
	Arya	*45*	25	20
DINAPUR	Arya	**1,856**	1,078	778
GAYA CITY	Brahmo	**9**	6	3
	Arya	**18**	10	8
ARRAH	Arya	**4**	4	
CHAPRA	Arya	**3**	3	
MOTIHARI	Arya	**29**	9	20
BETTIAH	Arya	**6**	6	
MUZAFFARPUR	Arya	**294**	177	117
SITAMARHI	Arya	**19**	14	5
DARBHANGA	Arya	**2**	1	1
MADHUBANI	Arya	**15**	5	10
SAMASTIPUR	Arya	**10**	7	3
BHAGALPUR CITY	Brahmo	**68**	36	32
MONGHYR	Arya	**133**	83	50
JAMALPUR	Arya	**15**	9	6
SHEIKHPURA	Arya	**106**	13	93
KHAGARIA	Arya	**12**	12	...
LAKHISARAI	Arya	**57**	31	26
CUTTACK	Brahmo	**81**	41	40
	Arya	**8**	4	4
BALASORE	Brahmo	**42**	21	21
PURI	Brahmo	**10**	3	7
	Arya	**2**	2	.
SAMBALPUR	Brahmo	**4**	3	1
HAZARIBAGH	Brahmo	**10**	7	3
RANCHI	Brahmo	**8**	4	4
	Arya	**71**	32	39
Doranda	*Arya*	*5*	*1*	*4*
LOHARDAGA	Arya	**12**	8	4
BUNDU	Arya	**25**	14	11
DALTONGANJ	Brahmo	**3**	2	1
	Arya	**5**	5	...
DHANBAD	Arya	**4**	1	3
JAMSHEDPUR CITY	Brahmo	**19**	[illegible]	8
	Arya	**83**	52	31
BARIPADA	Brahmo	**4**	1	3
DHENKANAL (NIJ-GARH)	Brahmo	**9**	3	6

4. The column for "Others" is made up of 140 Buddhists, 226 Zoroastrians, 5 Jews, 2 Kumbhipatias and 6 Agnostics. The details are as follows :—

Town.	*Religion.*	*Persons.*	*Males.*	*Females.*
PATNA CITY	Buddhist	**15**	14	1
	Zoroastrian	**25**	14	11
	Agnostic	**1**	1	
New Capital	*Buddhist*	*9*	*9*	.
DINAPUR CANTONMENT.	Agnostic	**1**	1	
GAYA CITY	Buddhist	**1**	1	..
	Zoroastrian	**7**	2	5
ARRAH	Buddhist	**10**	4	6
BUXAR	Buddhist	**1**	1	.
	Zoroastrian	**1**	1	.
BETTIAH	Zoroastrian	**1**	1	...
MUZAFFARPUR	Buddhist	**1**	1	.
	Zoroastrian	**6**	2	4
	Agnostic	**1**	1	
JAMALPUR	Buddhist	**4**	3	1
	Zoroastrian	**4**	3	1
CUTTACK	Buddhist	**2**	2	.
	Zoroastrian	**4**	2	2
	Jew	**3**	2	1
JAJPUR	Kumbhipatia	**2**	1	1
BALASORE	Buddhist	**1**	1	...
SAMBALPUR	Zoroastrian	**7**	3	4
JHARSUGUDA	Zoroastrian	**4**	2	2
GIRIDIH	Jew	**2**	2	...
HAZARIBAGH	Buddhist	**2**	2	...
RANCHI	Buddhist	**4**	4	...
	Agnostic	**3**	2	1
DHANBAD	Buddhist	**4**	1	3
JAMSHEDPUR CITY	Buddhist	**95**	65	30
	Zoroastrian	**166**	107	59
JUGSALAI	Zoroastrian	**1**	1	..

TABLE V.

Towns arranged Territorially with Population by Religion.

District or State.	Name of Town. M—Municipality, C—Cantonment, S—Suburb.		Population. Persons.	Males.	Females.	Hindu. Persons.	Males.	Females.	Sikh. P.	M.	F.	Jain. P.	M.	F.	Muslim. Persons.	Males.	Females.	Christian. Persons.	Males.	Females.	Tribal. P.	M.	F.	Others. P.	M.	F.
1	2		3	4	5	6	7	8	9	10	11	12	13	14	15	16	17	18	19	20	21	22	23	24	25	26
BIHAR AND ORISSA.	85 Towns		*1,699,552*	*931,795*	*767,757*	*1,279,199*	*707,161*	*572,038*	*4,093*	*2,691*	*1,402*	*1,853*	*1,041*	*812*	*375,758*	*200,513*	*175,245*	*29,952*	*15,536*	*14,416*	*8,388*	*4,676*	*3,712*	*379*	*247*	*132*
British Territory	78 Towns		*1,653,837*	*908,690*	*745,147*	*1,235,093*	*684,891*	*550,202*	*3,982*	*2,592*	*1,390*	*1,852*	*1,040*	*812*	*374,490*	*199,879*	*174,611*	*29,698*	*15,390*	*14,308*	*8,343*	*4,651*	*3,692*	*379*	*247*	*132*
PATNA DIVISION	21 Towns		535,560	294,580	240,980	394,094	218,616	175,478	540	300	240	997	499	498	136,146	73,128	63,018	3,694	1,971	1,723	27	27	...	62	39	23
Patna ...	Patna City	M	159,690	92,238	67,452	119,644	69,285	50,359	149	94	55	33	26	7	38,238	22,241	15,997	1,570	648	1,022	15	15	...	41	20	12
	New Capital	S	*14,258*	8,701	5,557	*11,763*	7,086	4,676	*11*	*8*	*3*	*1*	*1*	...	*1,968*	*1,331*	*637*	*492*	*251*	*241*	*15*	*15*	...	*9*	*9*	...
	Bihar	M	46,994	24,532	22,462	27,240	14,189	13,051	...	...	...	14	7	7	19,736	10,336	9,400	4	...	4	...	...	...	...	...	...
	Dinapur	M	24,221	12,347	11,874	19,570	9,988	9,582	...	...	...	...	...	...	4,634	2,349	2,285	17	10	7	...	...	...	...	...	...
	Mokameh		14,260	7,389	6,871	12,201	6,336	5,875	...	...	...	...	...	...	2,059	963	1,096	...	...	...	...	...	...	...	...	...
	Dinapur Cantt	C	10,217	5,909	4,308	6,880	3,774	3,106	...	...	...	...	...	...	2,286	1,249	1,037	1,050	885	165	...	...	...	1	1	...
	Barh	M	9,750	5,179	4,571	7,417	4,024	3,393	...	...	...	...	...	...	2,320	1,152	1,168	13	3	10	...	...	...	...	...	...
	Fatwa		9,393	5,027	4,366	8,449	4,607	3,842	3	3	...	1	1	...	939	415	524	1	1	...	...	...	...	...	...	...
	Khagaul	M	7,412	4,119	3,293	5,741	3,212	2,529	...	...	...	...	...	...	1,596	868	728	75	30	36	...	...	...	...	...	...
Gaya ...	Gaya City	M	88,005	50,625	37,380	66,462	38,502	27,960	44	30	14	375	190	186	20,596	11,626	8,970	508	262	246	12	12	...	8	3	5
	Daudnagar	M	11,699	6,257	5,442	8,912	4,737	4,175	...	...	...	...	...	...	2,787	1,520	1,267	...	...	...	...	...	...	...	...	...
	Jahanabad		8,764	4,884	3,880	6,386	3,614	2,772	...	...	...	...	...	...	2,378	1,270	1,108	...	...	...	...	...	...	...	...	...
	Nawada		7,485	3,976	3,509	5,132	2,838	2,294	30	19	11	35	22	13	2,288	1,097	1,191	...	...	...	...	...	...	...	...	...
	Aurangabad		7,428	3,985	3,443	4,591	2,645	1,946	...	...	...	...	...	...	2,822	1,331	1,491	15	9	6	...	...	...	...	...	...
	Hisua		7,131	3,375	3,756	5,906	2,854	3,052	1	1	...	43	19	24	1,181	501	680	...	...	...	...	...	...	...	...	...
	Tikari	M	5,481	2,687	2,794	4,267	2,139	2,128	...	...	...	4	2	2	1,209	545	664	1	1	...	...	...	...	...	...	...
Shahabad ...	Arrah	M	48,922	26,635	22,287	35,793	19,866	15,927	...	...	...	492	232	260	12,432	6,439	5,993	195	94	101	...	...	...	10	4	6
	Sasaram	M	25,175	12,473	12,702	14,797	7,524	7,273	268	135	133	...	...	...	10,084	4,806	5,278	26	8	18	...	...	...	...	...	...
	Dumraon	M	14,421	7,602	6,819	12,206	6,456	5,752	...	...	...	...	...	...	2,162	1,121	1,041	51	25	26	...	...	...	...	...	...
	Buxar	M	13,449	7,430	6,019	10,528	5,884	4,644	23	15	8	...	...	...	2,753	1,455	1,298	143	74	69	...	...	...	2	2	...
	Jagdispur	M	9,661	4,791	4,870	7,548	3,751	3,797	...	...	...	...	...	...	2,112	1,039	1,073	1	1	...	...	...	...	...	...	...
	Bhabua	M	6,002	3,220	2,782	4,422	2,401	2,021	22	3	19	...	...	...	1,534	805	729	24	11	13	...	...	...	...	...	...
TIRHUT DIVISION.	15 Towns		303,025	165,946	137,079	221,643	123,688	97,955	20	13	7	26	15	11	78,488	40,867	37,621	2,833	1,352	1,481	6	6	...	9	5	4
Saran ...	Chapra	M	47,448	25,934	21,514	35,873	19,888	15,985	...	...	...	6	6	...	11,505	6,006	5,409	64	34	30	...	...	...	...	...	...
	Siwan	M	14,215	7,981	6,234	8,674	5,101	3,573	...	...	...	...	...	...	5,519	2,869	2,650	22	11	11	...	...	...	...	...	...
	Revelganj	M	8,812	4,287	4,525	7,373	3,632	3,741	...	...	...	...	...	...	1,439	655	784	...	...	...	...	...	...	...	...	...
Champaran ...	Bettiah	M	27,941	14,650	13,283	16,723	9,198	7,525	9	7	2	...	...	...	9,495	4,690	4,805	1,713	763	950	...	...	...	1	1	...
	Motihari	M	17,545	10,526	7,019	12,709	7,956	4,753	...	...	...	3	3	...	4,729	2,526	2,203	104	41	63	...	...	...	...	...	...
Muzaffarpur ...	Muzaffarpur	M	42,812	24,841	17,971	30,648	18,340	12,308	1	1	...	...	...	...	11,801	6,345	5,456	348	145	203	6	6	...	8	4	4
	Hajipur	M	19,299	9,936	9,363	15,794	8,218	7,576	...	...	...	...	...	...	3,495	1,716	1,779	10	2	8	...	...	...	...	...	...
	Sitamarhi	M	10,701	6,255	4,446	8,755	5,189	3,566	...	...	...	9	2	7	1,895	1,046	849	42	18	24	...	...	...	...	...	...
	Lalganj	M	9,192	4,676	4,516	7,709	3,956	3,753	10	5	5	...	...	...	1,473	715	758	...	...	...	...	...	...	...	...	...
	Muzaffarpur Cantt.	C	237	209	28	40	35	5	...	...	...	...	...	...	46	39	7	151	135	16	...	...	...	...	...	...
Darbhanga ...	Darbhanga	M	60,676	32,274	28,402	42,217	22,769	19,448	...	...	...	...	...	...	18,308	9,432	8,876	151	73	78	...	...	...	...	...	...
	Madhubani	M	18,789	9,946	8,843	13,300	7,086	6,214	...	...	...	...	...	...	5,483	2,857	2,626	6	3	3	...	...	...	...	...	...
	Samastipur	M	9,891	6,101	3,790	7,390	4,602	2,788	...	...	...	...	...	...	2,280	1,373	907	221	126	95	...	...	...	...	...	...
	Rosera	M	8,869	4,533	4,336	6,458	4,296	4,162	...	...	...	8	4	4	402	232	170	1	1	...	...	...	...	...	...	...
	Jaynagar		6,598	3,788	2,810	5,980	3,422	2,558	...	...	...	...	...	...	618	366	253	...	...	...	...	...	...	...	...	...
BHAGALPUR DIVISION.	17 Towns		313,532	172,962	140,570	234,551	130,432	104,119	16	13	3	223	162	61	74,653	39,956	34,697	3,232	1,754	1,478	949	639	210	8	6	2
Bhagalpur ...	Bhagalpur City	M	83,847	46,868	36,979	58,348	33,299	25,049	...	...	...	69	37	32	24,555	12,946	11,609	769	493	276	106	93	13	...	...	...
	Colgong	M	5,233	2,632	2,601	3,985	2,040	1,945	...	...	...	...	...	...	1,236	585	651	12	7	5	...	...	...	...	...	...

MONGHYR ...	Monghyr	M	52,863	27,843	25,020	40,926	21,691	19,235	...	...		1	1	...	11,812	6,102	5,710	124	49	75	...	...	...	...	...	...
	Jamalpur	M	30,346	16,378	13,968	24,256	13,077	11,179	...	...	...	...	...	...	4,888	2,606	2,282	1,194	689	505	...	...	...	8	6	2
	Sheikhpura		14,017	7,024	6,993	9,746	5,018	4,728	...	...	...	...	...	...	4,271	2,006	2,265	...	...	...	...	...	...	...	...	...
	Khagaria		12,230	6,408	5,822	10,704	5,680	5,024	...	...	...	...	...	...	1,514	724	790	12	4	8	...	...	...	...	...	...
	Lakhisarai		8,813	4,612	4,201	7,779	4,065	3,714	1	1	...	5	4	1	1,005	529	476	23	13	10	...	...	...	...	...	...
	Begusarai		7,739	4,384	3,355	6,384	3,615	2,769	...	...	...	...	...	...	1,341	763	578	14	6	8	...	...	...	...	...	...
PURNEA ...	Katihar	M	15,864	9,014	6,850	10,778	6,220	4,558	...	...	...	...	...	...	4,919	2,706	2,213	165	87	78	2	1	1	...	...	...
	Railway Settlt.	*S*	*3,054*	*2,021*	*1,033*	*2,124*	*1,426*	*698*	...	...	...	...	...	...	*774*	*515*	*259*	*154*	*79*	*75*	*2*	*1*	*1*	...	...	...
	Purnea	M	15,474	9,255	6,219	11,313	6,771	4,542	4	4	...	38	31	7	4,020	2,396	1,624	99	53	46	...	...	...	...	...	...
	Kishanganj	M	8,946	5,817	3,129	5,223	3,390	1,833	...	...	...	65	57	8	3,644	2,361	1,283	12	7	5	2	2	...	...	...	...
	Forbesganj	M	5,939	3,713	2,226	3,850	2,543	1,306	...	...	...	20	10	10	2,035	1,140	895	34	18	16	...	...	...	...	...	...
SANTAL PARGANAS ...	Sahibganj	M	15,883	8,530	7,353	11,926	6,422	5,504	11	8	3	...	...	...	3,731	2,001	1,730	161	72	89	54	27	27	...	...	...
	Deoghar	M	14,217	8,117	6,100	13,380	7,680	5,700	...	...	...	21	20	1	574	328	246	152	9	143	90	80	10	...	...	...
	Dumka	M	9,471	5,317	4,154	7,688	4,267	3,421	...	...	...	...	...	...	1,206	635	571	187	104	83	390	311	79	...	...	...
	Madhupur	M	8,965	4,997	3,968	5,773	3,255	2,518	...	...	...	4	2	2	2,846	1,559	1,287	251	129	122	91	52	39	...	...	...
	Rajmahal		3,685	2,053	1,632	2,492	1,397	1,095	...	...	...	...	...	...	1,056	569	487	23	14	9	114	73	41	...	...	...
ORISSA DIVISION	9 Towns		**191,429**	**102,777**	**88,652**	**160,520**	**87,438**	**73,082**	**49**	**31**	**18**	**54**	**28**	**26**	**26,892**	**13,468**	**13,424**	**3,604**	**1,651**	**1,953**	**287**	**148**	**139**	**23**	**13**	**10**
CUTTACK ...	Cuttack	M	65,263	36,357	28,906	52,853	30,217	22,636	4	4	...	31	16	15	9,956	5,145	4,811	2,400	960	1,440	10	9	1	9	6	3
	Kendrapara	M	12,620	6,237	6,383	10,327	5,165	5,162	...	...	...	...	...	...	2,276	1,065	1,211	17	7	10	...	...	...	...	...	...
	Jajpur	M	10,673	5,274	5,399	9,738	4,794	4,944	...	...	...	...	...	...	929	478	451	4	1	3	...	...	...	2	1	1
BALASORE ...	Bhadrakh		18,283	8,943	9,340	10,689	5,464	5,225	...	...	...	...	...	...	7,580	3,472	4,108	14	7	7	...	...	...	...	...	...
	Balasore	M	17,843	10,133	7,710	13,608	7,894	5,714	8	4	4	...	...	...	3,615	1,893	1,722	487	278	209	124	63	61	1	1	...
PURI ...	Puri	M	37,568	20,703	16,865	36,891	20,239	16,652	2	2	...	...	...	...	475	344	131	200	118	82	...	...	...	...	...	...
SAMBALPUR ...	Sambalpur	M	15,017	7,716	7,301	13,580	6,971	6,609	6	3	3	...	...	...	1,148	590	558	242	136	106	34	13	21	7	3	4
	Bargarh		7,085	3,616	3,469	6,879	3,507	3,372	3	3	...	...	...	...	149	81	68	54	25	29	...	...	...	...	...	...
	Jharsuguda		7,077	3,798	3,279	5,955	3,187	2,768	26	15	11	23	12	11	764	400	364	186	119	67	119	63	56	4	2	2
CHOTA NAGPUR DIVISION.	16 Towns		**310,291**	**172,425**	**137,866**	**224,285**	**124,717**	**99,568**	**3,357**	**2,235**	**1,122**	**552**	**336**	**216**	**58,311**	**32,460**	**25,851**	**16,335**	**8,662**	**7,673**	**7,174**	**3,831**	**3,343**	**277**	**184**	**93**
HAZARIBAGH ...	Giridih	M	21,122	11,122	10,000	15,202	8,000	7,202	...	..	...	47	27	20	5,654	2,987	2,667	192	94	98	25	13	13	2	2	...
	Hazaribagh	M	20,977	10,903	10,074	14,648	7,682	6,966	18	14	4	213	111	102	4,975	2,510	2,465	860	455	405	261	129	132	2	2	...
	Chatra	M	8,758	4,312	4,446	6,303	3,140	3,163	1	1	...	24	15	9	2,409	1,147	1,262	19	7	12	2	2	...	...	...	...
RANCHI ...	Ranchi	M	50,517	26,918	23,599	27,717	16,135	13,582	8	5	3	77	44	33	12,096	6,139	5,957	7,566	4,011	3,555	3,046	1,578	1,468	7	6	1
	Doranda	*S*	*6,721*	*3,399*	*3,322*	*4,091*	*2,117*	*1,974*	*8*	*5*	*3*	...	...	...	*2,282*	*1,112*	*1,170*	*339*	*164*	*175*	*1*	*1*	...	...	...	...
	Lohardaga	M	7,577	3,816	3,761	4,840	2,460	2,380	...	...	...	...	...	...	2,001	972	1,029	376	192	184	360	192	168	...	...	...
	Bundu		6,487	3,273	3,214	6,149	3,099	3,050	1	1	...	...	...	...	293	152	141	5	3	2	39	18	21	...	...	...
PALAMAU ...	Daltonganj	M	12,040	6,601	5,439	9,461	5,340	4,121	3	1	2	9	8	1	2,369	1,175	1,194	140	45	95	58	32	26	...	...	...
	Garhwa		11,985	5,943	6,042	10,023	4,948	5,075	...	...	...	...	...	..	1,928	979	949	...	...	...	34	16	18	...	...	...
MANBHUM ...	Purulia	M	25,974	14,388	11,586	22,128	12,337	9,791	...	..	...	...	...	...	2,964	1,596	1,368	879	452	427	3	3	...	...	...	...
	Dhanbad	M	16,356	9,882	6,474	12,202	7,337	4,865	...	...	...	...	...	...	3,381	2,137	1,244	725	388	337	44	19	26	4	1	3
	Railway Settlt.	*S*	*4,664*	*2,989*	*1,675*	*2,910*	*1,911*	*999*	...	...	...	...	...	...	*1,219*	*790*	*429*	*542*	*288*	*254*	...	...	...	...	...	...
	Raghunathpur	M	7,139	3,654	3,485	6,765	3,469	3,296	...	...	...	...	...	...	320	177	143	54	8	46	...	...	...	...	...	...
	Jhalda	M	6,924	3,470	3,454	6,560	3,285	3,275	..	...	...	...	...	...	322	162	160	42	23	19	...	...	...	...	...	...
SINGHBHUM ...	Jamshedpur City		83,738	51,137	32,601	60,494	36,395	24,099	3,130	2,091	1,039	175	126	49	13,797	9,126	4,671	3,748	2,091	1,657	2,133	1,136	997	261	172	89
	Chakradharpur	M	11,191	6,215	4,976	7,513	4,203	3,310	5	3	3	..	...	..	2,232	1,222	1,010	1,054	572	482	381	210	171	...	...	...
	Railway Settlt.	*S*	*4,033*	*2,415*	*1,618*	*2,763*	*1,670*	*1,093*	...	...	...	...	...	...	*495*	*308*	*187*	*737*	*403*	*334*	*39*	*34*	*5*	...	...	...
	Chaibassa	M	10,785	5,716	5,069	8,031	4,219	3,812	5	4	1	1	1	...	1,699	906	793	595	274	321	454	312	142	...	...	...
	Jugsalai		8,721	5,075	3,646	6,249	3,668	2,581	186	116	70	6	4	2	1,865	1,067	798	80	47	33	334	172	162	1	1	...
Feudatory States	**7 Towns**		*45,715*	*23,105*	*22,610*	*44,106*	*22,270*	*21,836*	*41*	*29*	*12*	*1*	*1*	...	*1,268*	*634*	*634*	*254*	*146*	*108*	*45*	*25*	*20*	...	...	...
MAYURBHANJ ...	Baripada		6,193	3,513	2,680	5,817	3,313	2,504	...	...	...	1	1	...	337	176	161	38	23	15	...	...	...	...	...	...
DHENKANAL ...	Dhenkanal (Nijgarh)		7,480	3,993	3,487	7,132	3,824	3,308	...	...	...	...	...	...	327	159	168	21	10	11	...	...	...	...	...	...
	Bhuban		6,563	3,001	3,562	6,550	2,994	3,556	...	...	...	...	...	...	13	[illegible]	6	...	...	...	...	...	...	...	...	...
SONPUR ...	Sonpur (Nijgarh)		8,506	4,224	4,282	8,282	4,112	4,170	5	4	1	...	...	...	216	107	109	3	1	2	...	...	...	...	...	...
	Binka		3,326	1,540	1,786	3,309	1,526	1,783	...	...	...	...	...	...	4	4	...	...	...	...	13	10	3	...	...	...
PATNA ...	Bolangir		6,473	3,272	3,201	6,159	3,093	3,066	4	4	...	...	...	...	118	63	55	192	112	80	...	...	...	...	...	...
KALAHANDI ...	Bhawanipatna		7,174	3,562	3,612	6,857	3,408	3,449	32	21	11	...	...	...	253	118	135	...	...	...	32	15	17	...	...	...

TABLE VI.

BIRTHPLACE.

This table, which corresponds with Table XI of 1921, shows the birth-places of the population enumerated in the province It is divided into two parts. Part I contains the statistics for the province as a whole and for the various districts and states; while Part II gives similar information for the four cities.

2. In Part I birthplaces returned by small numbers of persons have been clubbed together in their respective classes. Details of these are given below :—

BORN IN	Persons	Males	Females
1	2	3	4
A.—II (b) Other Provinces and States in India—			
(i) Other provinces	**21**	**15**	**6**
Andamans and Nicobars	4	3	1
Baluchistan	11	6	5
Coorg	6	6	
(ii) Other Indian States	**270**	**181**	**89**
Assam States (Manipur and tribal areas)	6	2	4
Baluchistan States	5	5	
Baroda State	63	37	26
Kashmir State	92	65	27
Sikkim State	26	15	11
Western India Agency	78	57	21
B.—Other Asiatic Countries—			
Within British Dominions	**24**	**14**	**10**
Ceylon	20	11	9
Straits Settlements and Malaya	2	1	1
Elsewhere ...	2	2	
D.—Africa—			
Within British Dominions	**7**	**2**	**5**
British East Africa	2		2
Cape Colony	1	1	
Mauritius	2	1	1
Natal ..	2		2
Outside British Dominions	**2**	**2**	
Egypt	1	1	
Mozambique	1	1	
F.—Australasia—			
Within British Dominions	**25**	**10**	**15**
Australia	21	9	12
New Zealand	3	1	2
Tasmania	1		1

3. Throughout this table the phrase " Within British Dominions " should be taken to mean " Within the British Empire and Mandated Territories. "

TABLE VI.

BIRTHPLACE. PART I—DISTRICTS AND STATES.

BORN IN	TOTAL			ENUMERATED IN: Patna			Gaya			Shahabad			Saran.			Champaran.		
	Persons	Males	Females	Persons	Males	Females	Persons	Males.	Females	Persons	Males	Females	Persons	Males	Females	Persons.	Males	Females
1	2	3	4	5	6	7	8	9	10	11	12	13	14	15	16	17	18	19
TOTAL POPULATION	*43,036,583*	*21,089,560*	*21,947,023*	*1,846,474*	*956,124*	*890,350*	*2,388,462*	*1,193,643*	*1,194,819*	*1,993,489*	*999,099*	*994,390*	*2,486,468*	*1,220,049*	*1,266,419*	*2,145,687*	*1,080,956*	*1,064,731*
A.—INDIA	*42,986,309*	*21,065,545*	*21,920,764*	*1,844,896*	*954,845*	*890,051*	*2,388,251*	*1,193,497*	*1,194,754*	*1,993,290*	*998,941*	*994,349*	*2,486,136*	*1,219,818*	*1,266,318*	*2,134,170*	*1,077,210*	*1,056,960*
I. BIHAR AND ORISSA	*41,819,746*	*20,824,212*	*20,995,534*	*1,829,807*	*945,502*	*884,305*	*2,382,872*	*1,190,169*	*1,192,703*	*1,962,164*	*986,288*	*975,876*	*2,460,614*	*1,210,890*	*1,249,724*	*2,110,699*	*1,065,622*	*1,045,077*
(a) British Territory	*37,322,068*	*18,608,361*	*18,713,707*	*1,829,764*	*945,476*	*884,288*	*2,382,850*	*1,190,163*	*1,192,687*	*1,962,156*	*986,285*	*975,871*	*2,460,611*	*1,210,887*	*1,249,724*	*2,110,698*	*1,065,622*	*1,045,076*
PATNA DIVISION ...	**6,203,110**	**3,148,210**	**3,054,900**	**1,771,749**	**918,349**	**853,400**	**2,364,437**	**1,183,483**	**1,180,954**	**1,949,515**	**981,776**	**967,739**	**7,222**	**2,932**	**4,290**	**1,090**	**763**	**327**
Patna ...	**1,789,588**	926,926	862,662	**1,722,939**	899,422	823,517	**20,419**	7,701	12,718	**12,591**	3,992	8,599	**4,124**	1,410	2,714	**585**	371	214
Gaya	**2,447,098**	1,224,858	1,222,240	**37,092**	13,822	23,270	**2,337,971**	1,173,431	1,164,540	**10,755**	3,254	7,501	**372**	217	155	**183**	140	43
Shahabad ...	**1,966,424**	996,426	969,998	**11,718**	5,105	6,613	**6,047**	2,351	3,696	**1,926,169**	974,530	951,639	**2,726**	1,305	1,421	**322**	252	70
TIRHUT DIVISION ..	**10,720,710**	**5,328,945**	**5,391,765**	**28,391**	**15,345**	**13,046**	**1,684**	**1,163**	**521**	**6,404**	**1,857**	**4,547**	**2,452,718**	**1,207,660**	**1,245,058**	**2,109,221**	**1,064,630**	**1,044,591**
Saran	**2,483,532**	1,233,512	1,250,020	**11,239**	5,858	5,381	**789**	583	206	**4,734**	1,660	3,074	**2,436,162**	1,204,412	1,231,750	**10,060**	6,729	3,331
Champaran	**2,100,081**	1,058,701	1,041,380	**798**	549	249	**73**	49	24	**228**	126	102	**3,286**	1,034	2,252	**2,072,527**	1,049,875	1,022,652
Muzaffarpur	**2,959,417**	1,453,931	1,505,486	**11,469**	6,229	5,240	**460**	293	167	**1,124**	461	663	**12,408**	1,874	10,534	**25,794**	7,556	18,238
Darbhanga ...	**3,177,680**	1,582,801	1,594,879	**4,885**	2,709	2,176	**362**	238	124	**318**	210	108	**862**	340	522	**840**	470	370
BHAGALPUR DIVISION ...	**8,672,446**	**4,376,435**	**4,296,011**	**27,126**	**10,119**	**17,007**	**8,091**	**2,025**	**6,066**	**1,036**	**676**	**360**	**551**	**247**	**304**	**255**	**155**	**100**
Monghyr	**2,340,992**	1,171,204	1,169,788	**24,967**	8,839	16,128	**7,704**	1,825	5,879	**332**	197	135	**322**	118	204	**118**	72	46
Bhagalpur	**2,270,046**	1,148,538	1,121,508	**1,516**	905	611	**222**	107	115	**378**	246	132	**169**	102	67	**89**	52	37
Purnea ...	**2,009,560**	1,030,137	979,423	**290**	183	107	**59**	31	28	**145**	111	34	**40**	13	27	**22**	11	11
Santal Parganas	**2,061,848**	1,036,556	1,025,292	**353**	192	161	**106**	62	44	**181**	122	59	**20**	14	6	**26**	20	6
ORISSA DIVISION ..	**5,306,155**	**2,552,305**	**2,753,850**	**752**	**565**	**187**	**83**	**60**	**23**	**109**	**82**	**27**	**22**	**13**	**9**	**18**	**9**	**9**
Cuttack	**2,193,591**	1,039,577	1,154,014	**383**	286	97	**44**	31	13	**44**	35	9	**11**	8	3	**13**	7	6
Balasore ...	**979,731**	473,205	506,526	**105**	74	31	**17**	17		**13**	4	9	**3**	3	..	**3**		3
Angul ...	**221,524**	109,563	111,961	**7**	3	4	**2**	2	..	**2**	2				..	..	...	
Puri ...	**1,026,968**	493,995	532,973	**129**	91	38	**4**	4		**20**	15	5	**7**	1	6	**2**	2	
Sambalpur ..	**884,341**	435,965	448,376	**128**	111	17	**16**	6	10	**30**	26	4	**1**	1		...	...	
CHOTA NAGPUR DIVISION ...	**6,419,647**	**3,202,466**	**3,217,181**	**1,746**	**1,098**	**648**	**8,555**	**3,432**	**5,123**	**5,092**	**1,894**	**3,198**	**98**	**35**	**63**	**114**	**65**	**49**
Hazaribagh	**1,502,815**	747,628	755,187	**443**	236	207	**4,544**	2,020	2,524	**133**	77	56	**27**	11	16	**19**	15	4
Ranchi	**1,580,867**	782,784	798,083	**775**	500	275	**165**	111	54	**113**	76	37	**37**	12	25	**77**	41	36
Palamau	**807,354**	403,532	403,822	**183**	125	58	**3,551**	1,160	2,391	**4,638**	1,591	3,047	**14**	1	13	**4**	4	
Manbhum ...	**1,662,373**	843,166	819,207	**291**	196	95	**259**	135	124	**171**	124	47	**13**	10	3	**10**	2	8
Singhbhum ...	**866,238**	425,356	440,882	**54**	41	13	**36**	6	30	**37**	26	11	**7**	1	6	**4**	3	1
(b) Bihar and Orissa States.	*4,497,678*	*2,215,851*	*2,281,827*	*43*	*26*	*17*	*22*	*6*	*16*	*8*	*3*	*5*	*3*	*3*		*1*		*1*
Orissa States	**4,322,318**	2,128,498	2,193,820	**36**	22	14	**7**	1	6	**5**	2	3	**1**	1			...	
Chota Nagpur States ..	**175,360**	87,353	88,007	**7**	4	3	**15**	5	10	**3**	1	2	**2**	2	..	**1**		1
II. OTHER PARTS OF INDIA.	*466,563*	*241,333*	*225,230*	*15,089*	*9,343*	*5,746*	*5,379*	*3,328*	*2,051*	*31,126*	*12,653*	*18,473*	*25,522*	*8,928*	*16,594*	*23,471*	*11,588*	*11,883*
(a) ADJACENT PROVINCES AND STATES.	*414,166*	*206,941*	*207,225*	*12,869*	*7,996*	*4,873*	*3,999*	*2,457*	*1,542*	*29,518*	*11,586*	*17,932*	*24,967*	*8,530*	*16,437*	*22,442*	*11,010*	*11,432*
(i) British Territory ...	**402,059**	**202,915**	**199,144**	**12,854**	**7,984**	**4,870**	**3,992**	**2,453**	**1,539**	**29,518**	**11,586**	**17,932**	**24,967**	**8,530**	**16,437**	**22,440**	**11,008**	**11,432**
Bengal	**157,504**	79,314	78,190	**6,535**	3,804	2,731	**1,539**	885	654	**1,362**	727	635	**935**	563	372	**691**	375	316
Central Provinces and Berar	**81,573**	41,535	40,038	**107**	57	50	**160**	89	71	**113**	47	66	**17**	10	7	**24**	20	4
Madras	**36,457**	16,829	19,628	**108**	58	50	**28**	13	15	**22**	17	5	**11**	9	2	**16**	12	4
United Provinces	**126,525**	65,237	61,288	**6,104**	4,065	2,039	**2,265**	1,466	799	**28,021**	10,795	17,226	**24,004**	7,948	16,056	**21,709**	10,601	11,108
(ii) Indian States	**12,107**	**4,026**	**8,081**	15	12	3	7	4	3			...	...			2	2	
Bengal States ...	**20**	12	8	10	7	3	3		3			..		.		...	...	.
Central Provinces States ...	**7,744**	2,330	5,414									...				.		.
Madras States (including Cochin and Travancore).	**4,329**	1,673	2,656	5	5		4	4	.		.	..	...					
United Provinces States ...	**14**	11	3	...	...	...	...	...	...	...	..	...	.	.	..	2	2	..

(b) OTHER PROVINCES AND STATES.	*50,926*	*33,814*	*17,112*	*2,127*	*1,291*	*836*	*1,379*	*871*	*508*	*1,608*	*1,067*	*541*	*598*	*385*	*143*	*1,017*	*571*	*446*
(i) British Territory ...	**25,576**	**18,024**	**7,552**	**1,170**	**756**	**414**	**513**	**376**	**137**	**453**	**338**	**115**	**365**	**296**	**69**	**210**	**163**	**47**
Ajmer-Merwara	123	87	36	6	5	1	1	...	1	1	1	...	...	...	...	3	...	3
Assam	2,024	1,466	558	114	70	44	22	16	6	49	37	12	19	4	15	14	9	5
Bombay (*including* Aden) ...	6,976	4,639	2,337	154	84	70	214	158	56	78	47	31	59	39	20	31	27	4
Burma	299	116	183	23	6	17	11	2	9	25	15	10	11	4	7	1	1	...
Delhi	359	251	108	104	61	43	16	10	6	7	6	1	9	9	...	2	1	1
N.-W. F. Province ...	824	760	64	23	19	4	14	11	3	115	107	8	1	1	...	15	15	...
Punjab	15,051	10,690	4,361	743	510	233	232	178	54	176	133	43	265	238	27	144	110	34
Other Provinces*	22	16	6	3	1	2	3	1	2	2	2	...	1	1	...	...	...	...
(ii) Indian States ...	**25,350**	**15,790**	**9,560**	**957**	**535**	**422**	**866**	**495**	**371**	**1,155**	**729**	**426**	**163**	**89**	**74**	**807**	**408**	**399**
Bombay States	440	353	87	...	...	...	...	...	...	34	24	10	1	1	...	...	...	...
Central India (*Agency*) ...	3,075	1,270	805	132	44	88	304	165	139	437	297	140	5	...	5	7	5	2
Gwalior State	184	101	83	5	4	1	47	...	47	2	2	...	...	...	...	...	...	...
Hyderabad State	468	272	196	60	22	38	7	4	3	8	3	5	1	1	...	5	3	2
Mysore State	403	261	142	19	12	7	86	73	13	7	3	4	6	3	3	2	1	1
N.-W. F. Province (*Agencies and Tribal areas*).	475	437	38	...	...	...	...	...	...	...	...	...	...	...	...	...	...	...
Punjab States	279	186	93	2	...	2	...	...	...	1	1	...	...	...	...	...	...	...
Rajputana (*Agency*) ...	20,756	12,729	8,027	723	441	282	422	253	169	665	398	267	150	84	66	783	393	390
Other Indian States* ...	270	181	89	16	12	4	...	...	...	1	1	...	...	...	...	10	6	4
(c) FRENCH AND PORTUGUESE SETTLEMENTS.	*285*	*169*	*116*	*7*	*7*	...	*1*	...	*1*	...	...	...	...	...	...	...		...
(d) INDIA, *unspecified* ...	*1,186*	*409*	*777*	*86*	*49*	*37*	...	...	...	...	...	...	*27*	*13*	*14*	*12*	*7*	*5*
B.—OTHER ASIATIC COUNTRIES.	*38,240*	*13,514*	*24,726*	*459*	*346*	*113*	*148*	*108*	*40*	*175*	*147*	*28*	*262*	*189*	*73*	*11,410*	*3,695*	*7,715*
Within British Dominions* ...	24	14	10	1	...	1	...	...	...	1	...	1	1	...	1	1	1	...
Outside British Dominions ...	38,213	13,497	24,716	456	344	113	148	108	40	174	147	27	261	189	72	11,409	3,694	7,715
Afghanistan	1,423	1,385	38	83	80	3	40	38	2	36	35	1	20	15	5	21	21	...
China	30	20	10	5	4	1	2	2	...	...	...	...	1	...	1	...	...	...
Nepal	36,586	11,981	24,605	350	256	94	105	67	38	135	111	24	240	174	66	11,372	3,657	7,715
Elsewhere	174	111	63	18	4	14	1	1	...	3	1	2	...	...	...	16	16	...
Asia, *unspecified*	3	3	...	2	2	...	...	...	...	...	...	...	...	...	...	...	...	...
C.—EUROPE	*3,413*	*2,320*	*1,093*	*1,092*	*919*	*173*	*57*	*35*	*22*	*11*	*7*	*4*	*59*	*38*	*21*	*92*	*41*	*51*
Within British Dominions ...	3,077	2,149	928	1,056	913	143	52	33	19	10	6	4	57	36	21	71	39	32
United Kingdom and Ireland.	3,070	2,143	927	1,055	912	143	52	33	19	10	6	4	57	36	21	71	39	32
Elsewhere	7	6	1	1	1	...	...	...	...	...	...	...	...	...	...	...	...	...
Outside British Dominions ...	331	166	165	36	6	30	5	2	3	1	1	...	2	2	...	21	2	19
Europe, *unspecified* ...	5	5	...	...	...	...	...	...	...	...	...	...	...	...	...	...	...	...
D.—AFRICA	*43*	*27*	*16*	*8*	*4*	*4*	*1*	*1*	...	*1*	...	*1*	*4*	*2*	*2*	...	...	...
Within British Dominions* ...	7	2	5	4	1	3	...	...	...	1	...	1	...	...	...	...	...	...
Outside British Dominions*	2	2	...	1	1	...	...	...	...	...	...	...	...	...	...	...	...	...
Africa, *unspecified* ...	34	23	11	3	2	1	1	1	...	...	...	...	4	2	2	...	...	...
E.—AMERICA	*230*	*119*	*111*	*12*	*7*	*5*	*3*	...	*3*	*12*	*4*	*8*	*6*	*2*	*4*	*14*	*9*	*5*
Within British Dominions ...	9	3	6	1	...	1	...	...	...	...	...	...	5	2	3	...	...	...
Canada	9	3	6	1	...	1	...	...	...	...	...	...	5	2	3	...	...	...
Outside British Dominions ...	207	112	95	11	7	4	3	...	3	12	4	8	...	...	...	14	9	5
United States	203	111	92	9	7	2	3	...	3	12	4	8	...	...	...	14	9	5
Elsewhere	4	1	3	2	...	2	...	...	...	...	...	...	...	...	...	...	...	...
America, *unspecified* ...	14	4	10	...	...	...	...	...	...	...	...	...	1	...	1	...	...	...
F.—AUSTRALASIA ...	*32*	*13*	*19*	*7*	*3*	*4*	...	...	...	...	...	...	*1*	...	*1*	*1*	*1*	...
Within British Dominions* ...	25	10	15	1	...	1	...	...	...	...	...	...	1	...	1	1	1	...
Outside British Dominions ...	2	1	1	1	1	...	...	...	...	...	...	...	...	...	...	...	...	...
Australasia, *unspecified* ...	5	2	3	5	2	3	...	...	...	...	...	...	...	...	...	...	...	...
G.—BORN AT SEA ...	*1*	*1*	...	...	...	...	*1*	*1*	...	...	...	...	...	...	...	...	...	...
H.—BIRTHPLACE NOT RETURNED.	*1,315*	*1,021*	*294*	...	...	...	*1*	*1*	...	...	...	...	...	...	...	...	...	...

* For further details, *see* title-page of this table.

TABLE VI—*continued.*

BIRTHPLACE. PART I—DISTRICTS AND STATES.

BORN IN	MUZAFFARPUR Persons.	MUZAFFARPUR Males.	MUZAFFARPUR Females.	DARBHANGA Persons.	DARBHANGA Males.	DARBHANGA Females.	MONGHYR Persons.	MONGHYR Males.	MONGHYR Females.
1	20	21	22	23	24	25	26	27	28
TOTAL POPULATION	*2,941,025*	*1,443,847*	*1,497,178*	*3,166,094*	*1,570,959*	*1,595,135*	*2,287,154*	*1,145,797*	*1,141,357*
A.—INDIA	*2,931,394*	*1,441,606*	*1,489,788*	*3,157,718*	*1,569,297*	*1,588,421*	*2,286,685*	*1,145,462*	*1,141,223*
I. BIHAR AND ORISSA	2,927,042	1,439,037	1,488,005	3,153,993	1,567,048	1,586,945	2,279,404	1,140,983	1,138,421
(a) British Territory	2,927,042	1,439,037	1,488,005	3,153,982	1,567,046	1,586,936	2,279,403	1,140,983	1,138,420
PATNA DIVISION	4,776	2,007	2,769	3,923	1,304	2,619	19,008	7,799	11,209
Patna	3,602	1,310	2,292	3,044	951	2,093	11,768	4,765	7,003
Gaya	453	215	238	253	144	109	6,075	2,230	3,845
Shahabad	721	482	239	353	229	134	1,165	804	361
TIRHUT DIVISION	2,921,356	1,437,234	1,484,122	3,128,462	1,560,319	1,568,143	18,260	7,479	10,781
Saran	6,363	3,961	2,402	2,457	1,709	748	1,356	1,056	300
Champaran	21,923	6,427	15,496	460	272	188	134	85	49
Muzaffarpur	2,863,849	1,419,455	1,444,394	32,017	8,943	23,074	1,749	1,099	650
Darbhanga	29,221	7,391	21,830	3,093,528	1,549,395	1,544,133	15,021	5,208	9,813
BHAGALPUR DIVISION	1,655	610	1,045	21,798	5,364	16,434	2,239,430	1,125,022	1,114,408
Monghyr	1,230	407	823	16,831	3,660	13,171	2,213,983	1,116,106	1,097,877
Bhagalpur	313	144	169	4,820	1,636	3,184	22,241	7,823	14,418
Purnea	83	43	40	142	71	71	656	329	327
Santal Parganas	29	16	13	15	7	8	2,570	764	1,806
ORISSA DIVISION	47	26	21	20	13	7	53	34	19
Cuttack	20	14	6	11	5	6	36	26	10
Balasore	3	1	2	6	5	1	1	1	
Angul	2	1	1			...			
Puri	10	5	5	3	3	..	11	4	7
Sambalpur	12	5	7			..	5	3	2
CHOTA NAGPUR DIVISION	108	60	48	79	46	33	2,631	649	1,982
Hazaribagh	25	14	11	18	6	12	2,339	528	1,816
Ranchi	29	10	10	27	22	5	45	19	26
Palamau	27	11	16	6	1	5	30	21	9
Manbhum	24	16	8	17	7	10	200	76	124
Singhbhum	3		3	1		1	17	10	7
(b) Bihar and Orissa States.		..	...	11	2	9	2		2
Orissa States		.		2	2	...	1	...	1
Chota Nagpur States	..	...	...	9	..	9	1	..	1
II. OTHER PARTS OF INDIA.	*4,352*	*2,569*	*1,783*	*3,792*	*2,316*	*1,476*	*7,281*	*4,479*	*2,802*
(a) ADJACENT PROVINCES AND STATES.	*3,122*	*1,859*	*1,263*	*2,603*	*1,574*	*1,029*	*5,813*	*3,584*	*2,229*
(i) British Territory	3,121	1,859	1,262	2,600	1,571	1,029	5,812	3,584	2,228
Bengal	1,250	662	588	1,097	618	479	3,276	1,885	1,391
Central Provinces and Berar	52	29	23	18	10	8	92	57	35
Madras	18	14	4	43	36	7	86	46	41
United Provinces	1,801	1,154	647	1,442	907	535	2,358	1,597	761
(ii) Indian States	1		1	3	3	..	1	...	1
Bengal States	.		..	..	...	...	1	..	1
Madras States (including Cochin and Travancore).	1		1	3	3	...	...	...	...

BORN IN	BHAGALPUR Persons.	BHAGALPUR Males.	BHAGALPUR Females.	PURNEA Persons.	PURNEA Males.	PURNEA Females.	SANTAL PARGANAS Persons.	SANTAL PARGANAS Males.	SANTAL PARGANAS Females.
1	29	30	31	32	33	34	35	36	37
TOTAL POPULATION	*2,234,632*	*1,130,584*	*1,104,048*	*2,186,543*	*1,129,681*	*1,056,862*	*2,051,472*	*1,025,921*	*1,025,551*
A.—INDIA	*2,233,022*	*1,129,978*	*1,103,044*	*2,184,336*	*1,128,345*	*1,055,991*	*2,051,260*	*1,025,802*	*1,025,458*
I. BIHAR AND ORISSA	2,224,087	1,124,304	1,099,783	2,146,864	1,108,351	1,038,513	2,026,199	1,014,509	1,011,690
(a) British Territory	2,224,087	1,124,304	1,099,783	2,146,864	1,108,351	1,038,513	2,026,199	1,014,509	1,011,690
PATNA DIVISION	4,733	3,222	1,511	5,062	3,219	1,843	3,685	2,224	1,461
Patna	1,570	1,078	492	1,523	987	536	915	544	371
Gaya	668	382	286	1,063	655	408	671	406	265
Shahabad	2,495	1,762	733	2,486	1,647	839	2,099	1,274	825
TIRHUT DIVISION	22,250	9,773	12,477	24,400	17,859	6,541	1,324	1,018	306
Saran	1,946	1,443	503	3,668	2,959	709	582	476	106
Champaran	257	213	44	695	527	168	26	17	9
Muzaffarpur	2,684	1,987	697	6,227	4,774	1,458	378	297	81
Darbhanga	17,363	6,129	11,234	13,810	9,599	4,211	338	228	110
BHAGALPUR DIVISION	2,196,145	1,110,635	1,085,510	2,115,932	1,065,872	1,050,060	2,016,895	1,008,959	1,007,936
Monghyr	27,430	16,597	10,833	14,969	6,812	8,157	2,651	1,051	1,600
Bhagalpur	2,149,254	1,092,109	1,057,145	76,570	40,020	36,550	12,960	4,424	8,536
Purnea	5,749	3,191	2,558	2,069,129	1,094,443	974,686	3,069	1,564	1,505
Santal Parganas	14,722	6,738	6,984	25,314	13,247	12,007	1,997,685	1,001,800	995,885
ORISSA DIVISION	216	179	37	29	25	4	135	95	40
Cuttack	101	90	11	18	15	3	103	80	23
Balasore	12	8	4				4	3	1
Angul	17	17	...	..			..	...	...
Puri	59	39	20	11	10	1	18	10	8
Sambalpur	27	25	2	...	.		10	2	8
CHOTA NAGPUR DIVISION	643	395	248	1,381	676	705	3,153	1,206	1,947
Hazaribagh	277	127	150	51	31	20	1,446	476	970
Ranchi	154	103	51	1,038	504	534	139	63	76
Palamau	9	7	2	196	94	102	1		1
Manbhum	165	135	30	13	7	6	1,414	515	899
Singhbhum	32	23	9	83	40	43	152	151	1
(b) Bihar and Orissa States.	..	...	...				..	..	.
Orissa States	...	...	...	..	.	.	...	...	...
Chota Nagpur States	...	..	...	...	..	...	..	...	...
II. OTHER PARTS OF INDIA.	*8,935*	*5,674*	*3,261*	*37,472*	*19,994*	*17,478*	*26,068*	*12,300*	*13,768*
(a) ADJACENT PROVINCES AND STATES.	*6,760*	*4,175*	*2,585*	*35,467*	*18,421*	*17,046*	*24,790*	*11,525*	*13,265*
(i) British Territory	6,763	4,178	2,585	35,467	18,421	17,046	24,789	11,524	13,265
Bengal	3,450	1,823	1,627	28,913	14,878	14,035	21,066	9,980	11,086
Central Provinces and Berar	30	14	16	449	259	190	31	16	15
Madras	13	11	2	7	2	5	6	4	2
United Provinces	3,170	2,330	840	5,097	3,391	1,616	3,106	1,844	1,262
(ii) Indian States	..		...	..		..	1	1	...
Bengal States	...	...	...	..	...	..	...	...	..
Madras States (including Cochin and Travancore).	.	...	..	...	..	...	1	1	...

(b) OTHER PROVINCES AND STATES.	*1,320*	*765*	*515*	*1,095*	*662*	*433*	*1,468*	*895*	*573*	*2,172*	*1,496*	*676*	*2,005*	*1,573*	*432*	*1,278*	*775*	*503*
(i) British Territory ...	**378**	**238**	**140**	**310**	**225**	**85**	**468**	**344**	**124**	**368**	**301**	**67**	**606**	**514**	**92**	**327**	**245**	**82**
Ajmer-Marwara	1	...	1	...	...	...	2	2	...	...	...	...	...	...	...	...	...	...
Assam	34	19	15	6	4	2	21	17	4	9	3	3	12	5	7	27	20	7
Bombay (*including* Aden) ...	75	23	52	65	48	17	96	59	37	66	45	21	204	178	26	37	26	11
Burma	2	1	1	9	5	4	1	1	...	5	3	2	3	1	2	5	1	4
Delhi	4	3	1	4	3	1	41	28	13	2	1	1	...	...	...	6	5	1
N.-W. F. Province ...	15	12	3	32	18	14	21	20	1	...	...	...	53	53	...	6	6	...
Punjab	242	175	67	194	147	47	286	217	69	286	249	37	334	277	57	246	187	59
(ii) Indian States ...	**847**	**472**	**375**	**785**	**437**	**348**	**1,000**	**551**	**449**	**1,804**	**1,195**	**609**	**1,399**	**1,059**	**340**	**951**	**530**	**421**
Bombay States	...	...	...	2	2	...	1	1	...	...	...	...	...	...	...	...	...	...
Central India (*Agency*) ...	6	4	2	6	1	5	6	3	3	2	2	...	3	3	...	...	...	...
Gwalior State	...	...	...	2	...	2	11	8	3	44	34	10	6	6	...	3	...	3
Hyderabad State	...	...	...	...	...	...	5	4	1	...	...	...	3	1	2	...	...	...
Mysore State	8	3	5	6	5	1	2	2	...	3	2	1	6	4	2	2	1	1
Punjab States	...	...	...	5	5	...	...	...	...	...	...	...	...	...	...	2	2	...
Rajputana (*Agency*) ...	812	451	361	757	421	336	974	532	443	1,752	1,155	597	1,390	1,044	336	942	526	416
Other Indian States ...	21	14	7	7	3	4	1	1	...	3	2	1	1	1	...	2	1	1
(d) INDIA, *unspecified* ...	*10*	*5*	*5*	*27*	*13*	*14*	...	...	...	...	...	...	...	...	...	...	...	...
B.—OTHER ASIATIC COUNTRIES.	*9,420*	*2,071*	*7,349*	*8,989*	*1,611*	*6,678*	*265*	*228*	*37*	*1,479*	*530*	*949*	*2,140*	*1,303*	*837*	*41*	*39*	*2*
Within British Dominions ...	2	2	...	...	...	...	...	...	...	...	...	...	...	...	...	...	...	...
Outside British Dominions ...	**9,418**	2,069	7,349	**8,289**	1,611	6,678	**265**	238	37	**1,479**	530	949	**2,140**	1,303	837	**41**	39	2
Afghanistan	*22*	*22*	...	*21*	*21*	...	*58*	*53*	...	*70*	*70*	...	*372*	*371*	*1*	*17*	*17*	...
China	...	...	...	...	...	...	*4*	*3*	*1*	...	...	...	...	...	...	*5*	*3*	*2*
Nepal	*9,394*	*2,045*	*7,349*	*8,268*	*1,590*	*6,678*	*207*	*171*	*36*	*1,405*	*459*	*946*	*1,759*	*926*	*833*	*17*	*17*	...
Elsewhere	*2*	*2*	...	...	...	...	*1*	*1*	...	*4*	*1*	*3*	*9*	*6*	*3*	*2*	*2*	...
C.—EUROPE	*201*	*168*	*33*	*83*	*49*	*34*	*190*	*107*	*83*	*64*	*43*	*21*	*67*	*33*	*34*	*147*	*69*	*78*
Within British Dominions ...	**199**	167	32	**83**	49	34	**184**	106	78	**61**	41	20	**63**	33	30	**102**	53	49
United Kingdom and Ireland	*199*	*167*	*32*	*83*	*49*	*34*	*184*	*106*	*78*	*61*	*41*	*20*	*60*	*30*	*30*	*102*	*53*	*49*
Elsewhere	...	...	...	...	...	...	...	...	...	...	...	...	*3*	*3*	...	...	...	...
Outside British Dominions ...	2	1	1	...	...	...	6	1	5	3	2	1	4	...	4	45	16	29
D.—AFRICA	*5*	*1*	*4*	*2*	*2*	...	...	...	...	...	...	...	...	...	...	...	...	...
Within British Dominions ...	1	1	...	...	...	...	...	...	...	...	...	...	...	...	...	...	...	...
Outside British Dominions ...	...	...	...	1	1	...	...	...	...	...	...	...	...	...	...	...	...	...
Africa, *unspecified* ...	4	...	4	1	1	...	...	...	...	...	...	...	...	...	...	...	...	...
E.—AMERICA	*3*	*1*	*2*	*2*	...	*2*	*8*	...	*8*	*11*	*6*	*5*	...	...	...	*22*	*10*	*12*
Within British Dominions ...	...	...	...	...	...	...	...	...	...	2	...	2	...	...	...	...	...	...
Canada	...	...	...	...	...	...	...	...	...	*2*	...	*2*	...	...	...	...	...	...
Outside British Dominions ...	3	1	3	2	...	3	8	...	8	9	6	3	...	...	...	22	10	12
United States	*3*	*1*	*2*	*2*	...	*2*	*8*	...	*8*	*9*	*6*	*3*	...	...	...	*22*	*10*	*12*
F.—AUSTRALASIA ...	*2*	...	*2*	...	...	...	*6*	...	*6*	...	...	...	...	...	...	*2*	*1*	*1*
Within British Dominions ...	2	...	2	...	...	...	6	...	6	...	...	...	...	...	...	2	1	1
H.—BIRTHPLACE NOT RETURNED.	...	...	...	...	...	...	...	...	...	*56*	*27*	*29*	...	...	...	...	...	...

TABLE VI—*continued.*

BIRTHPLACE. PART I—DISTRICTS AND STATES.

BORN IN	ENUMERATED IN																	
	CUTTACK			BALASORE			ANGUL			PURI			SAMBALPUR			HAZARIBAGH		
	Persons	Males	Females	Persons	Males	Females	Persons	Males	Females	Persons	Males	Females	Persons	Males	Females	Persons	Males	Females
1	38	39	40	41	42	43	44	45	46	47	48	49	50	51	52	53	54	55
TOTAL POPULATION ..	*2,176,707*	*1,028,134*	*1,148,573*	*990,600*	*480,518*	*510,082*	*222,736*	*108,925*	*113,811*	*1,035,154*	*500,214*	*534,940*	*880,945*	*431,460*	*449,485*	*1,517,357*	*751,956*	*765,401*
A.—INDIA	*2,176,524*	*1,027,994*	*1,148,530*	*990,488*	*480,427*	*510,061*	*222,721*	*108,919*	*113,802*	*1,035,017*	*500,113*	*534,904*	*880,829*	*431,370*	*449,459*	*1,516,646*	*751,464*	*765,182*
I. BIHAR AND ORISSA	*2,170,136*	*1,024,258*	*1,145,878*	*977,144*	*474,179*	*502,965*	*218,559*	*107,966*	*110,593*	*1,021,763*	*493,486*	*528,277*	*859,370*	*422,188*	*437,182*	*1,491,834*	*737,508*	*754,326*
(a) British Territory	*2,154,248*	*1,019,752*	*1,134,496*	*965,099*	*470,331*	*494,768*	*205,884*	*104,394*	*101,490*	*1,015,898*	*492,588*	*523,310*	*836,648*	*414,820*	*421,828*	*1,491,808*	*737,493*	*754,315*
PATNA DIVISION	240	154	86	188	146	42	16	8	8	187	133	54	176	96	80	14,575	6,735	7,840
Patna	87	60	27	61	49	12				91	56	35	50	17	33	1,043	680	363
Gaya	39	28	11	55	46	9	14	6	8	71	55	16	63	35	28	12,770	5,561	7,209
Shahabad	114	66	48	72	51	21	2	2		25	22	3	63	44	19	762	494	268
TIRHUT DIVISION	118	87	31	95	76	19	7	5	2	89	76	13	88	58	30	917	676	241
Saran	58	28	30	14	13	1	3	3		7	6	1	46	26	20	515	402	113
Champaran	3	2	1	30	15	15	4	2	2	27	23	4	4	3	1	91	64	27
Muzaffarpur	37	30	7	12	12		..	.		27	23	4	21	15	6	191	123	68
Darbhanga	20	17	3	39	36	3				28	24	4	17	14	3	190	87	33
BHAGALPUR DIVISION	74	54	20	34	28	6				74	49	25	71	51	20	7,447	2,914	4,533
Monghyr	13	11	2	20	19	1				44	26	18	35	24	11	3,591	1,579	2,012
Bhagalpur	41	24	17	6	5	1		..		23	18	5	20	15	5	280	153	127
Purnea	12	11	1	5	3	2				5	3	2		..	.	20	13	7
Santal Parganas	8	8	..	3	1	2			.	2	2		16	13	3	3,556	1,169	2,387
ORISSA DIVISION	2,152,262	1,018,560	1,133,702	964,724	470,036	494,688	205,815	104,340	101,475	1,015,384	492,230	523,154	835,764	414,299	421,465	1,509	913	596
Cuttack	2,132,135	1,014,319	1,117,816	10,853	3,782	7,071	1,057	730	327	16,804	5,273	11,531	1,421	952	469	94	66	28
Balasore	6,141	1,185	4,956	953,376	465,918	487,458	54	34	20	414	253	161	74	54	20	34	31	3
Angul	127	83	44	28	24	4	204,431	103,384	101,047	37	30	7	356	204	152	3	2	1
Puri	13,454	2,703	10,751	439	293	146	161	128	33	998,002	486,604	511,398	280	183	97	24	21	3
Sambalpur	405	270	135	29	20	9	112	64	48	127	70	57	833,633	402,906	430,727	1,354	793	561
CHOTA NAGPUR DIVISION	1,554	897	657	58	45	13	46	41	5	164	100	64	549	316	233	1,467,360	726,255	741,105
Hazaribagh	65	49	16	22	21	1	8	8		26	15	11	61	46	15	1,451,248	719,583	731,665
Ranchi	94	65	29	2	1	1	7	6	1	19	13	6	121	62	59	4,692	2,107	2,585
Palamau				1	1			...		2	1	1	8	4	4	1,551	764	787
Manbhum	61	52	9	16	11	5	13	13		64	44	20	110	36	74	7,806	2,676	5,130
Singhbhum	1,334	731	603	17	11	6	18	14	4	53	37	26	249	168	81	2,063	1,125	938
(b) Bihar and Orissa States.	*15,888*	*4,506*	*11,382*	*12,045*	*3,848*	*8,197*	*12,675*	*3,572*	*9,103*	*5,865*	*898*	*4,967*	*22,722*	*7,368*	*15,354*	*26*	*15*	*11*
Orissa States	15,887	4,506	11,381	12,044	3,847	8,197	12,675	3,572	9,103	5,858	896	4,962	22,711	7,365	15,346	13	10	3
Chota Nagpur States	1		1	1	1		...	...	.	7	2	5	11	3	8	13	5	8
II. OTHER PARTS OF INDIA.	*6,388*	*3,736*	*2,652*	*13,344*	*6,248*	*7,096*	*4,162*	*953*	*3,209*	*13,254*	*6,627*	*6,627*	*21,459*	*9,182*	*12,277*	*24,812*	*13,956*	*10,856*
(a) ADJACENT PROVINCES AND STATES.	*4,792*	*2,729*	*2,063*	*12,307*	*5,521*	*6,786*	*4,047*	*884*	*3,163*	*12,266*	*5,950*	*6,316*	*18,777*	*7,530*	*11,247*	*21,504*	*11,900*	*9,604*
(i) British Territory ..	4,780	2,717	2,063	12,299	5,518	6,781	4,047	884	3,163	12,258	5,944	6,314	13,669	6,155	7,514	21,503	11,899	9,604
Bengal ...	1,995	1,055	940	11,235	4,766	6,469	113	51	62	2,398	1,274	1,124	599	349	250	4,203	2,368	1,835
Central Provinces and Berar	113	55	58	56	35	21	7	5	2	1,185	622	563	11,472	4,894	6,578	14,966	8,054	6,912
Madras ...	2,386	1,398	988	684	424	260	3,914	815	3,099	8,088	3,593	4,495	692	352	340	355	249	106
United Provinces .	286	209	77	324	293	31	13	13	...	587	455	132	906	560	346	1,979	1,228	751
(ii) Indian States ...	12	12	...	8	3	5			...	8	6	2	5,108	1,375	3,733	1	1	
Bengal States . .	1	1	.	...	..	...			...	4	3	1					..	.
Central Provinces States	11	11	...	1	.	1		..		3	3	..	5,105	1,374	3,731	.	.	..
Madras States (*excluding* Cochin and Travancore)			...	7	3	4	.	...	.	1	..	1	3	1	2	1	1	..

(b) OTHER PROVINCES AND STATES	*1,596*	*1,007*	*589*	*1,036*	*726*	*310*	*115*	*69*	*46*	*983*	*677*	*311*	*2,682*	*1,652*	*1,030*	*3,986*	*3,039*	*1,947*
(i) **British Territory** ...	**739**	**496**	**243**	**427**	**272**	**155**	**101**	**57**	**44**	**342**	**215**	**127**	**1,163**	**769**	**394**	**1,673**	**1,029**	**644**
Ajmer-Merwara ...	1	1	.	6	8	...	...	..	..	2	1	1	..	...		5	5	..
Assam ...	36	22	14	5	5	...	40	19	31	45	31	14	35	23	12	56	38	18
Bombay (*including* Aden)	370	250	120	237	131	106	14	8	6	110	48	63	370	253	117	932	560	373
Burma ...	11	7	4		.				..	14	6	8	8	6	2	20	8	13
Delhi ...	5	4	1			..				9	8	1	22	16	6	23	11	13
N.-W. F. Province ...	2		2							27	22	5	5	4	1	25	19	6
Punjab ...	313	212	101	179	130	49	47	10	17	135	99	36	723	407	266	606	383	223
Other Provinces ...	1		1		.	.				...	..	...	...	...	.	6	5	1
(ii) **Indian States** .	**857**	**511**	**346**	**609**	**454**	**155**	**14**	**12**	**2**	**646**	**462**	**184**	**1,519**	**883**	**636**	**1,613**	**1,010**	**603**
Bombay States ...	87	87		59	29	30		..		42	36	6	124	94	30			
Central India (*Agency*) ...	7	2	5	5	5	...			.	179	145	34	122	62	60	233	207	26
Gwalior State ...	4	4			..	.			.	22	15	7	13	12	6	4	4	
Hyderabad State .	22	11	11	16	14	2			..	55	41	14	15	9	6	2	1	1
Mysore State ...	10	7	3	9	4	5		.	...	48	35	13	14	6	8	38	25	13
N.-W. F. Province (*Agencies and Tribal areas*)		..	..	31	31					..	.		..	...	.	.		.
Punjab States .	1	1		1		1			.	14	12	2	25	14	11	...		
Rajputana (*Agency*) .	695	382	313	475	350	125	14	13	2	273	169	104	1,192	680	512	1,326	768	558
Other Indian States .	31	17	14	13	11	2		...	...	13	9	4	9	6	3	10	5	5
(c) FRENCH AND PORTUGUESE SETTLEMENTS.	...	...	..	*1*	*1*			.	.	..	...		...	..	.	*5*		*5*
(d) INDIA, *unspecified*	.	...	...	...	...	.		..	..	..	...	.	...	...		*17*	*17*	.
B.—OTHER ASIATIC COUNTRIES.	*127*	*117*	*10*	*80*	*73*	*7*	*2*	...	*2*	*109*	*84*	*25*	*105*	*82*	*23*	*544*	*408*	*136*
Within British Dominions .	2	1	1	..		..			...	1	1	...	1	1	...	1	1	...
Outside British Dominions ..	125	116	9	80	73	7	2	..	2	108	83	25	104	81	23	543	407	136
Afghanistan .	73	73	...	42	42				.	28	27	1	60	51	9	65	65	..
China ..			.		..		2		2							1	...	1
Nepal .	52	43	9	38	31	7		..		78	55	23	39	28	11	471	336	135
Elsewhere .	...	...	..	...	..	...	.	.	.	2	1	1	5	2	3	6	6	
C.—EUROPE ..	*52*	*21*	*31*	*13*	*9*	*4*	*13*	*6*	*7*	*20*	*13*	*7*	*10*	*7*	*3*	*145*	*82*	*63*
Within British Dominions .	39	18	21	12	9	3	12	6	6	16	9	7	10	7	3	137	75	62
United Kingdom and Ireland	39	18	21	12	9	3	12	6	6	16	9	7	10	7	3	136	75	61
Elsewhere ...	...	...	..	...	...		...	...	.	..	...	...	..	...	.	*1*	..	*1*
Outside British Dominions ..	13	3	10	1		1	1		1	4	4	...	..	...	...	6	5	1
Europe, *unspecified* .	...	...	..	...			.		...	...	...	...	..	..	...	2	2	.
D.—AFRICA ...	*1*	—	*1*	*1*	*1*		.	...	...	*3*	*2*	*1*	*1*	*1*	..	*4*	*2*	*2*
Within British Dominions .	..				...	..	.	.	...	1	...	1	...	...	...	..	...	...
Africa, *unspecified* ..	1	.	1	1	1	...	..	...	...	2	2	...	1	1	...	4	2	2
E.—AMERICA ..	*3*	*2*	*1*	*18*	*8*	*10*	..	...	...	*4*	*2*	*2*	...	..	.	*3*	..	*3*
Outside British Dominions .	3	2	1	5	4	1	...	...	...	4	2	2		.	...	3	..	3
United States ..	3	2	1	5	4	1	..	...	.	4	2	2	...	...	..	3	...	3
America, *unspecified* ..	...	...		13	4	9	...	..	...	...	...	..	...	...	.	..	...	...
F.—AUSTRALASIA ...	...		.	...	...	...	...	...	...	*1*	.	*1*		.	..	...	...	...
Within British Dominions .	...	...	...	.	...	..	..	...	...	1	...	1	...	...	...	...	...	...
H.—BIRTHPLACE NOT RETURNED.	...	...	...	...	...	...	...	...	...	...	...	...	...	...	...	*15*	...	*15*

TABLE VI—*continued.*

BIRTHPLACE. PART I—DISTRICTS AND STATES.

BORN IN	Enumerated in Ranchi: Persons	Males	Females	Palamau: Persons	Males	Females	Manbhum: Persons	Males	Females
1	56	57	58	59	60	61	62	63	64
TOTAL POPULATION	*1,567,149*	*777,063*	*790,086*	*818,736*	*409,778*	*408,958*	*1,810,890*	*940,009*	*870,881*
A.—INDIA	*1,566,558*	*776,728*	*789,830*	*818,632*	*409,706*	*408,926*	*1,809,019*	*938,595*	*870,424*
I. BIHAR AND ORISSA	*1,558,318*	*772,357*	*785,961*	*813,045*	*406,847*	*406,198*	*1,744,571*	*901,252*	*843,319*
(a) British Territory	*1,557,453*	*772,073*	*785,382*	*813,039*	*406,843*	*406,196*	*1,744,596*	*901,292*	*843,304*
PATNA DIVISION	3,655	2,415	1,240	13,128	6,069	7,059	27,407	19,372	8,035
Patna	436	309	127	253	177	76	2,736	1,862	874
Gaya	2,487	1,602	885	9,983	4,437	5,546	20,882	14,740	6,183
Shahabad	732	504	228	2,892	1,455	1,437	3,789	2,761	1,028
TIRHUT DIVISION	307	710	97	279	212	67	2,363	1,734	629
Saran	415	371	44	181	138	43	1,791	1,318	473
Champaran	41	35	6	15	11	4	51	29	22
Muzaffarpur	221	196	25	41	35	6	323	228	95
Darbhanga	130	108	22	42	28	14	198	159	39
BHAGALPUR DIVISION	474	360	114	99	64	35	32,742	20,979	11,763
Monghyr	107	64	43	61	47	14	24,227	16,114	8,113
Bhagalpur	253	227	26	15	9	6	1,543	1,268	275
Purnea	15	8	7	13	2	11	69	52	17
Santal Parganas	99	61	38	10	6	4	6,933	3,545	3,358
ORISSA DIVISION	1,142	574	568	32	19	13	1,120	869	251
Cuttack	813	391	422	11	9	2	356	212	114
Balasore	12	9	3		...	..	56	32	24
Angul	6	1	5		.		1	1	..
Puri	29	21	8	4	1	3	94	70	24
Sambalpur	282	152	130	17	9	8	613	524	89
CHOTA NAGPUR DIVISION	1,551,377	768,014	783,363	799,501	400,479	399,022	1,680,894	858,268	822,626
Hazaribagh	4,810	1,695	3,115	2,701	1,030	1,671	32,535	20,300	12,235
Ranchi	1,538,466	763,937	774,529	2,227	959	1,268	4,961	1,524	3,437
Palamau	1,979	838	1,141	794,490	398,441	396,049	520	360	160
Manbhum	4,611	1,083	3,528	70	42	28	1,639,976	834,831	805,145
Singhbhum	1,511	461	1,050	13	7	6	2,902	1,253	1,649
(b) Bihar and Orissa States.	*863*	*284*	*579*	*6*	*4*	*2*	*45*	*30*	*15*
Orissa States	863	284	579	6	4	2	44	30	14
Chota Nagpur States	.	...	...	...		...	1	...	1
II. OTHER PARTS OF INDIA.	*8,240*	*4,371*	*3,869*	*5,387*	*2,859*	*2,728*	*64,448*	*37,343*	*27,105*
(a) ADJACENT PROVINCES AND STATES.	*6,951*	*3,658*	*3,293*	*5,152*	*2,604*	*2,548*	*57,970*	*32,907*	*25,063*
(i) British Territory	6,949	3,657	3,292	5,151	2,603	2,548	57,966	32,904	25,062
Bengal	3,535	1,905	1,630	514	312	202	33,244	16,914	16,330
Central Provinces and Berar	2,199	791	1,408	2,328	1,087	1,241	13,418	7,813	5,605
Madras	90	53	37	2	2	..	1,442	788	654
United Provinces	1,125	908	217	2,307	1,202	1,105	9,862	7,389	2,473
(ii) Indian States	2	1	1	1	1	..	4	3	1
Bengal States	...	...	...	.		.	...	...	...
Central Provinces States	...	.	..			...	1	...	1
Madras States (*including* Cochin *and* Travancore).	2	1	1	1	1	...	3	3	...
United Provinces States	...	.	...	..	...	...	...	...	...

BORN IN	Enumerated in Singhbhum: Persons	Males	Females	Orissa States: Persons	Males	Females	Chota Nagpur States: Persons	Males	Females
1	65	66	67	68	69	70	71	72	73
TOTAL POPULATION	*929,802*	*469,421*	*460,381*	*4,465,385*	*2,196,691*	*2,268,694*	*186,622*	*91,731*	*94,891*
A.—INDIA	*927,043*	*467,263*	*459,780*	*4,465,098*	*2,196,471*	*2,268,627*	*186,576*	*91,694*	*94,882*
I. BIHAR AND ORISSA	*861,196*	*428,368*	*432,828*	*4,415,918*	*2,173,298*	*2,242,620*	*185,154*	*90,809*	*94,345*
(a) British Territory	*851,506*	*424,259*	*427,247*	*173,630*	*69,417*	*104,213*	*9,679*	*3,513*	*6,166*
PATNA DIVISION	5,698	4,010	1,688	2,504	1,643	861	436	351	85
Patna	1,294	893	401	413	294	119	44	38	16
Gaya	2,992	2,060	932	1,903	1,212	691	320	261	59
Shahabad	1,412	1,057	355	188	167	21	72	62	10
TIRHUT DIVISION	1,997	1,579	418	220	157	63	60	38	22
Saran	1,119	897	222	21	17	4	6	5	1
Champaran	137	103	34	69	38	31	2	2	...
Muzaffarpur	303	248	55	63	39	24	19	14	5
Darbhanga	438	331	107	67	63	4	33	17	16
BHAGALPUR DIVISION	1,905	1,320	585	466	184	282	66	48	18
Monghyr	1,357	889	468	386	136	250	52	39	13
Bhagalpur	288	217	71	42	25	17	13	9	4
Purnea	14	7	7	32	18	14	1	...	1
Santal Parganas	246	207	39	4	3	1	..	...	...
ORISSA DIVISION	9,047	6,179	2,868	117,495	42,966	74,529	377	219	158
Cuttack	4,069	3,273	796	25,050	9,840	15,210	144	103	41
Balasore	1,050	407	643	18,302	5,148	13,154	51	18	33
Angul	17	14	3	16,486	5,794	10,692	2	1	1
Puri	665	519	146	13,562	3,236	10,326	41	33	8
Sambalpur	3,306	1,966	1,340	44,095	18,048	26,047	139	61	78
CHOTA NAGPUR DIVISION	832,859	411,171	421,688	52,945	24,467	28,478	8,740	2,857	5,883
Hazaribagh	1,169	783	386	785	519	266	55	41	14
Ranchi	8,626	3,764	4,862	18,296	8,666	9,630	748	201	547
Palamau	123	92	31	19	14	5	2	2	..
Manbhum	4,197	1,861	2,336	1,500	725	775	1,372	469	903
Singhbhum	818,744	404,571	414,173	32,345	14,543	17,802	6,563	2,144	4,419
(b) Bihar and Orissa States.	*9,690*	*4,109*	*5,581*	*4,242,288*	*2,103,881*	*2,138,407*	*175,475*	*87,296*	*88,179*
Orissa States	9,389	3,954	5,435	4,241,793	2,103,660	2,138,133	983	342	641
Chota Nagpur States	301	155	146	495	221	274	174,492	86,954	87,538
II. OTHER PARTS OF INDIA.	*65,847*	*38,895*	*26,952*	*49,180*	*23,173*	*26,007*	*1,422*	*885*	*537*
(a) ADJACENT PROVINCES AND STATES.	*52,684*	*29,812*	*22,872*	*44,295*	*20,072*	*24,223*	*1,068*	*654*	*414*
(i) British Territory	52,669	29,802	22,867	37,382	17,485	19,897	1,063	649	414
Bengal	19,866	10,690	9,176	7,606	3,330	4,276	502	320	182
Central Provinces and Berar	16,395	8,470	7,925	18,165	9,007	9,158	185	103	82
Madras	7,995	4,575	3,420	10,271	4,258	6,013	180	101	79
United Provinces	8,413	6,067	2,346	1,340	890	450	196	125	71
(ii) Indian States	15	10	5	6,913	2,587	4,326	5	5	..
Bengal States	.	.	...	1	1	...		...	...
Central Provinces States	7	4	3	2,611	933	1,678	5	5	...
Madras States (*including* Cochin *and* Travancore).	6	6	...	4,291	1,644	2,647	...	...	...
United Provinces States	2	...	2	10	9	1	...	...	...

(b) OTHER PROVINCES AND STATES.	*1,234*	*708*	*576*	*435*	*255*	*180*	*6,246*	*4,310*	*1,936*	*12,122*	*8,748*	*3,374*	*4,885*	*3,101*	*1,784*	*354*	*231*	*123*
(i) **British Territory** ...	590	425	185	145	100	45	2,955	2,089	866	9,404	6,822	2,582	2,673	1,821	852	201	138	63
Ajmer-Marwara ...	...	...	...	...	...	...	93	65	28	...	...	..	2	1	1	...	...	...
Assam ...	186	103	83	10	7	3	154	106	40	900	780	130	226	136	90	4	3	1
Bombay (*including* Aden) ...	248	210	88	54	32	23	1,442	971	471	1,284	889	395	670	509	161	66	44	22
Burma ...	11	3	9	...	...	..	18	17	1	75	6	69	45	24	21	...	...	...
Delhi ...	4	4	...	...	...	..	6	2	4	45	35	10	49	44	5	1	...	1
N.-W. F. Province ...	...	...	...	2	2	.	...	...	...	426	421	5	49	29	11	2	1	1
Punjab ...	140	108	35	79	50	20	1,242	929	313	6,674	4,091	1,983	1,637	1,074	563	128	90	38
Other Provinces ...	1	1	...	...	...	..	...	...	...	...	...	..	4	4	...	...	...	..
(ii) **Indian States** ...	694	283	411	290	155	135	3,291	2,221	1,070	2,718	1,926	792	2,212	1,280	932	153	93	60
Bombay States ...	...	...	..	...	...	...	..	...	..	...	...	...	81	61	20	9	8	1
Central India (*Agency*) ...	11	7	4	42	1	41	30	12	18	335	217	148	151	74	77	22	14	8
Gwalior States ...	1	...	1	1	1	...	1	1	...	2	3	...	11	8	3	...	...	...
Hyderabad States ...	6	4	2	..	...	...	11	4	7	215	121	94	32	26	6	5	3	2
Mysore States ...	2	...	2	...	..	...	20	20	...	84	38	46	15	7	8	16	10	6
N.-W. F. Province (*Agencies and Tribal areas*).	4	1	3	...	...	...	440	405	35	...	...	...	...	...	...	...	...	...
Punjab States ...	...	...	...	23	20	3	...	...	...	15	8	7	187	121	66	3	2	1
Rajputana (*Agency*) ...	666	267	399	222	133	90	2,777	1,772	1,005	1,987	1,503	484	1,676	943	733	93	53	40
Other Indian States ...	4	4	...	2	1	1	12	7	5	50	37	13	59	40	19	5	3	2
(c) FRENCH AND PORTUGUESE SETTLEMENTS.	*5*	*5*	...	...	...	...	*232*	*126*	*106*	*34*	*30*	*4*	..	...	...	...	...	...
(d) INDIA, *unspecified* ...	...	...	...	...	...	...	...	...	.	*1,007*	*305*	*702*	...	...	...	...	...	...
B.—OTHER ASIATIC COUNTRIES.	*260*	*155*	*105*	*75*	*52*	*23*	*1,075*	*790*	*285*	*1,527*	*1,287*	*240*	*212*	*169*	*43*	*36*	*30*	*6*
Within British Dominions ...	3	1	2	...	...	...	3	2	1	5	2	3	2	2	...	...	...	...
Outside British Dominions ...	256	153	103	75	52	23	1,072	788	284	1,522	1,385	237	210	167	43	36	30	6
Afghanistan ...	*31*	*26*	*5*	*23*	*23*	...	*147*	*143*	*4*	*133*	*136*	*2*	*54*	*49*	*5*	*7*	*7*	...
China ...	*6*	*5*	*1*	*1*	*1*	...	*2*	*2*	...	.	...	...	*1*	...	*1*	...	...	...
Nepal ...	*212*	*120*	*92*	*46*	*27*	*19*	*852*	*596*	*256*	*1,370*	*1,137*	*233*	*147*	*112*	*35*	*29*	*23*	*6*
Elsewhere ...	*7*	*3*	*5*	*5*	*1*	*4*	*71*	*47*	*24*	*14*	*12*	*3*	*8*	*6*	*2*	...	...	...
Asia, *unspecified* ...	1	1	...	...	...	...	...	...	...	...	...	...	...	...	...	...	...	...
C.—EUROPE ...	*307*	*163*	*144*	*26*	*17*	*9*	*345*	*216*	*129*	*344*	*227*	*117*	*59*	*47*	*22*	*6*	*3*	*3*
Within British Dominions ...	189	93	97	24	15	9	328	204	124	324	209	115	42	26	16	6	3	3
United Kingdom and Ireland	*187*	*90*	*97*	*24*	*15*	*9*	*328*	*204*	*124*	*324*	*209*	*115*	*42*	*26*	*16*	*6*	*3*	*3*
Elsewhere ...	*2*	*2*	...	...	...	...	...	..	...	...	...	...	...	...	...	...	...	...
Outside British Dominions ...	118	71	47	2	2	...	17	12	5	17	15	2	27	21	6	...	...	...
Europe, *unspecified* ...	...	...	...	...	...	...	...	...	...	3	3	...	...	...	...	...	...	...
D.—AFRICA *unspecified* ...	*2*	*2*	...	*2*	*2*	...	...	...	...	*6*	*6*	...	*2*	*1*	*1*	...	...	...
E.—AMERICA ...	*16*	*12*	*4*	*1*	*1*	...	*8*	*8*	...	*80*	*44*	*36*	*1*	...	*1*	*3*	*3*	...
Within British Dominions ...	1	1	..	...	...	...	...	...	...	...	...	...	...	...	...	...	...	...
Canada ...	*1*	*1*	...	...	...	..	...	...	...	...	...	...	...	...	...	...	...	...
Outside British Dominions ...	15	11	4	1	1	...	8	8	...	80	44	36	1	...	1	3	3	...
United States ...	*14*	*11*	*3*	...	...	...	*8*	*8*	...	*80*	*44*	*36*	*1*	...	*1*	*3*	*3*	...
Elsewhere ...	*1*	...	*1*	*1*	*1*	...	...	...	...	...	...	...	...	...		...	...	...
F.—AUSTRALASIA ..	*6*	*3*	*3*	...	...	...	*1*	*1*	...	*1*	...	*1*	*3*	*3*	...	*1*	*1*	...
Within British Dominions ..	5	3	2	...	...	..	1	1	...	1	...	1	3	3	...	1	1	...
Outside British Dominions ...	1	...	1	...	...	...	...	...	...	...	...	...	...	...	...	...	...	...
H.—BIRTHPLACE NOT RETURNED.	...	...	...	...	...	...	*442*	*399*	*43*	*801*	*594*	*207*	...	...	..	...	...	...

TABLE VI—*concluded.*

BIRTHPLACE — PART II.—CITIES.

BORN IN	TOTAL.			ENUMERATED IN — Patna City.			Gaya City.			Bhagalpur City.			Jamshedpur City.		
	Persons	Males.	Females	Persons	Males	Females.	Persons.	Males	Females	Persons	Males.	Females	Persons.	Males	Females.
1	2	3	4	5	6	7	8	9	10	11	12	13	14	15	16
TOTAL CITY POPULATION	*415,280*	*240,868*	*174,412*	*159,690*	*92,238*	*67,452*	*88,005*	*50,625*	*37,380*	*83,847*	*46,868*	*36,979*	*83,738*	*51,137*	*32,601*
A.—INDIA	*412,916*	*239,205*	*173,711*	*159,909*	*91,924*	*67,985*	*87,837*	*50,511*	*37,326*	*83,764*	*46,809*	*36,955*	*82,106*	*49,961*	*32,145*
I. BIHAR AND ORISSA	*353,603*	*202,391*	*151,212*	*150,240*	*86,580*	*63,660*	*84,659*	*48,535*	*36,124*	*80,606*	*44,772*	*35,834*	*38,098*	*22,504*	*15,594*
(a) British Territory	*352,756*	*201,907*	*150,849*	*150,230*	*86,572*	*63,658*	*84,645*	*48,532*	*36,113*	*80,606*	*44,772*	*35,834*	*37,275*	*22,031*	*15,244*
PATNA DIVISION	224 179	128,133	96,046	136,969	77,710	59,259	82 652	47,050	35,602	1,253	988	265	3,305	2,385	920
Patna ..	132 361	74,624	57,737	128 919	72,199	56,720	2,038	1,426	612	625	461	164	779	538	241
Gaya ..	86 368	49 419	36,949	4 875	3 254	1,621	79,736	44,929	34,807	197	141	56	1,560	1,095	465
Shahabad	5,450	4,090	1,360	3,175	2,257	918	878	695	183	431	386	45	966	752	214
TIRHUT DIVISION	12,554	9,005	3,549	8,594	5,813	2,781	745	620	125	1,692	1,389	303	1,523	1,183	340
Saran	4 423	3,266	1,157	2 985	2 129	856	358	303	55	284	210	74	786	624	162
Champaran	889	768	121	449	301	148	35	31	4	279	272	7	126	94	32
Muzaffarpur	4 783	3 226	1,557	3,928	2 481	1 447	183	151	32	416	364	52	256	210	46
Darbhanga	2 459	1 815	644	1,232	882	350	169	135	34	703	543	160	355	255	100
BHAGALPUR DIVISION	81,975	45,121	36,854	2,719	1,703	1,016	580	395	185	77,146	41,966	35,180	1,530	1,057	473
Monghyr	4 799	3 216	1 583	1,443	906	537	444	308	136	1,822	1 304	518	1,090	608	392
Bhagalpur ..	74 743	39 974	34 769	861	519	342	76	46	30	73,582	39 240	34 342	224	169	55
Purnea	629	485	144	177	126	51	22	13	9	422	341	81	8	5	3
Santal Parganas	1 804	1 446	358	238	152	86	38	28	10	1,320	1,081	239	208	185	23
ORISSA DIVISION	6,278	4,753	1,525	597	421	176	65	47	18	206	173	33	5,410	4,112	1,298
Cuttack	3 798	3,095	703	364	274	90	37	26	11	99	88	11	3,298	2,710	588
Balasore	294	236	58	88	55	33	11	11		10	7	3	185	160	25
Angul	30	25	5	6	2	4	2	2		17	17		5	4	1
Puri	573	450	123	95	61	34	4	4		54	36	18	420	349	71
Sambalpur	1,583	947	636	44	29	15	11	4	7	26	25	1	1,502	889	613
CHOTA NAGPUR DIVISION	27,770	14,895	12 875	1 351	925	426	603	420	183	369	256	53	25,507	13,294	12,213
Hazaribagh ...	1 245	865	380	224	157	67	245	172	73	63	54	9	713	482	231
Ranchi	2 562	1,520	1 042	731	480	251	44	24	20	121	84	37	1,666	932	734
Palamau	431	315	116	153	106	47	213	153	60	5	5		60	51	9
Manbhum	2 456	1,354	1,102	201	145	56	93	69	24	94	90	4	2,068	1,050	1,018
Singhbhum	21,076	10,841	10,235	42	37	5	8	2	6	26	23	3	21,000	10,779	10,221
(b) Bihar and Orissa States	*847*	*484*	*363*	*10*	*8*	*2*	*14*	*3*	*11*	..		..	*833*	*473*	*350*
Orissa States	590	342	248	6	5	1	4		4				580	337	243
Chota Nagpur States	257	142	115	4	3	1	10	3	7	..			253	136	107
II. OTHER PARTS OF INDIA	*59,313*	*36,814*	*22,499*	*8,969*	*5,344*	*3,625*	*3,178*	*1,976*	*1,202*	*3,158*	*2,037*	*1,121*	*44,008*	*27,457*	*16,551*
(a) ADJACENT PROVINCES AND STATES	*47,299*	*28,331*	*18,968*	*7,691*	*4,611*	*3,080*	*2,413*	*1,490*	*923*	*2,270*	*1,390*	*880*	*34,925*	*20,840*	*14,085*
(i) British Territory	47,285	28,318	18 967	7 688	4 608	3,080	2 409	1,486	923	2 270	1 390	880	34,918	20,834	14,084
Bengal	16,977	10 460	6 517	4,411	2 531	1,880	973	582	391	1,762	993	769	9,831	6,354	3,477
Central Provinces and Berar	12 555	6 400	6 155	54	21	33	61	41	20	6	5	1	12,434	6,333	6,101
Madras ...	6,593	3 619	2,974	70	34	36	17	7	10	8	6	2	6,498	3,572	2,926
United Provinces ..	11,160	7,839	3,321	3,153	2,022	1,131	1,358	856	502	494	386	108	6,155	4,575	1,580
(ii) Indian States ..	14	13	1	3	3	..	4	4	..	..	...	..	7	6	1
Central Provinces States	1		1			...				...		...	1	...	1
Madras States (*including* Cochin *and* Travancore)	13	13	..	3	3	...	4	4	..	...	...	...	6	6	...

(b) OTHER PROVINCES AND STATES.	*11,773*	*8,372*	*3,409*	*1,368*	*723*	*545*	*764*	*486*	*278*	*588*	*647*	*241*	*8,853*	*6,515*	*2,338*
(i) **British Territory** ...	8,752	6,325	2,427	664	419	245	384	268	116	193	169	24	7,511	5,469	2,042
Ajmer-Marwara	3	2	1	3	2	1	...	...	...	...	...	...	...	...	...
Assam	808	668	140	94	59	35	12	7	5	2	2	...	700	600	100
Baluchistan	6	2	4	3	1	2	3	1	2	...	...	...	...	...	...
Bombay (*including* Aden) ...	1,290	905	385	97	47	50	192	138	54	20	19	1	981	701	280
Burma	38	9	29	12	4	8	5	...	5	5	3	2	16	2	14
Delhi	76	50	26	39	28	11	12	6	6	2	1	1	23	15	8
N.-W. F. Province	375	367	8	13	9	4	3	...	3	...	...	...	359	358	1
Punjab	6,156	4,322	1,834	403	269	134	157	116	41	164	144	20	5,432	3,793	1,639
(ii) **Indian States**	3,021	2,046	975	604	304	300	380	218	162	695	478	217	1,342	1,046	296
Baroda State	1	...	1	1	...	1	...	...	...	...	...	...	...	...	...
Central India (*Agency*) ...	299	141	158	116	30	86	21	...	21	...	...	...	162	111	51
Gwalior State	47	...	47	...	...	...	47	...	47	...	...	...	...	...	...
Hyderabad State	213	110	103	53	16	37	4	4	...	...	...	...	156	90	66
Kashmir State	14	13	1	7	7	...	...	...	...	2	1	1	5	5	...
Mysore State	114	90	24	15	8	7	84	73	11	1	1	...	14	8	6
Punjab States	2	...	2	2	...	2	...	...	...	...	...	...	...	...	...
Rajputana (*Agency*)	2,331	1,692	639	410	243	167	224	141	83	692	476	216	1,005	833	173
(c) FRENCH AND PORTUGUESE SETTLEMENTS.	*40*	*35*	*5*	*5*	*5*	...	*1*	...	*1*	...	...	...	*34*	*30*	*4*
(d) INDIA, *unspecified* ...	*201*	*77*	*124*	*5*	*5*	...	...	...	...	...	...		*196*	*72*	*124*
B.—OTHER ASIATIC COUNTRIES.	*948*	*722*	*226*	*306*	*233*	*73*	*107*	*78*	*29*	*52*	*41*	*11*	*483*	*370*	*113*
Within British Dominions ...	3	1	2	...	...	...	...	...	...	...	...	...	3	1	2
Ceylon	*3*	*1*	*2*	...	...	...	...	...	...	...	...	...	*3*	*1*	*2*
Outside British Dominions ...	943	719	224	304	231	73	107	78	29	52	41	11	480	369	111
Afghanistan	*110*	*107*	*3*	*63*	*60*	*3*	*30*	*30*	...	*14*	*14*	...	*3*	*3*	...
China	*5*	*4*	*1*	*4*	*3*	*1*	*1*	*1*	...	...	...	...	...	...	...
Nepal	*808*	*596*	*212*	*232*	*167*	*65*	*76*	*47*	*29*	*36*	*27*	*9*	*464*	*355*	*109*
Elsewhere	*20*	*12*	*8*	*5*	*1*	*4*	...	...	...	*2*	...	*2*	*13*	*11*	*2*
Asia, *unspecified*	2	2	...	2	2	...	...	...	...	...	...	...	...	...	...
C.—EUROPE	*516*	*292*	*224*	*167*	*78*	*89*	*55*	*33*	*22*	*27*	*14*	*13*	*267*	*167*	*100*
Within British Dominions ...	468	277	191	138	77	61	50	31	19	26	13	13	254	156	98
United Kingdom and Ireland ...	*468*	*277*	*191*	*138*	*77*	*61*	*50*	*31*	*19*	*26*	*13*	*13*	*254*	*156*	*98*
Outside British Dominions ...	48	15	33	29	1	28	5	2	3	1	1	...	13	11	2
D.—AFRICA	*6*	*3*	*3*	*4*	*1*	*3*	*1*	*1*	...	...	...	...	*1*	*1*	...
Within British Dominions ...	3	...	3	3	...	3	...	...	...	...	...	...	...	...	...
British East Africa ...	*2*	...	*2*	*2*	...	*2*	...	...	...	...	...	...	...	...	...
Mauritius	*1*	...	*1*	*1*	...	*1*	...	...	...	...	...	...	...	...	...
Africa, *unspecified*	3	3	...	1	1	...	1	1	...	...	...	...	1	1	...
E.—AMERICA	*88*	*49*	*39*	*1*	*1*	...	*3*	...	*3*	*4*	*4*	...	*80*	*44*	*36*
Outside British Dominions ...	88	49	39	1	1	...	3	...	3	4	4	...	80	44	36
United States	*88*	*49*	*39*	*1*	*1*	...	*3*	...	*3*	*4*	*4*	...	*80*	*44*	*36*
F.—AUSTRALASIA	*3*	*1*	*2*	*3*	*1*	*2*	...	...	...	...	...	...	...	...	...
Australasia, *unspecified* ...	3	1	2	3	1	2	...	...	...	...	...	...	...	...	...
G.—BORN AT SEA	*1*	*1*	...	...	...	...	*1*	*1*	...	...	...	...	...	...	...
H.—BIRTHPLACE NOT RETURNED.	*802*	*595*	*207*	...	...	...	*1*	*1*	...	...	...	...	*801*	*594*	*207*

TABLE VII.

AGE, SEX AND CIVIL CONDITION.

This table shows the distribution of the population by age, sex and civil condition. It is divided into three parts. Part I shows the distribution, for the whole province (including the Feudatory States), of the total population and of each religion. Part II shows the distribution, for each district and for the states, of the total population and of the (numerically) most important religions. Part III gives similar information for cities. In Parts II and III the age statistics are given in less detail than in the provincial summary.

2. The age-groups are shown as 5—10, 10—15 and so on. The second figure of each group denotes the age *not yet reached*. For instance the group 5—10 includes all persons aged 5, 6, 7, 8 or 9 years, but not those aged 10. The age of each person was reckoned from the *nearest* birthday, and not (as in 1921) from the number of *completed* years.

3. Divorced persons have been entered as "widowed". Persons recognized by custom as married have been shown as such, even though they have not gone through any formal ceremony.

TABLE VII.

Age, Sex and Civil Condition. **Part I—Provincial Summary.**

Age.	Population.			Unmarried.			Married.			Widowed.		
	Persons.	Males.	Females.	Persons.	Males.	Females.	Persons.	Males.	Females.	Persons.	Males.	Females.
1	2	3	4	5	6	7	8	9	10	11	12	13
ALL RELIGIONS.	*42,329,583*	*21,082,560*	*21,247,023*	*15,492,620*	*8,864,449*	*6,628,171*	*22,332,909*	*11,145,652*	*11,187,257*	*4,504,054*	*1,072,459*	*3,431,595*
0—1 ...	1,086,440	537,892	543,548	1,077,284	533,695	543,589	8,932	4,123	4,809	224	74	150
1—2 ...	1,159,900	559,991	599,909	1,144,131	553,415	590,716	15,382	6,429	8,953	387	147	240
2—3	1,353,570	643,610	710,960	1,319,752	629,922	689,830	32,918	12,402	20,516	900	286	614
3—4 ...	1,422,918	692,398	730,520	1,337,605	661,533	676,072	82,708	30,079	52,629	2,605	786	1,819
4—5 ...	1,372,830	688,391	684,439	1,248,555	643,453	605,102	120,231	43,673	76,558	4,044	1,265	2,779
Total 0—5 ...	*6,395,658*	*3,121,282*	*3,274,376*	*6,127,327*	*3,022,018*	*3,105,309*	*260,171*	*96,706*	*163,465*	*8,160*	*2,558*	*5,602*
5—10 ...	5,712,201	2,967,590	2,744,611	4,445,001	2,470,673	1,974,328	1,232,973	485,247	747,726	34,227	11,670	22,557
10—15 ...	4,893,370	2,585,364	2,308,016	3,054,823	1,856,319	1,198,504	1,788,722	711,270	1,077,452	49,825	17,765	32,060
15—20 ...	3,592,040	1,758,533	1,833,507	888,645	695,401	193,244	2,607,451	1,031,019	1,576,433	95,944	32,113	63,831
20—25 ...	3,757,537	1,797,417	1,960,120	503,103	428,884	74,219	3,103,157	1,319,723	1,783,434	151,277	48,610	102,467
25—30 ...	3,713,468	1,818,164	1,895,304	184,656	156,910	27,746	3,248,661	1,583,029	1,665,632	280,151	78,225	201,926
30—35 ...	3,408,134	1,691,464	1,716,670	114,935	95,077	19,858	2,938,303	1,507,135	1,431,168	354,896	89,252	265,644
35—40 ...	2,701,577	1,353,042	1,348,535	58,987	47,609	11,378	2,154,567	1,200,621	953,946	488,023	104,812	383,211
40—45 ...	2,316,018	1,165,561	1,150,457	42,616	34,269	8,347	1,746,117	1,017,299	728,818	527,285	113,093	413,202
45—50 ...	1,771,606	905,819	866,287	25,287	20,603	4,684	1,177,284	758,223	419,061	569,035	126,493	442,542
50—55 ...	1,407,604	710,709	696,895	18,727	15,046	3,681	874,851	579,158	295,693	514,026	116,505	397,521
55—60 ..	988,077	405,643	582,434	10,842	8,417	2,425	504,514	352,928	151,586	472,721	104,298	368,423
60—65 ...	787,656	355,250	432,406	7,996	6,009	1,987	361,358	259,617	101,741	418,302	89,624	328,676
65—70 ...	351,685	155,799	195,886	3,486	2,618	868	143,003	104,019	38,984	205,196	49,162	156,034
70 and over...	532,952	231,433	301,519	6,189	4,596	1,593	191,777	139,658	52,119	334,986	87,179	247,807
HINDUS BRAHMANIC	*35,199,144*	*17,552,329*	*17,646,815*	*13,557,465*	*7,236,541*	*5,320,924*	*18,750,877*	*9,379,493*	*9,371,384*	*3,890,802*	*936,295*	*2,954,507*
0—1 ...	890,264	441,065	449,199	883,453	437,984	445,469	6,632	3,018	3,614	179	63	116
1—2 ...	952,935	460,017	492,918	941,000	455,015	485,985	11,616	4,875	6,741	319	127	192
2—3 ...	1,106,489	534,877	581,612	1,080,078	514,852	565,226	25,652	9,780	15,872	759	245	514
3—4 ...	1,157,357	563,085	594,272	1,088,030	537,804	550,226	67,106	24,622	42,484	2,221	659	1,562
4—5 ...	1,113,306	558,937	554,379	1,011,397	531,891	489,506	98,513	36,005	62,508	3,396	1,081	2,305
Total 0—5 ...	*5,220,351*	*2,547,971*	*2,672,380*	*5,003,958*	*2,467,546*	*2,536,412*	*209,519*	*78,300*	*131,219*	*6,874*	*2,125*	*4,749*
5—10 ...	4,670,499	2,429,215	2,241,284	3,596,756	2,005,659	1,591,097	1,043,650	413,203	630,447	30,093	10,353	19,740
10—15 ...	4,022,320	2,130,304	1,892,016	2,462,458	1,507,832	954,626	1,516,203	606,706	909,497	43,659	15,766	27,893
15—20 ...	2,986,673	1,470,638	1,516,035	709,112	570,795	138,317	2,194,840	872,016	1,322,824	82,721	27,827	54,894
20—25 ...	3,138,451	1,508,583	1,629,868	403,937	355,416	48,521	2,604,212	1,111,113	1,493,099	130,302	42,054	88,248
25—30 ...	3,107,504	1,525,997	1,581,507	147,815	130,059	17,756	2,718,825	1,328,426	1,390,399	240,864	67,512	173,352
30—35 ...	2,860,109	1,422,176	1,437,933	92,617	79,589	13,028	2,461,933	1,265,013	1,196,920	305,559	77,574	227,985
35—40 ...	2,277,637	1,140,154	1,137,483	48,230	41,051	7,179	1,807,932	1,007,493	800,439	421,475	91,610	329,865
40—45 ...	1,960,731	985,900	974,831	34,922	29,891	5,031	1,469,339	855,896	613,443	456,470	100,113	356,357
45—50 ...	1,594,523	768,053	736,470	20,612	17,790	2,832	990,545	638,926	351,619	493,366	111,337	382,029
50—55 ...	1,195,731	603,259	592,472	15,034	12,855	2,179	734,430	487,709	246,721	446,267	102,695	343,572
55—60 ...	840,365	395,487	444,878	8,551	7,201	1,350	422,777	296,769	126,008	409,037	91,517	317,520
60—65 ...	669,234	300,929	368,305	6,200	5,081	1,119	301,502	217,414	84,088	361,532	78,434	283,098
65—70 ...	298,701	131,624	167,077	2,671	2,145	526	118,993	86,665	32,328	177,037	42,814	134,223
70 and over ..	446,315	192,039	254,276	4,592	3,631	961	156,177	113,844	42,333	285,546	74,564	210,982
HINDUS BRAHMO.	*445*	*232*	*213*	*254*	*144*	*110*	*157*	*79*	*78*	*34*	*9*	*25*
0—1 ...	13	0	4	13	9	4	...	...	...	...	...	...
1—2 ...	10	5	5	10	5	5	..	...	...	...	...	...
2—3 ...	13	6	7	13	6	7	...	...	...	..	...	...
3—4 ...	9	3	6	9	3	6	...	...	...	...	...	...
4—5 ...	19	10	9	19	10	9	...	...	...	...	..	...
Total 0—5 ..	*64*	*33*	*31*	*64*	*33*	*31*	..	...	...	...	...	...
5—10 ...	53	26	27	51	26	25	1	...	1	1	...	1
10—15 ...	55	27	28	51	26	25	4	1	3	...	...	...
15—20 ...	46	23	23	32	18	14	14	5	9	...	...	...
20—25 ...	33	18	15	19	12	7	14	6	8	..	...	...
25—30 ...	51	27	24	15	11	4	30	14	16	6	2	4
30—35 ...	33	17	16	9	7	2	23	10	13	1	...	1
35—40 ...	24	12	12	7	6	1	16	6	10	1	...	1
40—45 ...	19	11	8	3	3	...	15	8	7	1	...	1
45—50 ...	24	16	8	2	2	...	16	11	5	6	3	3
50—55 ...	16	10	6	.	...	...	11	9	2	5	1	4
55—60 ...	12	7	5	1	...	1	7	6	1	4	1	3
60—65 ...	2	1	1	..	...	...	1	1	..	1	...	1
65—70 ..	7	2	5	...	...	...	3	1	2	4	1	3
70 and over...	6	2	4	...	...	...	2	1	1	4	1	3
HINDUS ARYA.	*6,763*	*3,704*	*3,059*	*2,387*	*1,429*	*958*	*3,660*	*2,036*	*1,624*	*716*	*239*	*477*
0—1 ...	186	83	104	186	83	104	...	...	...	..	...	...
1—2 ...	165	80	85	165	80	85	...	...	...	...	...	...
2—3 ...	189	96	93	188	93	92	1	...	1	...	...	...
3—4 ...	204	105	99	193	97	93	10	7	3	1	1	...
4—5 ...	235	130	106	206	109	97	24	16	8	5	4	1
Total 0—5 ...	*979*	*499*	*487*	*938*	*464*	*474*	*35*	*23*	*12*	*6*	*5*	*1*
5—10 ...	875	489	386	694	398	296	173	85	88	8	6	2
10—15 ...	775	441	334	486	318	168	285	123	162	4	...	4
15—20 ...	648	343	302	147	131	16	481	210	271	20	5	15
20—25 ...	650	348	302	74	71	3	550	269	281	26	8	18
25—30 ...	588	340	248	25	24	1	526	303	223	37	13	24
30—35 ...	522	307	216	11	11	...	469	284	185	43	12	31
35—40 ...	395	229	166	8	8	...	324	199	125	63	22	41
40—45 ...	316	177	139	3	3	...	242	150	92	71	24	47
45—50 ...	280	154	128	1	1	...	192	124	68	87	29	58
50—55 ...	227	119	108	..	...	...	148	94	54	79	25	54
55—60 ..	192	102	90	..	...	...	109	76	33	83	26	57
60—65 ...	144	77	67		...	...	71	54	17	73	23	50
65—70 ..	66	30	36	...	...	...	26	19	7	40	11	29
70 and over...	105	53	52	...	..	...	29	23	6	76	30	46
SIKHS ...	*5,869*	*3,760*	*2,109*	*2,169*	*1,443*	*726*	*3,414*	*2,198*	*1,216*	*286*	*119*	*167*
0—1 ...	157	77	80	157	77	80	...	...	...	...	...	...
1—2 ...	153	78	75	153	78	75	...	...	...	...	...	...
2—3 ...	168	85	83	167	84	83	1	1	...	...	...	...
3—4 ...	142	75	67	142	75	67	...	...	...	...	...	...
4—5 ...	159	79	71	148	78	70	2	1	1	...	...	...
Total 0—5 ..	*770*	*394*	*376*	*767*	*392*	*375*	*3*	*2*	*1*	...	...	...
5—10 ...	560	321	239	528	313	215	32	8	24	...	...	...
10—15	496	301	195	387	262	125	107	38	69	2	1	1
15—20 ...	626	373	253	182	174	8	437	195	242	7	4	3
20—25 ...	778	475	303	148	147	1	620	322	298	10	6	4
25—30 ...	725	500	225	76	74	2	630	416	214	19	10	9
30—35	618	457	161	48	48		547	400	147	23	9	14
35—40	417	300	108	15	15		368	278	90	34	16	18
40—45 ...	301	222	79	5	5	...	261	200	61	35	17	18
45—50 ..	214	159	55	5	5	...	167	135	32	42	19	23
50—55 ...	140	105	35	1	1	...	109	91	18	30	13	17
55—60 ..	86	65	21	3	3		60	53	7	23	9	14
60—65 ...	67	48	19	2	2		42	38	4	23	8	15
65—70 ...	27	11	16	2	2		12	7	5	13	2	11
70 and over...	44	20	24	...	...	.	19	15	4	25	5	20

TABLE VII—*continued.*

Age, Sex and Civil Condition. **Part I—Provincial Summary.**

Age.	Population.			Unmarried.			Married.			Widowed.		
	Persons.	Males.	Females.	Persons.	Males.	Females.	Persons.	Males.	Females.	Persons.	Males.	Females.
1	2	3	4	5	6	7	8	9	10	11	12	13
JAINS	***4,052***	***2,224***	***1,828***	***1,495***	***885***	***610***	***2,146***	***1,229***	***917***	***411***	***110***	***301***
0—1	89	40	49	89	40	40	...	...	...	...	...	...
1—2	89	41	48	89	41	48		...		...	...	...
2—3	127	56	71	123	54	60	4	2	2	...	...	...
3—4	99	42	57	97	41	55	2	1	1	...	...	...
4—5	125	63	62	113	54	50	12	9	3	...	...	...
Total 0—5	*529*	*242*	*287*	*511*	*230*	*281*	*18*	*12*	*6*	...	...	...
5—10	478	256	222	398	210	188	80	46	34		...	...
10—15	469	271	198	322	199	123	143	71	72	4	1	3
15—20	425	245	180	116	101	15	298	141	157	11	3	8
20—25	418	247	171	65	64	1	334	175	159	19	8	11
25—30	346	205	141	35	34	1	285	161	124	26	10	16
30—35	306	172	134	16	16	...	260	149	111	30	7	23
35—40	282	156	126	10	9	1	228	138	90	44	9	35
40—45	232	129	103	8	8		183	113	70	41	8	33
45—50	176	105	71	5	5	...	117	53	64	54	17	37
50—55	142	82	60	4	4		94	67	27	44	11	33
55—60	103	55	48	2	2	...	57	39	18	44	14	30
60—65	67	30	37		...	...	29	19	10	38	11	27
65—70	38	17	21	2	2	...	13	10	3	23	5	18
70 and over	41	12	29	1	1		7	5	2	33	6	27
BUDDHISTS	***2,305***	***1,236***	***1,060***	***786***	***475***	***311***	***1,325***	***706***	***619***	***184***	***54***	***180***
0—1	72	31	41	72	31	41		...	...		...	...
1—2	62	34	28	62	34	28		...	...	...	...	...
2—3	65	30	35	65	30	35		...	...		...	...
3—4	57	27	30	57	27	30				...	...	...
4—5	63	34	29	62	33	29	1	1		...	...	...
Total 0—5	*319*	*156*	*163*	*318*	*155*	*163*	*1*	*1*			...	...
5—10	245	124	121	203	116	87	40	6	33	2	...	3
10—15	210	104	106	134	85	40	73	19	54	3		3
15—20	222	111	111	58	47	9	163	61	102	6	3	3
20—25	250	128	122	43	40	3	204	87	117	3	1	2
25—30	228	135	93	21	19	2	203	114	89	4	2	2
30—35	203	124	79	8	8		188	112	76	7	4	3
35—40	160	92	68	1	1	...	146	87	59	13	4	9
40—45	129	76	53	1	1	...	112	72	40	16	3	13
45—50	105	66	39	2	2	...	81	58	23	22	6	16
50—55	87	48	39	2	1	1	55	39	16	30	8	22
55—60	57	29	28	...			26	19	7	31	10	21
60—65	41	21	20		...	...	19	15	...	22	6	16
65—70	15	9	6	...	...	...	6	6		9	3	6
70 and over	24	12	12	...	...	...	8	8		16	4	12
ZOROASTRIANS	***264***	***159***	***105***	***130***	***85***	***45***	***128***	***73***	***55***	***6***	***1***	***5***
0—1	6	2	4	6	2	4		...	...	...	...	...
1—2	2	1	1	2	1	1					...	
2—3	7	4	3	7	4	3				...		...
3—4	2	2	...	2	2	...	...	...	...	...	...	...
4—5	11	5	6	11	5	6	...	...	...	...	...	...
Total 0—5	*28*	*14*	*14*	*28*	*14*	*14*		...	...		...	...
5—10	23	11	12	22	10	12	1	1				...
10—15	21	10	11	20	10	10	1	...	1		...	...
15—20	24	15	9	17	13	4	7	2	5			
20—25	21	15	6	15	12	3	6	...	3		...	...
25—30	32	22	10	15	14	1	17	5	[illegible]			...
30—35	25	15	10	10	9	1	15	6	9		...	...
35—40	28	17	11	3	3	...	25	14	11		...	...
40—45	20	12	8	...	...	...	20	13	8		...	...
45—50	14	10	4	...	...	...	13	10	3	1	...	1
50—55	14	7	7		...	...	12	7	5	2	...	2
55—60	6	4	2	...	...	...	5	4	1	1	...	1
60—65	3	3	...	...	...	...	3	3				...
65—70	3	3	...		...	...	2	3	...	1	1	...
70 and over	2	1	1				1	1		1	...	1
MUSLIMS	***4,284,306***	***2,123,112***	***2,161,194***	***1,515,822***	***875,913***	***639,909***	***2,359,322***	***1,160,987***	***1,198,335***	***409,162***	***86,212***	***322,950***
0—1	100,613	50,133	50,480	99,410	49,549	49,[illegible]	1,164	573	591	39	11	28
1—2	118,288	57,246	61,042	115,702	56,252	59,450	2,526	979	1,547	60	15	45
2—3	141,152	66,928	74,224	135,506	65,063	70,443	5,520	1,836	3,691	126	36	90
3—4	153,521	74,590	78,931	140,331	70,212	70,119	12,865	4,262	8,603	325	116	209
4—5	153,353	76,622	76,731	134,502	70,327	64,275	18,334	6,196	12,138	517	199	318
Total 0—5	*666,927*	*325,519*	*341,408*	*625,451*	*311,303*	*314,148*	*40,409*	*13,839*	*26,570*	*1,067*	*377*	*690*
5—10	620,769	338,282	297,487	456,833	350,993	105,840	160,634	61,154	99,480	3,302	1,135	2,167
10—15	516,168	273,081	243,187	294,253	186,601	107,092	217,398	[illegible]	133,551	4,537	1,583	2,954
15—20	357,581	171,211	186,370	70,277	58,603	11,674	278,833	109,844	169,011	8,471	2,786	5,685
20—25	377,410	175,166	202,244	35,363	34,047	1,336	325,275	136,869	188,406	13,773	4,270	9,503
25—30	369,020	175,136	193,884	13,131	11,338	1,793	329,899	157,255	172,644	25,990	6,543	19,447
30—35	335,313	162,956	172,357	7,510	6,222	1,288	294,439	149,513	144,926	33,364	7,221	26,143
35—40	262,407	130,260	132,147	3,468	2,370	1,198	214,192	120,030	94,162	44,752	7,960	36,792
40—45	222,058	111,484	110,574	2,363	1,410	953	171,266	101,517	69,749	48,429	8,557	39,872
45—50	167,980	86,735	81,245	1,282	982	300	115,398	76,890	38,508	50,800	9,363	41,437
50—55	129,541	66,282	64,259	1,025	756	230	84,225	57,147	27,078	44,291	8,379	35,912
55—60	92,177	44,327	47,850	571	387	184	50,497	36,098	11,999	41,109	7,841	33,267
60—65	74,577	34,454	40,123	403	318	155	37,278	27,090	10,198	36,836	7,056	29,780
65—70	35,649	16,687	18,962	266	213	53	16,135	12,056	4,079	19,248	4,418	14,830
70 and over	56,729	26,582	30,147	591	490	101	22,944	17,370	5,574	33,194	8,722	24,472
CHRISTIANS	***416,726***	***207,185***	***209,541***	***223,692***	***118,278***	***105,414***	***166,760***	***82,512***	***84,248***	***26,274***	***6,395***	***19,879***
0—1	15,025	7,860	7,686	14,989	7,381	7,608	36	8	28		...	...
1—2	13,669	6,716	6,953	13,619	6,698	6,921	49	17	32	1	1	...
2—3	15,628	7,620	8,008	15,550	7,586	7,964	75	33	42	3	1	2
3—4	15,938	7,874	8,064	15,790	7,806	7,984	143	69	74	5	...	5
4—5	15,139	7,011	7,525	14,913	7,503	7,410	216	108	108	10	3	7
Total 0—5	*75,399*	*37,213*	*38,186*	*74,861*	*36,973*	*37,888*	*519*	*235*	*284*	*19*	*5*	*14*
5—10	62,524	31,962	30,562	60,457	31,335	29,122	2,028	619	1,409	39	8	31
10—15	54,597	27,859	26,738	50,306	30,726	25,564	4,226	1,119	3,107	63	15	48
15—20	37,745	17,949	19,796	21,164	12,533	8,631	16,253	5,333	10,920	328	83	245
20—25	35,722	17,026	18,696	10,714	7,002	3,712	24,353	9,820	14,533	655	204	451
25—30	33,494	16,737	16,757	2,891	1,849	1,042	29,078	14,420	14,658	1,525	468	1,057
30—35	29,560	14,868	14,692	1,425	900	525	26,202	13,434	12,768	1,933	534	1,399
35—40	21,987	11,211	10,776	621	347	274	18,607	10,226	8,381	2,769	635	2,121
40—45	18,254	9,302	8,952	449	245	204	14,949	8,395	6,554	2,856	662	2,194
45—50	13,967	7,171	6,796	241	119	122	10,538	6,287	4,251	3,188	765	2,423
50—55	11,674	6,002	5,772	177	93	84	8,401	5,064	3,337	3,096	745	2,351
55—60	8,383	3,855	4,528	134	64	70	4,850	3,036	1,814	3,399	755	2,644
60—65	6,658	3,049	3,609	105	41	64	3,540	2,367	1,173	3,013	641	2,372
65—70	2,661	1,254	1,407	57	23	34	1,376	939	437	1,228	292	936
70 and over	4,101	1,827	2,274	88	29	59	1,840	1,218	622	2,173	590	1,583

TABLE VII—*continued.*

AGE, SEX AND CIVIL CONDITION. **PART I—PROVINCIAL SUMMARY.**

AGE.	POPULATION			UNMARRIED			MARRIED			WIDOWED.		
	Persons	Males	Females	Persons	Males	Females	Persons	Males	Females	Persons	Males	Females.
1	2	3	4	5	6	7	8	9	10	11	12	13
TRIBAL	***2,409,409***	***1,188,440***	***1,220,969***	***1,188,284***	***629,172***	***559,112***	***1,044,961***	***516,250***	***528,711***	***176,164***	***43,018***	***133,146***
0—1	**80,006**	39 061	40,945	**78,900**	38 537	40,363	**1,100**	524	576	**6**	.	6
1—2	**74,521**	35 771	38,750	**73,323**	35,209	38,114	**1,191**	558	633	**7**	4	3
2—3	**89,725**	43,903	45,822	**88,048**	42,142	45 906	**1,665**	757	908	**12**	4	8
3—4	**95,581**	46,590	48,991	**92,946**	45,462	47,484	**2,582**	1,118	1,464	**53**	10	43
4—5	**90,419**	44,903	45,516	**87,174**	43,538	43,636	**3,129**	1,337	1,792	**116**	28	88
Total 0—5	*430,252*	*209,228*	*221,024*	*420,391*	*204,988*	*215,503*	*9,667*	*4,294*	*5,373*	*194*	*46*	*148*
5—10	**356,137**	181,881	174,256	**329,024**	171,591	157,433	**26,331**	10,122	16,209	**782**	168	614
10—15	**298,229**	152,980	145,240	**246,398**	134,244	1[illegible]8,154	**50,278**	18,346	31,932	**1,553**	399	1,154
15—20	**208,031**	97,615	110,416	**87,537**	52,982	[illegible]4 555	**116 114**	43,231	72,883	**4,380**	1,402	2,978
20—25	**203,783**	95,402	108,381	**49,720**	32,090	17,[illegible]30	**147,573**	61,053	86,520	**6,490**	2,259	4,231
25—30	**201,454**	99,051	102 403	**20,629**	13,485	7,144	**169,146**	81,901	87,445	**11,679**	3,665	8,014
30—35	**181,414**	90,353	9[illegible],061	**13,275**	8 262	5 013	**154,203**	78,200	76,008	**13,936**	3,891	10,045
35—40	**138,204**	70,580	67 624	**6,823**	[illegible],494	2,7[illegible]	**112,701**	62,134	50 567	**18,880**	4,552	14,328
40—45	**113,936**	58,244	55,702	**4,860**	2 7 2	2,158	**89,710**	50,943	35,767	**19,366**	4 609	14,757
45—50	**84,303**	42,837	4[illegible]	**3,136**	1,[illegible]07	1,4[illegible]	**59,702**	[illegible],[illegible]87	23 515	**21,465**	4,053	16,512
50—55	**70,018**	34,855	3[illegible] 133	**2,483**	1,335	1,148	**47,355**	28,923	18,432	**20,180**	4,627	15,553
55—60	**46,689**	21,706	24,983	**1,579**	759	820	**26,124**	16,826	9,298	**18,986**	4,121	14,865
60—65	**36,858**	16 634	20,224	**1,225**	566	659	**18,871**	12 624	6,247	**16,762**	3,444	13,318
65—70	**14,517**	6,161	8,356	**488**	233	255	**6,436**	4,313	2 123	**7,593**	1,615	5,978
70 and over	**25,584**	10,884	14,700	**916**	441	473	**10,750**	7,173	3,577	**13,918**	3,267	10,651
JEWS	***24***	***15***	***9***	***16***	***12***	***4***	***6***	***3***	***3***	***2***		***2***
10—15	**1**	1		**1**	1					..	...	...
15—20	**2**	1	1	**1**		1	**1**	1				...
20—25	**2**	1	1	**2**	1	1						...
25—30	**2**	2		**2**	2						..	...
30—35	**4**	3	1	**3**	3		**1**		1		.	...
35—40	**8**	4	4	**4**	3	1	**3**	1	2	**1**	...	1
40—45	**3**	2	1	**2**	1	1	**1**	1			...	
45—50	**1**		1							**1**	.	1
60—65	**1**	1		**1**	1					..		...
KUMBHIPATIAS	***271***	***153***	***118***	***113***	***65***	***48***	***145***	***81***	***64***	***13***	***7***	***6***
0—1	**9**	3	6	**9**	3	6				..	...	...
1—2	**6**	2	4	**6**	2	4				..	.	...
2—3	**6**	4	2	**6**	4	2					..	...
3—4	**8**	5	3	**8**	[illegible]	3		..	..		.	...
4—5	**10**	5	5	**10**	5	5		.	.	...	.	...
Total 0—5	*39*	*19*	*20*	*39*	*19*	*20*		..		..	...	...
5—10	**37**	22	15	**34**	21	13	**3**	1	2	.	..	..
10—15	**29**	16	13	**25**	16	9	**4**	...	4		.	...
15—20	**16**	5	11	**6**	3	3	**10**	2	8			...
20—25	**16**	6	10	**1**	.	1	**15**	6	9			...
25—30	**23**	11	12	**1**	.		**21**	10	11	**1**		1
30—35	**25**	16	9	**3**	2	1	**22**	14	8		..	...
35—40	**24**	15	9	**1**	1		**22**	13	9	**1**	1	...
40—45	**19**	12	7				**19**	12	7			...
45—50	**17**	11	6	**1**		1	**13**	10	3	**3**	1	2
50—55	**14**	10	4	**1**	.		**11**	8	3	**2**	1	1
55—60	**7**	6	1	**1**	.		**2**	2		**4**	3	1
60—65	**4**	3	1				**2**	2		**2**	1	1
65—70	**1**	1					**1**	1			.	...
INDEFINITE BELIEFS	***15***	***12***	***3***	***7***	***7***		***8***	***5***	***3***		..	...
2—3	**1**	1		**1**	1			..				
5—10	**1**	1		**1**	1		.		.		.	...
15—20	**1**	1		**1**	1						..	..
20—25	**3**	2	.	**2**	2		**1**		1		..	..
25—30	**1**	1					**1**	1			...	.
30—35	**1**		1				**1**		1			.
35—40	**4**	3	1	**1**	1		**3**	2	1		.	..
45—50	**2**	2					**2**	2		..	.	...
70 and over	**1**	1		**1**	1						.	...

TABLE VII—*continued.*

Age, Sex and Civil Condition. — **Part II—Details for Districts.**

Age.	Population. Persons	Population. Males	Population. Females	Unmarried. Persons	Unmarried. Males	Unmarried. Females.	Married. Persons.	Married. Males.	Married. Females.	Widowed. Persons.	Widowed. Males	Widowed. Females.
1	2	3	4	5	6	7	8	9	10	11	12	13
PATNA.												
ALL RELIGIONS ..	*1,846,474*	*956,124*	*890,350*	*621,596*	*360,432*	*261,164*	*1,008,198*	*522,861*	*485,337*	*216,680*	*72,831*	*143,849*
0—1 ...	41,648	20,369	21,280	41,565	20,351	21,214	82	16	66	1	1	...
1—2	48,154	23,020	25,134	47,959	22,948	25,011	190	71	119	5	1	4
2—3 .	54,009	25,433	28,576	53,502	25,192	28 310	492	236	256	15	5	10
3—4	56,527	27,550	28,977	54,177	26,436	27 741	2,311	1,103	1,208	39	11	28
4—5 ..	55,698	28,367	27,331	51,747	26,501	25,246	3,884	1,847	2,037	67	19	48
Total 0—5	*256,036*	*124,739*	*131,298*	*248,950*	*121,428*	*127,522*	*6,959*	*3 273*	*3 686*	*127*	*37*	*90*
5—10 ..	228,998	122,487	106,511	180,103	99,497	80,606	47 978	20,680	27,298	917	310	607
10—15 ..	199,381	106,407	92,974	118,338	74 195	44,143	79,449	33 622	45,827	1,594	590	1,004
15—20	158,161	82 465	75,696	30,559	25,983	4,576	123,686	54,838	68,848	3,916	1,644	2,272
20—30 .	320,769	167,290	153,479	26,811	25,120	1,691	276,051	135,032	141,019	17,907	7,138	10,769
30—40	258,901	133,853	125,048	8,929	8,586	343	215,578	113,620	101,958	34,394	11,647	22,747
40—50 .	192,982	102,269	90,713	4,402	4,253	160	139,334	81,665	57,669	49,246	16,352	32,894
50—60	125,492	67,076	58,416	2,228	2,165	63	74,389	48,738	25,651	48,875	16,173	32,702
60 and over	105,754	51,539	54,215	1,276	1,206	70	44,774	31,393	13,381	59,704	18,940	40,764
HINDUS ..	*1,630,829*	*852 682*	*787,147*	*537,514*	*312,105*	*225,409*	*907,953*	*473,040*	*434,913*	*195,062*	*67,537*	*127,525*
0—1	37,100	18,103	16,996	37,017	18,085	18,932	82	16	66	1	1	...
1—2	42,693	20,347	22,346	42,504	21,278	22,226	184	66	118	5	1	4
2—3	47,731	22,529	25,202	47,271	23 297	21,974	447	228	219	13	4	9
3—4 ..	49,936	24,481	25,455	47 904	23,417	24,487	1,996	1,054	942	36	10	26
4—5 .	48 992	25,149	23,813	45 691	23,373	22,228	3,330	1 759	1,571	61	17	44
Total 0—5	*226,452*	*110 608*	*115,844*	*220 297*	*107 460*	*112,847*	*6,039*	*3,125*	*2,914*	*116*	*33*	*83*
5—10	201,257	100 923	94,934	155,659	86,366	69,293	44,727	19,665	25,062	871	294	579
10—15	175,219	93 726	81,493	99,793	61,337	38 456	73,910	31,836	42 064	1,516	563	953
15—20	139,927	72,996	66 941	24,149	20,886	3,264	112,212	50,593	61,619	3,566	1,517	2,049
20—30 .	285,537	149,525	136,012	21,953	20 805	1,148	247,348	122,129	125,219	16,236	6,591	9,645
30—40 .	231,991	120,006	111,135	8,170	7,010	160	192,007	102 084	90 773	30,981	10,893	20,088
40—50 ...	172,621	92,036	80,585	4,189	4,099	90	124,266	72 673	51,593	44,166	15,264	28,902
50—60	112,339	60 329	52 010	2,119	2,092	27	66,377	43 233	23,144	43,833	15,004	28 820
60 and over ..	94,496	43,273	45 223	1,182	1,160	22	39,537	27,732	11 805	53,777	17,381	36,396
MUSLIMS ...	*202,653*	*101,173*	*101,480*	*81,433*	*46,696*	*34,757*	*99,796*	*49,242*	*50,554*	*21,406*	*5,237*	*16,169*
0—1	4,462	2,233	2,239	4,462	2,223	2,239		...				...
1—2 .	5,393	2 641	2,752	5,387	2,638	2 749	6	3	3			...
2—3	6,204	2 867	3,337	6,157	2 858	3 299	45	8	37	2	1	1
3—4	6,517	3,035	3 482	6,199	2,985	3,214	315	49	266	3	1	2
4—5	6 623	3,179	3 444	6,063	3,089	2,974	554	88	468	6	2	4
Total 0—5 ...	*29 199*	*13,945*	*15,254*	*28 268*	*13 793*	*14,475*	*920*	*148*	*772*	*11*	*4*	*7*
5—10 ...	27,332	13,989	13,343	24,037	12,957	11,080	3,249	1,014	2,235	46	18	28
10—15 ...	23,743	12,495	11,248	18,133	10 674	7,459	5,532	1,794	3,738	78	27	51
15—20 ...	17,714	9 139	8 575	5,971	4 792	1,179	11,396	4,221	7,175	347	126	221
20—30 ...	34,179	17,020	17,159	4,106	3,681	425	28,419	12,796	15,623	1,654	543	1,111
30—40 .	26,361	12,689	13,672	613	568	45	22,377	11,377	11,000	3,371	744	2,627
40—50 ...	20,007	10 032	9,975	164	127	37	14,811	8,831	5,980	5,032	1,074	3,958
50—60 ...	12,978	6 651	6,327	86	62	24	7,900	5 430	2 470	4,992	1,159	3,833
60 and over ...	11,142	5,215	5,927	75	41	33	5,192	3,631	1,561	5,875	1,542	4,333
GAYA.												
ALL RELIGIONS ...	*2,388,462*	*1,193,643*	*1,194,819*	*796,766*	*457,823*	*338,943*	*1,312,983*	*647,032*	*665,951*	*278,713*	*88,788*	*189,925*
0—1	63,171	30,936	32,235	63,047	30,860	32,187	121	75	46	3	1	2
1—2	70,506	33,705	36,801	70,062	33 485	36,577	436	218	218	8	2	6
2—3 ...	79,178	37,161	42,017	78,134	36,718	41,416	1,016	433	583	28	10	18
3—4	81,447	39,648	41,799	77,893	38,308	39,585	3,440	1,304	2,136	114	36	78
4—5	77,168	39,214	37,954	71,458	37,101	34,357	5,515	2,051	3,464	195	62	133
Total 0—5	*371,470*	*180,664*	*190,806*	*360 594*	*176,472*	*184,122*	*10,528*	*4,081*	*6,447*	*348*	*111*	*237*
5—10 ...	308 482	160,938	147,544	225,757	127,754	98,003	80,358	32 385	47,973	2,367	799	1,568
10—15	263,576	138,647	124,929	134,729	85 632	49,097	125,328	51,705	73,623	3,519	1,310	2,209
15—20	199,040	96,990	102,050	29,440	25,686	3,754	163,744	68,950	94 794	5,856	2,354	3,502
20—30	416,899	203,120	213,779	26,720	24,730	1,990	364,385	168,700	195 685	25,794	9,690	16,104
30—40	335,100	167,308	167,797	10,880	9,737	1,143	275,748	141 521	134,227	48,472	16,045	32,427
40—50 ...	237,689	121,776	115,913	5,507	4,789	718	166,446	96,060	70,386	65,736	20,927	44,809
50—60 ...	147,243	74,243	73,000	2,158	2,088	70	83,225	53,280	29,945	61,860	18,875	42,985
60 and over .	108,963	49,962	59,001	981	935	46	43,221	30,350	12,871	64,761	18,677	46,084
HINDUS ...	*2,133,541*	*1,075,495*	*1,058,046*	*704,501*	*406,532*	*297,969*	*1,178,333*	*586,012*	*592,321*	*250,207*	*82,951*	*167,256*
0—1 ...	56,537	27,669	28,868	56,425	27 604	28,821	109	64	45	3	1	2
1—2 ..	62,982	30,051	32,931	62,563	29,862	32,701	393	188	205	6	1	5
2—3 ...	70,578	33,101	37,477	69,647	32,724	36 923	906	369	537	25	8	17
3—4 ...	72,627	35,418	37,209	69,442	34,222	35,220	3,080	1,162	1,918	105	34	71
4—5 ..	68,589	34,919	33,670	63,469	33,014	30,455	4,944	1,848	3,096	176	57	119
Total 0—5 .	*331,293*	*161,158*	*170,135*	*321 546*	*157,426*	*164,120*	*9,432*	*3,631*	*5,801*	*315*	*101*	*214*
5—10 ...	273,704	143,188	130,516	198,594	112,633	85,961	72,891	29,808	43,083	2,219	747	1,472
10—15 ...	234,122	123,790	110 332	117,312	74,912	42,400	113,544	47,650	65 894	3,266	1,228	2,038
15—20 .	178,216	87,828	90,386	25,361	22,333	3,028	147,566	63,287	84,279	5,289	2,208	3,081
20—30	374,594	185,108	189,486	23,987	22,379	1,608	327,336	153,594	173,742	23,271	9,135	14,136
30—40 ...	301,257	152,844	148 413	9,930	9 369	561	247,386	128,312	119,074	43,941	15,163	28,778
40—50 ..	212,679	110,232	102 447	4,819	4,614	205	148,536	85,869	62,667	59,324	19,749	39,575
50—60	131,723	66,989	64,734	2,047	2,002	45	74,257	47,358	26,899	55,419	17,629	37,790
60 and over .	95,953	44,358	51,595	905	864	41	37,885	26,503	11,382	57,163	16,991	40,172
MUSLIMS ...	*253,560*	*117,436*	*136,124*	*91,800*	*51,051*	*40,749*	*133,413*	*60,592*	*72,821*	*28,347*	*5,793*	*22,554*
0—1 ...	6,605	3,257	3,348	6,593	3,246	3,347	12	11	1	...	...	...
1—2 ...	7,515	3,641	3,874	7,470	3,610	3,860	43	30	13	2	1	1
2—3 ...	8,566	4,045	4 521	8,454	3,980	4 474	109	69	40	3	2	1
3—4 ...	8,792	4,218	4,574	8,424	4,075	4,349	359	141	218	9	2	7
4—5 ...	8,543	4,276	4,267	7,958	4,073	3,885	566	198	368	19	5	14
Total 0—5 ...	*40,021*	*19,437*	*20,584*	*38,899*	*18,984*	*19,915*	*1,089*	*443*	*646*	*33*	*10*	*23*
5—10 ...	34,647	17,677	16,970	27,054	15,068	11,986	7,445	2,557	4,888	148	52	96
10—15 .	29,333	14,789	14,544	17,338	10,678	6,660	11,742	4,029	7,713	253	82	171
15—20 ...	20,695	9,100	11,595	4,042	3,331	711	16,091	5,624	10,467	562	145	417
20—30 ...	42,035	17,873	24,162	2 686	2,319	367	36,843	15,004	21,839	2,506	550	1,956
30—40 ...	33,609	14,335	19,274	929	354	575	28,180	13,105	15,075	4,500	876	3,624
40—50 ...	24,831	11,445	13,386	676	167	509	17,786	10,113	7,673	6,369	1,105	5,264
50—60	15,426	7,199	8,227	103	82	21	8,915	5,881	3,034	6,408	1,236	5,172
60 and over .	12,963	5,581	7,382	73	68	5	5,322	3,836	1,486	7,568	1,677	5,891

TABLE VII—*continued.*

AGE, SEX AND CIVIL CONDITION. PART II—DETAILS FOR DISTRICTS.

Age.	Population.			Unmarried.			Married.			Widowed.		
	Persons.	Males	Females	Persons	Males.	Females	Persons	Males	Females.	Persons	Males	Females.
1	2	3	4	5	6	7	8	9	10	11	12	13
SHAHABAD.												
ALL RELIGIONS	*1,993,489*	*999,099*	*994,390*	*689,473*	*404,240*	*285,233*	*1,052,116*	*523,859*	*528,257*	*251,900*	*71,000*	*180,900*
0—1 ...	45,794	23,086	22,708	45 272	22,960	22,310	469	283	186	7	3	4
1—2 ...	54,344	26,056	28,288	53 706	25,754	27,952	625	298	327	13	4	9
2—3 ...	61,344	28,658	32,686	60,283	28,184	32,099	1,042	468	574	19	6	13
3—4 ...	63,127	30,710	32,417	60 564	29,670	30,894	2 479	1,020	1,459	84	20	64
4—5 ...	62,639	31,739	30,900	58,765	30,200	28,565	3,720	1,502	2,218	154	37	117
Total 0—5 ..	*287,248*	*140,249*	*146,999*	*278,696*	*136,668*	*142,028*	*8,275*	*3,511*	*4,764*	*277*	*70*	*207*
5—10 ...	258,364	136,628	121,736	199 013	111,244	87 769	58 210	24,974	33,236	1,141	410	731
10—15 ...	227,313	122,886	104,827	128 228	80,105	48,123	97,399	42,016	55,383	1,886	765	1,121
15—20 ...	179,346	91,279	88,067	32 434	28,096	4 338	141,990	61,221	80,769	4 922	1,962	2,960
20—30 ..	364,623	182,296	182,327	30 910	28,982	1,928	309,410	144,543	164,867	24 303	8,771	15,532
30—40 .	280,697	141,951	141,745	11 673	11,050	623	225 623	116,340	109,283	49,301	14,461	34,840
40—50 ..	192,413	95,234	97,179	5 021	4,786	235	124 494	73,100	51,394	62,898	17,348	45,550
50—60 ..	112,507	53,618	58,889	2 275	2,171	104	56,963	37,483	19 480	53 269	13,964	39,305
60 and over ..	84,878	35,058	49,820	1,223	1,138	85	29,752	20,671	9,081	53,903	13,249	40,654
HINDUS ...	*1,838,862*	*924,282*	*914,580*	*634,185*	*373,113*	*261,072*	*968,627*	*484,125*	*484,502*	*236,050*	*67,044*	*169,006*
0—1 ...	41,866	21,083	20 783	41,490	20 885	20,605	370	195	175	6	3	3
1—2 ..	49,895	23,922	25 973	49,312	23,653	25,659	571	266	305	12	3	9
2—3 ...	56,258	26,293	29,965	55,289	25,867	29,422	953	422	531	16	4	12
3—4 ...	57,795	28,131	29,664	55,448	27,175	28,273	2,268	939	1,329	79	17	62
4—5 ...	57,346	29,096	28,250	53,807	27,674	26,133	3,395	1,390	2,005	144	32	112
Total 0—5 ...	*263,160*	*128,525*	*134,635*	*255,346*	*125,254*	*130,092*	*7,557*	*3,212*	*4,345*	*257*	*59*	*198*
5—10 ...	236,719	125,313	111,406	182,406	101,074	80,472	53,238	22,957	30,281	1,075	382	693
10—15	208 671	112,951	95,720	117,579	73,480	44,099	89,316	38,750	50,566	1,776	721	1,055
15—20	165,339	84 592	80,747	29,917	26,046	3 871	130,778	56,701	74,078	4,643	1,845	2,798
20—30 ...	338,934	170,837	167,197	29,259	27,575	1,684	285,829	134,204	151,125	22 946	8,258	14,688
30—40	266 747	132,703	134,044	11 372	10,836	536	208 721	108,016	100,655	46 654	13,801	32,853
40—50	178 575	88,675	89,900	4,903	4 700	203	114 560	67,481	47,079	59 112	16,494	42,618
50—60	103 963	49 639	54,324	2,232	2,144	88	51,926	34,274	17 652	49 805	13,201	36,604
60 and over ...	77,654	31,847	45,807	1,171	1,104	67	26,701	18,460	8,241	49,782	12,283	37,499
MUSLIMS ..	*151,368*	*73,260*	*78,108*	*54,033*	*30,451*	*23,582*	*81,802*	*38,915*	*42,887*	*15,533*	*3,894*	*11,639*
0—1 ..	3,846	1,964	1,882	3,806	1,936	1,870	39	28	11	1	..	1
1—2 ..	4,346	2,085	2,261	4,291	2,052	2 239	54	33	23	1	1	..
2—3 ..	4,975	2,317	2,658	4 884	2,269	2,615	88	46	42	3	2	1
3—4 .	5 227	2,530	2,697	5.017	2,448	2,569	205	79	126	5	3	2
4—5 ...	5,179	2,586	2,593	4,857	2,474	2,383	312	107	205	10	5	5
Total 0—5 ...	*23,573*	*11,482*	*12,091*	*22,855*	*11,179*	*11,676*	*698*	*292*	*406*	*20*	*11*	*9*
5—10 ...	21,175	11,067	10,108	16 255	9,076	7,179	4,857	1 963	2,894	63	28	35
10—15 ...	18,425	9,719	8,706	10 404	6,484	3,920	7 914	3,191	4,723	107	44	63
15—20 ..	13,702	6,541	7,161	2,440	2,003	437	10 988	4,423	6,565	274	115	159
20—30 .	26,058	12,011	14,047	1,590	1,367	223	23,136	10,141	12,995	1 332	503	829
30—40 ..	19 427	8,960	10,467	288	204	84	16 559	8,112	8 447	2 580	644	1,936
40—50	13,548	6,425	7,123	109	79	30	9 732	5,506	4,226	3,707	840	2,867
50—60 .	8 367	3,894	4,473	43	27	16	4 917	3,115	1,802	3,407	752	2,655
60 and over ..	7,093	3,161	3,932	49	32	17	3,001	2,172	829	4,043	957	3,086
SARAN.												
ALL RELIGIONS ..	*2,486,468*	*1,220,049*	*1,266,419*	*975,934*	*560,014*	*415,920*	*1,221,012*	*585,799*	*635,213*	*289,522*	*74,236*	*215,286*
0—1 ...	47,884	24,355	23,529	47 399	23,970	23,420	476	283	194	9	3	6
1—2 ...	61,901	30,379	31,522	61 040	29,975	31,065	849	398	451	12	6	6
2—3 ...	71,571	34,037	37,534	70 266	33,472	36,794	1,276	554	722	29	11	18
3—4 ...	77,786	37,718	40,068	75 652	36,833	38,819	2,035	859	1,176	99	26	73
4—5 ...	79,323	39,653	39,670	76,475	38,456	38,019	2,685	1,155	1,530	163	42	121
Total 0—5 .	*338,465*	*166,042*	*172,423*	*330,832*	*162,706*	*168,126*	*7,391*	*3,248*	*4,073*	*312*	*88*	*224*
5—10 ..	343,022	181,148	161,874	304,160	165 866	138,204	37,880	15,010	22,870	982	272	710
10—15	296 985	161,529	135,356	220 814	131,567	89,247	74 509	29,470	45,039	1,562	492	1,070
15—20	202.717	102,743	99,981	54,738	43,088	11,650	143,649	58,161	85,488	4 330	1,484	2,846
20—30	413,880	193,166	220 714	42,463	36,498	5,965	347,338	149,985	197,353	24 079	6,683	17,396
30—40 ...	364,310	165,923	198,387	13,372	12,008	[illegible]	298,195	141,675	156,520	52 743	14,240	38,503
40—50 ...	256 068	122,839	133 229	5 569	4,918	[illegible]	178 462	100,261	78,201	72 087	17,707	54 430
50—60 ...	152 221	71,327	78,894	2,452	2,045	407	84 941	54,610	30,312	64 848	16,663	48,105
60 and over ...	118,900	53,343	65,556	1,554	1,268	286	48,717	33,357	15,360	68,629	18,717	49,912
HINDUS ...	*2,176,984*	*1,072,048*	*1,104,936*	*850,824*	*489,774*	*361,050*	*1,066,267*	*515,378*	*550,889*	*259,893*	*66,896*	*192,997*
0—1 ..	41,284	20,803	20,481	40 951	20,648	20 303	327	154	173	6	1	5
1—2	53 369	26,086	27,283	52,703	25,828	26,877	657	254	403	9	4	5
2—3 ..	61 589	29,145	32,444	60 553	28,760	31,793	1 011	373	638	25	7	18
3—4 ...	67 085	32,453	34,632	65 270	31,731	33 539	1 728	701	1,027	87	21	66
4—5 .	68,511	34,210	34,301	66,041	33,187	32,854	2 325	985	1,340	145	38	107
Total 0—5 ..	*291,838*	*142,697*	*149,141*	*285,518*	*140,154*	*145,364*	*6,048*	*2,472*	*3,576*	*272*	*71*	*201*
5—10 ...	296 917	156,903	140,014	263 925	143,838	120,087	32,120	12,827	19,293	872	238	634
10—15 ..	257,510	140,541	116,969	192,468	114,611	77,857	63 670	28,499	35,171	1,372	431	941
15—20 ...	177 002	90,612	86,390	48 560	38,246	10,314	124,586	51,038	73,548	3,856	1,328	2,528
20—30 ...	363 629	170,553	193,076	38 767	33,467	5,300	303 605	132,007	170,598	21 257	6,089	15,818
30—40 ...	322 810	147,894	174,416	12 624	11,449	1,175	262 145	126,266	135,879	47 541	11,119	36,422
40—50 ..	227,440	109,598	117,842	5 294	4 801	493	157 324	88,770	68,546	64 822	16,018	48,804
50—60	135,248	65,209	70,039	2,230	1,993	237	74 777	48,194	26,583	58,241	15,022	43,219
60 and over ...	105,090	47,041	58,049	1,438	1,225	213	42,592	29,186	13,406	61,060	16,630	44,430
MUSLIMS ...	*309,005*	*147.708*	*161,302*	*124,870*	*70,067*	*54,803*	*154,524*	*70,301*	*84,223*	*29,611*	*7,335*	*22,276*
0—1 ...	6,593	3,449	3,144	6 441	3,319	3,122	149	128	21	3	2	1
1—2 ...	8 520	4,288	4,232	8 325	4,142	4,183	192	144	48	3	2	1
2—3 ..	9,963	4,880	5,083	9 694	4,700	4,994	265	176	89	4	4	...
3—4 ...	10,684	5,254	5,430	10 365	5,091	5,274	307	158	149	12	5	7
4—5 ...	10,795	5,434	5,361	10,419	5,261	5,158	358	169	189	18	4	14
Total 0—5 ...	*46,555*	*23,305*	*23,250*	*45,244*	*22,513*	*22,731*	*1,271*	*775*	*496*	*40*	*17*	*23*
5—10 .	46,055	24,211	21,844	40 188	21,995	18,193	5,757	2,182	3,575	110	34	76
10—15 ..	39 331	20,954	18,377	28,306	16,923	11,383	10 835	3,970	6,865	190	61	129
15—20 ..	25 672	14,090	11,582	6,150	4,818	1,332	19,048	7,116	11,932	474	156	318
20—30 ...	50,152	21,555	28,597	3,662	3,014	648	44,268	17,897	26,371	2,222	644	1,578
30—40	41 927	17,985	23,942	736	550	186	35 992	16,315	19,677	5,199	1,120	4,079
40—50 ..	28 572	13,211	15,361	270	163	107	21,092	11,460	9,632	7,210	1,588	5,622
50—60 ...	16,947	8,100	8,847	199	49	150	10,145	6,421	3,724	6,603	1,630	4,973
60 and over ...	13,794	6,291	7,503	115	42	73	6,116	4,165	1,951	7,563	2,085	5,478

TABLE VII—*continued.*

Age.	Population. Persons.	Population. Males.	Population. Females.	Unmarried. Persons.	Unmarried. Males.	Unmarried. Females.	Married. Persons.	Married. Males.	Married. Females.	Widowed. Persons.	Widowed. Males.	Widowed. Females.
1	2	3	4	5	6	7	8	9	10	11	12	13
CHAMPARAN.												
ALL RELIGIONS ...	*2,145,687*	*1,080,956*	*1,064,731*	*805,317*	*456,210*	*349,107*	*1,128,438*	*567,481*	*560,957*	*211,932*	*57,265*	*154,667*
0—1 ...	47,507	23,040	24,467	47,071	22,885	24,186	426	153	273	10	2	8
1—2 ...	58,693	27,773	30,920	57,953	27,521	30,432	729	252	477	11	...	11
2—3 ...	66,425	30,804	35,621	65,124	30,333	34,791	1,268	467	801	33	4	29
3—4 ...	70,307	33,370	36,937	67,844	32,435	35,409	2,363	913	1,450	100	22	78
4—5 ...	69,424	33,995	35,429	66,160	32,755	33,405	3,113	1,202	1,911	151	38	113
Total 0—5 ...	*312,356*	*148,982*	*163,374*	*304,152*	*145,929*	*158,223*	*7,899*	*2,987*	*4,912*	*305*	*66*	*239*
5—10 ...	293,046	151,774	141,272	243,352	132,681	110,671	48,565	18,763	29,802	1,129	330	799
10—15 ...	247,738	133,745	114,093	166,450	100,333	66,118	79,527	31,816	47,711	1,761	597	1,164
15—20 ...	170,008	86,856	83,152	39,938	32,225	7,713	126,154	53,074	73,080	3,916	1,557	2,359
20—30 ...	376,456	186,395	190,061	33,459	29,541	3,918	323,540	149,706	173,834	19,457	7,148	12,309
30—40 ...	331,346	166,607	164,739	11,275	9,755	1,520	279,342	145,168	134,174	40,729	11,684	29,045
40—50 ...	216,563	112,822	103,741	4,233	3,678	555	159,120	95,449	63,671	53,210	13,695	39,515
50—60 ...	117,528	58,644	59,884	1,524	1,291	233	69,569	46,236	23,333	46,435	11,117	35,318
60 and over ...	80,646	36,131	44,515	934	778	156	34,722	24,281	10,440	44,090	11,071	33,019
HINDUS ...	*1,787,274*	*903,010*	*884,264*	*676,292*	*384,614*	*291,678*	*931,949*	*468,935*	*462,314*	*179,733*	*49,461*	*130,272*
0—1 ...	39,330	19,075	20,255	38,991	18,953	20,038	332	121	211	7	1	6
1—2 ...	48,435	22,880	25,555	47,846	22,680	25,166	581	200	381	8	...	8
2—3 ...	54,853	25,350	29,503	53,821	24,963	28,858	1,004	384	620	28	3	25
3—4 ...	57,919	27,475	30,444	56,010	26,726	29,287	1,821	730	1,091	85	19	66
4—5 ...	57,177	28,036	29,141	54,696	27,068	27,628	2,355	936	1,419	126	32	94
Total 0—5 ...	*257,714*	*123,816*	*134,898*	*251,367*	*120,390*	*130,977*	*6,093*	*2,371*	*3,722*	*254*	*55*	*199*
5—10 ...	241,936	125,498	116,438	203,533	110,788	92,745	37,437	14,427	23,010	966	283	683
10—15 ...	205,037	110,106	94,931	140,737	84,636	56,101	62,773	24,950	37,823	1,527	520	1,007
15—20 ...	141,072	72,501	68,571	34,597	28,017	6,580	103,152	43,145	60,007	3,323	1,339	1,984
20—30 ...	314,162	156,540	157,622	29,600	26,355	3,245	268,152	134,048	144,104	16,410	6,137	10,273
30—40 ...	278,384	140,472	137,912	10,298	9,036	1,262	233,527	121,289	112,238	34,559	10,147	24,412
40—50 ...	182,504	95,430	87,174	3,904	3,443	461	133,429	80,081	53,348	45,261	11,896	33,365
50—60 ...	98,901	49,479	49,422	1,399	1,217	182	58,000	38,621	19,438	39,433	9,631	29,802
60 and over ...	67,474	30,178	37,296	857	732	125	28,617	19,993	8,624	38,000	9,453	28,547
MUSLIMS ...	*354,235*	*175,988*	*178,247*	*126,569*	*70,437*	*56,132*	*195,808*	*97,815*	*97,993*	*31,858*	*7,736*	*24,122*
0—1 ...	8,055	3,902	4,153	7,958	3,869	4,089	94	32	62	3	1	2
1—2 ...	10,123	4,828	5,295	9,972	4,776	5,196	148	52	96	3	...	3
2—3 ...	11,440	5,392	6,048	11,171	5,308	5,863	264	83	181	5	1	4
3—4 ...	12,261	5,839	6,422	11,704	5,653	6,051	542	183	359	15	3	12
4—5 ...	12,109	5,895	6,214	11,326	5,623	5,703	758	266	492	25	6	19
Total 0—5 ...	*53,988*	*25,856*	*28,132*	*52,131*	*25,229*	*26,902*	*1,806*	*616*	*1,190*	*51*	*11*	*40*
5—10 ...	50,471	25,979	24,492	39,194	21,601	17,593	11,117	4,332	6,785	160	46	114
10—15 ...	42,101	23,354	10,747	25,145	15,420	9,725	16,724	6,858	9,866	232	76	156
15—20 ...	28,553	14,174	14,379	5,059	4,068	991	22,904	8,888	10,016	500	218	378
20—30 ...	61,660	29,571	32,089	3,652	3,090	562	54,987	25,476	29,511	3,021	1,005	2,016
30—40 ...	52,431	25,879	26,552	903	690	213	45,415	23,663	21,752	6,113	1,526	4,587
40—50 ...	33,620	17,230	16,390	307	226	81	25,445	15,220	10,225	7,868	1,784	6,084
50—60 ...	18,403	9,056	9,347	110	69	41	11,371	7,519	3,852	6,922	1,468	5,454
60 and over ...	13,008	5,989	7,119	68	44	24	6,039	4,343	1,796	6,901	1,602	5,299
MUZAFFARPUR.												
ALL RELIGIONS ...	*2,941,025*	*1,443,847*	*1,497,178*	*1,009,674*	*584,333*	*425,341*	*1,579,897*	*775,935*	*803,962*	*351,454*	*83,579*	*267,875*
0—1 ...	61,104	30,409	30,695	60,516	30,061	30,455	556	338	218	32	10	22
1—2 ...	69,686	33,528	36,158	68,581	32,931	35,650	1,072	581	491	33	16	17
2—3 ...	84,100	39,478	44,643	81,796	38,586	43,210	2,261	869	1,392	63	23	40
3—4 ...	92,836	44,624	48,212	87,169	42,598	44,671	5,451	1,962	3,489	216	64	152
4—5 ...	94,903	47,060	47,843	86,718	44,051	42,667	7,833	2,905	4,928	352	104	248
Total 0—5 ...	*402,649*	*195,099*	*207,550*	*384,780*	*188,227*	*196,553*	*17,173*	*6,655*	*10,518*	*696*	*217*	*479*
5—10 ...	403,824	211,268	192,556	308,855	171,888	136,967	91,766	38,113	53,653	3,203	1,267	1,936
10—15 ...	341,461	183,089	158,372	203,376	125,230	78,146	133,568	55,859	77,709	4,517	2,000	2,517
15—20 ...	225,506	112,136	113,370	44,225	37,028	7,197	174,216	71,877	102,339	7,065	3,231	3,834
20—30 ...	490,570	235,481	255,089	39,585	35,894	3,691	420,548	188,665	231,883	30,437	10,922	19,515
30—40 ...	434,295	208,449	225,846	17,698	16,179	1,519	355,123	177,660	177,163	61,474	14,610	46,864
40—50 ...	311,830	149,842	161,988	6,980	6,279	701	220,685	136,270	94,415	84,165	17,298	66,873
50—60 ...	188,800	88,676	100,124	2,766	2,428	338	106,478	70,048	36,435	77,556	16,205	61,351
60 and over ...	142,090	59,807	82,283	1,409	1,189	220	58,340	40,793	17,547	82,341	17,834	64,507
HINDUS ...	*2,549,006*	*1,258,489*	*1,290,517*	*873,465*	*507,263*	*366,202*	*1,367,084*	*676,165*	*690,919*	*308,457*	*75,061*	*233,396*
0—1 ...	52,087	25,880	26,207	51,562	25,558	26,004	498	314	184	27	8	19
1—2 ...	59,499	28,631	30,868	58,536	28,091	30,445	935	527	408	28	13	15
2—3 ...	72,196	33,836	38,360	70,130	33,028	37,102	2,012	700	1,282	54	18	36
3—4 ...	79,765	38,304	41,461	74,769	36,492	38,277	4,807	1,767	3,050	189	55	134
4—5 ...	81,529	40,455	41,074	74,385	37,787	36,598	6,840	2,578	4,262	304	90	214
Total 0—5 ...	*345,076*	*167,106*	*177,970*	*329,382*	*160,956*	*168,426*	*15,092*	*5,966*	*9,126*	*602*	*184*	*418*
5—10 ...	347,575	182,189	165,386	266,253	147,993	118,260	78,486	33,070	45,416	2,836	1,126	1,710
10—15 ...	294,712	158,427	136,285	176,109	108,258	67,851	114,574	48,374	66,200	4,029	1,795	2,234
15—20 ...	195,864	98,188	97,676	38,928	32,734	6,194	150,668	62,561	88,107	6,268	2,893	3,375
20—30 ...	426,387	207,147	219,240	35,820	32,725	3,095	363,800	164,670	199,130	26,767	9,752	17,015
30—40 ...	378,448	183,573	194,875	16,331	15,047	1,284	308,045	155,306	152,739	54,072	13,220	40,852
40—50 ...	272,756	132,134	140,622	6,681	6,078	603	192,112	110,394	81,718	73,963	15,062	58,901
50—60 ...	165,022	77,830	87,202	2,653	2,357	296	94,099	60,834	33,265	68,270	14,630	53,641
60 and over ...	123,166	51,905	71,261	1,308	1,115	193	50,208	34,990	15,218	71,650	15,800	55,850
MUSLIMS ...	*391,091*	*184,852*	*206,239*	*135,686*	*76,739*	*58,947*	*212,452*	*99,611*	*112,841*	*42,953*	*8,502*	*34,451*
0—1 ...	9,000	4,519	4,481	8,937	4,493	4,444	58	24	34	5	2	3
1—2 ...	10,172	4,890	5,282	10,030	4,833	5,197	137	54	83	5	3	2
2—3 ...	11,906	5,636	6,270	11,648	5,552	6,096	249	79	170	9	5	4
3—4 ...	13,054	6,314	6,740	12,383	6,100	6,283	644	205	439	27	9	16
4—5 ...	13,349	6,595	6,754	12,308	6,254	6,054	993	327	666	48	14	34
Total 0—5 ...	*57,481*	*27,954*	*29,527*	*55,306*	*27,232*	*28,074*	*2,081*	*689*	*1,392*	*94*	*33*	*61*
5—10 ...	56,156	29,035	27,121	42,512	23,853	18,659	13,277	5,041	8,236	367	141	226
10—15 ...	46,666	24,023	22,043	27,190	16,935	10,255	18,986	7,463	11,506	488	205	283
15—20 ...	29,554	13,906	15,648	5,244	4,264	980	23,514	9,304	14,210	796	338	458
20—30 ...	63,931	28,177	35,754	3,628	3,063	575	56,638	23,956	33,683	3,665	1,168	2,497
30—40 ...	55,608	24,702	30,906	1,320	1,088	232	46,985	22,316	24,669	7,393	1,388	6,005
40—50 ...	38,978	17,047	21,331	277	181	96	28,511	15,942	12,669	10,190	1,624	8,566
50—60 ...	23,733	10,831	12,902	110	69	41	14,346	9,189	5,157	9,277	1,573	7,704
60 and over ...	18,894	7,887	11,007	99	64	35	8,112	5,791	2,321	10,683	2,032	8,651

TABLE VII—*continued.*

Age, Sex and Civil Condition. | **Part II—Details for Districts.**

Age.	Population. Persons.	Males.	Females.	Unmarried. Persons.	Males.	Females.	Married. Persons.	Males.	Females.	Widowed. Persons.	Males.	Females.
1	2	3	4	5	6	7	8	9	10	11	12	13
DARBHANGA.												
ALL RELIGIONS ...	*3,166,094*	*1,570,959*	*1,595,135*	*790,484*	*463,752*	*326,732*	*2,010,541*	*1,012,350*	*998,191*	*365,069*	*94,857*	*270,212*
0—1 ...	57,275	28,958	28,317	56,643	28,694	27,949	592	252	340	40	12	28
1—2 ...	75,798	37,012	38,786	73,521	36,039	37,482	2,143	916	1,227	134	57	77
2—3 ...	93,312	44,807	48,505	86,387	41,936	44,451	6,596	2,757	3,839	329	114	215
3—4 ...	104,352	51,135	53,217	83,933	42,948	40,985	19,630	7,916	11,714	789	271	518
4—5 ...	105,284	52,627	52,657	74,751	40,471	34,280	29,407	11,748	17,659	1,126	408	718
Total 0—5 ...	*436,021*	*214,539*	*221,482*	*375,285*	*190,088*	*185,147*	*58,368*	*23,589*	*34,779*	*2,418*	*862*	*1,556*
5—10 ...	446,737	233,332	213,405	223,618	131,623	91,995	214,468	98,216	116,252	8,651	3,493	5,158
10—15 ...	377,234	200,080	177,154	125,373	82,888	42,485	241,741	112,686	129,055	10,120	4,506	5,614
15—20 ...	246,660	119,588	127,072	25,713	22,851	2,862	210,961	91,085	118,976	9,986	4,752	5,284
20—30 ...	544,467	260,210	284,257	24,351	22,155	2,196	483,185	224,758	258,327	37,031	13,297	23,734
30—40 ...	471,054	231,328	239,726	9,207	7,998	1,200	396,037	207,541	188,496	65,810	15,759	50,021
40—50 ...	321,723	160,371	161,352	3,728	3,369	359	235,759	139,664	96,095	82,236	17,338	64,898
50—60 ...	187,019	90,928	96,091	1,692	1,519	173	111,271	72,930	38,341	74,056	16,479	57,577
60 and over ...	135,179	60,583	74,596	1,567	1,261	306	58,351	40,981	17,870	74,761	18,341	56,420
HINDUS ...	*2,725,427*	*1,354,928*	*1,370,499*	*657,204*	*387,147*	*270,057*	*1,746,940*	*882,580*	*864,360*	*321,283*	*85,201*	*236,082*
0—1 ...	48,667	24,662	24,005	48,113	24,447	23,066	517	204	313	37	11	26
1—2 ...	64,704	31,587	33,117	62,715	30,796	31,919	1,869	737	1,132	120	54	66
2—3 ...	79,685	38,174	41,511	73,550	35,713	37,837	5,828	2,353	3,475	307	108	199
3—4 ...	88,992	43,484	45,508	70,685	36,191	34,494	17,595	7,060	10,535	712	233	479
4—5 ...	89,554	44,660	44,894	62,100	33,740	28,360	26,464	10,580	15,884	990	340	650
Total 0—5 ...	*371,602*	*182,567*	*189,035*	*317,163*	*160,887*	*156,276*	*52,273*	*20,934*	*31,339*	*2,166*	*746*	*1,420*
5—10 ...	381,833	159,409	182,424	182,611	107,922	74,689	191,213	88,273	102,940	8,009	3,214	4,795
10—15 ...	323,543	171,819	151,724	100,747	67,183	33,564	213,444	100,496	112,148	9,352	4,140	5,212
15—20 ...	212,278	103,540	108,738	21,391	19,250	2,141	181,852	79,948	101,104	9,035	4,342	4,693
20—30 ...	470,647	225,983	244,664	21,201	19,480	1,721	415,778	194,395	221,383	33,068	12,108	20,960
30—40 ...	408,299	201,504	206,795	8,122	7,163	959	342,119	179,983	162,136	58,058	14,358	43,700
40—50 ...	279,872	130,760	140,112	3,290	3,009	281	204,268	121,021	83,247	72,314	15,730	56,584
50—60 ...	162,663	79,144	83,519	1,505	1,358	147	96,117	62,895	33,222	65,641	14,891	50,150
60 and over ...	115,290	51,202	64,088	1,174	895	279	49,876	34,635	15,241	64,240	15,672	48,568
MUSLIMS ...	*440,037*	*215,663*	*224,374*	*133,024*	*76,440*	*56,584*	*263,264*	*129,579*	*133,685*	*43,749*	*9,644*	*34,105*
0—1 ...	8,595	4,288	4,307	8,517	4,239	4,278	75	48	27	3	1	2
1—2 ...	11,080	5,416	5,664	10,792	5,224	5,568	274	179	95	14	3	11
2—3 ...	13,607	6,621	6,986	12,817	6,211	6,606	768	404	364	22	6	16
3—4 ...	15,344	7,642	7,702	13,232	6,748	6,484	2,035	856	1,179	77	38	39
4—5 ...	15,710	7,954	7,756	12,632	6,719	5,913	2,942	1,167	1,775	136	68	68
Total 0—5 ...	*64,336*	*31,921*	*32,415*	*57,950*	*29,151*	*28,839*	*6,094*	*2,654*	*3,440*	*252*	*116*	*136*
5—10 ...	64,845	33,886	30,959	40,952	23,666	17,286	23,251	9,941	13,310	642	279	363
10—15 ...	53,648	28,224	25,414	24,589	15,680	8,909	28,291	12,188	16,103	768	366	402
15—20 ...	34,335	16,022	18,313	4,269	3,555	714	29,485	12,027	17,058	951	410	541
20—30 ...	74,293	34,158	40,135	3,110	2,649	461	67,224	30,522	36,702	3,959	1,187	2,772
30—40 ...	62,653	29,770	32,883	1,073	827	246	53,853	27,513	26,820	7,747	1,430	6,317
40—50 ...	41,763	20,554	21,209	434	358	76	31,416	18,591	12,826	9,913	1,605	8,308
50—60 ...	24,304	11,755	12,549	186	160	26	15,112	10,010	5,102	9,666	1,555	7,421
60 and over ...	19,860	9,363	10,497	391	364	27	8,958	6,353	2,625	10,511	2,666	7,845
MONGHYR.												
ALL RELIGIONS ...	*2,287,154*	*1,145,797*	*1,141,357*	*684,336*	*405,749*	*278,587*	*1,364,830*	*674,937*	*689,893*	*237,988*	*65,111*	*172,877*
0—1 ...	54,278	26,736	27,542	53,550	26,372	27,178	696	353	343	32	11	21
1—2 ...	64,489	31,083	33,406	63,140	30,517	32,623	1,302	548	754	47	18	20
2—3 ...	71,797	33,958	37,839	68,917	32,919	35,998	2,869	1,008	1,861	71	31	40
3—4 ...	77,515	37,074	39,541	69,479	35,273	34,206	7,842	2,623	5,219	194	78	116
4—5 ...	75,564	38,458	37,006	63,454	34,468	28,986	11,750	3,910	7,840	300	120	160
Total 0—5 ...	*343,583*	*168,249*	*175,334*	*318,540*	*159,549*	*158,991*	*24,399*	*8,442*	*15,957*	*644*	*258*	*356*
5—10 ...	313,187	164,928	148,259	195,434	116,846	78,588	114,966	46,919	68,047	2,787	1,163	1,624
10—15 ...	264,682	141,058	123,624	112,537	75,647	36,890	148,404	63,707	84,697	3,741	1,644	2,097
15—20 ...	178,438	87,191	91,247	22,393	19,949	2,444	150,961	66,007	85,894	5,084	2,175	2,909
20—30 ...	377,848	181,122	196,726	20,659	19,592	1,067	337,018	154,478	182,540	20,171	7,062	13,119
30—40 ...	322,809	160,226	162,583	8,192	7,874	318	276,824	142,111	134,713	37,793	10,221	27,572
40—50 ...	230,067	118,837	111,280	3,754	3,605	149	173,658	101,780	71,878	52,655	13,452	39,203
50—60 ...	143,544	72,753	70,791	1,864	1,791	73	88,335	57,451	30,884	53,295	13,511	39,784
60 and over ...	112,896	51,433	61,563	963	876	87	50,215	34,922	15,293	61,818	15,635	46,183
HINDUS ...	*2,049,192*	*1,031,465*	*1,017,727*	*598,040*	*356,485*	*241,555*	*1,235,888*	*614,378*	*621,010*	*215,764*	*60,602*	*155,162*
0—1 ...	48,404	23,894	24,510	47,767	23,567	24,200	615	316	299	22	11	11
1—2 ...	57,171	27,638	29,533	55,969	27,119	28,850	1,168	501	667	34	18	16
2—3 ...	63,656	30,163	33,493	61,047	29,222	31,825	2,548	912	1,636	61	29	32
3—4 ...	68,770	33,743	35,027	61,356	31,265	30,091	7,235	2,404	4,831	179	74	105
4—5 ...	66,847	34,135	32,712	55,703	30,422	25,281	10,870	3,501	7,269	274	112	162
Total 0—5 ...	*304,848*	*149,573*	*155,275*	*281,842*	*141,595*	*140,247*	*22,436*	*7,734*	*14,702*	*570*	*244*	*326*
5—10 ...	278,288	146,723	131,565	169,601	102,086	67,515	106,650	43,521	62,529	2,637	1,116	1,521
10—15 ...	236,646	126,097	109,940	96,255	65,424	30,831	136,241	59,093	77,148	3,550	1,580	1,970
15—20 ...	160,805	78,790	81,215	18,790	17,061	1,729	136,515	59,677	76,838	4,760	2,052	2,648
20—30 ...	339,660	164,344	175,316	17,976	17,182	794	303,339	140,556	162,783	18,345	6,606	11,739
30—40 ...	291,327	145,766	145,561	7,722	7,503	219	249,379	128,682	120,697	34,226	9,581	24,645
40—50 ...	207,854	107,907	99,947	3,477	3,367	110	156,760	91,957	64,743	47,677	12,583	35,094
50—60 ...	129,752	65,996	63,756	1,571	1,521	50	79,805	51,929	27,876	48,376	12,546	35,830
60 and over ...	101,412	46,269	55,143	806	746	60	44,923	31,229	13,694	55,683	14,294	41,389
MUSLIMS ...	*228,497*	*109,408*	*119,089*	*82,179*	*46,980*	*35,199*	*124,684*	*58,125*	*66,559*	*21,634*	*4,303*	*17,331*
0—1 ...	5,584	2,699	2,885	5,498	2,664	2,834	76	35	41	10	...	10
1—2 ...	7,011	3,306	3,705	6,870	3,261	3,609	128	45	83	13	...	13
2—3 ...	7,809	3,649	4,160	7,546	3,556	3,990	253	91	162	10	2	8
3—4 ...	8,388	4,061	4,327	7,782	3,846	3,936	591	211	380	15	4	11
4—5 ...	8,305	4,193	4,112	7,424	3,886	3,538	855	299	556	26	8	18
Total 0—5 ...	*37,097*	*17,908*	*19,189*	*35,120*	*17,213*	*17,907*	*1,903*	*681*	*1,222*	*74*	*14*	*60*
5—10 ...	33,512	17,465	16,047	24,660	14,116	10,544	8,707	3,304	5,403	145	45	100
10—15 ...	27,510	14,336	13,174	15,475	9,733	5,742	11,856	4,543	7,307	185	60	125
15—20 ...	17,683	8,023	9,660	3,353	2,703	650	13,962	5,202	8,760	388	118	250
20—30 ...	36,568	15,966	20,602	2,460	2,235	225	[illegible]	18,710	10,043	1,750	431	1,334
30—40 ...	30,136	13,758	16,378	407	303	66	[illegible]	12,798	19,445	3,466	598	2,869
40—50 ...	21,044	10,412	10,632	257	226	31	16,237	9,366	6,871	4,850	620	4,030
50—60 ...	13,346	6,516	6,830	281	263	18	8,267	5,323	2,944	4,798	930	3,868
60 and over ...	11,381	5,024	6,377	146	129	17	5,162	3,598	1,564	5,993	1,297	4,096

TABLE VII—*continued.*

AGE, SEX AND CIVIL CONDITION. | **PART II—DETAILS FOR DISTRICTS.**

Age.	Population.			Unmarried.			Married.			Widowed.		
	Persons.	Males.	Females.	Persons.	Males.	Females.	Persons.	Males.	Females.	Persons.	Males.	Females.
1	2	3	4	5	6	7	8	9	10	11	12	13
BHAGALPUR.												
ALL RELIGIONS ...	*2,234,632*	*1,130,584*	*1,104,048*	*650,361*	*381,553*	*268,808*	*1,343,542*	*683,666*	*659,876*	*240,729*	*65,365*	*175,364*
0—1 ...	48,489	23,894	24,595	47,994	23,614	24,380	478	269	209	17	11	6
1—2 ...	56,358	27,193	29,167	55,521	26,840	28,681	812	338	474	26	14	12
2—3 ...	70,187	33,248	36,939	67,700	32,266	35,434	2,411	953	1,458	76	29	47
3—4 ...	79,447	38,969	40,478	70,689	35,839	34,850	8,542	3,062	5,480	216	68	148
4—5 ...	78,275	39,740	38,535	64,652	34,977	29,675	13,314	4,669	8,645	309	94	215
Total 0—5 ...	*332,757*	*163,043*	*169,714*	*306,556*	*153,536*	*153,020*	*25,557*	*9,291*	*16,266*	*644*	*216*	*428*
5—10 ...	320,396	168,799	151,597	194,250	116,731	77,519	122,911	50,893	72,018	3,235	1,175	2,060
10—15 ...	265,198	141,432	123,766	108,890	74,123	34,737	151,721	65,476	86,245	4,587	1,833	2,754
15—20 ...	179,452	87,231	92,218	20,077	17,780	2,397	153,184	66,832	86,352	6,191	2,622	3,569
20—30 ...	392,889	192,151	200,738	14,811	13,871	940	353,044	169,196	183,848	25,034	9,084	15,950
30—40 ...	326,907	168,417	158,490	3,754	3,568	186	278,051	152,144	125,907	45,102	12,705	32,397
40—50 ...	209,858	110,812	99,046	1,258	1,216	42	153,561	95,604	57,957	55,009	13,966	41,043
50—60 ...	118,920	59,064	59,856	472	452	20	69,048	47,332	21,716	49,400	11,880	37,520
60 and over ...	88,255	39,032	49,223	263	246	17	36,465	26,902	9,563	51,527	11,884	39,643
HINDUS ...	*1,980,202*	*1,002,604*	*977,598*	*569,926*	*334,059*	*235,867*	*1,193,423*	*608,149*	*585,274*	*216,913*	*60,456*	*156,457*
0—1 ...	42,754	21,053	21,702	42,348	20,789	21,559	391	264	127	15	9	6
1—2 ...	49,462	23,840	25,622	48,794	23,583	25,211	644	295	349	24	13	11
2—3 ...	61,589	29,176	32,413	59,511	28,294	31,217	2,031	857	1,174	47	25	22
3—4 ...	69,762	34,234	35,528	62,194	31,450	30,744	7,383	2,723	4,660	175	61	114
4—5 ...	68,688	34,910	33,778	56,802	30,704	26,098	11,605	4,152	7,453	281	86	195
Total 0—5 ...	*292,255*	*143,212*	*149,043*	*269,649*	*134,767*	*134,882*	*22,064*	*8,251*	*13,813*	*543*	*194*	*349*
5—10 ...	282,239	143,730	138,509	169,908	102,039	67,869	109,416	45,585	63,831	2,915	1,105	1,810
10—15 ...	234,328	125,006	109,322	94,708	64,479	30,229	135,454	58,789	76,665	4,166	1,738	2,428
15—20 ...	159,142	77,419	81,723	17,268	15,823	1,445	136,202	59,633	76,569	5,672	2,463	3,209
20—30 ...	349,379	171,216	178,163	13,037	12,283	754	313,578	150,483	163,095	22,764	8,450	14,314
30—40 ...	291,478	150,564	140,914	3,461	3,326	135	247,255	135,379	111,876	40,762	11,859	28,903
40—50 ...	187,079	98,862	88,217	1,216	1,188	28	136,389	84,722	51,667	49,474	12,952	36,522
50—60 ...	106,080	53,185	52,895	435	420	15	61,153	41,834	19,319	44,492	10,931	33,561
60 and over ...	78,282	34,461	43,821	244	234	10	31,912	23,463	8,449	46,126	10,764	35,362
MUSLIMS ...	*249,436*	*125,257*	*124,179*	*77,941*	*46,068*	*31,873*	*147,961*	*74,382*	*73,579*	*23,534*	*4,807*	*18,727*
0—1 ...	5,614	2,770	2,844	5,526	2,754	2,772	86	14	72	2	2	...
1—2 ...	6,760	3,287	3,473	6,592	3,245	3,347	166	41	125	2	1	1
2—3 ...	8,458	4,010	4,448	8,051	3,910	4,141	378	96	282	29	4	25
3—4 ...	9,526	4,661	4,865	8,339	4,316	4,023	1,146	338	808	41	7	34
4—5 ...	9,404	4,746	4,658	7,673	4,194	3,479	1,704	545	1,159	27	7	20
Total 0—5 ...	*39,762*	*19,474*	*20,288*	*36,181*	*18,419*	*17,762*	*3,480*	*1,034*	*2,446*	*101*	*21*	*80*
5—10 ...	37,331	19,609	17,722	23,597	14,271	9,326	13,416	5,269	8,147	318	69	249
10—15 ...	30,155	16,012	14,143	13,576	9,267	4,309	16,160	6,651	9,509	419	94	325
15—20 ...	19,867	9,578	10,289	2,599	2,315	284	10,757	7,106	3,651	511	157	354
20—30 ...	42,666	20,496	22,170	1,623	1,481	142	38,800	18,391	20,409	2,243	624	1,619
30—40 ...	34,822	17,530	17,292	257	223	34	30,265	16,478	13,787	4,300	829	3,471
40—50 ...	22,398	11,722	10,676	61	52	9	16,858	10,674	6,184	5,479	996	4,483
50—60 ...	12,620	6,352	6,268	34	31	3	7,741	5,392	2,349	4,845	929	3,916
60 and over ...	9,815	4,484	5,331	13	9	4	4,484	3,467	1,017	5,318	1,088	4,230
PURNEA.												
ALL RELIGIONS ...	*2,186,543*	*1,129,681*	*1,056,862*	*766,410*	*459,310*	*307,100*	*1,194,856*	*616,117*	*578,738*	*225,278*	*54,254*	*171,024*
0—1 ...	43,592	21,999	21,593	43,211	21,504	21,707	372	191	181	9	4	5
1—2 ...	55,151	26,210	28,941	53,950	25,830	28,120	1,183	375	808	18	5	13
2—3 ...	70,821	33,812	37,009	68,002	32,161	35,841	2,761	674	2,087	58	17	41
3—4 ...	79,844	38,228	41,616	73,197	36,540	36,657	5,999	1,045	4,954	148	43	105
4—5 ...	80,349	39,674	40,675	70,917	37,234	33,683	9,220	2,380	6,840	212	60	152
Total 0—5 ...	*329,757*	*158,663*	*171,094*	*309,277*	*153,269*	*156,008*	*20,035*	*5,265*	*14,770*	*445*	*129*	*316*
5—10 ...	320,666	167,412	153,254	233,897	138,350	95,547	84,673	28,450	56,223	2,096	612	1,484
10—15 ...	261,294	139,940	121,354	147,189	98,976	48,213	111,073	40,094	70,979	3,032	870	2,162
15—20 ...	182,291	87,582	94,709	37,307	32,875	4,432	139,438	53,193	86,245	5,546	1,514	4,032
20—30 ...	400,367	194,332	206,035	30,966	28,880	2,086	342,164	158,095	184,069	27,237	7,357	19,880
30—40 ...	326,558	177,252	149,306	5,694	5,160	534	269,186	160,006	109,180	51,678	12,086	39,592
40—50 ...	198,711	114,553	84,158	1,370	1,201	169	140,372	100,497	39,875	56,969	12,855	44,114
50—60 ...	99,594	55,213	44,381	442	385	57	57,606	45,343	12,263	41,546	9,485	32,061
60 and over ...	67,305	34,734	32,571	268	214	54	30,308	25,174	5,134	36,729	9,346	27,383
HINDUS ...	*1,285,314*	*665,451*	*619,863*	*443,196*	*262,403*	*180,793*	*701,217*	*364,278*	*336,939*	*140,901*	*38,770*	*102,131*
0—1 ...	25,712	12,737	12,975	25,529	12,603	12,926	180	130	50	4	2	2
1—2 ...	31,851	15,139	16,712	31,381	14,899	16,482	461	237	224	9	3	6
2—3 ...	40,909	18,956	21,953	39,938	18,625	21,313	937	320	617	34	11	23
3—4 ...	45,886	21,988	23,898	43,136	21,211	21,925	2,665	751	1,914	85	26	59
4—5 ...	45,648	22,634	23,014	41,478	21,507	19,971	4,053	1,092	2,961	117	35	82
Total 0—5 ...	*190,007*	*91,452*	*98,555*	*181,463*	*88,846*	*92,617*	*8,296*	*2,530*	*5,766*	*249*	*77*	*172*
5—10 ...	184,661	96,304	88,357	136,342	80,039	56,303	46,882	15,842	31,040	1,437	423	1,014
10—15 ...	150,532	80,207	70,325	84,519	56,526	27,993	63,870	23,050	40,820	2,143	631	1,512
15—20 ...	104,088	49,765	54,323	19,571	17,264	2,307	80,803	31,399	49,404	3,714	1,102	2,612
20—30 ...	233,461	114,115	119,346	16,343	15,229	1,114	200,272	93,807	106,465	16,846	5,079	11,767
30—40 ...	195,628	106,781	88,847	3,464	3,169	295	161,238	95,110	66,128	30,926	8,502	22,424
40—50 ...	121,611	70,611	51,000	963	869	94	86,180	60,494	25,686	34,448	9,228	25,220
50—60 ...	61,993	34,357	27,636	337	300	37	35,306	27,082	8,224	26,350	6,975	19,375
60 and over ...	43,333	21,859	21,474	175	142	33	18,370	14,964	3,406	24,788	6,753	18,035
MUSLIMS ...	*886,368*	*456,347*	*430,021*	*315,967*	*192,874*	*123,093*	*480,914*	*248,298*	*232,616*	*83,487*	*15,175*	*68,312*
0—1 ...	17,568	8,813	8,755	17,373	8,751	8,622	191	60	131	4	2	2
1—2 ...	22,795	10,850	11,945	22,069	10,712	11,357	717	136	581	9	2	7
2—3 ...	29,261	13,597	15,664	27,424	13,243	14,181	1,813	348	1,465	24	6	18
3—4 ...	33,279	15,899	17,380	29,404	15,003	14,401	3,812	879	2,933	63	17	46
4—5 ...	34,637	16,699	17,938	28,811	15,410	13,401	5,132	1,264	3,868	94	25	69
Total 0—5 ...	*136,940*	*65,858*	*71,082*	*126,081*	*63,119*	*61,962*	*11,665*	*2,687*	*8,978*	*194*	*52*	*142*
5—10 ...	133,645	69,864	63,781	95,418	57,163	38,255	37,572	12,513	25,059	655	188	467
10—15 ...	108,951	58,766	50,185	61,233	41,612	19,621	46,837	16,917	29,920	881	237	644
15—20 ...	76,981	37,203	39,778	17,295	15,273	2,022	57,881	21,524	36,357	1,805	406	1,399
20—30 ...	164,505	79,036	85,469	14,266	13,349	917	139,954	63,443	76,511	10,285	2,244	8,041
30—40 ...	128,932	69,355	59,577	2,148	1,927	221	106,200	63,903	42,297	20,584	3,525	17,059
40—50 ...	75,854	43,155	32,699	353	289	64	53,197	39,320	13,877	22,304	3,546	18,758
50—60 ...	37,003	20,463	16,540	93	76	17	21,888	17,941	3,947	15,022	2,446	12,576
60 and over ...	23,557	12,647	10,910	80	66	14	11,720	10,050	1,670	11,757	2,531	9,226

TABLE VII—*continued.*

AGE, SEX AND CIVIL CONDITION. | **PART II—DETAILS FOR DISTRICTS.**

Age.	Population.			Unmarried.			Married.			Widowed.		
	Persons.	Males.	Females.	Persons.	Males.	Females.	Persons.	Males.	Females.	Persons.	Males.	Females.
1	2	3	4	5	6	7	8	9	10	11	12	13
SANTAL PARGANAS.												
ALL RELIGIONS ...	*2,051,472*	*1,025,921*	*1,025,551*	*809,104*	*451,908*	*357,196*	*1,071,501*	*533,792*	*537,709*	*170,867*	*40,221*	*130,646*
0—1 ...	59,991	29,461	30,530	56,973	28,229	28,744	3,003	1,229	1,774	15	3	12
1—2 ...	59,379	28,646	30,733	56,267	27,402	28,865	3,096	1,239	1,857	16	5	11
2—3 ...	70,597	33,810	36,787	66,219	32,169	34,050	4,331	1,632	2,699	47	9	38
3—4 ...	77,606	38,205	39,401	70,408	35,530	34,878	7,058	2,645	4,413	140	30	110
4—5 ...	75,909	38,330	37,579	66,968	35,005	31,963	8,731	3,273	5,458	210	52	158
Total 0—5 ...	*343,482*	*168,452*	*175,030*	*316,835*	*158,335*	*158,500*	*26,219*	*10,018*	*16,201*	*428*	*99*	*329*
5—10 ...	300,235	156,042	144,193	231,249	130,039	101,210	67,557	25,639	41,918	1,429	364	1,065
10—15 ...	247,962	130,043	117,919	153,796	92,910	60,886	91,942	36,516	55,426	2,224	617	1,607
15—20 ...	172,519	82,581	89,938	42,593	28,796	13,797	125,209	52,390	72,819	4,717	1,395	3,322
20—30 ...	357,675	172,307	185,368	37,933	24,889	13,044	300,111	142,067	158,044	19,631	5,351	14,280
30—40 ...	279,418	142,126	137,292	14,825	9,030	5,795	232,246	126,473	100,773	32,347	7,623	24,724
40—50 ...	174,975	90,152	84,823	6,867	4,416	2,451	128,893	76,980	51,913	39,215	8,756	30,459
50—60 ...	104,269	51,464	52,805	3,219	2,107	1,032	64,799	41,282	23,517	36,251	7,985	28,266
60 and over ...	70,937	32,754	38,183	1,787	1,296	491	34,525	23,427	11,098	34,625	8,031	26,594
HINDUS ...	*949,198*	*475,601*	*473,597*	*322,044*	*186,185*	*135,859*	*531,321*	*268,067*	*263,254*	*95,833*	*21,349*	*74,484*
0—1 ...	26,732	13,104	13,628	24,967	12,477	12,490	1,755	625	1,130	10	2	8
1—2 ...	26,727	12,942	13,785	24,922	12,315	12,607	1,793	623	1,170	12	4	8
2—3 ...	31,484	15,078	16,406	28,822	14,216	14,606	2,622	854	1,708	40	8	32
3—4 ...	34,632	17,103	17,529	30,158	15,674	14,484	4,369	1,407	2,962	105	22	83
4—5 ...	33,433	16,993	16,440	27,875	15,232	12,643	5,415	1,727	3,688	143	34	109
Total 0—5 ...	*153,008*	*75,220*	*77,788*	*136,744*	*69,914*	*66,830*	*15,954*	*5,236*	*10,718*	*310*	*70*	*240*
5—10 ...	133,305	69,939	63,366	89,871	54,169	35,702	42,475	15,524	26,951	959	246	713
10—15 ...	110,113	58,566	51,547	54,802	36,651	18,151	53,970	21,526	32,444	1,341	389	952
15—20 ...	78,433	37,929	40,504	13,953	10,421	3,532	61,994	26,805	35,189	2,486	703	1,783
20—30 ...	169,967	81,374	88,593	15,040	9,112	5,928	143,865	69,638	74,227	11,062	2,624	8,438
30—40 ...	135,851	69,081	66,820	6,717	3,258	3,459	110,386	61,818	48,568	18,748	3,955	14,793
40—50 ...	85,367	43,928	41,439	3,006	1,555	1,451	59,569	37,503	22,066	22,792	4,870	17,922
50—60 ...	49,476	24,394	25,082	1,269	710	559	28,236	19,361	8,875	19,971	4,323	15,648
60 and over ...	33,678	15,220	18,458	642	305	247	14,872	10,656	4,216	18,164	4,169	13,995
MUSLIMS ...	*223,702*	*112,839*	*110,863*	*81,149*	*45,826*	*35,323*	*126,887*	*63,913*	*62,974*	*15,666*	*3,100*	*12,566*
0—1 ...	6,797	3,422	3,375	6,521	3,275	3,246	273	146	127	3	1	2
1—2 ...	7,124	3,483	3,641	6,812	3,333	3,479	311	150	161	1	...	1
2—3 ...	8,277	3,989	4,288	7,765	3,769	3,996	509	220	289	3	...	3
3—4 ...	8,985	4,507	4,478	7,947	4,026	3,921	1,025	478	547	13	3	10
4—5 ...	9,034	4,700	4,334	7,629	4,031	3,598	1,381	663	718	24	6	18
Total 0—5 ...	*40,217*	*20,101*	*20,116*	*36,674*	*18,434*	*18,240*	*3,499*	*1,657*	*1,842*	*44*	*10*	*34*
5—10 ...	34,958	18,414	16,544	24,353	14,008	10,255	10,443	4,265	6,178	162	51	111
10—15 ...	27,943	14,825	13,118	14,211	9,082	5,120	13,503	5,669	7,834	229	74	155
15—20 ...	18,580	8,897	9,683	2,361	1,829	532	15,804	6,950	8,854	415	118	297
20—30 ...	39,285	19,080	20,205	2,117	1,471	646	35,406	17,153	18,253	1,762	456	1,306
30—40 ...	28,839	14,547	14,292	802	499	303	25,058	13,507	11,551	2,979	541	2,438
40—50 ...	17,142	8,774	8,368	348	221	127	13,160	7,959	5,201	3,634	594	3,040
50—60 ...	9,810	4,592	4,918	186	121	65	6,392	4,213	2,179	3,232	558	2,674
60 and over ...	6,928	3,309	3,619	97	71	26	3,622	2,540	1,082	3,209	698	2,511
TRIBAL ...	*865,128*	*430,935*	*434,193*	*400,394*	*216,602*	*183,792*	*406,219*	*198,746*	*207,473*	*58,515*	*15,587*	*42,928*
0—1 ...	26,072	12,748	13,324	25,095	12,290	12,805	975	458	517	2	...	2
1—2 ...	25,164	12,032	13,132	24,169	11,565	12,604	992	466	526	2	1	2
2—3 ...	30,447	14,568	15,879	29,243	14,009	15,234	1,200	558	642	4	1	3
3—4 ...	33,580	16,412	17,168	31,898	15,651	16,247	1,660	756	904	22	5	17
4—5 ...	32,989	16,406	16,581	31,019	15,521	15,498	1,927	875	1,052	43	12	31
Total 0—5 ...	*148,252*	*72,168*	*76,084*	*141,424*	*69,036*	*72,388*	*6,754*	*3,113*	*3,641*	*74*	*19*	*55*
5—10 ...	129,982	66,716	63,266	115,718	60,851	54,867	13,956	5,798	8,158	308	67	241
10—15 ...	108,127	55,821	52,306	83,788	46,434	37,354	23,687	9,233	14,454	652	154	498
15—20 ...	74,297	35,215	39,082	25,642	16,221	9,421	46,855	18,425	28,430	1,800	569	1,231
20—30 ...	146,040	70,680	75,360	20,333	14,030	6,303	118,988	54,412	64,570	6,719	2,238	4,481
30—40 ...	112,977	57,662	55,315	7,215	5,221	1,994	95,297	49,357	45,940	10,465	3,084	7,381
40—50 ...	71,335	36,854	34,481	3,485	2,624	861	55,251	30,974	24,277	12,599	3,258	9,349
50—60 ...	44,303	21,844	22,459	1,749	1,357	392	29,702	17,417	12,285	12,852	3,070	9,782
60 and over ...	29,815	13,075	15,840	1,040	828	212	15,729	10,017	5,712	13,046	3,130	9,916
CUTTACK.												
ALL RELIGIONS ...	*2,176,707*	*1,028,134*	*1,148,573*	*904,777*	*528,284*	*376,493*	*975,675*	*460,519*	*515,156*	*296,255*	*39,331*	*256,924*
0—1 ...	56,582	28,138	28,444	56,579	28,138	28,441	3	...	3	...	...	...
1—2 ...	56,890	27,760	29,130	56,883	27,759	29,124	7	1	6	...	...	...
2—3 ...	62,197	29,918	32,279	62,175	29,912	32,263	19	6	13	3	...	3
3—4 ...	57,858	28,399	29,459	57,737	28,357	29,380	111	41	70	10	1	9
4—5 ...	51,740	26,169	25,571	51,529	26,092	25,437	197	75	122	14	2	12
Total 0—5 ...	*285,267*	*140,384*	*144,883*	*284,903*	*140,258*	*144,645*	*337*	*123*	*214*	*27*	*3*	*24*
5—10 ...	247,574	126,358	121,216	236,773	124,819	111,954	10,512	1,623	8,969	289	16	273
10—15 ...	237,641	122,309	115,332	208,773	118,427	90,346	28,016	3,824	24,192	852	58	794
15—20 ...	211,103	101,918	109,185	98,248	76,916	21,332	107,955	24,633	83,322	4,900	370	4,530
20—30 ...	397,584	179,997	217,587	66,450	60,281	6,169	304,326	116,972	187,354	26,808	2,744	24,064
30—40 ...	319,694	142,948	176,746	6,348	5,173	1,175	256,199	132,414	123,785	57,147	5,361	51,786
40—50 ...	234,686	106,780	127,809	1,893	1,346	547	156,281	96,634	59,647	76,514	8,809	67,705
50—60 ...	150,654	68,894	81,760	877	669	208	78,858	57,276	21,582	70,919	10,950	59,969
60 and over ...	92,502	38,537	53,965	512	395	117	33,191	27,122	6,069	58,799	11,020	47,779
HINDUS ...	*2,106,830*	*996,424*	*1,110,406*	*874,228*	*510,681*	*363,547*	*944,810*	*447,145*	*497,665*	*287,792*	*38,598*	*249,194*
0—1 ...	54,794	27,243	27,551	54,791	27,243	27,548	3	...	3	...	...	...
1—2 ...	55,157	26,887	28,270	55,151	26,887	28,264	6	...	6	...	...	...
2—3 ...	60,233	28,967	31,266	60,212	28,961	31,251	18	6	12	3	...	3
3—4 ...	56,008	27,484	28,524	55,889	27,443	28,446	109	40	69	10	1	9
4—5 ...	50,092	25,336	24,756	49,886	25,262	24,624	192	72	120	14	2	12
Total 0—5 ...	*276,284*	*135,917*	*140,367*	*275,929*	*135,796*	*140,133*	*328*	*118*	*210*	*27*	*3*	*24*
5—10 ...	239,036	121,990	117,046	228,462	120,495	107,967	10,291	1,480	8,811	283	15	268
10—15 ...	229,134	117,994	111,140	201,241	114,208	87,033	27,066	3,730	23,336	827	56	771
15—20 ...	203,846	98,724	105,122	94,989	74,404	20,585	104,086	23,958	80,128	4,771	362	4,409
20—30 ...	384,480	174,640	209,840	64,290	58,411	5,879	294,153	113,554	180,599	26,037	2,675	23,362
30—40 ...	310,020	138,955	171,065	6,125	5,012	1,113	248,531	128,701	119,830	55,364	5,242	50,122
40—50 ...	227,692	103,701	123,991	1,834	1,313	521	151,649	93,817	57,832	74,209	8,661	65,548
50—60 ...	146,531	67,033	79,498	860	656	204	76,589	55,582	21,007	69,082	10,795	58,287
60 and over ...	89,807	37,380	52,427	498	386	112	32,117	26,205	5,912	57,192	10,789	46,403

TABLE VII—*continued.*

AGE, SEX AND CIVIL CONDITION. | **PART II—DETAILS FOR DISTRICTS.**

Age.	Population.			Unmarried.			Married.			Widowed.		
	Persons.	Males.	Females.	Persons.	Males.	Females.	Persons.	Males.	Females.	Persons.	Males.	Females.
1	2	3	4	5	6	7	8	9	10	11	12	13
CUTTACK—concluded.												
MUSLIMS ...	*66,104*	*29,965*	*36,139*	*28,518*	*16,674*	*11,844*	*29,432*	*12,622*	*16,810*	*8,154*	*669*	*7,485*
0—1 ...	1,697	850	847	1,697	850	847	...	...	...	...	...	...
1—2 ...	1,663	839	824	1,662	838	824	1	1	...	...	...	...
2—3 ...	1,885	916	969	1,884	916	968	1	...	1	...	...	...
3—4 ...	1,769	878	891	1,767	877	890	2	1	1	...	...	...
4—5 ...	1,556	791	765	1,551	788	763	5	3	2	...	...	...
Total 0—5 ...	*8,570*	*4,274*	*4,296*	*8,561*	*4,269*	*4,292*	*9*	*5*	*4*	...	...	...
5—10 ...	8,065	4,178	3,887	7,864	4,141	3,723	196	37	159	5	...	5
10—15 ...	7,979	4,114	3,865	7,064	4,036	3,028	892	77	815	23	1	22
15—20 ...	6,759	2,970	3,789	2,920	2,344	576	3,716	619	3,097	123	7	116
20—30 ...	12,424	5,018	7,406	1,886	1,707	179	9,792	3,248	6,514	746	63	683
30—40 ...	9,197	3,756	5,441	164	132	32	7,297	3,512	3,785	1,736	112	1,624
40—50 ...	6,664	2,820	3,844	38	28	10	4,374	2,652	1,722	2,252	140	2,112
50—60 ...	3,921	1,759	2,162	12	10	2	2,147	1,608	539	1,762	141	1,621
60 and over ...	2,525	1,076	1,449	9	7	2	1,009	864	145	1,507	205	1,302
BALASORE.												
ALL RELIGIONS ...	*990,600*	*480,518*	*510,082*	*380,120*	*235,652*	*144,468*	*457,335*	*220,697*	*236,638*	*153,145*	*24,169*	*128,976*
0—1 ...	23,267	11,572	11,695	23,265	11,572	11,693	2	...	2	...	...	...
1—2 ...	24,367	11,981	12,386	24,358	11,979	12,379	8	2	6	1	...	1
2—3 ...	26,881	12,998	13,883	26,854	12,987	13,867	25	11	14	2	...	2
3—4 ...	25,476	12,429	13,047	25,345	12,407	12,938	124	22	102	7	...	7
4—5 ...	22,997	11,532	11,465	22,767	11,503	11,264	216	28	188	14	1	13
Total 0—5 ...	*122,988*	*60,512*	*62,476*	*122,589*	*60,448*	*62,141*	*375*	*63*	*312*	*24*	*1*	*23*
5—10 ...	107,241	55,579	51,662	97,689	54,617	43,072	9,284	947	8,337	268	15	253
10—15 ...	101,140	53,374	47,766	81,596	50,888	30,708	18,882	2,451	16,431	662	35	627
15—20 ...	97,909	47,354	50,555	39,807	33,806	6,001	54,731	13,288	41,443	3,371	260	3,111
20—30 ...	197,627	91,746	105,881	32,708	30,719	1,989	147,001	58,985	88,016	17,918	2,042	15,876
30—40 ...	159,974	75,573	84,401	4,263	3,905	358	120,461	67,587	52,874	35,250	4,381	30,869
40—50 ...	108,549	52,101	56,448	953	833	120	66,024	44,893	21,132	41,572	6,466	35,106
50—60 ...	62,557	29,692	32,865	341	286	55	29,512	23,088	6,424	32,704	6,318	26,386
60 and over ...	32,615	14,197	18,418	174	150	24	11,065	9,396	1,669	21,376	4,651	16,725
HINDUS ...	*944,681*	*457,943*	*486,738*	*360,519*	*224,314*	*136,205*	*435,872*	*210,112*	*225,760*	*148,290*	*23,517*	*124,773*
0—1 ...	21,964	10,962	11,002	21,962	10,962	11,000	2	...	2	...	...	...
1—2 ...	23,055	11,362	11,693	23,047	11,360	11,687	7	2	5	1	...	1
2—3 ...	25,400	12,300	13,100	25,373	12,289	13,084	25	11	14	2	...	2
3—4 ...	24,005	11,713	12,292	23,876	11,691	12,185	122	22	100	7	...	7
4—5 ...	21,650	10,864	10,786	21,427	10,836	10,591	210	37	183	13	1	12
Total 0—5 ...	*116,074*	*57,201*	*58,873*	*115,685*	*57,138*	*58,547*	*366*	*69*	*304*	*23*	*1*	*22*
5—10 ...	101,637	52,680	48,957	92,340	51,753	40,587	9,037	913	8,124	260	14	246
10—15 ...	96,174	50,777	45,397	77,407	40,384	37,023	18,128	2,359	15,769	639	34	605
15—20 ...	93,326	45,305	48,021	38,120	32,430	5,690	51,942	12,627	39,315	3,264	240	3,018
20—30 ...	188,317	87,432	100,885	31,423	29,586	1,837	139,556	55,904	83,652	17,338	1,942	15,396
30—40 ...	153,098	72,317	80,781	4,118	3,784	334	114,828	64,284	50,544	34,152	4,249	29,903
40—50 ...	104,304	50,002	54,302	928	812	116	63,130	42,870	20,260	40,246	6,320	33,926
50—60 ...	60,342	28,589	31,753	330	280	50	28,307	22,128	6,179	31,705	6,181	25,524
60 and over ...	31,409	13,640	17,769	168	147	21	10,578	8,965	1,613	26,663	4,528	22,135
MUSLIMS ...	*31,735*	*15,661*	*16,074*	*12,817*	*7,664*	*5,153*	*15,301*	*7,535*	*7,766*	*3,617*	*462*	*3,155*
0—1 ...	838	394	444	838	394	444	...	...	...	...	...	...
1—2 ...	855	400	455	854	400	454	1	...	1	...	...	...
2—3 ...	939	450	489	939	450	489	...	...	...	...	...	...
3—4 ...	912	452	460	909	452	457	2	...	2	1	...	1
4—5 ...	830	410	420	824	409	415	6	1	5	...	...	...
Total 0—5 ...	*4,374*	*2,106*	*2,268*	*4,364*	*2,105*	*2,259*	*9*	*1*	*8*	*1*	...	*1*
5—10 ...	3,645	1,913	1,732	3,455	1,893	1,562	183	19	164	7	1	6
10—15 ...	3,384	1,798	1,586	2,816	1,740	1,076	551	58	493	17	...	17
15—20 ...	3,285	1,479	1,806	1,189	1,010	179	2,021	461	1,560	75	8	67
20—30 ...	6,582	3,069	3,513	882	821	61	5,286	2,183	3,103	414	65	349
30—40 ...	4,846	2,408	2,342	91	78	13	3,922	2,328	1,594	827	22	785
40—50 ...	3,070	1,544	1,526	14	12	2	2,044	1,429	615	1,012	103	909
50—60 ...	1,647	809	838	5	4	1	893	708	185	749	97	652
60 and over ...	908	445	463	1	1	...	392	348	44	515	96	419
ANGUL.												
ALL RELIGIONS ...	*222,736*	*108,925*	*113,811*	*98,936*	*54,368*	*44,568*	*104,387*	*51,741*	*52,646*	*19,413*	*2,816*	*16,597*
0—1 ...	8,188	3,997	4,191	8,184	4,083	4,101	4	4	...	...	...	...
1—2 ...	7,095	3,436	3,659	7,075	3,436	3,639	20	10	10	...	...	...
2—3 ...	7,843	3,774	4,069	7,800	3,756	4,044	41	18	23	2	...	2
3—4 ...	7,531	3,691	3,840	7,470	3,669	3,801	59	22	37	2	...	2
4—5 ...	7,101	3,545	3,556	7,019	3,517	3,502	77	27	50	5	1	4
Total 0—5 ...	*37,758*	*18,443*	*19,315*	*37,548*	*18,361*	*19,187*	*201*	*81*	*120*	*9*	*1*	*8*
5—10 ...	28,427	14,182	14,245	26,383	13,726	12,657	2,002	452	1,550	42	4	38
10—15 ...	24,258	12,347	11,911	20,257	11,311	8,946	3,922	1,037	2,885	79	9	70
15—20 ...	18,317	8,958	9,359	7,873	5,565	2,308	10,154	3,520	6,634	290	73	217
20—30 ...	39,564	18,893	20,671	5,682	4,572	1,110	32,404	13,936	18,468	1,478	385	1,093
30—40 ...	33,654	16,676	16,978	781	562	219	29,338	15,580	13,758	3,535	525	3,010
40—50 ...	21,385	10,609	10,776	242	154	88	15,963	9,869	6,094	5,180	586	4,594
50—60 ...	12,263	5,807	6,456	99	66	33	7,338	5,129	2,209	4,826	612	4,214
60 and over ...	7,110	3,010	4,100	71	51	20	3,065	2,338	727	3,974	621	3,353
HINDUS ...	*163,663*	*80,344*	*83,319*	*70,503*	*39,524*	*30,979*	*78,960*	*38,944*	*40,016*	*14,200*	*1,876*	*12,324*
0—1 ...	6,483	3,165	3,318	6,479	3,161	3,318	4	4	...	...	...	...
1—2 ...	5,634	2,754	2,880	5,617	2,744	2,873	17	10	7	...	...	...
2—3 ...	6,071	2,941	3,130	6,040	2,926	3,114	29	15	14	2	...	2
3—4 ...	5,602	2,754	2,848	5,560	2,740	2,820	40	14	26	2	...	2
4—5 ...	5,293	2,647	2,646	5,236	2,631	2,605	55	16	39	2	...	2
Total 0—5 ...	*29,083*	*14,261*	*14,822*	*28,932*	*14,202*	*14,730*	*145*	*59*	*86*	*6*	...	*6*
5—10 ...	21,064	10,496	10,568	19,181	10,120	9,061	1,848	374	1,474	35	2	33
10—15 ...	17,599	9,031	8,568	13,961	8,130	5,831	3,571	893	2,678	67	8	59
15—20 ...	13,325	6,623	6,702	4,622	3,737	885	8,493	2,835	5,658	210	51	159
20—30 ...	29,512	14,252	15,260	3,298	2,970	328	25,186	11,039	14,147	1,028	243	785
30—40 ...	24,024	11,996	12,028	322	266	56	21,141	11,443	9,698	2,561	317	2,244
40—50 ...	14,952	7,295	7,657	121	81	40	11,060	6,849	4,211	3,771	365	3,406
50—60 ...	8,740	4,061	4,679	41	29	12	5,160	3,615	1,545	3,539	407	3,132
60 and over ...	5,364	2,339	3,025	25	19	6	2,856	1,837	519	2,983	483	2,500

TABLE VII—*continued.*

AGE, SEX AND CIVIL CONDITION. **PART II—DETAILS FOR DISTRICTS.**

Age.	Population. Persons.	Population. Males.	Population. Females.	Unmarried. Persons.	Unmarried. Males.	Unmarried. Females.	Married. Persons.	Married. Males.	Married. Females.	Widowed. Persons.	Widowed. Males.	Widowed. Females.
1	2	3	4	5	6	7	8	9	10	11	12	13
ANGUL—concluded.												
TRIBAL ...	*58,473*	*28,249*	*30,224*	*28,157*	*14,674*	*13,483*	*25,143*	*12,645*	*12,498*	*5,173*	*930*	*4,243*
0—1 ...	1,681	822	859	1,681	822	859	...	...	...	...	...	...
1—2 ...	1,444	675	769	1,441	675	766	3	...	3	...	...	...
2—3 ...	1,759	828	931	1,747	825	922	12	3	9	...	...	...
3—4 ...	1,915	930	985	1,896	922	974	19	8	11	...	...	...
4—5 ...	1,789	888	901	1,765	876	889	21	11	10	3	1	2
Total 0—5 ...	*8,588*	*4,143*	*4,445*	*8,530*	*4,120*	*4,410*	*55*	*22*	*33*	*3*	*1*	*2*
5—10 ...	7,295	3,647	3,648	7,136	3,567	3,569	152	78	74	7	2	5
10—15 ...	6,600	3,284	3,316	6,245	3,149	3,096	343	134	209	12	1	11
15—20 ...	4,935	2,308	2,627	3,223	1,807	1,416	1,632	479	1,153	80	22	58
20—30 ...	9,923	4,564	5,359	2,347	1,569	778	7,129	2,854	4,275	447	141	306
30—40 ...	9,545	4,629	4,016	454	323	131	8,127	4,103	4,024	964	203	761
40—50 ...	6,364	3,271	3,093	120	72	48	4,847	2,980	1,867	1,397	219	1,178
50—60 ...	3,492	1,736	1,756	56	35	21	2,156	1,498	658	1,280	203	1,077
60 and over ...	1,731	667	1,064	46	32	14	702	497	205	983	138	845
PURI.												
ALL RELIGIONS ...	*1,035,154*	*500,214*	*534,940*	*421,949*	*242,918*	*179,031*	*491,468*	*240,003*	*251,465*	*121,737*	*17,293*	*104,444*
0—1 ...	26,490	13,007	13,483	26,490	13,007	13,483	...	...	...	...	...	...
1—2 ...	26,792	12,958	13,834	26,792	12,958	13,834	..	...	...	...	...	...
2—3 ...	30,859	14,711	16,148	30,859	14,711	16,148	...	...	...	...	...	...
3—4 ...	29,451	14,224	15,227	29,423	14,217	15,206	27	7	20	1	..	1
4—5 ...	26,828	13,288	13,540	26,764	13,272	13,402	58	16	43	6	...	6
Total 0—5 ...	*140,420*	*68,188*	*72,232*	*140,328*	*68,165*	*72,163*	*85*	*23*	*62*	*7*	...	*7*
5—10 ...	121,056	60,989	60,067	115,339	60,444	54,895	5,600	540	5,060	117	5	112
10—15 ...	111,591	57,009	54,402	95,744	55,220	40,524	15,518	1,865	13,653	329	14	315
15—20 ...	96,961	46,402	50,559	39,120	31,432	7,688	56,178	14,821	41,357	1,663	140	1,514
20—30 ...	189,209	87,441	101,768	26,662	23,936	2,726	153,276	62,400	90,876	9,271	1,105	8,166
30—40 ...	152,045	72,088	79,957	2,923	2,283	640	127,114	67,638	59,476	22,008	2,167	19,841
40—50 ...	112,332	54,853	57,479	1,048	806	242	78,471	50,258	28,213	32,813	3,789	29,024
50—60 ...	71,551	34,998	36,553	484	393	91	39,741	29,613	10,128	31,326	4,992	26,334
60 and over ...	39,989	18,156	21,833	301	239	62	15,485	12,845	2,640	24,203	5,072	19,131
HINDUS ...	*1,011,079*	*488,555*	*522,524*	*410,796*	*236,575*	*174,221*	*480,912*	*234,944*	*245,968*	*119,371*	*17,036*	*102,335*
0—1 ...	25,814	12,684	13,130	25,814	12,684	13,130	...	...		...	...	...
1—2 ...	26,119	12,627	13,493	26,119	12,627	13,402	...		...	...	...	...
2—3 ...	30,076	14,315	15,761	30,076	14,315	15,761	...	...	...	...	...	...
3—4 ...	28,657	13,827	14,830	28,629	13,820	14,809	27	7	20	1	...	1
4—5 ...	26,076	12,912	13,164	26,016	12,806	13,120	56	16	40	4	...	4
Total 0—5 ...	*136,742*	*66,365*	*70,377*	*136,654*	*66,349*	*70,312*	*83*	*23*	*60*	*5*	...	*5*
5—10 ...	117,906	59,391	58,515	112,258	58,865	53,393	5,539	522	5,017	109	4	105
10—15 ...	108,850	55,692	53,158	93,266	53,846	39,420	15,268	1,835	13,433	316	11	305
15—20 ...	94,701	45,350	49,351	38,097	30,631	7,466	54,974	14,574	40,400	1,630	145	1,485
20—30 ...	184,926	85,477	99,449	25,916	23,280	2,627	149,916	61,107	88,809	9,094	1,081	8,013
30—40 ...	148,649	70,457	78,192	2,812	2,192	620	124,276	66,134	58,143	21,561	2,131	19,430
40—50 ...	109,991	53,712	56,279	1,027	793	234	76,788	49,183	27,605	32,176	3,736	28,440
50—60 ...	70,165	34,323	35,842	475	387	88	38,924	29,003	9,921	30,766	4,933	25,833
60 and over ...	39,149	17,788	21,361	291	230	61	15,144	12,563	2,581	23,714	4,995	18,719
MUSLIMS ...	*22,518*	*10,875*	*11,643*	*10,320*	*5,882*	*4,438*	*9,978*	*4,768*	*5,210*	*2,220*	*225*	*1,995*
0—1 ...	618	298	320	618	298	320	...	...	...	...	...	...
1—2 ...	633	308	325	633	308	325	...	...	...	...	...	...
2—3 ...	739	370	369	739	370	369	...	...	...	...	...	...
3—4 ...	749	373	376	749	373	376	...	...	..	...	...	...
4—5 ...	709	356	353	705	356	349	2	...	2	2	...	2
Total 0—5 ...	*3,448*	*1,705*	*1,743*	*3,444*	*1,705*	*1,739*	*2*	...	*2*	*2*	...	*2*
5—10 ...	2,954	1,497	1,457	2,889	1,480	1,409	57	16	41	8	1	7
10—15 ...	2,564	1,313	1,251	2,307	1,283	1,024	244	27	217	13	3	10
15—20 ...	2,097	974	1,123	911	736	175	1,154	234	920	32	4	28
20—30 ...	4,004	1,824	2,180	642	576	66	3,194	1,225	1,969	168	23	145
30—40 ...	3,182	1,529	1,653	99	81	18	2,659	1,416	1,243	424	32	392
40—50 ...	2,172	1,051	1,121	15	10	5	1,564	998	566	593	43	550
50—60 ...	1,315	638	677	6	4	2	775	579	196	534	55	479
60 and over ...	782	344	438	7	7	...	329	273	56	446	64	382
SAMBALPUR.												
ALL RELIGIONS ...	*880,945*	*431,460*	*449,485*	*327,300*	*178,721*	*148,579*	*468,447*	*233,585*	*234,862*	*85,198*	*19,154*	*66,044*
0—1 ...	27,280	13,366	13,914	27,280	13,366	13,914	...	...	...	...	...	...
1—2 ...	22,894	11,119	11,775	22,892	11,117	11,775	2	2	...	...	...	...
2—3 ...	24,414	11,663	12,751	24,408	11,658	12,750	6	5	1	...	...	...
3—4 ...	25,119	12,197	12,922	25,032	12,172	12,860	84	25	59	3	...	3
4—5 ...	24,349	12,095	12,254	24,172	12,045	12,127	167	47	120	10	3	7
Total 0—5 ...	*124,056*	*60,440*	*63,616*	*123,784*	*60,358*	*63,426*	*259*	*79*	*180*	*13*	*3*	*10*
5—10 ...	109,285	55,292	53,993	97,565	51,888	45,677	11,592	3,385	8,207	128	19	109
10—15 ...	98,878	51,492	47,386	73,984	42,387	31,597	24,529	9,044	15,485	365	61	304
15—20 ...	76,520	36,808	39,712	19,195	13,978	5,217	55,815	22,388	33,427	1,510	442	1,068
20—30 ...	158,922	76,786	82,136	9,961	8,296	1,665	142,071	66,023	76,048	6,890	2,467	4,423
30—40 ...	129,654	64,516	65,138	1,651	1,114	537	114,519	59,950	54,569	13,484	3,452	10,032
40—50 ...	90,627	44,848	45,779	622	402	220	69,894	40,089	29,805	20,111	4,357	15,754
50—60 ...	54,635	25,595	29,040	316	181	135	33,851	21,430	12,421	20,468	3,984	16,484
60 and over ...	38,368	15,683	22,685	222	117	105	15,917	11,197	4,720	22,229	4,369	17,860
HINDUS ...	*870,178*	*426,029*	*444,149*	*322,991*	*176,002*	*146,989*	*463,643*	*231,054*	*232,589*	*84,944*	*18,973*	*65,971*
0—1 ...	26,955	13,209	13,746	26,955	13,209	13,746	...	...	...	...	...	...
1—2 ...	22,608	10,972	11,636	22,606	10,970	11,636	2	2	...	...	...	...
2—3 ...	24,091	11,510	12,581	24,085	11,505	12,580	6	5	1	...	...	...
3—4 ...	24,790	12,037	12,753	24,703	12,012	12,691	84	25	59	3	...	3
4—5 ...	24,017	11,923	12,094	23,844	11,875	11,969	164	46	118	9	2	7
Total 0—5 ...	*122,461*	*59,651*	*62,810*	*122,193*	*59,571*	*62,622*	*256*	*78*	*178*	*12*	*2*	*10*
5—10 ...	107,851	54,557	53,294	96,164	51,168	44,996	11,559	3,370	8,189	128	19	109
10—15 ...	97,589	50,843	46,746	72,794	41,765	31,029	24,431	9,017	15,414	364	61	303
15—20 ...	75,590	36,338	39,252	18,727	13,668	5,059	55,366	22,230	33,136	1,497	440	1,057
20—30 ...	157,006	75,818	81,188	9,668	8,063	1,605	140,534	65,308	75,226	6,804	2,447	4,357
30—40 ...	128,116	63,723	64,393	1,608	1,081	527	110,100	[illegible]	53,956	13,315	3,415	9,900
40—50 ...	90,580	44,309	45,271	611	396	215	69,092	39,593	29,499	19,877	4,320	15,557
50—60 ...	54,037	25,292	28,745	306	174	132	33,485	21,176	12,309	20,246	3,942	16,304
60 and over ...	37,948	15,498	22,450	220	116	104	15,727	11,055	4,672	22,001	4,327	17,674

TABLE VII—*continued.*

AGE, SEX AND CIVIL CONDITION. **PART II—DETAILS FOR DISTRICTS.**

AGE.	POPULATION.			UNMARRIED.			MARRIED.			WIDOWED.		
	Persons.	Males.	Females.	Persons.	Males.	Females.	Persons.	Males.	Females.	Persons.	Males.	Females.
1	2	3	4	5	6	7	8	9	10	11	12	13
SAMBALPUR—concluded.												
MUSLIMS ...	*3,813*	*2,008*	*1,805*	*1,485*	*877*	*608*	*1,904*	*1,078*	*831*	*434*	*58*	*366*
0—1 ...	99	49	50	99	49	50	...	...	...	...	...	...
1—2 ...	86	47	39	86	47	39	...	...	...	...	...	...
2—3 ...	88	41	47	88	41	47	...	...	...	...	...	...
3—4 ...	88	43	45	88	43	45	...	...	...	...	...	...
4—5 ...	88	50	38	85	49	36	2	...	2	1	1	...
Total 0—5 ...	*449*	*230*	*219*	*446*	*229*	*217*	*2*	...	*2*	*1*	*1*	...
5—10 ...	399	208	191	384	203	181	15	5	10	...	...	...
10—15 ...	382	193	189	342	183	159	40	10	30	...	...	...
15—20 ...	362	195	167	160	121	39	196	74	122	6	...	6
20—30 ...	791	443	348	122	113	9	631	323	308	38	7	31
30—40 ...	626	346	280	20	19	1	524	313	211	82	14	68
40—50 ...	416	211	205	5	4	1	302	196	106	109	11	98
50—60 ...	227	116	111	6	5	1	129	99	30	92	12	80
60 and over ...	161	66	95	...	...	...	65	53	12	96	13	83
HAZARIBAGH.												
ALL RELIGIONS ...	*1,517,357*	*751,956*	*765,401*	*533,115*	*303,896*	*229,219*	*841,516*	*414,409*	*427,107*	*142,726*	*33,651*	*109,075*
0—1 ...	49,704	23,999	25,705	48,996	23,727	25,269	689	270	419	19	2	17
1—2 ...	47,884	22,832	25,052	46,828	22,415	24,413	1,035	404	631	21	3	18
2—3 ...	56,878	26,872	30,006	54,431	26,093	28,338	2,411	776	1,636	36	4	32
3—4 ...	60,665	29,553	31,112	55,304	27,962	27,342	5,227	1,542	3,685	134	49	85
4—5 ...	55,385	27,816	27,569	48,068	25,641	22,427	7,093	2,081	5,012	224	94	130
Total 0—5 ...	*270,516*	*131,062*	*139,454*	*253,627*	*125,838*	*127,789*	*16,455*	*5,072*	*11,383*	*434*	*152*	*282*
5—10 ...	216,827	112,321	104,506	151,707	88,417	63,290	63,363	23,351	40,012	1,757	553	1,204
10—15 ...	178,083	93,172	84,911	91,264	59,152	32,112	84,405	33,296	51,109	2,414	724	1,690
15—20 ...	128,091	61,295	66,796	19,535	16,075	3,460	104,711	44,018	60,693	3,845	1,202	2,643
20—30 ...	270,792	128,829	141,963	12,885	11,174	1,711	241,883	113,177	128,706	16,024	4,478	11,546
30—40 ...	211,215	105,265	105,950	2,010	1,193	406	179,838	96,852	82,986	28,758	6,290	22,468
40—50 ...	128,997	66,548	62,449	893	702	191	93,497	58,126	35,371	34,607	7,720	26,887
50—60 ...	71,018	35,369	35,649	381	274	107	40,678	28,157	12,521	29,959	6,938	23,021
60 and over ...	41,818	18,095	23,723	204	141	63	16,686	12,360	4,326	24,928	5,594	19,334
HINDUS ...	*1,208,099*	*597,528*	*610,571*	*413,737*	*237,427*	*176,310*	*675,902*	*332,124*	*343,778*	*118,460*	*27,977*	*90,483*
0—1 ...	39,141	19,007	20,134	38,542	18,779	19,763	584	226	358	15	2	13
1—2 ...	37,471	17,876	19,595	36,660	17,541	19,119	795	333	462	16	2	14
2—3 ...	44,439	21,008	23,431	42,448	20,353	22,095	1,960	653	1,307	31	2	29
3—4 ...	47,331	23,040	24,291	42,970	21,775	21,195	4,260	1,234	3,026	101	31	70
4—5 ...	42,893	21,548	21,345	37,039	19,879	17,160	5,691	1,609	4,082	163	60	103
Total 0—5 ...	*211,275*	*102,479*	*108,796*	*197,659*	*98,327*	*99,332*	*13,290*	*4,055*	*9,235*	*326*	*97*	*229*
5—10 ...	169,650	87,814	81,836	116,846	68,618	48,228	51,428	18,753	32,675	1,376	443	933
10—15 ...	140,592	73,484	67,108	70,199	45,931	24,268	68,450	26,936	41,514	1,943	617	1,326
15—20 ...	102,607	49,129	53,478	15,115	12,623	2,492	84,295	35,517	48,778	3,197	989	2,208
20—30 ...	218,856	103,532	115,324	10,382	9,095	1,287	194,793	90,821	103,972	13,681	3,616	10,065
30—40 ...	171,166	84,880	86,286	2,251	1,853	398	144,330	77,684	66,646	24,585	5,343	19,242
40—50 ...	104,125	53,600	50,525	789	624	165	74,188	46,476	27,712	29,148	6,500	22,648
50—60 ...	57,188	28,321	28,867	331	243	88	32,076	22,300	9,769	24,779	5,769	19,010
60 and over ...	32,640	14,289	18,351	165	113	52	13,050	9,573	3,477	19,425	4,603	14,822
MUSLIMS ...	*171,694*	*84,799*	*86,895*	*57,833*	*32,690*	*25,143*	*100,740*	*49,144*	*51,596*	*13,121*	*2,965*	*10,156*
0—1 ...	5,818	2,821	2,997	5,755	2,802	2,953	59	19	40	4	...	4
1—2 ...	5,734	2,735	2,999	5,537	2,686	2,851	192	48	144	5	1	4
2—3 ...	6,853	3,216	3,637	6,476	3,132	3,344	373	82	291	4	2	2
3—4 ...	7,302	3,584	3,718	6,321	3,097	3,194	753	239	514	28	18	10
4—5 ...	6,821	3,472	3,349	5,708	3,062	2,646	1,065	378	687	48	32	16
Total 0—5 ...	*32,528*	*15,828*	*16,700*	*29,997*	*15,009*	*14,988*	*2,442*	*766*	*1,676*	*89*	*53*	*36*
5—10 ...	25,997	13,488	12,509	16,466	9,658	6,808	9,306	3,740	5,566	225	90	135
10—15 ...	20,688	10,702	9,986	8,799	5,827	2,972	11,654	4,803	6,851	235	72	163
15—20 ...	14,286	6,673	7,613	1,446	1,260	186	12,467	5,298	7,169	373	115	258
20—30 ...	29,550	13,753	15,797	873	758	115	27,367	12,625	14,742	1,310	370	940
30—40 ...	22,187	10,863	11,324	151	104	47	19,748	10,284	9,464	2,288	475	1,813
40—50 ...	13,622	7,045	6,577	48	37	11	10,464	6,378	4,086	3,110	630	2,480
50—60 ...	7,880	4,085	3,795	22	13	9	4,910	3,428	1,482	2,898	594	2,304
60 and over ...	5,006	2,412	2,594	31	24	7	2,382	1,822	560	2,593	566	2,027
TRIBAL ...	*133,156*	*67,192*	*65,964*	*59,305*	*32,472*	*26,833*	*62,954*	*32,073*	*30,881*	*10,897*	*2,647*	*8,250*
0—1 ...	4,621	2,113	2,506	4,575	2,088	2,487	46	25	21	...	...	...
1—2 ...	4,559	2,150	2,409	4,511	2,127	2,384	48	23	25	...	...	...
2—3 ...	5,451	2,585	2,866	5,373	2,540	2,097	77	39	38	1	...	1
3—4 ...	5,902	2,871	3,031	5,683	2,802	2,881	214	69	145	5	...	5
4—5 ...	5,545	2,731	2,814	5,200	2,639	2,561	332	90	242	13	2	11
Total 0—5 ...	*26,078*	*12,450*	*13,628*	*25,342*	*12,202*	*13,140*	*717*	*246*	*471*	*19*	*2*	*17*
5—10 ...	20,650	10,722	9,928	17,885	9,854	8,031	2,611	848	1,763	154	20	134
10—15 ...	16,275	8,670	7,605	11,786	7,102	4,684	4,256	1,533	2,723	233	35	198
15—20 ...	10,718	5,241	5,477	2,669	1,992	677	7,782	3,151	4,632	266	98	168
20—30 ...	21,475	11,050	10,425	1,376	1,142	234	19,099	9,429	9,670	1,060	470	590
30—40 ...	17,234	9,154	8,080	173	133	40	15,227	8,566	6,661	1,834	455	1,379
40—50 ...	10,836	5,662	5,174	44	31	13	8,513	5,057	3,456	2,279	574	1,705
50—60 ...	5,819	2,903	2,916	22	12	10	3,561	2,329	1,232	2,236	562	1,674
60 and over ...	4,071	1,340	2,731	8	4	4	1,187	914	273	2,876	422	2,454
RANCHI.												
ALL RELIGIONS ...	*1,567,149*	*777,063*	*790,086*	*709,067*	*382,859*	*326,208*	*727,013*	*360,030*	*366,983*	*131,069*	*34,174*	*96,895*
0—1 ...	55,086	26,795	28,291	54,851	26,671	28,180	226	119	107	9	5	4
1—2 ...	51,768	24,963	26,805	51,402	24,802	26,600	355	156	199	11	5	6
2—3 ...	60,319	29,133	31,186	59,624	28,853	30,771	677	271	406	18	9	9
3—4 ...	61,933	30,503	31,430	60,552	29,964	30,588	1,371	520	851	70	19	51
4—5 ...	56,929	28,512	28,417	54,948	27,777	27,171	1,860	703	1,157	121	32	89
Total 0—5 ...	*286,095*	*139,906*	*146,189*	*281,377*	*136,067*	*145,310*	*4,489*	*1,769*	*2,720*	*229*	*70*	*159*
5—10 ...	227,866	116,620	111,246	203,395	108,266	95,129	23,878	8,209	15,669	593	145	448
10—15 ...	191,080	99,065	92,015	146,893	83,232	63,661	44,127	15,568	28,559	960	265	695
15—20 ...	132,593	63,817	68,776	43,104	29,205	13,899	66,767	33,631	33,136	2,632	891	1,741
20—30 ...	258,668	125,249	133,419	26,088	18,980	7,108	220,472	102,304	118,168	12,108	3,965	8,143
30—40 ...	203,619	102,755	100,864	4,926	3,251	1,675	174,671	92,844	81,827	23,022	5,660	17,362
40—50 ...	131,058	66,633	64,425	1,634	992	642	98,424	57,507	40,917	31,610	8,144	23,466
50—60 ...	81,230	39,358	41,872	869	463	406	47,722	31,618	16,104	30,639	7,277	23,362
60 and over ...	54,040	23,660	30,380	701	323	378	18,463	10,580	7,883	28,876	6,757	22,119

TABLE VII—*continued.*

Age, Sex and Civil Condition. **Part II—Details for Districts.**

Age.	Population. Persons.	Males.	Females.	Unmarried. Persons.	Males.	Females.	Married. Persons.	Males.	Females.	Widowed. Persons.	Males.	Females.
1	2	3	4	5	6	7	8	9	10	11	12	13
RANCHI—concluded.												
HINDUS ...	*869,492*	*433,323*	*436,169*	*367,697*	*202,676*	*165,021*	*429,892*	*210,359*	*219,533*	*78,903*	*20,288*	*58,615*
0—1 ...	29,948	14,438	15,530	29,794	14,340	15,454	145	83	63	9	5	4
1—2 ...	28,428	13,662	14,766	28,187	13,545	14,642	234	114	120	7	3	4
2—3 ...	33,095	16,022	17,073	32,612	15,918	16,694	471	197	274	12	7	5
3—4 ...	34,014	16,755	17,259	33,030	16,389	16,641	935	351	584	49	15	34
4—5 ...	30,908	15,498	15,410	29,585	15,020	14,565	1,239	456	783	84	22	62
Total 0—5 ...	*156,393*	*76,365*	*80,028*	*153,208*	*75,112*	*78,096*	*3,024*	*1,201*	*1,823*	*161*	*52*	*109*
5—10 ...	123,069	63,152	59,917	106,174	57,505	48,669	16,472	5,542	10,930	423	105	318
10—15 ...	102,751	63,393	40,359	72,780	43,885	29,895	29,306	10,332	18,974	665	175	490
15—20 ...	72,950	35,640	37,310	18,649	14,174	4,475	52,619	20,907	31,712	1,682	559	1,123
20—30 ...	147,493	72,134	75,360	12,226	9,913	2,313	127,823	59,841	67,982	7,444	2,370	5,074
30—40 ...	116,621	59,509	57,112	2,796	2,018	778	98,993	53,411	45,582	14,832	4,080	10,752
40—50 ...	74,814	38,334	36,480	934	609	325	54,946	32,792	22,154	18,934	4,033	14,001
50—60 ...	45,245	21,928	23,317	508	272	236	26,731	17,464	9,267	18,006	4,192	13,814
60 and over ...	30,156	12,879	17,277	422	188	234	12,978	8,860	4,100	16,756	3,832	12,934
MUSLIMS ...	*66,047*	*33,778*	*32,269*	*23,634*	*13,564*	*10,070*	*37,207*	*18,954*	*18,253*	*5,206*	*1,260*	*3,946*
0—1 ...	2,190	1,078	1,112	2,173	1,066	1,107	17	12	5	...	...	...
1—2 ...	2,133	1,064	1,069	2,103	1,055	1,048	29	9	20	1	...	1
2—3 ...	2,587	1,263	1,324	2,518	1,247	1,271	67	16	51	2	...	2
3—4 ...	2,644	1,316	1,328	2,429	1,240	1,180	212	67	145	3	...	3
4—5 ...	2,437	1,241	1,196	2,098	1,126	972	333	113	220	6	2	4
Total 0—5 ...	*11,991*	*5,962*	*6,029*	*11,321*	*5,743*	*5,578*	*658*	*217*	*441*	*12*	*2*	*10*
5—10 ...	9,665	5,101	4,564	6,662	3,872	2,790	2,965	1,220	1,745	38	9	29
10—15 ...	7,989	4,267	3,722	3,987	2,575	1,412	3,942	1,674	2,268	60	18	42
15—20 ...	5,802	2,807	2,905	853	710	143	4,813	2,042	2,771	136	55	81
20—30 ...	11,493	5,735	5,768	576	477	99	10,437	5,094	5,343	480	154	326
30—40 ...	8,285	4,377	3,908	120	100	20	7,252	4,040	3,212	913	237	676
40—50 ...	5,434	2,905	2,529	61	43	18	4,141	2,575	1,566	1,232	287	945
50—60 ...	3,147	1,582	1,565	36	29	7	1,940	1,300	640	1,171	253	918
60 and over ...	2,241	1,052	1,189	18	15	3	1,059	792	267	1,164	245	919
CHRISTIANS ...	*262,608*	*130,114*	*132,494*	*141,771*	*74,492*	*67,279*	*104,095*	*51,334*	*52,761*	*16,742*	*4,288*	*12,454*
0—1 ...	9,618	4,711	4,907	9,591	4,705	4,886	27	6	21	...	...	...
1—2 ...	8,849	4,327	4,522	8,807	4,313	4,494	41	13	28	1	1	...
2—3 ...	10,114	4,892	5,222	10,047	4,863	5,184	66	28	38	1	1	...
3—4 ...	10,351	5,103	5,248	10,245	5,056	5,189	102	47	55	4	...	4
4—5 ...	9,795	4,933	4,852	9,664	4,870	4,794	123	61	62	8	2	6
Total 0—5 ...	*48,727*	*23,966*	*24,761*	*48,354*	*23,807*	*24,547*	*359*	*155*	*204*	*14*	*4*	*10*
5—10 ...	40,124	20,619	19,505	39,352	20,298	19,054	746	315	431	26	6	20
10—15 ...	34,873	17,944	16,929	32,605	17,307	15,298	2,231	628	1,603	37	9	28
15—20 ...	23,459	11,140	12,319	12,947	7,753	5,194	10,313	3,332	6,981	199	55	144
20—30 ...	42,320	20,328	21,992	7,082	4,593	2,489	33,863	15,295	18,568	1,375	440	935
30—40 ...	31,759	15,949	15,810	864	480	384	27,941	14,694	13,247	2,954	775	3,179
40—50 ...	19,774	9,944	9,830	288	135	153	15,677	8,834	6,843	3,809	975	2,834
50—60 ...	12,978	6,235	6,743	144	66	78	8,590	5,160	3,430	4,244	1,009	3,235
60 and over ...	8,594	3,989	4,605	135	53	82	4,375	3,021	1,454	4,084	1,015	3,069
TRIBAL ...	*368,247*	*179,477*	*188,770*	*175,715*	*91,974*	*83,741*	*162,394*	*79,181*	*83,213*	*30,138*	*8,329*	*21,810*
0—1 ...	13,314	6,570	6,744	13,277	6,552	6,725	37	18	19	...	...	...
1—2 ...	12,341	5,903	6,438	12,288	5,882	6,406	51	20	31	2	1	1
2—3 ...	14,497	6,946	7,551	14,422	6,915	7,507	72	30	42	3	1	2
3—4 ...	14,063	7,319	7,644	14,828	7,260	7,568	121	55	66	14	4	10
4—5 ...	13,768	6,830	6,938	13,583	6,752	6,831	162	72	90	23	6	17
Total 0—5 ...	*68,883*	*33,568*	*35,315*	*68,398*	*33,361*	*35,037*	*443*	*195*	*248*	*42*	*12*	*30*
5—10 ...	54,925	27,707	27,218	51,148	26,557	24,591	3,671	1,125	2,546	106	25	81
10—15 ...	46,282	23,420	22,862	37,475	20,434	17,041	8,609	2,923	5,686	198	63	135
15—20 ...	30,310	14,194	16,116	10,729	6,644	4,085	18,967	7,328	11,639	614	222	392
20—30 ...	57,237	27,004	30,233	6,187	3,980	2,207	48,247	23,024	26,233	2,803	1,000	1,803
30—40 ...	46,828	22,861	23,967	1,135	644	401	40,384	20,649	19,735	5,309	1,568	3,741
40—50 ...	30,952	15,408	15,544	338	193	145	23,599	13,269	10,330	7,015	1,946	5,069
50—60 ...	19,818	9,591	10,227	181	96	85	12,434	7,675	4,759	7,203	1,820	5,383
60 and over ...	13,012	5,724	7,288	124	65	59	6,040	3,093	2,947	6,848	1,666	5,182
PALAMAU.												
ALL RELIGIONS ...	*818,736*	*409,778*	*408,958*	*295,632*	*163,406*	*132,226*	*452,043*	*227,347*	*224,696*	*71,061*	*19,025*	*52,036*
0—1 ...	28,038	13,767	14,271	27,706	13,619	14,087	328	146	182	4	2	2
1—2 ...	27,197	13,007	14,190	26,643	12,744	13,899	547	259	288	7	4	3
2—3 ...	30,653	14,501	16,152	29,566	14,064	15,502	1,070	432	638	17	5	12
3—4 ...	32,298	15,764	16,534	29,741	14,759	14,982	2,504	993	1,511	53	12	41
4—5 ...	31,387	15,843	15,544	27,688	14,345	13,343	3,611	1,475	2,130	88	23	65
Total 0—5 ...	*149,573*	*72,882*	*76,691*	*141,344*	*69,531*	*71,813*	*8,060*	*3,305*	*4,755*	*169*	*46*	*123*
5—10 ...	118,657	61,680	56,977	84,674	47,225	37,449	33,319	14,194	19,125	664	261	403
10—15 ...	96,574	50,866	45,708	49,116	30,232	18,884	46,433	20,192	26,241	1,025	442	583
15—20 ...	69,772	33,977	35,795	10,283	8,051	2,232	57,548	25,131	32,417	1,941	795	1,146
20—30 ...	143,597	69,851	73,746	7,192	5,980	1,212	128,576	61,159	67,417	7,829	2,712	5,117
30—40 ...	111,871	56,258	55,613	1,890	1,408	392	95,836	50,896	44,940	14,145	3,864	10,281
40—50 ...	69,312	36,171	33,141	702	577	125	51,315	31,260	20,055	17,295	4,334	12,961
50—60 ...	35,366	17,776	17,590	246	201	45	20,917	14,221	6,696	14,203	3,354	10,849
60 and over ...	24,014	10,317	13,697	185	111	74	10,039	6,989	3,050	13,790	3,217	10,573
HINDUS ...	*669,961*	*335,519*	*334,442*	*237,361*	*132,341*	*105,020*	*372,789*	*187,266*	*185,523*	*59,811*	*15,912*	*43,899*
0—1 ...	22,660	11,111	11,549	22,364	10,982	11,382	293	127	166	3	2	1
1—2 ...	21,998	10,498	11,500	21,528	10,273	11,255	464	222	242	6	3	3
2—3 ...	24,825	11,745	13,080	23,955	11,379	12,576	861	363	498	9	3	6
3—4 ...	26,018	12,640	13,378	24,068	11,907	12,161	1,906	723	1,183	44	10	34
4—5 ...	25,106	12,525	12,581	22,316	11,484	10,832	2,714	1,023	1,691	76	18	58
Total 0—5 ...	*120,607*	*58,519*	*62,088*	*114,231*	*56,025*	*58,206*	*6,238*	*2,458*	*3,780*	*138*	*36*	*102*
5—10 ...	96,527	50,159	46,368	67,874	38,155	29,719	28,076	11,775	16,301	577	229	348
10—15 ...	79,367	42,067	37,300	38,858	24,515	14,343	39,638	17,170	22,468	971	491	480
15—20 ...	57,220	28,016	29,204	7,915	6,495	1,420	47,667	20,860	26,807	1,638	661	977
20—30 ...	110,019	57,617	60,702	5,879	5,021	858	105,756	50,308	55,448	6,684	2,288	4,396
30—40 ...	92,160	46,434	45,726	1,635	1,336	299	78,521	41,839	36,682	12,004	3,259	8,745
40—50 ...	57,258	29,836	27,422	610	515	95	41,938	25,656	16,282	14,710	3,665	11,045
50—60 ...	29,061	14,603	14,450	208	181	27	16,986	11,625	5,361	11,867	2,796	9,071
60 and over ...	19,442	8,269	11,173	151	98	53	7,969	5,575	2,394	11,322	2,596	8,726

TABLE VII—*continued.*

AGE, SEX AND CIVIL CONDITION. | **PART II—DETAILS FOR DISTRICTS.**

Age.	Population. Persons.	Males.	Females.	Unmarried. Persons.	Males.	Females.	Married. Persons.	Males.	Females.	Widowed. Persons.	Males.	Females.
1	2	3	4	5	6	7	8	9	10	11	12	13
PALAMAU—concluded.												
MUSLIMS ...	*74,501*	*37,369*	*37,132*	*24,218*	*13,427*	*10,791*	*43,917*	*22,440*	*21,477*	*6,366*	*1,502*	*4,864*
0—1 ...	2,552	1,264	1,288	2,539	1,260	1,279	13	4	9	...	...	...
1—2 ...	2,409	1,180	1,229	2,358	1,160	1,198	51	20	31	...	...	...
2—3 ...	2,684	1,287	1,397	2,532	1,244	1,288	148	43	105	4	...	4
3—4 ...	3,018	1,561	1,457	2,515	1,331	1,184	496	228	268	7	2	5
4—5 ...	3,151	1,749	1,402	2,371	1,345	1,026	772	400	372	8	4	4
Total 0—5 ...	*13,814*	*7,041*	*6,773*	*12,315*	*6,340*	*5,975*	*1,480*	*695*	*785*	*19*	*6*	*13*
5—10 ...	10,965	5,741	5,224	6,783	3,789	2,994	4,110	1,924	2,186	72	28	44
10—15 ...	8,563	4,304	4,259	3,652	2,124	1,528	4,797	2,137	2,660	114	43	71
15—20 ...	6,448	3,154	3,294	723	612	111	5,561	2,476	3,085	164	66	98
20—30 ...	12,839	6,336	6,503	537	436	101	11,681	5,701	5,980	621	199	422
30—40 ...	9,792	4,833	4,959	139	83	56	8,441	4,476	3,965	1,212	274	938
40—50 ...	6,230	3,225	3,005	40	29	11	4,726	2,881	1,845	1,464	315	1,140
50—60 ...	3,378	1,667	1,711	15	10	5	2,043	1,390	653	1,320	267	1,053
60 and over ...	2,472	1,068	1,404	14	4	10	1,078	760	318	1,380	304	1,076
TRIBAL ...	*65,647*	*32,632*	*33,015*	*29,510*	*15,251*	*14,259*	*31,814*	*15,952*	*15,862*	*4,323*	*1,429*	*2,894*
0—1 ...	2,408	1,177	1,231	2,385	1,162	1,223	22	15	7	1	...	1
1—2 ...	2,473	1,183	1,290	2,440	1,165	1,275	32	17	15	1	1	...
2—3 ...	2,777	1,300	1,477	2,714	1,272	1,442	61	26	35	2	2	...
3—4 ...	2,894	1,383	1,511	2,794	1,341	1,453	99	42	57	1	...	1
4—5 ...	2,784	1,388	1,396	2,661	1,335	1,326	119	52	67	4	1	3
Total 0—5 ...	*13,336*	*6,431*	*6,905*	*12,994*	*6,275*	*6,719*	*333*	*152*	*181*	*9*	*4*	*5*
5—10 ...	9,862	5,122	4,740	8,761	4,625	4,136	1,086	493	593	15	4	11
10—15 ...	7,557	3,959	3,598	5,637	3,083	2,554	1,884	861	1,023	36	15	21
15—20 ...	5,400	2,457	2,943	1,308	738	570	3,960	1,655	2,305	132	64	68
20—30 ...	11,147	5,269	5,878	628	419	209	10,029	4,641	5,388	490	209	281
30—40 ...	8,801	4,432	4,369	100	64	36	7,882	4,075	3,807	819	293	526
40—50 ...	5,187	2,775	2,412	49	30	19	4,138	2,427	1,711	1,000	318	682
50—60 ...	2,548	1,329	1,219	17	9	8	1,654	1,076	578	877	244	633
60 and over ...	1,809	858	951	16	8	8	848	572	276	345	278	667
MANBHUM.												
ALL RELIGIONS ...	*1,810,890*	*940,009*	*870,881*	*626,072*	*369,819*	*256,253*	*1,009,980*	*533,055*	*476,925*	*174,838*	*37,135*	*137,703*
0—1 ...	52,481	27,340	25,141	52,113	27,166	24,947	357	172	185	11	2	9
1—2 ...	46,973	22,917	24,056	46,124	22,592	23,532	825	318	507	24	7	17
2—3 ...	59,313	28,206	31,107	57,255	27,463	29,792	2,011	734	1,277	47	9	38
3—4 ...	61,297	29,834	31,463	56,986	28,381	28,605	4,170	1,418	2,752	141	35	106
4—5 ...	56,640	28,551	28,089	50,850	26,649	24,201	5,556	1,835	3,721	234	67	167
Total 0—5 ...	*276,704*	*136,848*	*139,856*	*263,928*	*132,851*	*131,077*	*12,919*	*4,477*	*8,442*	*457*	*120*	*337*
5—10 ...	232,094	121,543	110,551	176,082	102,372	73,710	54,587	18,832	35,755	1,425	339	1,086
10—15 ...	203,028	107,701	95,327	117,794	77,044	40,750	82,874	29,099	53,775	2,360	558	1,802
15—20 ...	171,303	84,450	86,853	33,591	28,278	5,313	132,071	54,902	77,169	5,641	1,270	4,371
20—30 ...	349,986	180,179	169,807	26,674	22,947	3,727	302,756	152,555	150,201	20,556	4,677	15,879
30—40 ...	264,726	146,833	117,893	5,848	4,647	1,201	225,306	135,194	90,112	33,572	6,992	26,580
40—50 ...	162,657	88,763	73,894	1,704	1,426	278	119,317	78,816	40,501	41,636	8,521	33,115
50—60 ...	91,649	46,893	44,756	655	537	118	54,219	38,731	15,488	36,775	7,625	29,150
60 and over ...	58,743	26,799	31,944	396	317	79	25,931	19,449	6,482	32,416	7,033	25,383
HINDUS ...	*1,592,537*	*824,012*	*768,515*	*546,101*	*324,488*	*221,613*	*890,937*	*468,637*	*422,300*	*155,489*	*30,887*	*124,602*
0—1 ...	46,369	24,321	22,048	46,040	24,165	21,875	319	154	165	10	2	8
1—2 ...	41,252	20,151	21,101	40,027	19,988	20,039	703	258	445	22	5	17
2—3 ...	51,964	24,696	27,268	50,236	24,103	26,133	1,684	585	1,099	44	8	36
3—4 ...	53,632	26,137	27,495	49,953	24,942	25,011	3,550	1,165	2,385	129	30	99
4—5 ...	49,531	25,044	24,487	44,568	23,465	21,103	4,758	1,526	3,232	205	53	152
Total 0—5 ...	*242,748*	*120,349*	*122,399*	*231,324*	*116,563*	*114,761*	*11,014*	*3,688*	*7,326*	*410*	*98*	*312*
5—10 ...	203,669	106,775	96,894	153,705	89,984	63,721	48,746	16,539	32,207	1,218	252	966
10—15 ...	178,071	94,335	83,736	102,053	67,423	34,630	74,064	26,542	47,522	1,954	370	1,584
15—20 ...	151,018	74,036	76,982	28,702	24,590	4,112	117,481	48,537	68,944	4,835	909	3,926
20—30 ...	308,831	158,217	150,614	22,730	19,770	2,960	268,070	134,772	133,298	18,031	3,675	14,356
30—40 ...	232,821	128,713	104,108	5,125	4,102	1,023	197,752	118,842	78,910	29,944	5,769	24,175
40—50 ...	142,933	77,469	65,464	1,533	1,299	234	104,093	68,937	35,156	37,307	7,233	30,074
50—60 ...	80,650	40,838	39,812	583	478	105	47,107	33,795	13,312	32,960	6,565	26,395
60 and over ...	51,786	23,280	28,506	346	279	67	22,610	16,983	5,626	28,830	6,016	22,814
MUSLIMS ...	*111,377*	*61,712*	*49,665*	*34,516*	*20,445*	*14,071*	*67,715*	*38,236*	*29,479*	*9,146*	*3,031*	*6,115*
0—1 ...	2,903	1,464	1,439	2,880	1,402	1,486	22	12	10	1	...	1
1—2 ...	2,746	1,361	1,385	2,670	1,326	1,344	75	34	41	1	1	...
2—3 ...	3,591	1,746	1,845	3,400	1,671	1,729	189	74	115	2	1	1
3—4 ...	3,672	1,777	1,895	3,254	1,628	1,626	411	145	266	7	4	3
4—5 ...	3,448	1,701	1,747	2,861	1,494	1,367	571	197	374	16	10	6
Total 0—5 ...	*16,360*	*8,049*	*8,311*	*15,065*	*7,571*	*7,494*	*1,268*	*462*	*806*	*27*	*16*	*11*
5—10 ...	13,937	7,279	6,658	9,532	6,551	3,071	4,298	1,674	3,024	117	54	63
10—15 ...	12,328	6,761	5,567	6,192	4,135	2,057	5,918	2,508	3,410	218	118	100
15—20 ...	10,506	5,692	4,814	1,735	1,486	249	8,381	3,996	4,365	390	210	180
20—30 ...	22,550	13,639	9,911	1,573	1,358	215	19,757	10,796	8,961	1,220	455	765
30—40 ...	17,004	10,265	6,739	335	272	63	14,920	9,379	5,541	1,749	614	1,135
40—50 ...	10,127	6,134	3,993	72	55	17	7,947	5,442	2,505	2,108	637	1,471
50—60 ...	5,289	3,100	2,189	12	9	3	3,545	2,655	890	1,732	445	1,287
60 and over ...	3,276	1,784	1,492	10	8	2	1,681	1,324	357	1,585	452	1,133
TRIBAL ...	*99,160*	*50,253*	*48,907*	*42,064*	*23,016*	*10,048*	*47,485*	*24,163*	*23,322*	*9,611*	*3,074*	*6,537*
0—1 ...	2,972	1,433	1,539	2,965	1,429	1,536	7	4	3	...	...	...
1—2 ...	2,764	1,298	1,466	2,723	1,274	1,449	40	23	17	1	1	...
2—3 ...	3,539	1,651	1,888	3,407	1,580	1,827	131	71	00	1	...	1
3—4 ...	3,780	1,810	1,970	3,575	1,707	1,868	200	102	98	5	1	4
4—5 ...	3,433	1,691	1,742	3,211	1,585	1,626	210	103	107	12	3	9
Total 0—5 ...	*16,488*	*7,883*	*8,605*	*15,881*	*7,575*	*8,306*	*588*	*303*	*285*	*19*	*5*	*14*
5—10 ...	13,640	7,061	6,579	12,073	6,442	5,631	1,478	586	892	89	33	56
10—15 ...	11,884	6,240	5,644	8,914	5,168	3,746	2,782	1,002	1,780	188	70	118
15—20 ...	9,044	4,375	4,669	2,779	1,980	799	5,855	2,346	3,509	410	149	261
20—30 ...	17,083	8,521	8,562	1,981	1,541	440	13,840	6,480	7,360	1,262	500	762
30—40 ...	13,642	7,177	6,465	277	186	91	11,590	6,408	5,182	1,775	582	1,193
40—50 ...	8,731	4,686	4,045	73	54	19	6,601	4,015	2,586	2,057	617	1,440
50—60 ...	5,218	2,685	2,533	51	42	9	3,247	2,067	1,180	1,920	576	1,344
60 and over ...	3,426	1,625	1,805	35	28	7	1,504	1,056	448	1,891	541	1,350

TABLE VII—*continued.*

AGE, SEX AND CIVIL CONDITION. | **PART II—DETAILS FOR DISTRICTS.**

Age.	Population.			Unmarried.			Married.			Widowed.		
	Persons.	Males.	Females.	Persons.	Males.	Females.	Persons.	Males.	Females.	Persons.	Males.	Females.
1	2	3	4	5	6	7	8	9	10	11	12	13
SINGHBHUM.												
ALL RELIGIONS ...	*929,802*	*469,421*	*460,381*	*467,340*	*253,562*	*213,778*	*394,209*	*204,414*	*189,788*	*68,260*	*11,445*	*56,815*
0—1 ...	29,701	14,734	14,967	29,583	14,701	14,882	112	31	81	6	2	4
1—2 ...	27,231	13,282	13,949	27,085	13,239	13,846	140	43	103	...	...	...
2—3 ...	32,846	15,790	17,056	32,519	15,711	16,808	322	79	243	5	...	5
3—4 ...	34,159	16,746	17,413	33,442	16,526	16,916	692	219	473	25	1	24
4—5 ...	31,457	15,768	15,689	30,432	15,424	15,008	979	341	638	46	3	43
Total 0—5 ...	*155,394*	*76,320*	*79,074*	*153,061*	*75,601*	*77,460*	*2,251*	*713*	*1,538*	*82*	*6*	*76*
5—10 ...	127,216	65,601	61,615	118,141	62,969	55,172	8,865	2,615	6,250	210	17	193
10—15 ...	110,172	57,069	53,103	92,960	51,910	41,050	16,821	5,100	11,721	391	59	332
15—20 ...	88,201	42,356	45,845	41,763	25,826	15,937	45,073	16,240	28,833	1,365	290	1,075
20—30 ...	178,140	91,372	86,768	41,221	27,220	14,001	130,148	62,667	67,481	6,771	1,485	5,286
30—40 ...	127,733	67,512	60,221	12,043	6,880	5,163	102,122	58,283	43,839	13,568	2,349	11,219
40—50 ...	74,145	38,131	36,014	4,612	2,159	2,453	52,436	33,235	19,201	17,097	2,737	14,360
50—60 ...	41,591	19,764	21,827	2,177	710	1,467	24,372	16,732	7,640	15,042	2,322	12,720
60 and over ...	27,210	11,296	15,914	1,362	287	1,075	12,114	8,829	3,285	13,734	2,180	11,554
HINDUS ...	*460,075*	*237,465*	*222,610*	*200,074*	*114,146*	*85,928*	*223,911*	*117,822*	*106,089*	*36,090*	*5,497*	*30,593*
0—1 ...	13,801	6,912	6,889	13,691	6,879	6,812	106	31	75	4	2	2
1—2 ...	13,542	6,569	6,973	13,410	6,531	6,879	132	38	94	.	...	...
2—3 ...	15,992	7,632	8,360	15,758	7,571	8,187	230	61	169	4	...	4
3—4 ...	16,394	8,007	8,387	15,887	7,840	8,047	488	166	322	19	1	18
4—5 ...	15,092	7,587	7,505	14,338	7,329	7,009	723	256	467	31	2	29
Total 0—5 ...	*74,821*	*36,707*	*38,114*	*73,084*	*36,150*	*36,934*	*1,679*	*552*	*1,127*	*58*	*5*	*53*
5—10 ...	60,946	31,650	29,296	53,636	29,537	24,099	7,164	2,101	5,063	146	12	134
10—15 ...	52,402	27,555	24,847	39,743	23,657	16,086	12,403	3,871	8,532	256	27	229
15—20 ...	43,732	21,390	22,342	14,728	10,568	4,160	28,198	10,670	17,528	806	152	654
20—30 ...	92,581	49,281	43,300	13,673	10,742	2,931	75,166	37,730	37,436	3,742	809	2,933
30—40 ...	64,424	35,301	29,123	3,282	2,214	1,068	54,092	31,894	22,108	7,050	1,193	5,857
40—50 ...	37,246	19,906	17,340	1,287	972	315	26,877	17,664	9,213	9,082	1,270	7,812
50—60 ...	20,605	10,044	10,561	427	231	196	12,314	8,772	3,542	7,864	1,041	6,823
60 and over ...	13,318	5,631	7,687	214	75	139	6,018	4,568	1,450	7,086	988	6,098
MUSLIMS ...	*26,754*	*16,543*	*10,211*	*9,723*	*6,355*	*3,368*	*15,673*	*9,947*	*5,726*	*1,358*	*241*	*1,117*
0—1 ...	615	329	286	615	329	286	...	...	...	...	...	...
1—2 ...	647	330	317	646	329	317	1	1	.	...	...	...
2—3 ...	703	333	370	702	333	369	1	...	1	...	...	...
3—4 ...	708	345	363	702	341	361	6	4	2	...	...	...
4—5 ...	646	316	330	629	307	322	16	9	7	1	...	1
Total 0—5 ...	*3,319*	*1,653*	*1,666*	*3,294*	*1,639*	*1,655*	*24*	*14*	*10*	*1*	...	*1*
5—10 ...	2,604	1,420	1,184	2,332	1,323	1,009	263	96	167	9	1	8
10—15 ...	2,366	1,345	1,021	1,759	1,185	574	588	158	430	19	2	17
15—20 ...	2,881	1,689	1,192	935	868	67	1,901	815	1,086	45	6	39
20—30 ...	6,958	4,460	2,498	1,013	969	44	5,758	3,434	2,324	187	57	130
30—40 ...	4,722	3,417	1,305	266	253	13	4,178	3,112	1,066	278	52	226
40—50 ...	2,305	1,590	715	69	63	6	1,919	1,477	442	317	50	267
50—60 ...	992	636	356	39	39	...	704	561	143	249	36	213
60 and over ...	607	333	274	16	16	...	338	280	58	253	37	216
CHRISTIANS ...	*19,552*	*10,056*	*9,496*	*10,181*	*5,517*	*4,664*	*8,236*	*4,284*	*3,952*	*1,135*	*255*	*880*
0—1 ...	667	326	341	667	326	341	...	...	...	...	...	...
1—2 ...	663	329	334	663	329	334	...	...	..	...	...	...
2—3 ...	717	360	357	716	359	357	1	1	...	...	...	...
3—4 ...	729	374	355	726	372	354	3	2	1	...	...	...
4—5 ...	714	364	350	703	358	345	10	6	4	1	...	1
Total 0—5 ...	*3,490*	*1,753*	*1,737*	*3,475*	*1,744*	*1,731*	*14*	*9*	*5*	*1*	...	*1*
5—10 ...	2,668	1,371	1,297	2,607	1,347	1,260	58	24	34	3	...	3
10—15 ...	2,189	1,117	1,072	2,035	1,075	960	148	41	107	6	1	5
15—20 ...	1,733	822	911	971	588	383	749	232	517	13	2	11
20—30 ...	3,652	1,869	1,783	850	599	251	2,690	1,237	1,453	112	33	79
30—40 ...	2,778	1,502	1,276	162	113	49	2,395	1,346	1,049	221	43	178
40—50 ...	1,623	911	712	51	36	15	1,313	815	498	259	60	199
50—60 ...	874	452	422	20	13	7	589	381	208	265	58	207
60 and over ...	545	259	280	10	2	8	280	199	81	255	58	197
TRIBAL ...	*419,338*	*202,616*	*216,722*	*245,796*	*126,467*	*119,329*	*143,946*	*70,747*	*73,199*	*29,596*	*5,402*	*24,194*
0—1 ...	14,510	7,113	7,397	14,502	7,113	7,389	6	...	6	2	...	2
1—2 ...	12,272	5,998	6,274	12,259	5,994	6,265	13	4	9	...	...	...
2—3 ...	15,319	7,405	7,914	15,229	7,389	7,840	89	16	73	1	...	1
3—4 ...	16,232	7,908	8,364	16,031	7,921	8,110	195	47	148	6	...	6
4—5 ...	14,906	7,446	7,458	14,663	7,377	7,286	230	70	160	13	1	12
Total 0—5 ...	*73,239*	*35,932*	*37,307*	*72,684*	*35,794*	*36,890*	*533*	*137*	*396*	*22*	*1*	*21*
5—10 ...	60,653	30,956	29,697	59,222	30,558	28,664	1,379	394	985	52	4	48
10—15 ...	52,915	26,862	26,053	40,167	25,820	23,347	3,639	1,014	2,625	109	28	81
15—20 ...	39,385	18,169	21,216	24,973	13,656	11,317	13,914	4,386	9,528	498	127	371
20—30 ...	73,758	34,978	38,785	25,460	14,690	10,770	45,576	19,704	25,872	2,722	579	2,143
30—40 ...	55,031	26,674	28,357	8,277	4,245	4,032	40,750	21,380	19,870	6,004	1,049	4,955
40—50 ...	32,661	15,470	17,191	3,201	1,084	2,117	22,045	13,045	9,000	7,415	1,341	6,074
50—60 ...	19,003	8,538	10,465	1,691	427	1,264	10,662	6,931	3,731	6,650	1,180	5,470
60 and over ...	12,693	5,043	7,651	1,121	193	928	5,448	3,756	1,692	6,124	1,093	5,031
ORISSA STATES.												
ALL RELIGIONS ...	*4,465,385*	*2,196,691*	*2,268,694*	*2,041,235*	*1,118,593*	*922,642*	*2,039,937*	*1,014,109*	*1,025,828*	*384,913*	*63,989*	*320,324*
0—1 ...	153,725	75,815	77,910	153,725	75,815	77,910	...	...	...	...	...	...
1—2 ...	140,637	68,383	72,254	140,637	68,383	72,254	..	...	...	...	...	...
2—3 ...	161,121	77,512	83,609	161,046	77,402	83,554	73	20	53	2	...	2
3—4 ...	159,064	77,449	81,615	158,404	77,243	81,161	640	206	434	20	...	20
4—5 ...	146,942	73,123	73,819	145,755	72,742	73,013	1,144	378	766	43	3	40
Total 0—5 ...	*761,489*	*372,282*	*389,207*	*759,567*	*371,675*	*387,892*	*1,857*	*604*	*1,253*	*65*	*3*	*62*
5—10 ...	612,075	310,886	301,189	573,546	300,633	272,913	37,802	10,162	27,640	727	91	636
10—15 ...	524,072	271,036	253,036	439,064	246,837	192,227	83,300	23,004	59,396	1,708	295	1,413
15—20 ...	390,072	186,439	203,633	149,988	107,570	42,418	233,199	77,258	155,941	6,885	1,611	5,274
20—30 ...	798,282	381,918	416,364	97,969	77,927	20,042	667,172	295,858	371,314	60,141	8,133	26,008
30—40 ...	633,245	317,786	315,459	13,730	9,551	4,170	540,005	290,879	249,133	74,513	12,356	62,157
40—50 ...	395,263	197,860	197,403	4,379	2,693	1,686	289,676	180,424	109,252	101,228	14,743	86,485
50—60 ...	217,254	102,540	114,705	1,831	1,070	761	126,375	87,928	38,447	89,048	13,551	75,497
60 and over ...	133,613	56,935	77,078	1,161	637	524	55,554	42,092	13,462	76,898	13,206	63,692

TABLE VII—*continued*.

AGE, SEX AND CIVIL CONDITION. | **PART II—DETAILS FOR DISTRICTS.**

Age.	Population. Persons.	Population. Males.	Population. Females.	Unmarried. Persons.	Unmarried. Males.	Unmarried. Females.	Married. Persons.	Married. Males.	Married. Females.	Widowed. Persons.	Widowed. Males.	Widowed. Females.
1	2	3	4	5	6	7	8	9	10	11	12	13
ORISSA STATES—concluded.												
HINDUS ...	*4,067,176*	*1,999,547*	*2,067,629*	*1,834,368*	*1,009,688*	*824,680*	*1,875,424*	*931,211*	*944,213*	*357,384*	*58,648*	*298,736*
0—1 ...	138,575	68,343	70,232	138,575	68,343	70,232	...	...	...	...	...	...
1—2 ...	127,200	61,796	65,404	127,200	61,796	65,404	...	...	...	...	...	...
2—3 ...	145,311	69,812	75,499	145,239	69,795	75,444	70	17	53	2	...	2
3—4 ...	143,111	69,647	73,464	142,487	69,461	73,026	604	186	418	20	...	20
4—5 ...	132,188	65,807	66,381	131,078	65,465	65,613	1,071	340	731	39	2	37
Total 0—5 ...	*686,385*	*335,405*	*350,980*	*684,579*	*334,860*	*349,719*	*1,745*	*543*	*1,202*	*61*	*2*	*59*
5—10 ...	553,473	281,190	272,283	516,400	271,456	244,944	36,377	9,648	26,729	696	86	610
10—15 ...	475,201	246,183	229,018	394,488	223,262	171,226	79,095	22,644	56,451	1,618	277	1,341
15—20 ...	356,071	170,700	185,371	133,596	97,515	36,081	216,077	71,707	144,370	6,398	1,478	4,920
20—30 ...	729,863	349,198	380,665	86,797	70,246	16,551	612,393	271,533	340,860	30,673	7,419	23,254
30—40 ...	578,519	289,025	288,894	11,998	8,411	3,587	497,442	270,017	227,425	69,079	11,197	57,882
40—50 ...	363,661	181,257	182,404	3,881	2,416	1,465	265,331	165,292	100,039	94,449	13,549	80,900
50—60 ...	200,721	94,559	106,162	1,630	965	665	116,115	81,124	34,991	82,976	12,470	70,506
60 and over ...	123,282	51,430	71,852	999	557	442	50,849	38,703	12,146	71,434	12,170	59,264
CHRISTIANS ...	*74,468*	*36,878*	*37,590*	*41,676*	*21,636*	*20,040*	*28,453*	*14,337*	*14,116*	*4,339*	*905*	*3,434*
0—1 ...	2,910	1,434	1,476	2,910	1,434	1,476	...	...	...	...	...	...
1—2 ...	2,481	1,230	1,251	2,481	1,230	1,251	...	...	...	...	...	...
2—3 ...	2,951	1,496	1,455	2,951	1,496	1,455	...	...	...	...	...	...
3—4 ...	2,997	1,516	1,481	2,982	1,508	1,474	15	8	7	...	...	...
4—5 ...	2,717	1,360	1,357	2,687	1,344	1,343	30	16	14	...	...	...
Total 0—5 ...	*14,056*	*7,036*	*7,020*	*14,011*	*7,012*	*6,999*	*45*	*24*	*21*	...	...	...
5—10 ...	11,622	5,927	5,695	11,377	5,813	5,564	243	112	131	2	2	...
10—15 ...	10,207	5,202	5,005	9,677	5,023	4,654	522	176	346	8	3	5
15—20 ...	6,850	3,206	3,644	3,797	2,185	1,612	2,998	1,011	1,987	55	10	45
20—30 ...	12,266	5,924	6,342	2,387	1,363	1,024	9,526	4,472	5,054	353	89	264
30—40 ...	8,764	4,448	4,316	275	163	112	7,727	4,112	3,615	762	173	589
40—50 ...	5,360	2,702	2,658	94	47	47	4,266	2,466	1,800	1,000	189	811
50—60 ...	3,150	1,494	1,656	36	17	19	2,066	1,265	801	1,048	212	836
60 and over ...	2,193	939	1,254	22	13	9	1,060	699	361	1,111	227	884
TRIBAL ...	*304,502*	*150,172*	*154,330*	*157,358*	*82,720*	*74,638*	*126,408*	*63,306*	*63,102*	*20,736*	*4,146*	*16,590*
0—1 ...	11,669	5,759	5,910	11,669	5,759	5,910	...	...	...	...	...	...
1—2 ...	10,442	5,098	5,344	10,442	5,098	5,344	...	...	...	...	...	...
2—3 ...	12,271	5,913	6,358	12,268	5,910	6,358	3	3	...	...	...	...
3—4 ...	12,379	6,000	6,379	12,359	5,989	6,370	20	11	9	...	...	...
4—5 ...	11,486	5,687	5,799	11,444	5,666	5,778	39	20	19	3	1	2
Total 0—5 ...	*58,247*	*28,457*	*29,790*	*58,182*	*28,422*	*29,760*	*62*	*34*	*28*	*3*	*1*	*2*
5—10 ...	44,649	22,558	22,091	43,582	22,185	21,397	1,045	370	675	22	3	19
10—15 ...	36,627	18,578	18,049	33,225	17,560	15,665	3,330	1,003	2,327	72	15	57
15—20 ...	25,415	11,685	13,730	12,035	7,424	4,611	12,985	4,149	8,836	395	112	283
20—30 ...	52,378	24,798	27,580	8,300	6,000	2,420	42,111	18,325	23,786	1,958	584	1,374
30—40 ...	42,990	22,043	20,947	1,361	894	467	37,312	20,222	17,090	4,317	927	3,390
40—50 ...	24,359	12,848	11,511	380	211	169	18,656	11,700	6,956	5,323	937	4,386
50—60 ...	12,331	5,943	6,388	153	77	76	7,554	5,061	2,493	4,624	805	3,819
60 and over ...	7,506	3,262	4,244	131	58	73	3,353	2,442	911	4,022	762	3,260
CHOTA NAGPUR STATES.												
ALL RELIGIONS ...	*186,622*	*91,731*	*94,891*	*87,622*	*47,047*	*40,575*	*82,993*	*41,914*	*41,079*	*16,007*	*2,770*	*13,237*
0—1 ...	5,165	2,520	2,645	5,165	2,520	2,645	...	...	...	...	...	...
1—2 ...	5,712	2,759	2,953	5,712	2,759	2,953	...	...	...	...	...	...
2—3 ...	6,885	3,286	3,599	6,885	3,286	3,599	...	...	...	...	...	...
3—4 ...	7,213	3,478	3,735	7,164	3,466	3,698	49	12	37	...	...	...
4—5 ...	6,599	3,252	3,347	6,498	3,227	3,271	101	25	76	...	...	...
Total 0—5 ...	*31,574*	*15,295*	*16,279*	*31,424*	*15,258*	*16,166*	*150*	*37*	*113*	...	...	...
5—10 ...	26,926	13,783	13,143	24,019	12,778	11,241	2,837	995	1,842	70	10	60
10—15 ...	23,029	11,968	11,061	17,658	10,074	7,584	5,234	1,873	3,361	137	21	116
15—20 ...	17,060	8,124	8,936	6,631	4,252	2,379	10,057	3,802	6,255	372	70	302
20—30 ...	32,191	15,450	16,741	5,599	3,610	1,989	25,039	11,491	13,548	1,553	349	1,204
30—40 ...	24,986	12,661	12,325	1,401	734	667	20,511	11,371	9,140	3,074	556	2,518
40—50 ...	15,712	7,977	7,735	512	203	309	11,319	7,083	4,236	3,881	691	3,190
50—60 ...	8,776	4,051	4,725	221	81	140	5,108	3,417	1,691	3,447	553	2,894
60 and over ...	6,368	2,422	3,946	157	57	100	2,738	1,845	893	3,473	520	2,953
HINDUS ...	*127,702*	*63,461*	*64,241*	*55,240*	*30,572*	*24,668*	*61,040*	*30,883*	*30,157*	*11,422*	*2,006*	*9,416*
0—1 ...	3,485	1,712	1,773	3,485	1,712	1,773	...	...	...	...	...	...
1—2 ...	3,878	1,885	1,993	3,878	1,885	1,993	...	...	...	...	...	...
2—3 ...	4,666	2,230	2,436	4,666	2,230	2,436	...	...	...	...	...	...
3—4 ...	4,839	2,338	2,501	4,805	2,330	2,475	34	8	26	...	...	...
4—5 ...	4,400	2,178	2,222	4,332	2,162	2,170	68	16	52	...	...	...
Total 0—5 ...	*21,268*	*10,343*	*10,925*	*21,166*	*10,319*	*10,847*	*102*	*24*	*78*	...	...	...
5—10 ...	18,165	9,348	8,817	15,758	8,580	7,178	2,352	702	1,590	55	6	49
10—15 ...	15,587	8,183	7,404	11,176	6,673	4,503	4,306	1,498	2,808	105	12	93
15—20 ...	11,615	5,596	6,019	3,546	2,528	1,018	7,808	3,032	4,776	261	46	215
20—30 ...	22,238	10,785	11,453	2,620	1,905	715	18,509	8,633	9,876	1,107	245	862
30—40 ...	17,383	8,987	8,396	596	367	229	14,560	8,194	6,366	2,227	426	1,801
40—50 ...	10,889	5,637	5,252	226	117	109	7,924	5,012	2,912	2,739	508	2,231
50—60 ...	6,108	2,863	3,245	90	46	44	3,564	2,425	1,139	2,454	392	2,062
60 and over ...	4,451	1,721	2,730	62	37	25	1,915	1,313	602	2,474	371	2,103
TRIBAL ...	*56,098*	*26,746*	*29,352*	*31,293*	*15,877*	*15,416*	*20,409*	*10,147*	*10,262*	*4,396*	*722*	*3,674*
0—1 ...	1,609	775	834	1,609	775	834	...	...	...	...	...	...
1—2 ...	1,749	836	913	1,749	836	913	...	...	...	...	...	...
2—3 ...	2,116	1,010	1,106	2,116	1,010	1,106	...	...	...	...	...	...
3—4 ...	2,280	1,095	1,185	2,266	1,091	1,175	14	4	10	...	...	...
4—5 ...	2,105	1,027	1,078	2,074	1,018	1,056	31	9	22	...	...	...
Total 0—5 ...	*9,859*	*4,743*	*5,116*	*9,814*	*4,730*	*5,084*	*45*	*13*	*32*	...	...	...
5—10 ...	8,406	4,250	4,156	7,953	4,030	3,923	438	216	222	15	4	11
10—15 ...	7,134	3,627	3,507	6,276	3,270	2,997	826	339	487	32	9	23
15—20 ...	5,170	2,391	2,779	3,019	1,676	1,343	2,044	692	1,352	107	23	84
20—30 ...	9,391	4,353	5,038	2,930	1,667	1,263	6,041	2,589	3,452	420	97	323
30—40 ...	7,196	3,424	3,772	796	361	435	5,587	2,939	2,648	813	124	689
40—50 ...	4,555	2,180	2,375	281	81	200	3,189	1,927	1,262	1,085	172	913
50—60 ...	2,543	1,112	1,431	130	34	96	1,457	928	529	956	150	806
60 and over ...	1,844	666	1,178	94	19	75	782	504	278	968	143	825

TABLE VII—*continued.*

AGE, SEX AND CIVIL CONDITION. **PART III—DETAILS FOR CITIES.**

Age.	Population.			Unmarried.			Married.			Widowed.		
	Persons.	Males.	Females.	Persons.	Males.	Females.	Persons.	Males.	Females.	Persons.	Males.	Females.
1	2	3	4	5	6	7	8	9	10	11	12	13
PATNA CITY.												
ALL RELIGIONS ...	*159,690*	*92,238*	*67,452*	*54,936*	*34,338*	*20,598*	*87,006*	*51,847*	*35,159*	*17,748*	*6,053*	*11,695*
0—1 ...	2,953	1,427	1,526	2,893	1,419	1,474	59	7	52	1	1	...
1—2 ...	3,393	1,677	1,716	3,322	1,659	1,663	71	18	53	...	...	...
2—3 ...	4,054	1,990	2,064	3,980	1,940	2,040	72	50	22	2	...	2
3—4 ...	4,009	2,040	1,969	3,849	1,924	1,925	156	114	42	4	2	2
4—5 ...	3,850	2,042	1,808	3,636	1,885	1,751	207	153	54	7	4	3
Total 0—5 ...	*18,259*	*9,176*	*9,083*	*17,680*	*8,827*	*8,853*	*565*	*342*	*223*	*14*	*7*	*7*
5—10 ...	17,434	9,617	7,817	14,994	8,529	6,465	2,404	1,069	1,335	36	19	17
10—15 ...	17,326	10,031	7,295	12,004	7,690	4,314	5,240	2,306	2,934	82	35	47
15—20 ...	16,931	10,457	6,474	5,159	4,495	664	11,418	5,782	5,636	354	180	174
20—30 ...	32,325	19,971	12,354	4,049	3,816	233	26,627	15,318	11,309	1,649	837	812
30—40 ...	23,586	13,964	9,622	633	605	28	19,836	12,283	7,553	3,117	1,076	2,041
40—50 ...	16,733	9,734	6,999	233	214	19	12,018	8,218	3,800	4,482	1,302	3,180
50—60 ...	9,406	5,436	3,970	119	110	9	5,621	4,110	1,511	3,666	1,216	2,450
60 and over ...	7,690	3,852	3,838	65	52	13	3,277	2,419	858	4,348	1,381	2,967
HINDUS ...	*119,644*	*69,285*	*50,359*	*38,772*	*24,400*	*14,372*	*67,206*	*40,177*	*27,029*	*13,666*	*4,708*	*8,958*
0—1 ...	2,227	1,054	1,173	2,167	1,046	1,121	59	7	52	1	1	...
1—2 ...	2,576	1,274	1,302	2,505	1,256	1,249	71	18	53	...	...	...
2—3 ...	3,097	1,533	1,564	3,023	1,483	1,540	72	50	22	2	...	2
3—4 ...	3,064	1,573	1,491	2,911	1,464	1,447	150	108	42	3	1	2
4—5 ...	2,920	1,559	1,361	2,719	1,414	1,305	195	142	53	6	3	3
Total 0—5 ...	*13,884*	*6,993*	*6,891*	*13,325*	*6,663*	*6,662*	*547*	*325*	*222*	*12*	*5*	*7*
5—10 ...	12,997	7,233	5,764	10,815	6,259	4,556	2,150	959	1,191	32	15	17
10—15 ...	12,897	7,577	5,320	8,285	5,451	2,834	4,535	2,096	2,439	77	30	47
15—20 ...	12,600	7,865	4,735	3,147	2,871	276	9,160	4,849	4,311	293	145	148
20—30 ...	24,298	15,085	9,213	2,494	2,450	44	20,448	11,966	8,482	1,356	669	687
30—40 ...	17,917	10,616	7,301	428	428	...	15,049	9,334	5,715	2,440	854	1,586
40—50 ...	12,434	7,184	5,250	157	157	...	8,834	6,017	2,817	3,443	1,010	2,433
50—60 ...	6,938	3,984	2,954	83	83	...	4,114	2,951	1,163	2,741	950	1,791
60 and over ...	5,679	2,748	2,931	38	38	...	2,369	1,680	689	3,272	1,030	2,242
MUSLIMS ...	*38,238*	*22,241*	*15,997*	*15,094*	*9,599*	*5,495*	*19,166*	*11,330*	*7,836*	*3,978*	*1,312*	*2,666*
0—1 ...	676	348	328	676	348	328	...	...	...	...	...	...
1—2 ...	783	387	396	783	387	396	...	...	...	...	...	...
2—3 ...	919	438	481	919	438	481	...	...	...	...	...	...
3—4 ...	901	446	455	896	441	455	5	5	...	...	...	...
4—5 ...	889	468	421	874	454	420	13	12	1	2	2	...
Total 0—5 ...	*4,168*	*2,087*	*2,081*	*4,148*	*2,068*	*2,080*	*18*	*17*	*1*	*2*	*2*	...
5—10 ...	4,219	2,329	1,890	3,960	2,214	1,746	254	110	144	5	5	...
10—15 ...	4,206	2,408	1,798	3,502	2,195	1,307	699	208	491	5	5	...
15—20 ...	4,123	2,525	1,598	1,848	1,574	274	2,215	917	1,298	60	34	26
20—30 ...	7,693	4,753	2,940	1,395	1,307	88	6,015	3,280	2,735	283	166	117
30—40 ...	5,407	3,223	2,184	157	157	...	4,596	2,851	1,745	654	215	439
40—50 ...	4,091	2,432	1,659	48	48	...	3,031	2,102	929	1,012	282	730
50—60 ...	2,371	1,402	969	23	23	...	1,446	1,118	328	902	261	641
60 and over ...	1,960	1,082	878	13	13	...	892	727	165	1,055	342	713
GAYA CITY.												
ALL RELIGIONS ...	*88,005*	*50,625*	*37,380*	*25,377*	*15,733*	*9,644*	*52,643*	*31,766*	*20,877*	*9,985*	*3,126*	*6,859*
0—1 ...	1,795	901	894	1,789	895	894	6	6	...	...	...	...
1—2 ...	2,009	1,004	1,005	1,994	991	1,003	15	13	2	...	...	...
2—3 ...	2,210	1,135	1,075	2,177	1,121	1,056	32	14	18	1	...	1
3—4 ...	2,158	1,127	1,031	2,060	1,087	973	96	39	57	2	1	1
4—5 ...	1,954	1,036	918	1,801	969	832	147	64	83	6	3	3
Total 0—5 ...	*10,126*	*5,203*	*4,923*	*9,821*	*5,063*	*4,758*	*296*	*136*	*160*	*9*	*4*	*5*
5—10 ...	8,964	4,953	4,011	6,843	4,049	2,794	2,066	878	1,188	55	26	29
10—15 ...	8,649	4,938	3,711	5,032	3,349	1,683	3,527	1,543	1,984	90	46	44
15—20 ...	8,139	4,705	3,434	1,661	1,461	200	6,280	3,153	3,127	198	91	107
20—30 ...	17,738	10,528	7,210	1,433	1,285	148	15,396	8,845	6,551	909	398	511
30—40 ...	14,551	8,743	5,808	388	344	44	12,363	7,812	4,551	1,800	587	1,213
40—50 ...	10,269	6,240	4,029	129	116	13	7,602	5,407	2,195	2,538	717	1,821
50—60 ...	5,616	3,265	2,351	50	47	3	3,348	2,590	758	2,218	628	1,590
60 and over ...	3,953	2,050	1,903	20	19	1	1,765	1,402	363	2,168	629	1,539
HINDUS ...	*66,462*	*38,502*	*27,960*	*18,423*	*11,489*	*6,934*	*40,027*	*24,355*	*15,672*	*8,012*	*2,658*	*5,354*
0—1 ...	1,393	697	696	1,390	694	696	3	3	...	...	...	...
1—2 ...	1,536	764	772	1,528	758	770	8	6	2	...	...	...
2—3 ...	1,665	854	811	1,641	847	794	23	7	16	1	...	1
3—4 ...	1,604	842	762	1,534	818	716	68	23	45	2	1	1
4—5 ...	1,422	755	667	1,311	712	599	107	41	66	4	2	2
Total 0—5 ...	*7,620*	*3,912*	*3,708*	*7,404*	*3,829*	*3,575*	*209*	*80*	*129*	*7*	*3*	*4*
5—10 ...	6,534	3,621	2,913	4,876	2,910	1,966	1,611	688	923	47	23	24
10—15 ...	6,326	3,635	2,691	3,513	2,364	1,149	2,736	1,231	1,505	77	40	37
15—20 ...	6,096	3,563	2,533	1,118	1,007	111	4,820	2,478	2,342	158	78	80
20—30 ...	13,497	8,101	5,396	1,022	935	87	11,728	6,830	4,898	747	336	411
30—40 ...	11,243	6,832	4,411	317	284	33	9,464	6,037	3,427	1,462	511	951
40—50 ...	7,852	4,830	3,022	111	99	12	5,731	4,110	1,621	2,010	621	1,389
50—60 ...	4,282	2,475	1,807	44	43	1	2,468	1,902	566	1,770	530	1,240
60 and over ...	3,012	1,533	1,479	18	18	...	1,260	999	261	1,734	516	1,218
MUSLIMS ...	*20,596*	*11,626*	*8,970*	*6,629*	*4,089*	*2,540*	*12,089*	*7,093*	*4,996*	*1,878*	*444*	*1,434*
0—1 ...	382	196	186	378	192	186	4	4	...	...	...	...
1—2 ...	449	228	221	443	222	221	6	6	...	...	...	...
2—3 ...	522	270	252	512	263	249	10	7	3	...	...	...
3—4 ...	528	275	253	504	261	243	24	14	10	...	...	...
4—5 ...	508	267	241	470	248	222	37	19	18	1	...	1
Total 0—5 ...	*2,389*	*1,236*	*1,153*	*2,307*	*1,186*	*1,121*	*81*	*50*	*31*	*1*	...	*1*
5—10 ...	2,338	1,281	1,057	1,893	1,106	787	436	171	265	9	4	5
10—15 ...	2,239	1,258	981	1,464	959	505	762	293	469	13	6	7
15—20 ...	1,959	1,103	856	513	438	75	1,407	652	755	39	13	26
20—30 ...	4,058	2,339	1,719	379	332	47	3,525	1,947	1,578	154	60	94
30—40 ...	3,145	1,823	1,322	58	53	5	2,767	1,695	1,072	320	75	245
40—50 ...	2,299	1,342	957	15	15	...	1,782	1,239	543	502	88	414
50—60 ...	1,261	745	516	...	...	...	837	654	183	424	91	333
60 and over ...	908	499	409	...	...	...	492	392	100	416	107	309

TABLE VII—*concluded.*

AGE, SEX AND CIVIL CONDITION. **PART III—DETAILS FOR CITIES.**

Age.	Population			Unmarried			Married			Widowed.		
	Persons	Males	Females	Persons	Males	Females	Persons.	Males.	Females	Persons.	Males.	Females.
1	2	3	4	5	6	7	8	9	10	11	12	13
					BHAGALPUR CITY.							
ALL RELIGIONS ...	*83,847*	*46,868*	*36,979*	*27,212*	*16,448*	*10,764*	*48,697*	*28,450*	*20,247*	*7,938*	*1,970*	*5,968*
0—1 .	**1,841**	942	899	**1,780**	934	846	**61**	8	53	...	..	...
1—2 .	**1,939**	969	970	**1,857**	948	909	**82**	21	61	.	...	...
2—3 ...	**2,272**	1,147	1,125	**2,181**	1,105	1,076	**65**	38	27	**26**	4	22
3—4 ..	**2,409**	1,232	1,177	**2,183**	1,130	1,044	**196**	89	107	**30**	4	26
4—5 ...	**2,342**	1,176	1,166	**2,026**	1,044	982	**305**	139	176	**11**	3	8
Total 0—5 ...	*10,803*	*5,466*	*5,337*	*10,027*	*5,170*	*4,857*	*709*	*285*	*424*	*67*	*11*	*56*
5—10 ...	**10,272**	5,433	4,839	**7,495**	4,400	3,095	**2,730**	1,015	1,715	**47**	18	29
10—15 ..	**9,414**	5,078	4,336	**5,684**	3,565	2,119	**3,671**	1,493	2,178	**59**	20	39
15—20 ...	**8,221**	4,603	3,618	**2,102**	1,542	560	**5,971**	3,015	2,956	**148**	46	102
20—30 ...	**16,507**	9,507	7,000	**1,909**	1,803	106	**14,450**	9,100	5,350	**750**	214	544
30—40 ...	**12,494**	7,375	5,119	**354**	332	22	**10,645**	6,700	3,945	**1,495**	343	1,152
40—50 ...	**8,211**	5,000	3,211	**140**	136	4	**6,150**	4,421	1,729	**1,921**	443	1,478
50—60 ..	**4,496**	2,600	1,896	**19**	18	1	**2,825**	2,158	667	**1,652**	424	1,228
60 and over ...	**3,339**	1,716	1,623	**2**	2	...	**1,546**	1,263	283	**1,791**	451	1,340
HINDUS ...	*58,348*	*33,299*	*25,049*	*17,322*	*10,514*	*6,808*	*35,346*	*21,252*	*14,094*	*5,680*	*1,533*	*4,147*
0—1 ...	**1,255**	630	625	**1,245**	623	622	**10**	7	3			
1—2 .	**1,283**	634	649	**1,260**	619	641	**23**	15	8	...	...	...
2—3 ...	**1,459**	761	698	**1,410**	734	676	**49**	27	22		..	..
3—4 ...	**1,529**	792	737	**1,384**	739	645	**142**	52	90	**3**	1	2
4—5 ...	**1,482**	728	754	**1,256**	654	602	**219**	72	147	**7**	2	5
Total 0—5 ...	*7,008*	*3,546*	*3,463*	*6,555*	*3,369*	*3,186*	*443*	*173*	*270*	*10*	*3*	*7*
5—10 ...	**6,672**	3,472	3,200	**4,503**	2,697	1,806	**2,136**	761	1,375	**33**	14	19
10—15 ...	**6,315**	3,382	2,933	**3,474**	2,148	1,326	**2,803**	1,219	1,584	**38**	15	23
15—20 ...	**5,828**	3,379	2,449	**1,425**	975	450	**4,301**	2,309	1,033	**102**	36	66
20—30 .	**11,961**	7,182	4,779	**942**	905	37	**10,467**	6,111	4,356	**552**	166	386
30—40 ...	**9,029**	5,488	3,541	**285**	282	3	**7,672**	4,943	2,729	**1,072**	263	809
40—50 .	**5,922**	3,712	2,210	**122**	122	.	**4,406**	3,232	1,174	**1,394**	358	1,036
50—60 ...	**3,271**	1,933	1,338	**14**	14		**2,048**	1,572	476	**1,209**	347	862
60 and over ...	**2,342**	1,206	1,136	**2**	2		**1,070**	873	197	**1,270**	331	939
MUSLIMS ...	*24,555*	*12,946*	*11,609*	*9,341*	*5,537*	*3,804*	*13,019*	*6,999*	*6,020*	*2,195*	*410*	*1,785*
0—1 ...	**576**	305	271	**524**	303	221	**52**	3	50			
1—2 ..	**644**	328	316	**587**	324	263	**57**	4	53		.	
2—3 .	**801**	381	420	**759**	366	393	**16**	11	5	**26**	4	22
3—4 ..	**864**	434	430	**786**	395	391	**52**	36	16	**26**	3	23
4—5 ..	**847**	443	405	**757**	384	373	**85**	57	28	**5**	1	4
Total 0—5 ...	*[illegible]*	*[illegible]*	*1,840*	*3,413*	*[illegible]*	*1,641*	*[illegible]*	*110*	*163*	*57*	*8*	*49*
5—10 .	**3,427**	1,837	1,590	**2,840**	1,586	1,254	**571**	243	325	**16**	5	11
10—15 .	**2,900**	1,543	1,357	**2,037**	1,273	764	**843**	265	578	**20**	5	15
15—20 ...	**2,287**	1,146	1,141	**604**	508	96	**1,639**	629	1,010	**44**	9	35
20—30 .	**4,480**	2,330	2,150	**384**	342	42	**3,894**	1,940	1,954	**202**	48	154
30—40 ...	**3,355**	1,830	1,525	**50**	44	6	**2,899**	1,710	1,189	**406**	76	330
40—50 ..	**2,226**	1,243	983	**10**	9	1	**1,700**	1,158	542	**516**	79	437
50—60	**1,180**	636	544	**3**	3		**747**	562	185	**430**	71	359
60 and over ...	**968**	488	480				**464**	379	85	**504**	109	395
					JAMSHEDPUR CITY.							
ALL RELIGIONS ..	*83,738*	*51,137*	*32,601*	*30,451*	*20,025*	*10,426*	*49,090*	*30,273*	*18,817*	*4,197*	*839*	*3,358*
0—1	**1,899**	1,017	882	**1,882**	1,010	872	**17**	7	10	.	.	..
1—2 ...	**2,033**	1,012	1,021	**1,959**	998	961	**74**	14	60	.	..	..
2—3 ...	**2,329**	1,142	1,187	**2,244**	1,120	1,134	**84**	22	62	**1**	...	1
3—4 ..	**2,184**	1,114	1,070	**2,119**	1,075	1,044	**63**	39	24	**2**	...	2
4—5 ...	**1,893**	964	929	**1,807**	915	892	**82**	49	33	**4**	...	4
Total 0—5 .	*10,338*	*5,249*	*5,089*	*10,011*	*5,119*	*4,893*	*320*	*131*	*189*	*7*	.	*7*
5—10	**7,327**	4,004	3,323	**6,531**	3,698	2,833	**785**	305	480	**11**	1	10
10—15 ...	**6,421**	3,594	2,827	**4,792**	3,122	1,670	**1,608**	468	1,140	**21**	4	17
15—20	**9,220**	4,993	4,228	**3,066**	2,584	482	**6,050**	2,377	3,673	**104**	31	73
20—30 ...	**25,045**	16,233	8,812	**5,033**	4,586	447	**19,538**	11,485	8,053	**474**	162	312
30—40	**14,917**	10,775	4,142	**849**	788	61	**13,316**	9,784	3,532	**752**	203	549
40—50 ...	**6,313**	4,062	2,251	**115**	97	18	**4,996**	3,791	1,205	**1,202**	174	1,028
50—60	**2,654**	1,500	1,154	**35**	19	16	**1,782**	1,371	411	**837**	110	727
60 and over ..	**1,503**	728	775	**19**	13	6	**695**	561	134	**789**	154	635
HINDUS ...	*60,494*	*36,395*	*24,099*	*21,422*	*14,135*	*7,287*	*35,658*	*21,599*	*14,059*	*3,414*	*661*	*2,753*
0—1	**1,396**	777	619	**1,379**	770	609	**17**	7	10	..	..	..
1—2	**1,493**	750	743	**1,419**	730	689	**74**	14	60	-	..	
2—3 ...	**1,707**	841	866	**1,623**	820	803	**83**	21	62	**1**	..	1
3—4 ...	**1,597**	821	776	**1,534**	784	750	**61**	37	24	**2**	...	2
4—5 ..	**1,384**	718	666	**1,302**	672	630	**78**	46	32	**4**	.	4
Total 0—5 ..	*7,677*	*3,907*	*3,670*	*7,2 7*	*3,782*	*3,476*	*318*	*125*	*188*	*7*	..	*7*
5—10 ...	**5,338**	2,910	2,428	**4,646**	2,635	2,011	**684**	274	410	**8**	1	7
10—15 .	**4,623**	2,557	2,066	**3,315**	2,141	1,174	**1,295**	414	881	**13**	2	11
15—20 ...	**6,543**	3,469	3,074	**1,982**	1,696	286	**4,473**	1,717	2,726	**88**	26	62
20—30 ..	**18,184**	11,791	6,393	**3,608**	3,347	261	**14,192**	8,313	5,879	**384**	131	253
30—40	**10,596**	7,448	3,148	**473**	428	45	**9,530**	6,853	3,677	**593**	167	426
40—50 ...	**4,509**	2,728	1,781	**97**	79	18	**3,411**	2,524	887	**1,001**	125	876
50—60	**1,962**	1,039	923	**26**	14	13	**1,260**	946	314	**676**	79	597
60 and over ...	**1,162**	543	619	**18**	13	5	**500**	403	97	**644**	130	514
MUSLIMS ...	*13,797*	*9,126*	*4,671*	*4,743*	*3,275*	*1,468*	*8,576*	*5,757*	*2,819*	*478*	*94*	*384*
0—1 ..	**272**	136	136	**272**	136	136	...	..	.	...	...	.
1—2 ...	**273**	130	143	**273**	130	143		.		...	...	...
2—3 ...	**323**	154	169	**322**	153	169	**1**	1		...	...	...
3—4 ...	**307**	148	159	**306**	147	159	**1**	1		..	..	..
4—5 ...	**257**	115	142	**254**	112	142	**3**	3	.		..	..
Total 0—5 ..	*1,432*	*683*	*749*	*1,427*	*678*	*749*	*5*	*5*	..	..	...	...
5—10 ...	**1,107**	608	499	**1,012**	576	436	**92**	32	60	**3**		3
10—15 ...	**1,082**	631	451	**836**	597	239	**240**	33	207	**8**	1	5
15—20 ...	**1,590**	965	625	**582**	555	27	**995**	407	588	**13**	3	10
20—30 ...	**4,181**	2,862	1,319	**685**	668	17	**3,441**	2,175	1,266	**55**	19	36
30—40 ...	**2,657**	2,140	508	**201**	201	..	**2,365**	1,929	436	**91**	19	72
40—50 ...	**1,085**	819	266	...		...	**973**	797	176	**112**	22	90
50—60 ...	**424**	283	141	...	...	...	**324**	267	57	**100**	16	84
60 and over ..	**239**	126	113	.	...	...	**141**	112	29	**98**	14	84

TABLE VIII.

CIVIL CONDITION BY AGE.

FOR SELECTED CASTES AND TRIBES.

This table contains statistics, for selected castes and tribes, similar to those given in Table VII for the whole population. The age periods, however, are different in the two tables. In this respect again the present table differs slightly from Table XIV of 1921, with which it otherwise corresponds in form.

2. In the case of some of the selected castes, etc. complete statistics for the whole province have been shown ; in the case of others the statistics are for representative localities only. But in both cases the *natural* (and not the *administrative*) division has been taken as the unit of locality. The districts and states falling within each natural division of the province are reproduced below from Chapter I of the report volume :—

NORTH BIHAR—

- Saran.
- Champaran.
- Muzaffarpur.
- Darbhanga.
- Bhagalpur.
- Purnea.

SOUTH BIHAR—

- Patna.
- Gaya.
- Shahabad.
- Monghyr.

ORISSA—

- Cuttack.
- Balasore.
- Puri.

CHOTA NAGPUR PLATEAU—

- Hazaribagh.
- Ranchi.
- Palamau.
- Manbhum.
- Singhbhum.
- Santal Parganas.
- Angul.
- Sambalpur.
- Feudatory States.

TABLE VIII.

Civil condition by age for selected castes and tribes.

Caste or Tribe.	Locality (Natural Division or District).	Sex.	Population dealt with.	Unmarried. Total.	Unmarried. 0—6	Unmarried. 7—13	Unmarried. 14—16	Unmarried. 17—23	Unmarried. 24—43	Unmarried. 44 and over.	Married. Total.	Married. 0—6	Married. 7—13	Married. 14—16	Married. 17—23	Married. 24—43	Married. 44 and over.	Widowed. Total.	Widowed. 0—6	Widowed. 7—13	Widowed. 14—16	Widowed. 17—23	Widowed. 24—43	Widowed. 44 and over.
1	2	3	4	5	6	7	8	9	10	11	12	13	14	15	16	17	18	19	20	21	22	23	24	25
BABHAN [BHUMIHAR BRAHMAN] *Hindu.*	*Total*	Male	*462,377*	*214,283*	*67,813*	*67,701*	*17,885*	*21,294*	*31,947*	*8,143*	*208,265*	*1,507*	*7,592*	*10,612*	*29,899*	*99,758*	*58,897*	*39,829*	*57*	*262*	*290*	*1,261*	*12,431*	*25,528*
		Female	*414,126*	*120,200*	*65,441*	*48,210*	*4,122*	*1,526*	*715*	*186*	*194,735*	*1,898*	*12,804*	*16,160*	*40,002*	*94,514*	*29,357*	*99,191*	*141*	*579*	*802*	*3,334*	*33,272*	*61,063*
	North Bihar ...	Male	196,525	95,120	29,060	31,883	8,618	9,809	12,972	2,778	87,506	598	2,367	3,575	11,696	43,223	26,047	12,899	28	120	132	442	4,047	9,121
		Female	187,119	56,054	28,849	23,084	2,215	706	416	124	84,180	750	4,076	6,003	16,914	43,350	13,081	46,885	81	272	434	1,313	15,855	28,930
	South Bihar ...	Male	254,569	114,196	36,366	34,193	8,889	11,038	18,430	5,280	115,318	830	4,847	6,751	17,454	53,858	31,578	25,055	25	120	146	792	8,083	15,889
		Female	216,823	61,804	34,094	23,878	1,875	727	276	54	105,133	834	7,853	9,090	22,033	49,003	15,720	49,886	54	264	335	1,846	16,492	30,895
	Hazaribagh ...	Male	11,283	4,967	1,887	1,625	378	447	545	85	5,441	79	378	286	749	2,677	1,272	875	4	13	12	27	301	518
		Female	10,184	2,342	1,598	648	32	33	23	8	5,422	308	875	467	1,055	2,161	558	2,420	6	43	33	175	925	1,338
BRAHMAN *Hindu*	*Total*	Male	*1,069,759*	*488,664*	*167,269*	*161,792*	*51,108*	*54,244*	*44,551*	*9,700*	*503,895*	*3,087*	*14,458*	*20,648*	*72,570*	*259,590*	*133,612*	*77,200*	*118*	*377*	*735*	*2,583*	*23,434*	*49,953*
		Female	*1,031,528*	*283,573*	*165,847*	*105,587*	*7,278*	*2,570*	*1,771*	*520*	*498,236*	*4,415*	*49,002*	*46,978*	*111,852*	*227,112*	*58,877*	*249,219*	*369*	*2,033*	*2,964*	*12,069*	*93,105*	*139,179*
	North Bihar ...	Male	443,980	210,700	70,078	71,532	20,839	21,507	31,408	4,436	203,216	1,683	6,356	8,030	26,925	104,522	55,700	30,064	81	196	209	940	9,174	19,464
		Female	421,807	124,390	69,602	48,573	3,747	1,213	822	233	196,966	1,988	16,859	16,584	41,472	95,633	24,630	100,451	171	714	905	3,737	36,803	58,121
	South Bihar ...	Male	226,982	101,252	34,479	32,441	8,321	10,623	12,471	3,017	104,979	733	4,307	5,774	15,676	51,185	27,214	20,751	19	137	165	663	6,610	13,167
		Female	218,710	60,489	35,507	22,607	1,487	469	281	48	104,564	921	8,284	9,853	22,605	48,357	14,545	53,657	63	352	413	3,049	19,111	31,669
	Orissa ...	Male	189,263	86,449	26,087	27,843	13,579	12,860	5,243	837	87,966	37	728	2,517	13,907	46,313	24,464	14,848	2	9	260	606	4,071	9,900
		Female	199,248	43,779	25,373	16,817	1,069	295	181	44	98,509	173	12,469	11,164	24,328	41,327	9,048	56,960	9	526	1,042	3,099	22,848	38,536
	C. N. Plateau	Male	209,534	90,263	35,725	29,976	8,309	9,354	5,429	1,410	107,734	634	3,977	4,322	16,062	57,500	26,239	11,537	16	45	101	374	3,579	7,422
		Female	191,763	54,915	35,165	17,500	975	503	487	194	98,197	1,333	11,390	9,378	23,447	41,695	10,754	38,651	136	441	604	2,284	14,343	20,553
CHAMAR *Hindu*	*Total*	Male	*612,875*	*221,144*	*122,609*	*73,049*	*11,557*	*8,465*	*4,346*	*1,118*	*365,700*	*9,346*	*46,622*	*27,094*	*51,446*	*162,029*	*69,163*	*26,031*	*126*	*1,069*	*853*	*1,722*	*8,432*	*13,759*
		Female	*673,986*	*184,572*	*128,109*	*49,727*	*3,633*	*1,616*	*1,188*	*299*	*396,010*	*15,199*	*58,814*	*35,085*	*72,747*	*172,528*	*41,647*	*93,404*	*461*	*1,716*	*1,229*	*2,350*	*30,300*	*56,848*
	North Bihar ...	Male	334,524	117,951	63,631	40,659	6,655	4,954	2,445	607	202,131	5,911	26,353	14,607	26,937	89,665	38,658	14,442	128	725	533	1,014	4,838	7,204
		Female	373,077	100,918	67,085	29,452	2,339	1,081	721	240	216,938	9,140	31,553	18,252	38,458	96,655	23,880	55,221	299	1,069	848	1,673	17,889	33,443
	South Bihar ...	Male	179,450	63,830	38,141	19,592	2,643	1,789	1,273	392	107,035	2,184	14,270	8,635	15,880	45,256	20,804	8,585	39	251	239	408	2,546	5,012
		Female	198,967	52,452	39,200	12,104	542	281	307	18	120,008	3,665	18,330	11,246	22,075	51,685	13,007	26,507	69	448	234	731	8,273	16,752
	Cuttack ...	Male	7,632	3,928	1,167	1,387	605	650	87	12	3,522	...	25	53	444	2,064	936	182	...	1	1	2	58	120
		Female	9,322	2,897	1,335	1,210	274	56	17	5	4,275	2	127	467	1,137	2,151	391	2,150	..	1	8	101	844	1,196
	C. N. Plateau...	Male	91,969	35,435	20,650	11,411	1,654	1,072	541	107	53,012	1,251	5,974	3,799	8,179	26,044	8,765	2,822	29	92	80	208	990	1,423
		Female	92,620	28,305	20,489	6,961	478	198	143	36	54,789	2,392	8,804	5,120	11,077	23,027	4,369	9,526	93	198	139	345	3,294	5,457
GAURA *Hindu*	Orissa ...	Male	*124,303*	*64,197*	*22,586*	*20,481*	*8,218*	*9,870*	*2,790*	*252*	*54,978*	*15*	*673*	*1,887*	*5,486*	*31,470*	*15,447*	*5,128*	*1*	*75*	*164*	*203*	*1,355*	*3,330*
		Female	*139,967*	*44,866*	*23,471*	*17,330*	*2,976*	*774*	*273*	*42*	*62,859*	*47*	*3,597*	*4,360*	*16,485*	*32,141*	*6,299*	*32,242*	*3*	*134*	*409*	*778*	*11,970*	*18,948*
GOALA [AHIR, GOPA, YADAVA] *Hindu*	*Total*	Male	*1,765,379*	*634,811*	*315,266*	*217,900*	*38,201*	*33,149*	*25,679*	*4,616*	*1,007,020*	*18,484*	*107,238*	*68,107*	*140,284*	*465,361*	*207,546*	*123,548*	*745*	*2,903*	*2,327*	*6,691*	*44,447*	*66,435*
		Female	*1,689,762*	*457,279*	*307,257*	*131,780*	*10,148*	*4,535*	*2,822*	*737*	*976,282*	*32,206*	*142,391*	*83,678*	*171,288*	*430,543*	*116,176*	*256,201*	*1,250*	*4,643*	*3,277*	*8,276*	*81,291*	*157,464*
	North Bihar ...	Male	919,501	331,445	158,124	117,682	20,879	18,106	13,938	2,716	525,422	11,502	57,097	32,858	69,453	244,144	110,368	62,634	489	1,906	1,347	3,947	23,010	31,936
		Female	887,512	237,278	153,154	73,411	5,910	2,749	1,716	338	510,540	17,898	73,341	40,764	86,090	229,700	82,747	139,694	812	2,778	1,797	4,113	43,884	86,810
	South Bihar ...	Male	620,104	218,729	112,767	71,710	12,325	11,057	9,355	1,515	352,922	4,683	36,273	25,549	51,465	160,863	74,089	48,453	215	740	694	2,037	16,720	28,047
		Female	582,382	161,534	112,793	44,075	2,763	1,056	597	250	339,536	7,952	47,089	30,950	63,440	148,581	42,518	81,318	242	1,126	808	2,398	24,547	52,142
	C. N. Plateau*	Male	225,774	84,637	44,375	28,508	4,997	3,986	2,386	385	128,676	2,299	13,968	9,700	19,366	60,354	23,089	12,461	41	358	286	707	4,717	6,452
		Female	219,868	58,467	41,310	14,204	1,475	730	509	149	126,212	6,356	21,961	11,964	22,758	53,263	10,911	35,189	196	739	612	1,770	13,360	18,512
KARAN *Hindu*	Orissa ...	Male	*53,140*	*28,347*	*8,137*	*8,484*	*3,363*	*5,761*	*2,414*	*188*	*22,078*	*3*	*85*	*116*	*1,253*	*12,567*	*8,054*	*2,715*	...	*2*	*3*	*15*	*698*	*1,997*
		Female	*60,843*	*20,107*	*7,975*	*8,053*	*2,703*	*1,170*	*184*	*22*	*25,043*	*12*	*315*	*747*	*6,200*	*14,991*	*3,478*	*15,693*	*1*	*17*	*29*	*420*	*5,829*	*9,397*
KAYASTH *Hindu*	*Total*	Male	*161,988*	*78,397*	*26,107*	*25,134*	*8,026*	*9,782*	*7,305*	*2,043*	*71,253*	*425*	*1,977*	*2,485*	*8,525*	*36,984*	*20,857*	*12,338*	*15*	*59*	*128*	*481*	*3,472*	*8,183*
		Female	*149,155*	*51,349*	*26,612*	*20,671*	*2,910*	*721*	*337*	*98*	*65,799*	*676*	*2,944*	*4,896*	*14,849*	*33,257*	*9,177*	*32,007*	*41*	*140*	*168*	*1,099*	*10,848*	*19,711*
	North Bihar ...	Male	92,121	46,216	15,052	15,266	4,682	5,709	4,371	1,136	39,527	299	1,107	1,138	4,338	20,757	11,888	6,378	12	39	101	223	1,723	4,280
		Female	86,373	30,619	15,342	12,603	1,855	490	250	79	37,137	442	1,598	2,535	8,101	19,555	4,906	18,617	31	77	105	751	6,678	11,075
	South Bihar ...	Male	69,867	32,181	11,055	9,868	3,344	4,073	2,934	907	31,726	136	870	1,347	4,187	16,227	8,969	5,960	3	20	27	258	1,749	3,903
		Female	62,782	20,730	11,270	8,068	1,055	231	87	19	28,662	234	1,346	2,361	6,748	13,702	4,271	13,390	10	63	63	348	4,270	8,696
KHANDAIT *Hindu*	Orissa ...	Male	*402,631*	*210,171*	*65,667*	*65,907*	*28,591*	*38,919*	*10,667*	*420*	*172,683*	*43*	*610*	*2,431*	*19,590*	*90,917*	*59,092*	*19,777*	*1*	*3*	*16*	*1,160*	*5,564*	*13,033*
		Female	*458,354*	*163,671*	*70,013*	*66,078*	*20,037*	*5,946*	*1,312*	*285*	*205,938*	*78*	*2,255*	*19,832*	*56,987*	*99,774*	*97,017*	*88,745*	*8*	*82*	*285*	*2,542*	*31,952*	*53,876*

KOIRI [DANGI, KUSHWAHA KSHATRIYA] *Hindu*	*Total*	Male	*661,899*	*231,102*	*117,443*	*76,064*	*13,373*	*11,658*	*10,569*	*1,995*	*381,721*	*6,442*	*39,266*	*25,468*	*53,317*	*173,964*	*83,364*	*49,076*	*263*	*1,159*	*1,003*	*2,578*	*17,486*	*36,587*
		Female	*640,089*	*169,002*	*116,169*	*46,511*	*3,221*	*1,444*	*1,179*	*478*	*369,410*	*9,820*	*52,294*	*30,389*	*64,994*	*165,679*	*46,234*	*101,677*	*404*	*1,896*	*1,099*	*2,696*	*31,297*	*64,285*
	North Bihar	Male	351,691	124,225	60,301	42,670	7,671	6,666	5,827	1,181	242,749	3,638	21,073	12,626	26,943	93,939	45,530	24,717	175	772	599	1,405	8,867	12,809
		Female	340,511	92,378	59,593	28,178	2,271	1,087	870	384	194,526	5,484	25,039	14,571	32,015	89,716	25,962	53,607	299	1,305	602	1,314	16,264	33,923
	South Bihar ...	Male	245,315	83,473	43,323	26,323	4,638	4,275	4,313	701	140,354	1,753	13,778	10,128	20,674	68,031	31,090	21,488	52	291	333	913	7,659	12,241
		Female	234,686	59,414	43,258	14,873	780	545	183	75	136,369	2,589	19,514	13,385	34,783	60,044	17,054	38,903	63	507	386	1,087	11,030	24,032
	C. N. Plateau*	Male	64,893	23,404	13,919	7,062	1,064	417	439	113	38,618	1,051	4,415	2,714	5,800	17,994	6,644	2,871	36	96	71	171	960	1,537
		Female	64,892	17,210	13,318	3,465	170	112	126	9	38,515	1,707	6,841	3,433	7,206	15,020	3,228	9,167	43	184	111	205	3,104	5,430
MUNDA ..	Ranchi ...	Male	*189,445*	*103,532*	*44,912*	*35,618*	*10,447*	*8,637*	*4,198*	*370*	*78,716*	*272*	*1,296*	*2,680*	*9,401*	*44,594*	*20,473*	*7,197*	*14*	*32*	*71*	*274*	*2,490*	*4,316*
		Female	*196,975*	*92,414*	*46,114*	*32,107*	*7,814*	*4,384*	*1,723*	*272*	*81,867*	*331*	*2,626*	*5,235*	*16,577*	*44,377*	*12,721*	*22,694*	*40*	*92*	*204*	*586*	*7,373*	*14,399*
Hindu ...	...	Male	54,173	28,351	12,139	9,246	2,221	2,577	2,016	52	23,440	138	612	1,253	2,914	13,087	6,436	2,382	6	23	33	111	929	1,380
		Female	56,383	23,656	12,958	8,024	1,333	331	410	100	24,568	171	1,271	1,786	5,301	13,031	3,008	8,159	21	40	87	213	2,766	5,032
Christian ...		Male	48,282	27,385	11,044	9,829	3,228	3,567	669	58	19,246	44	186	208	2,350	11,285	5,184	1,651	3	4	8	43	508	1,065
		Female	48,959	25,033	11,546	8,584	2,760	1,507	563	73	19,360	66	193	736	4,096	10,671	3,600	4,566	5	10	9	91	1,436	3,015
Tribal religion ...	...	Male	86,990	47,796	31,039	16,543	4,908	3,563	1,513	160	36,030	90	499	1,129	4,287	30,222	9,853	3,164	5	5	30	120	1,053	1,951
		Female	91,683	43,725	21,610	15,490	3,721	2,046	750	99	37,939	104	1,163	2,713	7,181	30,675	6,104	9,969	14	42	108	382	3,171	6,352
MUSAHAR *Hindu*	*Total*	Male	*348,551*	*123,879*	*69,140*	*42,162*	*5,532*	*3,522*	*2,800*	*723*	*208,562*	*5,719*	*24,519*	*14,956*	*27,195*	*93,452*	*42,721*	*16,110*	*163*	*718*	*742*	*1,273*	*5,030*	*8,184*
		Female	*345,532*	*104,603*	*74,481*	*26,956*	*1,570*	*575*	*515*	*106*	*205,064*	*7,433*	*29,992*	*17,292*	*35,669*	*90,123*	*24,555*	*35,865*	*401*	*824*	*720*	*1,448*	*11,418*	*21,054*
	North Bihar ...	Male	204,497	75,772	40,152	26,500	4,000	2,584	1,887	550	119,158	3,421	13,217	8,592	15,657	54,871	33,397	9,567	111	401	542	874	3,235	4,314
		Female	205,452	64,232	44,203	17,515	1,225	768	411	90	118,147	4,312	16,886	9,055	20,938	53,823	13,233	23,073	211	555	572	1,118	7,822	12,800
	South Bihar ...	Male	144,054	48,107	28,988	15,563	1,532	938	913	173	89,404	2,298	11,302	6,364	11,538	38,578	10,324	6,543	53	227	200	309	1,705	3,870
		Female	140,080	40,371	30,278	9,441	345	187	104	16	86,917	3,121	13,106	7,337	14,731	37,300	11,332	12,792	190	360	148	335	3,506	8,254
ORAON ...	Ranchi ...	Male	*214,513*	*105,936*	*53,958*	*37,653*	*8,164*	*4,321*	*1,112*	*228*	*97,546*	*724*	*3,663*	*5,324*	*14,907*	*50,938*	*21,990*	*11,031*	*24*	*50*	*132*	*491*	*3,994*	*6,340*
		Female	*225,587*	*93,924*	*55,011*	*30,863*	*5,020*	*2,012*	*814*	*204*	*104,417*	*805*	*6,937*	*8,806*	*20,323*	*51,320*	*16,226*	*27,246*	*68*	*131*	*198*	*766*	*8,822*	*17,261*
Hindu ...	...	Male	79,412	37,358	21,080	13,018	1,911	925	347	77	37,642	383	1,864	2,554	5,958	18,826	8,058	4,412	14	16	61	236	1,607	2,418
		Female	84,352	31,474	19,914	10,053	875	330	237	75	41,795	383	3,470	3,994	7,181	20,090	6,677	11,083	32	70	97	367	3,657	6,860
Christian ...	...	Male	56,226	31,643	13,790	10,977	3,731	2,699	401	45	22,492	142	236	360	2,937	13,172	5,595	2,091	2	1	2	55	703	1,328
		Female	57,096	28,675	14,298	9,926	2,782	1,206	403	60	23,044	180	332	1,111	5,168	12,290	3,963	5,377	9	6	17	106	1,672	3,567
Tribal religion ...	...	Male	78,875	36,935	19,088	13,658	2,522	1,197	364	106	37,412	300	1,563	2,410	5,962	18,940	8,337	4,528	8	33	60	200	1,624	2,504
		Female	84,139	33,775	20,799	10,884	1,368	476	184	69	39,578	242	3,136	3,701	7,974	18,940	5,586	10,786	27	55	64	393	3,403	6,834
RAJPUT [CHHATRI, KSHATRIYA] *Hindu*	*Total*	Male	*729,105*	*357,035*	*113,959*	*112,201*	*31,827*	*39,509*	*48,162*	*11,377*	*517,293*	*2,091*	*10,531*	*14,111*	*41,994*	*160,025*	*88,541*	*54,777*	*173*	*474*	*706*	*1,938*	*17,230*	*34,956*
		Female	*659,823*	*199,303*	*107,781*	*77,328*	*8,377*	*2,931*	*2,069*	*817*	*303,244*	*3,336*	*20,979*	*23,797*	*65,129*	*148,597*	*41,406*	*157,276*	*219*	*1,021*	*1,255*	*6,080*	*55,540*	*93,131*
	North Bihar ...	Male	373,525	189,916	56,098	60,814	17,032	21,413	27,872	6,687	155,557	970	4,774	6,277	18,851	77,762	46,923	28,052	128	237	434	1,080	8,534	17,630
		Female	337,126	103,554	53,166	42,582	4,418	1,520	1,381	587	149,348	1,350	8,035	10,519	30,782	76,863	21,199	84,224	153	530	466	2,771	29,706	50,490
	South Bihar ...	Male	247,853	119,026	39,740	36,231	10,245	12,533	10,222	4,055	108,121	720	3,809	5,530	15,746	52,976	29,390	20,706	20	102	125	541	6,558	13,360
		Female	225,756	64,687	36,797	24,736	3,330	536	235	73	106,881	848	7,665	9,310	23,917	49,953	15,004	54,188	60	301	424	2,354	18,900	32,140
	C. N. Plateau...	Male	107,727	48,093	18,121	15,156	4,550	5,563	4,068	635	53,615	401	1,948	2,314	7,397	29,337	13,228	6,019	25	135	147	308	2,138	3,266
		Female	96,941	31,062	17,818	10,010	1,639	875	563	167	47,015	1,038	4,079	3,968	10,433	21,781	5,113	18,864	36	181	365	955	6,844	10,483
SANTAL ...	C. N. Plateau†	Male	*792,933*	*399,943*	*172,755*	*143,835*	*37,317*	*31,561*	*13,458*	*1,017*	*365,450*	*2,919*	*10,698*	*14,784*	*50,399*	*202,531*	*84,119*	*27,540*	*37*	*191*	*538*	*1,658*	*10,505*	*14,611*
		Female	*797,357*	*340,614*	*184,734*	*117,237*	*20,275*	*12,696*	*4,905*	*767*	*364,631*	*3,032*	*18,330*	*31,935*	*80,615*	*181,508*	*49,211*	*92,112*	*175*	*661*	*1,237*	*4,380*	*30,114*	*55,545*
Hindu ...	...	Male	247,799	130,215	53,406	44,570	14,088	12,516	5,195	440	110,367	572	2,411	3,338	15,480	63,884	24,682	7,217	3	27	91	467	2,830	3,799
		Female	248,615	107,566	67,346	36,485	6,867	4,764	1,797	301	107,818	498	4,700	10,008	26,451	54,366	11,215	33,237	50	173	375	1,601	11,640	19,399
Christian ...	...	Male	6,012	3,279	1,267	1,131	377	374	130	...	2,568	20	74	63	202	1,445	674	165	..	.	1	8	81	76
		Female	5,959	2,906	1,164	1,143	343	183	67	6	2,475	6	52	106	445	1,413	403	578	..	...	2	20	183	373
Tribal religion ...	...	Male	539,122	266,449	118,082	98,134	22,852	18,671	8,133	577	252,515	2,327	8,213	11,283	34,627	137,202	58,763	20,158	34	164	446	1,183	7,594	10,737
		Female	542,783	230,146	126,224	79,600	13,065	7,749	3,041	460	254,338	2,528	13,578	21,221	53,688	125,730	37,593	58,297	125	489	860	2,750	18,291	35,773
TANTI [TATWA] *Hindu*	*Total*	Male	*277,909*	*94,889*	*48,530*	*30,067*	*6,339*	*3,440*	*2,829*	*684*	*168,625*	*4,159*	*20,959*	*10,352*	*21,009*	*76,000*	*36,155*	*14,395*	*127*	*708*	*568*	*1,008*	*4,771*	*7,213*
		Female	*297,601*	*68,834*	*47,345*	*18,419*	*1,700*	*677*	*615*	*78*	*176,698*	*7,861*	*28,002*	*14,173*	*32,089*	*76,042*	*18,531*	*52,069*	*298*	*1,131*	*603*	*1,537*	*17,352*	*31,148*
	North Bihar ...	Male	161,311	50,896	28,606	16,105	3,490	1,752	1,551	364	101,987	3,028	14,812	7,206	13,825	44,612	10,504	8,928	111	542	456	757	3,152	3,908
		Female	171,132	38,223	27,809	9,014	607	277	370	56	104,901	5,021	18,920	8,606	17,646	43,634	10,465	28,306	264	911	440	942	9,208	16,543
	South Bihar ...	Male	56,344	16,730	10,655	4,752	485	401	333	204	37,260	1,106	5,863	3,755	4,580	14,927	8,000	2,854	16	162	106	184	850	1,536
		Female	62,355	12,784	9,905	2,486	124	123	138	8	40,019	2,180	7,208	3,244	6,156	16,364	4,768	9,552	33	169	76	196	2,714	6,364
	Orissa ...	Male	59,254	27,261	9,269	9,210	3,364	4,257	1,045	116	29,378	25	264	591	3,595	16,461	8,642	2,615	...	4	6	67	769	1,769
		Female	63,814	17,827	9,631	6,919	879	277	107	14	31,778	51	1,805	2,323	8,287	16,014	3,298	14,209	1	51	87	399	5,430	8,241
TELI *Hindu* ...	*Total*	Male	*531,797*	*194,405*	*99,432*	*66,823*	*11,869*	*9,982*	*5,783*	*1,216*	*305,827*	*5,287*	*31,599*	*20,724*	*45,086*	*141,783*	*61,348*	*31,565*	*168*	*735*	*627*	*1,832*	*11,530*	*16,673*
		Female	*528,336*	*145,369*	*97,673*	*41,220*	*2,999*	*1,971*	*1,093*	*406*	*303,606*	*9,723*	*45,984*	*25,995*	*58,548*	*131,656*	*31,700*	*79,368*	*237*	*1,347*	*915*	*2,180*	*25,414*	*49,275*
	North Bihar ...	Male	221,410	76,599	38,466	26,815	4,201	3,616	2,737	665	129,269	3,719	15,581	8,709	18,909	58,518	25,743	15,531	108	434	348	1,049	5,923	7,669
		Female	219,308	56,752	38,055	16,326	1,049	547	535	240	128,211	4,417	19,958	10,575	22,941	56,422	13,808	34,345	128	763	364	879	10,667	21,524
	South Bihar ...	Male	110,468	39,391	20,500	13,403	2,101	1,548	1,417	332	63,503	672	5,907	4,001	9,777	28,521	13,935	7,574	17	98	119	315	2,673	4,352
		Female	109,217	28,932	20,256	8,061	355	144	77	39	63,429	1,194	9,297	6,010	15,123	27,565	7,240	16,856	31	186	118	353	4,968	11,200
	C. N. Plateau...	Male	199,919	78,424	40,466	26,515	5,477	4,118	1,639	319	113,035	1,896	10,071	7,414	17,300	74,744	31,670	8,460	43	203	160	468	3,934	4,052
		Female	199,811	59,673	39,362	16,833	1,505	1,280	481	127	111,966	4,113	16,729	9,410	23,484	47,669	10,562	28,167	78	398	413	948	9,779	16,551

* Excluding Angul, Sambalpur and Feudatory States.

TABLE IX.

INFIRMITIES.

This table, which corresponds with Table XII of 1921, shows the distribution (1) by age and (2) by locality of persons suffering from insanity, deaf-mutism, total blindness and leprosy.

2. Persons suffering from more than one infirmity have been shown separately under each head, but they have been counted *only* once in the columns for "Population afflicted". Hence the figures in the latter columns do not agree exactly with the sum of the figures for the several infirmities. The following statement gives particulars of persons suffering from more than one infirmity :—

	Persons.	Males.	Females.
Total ...	***494***	***320***	***174***
Insane and blind	34	21	13
Insane and deaf-mutes ...	199	142	57
Insane and lepers	15	12	3
Deaf-mutes and blind	131	73	58
Deaf-mutes and lepers	43	22	21
Blind and lepers	69	48	21
Insane, blind and leper	1	1	...
Insane, deaf-mute and leper	1	...	1
Insane, blind, deaf-mute and leper ...	1	1	...

TABLE IX.

Infirmities. Distribution—(1) By Age and (2) By Locality.

(1) Age. (2) District or State.	Population Afflicted. Persons.	Males.	Females.	Insane. Persons.	Males.	Females.	Deaf-Mutes. Persons.	Males.	Females.	Blind. Persons.	Males.	Females.	Lepers. Persons.	Males.	Females.
1	2	3	4	5	6	7	8	9	10	11	12	13	14	15	16
All Ages and Localities.	*111,148*	*63,894*	*47,254*	*9,045*	*5,902*	*3,143*	*26,475*	*16,148*	*10,327*	*53,332*	*25,519*	*27,813*	*22,794*	*16,648*	*6,146*
0—1	441	219	222	7	3	4	189	83	106	236	129	107	9	4	5
1—2	600	323	277	8	6	2	231	111	120	350	201	149	11	5	6
2—3	816	442	374	11	7	4	313	154	159	467	368	109	27	14	13
3—4	1,111	644	467	20	14	6	512	294	218	558	324	234	25	14	11
4—5	1,449	855	594	62	38	24	700	420	280	636	370	266	58	31	27
Total 0—5	*4,417*	*2,483*	*1,934*	*108*	*68*	*40*	*1,945*	*1,062*	*883*	*2,247*	*1,292*	*955*	*130*	*68*	*62*
5—10	7,490	4,634	3,856	371	240	131	3,661	2,371	1,290	3,149	1,941	1,208	357	214	143
10—15	7,928	4,934	2,994	510	327	183	3,758	2,340	1,418	3,105	1,938	1,167	609	363	246
15—20	7,405	4,454	2,951	657	418	239	2,938	1,795	1,143	2,651	1,532	1,119	1,206	743	463
20—25	7,978	4,862	3,116	771	492	279	2,856	1,792	1,064	2,872	1,600	1,272	1,517	1,007	510
25—30	8,851	5,450	3,401	1,063	713	350	2,502	1,570	932	3,096	1,553	1,543	2,222	1,639	583
30—35	8,942	5,486	3,456	1,146	786	360	2,138	1,297	841	3,100	1,478	1,622	2,601	1,957	644
35—40	8,869	5,433	3,446	1,077	722	355	1,616	983	633	3,285	1,527	1,758	2,922	2,212	710
40—45	8,621	5,323	3,298	970	655	315	1,396	871	525	3,353	1,580	1,773	2,930	2,235	695
45—50	8,011	4,799	3,212	741	485	256	1,025	628	397	3,687	1,715	1,972	2,591	1,987	604
50—55	7,042	4,029	3,013	597	374	223	775	460	315	3,578	1,605	1,973	2,118	1,608	510
55—60	6,778	3,347	3,431	365	209	156	597	338	259	4,380	1,744	2,636	1,454	1,067	387
60—65	6,332	3,049	3,283	278	158	120	549	325	224	4,405	1,762	2,643	1,129	822	307
65—70	4,043	1,929	2,114	140	78	62	296	189	107	3,181	1,333	1,848	443	332	111
70 and over	8,441	3,692	4,749	251	177	74	423	227	196	7,243	2,919	4,324	565	394	171
British Territory	*98,869*	*57,237*	*41,632*	*8,264*	*5,416*	*2,848*	*24,003*	*14,709*	*9,294*	*47,754*	*23,018*	*24,736*	*19,329*	*14,408*	*4,921*
Patna Division	20,895	11,373	9,522	1,225	723	502	2,991	1,860	1,131	13,796	6,395	7,401	2,907	2,410	497
Patna	4,340	2,417	1,923	328	236	92	638	390	248	2,800	1,281	1,519	580	514	66
Gaya	9,240	5,101	4,139	426	203	223	1,271	780	491	5,768	2,693	3,075	1,786	1,431	355
Shahabad	7,315	3,8[illegible]	3,460	471	284	187	1,082	690	392	5,228	2,421	2,807	541	465	76
Tirhut Division	25,611	15,397	10,214	1,614	1,094	520	9,652	5,982	3,670	11,659	5,917	5,742	2,839	2,513	326
Saran	3,795	2,270	1,525	313	224	89	1,137	714	433	1,947	981	966	421	370	51
Champaran	6,695	3,943	2,752	287	193	94	3,359	2,029	1,330	2,437	1,189	1,248	649	560	89
Muzaffarpur	7,638	4,708	2,930	442	287	155	2,654	1,705	949	3,588	1,845	1,743	977	891	86
Darbhanga	7,483	4,476	3,007	572	390	182	2,502	1,534	968	3,687	1,902	1,785	792	692	100
Bhagalpur Division	15,809	9,283	6,526	1,142	689	453	4,198	2,481	1,717	6,791	3,443	3,348	3,711	2,691	1,020
Monghyr	3,742	2,167	1,575	262	154	108	665	383	282	2,327	1,223	1,104	489	407	82
Bhagalpur	3,204	1,936	1,268	193	134	60	790	479	311	1,498	748	750	729	591	138
Purnea	3,841	2,303	1,538	385	321	164	1,643	968	675	1,398	776	622	437	350	87
Santal Parganas	5,021	2,877	2,144	302	190	112	1,100	651	449	1,568	696	872	2,056	1,343	713
Orissa Division	15,585	9,756	5,829	1,457	939	518	2,670	1,726	944	5,596	2,805	2,791	5,924	4,328	1,596
Cuttack	6,777	4,274	2,503	705	456	249	883	582	301	2,673	1,371	1,302	2,545	1,891	654
Balasore	3,321	2,157	1,164	295	181	114	1,125	735	300	746	379	367	1,180	874	306
Angul	403	233	170	13	10	3	110	63	47	199	101	98	82	60	22
Puri	3,425	2,265	1,160	323	217	103	305	204	101	1,095	598	497	1,707	1,249	458
Sambalpur	1,659	827	832	121	75	46	247	142	105	883	356	527	410	254	156
Chota Nagpur Division ...	20,969	11,428	9,541	2,826	1,971	855	4,492	2,660	1,832	9,912	4,458	5,454	3,948	2,466	1,482
Hazaribagh	3,173	1,714	1,459	231	142	89	1,064	646	418	1,673	782	891	244	169	75
Ranchi	5,884	3,382	2,502	1,887	1,394	403	1,246	692	554	2,524	1,133	1,391	298	202	96
Palamau	2,530	1,254	1,276	165	98	67	409	232	177	1,767	812	955	221	129	92
Manbhum	8,433	4,570	3,863	447	282	165	1,614	997	617	3,394	1,455	1,939	3,032	1,877	1,155
Singhbhum	949	508	441	96	55	41	159	93	66	554	276	278	153	89	64
Feudatory States	*12,279*	*6,657*	*5,622*	*781*	*486*	*295*	*2,472*	*1,439*	*1,033*	*5,578*	*2,501*	*3,077*	*3,465*	*2,240*	*1,225*
Orissa States	12,141	6,588	5,553	761	472	289	2,453	1,427	1,026	5,506	2,475	3,031	3,436	2,223	1,213
Chota Nagpur States ...	138	69	69	20	14	6	19	12	7	72	26	46	29	17	12

TABLE X.

OCCUPATION OR MEANS OF LIVELIHOOD.

In this table all occupations returned at the census have been classified according to a scheme which comprises 4 main classes, 12 sub-classes, 55 orders and 195 groups. (Order no. 1 is further divided into 5 sub-orders.) This scheme differs but little from the one adopted at the last census, but in other respects there are important differences between the present table and the corresponding table (XVII) of 1921. The main points of difference are briefly indicated below :

(*a*) In 1921 the total population was divided into "actual workers" and "dependants". On the present occasion it has been divided into "earners", "working dependants" and "non-working dependants".

(*b*) Against each occupation in 1921 was shown the total number of persons *supported* by it i.e., both workers and dependants. This time only persons actually *following* an occupation, either as earners or as working dependants, have been shown against it, and no attempt has been made to distribute the non-working dependants between the various occupations by which they are supported.

(*c*) In 1921 the *principal* occupation only of each person was shown, except in the case of those persons whose subsidiary means of livelihood was agriculture. On this occasion an attempt has been made to record the subsidiary occupations of all persons who had more than one means of livelihood.

2. The table is divided into two parts. Part I contains complete statistics for each class, sub-class, order and group, separate figures being given for (*a*) the province as a whole, (*b*) British territory, and (*c*) the Feudatory States. Part II gives similar information in detail for each district and state, as well as for the four "cities"; but in this part groups which are numerically unimportant have not ordinarily been shown.

ERRATUM.

Against		Under	For	Read
Singhbhum	...	... Column 443	2,214	2,158
Do.	...	... „ 444	11	10
Do.	...	... „ 711	136	186

Group number.	OCCUPATION.	TOTAL FOLLOWING OCCUPATION.	As principal occupation.		As working dependants.		As subsidiary to other occupation.		TOTAL FOLLOWING OCCUPATION.	As principal occupation.		As working dependants.		As subsidiary to other occupation.		TOTAL FOLLOWING OCCUPATION.	As principal occupation.		As working dependants.		As subsidiary to other occupation.	
	(b) without subsidiary occupation																					
	Total working dependants ...		899,023		305,133		393,890			476,791		230,623		256,168			222,232		84,510		137,722	
	Total non-working dependants ...		24,719,412		8,843,607		15,875,805			22,134,540		7,935,501		14,209,039			2,584,872		918,106		1,666,766	
			Males.	Females.	Males.	Females.	Males.	Females.		Males.	Females.	Males.	Females.	Males.	Females.		Males.	Females.	Males.	Females.	Males.	Females.
1	2	3	4	5	6	7	8	9	10	11	13	13	14	15	16	17	18	19	20	21	22	23
	A.—PRODUCTION OF RAW MATERIALS ...	**14,672,521**	**9,074,985**	**3,606,285**	**260,610**	**280,189**	**705,079**	**145,473**	**12,872,569**	**8,577,374**	**3,236,152**	**181,287**	**171,073**	**589,346**	**117,337**	**1,799,952**	**1,097,511**	**370,133**	**79,323**	**109,116**	**115,733**	**28,136**
	I.—EXPLOITATION OF ANIMALS AND VEGETATION ...	**14,515,640**	**9,587,642**	**3,574,897**	**259,963**	**279,853**	**675,210**	**138,075**	**12,732,727**	**8,497,464**	**3,210,362**	**180,805**	**170,835**	**562,274**	**110,987**	**1,782,913**	**1,090,178**	**364,535**	**79,158**	**109,018**	**112,936**	**27,088**
	1. Pasture and Agriculture ...	**14,422,203**	**9,539,107**	**3,564,632**	**259,014**	**279,193**	**643,951**	**136,306**	**12,649,529**	**8,454,135**	**3,201,108**	**179,941**	**170,346**	**534,620**	**109,379**	**1,772,674**	**1,084,972**	**363,524**	**79,073**	**108,847**	**109,331**	**26,927**
	(a) *Ordinary Cultivation* ...	*14,052,091*	*9,340,898*	*3,535,019*	*197,708*	*267,149*	*539,553*	*132,069*	*12,400,422*	*8,310,190*	*3,176,200*	*144,811*	*164,289*	*499,385*	*106,054*	*1,651,669*	*1,030,408*	*348,819*	*53,397*	*102,867*	*90,178*	*26,005*
1	Non-cultivating proprietors taking rent in money or kind ...	172,394	98,060	19,270	1,151	1,485	50,118	2,310	159,015	89,788	16,552	1,140	1,458	47,933	2,147	13,376	8,272	2,718	11	27	2,185	163
2	Estate agents and managers of owners ...	1,801	1,048	13	1	...	780	4	1,766	1,027	8	1	...	726	4	35	21	10	...	...	4	...
3	Estate agents and managers of Government ...	345	249	2	...	...	88	6	322	230	3	...	...	84	6	23	19	...	...	...	4	...
4	Rent collectors, clerks, etc. ...	30,807	19,585	668	246	3	10,201	104	28,707	14,133	667	241	3	9,560	103	2,100	1,452	1	5	...	641	1
5	Cultivating owners ...	404,566	325,144	43,031	4,648	2,303	28,072	1,369	364,507	291,002	39,471	4,224	2,207	26,326	1,377	40,059	34,143	3,560	424	96	1,740	91
6	Tenant cultivators ...	9,194,673	6,806,034	1,866,835	69,231	96,339	238,317	43,937	8,304,690	8,129,666	1,778,433	65,241	94,507	205,174	31,570	820,083	676,369	90,402	3,980	3,833	33,143	12,367
7	Agricultural labourers ...	4,317,329	2,090,349	1,598,156	122,440	165,019	362,026	84,340	3,541,504	1,760,844	1,341,067	73,468	66,107	309,576	70,947	775,825	310,005	252,088	48,977	98,012	52,450	13,383
8	Cultivators of jhum, taungya and shifting areas	176	139	40	1	...	6	...	8	1	...	1	...	6	...	168	138	40	...	...	...	...
	(b) *Cultivation of special crops, fruit, etc. (Planters, managers, clerks and labourers)*	*21,109*	*9,658*	*3,972*	*580*	*119*	*6,445*	*334*	*20,306*	*9,095*	*3,746*	*577*	*118*	*6,437*	*333*	*803*	*563*	*226*	*3*	*1*	*9*	*1*
9	Cinchona ...	5	3	...	2	...	...	...	5	3	...	3	...	...	...	...	...	...	...	...	...	...
10	Coconut ...	276	37	1	3	...	234	2	276	37	1	2	...	234	2	...	...	...	...	...	...	...
11	Coffee ...	1	1	...	...	...	...	...	1	1	...	...	...	...	...	...	...	...	...	...	...	...
12	Ganja ...	...	...	...	...	...	...	...	...	...	...	...	...	...	...	...	...	...	...	...	...	...
13	Pan-vine ...	2,703	1,180	76	130	10	1,207	50	2,701	1,179	76	180	10	1,206	50	2	1	...	...	...	1	...
14	Rubber ...	...	...	...	...	...	...	...	...	...	...	...	...	...	...	...	...	...	...	...	...	...
15	Tea ...	614	260	224	4	2	104	30	593	235	213	3	2	100	30	21	16	1	1	...	4	...
16	Market gardeners, flower and fruit growers ...	17,519	8,187	3,671	392	107	4,901	252	18,730	7,640	3,440	390	106	4,397	351	780	547	235	2	1	4	1
	(c) *Forestry* ...	*16,943*	*6,841*	*3,661*	*151*	*795*	*4,039*	*1,456*	*12,367*	*4,758*	*2,803*	*124*	*448*	*3,226*	*1,016*	*4,576*	*2,085*	*858*	*37*	*353*	*813*	*440*
17	Forest officers, rangers, guards, etc. ...	1,899	1,393	17	3	...	484	2	951	616	10	2	...	315	2	948	777	1	1	...	169	...
18	Wood cutters and charcoal burners... ...	11,800	4,351	2,668	78	489	3,010	1,304	9,142	3,333	2,003	63	221	2,570	952	2,658	918	665	15	368	440	352
19	Collectors of forest produce ...	2,964	1,107	937	68	306	458	88	2,119	727	764	59	221	307	51	845	380	183	9	86	161	37
20	Collectors of lac ...	280	90	39	2	...	87	62	155	80	30	...	...	34	11	126	10	8	2	...	53	61
	(d) *Stock raising* ...	*315,840*	*181,064*	*31,643*	*60,546*	*11,065*	*29,420*	*2,103*	*213,611*	*139,451*	*18,318*	*34,915*	*5,495*	*23,640*	*1,892*	*102,229*	*51,613*	*13,424*	*25,631*	*5,570*	*5,780*	*211*
21	Cattle and buffalo breeders and keepers ...	93,035	47,166	18,397	11,127	4,400	11,038	907	74,309	43,523	8,069	8,529	2,878	10,433	877	18,726	3,643	10,339	2,598	1,523	606	30
22	Breeders of transport animals ...	123	64	...	...	...	59	...	121	63	...	...	...	58	...	2	1	...	...	...	1	...
23	Herdsmen, shepherds and breeders of other animals ...	222,682	133,834	13,245	49,410	6,605	18,323	1,196	139,181	85,865	10,149	26,380	2,617	13,149	1,015	83,501	47,969	3,096	23,033	4,048	5,174	181
	(e) *Raising of small animals and insects* ...	*16,290*	*946*	*338*	*29*	*65*	*14,488*	*354*	*2,893*	*643*	*141*	*14*	*9*	*1,982*	*84*	*13,397*	*303*	*197*	*15*	*56*	*12,556*	*270*
24	Birds, bees, etc. ...	35	12	4	4	...	5	10	17	9	2	...	...	5	1	18	3	2	4	...	...	9
25	Silkworms ...	716	23	110	...	55	455	73	77	17	11	...	1	41	7	639	6	99	...	54	414	66
26	Lac cultivation ...	15,499	911	224	25	10	14,028	271	2,729	617	128	14	8	1,886	70	12,740	294	96	11	2	13,149	195

No.	Occupation	1	2	3	4	5	6	7	8	9	10	11	12	13	14	15	16	17	18	19	20	21
	2.—Fishing and Hunting	**93,437**	**48,535**	**10,265**	**949**	**660**	**31,259**	**1,769**	**83,198**	**43,329**	**9,254**	**384**	**489**	**27,654**	**1,608**	**10,239**	**5,206**	**1,011**	**85**	**171**	**3,605**	**161**
27	Fishing and pearling	91,062	47,251	10,110	944	660	30,377	1,720	80,971	43,108	9,100	859	489	26,956	1,569	10,091	5,143	1,010	85	171	3,521	161
28	Hunting	2,375	1,284	165	5	...	882	49	2,227	1,221	154	5	...	706	49	148	63	1	...	...	84	...
	II.—EXPLOITATION OF MINERALS	**156,881**	**87,243**	**31,388**	**647**	**336**	**29,869**	**7,398**	**139,842**	**79,910**	**25,790**	**482**	**238**	**27,072**	**6,350**	**17,039**	**7,333**	**5,598**	**165**	**98**	**2,797**	**1,048**
	3.—Metallic Minerals	**12,987**	**4,908**	**4,319**	**324**	**85**	**2,478**	**873**	**1,733**	**836**	**289**	**218**	**36**	**311**	**43**	**11,254**	**4,072**	**4,030**	**106**	**49**	**2,167**	**830**
29	Gold	272	21	193	...	10	20	28	55	1	19	...	...	5	...	247	20	174	...	10	15	28
30	Iron	10,581	3,819	3,808	16	12	2,128	803	172	108	38	10	...	5	11	10,409	3,711	3,765	6	12	2,123	792
31	Lead, silver and zinc	507	143	105	...	7	243	9	507	143	105	..	7	343	9	...	...	...	...	...	...	...
32	Manganese	595	341	91	100	27	26	10	...	...	...	...	...	...	...	595	341	91	100	27	26	10
33	Tin and wolfram	386	144	2	208	29	1	1	386	145	2	208	29	1	1	...	...	...	...	...	...	...
34	Other metallic minerals	646	438	125	...	...	60	22	643	439	125	...	...	57	23	3	...	...	...	...	3	...
	4.—Non-Metallic Minerals	**143,894**	**82,335**	**27,069**	**323**	**251**	**27,391**	**6,525**	**138,109**	**79,074**	**25,501**	**264**	**202**	**26,761**	**6,307**	**5,785**	**3,261**	**1,568**	**59**	**49**	**630**	**218**
35	Coal	122,306	75,048	22,775	307	194	18,757	4,327	117,800	73,104	21,445	250	168	18,465	4,278	4,506	2,752	1,330	57	26	292	40
36	Petroleum	1	1	...	...	...	...	...	1	1	...	...	...	..	...	...	...	...	..	...	...	...
37	Building materials (including stone, materials for cement-manufacture and clays) ...	1,402	565	254	2	25	300	166	140	50	16	...	2	52	11	1,262	506	238	2	23	338	155
38	Mica	9,141	2,987	1,570	1	4	3,979	600	9,141	2,987	1,570	1	4	3,979	600	...	...	...	...	...	...	...
39	Precious and semi-precious stones	59	35	...	...	...	24	...	59	35	...	...	...	24	...	...	...	...	...	...	...	..
40	Salt, saltpetre and other saline substances ...	10,935	2,782	2,469	13	28	4,211	1,432	10,918	2,779	2,469	13	28	4,211	1,418	17	3	...	...	...	...	14
41	Other non-metallic minerals	50	19	1	..	...	30	...	50	19	1	...	...	30	..	...	...	...	...	...	...	...
	B.—PREPARATION AND SUPPLY OF MATERIAL SUBSTANCES ...	**2,653,041**	**1,179,660**	**736,171**	**16,128**	**71,507**	**549,327**	**100,248**	**2,272,989**	**1,056,897**	**593,541**	**12,746**	**46,519**	**479,889**	**83,397**	**380,052**	**122,763**	**142,630**	**3,382**	**24,988**	**69,438**	**16,851**
	III.—INDUSTRY	**1,611,627**	**709,271**	**455,066**	**10,586**	**51,946**	**332,121**	**52,637**	**1,362,017**	**623,405**	**365,935**	**8,824**	**32,481**	**289,017**	**42,355**	**249,610**	**85,866**	**89,131**	**1,762**	**19,465**	**43,104**	**10,282**
	5.—Textiles	**274,000**	**123,207**	**69,022**	**2,527**	**14,239**	**56,918**	**8,087**	**198,715**	**91,988**	**47,744**	**1,853**	**7,047**	**43,930**	**6,153**	**75,285**	**31,219**	**21,278**	**674**	**7,192**	**12,988**	**1,934**
42	Cotton ginning, cleaning and pressing ...	4,141	1,853	1,413	10	46	645	174	3,963	1,728	1,366	10	41	644	174	178	125	47	...	5	1	...
43	Cotton spinning, seizing and weaving ...	239,728	111,728	57,509	2,250	12,630	50,441	5,060	167,457	81,427	37,420	1,687	5,668	37,849	3,406	72,271	30,301	20,170	563	6,963	12,592	1,674
44	Jute pressing, spinning and weaving ...	7,151	1,447	1,530	8	335	2,784	1,047	7,911	1,424	1,468	7	335	3,741	1,036	140	23	62	1	...	43	11
45	Rope, twine, string and other fibres ...	9,252	1,255	4,705	97	1,001	893	1,301	8,515	1,015	4,394	97	943	878	1,288	737	240	411	...	58	15	13
46	Wool carding, spinning and weaving ...	5,766	3,142	1,299	30	33	1,191	131	5,762	3,142	1,236	30	33	1,190	131	4	...	3	...	...	1	...
47	Silk spinning and weaving	3,900	1,583	1,424	110	163	361	259	1,963	1,055	860	...	...	25	23	1,937	528	564	110	163	336	236
48	Hair (horse-hair), etc.	60	4	...	...	...	40	16	60	4	...	...	...	40	16	...	...	...	...	...	...	...
49	Dyeing, bleaching printing, preparation and sponging of textiles..	3,897	2,171	1,038	20	31	558	79	3,880	2,169	1,027	20	27	558	79	17	2	11	...	4	...	...
50	Lace, crepe, embroideries, fringes, etc., and insufficiently described textile industries ...	105	24	74	2	...	5	...	104	24	73	2	...	5	...	1	...	1	...	...	...	...
	6.—Hides, skins and hard materials from the animal kingdom ...	**6,224**	**3,128**	**1,178**	**39**	**75**	**1,460**	**344**	**6,042**	**3,084**	**1,100**	**39**	**63**	**1,444**	**312**	**182**	**44**	**78**	...	**12**	**16**	**32**
51	Working in leather	5,368	2,053	1,000	13	68	1,305	320	5,250	2,831	960	13	56	1,303	297	118	22	50	...	12	2	32
52	Furriers and persons occupied with feathers, and bristles; brush-makers	66	28	...	...	...	38	...	66	28	...	...	...	38	...	...	...	...	...	...	...	...
53	Bone, ivory, horn, shell, etc., workers (except buttons)	790	447	178	26	7	117	15	726	425	150	26	7	103	15	64	22	28	...	...	14	...
	7.—Wood	**187,327**	**82,080**	**51,335**	**1,358**	**5,976**	**38,616**	**7,962**	**150,037**	**71,962**	**36,909**	**1,205**	**2,889**	**31,893**	**5,069**	**37,290**	**10,118**	**14,336**	**153**	**3,087**	**6,723**	**2,873**
54	Sawyers	1,664	712	44	4	1	901	2	786	332	42	4	1	406	1	878	380	2	...	...	495	1
55	Carpenters, turners and joiners, etc. ...	67,848	41,600	2,604	558	81	22,636	379	62,489	39,372	2,531	539	81	19,610	356	5,359	2,228	73	19	...	3,016	23
56	Basket makers and other industries of woody materials, including leaves, and thatchers and builders working with bamboo, reeds or similar materials	117,815	39,768	48,687	796	5,894	15,089	7,581	86,762	32,258	34,426	662	2,807	11,877	4,732	31,053	7,510	14,261	134	3,087	3,213	2,849
	8.—Metals	**118,628**	**77,114**	**12,436**	**1,451**	**2,013**	**23,717**	**1,897**	**98,932**	**65,638**	**8,683**	**1,147**	**1,285**	**20,521**	**1,658**	**19,696**	**11,476**	**3,753**	**304**	**728**	**3,196**	**239**
57	Smelting, forging and rolling of iron and other metals	23,401	20,082	2,969	7	1	124	238	23,332	20,054	2,944	7	1	104	223	69	28	15	...	...	20	6
58	Makers of arms, guns, etc.	749	403	37	...	..	296	13	749	403	37	...	...	206	13	...	...	..	...	...	...	...
59	Blacksmiths, other workers in iron, makers of implements	76,382	43,054	7,656	1,185	1,86[illegible]	21,038	1,685	60,600	34,396	4,384	926	1,183	18,348	1,363	15,782	8,658	3,272	259	681	2,690	222
60	Workers in brass, copper and bell metal ...	17,397	13,153	1,608	250	11	2,158	61	13,557	10,366	1,199	205	65	1,672	60	3,840	2,787	464	45	47	486	11
61	Workers in other metals (except precious metals)	695	420	119	9	34	101	10	692	417	119	9	36	101	10	3	3	...	...	...	...	...
62	Workers in mints, die-sinkers, etc. ...	4	2	2	...	...	...	...	2	2	...	...	...	...	..	2	...	2	...	...	...	...

TABLE X—*continued.*

OCCUPATION OR MEANS OF LIVELIHOOD.

PART I—PROVINCIAL SUMMARY.

Group number.	OCCUPATION.	BIHAR AND ORISSA.							BRITISH TERRITORY.							FEUDATORY STATES.						
		TOTAL FOLLOWING OCCUPATION.	*As principal occupation.*		*As working dependants.*		*As subsidiary to other occupation.*		TOTAL FOLLOWING OCCUPATION.	*As principal occupation.*		*As working dependants.*		*As subsidiary to other occupation.*		TOTAL FOLLOWING OCCUPATION.	*As principal occupation.*		*As working dependants.*		*As subsidiary to other occupation.*	
			Males.	Females.	Males.	Females.	Males.	Females.		Males.	Females.	Males.	Females.	Males.	Females.		Males.	Females.	Males.	Females.	Males.	Females.
1	2	3	4	5	6	7	8	9	10	11	12	13	14	15	16	17	18	19	20	21	22	23
	9.—Ceramics	**156,552**	**67,691**	**43,470**	**1,324**	**3,079**	**35,539**	**5,449**	**135,095**	**59,477**	**36,924**	**1,111**	**2,227**	**30,170**	**5,186**	**21,457**	**8,214**	**6,546**	**218**	**852**	**5,369**	**263**
63	Potters and makers of earthen-ware	**148,690**	63,254	41,790	1,316	3,051	34,089	5,190	**127,758**	55,338	35,381	1,106	2,220	28,783	4,931	**20,932**	7,016	6,409	210	831	5,307	259
64	Brick and tile makers	**7,071**	4,022	1,460	8	26	1,316	239	**6,551**	3,724	1,325	5	5	1,257	235	**520**	298	135	3	21	59	4
65	Other workers in ceramics	**791**	415	220	...	2	134	20	**786**	415	218	...	2	131	20	**5**	...	2	...	...	3	...
	10.—Chemical products properly so called and analogous	**114,015**	**44,634**	**35,026**	**555**	**1,673**	**26,232**	**5,895**	**102,624**	**41,840**	**30,975**	**507**	**1,069**	**22,747**	**5,546**	**11,391**	**2,794**	**4,051**	**48**	**664**	**3,485**	**349**
66	Manufacture of matches, fire-works and other explosives	**271**	200	23	...	...	48	...	**257**	195	21	...	...	41	...	**14**	5	2	...	...	7	...
67	Manufacture of aerated and mineral waters and ice	**82**	36	20	...	...	4	13	**36**	33	...	...	...	3	...	**46**	3	20	...	...	1	13
68	Manufacture and refining of vegetable oils	**107,354**	41,353	33,747	488	1,620	24,453	5,693	**96,033**	38,570	29,732	440	957	20,976	5,358	**11,321**	2,783	4,015	48	663	3,477	335
69	Manufacture and refining of mineral oils	**536**	158	314	...	9	28	27	**536**	158	314	...	9	28	37	...	...	...	...	...	...	...
70	Others	**5,772**	2,887	913	67	44	1,699	163	**5,762**	2,894	908	67	43	1,699	161	**10**	3	5	...	1	...	1
	11.—Food industries	**239,232**	**53,843**	**132,657**	**748**	**17,218**	**23,336**	**11,430**	**195,076**	**48,743**	**105,731**	**628**	**12,163**	**20,337**	**7,474**	**44,156**	**5,100**	**26,926**	**120**	**5,055**	**2,999**	**3,956**
71	Rice pounders and huskers and flour grinders	**92,304**	3,198	63,683	198	13,267	6,209	6,749	**74,077**	2,897	52,052	189	9,234	6,053	3,653	**18,227**	301	11,631	9	3,033	157	3,096
72	Grain parchers, etc.	**104,526**	19,801	63,167	337	4,836	12,027	4,368	**79,028**	15,245	47,974	228	2,805	9,268	3,508	**25,498**	4,556	15,198	100	2,021	2,759	800
73	Butchers	**5,792**	4,284	709	31	16	599	63	**5,779**	4,274	799	31	16	596	63	**13**	10	...	...	...	3	...
74	Makers of sugar, molasses and gur	**1,290**	1,031	99	1	...	151	8	**1,286**	1,028	98	1	...	151	8	**4**	3	1	...	...	...	...
75	Sweetmeat and condiment makers	**10,162**	6,835	2,166	62	34	907	98	**10,039**	6,807	2,143	62	33	896	98	**63**	28	33	...	1	11	...
76	Toddy drawers	**17,916**	13,997	1,176	47	36	2,607	53	**17,897**	13,983	1,176	47	36	2,602	53	**19**	14	...	...	...	5	...
77	Brewers and distillers	**188**	147	8	...	...	33	...	**121**	93	8	...	...	20	...	**67**	54	...	...	...	13	...
78	Manufacturers of tobacco	**6,870**	4,432	1,491	67	39	764	87	**6,664**	4,292	1,465	65	39	716	87	**206**	130	26	2	...	48	...
79	Manufacturers of opium	**58**	26	7	...	...	21	4	**58**	26	7	...	...	21	4	...	...	...	...	...	...	...
80	Manufacturers of ganja	**14**	10	2	...	...	2	...	**14**	10	2	...	...	2	...	...	...	...	...	...	...	...
81	Others	**172**	92	69	5	...	16	...	**113**	88	7	5	...	13	...	**59**	4	52	...	...	3	...
	12.—Industries of dress and the toilet	**354,923**	**172,918**	**87,999**	**1,996**	**6,419**	**76,490**	**9,692**	**328,419**	**162,123**	**80,054**	**1,793**	**5,344**	**70,319**	**8,786**	**26,504**	**10,795**	**7,945**	**203**	**1,075**	**6,180**	**306**
82	Boot, shoe, sandal and clog makers	**46,661**	30,071	6,292	281	147	9,292	578	**45,835**	29,434	6,117	281	86	9,290	578	**826**	587	175	...	63	3	...
83	Tailors, milliners, dress-makers and darners	**36,919**	22,494	8,070	115	150	5,201	889	**36,428**	22,102	8,009	114	132	5,182	880	**491**	392	61	1	18	19	...
84	Embroiderers, hat-makers and makers of other articles of wear	**557**	274	116	...	24	119	24	**556**	273	116	...	24	119	24	**1**	1	...	...	...	...	...
85	Washing and cleaning	**139,965**	50,603	50,382	731	4,968	27,545	5,736	**122,562**	45,019	43,085	629	4,010	24,350	5,463	**17,403**	5,584	7,297	102	958	3,180	273
86	Barbers, hair dressers and wig-makers	**128,622**	68,970	21,778	856	1,104	34,116	1,799	**121,054**	64,709	21,461	756	1,073	31,228	1,767	**7,568**	4,301	317	100	31	2,887	33
87	Other industries connected with the toilet	**2,199**	606	1,361	13	26	227	66	**1,984**	476	1,266	13	20	144	65	**215**	30	95	...	6	83	1
	13.—Furniture industries	**255**	**61**	**165**	...	...	**11**	**18**	**255**	**61**	**165**	...	...	**11**	**18**	...	...	...	...	...	...	...
88	Cabinet-makers, carriage-painters, etc.	**201**	45	136	...	...	3	17	**201**	45	136	...	...	3	17	...	...	...	...	...	...	...
89	Upholsterers, tent-makers, etc.	**54**	16	29	...	...	8	1	**54**	16	29	...	...	8	1	...	...	...	...	...	...	...
	14.—Building industries	**38,509**	**22,727**	**7,274**	**85**	**584**	**6,660**	**1,179**	**33,758**	**21,638**	**5,172**	**70**	**40**	**5,916**	**922**	**4,751**	**1,089**	**2,102**	**15**	**544**	**744**	**257**
90	Lime burners, cement workers; excavators and well sinkers; stone cutters and dressers; brick layers and masons; builders (other than buildings made of bamboo or similar materials), painters, decorators of houses, tilers, plumbers, etc.	**38,509**	22,727	7,274	85	584	6,660	1,179	**33,758**	21,638	5,172	70	40	5,916	922	**4,751**	1,089	2,102	15	544	744	257
	15.—Construction of means of transport	**796**	**577**	**5**	**2**	...	**212**	...	**662**	**519**	**5**	**2**	...	**136**	...	**134**	**58**	...	...	...	**76**	...
91	Persons engaged in making, assembling or repairing motor vehicles or cycles	**472**	384	1	2	...	85	...	**442**	359	1	2	...	80	...	**30**	25	...	...	...	5	...
92	Carriage, cart, palki, etc. makers and wheel-wrights	**310**	181	4	...	...	125	...	**210**	153	4	...	...	54	...	**100**	20	...	...	...	71	...
93	Ship, boat, aeroplane builders	**14**	12	...	...	...	2	...	**10**	8	...	...	...	2	...	**4**	4	...	...	...	...	...
	16.—Production and transmission of physical force	**436**	**395**	**6**	**2**	...	**33**	...	**391**	**350**	**6**	**2**	...	**33**	...	**45**	**45**	...	...	...	...	...
94	Heat, light, electricity, motive power, etc., gas works and electric light and power	**436**	395	6	2	...	33	...	**391**	350	6	2	...	33	...	**45**	45	...	...	...	...	...

No.	Occupation																					
	17 —Miscellaneous and undefined industries	**120,730**	**60,896**	**14,493**	**499**	**670**	**42,888**	**1,284**	**112,011**	**55,982**	**12,377**	**467**	**414**	**41,560**	**1,211**	**8,719**	**4,914**	**2,116**	**32**	**256**	**1,328**	**73**
95	Printers, engravers, book binders etc	496	434	5	4		52	1	492	365	5	4		46		74	69				4	1
96	Makers of musical instruments	1,433	1,095	54	18	20	299	7	1,123	836	36	18	20	206	5	310	199	18			91	2
97	Makers of clocks and surgical or scientific instruments etc	227	204		1		22		225	202		1		22		2	2					
98	Makers of jewellery and ornaments	87,840	44,331	2,076	409	132	40 585	317	82,497	40,398	1,934	378	111	39,390	386	5,343	3 923	112	31	21	1 105	21
99	Other miscellaneous and undefined industries (toy making taxidermy, etc.)	9,264	5,339	2,436	39	68	1,143	239	9,242	5,319	2,435	39	68	1 145	230	22	20	1			1	
100	Scavenging	21,470	9,563	9,932	28	450	787	720	18,502	8 862	7,967	27	215	750	681	2,968	701	1 965	1	435	37	39
	IV —TRANSPORT	**132,612**	**110,257**	**20,215**	**1,239**	**1,949**	**46,407**	**2,545**	**157,536**	**99,019**	**12,959**	**478**	**433**	**42,411**	**2,236**	**25,076**	**11,238**	**7,256**	**761**	**1 516**	**3,996**	**309**
101	**18 —Transport by air**											..										
	19 —Transport by water	**15,801**	**11,197**	**493**	**110**	**92**	**3,857**	**52**	**12,118**	**8,600**	**478**	**104**	**90**	**2,797**	**49**	**3,683**	**3,597**	**15**	**6**	**2**	**1,060**	**3**
102	Ship owners boat owners and their employees officers mariners etc ship brokers boatmen and towmen	15,471	10,911	492	110	92	3,814	52	11,790	8 316	477	104	90	2,754	49	3,681	2 595	15	6	2	1 060	3
103	Persons (other than labourers) employed in harbours docks rivers and canals, including pilots	214	195				19		212	193				19		2	2					
104	Labourers employed on harbours docks rivers and canals	116	91	1			24		116	91	1	.		24								
	20 —Transport by road	**123,885**	**64,468**	**18,547**	**952**	**1,797**	**35,712**	**2,409**	**105,395**	**57,733**	**11,611**	**307**	**308**	**33,315**	**2,121**	**18,490**	**6,735**	**6,936**	**645**	**1,489**	**2,397**	**288**
105	Persons (other than labourers employed on the construction and maintenance of roads and bridges	335	227	54			40	14	279	181	54			30	14	56	[illegible]				0	
106	Labourers employed on roads and bridges	47,724	18,202	14 966	718	1 689	9,948	3 201	32,014	13,510	6,046	88	200	9,251	1,919	15,710	5 692	6,92[illegible]	630	1 489	607	282
107	Owners managers and employees (excluding personal servants) connected with mechanically driven vehicles (including trams)	3,715	2,873	16	11	35	772	2	3,645	2,819	15	11	35	763	2	70	60	1			9	
108	Owners managers and employees (excluding personal servants) connected with other vehicles	27,334	16,898	173	134	19	10,040	71	24,745	15 977	159	119	19	8 446	65	2,589	321	1	1		1 634	6
109	Palki, etc bearers and owners	21,792	9 454	70	61	36	12 154	17	21,739	9,449	69	61	36	12 107	17	53	5	1			17	
110	Pack elephant camel mule ass and bullock owners and drivers	9,685	7,701	182	10	6	1,754	32	9,680	7 696	182	10	6	1,754	32	5	5					
111	Porters and messengers	13,300	9,107	3,087	18	12	1,004	72	13,293	9,101	3,086	18	12	1 004	72	7	6	1				
	21.—Transport by rail	**40,015**	**32,367**	**1,155**	**71**	**60**	**6,283**	**79**	**37,537**	**30,714**	**850**	**65**	**35**	**5,812**	**61**	**2,478**	**1,653**	**305**	**6**	**25**	**471**	**18**
112	Railway employees of all kinds other than coolies	22,950	19,800	197	46	14	2,873	20	21,524	18,813	153	41	12	2,487	15	1,426	987	44	5	2	386	2
113	Labourers employed on railway construction and maintenance and coolies and porters employed on railway premises	17,065	13,567	958	25	46	3 410	59	16,013	11,901	697	24	33	3,325	43	1,052	666	261	1	33	85	16
	22. Post office, telegraph and telephone services	**2,911**	**2,225**	**20**	**106**		**555**	**5**	**2,486**	**1,972**	**20**	**2**		**487**	**5**	**425**	**253**		**104**		**68**	...
114	Post office telegraph and telephone services	2,911	2 225	20	106		555	5	2,486	1 972	20	2		487	5	425	253		104		68	
	V —TRADE	**858 802**	**360,132**	**260,890**	**4,303**	**17,612**	**170,799**	**45,066**	**753,436**	**334,473**	**214,647**	**3,444**	**13,605**	**148,461**	**38,806**	**105,366**	**25,659**	**46,243**	**859**	**4,007**	**22,338**	**6,260**
	23.—Banks, establishments of credit, exchange and insurance	**19,987**	**7,054**	**667**	**122**	**75**	**11,696**	**373**	**18,601**	**6,713**	**636**	**113**	**72**	**10,720**	**347**	**1,386**	**341**	**31**	**9**	**3**	**976**	**26**
115	Bank managers money lenders exchange and insurance agents money changers and brokers and their employees	19,987	7,054	667	122	75	11 696	373	18,601	6,713	636	113	72	10,720	347	1,386	341	31		3	976	26
	24.—Brokerage commission and export	**1,208**	**682**	**236**	**15**	**7**	**267**	**1**	**1,053**	**562**	**230**	**15**	**5**	**241**		**155**	**120**	**6**		**2**	**26**	**1**
116	Brokers commission agents commercial travellers warehouse owners and employees	1,208	683	236	15	7	267	1	1,053	562	230	15	5	241		155	120	6		2	26	1
	25 —Trade in textiles	**26,220**	**16,615**	**3,178**	**140**	**357**	**5,600**	**330**	**21,328**	**13,682**	**2,687**	**93**	**324**	**4,278**	**264**	**4,892**	**2,933**	**491**	**47**	**33**	**1,322**	**66**
117	Trade in piece goods wool cotton silk hair and other textiles	26,220	16 615	3,178	140	357	5,600	330	21,328	13 682	2 687	93	324	4 278	264	4,892	2 933	491	47	33	1 322	66
	26. Trade in skins, leather and furs	**8,428**	**4,675**	**1,080**	**68**	**92**	**2,252**	**261**	**8,152**	**4,468**	**1,057**	**36**	**84**	**2,246**	**261**	**276**	**207**	**23**	**32**	**8**	**6**	
118	Trade in skins leather furs feathers horn, etc and the articles made from these	8,428	4 675	1 080	68	92	2 252	261	8,152	4,468	1,057	36	84	2 246	261	276	207	23	32	8	6	
	27 —Trade in wood	**33,818**	**5,562**	**5,918**	**542**	**616**	**11,307**	**9,873**	**30,813**	**4,811**	**4,994**	**420**	**491**	**10,406**	**9,691**	**3,005**	**751**	**924**	**122**	**125**	**901**	**182**
119	Trade in wood (not fire wood)	29,076	4 147	4,158	399	451	10,291	9 630	28,391	3 933	4 120	397	451	9,877	9,608	685	309	38	2		414	22
120	Trade in barks	545	456	31		1	50	7	545	453	31		1	50	7							
121	Trade in bamboos and canes	3,481	862	1 462	143	148	736	130	1,565	373	733	33	37	339	65	1,916	484	729	130	121	397	65
122	Trade in thatches and other forest produce	716	97	267	.	16	230	106	312	39	110	.	12	140	11	404	58	157		4	90	95

TABLE X—*continued.*

OCCUPATION OR MEANS OF LIVELIHOOD. PART I—PROVINCIAL SUMMARY.

Group number.	OCCUPATION.	BIHAR AND ORISSA.							BRITISH TERRITORY.							FEUDATORY STATES.						
		TOTAL FOLLOWING OCCUPATION.	*As principal occupation.*		*As working dependants.*		*As subsidiary to other occupation.*		TOTAL FOLLOWING OCCUPATION.	*As principal occupation.*		*As working dependants.*		*As subsidiary to other occupation.*		TOTAL FOLLOWING OCCUPATION.	*As principal occupation.*		*As working dependants.*		*As subsidiary to other occupation.*	
			Males.	Females.	Males.	Females.	Males.	Females.		Males.	Females.	Males	Females.	Males.	Females.		Males.	Females.	Males.	Females.	Males.	Females.
1	2	3	4	5	6	7	8	9	10	11	12	13	14	15	16	17	18	19	20	21	22	23
	28.—Trade in Metals	**1,045**	**578**	**223**	**38**	...	**189**	**17**	**726**	**444**	**100**	**9**	...	**156**	**17**	**319**	**134**	**123**	**29**	...	**33**	...
123	Trade in metals, machinery, knives, tools, etc.	1,045	578	223	38	...	189	17	726	444	100	9	...	156	17	319	134	123	29	...	33	...
	29.—Trade in Pottery, Bricks and Tiles ...	**4,606**	**1,183**	**1,650**	**54**	**178**	**1,315**	**228**	**4,287**	**1,169**	**1,536**	**52**	**164**	**1,149**	**217**	**321**	**14**	**114**	**2**	**14**	**166**	**11**
124	Trade in pottery, bricks and tiles	4,606	1,183	1,650	54	178	1,315	228	4,287	1,169	1,536	52	164	1,149	217	321	14	114	2	14	166	11
	30.—Trade in Chemical Products	**5,031**	**2,912**	**573**	**9**	**11**	**1,464**	**62**	**4,378**	**2,715**	**384**	**9**	**11**	**1,203**	**56**	**653**	**197**	**189**	...	...	**261**	**6**
125	Drugs, dyes, paints, petroleum, explosives, etc.	5,031	2,912	573	9	11	1,464	62	4,378	2,715	384	9	11	1,203	56	653	197	189	...	...	261	6
	31.—Hotels, Cafes, Restaurants, etc.	**32,330**	**15,737**	**10,848**	**110**	**172**	**4,582**	**881**	**28,964**	**13,956**	**10,512**	**53**	**149**	**3,509**	**785**	**3,366**	**1,781**	**336**	**57**	**23**	**1,073**	**96**
126	Vendors of wine, liquors, aerated waters and ice	29,446	14,493	9,831	102	109	4,196	715	26,120	12,739	9,497	45	86	3,133	620	3,326	1,754	334	57	23	1,063	96
127	Owners and managers of hotels, cook shops, sarais, etc. (and employés)	2,667	1,106	973	4	59	362	164	2,627	1,078	971	4	50	352	163	40	27	2	...	...	10	1
128	Hawkers of drink and food-stuffs	217	139	44	4	4	24	2	217	139	44	4	4	24	2	...	...	...	...	...	...	...
	32.—Other Trade in Food-stuffs	**463,592**	**162,447**	**176,593**	**1,739**	**11,474**	**94,108**	**23,231**	**391,572**	**147,572**	**135,885**	**1,439**	**8,361**	**79,268**	**19,107**	**72,020**	**14,875**	**34,708**	**300**	**3,113**	**14,900**	**4,124**
129	Grain and pulse dealers	86,804	36,094	29,988	221	1,303	16,684	3,614	63 827	33,049	16,773	155	1,005	12,118	1,727	22,977	3,045	14,215	66	298	3,466	1,887
130	Dealers in sweetmeats, sugar and spices	28 697	17,676	5,761	90	268	4,557	345	27,408	17,027	5,476	81	243	4,244	337	1,289	649	285	9	25	313	8
131	Dealers in dairy product, eggs and poultry	116 430	35,552	55,035	274	4,370	21,739	9,460	109 887	25,220	50,360	266	3,538	21,178	9,316	6,543	323	4,675	8	832	561	144
132	Dealers in animals for food	892	506	43	1	1	337	4	882	496	43	1	1	337	4	10	10	...	...		...	...
133	Dealers in fodder for animals	5,298	1,257	2,536	25	268	598	614	4,494	1,034	2,315	25	193	367	560	804	223	221	...	75	231	54
134	Dealers in other food-stuffs	220,005	78,469	76,264	1,077	5,219	49,885	9,091	180,011	68,024	61,029	864	3,342	39,688	7,064	39,994	10,445	15,235	213	1,877	10,197	2,027
135	Dealers in tobacco	4,830	2,463	913	48	45	1,262	99	4,566	2,350	841	44	39	1,194	98	264	113	72	4	6	68	1
136	Dealers in opium	157	107	6	...	...	44	...	90	59	5	...	...	26	...	67	48	1	...	...	18	...
137	Dealers in ganja	479	323	47	3	...	102	4	407	304	48	3	...	56	1	72	19	4	...	...	46	3
	33.—Trade in Clothing and Toilet articles ...	**6,075**	**3,514**	**1,344**	**26**	**42**	**918**	**231**	**4,546**	**2,656**	**1,077**	**20**	**9**	**565**	**219**	**1,529**	**858**	**267**	**6**	**33**	**353**	**12**
138	Trade in ready-made clothing and other articles of dress and the toilet (hats, umbrellas, socks, ready-made shoes, perfumes, etc.)	6,075	3,514	1,344	26	42	918	231	4,546	2,656	1,077	20	9	565	219	1,529	858	267	6	33	353	12
	34.—Trade in Furniture	**2,393**	**1,519**	**349**	**6**	**14**	**427**	**78**	**2,186**	**1,448**	**264**	**6**	**13**	**407**	**50**	**205**	**71**	**85**	...	**1**	**20**	**28**
139	Trade in furniture, carpets, curtains and bedding	621	274	194	...	9	106	38	516	270	119	...	9	102	16	105	4	75	...	...	4	22
140	Hardware, cooking utensils, porcelain, crockery, glassware, bottles, articles for gardening, etc.	1,772	1,245	155	6	5	321	40	1,672	1,178	145	6	4	305	34	100	67	10	...	1	16	6
	35.—Trade in Building Materials	**916**	**272**	**273**	**12**	**10**	**195**	**154**	**898**	**267**	**262**	**12**	**10**	**193**	**154**	**18**	**5**	**11**	...	...	**2**	...
141	Trade in building materials (other than bricks, tiles and woody materials)	916	273	273	12	10	195	154	898	267	262	12	10	193	154	18	5	11	...	...	2	...
	36.—Trade in Means of Transport	**5,072**	**3,080**	**218**	**6**	**2**	**1,804**	**42**	**5,000**	**2,978**	**193**	**6**	**2**	**1,779**	**42**	**72**	**22**	**25**	...	...	**25**	...
142	Dealers and hirers in mechanical transport, motors, cycles, etc.	77	73	...	...	...	4	...	76	72	...	...	...	4	...	1	1	...	...	...	...	...
143	Dealers and hirers in other carriages, carts, boats, etc. ...	895	313	30	.	1	552	...	856	308	4	...	1	550	...	37	10	25	...	...	2	...
144	Dealers and hirers of elephants, camels, horses, cattle, asses, mules, etc.	4,100	3,614	189	6	1	1,248	42	4,066	3,603	180	6	1	1,225	42	34	11	...	...	...	23	...
	37.—Trade in fuel	**54,317**	**8,831**	**29,749**	**233**	**3,618**	**5,956**	**5,930**	**39,778**	**6,572**	**21,527**	**211**	**3,062**	**4,085**	**4,321**	**14,539**	**2,259**	**8,222**	**22**	**556**	**1,871**	**1,609**
145	Dealers in fire-wood, charcoal, coal, cowdung, etc.	54,317	8,831	29,740	233	3,618	5,956	5,930	39,778	6,572	21,527	211	3,062	4,085	4,321	14,539	2,259	8,222	22	556	1,871	1,609

No.	Occupation																					
	38.—Trade in Articles of Luxury and those pertaining to Letters and the Arts and Sciences	17,273	9,908	4,946	216	240	2,332	531	15,880	8,271	4,739	78	157	2,181	453	1,393	737	207	137	83	151	78
146	Dealers in precious stones, jewellery (real and imitation), clocks, optical instruments, etc.	1,222	940	90	56	13	118	6	877	688	36	...	19	85	6	345	253	4	56	...	33	...
147	Dealers in common bangles, bead, necklaces, fans, small articles, toys, hunting and fishing tackles, flowers, etc. ...	13,696	6,300	4,595	153	208	1,938	503	12,843	5,976	4,305	71	123	1,850	435	853	324	200	81	82	88	78
148	Publishers, book-sellers, stationers, dealers in music, pictures, musical instruments and curiosities	2,355	1,768	261	8	20	276	22	2,160	1,607	258	8	19	346	32	195	161	3	...	1	30	...
	39.—Trade of other sorts	176,489	116,543	29,045	967	704	26,387	2,848	175,272	116,189	28,564	871	691	26,135	2,832	1,217	354	481	96	13	252	21
149	Dealers in rags, stable refuse, etc.	3	3	...	...	...	...	...	3	3	...	...	...	...	...	...	...	...	...	...	...	...
150	General store-keepers and shop-keepers otherwise unspecified ...	169,862	112,634	27,900	931	663	25,003	2,723	168,665	112,292	27,434	835	640	24,753	2,702	1,197	342	475	96	13	250	21
151	Itinerant traders, pedlars and hawkers (of other than food, etc.)	2,291	1,321	728	8	6	178	50	2,276	1,316	723	8	6	176	50	13	5	6	...	...	2	...
152	Other trades (including farmers of pounds, tools and markets) ...	4,333	3,585	408	28	36	1,206	70	4,326	3,578	408	28	36	1,206	70	7	7	...	...	...	...	...
	C.—PUBLIC ADMINISTRATION AND LIBERAL ARTS	333,249	187,991	24,313	2,636	1,224	118,156	3,929	288,677	164,531	23,163	2,419	1,123	93,640	3,791	44,572	23,460	1,150	217	91	19,516	138
	VI.—PUBLIC FORCE	57,938	36,683	1	128	...	21,126	...	44,361	27,814	1	111	...	16,435	...	13,577	8,869	...	17	...	4,691	...
	40.—Army	1,034	1,025	1	...	...	8	...	1,034	1,025	1	...	...	8	...	...	...	...	...	...	...	...
153	Army (Imperial)	1,010	1,003	1	...	...	6	...	1,010	1,003	1	...	...	6	...	...	...	...	...	...	...	...
154	Army (Indian States)	24	22	...	...	...	2	...	24	22	...	...	...	2	...	...	...	...	...	...	...	...
155	**41.—Navy**	...	...	...	...	...	...	...	...	...	...	...	...	...	...	...	...	...	...	...	...	...
156	**42.—Air force**	...	...	...	...	...	...	...	...	...	...	...	...	...	...	...	...	...	...	...	...	...
	43.—Police	56,904	35,658	...	128	...	21,118	...	43,327	26,789	...	111	...	16,427	...	13,577	8,869	...	17	...	4,691	...
157	Police	17,751	15,197	...	33	...	2,521	...	13,571	11,332	...	32	...	2,207	...	4,180	3,865	...	1	...	314	...
158	Village watchmen	39,153	20,461	...	95	...	18,597	...	29,756	15,457	...	79	...	14,220	...	9,397	5,004	...	16	...	4,377	...
	VII.—PUBLIC ADMINISTRATION	26,502	16,483	382	346	174	9,066	51	17,847	13,414	305	322	174	3,595	37	8,655	3,069	77	24	...	5,471	14
	44.—Public Administration	26,502	16,483	382	346	174	9,066	51	17,847	13,414	305	322	174	3,595	37	8,655	3,069	77	24	...	5,471	14
159	Service of the State	14,568	11,693	209	53	172	2,400	32	14,153	11,293	200	43	172	2,404	32	415	400	...	10	...	5	...
160	Service of Indian and Foreign States	5,614	2,076	36	18	1	3,480	3	336	224	12	5	1	91	3	5,278	1,853	24	13	...	3,380	...
161	Municipal and other local (not village) service	1,224	824	54	234	...	112	...	1,211	814	54	234	...	109	...	13	10	...	...	...	3	...
162	Village officials and servants other than watchmen	5,096	1,890	83	41	1	3,065	16	2,147	1,083	30	40	1	991	2	2,949	807	53	1	...	2,074	14
	VIII.—PROFESSIONS AND LIBERAL ARTS ...	248,809	134,825	23,930	2,162	1,050	82,964	3,878	226,469	123,303	22,857	1,986	959	73,610	3,754	22,340	11,522	1,073	176	91	9,354	124
	45.—Religion	136,033	71,634	8,239	1,257	631	52,435	1,787	123,908	65,911	7,590	1,138	609	46,912	1,748	12,125	5,723	699	119	22	5,523	39
163	Priests, ministers, etc.	114,838	61,056	7,482	1,043	599	42,983	1,675	107,717	57,576	6,843	955	580	40,113	1,650	7,121	3,480	639	88	19	2,870	25
164	Monks, nuns, religious mendicants	2,875	1,988	537	48	8	287	7	2,873	1,987	537	48	8	286	7	2	1	...	...	...	1	...
165	Other religious workers	1,954	969	135	40	5	777	20	1,752	856	102	48	5	713	28	292	113	23	1	...	64	1
166	Servants in religious edifices, burial and burning grounds, pilgrim conductors, circumcisers, etc.	16,366	7,621	145	117	19	8,388	76	11,566	5,492	108	87	16	5,800	63	4,800	2,129	37	30	3	2,588	13
	46.—Law	9,734	8,074	33	22	...	1,592	13	9,669	8,028	33	22	...	1,573	13	65	46	...	...	...	19	...
167	Lawyers of all kinds, including Qazis, Law Agents and Mukhtiars	6,055	5,210	3	3	...	839	...	6,002	5,170	3	3	...	826	...	53	40	...	...	...	13	...
168	Lawyers' clerks, petition writers, etc.	3,679	2,864	30	19	...	753	13	3,667	2,858	30	19	...	747	13	12	6	...	...	...	6	...
	47.—Medicine	24,798	7,411	11,836	58	213	3,568	1,712	23,442	6,847	11,739	41	212	2,904	1,699	1,356	564	97	17	1	664	13
169	Registered medical practioners, including oculists	4,293	3,312	214	14	...	733	30	4,185	3,232	212	14	...	717	30	108	90	2	...	...	16	...
170	Other persons practising the healing arts without being registered	4,853	2,333	151	21	9	2,306	33	4,054	2,101	148	19	9	1,746	31	799	232	3	2	...	560	3
171	Dentists	79	71	1	...	...	7	...	79	71	1	...	...	7	...	...	...	...	...	...	...	...
172	Midwives, vaccinators, compounders, nurses, masseurs, etc. ...	15,085	1,311	11,453	22	204	436	1,659	14,713	1,113	11,361	7	203	381	1,648	372	198	92	15	1	55	11
173	Veterinary surgeons	488	384	17	1	...	86	...	411	340	17	1	...	53	...	77	44	...	...	...	33	...
	48.—Instruction	40,166	29,167	1,444	401	52	9,033	69	35,704	25,681	1,310	380	52	8,216	65	4,462	3,486	134	21	...	817	4
174	Professors and teachers of all kinds	34,530	23,910	1,339	397	48	8,768	68	30,213	20,523	1,227	376	48	7,975	65	4,317	3,388	112	21	...	793	3
175	Clerks and servants connected with education	5,636	5,257	105	4	4	265	1	5,491	5,159	83	4	4	241	...	145	98	22	...	...	24	1

TABLE X—*continued.*

OCCUPATION OR MEANS OF LIVELIHOOD. PART I—PROVINCIAL SUMMARY.

Group number.	OCCUPATION.	BIHAR AND ORISSA. Total following occupation.	As principal occupation. Males.	As principal occupation. Females.	As working dependants. Males.	As working dependants. Females.	As subsidiary to other occupation. Males.	As subsidiary to other occupation. Females.	BRITISH TERRITORY. Total following occupation.	As principal occupation. Males.	As principal occupation. Females.	As working dependants. Males.	As working dependants. Females.	As subsidiary to other occupation. Males.	As subsidiary to other occupation. Females.	FEUDATORY STATES. Total following occupation.	As principal occupation. Males.	As principal occupation. Females.	As working dependants. Males.	As working dependants. Females.	As subsidiary to other occupation. Males.	As subsidiary to other occupation. Females.
1	2	3	4	5	6	7	8	9	10	11	12	13	14	15	16	17	18	19	20	21	22	23
	49.—Letters, Arts and Sciences (other than 44)	**38,078**	**18,539**	**2,328**	**424**	**154**	**16,336**	**297**	**33,746**	**16,836**	**2,185**	**405**	**86**	**14,005**	**229**	**4,332**	**1,703**	**143**	**19**	**68**	**2,331**	**68**
176	Public scribes, stenographers, etc.	**296**	178	1	1	.	116	...	**275**	168	1	1	...	105		**21**	10	...	.	..	11	...
177	Architects, surveyors, engineers and their employees (not being State servants)	**2,268**	1,683	3	12	...	588	3	**1,435**	1,053	1	11	...	368	2	**833**	610	2	1		230	...
178	Authors, editors, journalists and photographers	**435**	346	43	10	6	30	...	**427**	342	43	10	6	26	...	**8**	4	.	.	...	4	...
179	Artists, sculptors and image-makers	**402**	221	61	4	2	106	8	**262**	130	55	...	...	71	6	**140**	91	6	4	2	35	2
180	Scientists (astronomers, botanists, etc.)	**10**	4	...	...	...	6	...	**8**	2	...	...	...	6	...	**2**	2	...	...	..	..	..
181	Horoscope casters, astrologers, fortune-tellers, wizards, witches and mediums	**1,541**	577	59	13	3	882	7	**1,201**	431	58	11	3	692	7	**340**	146	1	3	1	190	...
182	Musicians (composers and performers other than military), actors, dancers, etc.	**31,977**	14,651	2,059	383	143	14,468	273	**29,114**	13,913	1,927	371	78	12,618	207	**2,863**	738	132	12	65	1,850	66
183	Managers and employees of places of public entertainments, race courses, societies, clubs	**153**	136	7	...	...	10	...	**151**	134	7	...	...	10	...	**2**	2	..	...	...	...	...
184	Conjurors, acrobats, reciters, exhibitors of curiosities and wild animals, etc.	**996**	763	95	1		130	7	**873**	663	93	1	...	109	7	**123**	100	2	.	...	21	...
	D.—MISCELLANEOUS	**1,780,825**	**891,284**	**610,559**	**25,759**	**40,970**	**166,059**	**46,194**	**1,673,654**	**849,212**	**565,375**	**24,171**	**37,443**	**154,383**	**43,070**	**107,171**	**42,072**	**45,184**	**1,588**	**3,527**	**11,676**	**3,124**
	IX.—PERSONS LIVING ON THEIR INCOME	**2,856**	**1,460**	**415**	**25**	**22**	**897**	**37**	**2,584**	**1,338**	**351**	**94**	**17**	**825**	**29**	**272**	**122**	**64**	**1**	**5**	**72**	**8**
	50.—Persons living principally on their income	**2,856**	**1,460**	**415**	**25**	**22**	**897**	**37**	**2,584**	**1,338**	**351**	**24**	**17**	**825**	**29**	**272**	**122**	**64**	**1**	**5**	**72**	**8**
185	Proprietors (other than of agricultural land), fund and scholarships holders and pensioners	**2,856**	1,460	415	25	22	897	37	**2,584**	1,338	351	24	17	825	29	**272**	122	64	1	5	72	8
	X.—DOMESTIC SERVICE	**241,266**	**94,093**	**78,155**	**5,272**	**29,368**	**25,092**	**9,286**	**212,405**	**82,211**	**63,712**	**5,179**	**28,544**	**23,798**	**8,961**	**28,861**	**11,882**	**14,443**	**93**	**824**	**1,294**	**325**
	51.—Domestic Service	**241,266**	**94,093**	**78,155**	**5,272**	**29,368**	**25,092**	**9,286**	**212,405**	**82,211**	**63,712**	**5,179**	**28,544**	**23,798**	**8,961**	**28,861**	**11,882**	**14,443**	**93**	**824**	**1,294**	**325**
186	Private motor-drivers and cleaners	**2,398**	2,012	23	17	.	345	1	**2,221**	1,873	23	17	..	307	1	**177**	139				38	...
187	Other domestic service	**238,868**	92,081	78,132	5,255	29,368	24,747	9,285	**210,184**	80,338	63,689	5,162	28,544	23,401	8,960	**28,684**	11,743	14,443	93	824	1,256	325
	XI. INSUFFICIENTLY DESCRIBED OCCUPATIONS	**1,434,088**	**747,990**	**499,472**	**8,099**	**10,414**	**132,252**	**35,861**	**1,372,509**	**726,654**	**474,731**	**7,408**	**8,037**	**122,516**	**33,163**	**61,579**	**21,336**	**24,741**	**691**	**2,377**	**9,736**	**2,698**
	52.—General terms which do not indicate a definite occupation	**1,434,088**	**747,990**	**499,472**	**8,099**	**10,414**	**132,252**	**35,861**	**1,372,509**	**726,654**	**474,731**	**7,408**	**8,037**	**122,516**	**33,163**	**61,579**	**21,336**	**24,741**	**691**	**2,377**	**9,736**	**2,698**
188	Manufacturers, business-men and contractors otherwise unspecified	**15,695**	11,681	1,316	69	84	2,343	202	**14,924**	11,201	1,302	32	83	2,164	142	**771**	480	14	37	1	170	60
189	Cashiers, accountants, book-keepers, clerks and other employees, in unspecified offices and warehouses and shops....	**240,784**	185,962	20,900	1,046	431	31,006	1,440	**240,123**	185,609	20,810	1,033	416	30,836	1,410	**661**	353	81	12	15	170	30
190	Mechanics otherwise unspecified	**3,219**	2,659	37	4	7	308	4	**3,167**	3,807	37	4	7	308	4	**52**	52		.	...		...
191	Labourers and workmen otherwise unspecified	**1,174,390**	547,488	477,219	6,981	9,892	98,595	34,215	**1,114,295**	527,037	452,573	6,330	7,631	89,208	31,607	**60,095**	20,451	24,046	642	2,361	9,387	2,608
	XII.—UNPRODUCTIVE	**102,615**	**47,741**	**32,517**	**12,363**	**1,166**	**7,818**	**1,010**	**86,156**	**39,009**	**26,581**	**11,560**	**845**	**7,244**	**917**	**16,459**	**8,732**	**5,936**	**803**	**321**	**574**	**93**
192	**53.—Inmates of jails, asylums and alms houses (a)**	**11,538**	..	.	**11,235**	**303**	**[4,439]**	**[1,018]**	**10,719**	...	...	**10,470**	**249**	**[4,248]**	**[1,005]**	**819**	.	.	**765**	**54**	**[191]**	**[13]**
	54.—Beggars, vagrants, prostitutes	**90,520**	**47,451**	**32,503**	**1,126**	**863**	**7,569**	**1,008**	**74,895**	**38,733**	**26,567**	**1,088**	**596**	**6,996**	**915**	**15,625**	**8,718**	**5,936**	**38**	**267**	**573**	**93**
193	Beggars and vagrants	**88,313**	47,368	30,636	1,126	853	7,534	796	**72,782**	38,651	24,782	1,088	587	6,961	713	**15,531**	8,717	5,854	38	266	573	83
194	Procurers and prostitutes	**2,207**	83	1,867	...	10	35	312	**2,113**	82	1,785	...	9	35	202	**94**	1	82	..	1	...	10
195	**55.—Other unclassified non-productive industries**	**557**	**290**	**14**	**2**	...	**249**	**2**	**542**	**276**	**14**	**2**	...	**248**	**2**	**15**	**14**	.	...	..	**1**	...

(a) Persons undergoing rigorous imprisonment in jails have been treated as "working dependants". All other inmates of jails, asylums, etc., have been treated as "non-working dependants", but their number is here shown for convenience in the columns headed "As subsidiary to other occupation".

TABLE X—*continued.*

OCCUPATION OR MEANS OF LIVELIHOOD.

PART II—DETAILS FOR DISTRICTS AND CITIES.

TOTAL OF ALL CLASSES.

DISTRICT, STATE OR CITY.	TOTAL POPULATION. Persons.	Earners. Males.	Earners. Females.	Working dependants. Males.	Working dependants. Females	Non-working dependants. Males.	Non-working dependants. Females.	Earners with a subsidiary occupation. Males.	Earners with a subsidiary occupation. Females.
1	2	3	4	5	6	7	8	9	10
BIHAR AND ORISSA	**42,329,583**	**11,933,820**	**4,977,328**	**305,133**	**393,890**	**8,843,607**	**15,875,805**	**1,533,621**	**295,844**
British Territory	**37,677,576**	**10,648,014**	**4,418,231**	**220,623**	**256,168**	**7,925,501**	**14,209,039**	**1,317,258**	**247,595**
PATNA DIVISION	**6,228,425**	**1,883,259**	**901,378**	**9,338**	**4,478**	**1,256,299**	**2,173,703**	**135,406**	**31,239**
Patna	1,846,474	576,814	241,862	3,567	632	375,753	647,856	39,292	7,116
Gaya	2,388,462	699,746	351,108	4,237	3,229	489,080	840,482	44,835	13,635
Shahabad	1,993,489	606,699	308,408	1,544	617	390,856	685,365	51,279	10,488
TIRHUT DIVISION	**10,739,274**	**3,096,413**	**1,161,620**	**17,714**	**48,487**	**2,201,684**	**4,213,356**	**403,074**	**85,004**
Saran	2,486,468	704,568	340,511	2,868	5,731	512,623	930,177	92,335	29,437
Champaran	2,145,687	664,828	280,109	4,882	7,708	411,236	766,919	82,380	24,451
Muzaffarpur	2,941,025	846,645	282,780	3,017	28,769	504,186	1,185,629	129,253	20,955
Darbhanga	3,166,094	880,372	248,220	6,947	6,284	683,640	1,340,631	99,106	10,161
BHAGALPUR DIVISION	**8,759,801**	**2,605,393**	**1,199,736**	**27,365**	**26,895**	**1,799,225**	**3,110,187**	**169,987**	**61,114**
Monghyr	2,987,154	695,973	340,358	5,384	11,330	444,490	789,609	34,828	9,651
Bhagalpur	2,234,632	639,520	282,375	8,080	8,137	483,064	813,536	35,399	6,992
Purnea	2,186,543	644,062	122,724	2,524	872	483,095	923,266	14,419	1,213
Santal Parganas	3,051,472	635,838	455,279	11,447	6,556	388,636	583,716	55,343	43,358
ORISSA DIVISION	**5,306,142**	**1,499,909**	**474,373**	**72,822**	**69,298**	**977,350**	**2,213,220**	**365,546**	**26,588**
Cuttack	2,176,707	604,043	156,891	4,419	16,156	419,672	973,526	158,373	8,188
Balasore	990,600	279,965	87,708	18,189	4,551	182,444	417,822	89,905	8,251
Angul	222,736	68,954	41,958	1,344	190	38,627	71,663	12,220	1,527
Puri	1,035,154	298,374	79,357	14,668	15,733	187,173	439,859	68,136	6,870
Sambalpur	880,945	247,673	106,459	34,352	32,668	149,436	310,358	36,912	6,752
CHOTA NAGPUR DIVISION	**6,643,934**	**1,563,940**	**690,124**	**93,314**	**107,010**	**1,690,973**	**2,498,578**	**243,245**	**43,650**
Hazaribagh	1,517,357	385,499	208,499	2,217	2,222	364,240	554,688	58,275	11,680
Ranchi	1,567,149	237,763	132,377	54,646	85,931	464,654	571,778	40,611	8,308
Palamau	818,736	223,864	136,124	13,563	8,053	173,411	264,781	33,166	7,072
Manbhum	1,810,890	494,061	154,875	17,171	5,990	428,787	730,016	81,516	9,742
Singhbhum	929,802	222,763	28,249	6,777	4,814	239,881	377,318	34,677	5,948
Feudatory States	**4,652,007**	**1,285,806**	**559,097**	**84,510**	**137,722**	**918,106**	**1,666,766**	**216,363**	**48,249**
Orissa States	4,465,385	1,232,789	520,025	82,654	134,581	881,218	1,614,088	201,533	42,583
Chota Nagpur States	186,622	53,017	39,072	1,856	3,141	36,888	52,678	14,830	5,666
Cities	**415,280**	**150,216**	**29,732**	**4,499**	**330**	**86,153**	**144,350**	**5,989**	**596**
Patna City	159,690	54,947	11,489	545	43	36,746	55,920	1,684	39
Gaya City	88,005	34,294	6,880	1,821	22	14,510	30,478	680	10
Bhagalpur City	83,847	26,106	5,785	1,985	210	18,774	30,984	2,356	84
Jamshedpur City	83,738	34,869	5,578	145	55	16,123	26,908	1,269	463

CLASS A.—PRODUCTION OF RAW MATERIALS. / ***SUB-CLASS I.—EXPLOITATION OF ANIMALS AND VEGETATION.***

DISTRICT, STATE OR CITY.	Class A. Earners (principal occupation). Males.	Class A. Earners (principal occupation). Females.	Class A. Working dependants. Males.	Class A. Working dependants. Females.	Class A. Earners (subsidiary occupation). Males.	Class A. Earners (subsidiary occupation). Females.	Sub-class I. Earners (principal occupation). Males.	Sub-class I. Earners (principal occupation). Females.	Sub-class I. Working dependants. Males.	Sub-class I. Working dependants. Females.	Sub-class I. Earners (subsidiary occupation). Males.	Sub-class I. Earners (subsidiary occupation). Females.
1	11	12	13	14	15	16	17	18	19	20	21	22
BIHAR AND ORISSA	**9,374,885**	**3,606,285**	**260,610**	**280,189**	**705,079**	**145,473**	**9,587,642**	**3,574,897**	**259,963**	**279,853**	**675,210**	**138,075**
British Territory	**8,577,374**	**3,236,152**	**181,287**	**171,073**	**589,346**	**117,337**	**8,497,464**	**3,210,362**	**180,805**	**170,835**	**562,274**	**110,987**
PATNA DIVISION	**1,302,205**	**574,180**	**2,809**	**3,630**	**77,371**	**15,794**	**1,302,135**	**573,957**	**2,809**	**3,630**	**77,866**	**15,791**
Patna	364,359	137,622	570	487	22,553	2,900	364,350	137,400	570	487	22,553	2,900
Gaya	475,128	207,257	2,131	2,565	27,482	7,519	475,112	207,357	2,131	3,535	27,482	7,519
Shahabad	462,718	229,301	108	578	27,837	5,375	462,673	229,291	108	578	27,833	5,372
TIRHUT DIVISION	**2,741,934**	**971,845**	**10,601**	**16,464**	**191,347**	**42,963**	**2,739,102**	**969,451**	**10,588**	**16,435**	**186,874**	**41,515**
Saran	638,959	297,059	1,873	4,858	35,690	14,054	638,465	293,772	1,870	4,548	35,024	13,651
Champaran	610,324	261,107	4,443	7,183	36,354	14,453	610,078	360,856	4,440	7,182	35,918	14,333
Muzaffarpur	766,302	236,586	1,131	1,694	74,528	10,098	764,510	234,844	1,129	1,080	71,287	9,251
Darbhanga	726,349	177,093	3,154	2,720	44,766	4,358	726,049	176,970	3,149	2,725	44,645	4,350
BHAGALPUR DIVISION	**2,095,217**	**921,108**	**22,134**	**22,215**	**58,621**	**29,746**	**2,094,882**	**920,918**	**22,133**	**22,215**	**58,083**	**29,645**
Monghyr	459,387	194,090	3,980	9,073	12,385	3,806	459,371	194,033	3,080	9,073	12,380	3,806
Bhagalpur	511,519	222,496	5,215	6,499	13,601	3,182	511,470	222,477	5,214	6,409	13,574	3,182
Purnea	558,120	106,586	2,073	464	7,403	740	558,095	106,548	3,078	464	7,403	740
Santal Parganas	566,191	397,936	10,864	6,179	25,232	22,018	565,946	397,800	10,861	6,179	24,727	21,017
ORISSA DIVISION	**1,190,914**	**216,269**	**63,921**	**31,849**	**146,941**	**8,702**	**1,190,657**	**216,160**	**63,930**	**31,849**	**146,896**	**8,702**
Cuttack	473,633	61,931	3,609	1,468	57,763	2,311	473,630	61,931	3,609	1,468	57,763	2,311
Balasore	244,545	44,342	14,313	767	33,000	677	244,544	44,342	14,313	767	33,000	677
Angul	58,831	31,896	1,277	107	6,624	938	58,830	31,896	1,276	107	6,612	938
Puri	218,921	22,693	11,825	3,401	35,634	1,360	218,918	23,692	11,825	3,401	35,632	1,359
Sambalpur	194,984	55,407	32,907	26,106	13,920	3,417	194,735	55,299	32,907	26,106	13,889	3,417
CHOTA NAGPUR DIVISION	**1,247,104**	**552,750**	**61,812**	**96,915**	**114,566**	**20,132**	**1,170,688**	**529,876**	**61,345**	**96,706**	**92,555**	**15,334**
Hazaribagh	331,190	174,947	1,369	1,837	15,996	5,787	316,905	107,909	1,331	1,822	11,100	4,027
Ranchi	187,863	111,218	50,644	79,667	15,199	2,862	187,852	111,218	50,644	79,649	18,104	2,861
Palamau	187,387	113,198	9,249	7,541	11,403	1,810	187,327	113,198	9,348	7,541	11,388	1,810
Manbhum	390,824	94,774	15,154	3,972	46,430	6,053	332,914	80,646	14,930	3,830	32,477	3,852
Singhbhum	149,840	58,613	5,413	3,908	20,538	3,620	145,600	56,905	5,103	3,874	19,396	2,784
Feudatory States	**1,097,511**	**370,133**	**79,323**	**109,116**	**115,733**	**28,136**	**1,090,178**	**364,535**	**79,158**	**109,018**	**112,936**	**27,088**
Orissa States	1,052,322	338,194	77,820	106,637	107,119	24,447	1,045,039	332,649	77,655	106,543	104,328	23,400
Chota Nagpur States	45,189	31,939	1,503	2,479	8,614	3,689	45,139	31,886	1,503	2,475	8,608	3,688
Cities	**25,541**	**2,810**	**638**	**53**	**2,572**	**89**	**25,293**	**2,798**	**637**	**53**	**2,572**	**89**
Patna City	7,986	1,506	144	5	1,147	2	7,986	1,506	144	5	1,147	2
Gaya City	11,465	716	427	9	505	3	11,465	716	427	9	505	3
Bhagalpur City	4,137	352	33	11	513	8	4,117	345	37	11	512	8
Jamshedpur City	1,953	237	29	28	408	76	1,725	232	29	28	408	76

TABLE X—continued.

OCCUPATION OR MEANS OF LIVELIHOOD. PART II—DETAILS FOR DISTRICTS AND CITIES.

DISTRICT, STATE OR CITY.	ORDER 1.—PASTURE AND AGRICULTURE. Earners (principal occupation). Males.	Females.	Working dependants. Males.	Females.	Earners (subsidiary occupation). Males.	Females.	Sub-order 1 (a)—Ordinary cultivation. TOTAL OF SUB-ORDER 1(a). Earners (principal occupation). Males.	Females.	Working dependants. Males.	Females.	Earners (subsidiary occupation). Males.	Females.
1	23	24	25	26	27	28	29	30	31	32	33	34
BIHAR AND ORISSA	**9,539,107**	**3,564,632**	**259,014**	**279,193**	**643,951**	**136,306**	**9,340,598**	**3,525,019**	**197,708**	**267,149**	**589,558**	**132,059**
British Territory ..	**8,454,135**	**3,201,108**	**179,941**	**170,340**	**534,620**	**109,379**	**8,310,190**	**3,176,200**	**144,311**	**164,282**	**499,385**	**106,054**
PATNA DIVISION ..	**1,309,785**	**573,289**	**2,804**	**3,830**	**77,534**	**15,729**	**1,285,250**	**568,171**	**2,772**	**3,609**	**76,173**	**15,422**
Patna ...	364,187	237,367	57	447	22,331?	2,90[illegible]	[illegible]1,912	131,614	557	444	22,269	2,808
Gaya ...	474,960	207,068	2,120	2,562	27,455?	7,494	467,714?	204,951	2,107	2,568	27,078	7,490
Shahabad ...	461,040?	228,890?	1?8	[illegible]	[illegible]	5,330	455,622?	226,601	108	572	26,826	5,149
TIRHUT DIVISION ..	**2,728,735**	**964,823**	**10,486**	**16,331**	**176,080**	**40,466**	**2,717,686**	**962,182**	**9,625**	**15,740**	**172,250**	**40,025**
Saran ...	[illegible]	[illegible]6,274	1,862?	[illegible]	34,[illegible]	13,447	[illegible]	[illegible]	1,845	4,878	33,542	13,289
Champaran ...	[illegible]	240,402?	[illegible]	7,1[illegible]	[illegible]	4,0[illegible]	605,754	240,501?	4,401	7,162	32,938	13,991
Muzaffarpur ...	[illegible]	[illegible]	[illegible]	1,62[illegible]	[illegible]	8,9[illegible]	[illegible]	286,891	405	1,173	65,133	8,782
Darbhanga ...	[illegible]	175,545?	5,106	2,68[illegible]	41,[illegible]32	3,986?	718,523	274,839?	2,974	2,550	40,647	3,963
BHAGALPUR DIVISION ..	**2,084,182**	**919,310**	**22,094**	**22,197**	**56,016**	**29,445**	**2,046,264**	**915,640**	**13,614**	**19,682**	**47,657**	**28,012**
Monghyr ...	457,183?	193,504	[illegible]	9,[illegible]	12,22[illegible]	3,602?	[illegible]	192,442?	3,918	9,019	11,828	3,643
Bhagalpur ...	[illegible]	221,[illegible]	7,205?	6,447	12,513	[illegible]	[illegible]3,757	221,171	6,162	6,486	11,897	3,097
Purnea ...	582,716?	106,383?	2,076	461	7,[illegible]	79[illegible]	582,344	106,008	1,924	462	6,561	725
Santal Parganas ...	565,014?	397,528	10,655	6,17[illegible]	24,2[illegible]	21,731?	[illegible]5,008	396,025	2,810	3,715	17,376	20,547
ORISSA DIVISION ...	**1,173,047**	**214,465**	**63,401**	**31,699**	**134,215**	**8,472**	**1,126,690**	**204,242**	**54,212**	**30,433**	**121,154**	**7,958**
Cuttack ...	468,369	61,771	3,756?	1,449	[illegible]	2,291?	447,[illegible]01	50,395	1,523	911	47,336	2,079
Balasore ...	240,575?	43,836?	14,072	726	28,142	682?	335,559	42,009	12,598	5[illegible]	26,281	573
Angul ...	58,749	31,865?	[illegible],275	1[illegible]7	6,[illegible]	985?	54,516	30,969	79	26	5,[illegible]	913
Puri ...	31[illegible]	42,399	11,64[illegible]	3,300?	34,401?	1,337?	302,976	21,336	9,255?	3,104	31,806	1,144
Sambalpur ...	192,073	54,591	39,[illegible]	[illegible]	1[illegible]87	4,272	155,[illegible]	53,633	30,754	35,656?	10,875	3,249
CHOTA NAGPUR DIVISION	**1,167,386**	**529,221**	**81,156**	**96,489**	**90,781**	**15,267**	**1,134,300**	**526,015**	**64,088**	**94,818**	**82,151**	**14,687**
Hazaribagh ...	316,702	167,643?	1,931?	1,832?	19,737	4,010?	314,164?	167,285	1,271	1,814	9,372	3,927
Ranchi ...	1[illegible],092	111,121	50,593?	79,641	17,[illegible]	2,[illegible]	[illegible],449	110,295	47,397	78,964	15,306	2,539
Palamau ...	157,218?	11[illegible],771	9,248	7,741	11,218?	[illegible]	[illegible],155	112,543?	8,314	7,369	9,763	1,739
Manbhum ...	331,247?	80,276	14,518	3,75[illegible]	11,568?	3,821?	317,473	79,538	4,150	3,158	29,355	3,683
Singhbhum ...	145,047	56,805	5,166	3,829?	19,982?	2,7[illegible]	110,019	56,354	2,656	3,515	18,395	2,749
Feudatory States	**1,084,972**	**363,524**	**79,073**	**108,847**	**109,331**	**26,927**	**1,030,408**	**348,819**	**53,397**	**102,867**	**90,173**	**26,005**
Orissa States	1,040,019?	[illegible]1,672	77,771?	101,37[illegible]	100,857?	23,25[illegible]	998,838?	317,709	52,751	100,463	82,790	22,374
Chota Nagpur States	44,953?	31,852?	1,302?	7,470?	[illegible],474	3,372?	41,515?	31,020	646	2,404	7,383	3,631
Cities	**35,122**	**2,749**	**632**	**48**	**2,565**	**88**	**24,082**	**2,583**	**628**	**46**	**2,371**	**84**
Patna City .	[illegible],097	1,402	44	5	1,[illegible]44	2	7,750	1,447	144	5	1,136	2
Gaya City ..	11,485	706	437	9	506	3	11,217	644	435	9	451	...
Bhagalpur City ..	3,995?	333	37	11	509	8	3,760	309	35	11	462	7
Jamshedpur City ...	1,696	215	24	23	407	75	1,325	183	24	21	293	75

DISTRICT, STATE OR CITY.	Group 1.—Non-cultivating proprietors taking rent in money or kind. Earners (principal occupation). Males.	Females.	Working dependants. Males.	Females.	Earners (subsidiary occupation). Males.	Females.	Group 4.—Rent collectors, clerks, etc. Earners (principal occupation). Males.	Females.	Working dependants. Males.	Females.	Earners (subsidiary occupation). Males.	Females.
1	35	36	37	38	39	40	41	42	43	44	45	46
BIHAR AND ORISSA	**98,060**	**19,270**	**1,151**	**1,485**	**50,118**	**2,310**	**19,585**	**668**	**246**	**3**	**10,201**	**104**
British Territory ..	**89,788**	**16,552**	**1,140**	**1,458**	**47,933**	**2,147**	**18,133**	**667**	**241**	**3**	**9,560**	**103**
PATNA DIVISION ..	**27,942**	**5,731**	**281**	**194**	**10,214**	**564**	**6,451**	**304**	**51**	**1**	**1,813**	**51**
Patna ...	10,889	1,507	182	60	4,146	249	3,069?	163	...	...	671	28
Gaya ...	8,577	1,751?	143	41	2,954	108	3,095	236	51	1	646	17
Shahabad ...	8,376	2,843?	6	203?	3,814?	207	1,287	5	.	...	507	6
TIRHUT DIVISION ..	**23,660**	**2,725**	**177**	**112**	**14,901**	**522**	**3,895**	**141**	**18**	**...**	**3,965**	**26**
Saran ...	5,572	484	45	107	3,040?	145	630?	96	5	...	842	13
Champaran ...	1,297	133?	8	8	772	28	404	..	..	...	730	6
Muzaffarpur ...	9,939	1,468		2	7,102	279	2,054	45	11	...	1,5[illegible]	7
Darbhanga ...	6,852	650?	124	..	3,097	73	807	.	2	..	570	..
BHAGALPUR DIVISION ..	**19,279**	**3,127**	**290**	**687**	**3,349**	**141**	**1,369**	**63**	**..**	**...**	**458**	**7**
Monghyr ...	5,190	2,571	107	624	1,952	99?	380	62	.	...	79	7
Bhagalpur ...	2,776	345	27	60	668?	15	250	..	..		112	.
Purnea ...	2,607	178	26	3	564	21	540	1	...	..	119	...
Santal Parganas ...	8,607?	32	50	...	167	6	199	...	...	...	148	...
ORISSA DIVISION ...	**11,645**	**3,513**	**91**	**38**	**10,142**	**504**	**5,227**	**18**	**170**	**2**	**2,714**	**4**
Cuttack ...	6,654	1,513	28	4	5,169	227	2,388	1	6	...	1,141	...
Balasore ...	1,888	460	11	4	1,841	83?	720	2	5	1	746	4
Angul ...	977?	652	1		651?	74	...	...	.	..	311?	...
Puri ...	2,297	568	43	19	1,553?	54	1,883	...	156	.	444	...
Sambalpur ...	339	297	9	11	862	66	236	15	...	1	73	...
CHOTA NAGPUR DIVISION	**7,262**	**1,456**	**301**	**427**	**9,327**	**416**	**1,191**	**51**	**2**	**...**	**610**	**15**
Hazaribagh ...	1,891	280	27	12	1,054	47	402	18	..	.	236?	9
Ranchi ...	1,831?	654	148	384?	1,669?	60	96	7	..	...	14	3
Palamau ...	1,312	133	47	[illegible]	2,835?	197	459	26	1?	...	135?	2
Manbhum ...	1,900	345	77	27	3,445	168	128	1	..	...	75	.
Singhbhum ...	383	45	2	3	291	14	106	5	1	...	130?	1
Feudatory States	**8,272**	**2,718**	**11**	**27**	**2,185**	**163**	**1,452**	**1**	**5**	**..**	**641**	**1**
Orissa States	8,004	2,672	3	17	2,141?	163	1,452	1	5	..	641	1
Chota Nagpur States	268	46?	8	10	44		.	..	...	...	...	..
Cities	**3,587**	**379**	**212**	**13**	**660**	**1**	**73**	**17**	**...**	**..**	**4**	**...**
Patna City .	1,767	264	103	1	454?	..	20	...	...	...	1	...
Gaya City ..	1,227	64	106	3	55	.	45	16	..	...	3	...
Bhagalpur City ..	384	47	3	9	65	1	1	.	...	...	...	...
Jamshedpur City ...	180	4	...	...	36	.	7	1	...	...	...	...

TABLE X—*continued.*

Occupation or Means of Livelihood. Part II—Details for Districts and Cities.

District, State or City.	*Sub-order 1(a)—Ordinary cultivation—concluded.* Group 5.—Cultivating owners. Earners (principal occupation). Males.	Females.	Working dependants. Males.	Females.	Earners (subsidiary occupation). Males.	Females.	Group 6.—Tenant cultivators. Earners (principal occupation). Males.	Females.	Working dependants. Males.	Females.	Earners (subsidiary occupation). Males.	Females.	Group 7.—Agricultural labourers. Earners (principal occupation). Males.	Females.	Working dependants. Males.	Females.	Earners (subsidiary occupation). Males.	Females.	*Sub-order 1(b)—Cultivation of special crops, fruit, etc.* Total of Sub-order 1 (b). Earners (principal occupation). Males.	Females.	Working dependants. Males.	Females.	Earners (subsidiary occupation). Males.	Females.
1	47	48	49	50	51	52	53	54	55	56	57	58	59	60	61	62	63	64	65	66	67	68	69	70
BIHAR AND ORISSA	**325,144**	**43,031**	**4,648**	**2,303**	**28,072**	**1,368**	**6,806,034**	**1,868,835**	**69,221**	**98,339**	**238,317**	**43,927**	**2,090,349**	**1,593,155**	**122,440**	**165,019**	**262,096**	**84,340**	**9,658**	**3,972**	**580**	**119**	**6,446**	**334**
British Territory ...	**291,002**	**39,471**	**4,224**	**2,207**	**26,326**	**1,277**	**6,129,665**	**1,778,433**	**65,241**	**94,507**	**205,174**	**31,570**	**1,780,344**	**1,341,067**	**73,463**	**66,107**	**209,576**	**70,947**	**9,095**	**3,746**	**577**	**118**	**6,437**	**333**
Patna Division ...	**17,246**	**2,467**	**72**	**24**	**2,057**	**53**	**960,743**	**278,383**	**2,168**	**2,918**	**44,630**	**7,465**	**272,771**	**281,196**	**200**	**472**	**17,416**	**7,289**	**3,031**	**1,561**	**6**	**1**	**175**	**58**
Patna	2,567	333	...	9	498	2	285,137	81,516	415	383	12,513	1,247	61,445	53,095	10	42	4,441	1,277	956	359	..	...	47	11
Gaya	3,039	700	64	1	451	3	369,658	111,740	1,666	2,268	18,964	4,316	93,053	90,909	188	242	4,773	2,986	1,089	494	6	1	78	22
Shahabad	11,642	1,434	8	14	1,108	48	315,948	85,127	87	267	13,153	1,902	118,273	137,192	7	188	8,242	3,026	986	708	..	...	50	25
Tirhut Division ...	**90,517**	**19,431**	**153**	**79**	**9,589**	**603**	**2,021,615**	**591,126**	**3,934**	**6,796**	**56,691**	**5,511**	**577,356**	**348,703**	**5,342**	**8,753**	**86,785**	**33,354**	**1,367**	**532**	**40**	**37**	**853**	**111**
Saran ...	13,969	1,556	38	41	2,096	78	572,103	235,453	695	2,553	9,503	1,729	45,384	58,406	1,002	2,106	17,880	11,322	309	239	...	25	188	52
Champaran ...	25,460	6,849	13	...	524	57	452,977	157,942	2,528	4,179	4,659	509	125,465	95,385	1,552	3,000	36,136	13,336	103	15	...	...	80	12
Muzaffarpur ...	27,840	3,604	...	37	4,549	302	485,486	102,952	17	32	22,227	1,800	231,050	122,922	877	1,101	38,006	6,308	642	124	3	3	346	36
Darbhanga ...	24,238	7,422	102	1	3,420	165	511,049	94,779	694	33	19,302	1,413	175,457	71,958	2,051	2,546	15,233	2,313	323	154	37	9	239	11
Bhagalpur Division ...	**40,240**	**6,554**	**651**	**496**	**2,466**	**126**	**1,499,524**	**565,876**	**9,370**	**15,687**	**17,538**	**10,891**	**485,807**	**340,017**	**3,302**	**2,812**	**23,839**	**16,846**	**1,253**	**995**	**4**	**20**	**329**	**29**
Monghyr ...	12,620	3,659	318	103	852	34	357,079	192,551	3,086	7,750	8,225	1,775	77,376	57,508	317	543	714	1,737	572	568	3	20	20	7
Bhagalpur	7,814	1,935	308	375	511	77	331,580	62,599	3,399	4,464	4,479	671	161,330	136,289	1,226	1,587	6,126	2,384	324	307	1	...	75	20
Purnea	19,645	930	24	18	1,057	21	303,632	15,115	316	199	2,347	89	205,807	89,760	1,565	244	2,471	594	268	93	...	...	183	...
Santal Parganas ...	161	30	1	2	40	4	506,633	330,613	2,369	3,274	2,487	8,356	41,304	56,350	190	439	14,528	12,181	89	37	...	...	51	2
Orissa Division ...	**87,970**	**4,611**	**2,402**	**393**	**7,827**	**153**	**767,185**	**72,288**	**7,876**	**5,611**	**44,386**	**1,989**	**254,192**	**123,814**	**43,672**	**24,389**	**55,622**	**5,308**	**2,644**	**515**	**486**	**55**	**4,676**	**73**
Cuttack	18,111	942	37	8	3,224	60	312,326	15,779	280	58	17,820	632	107,878	38,155	1,181	841	20,019	1,360	899	270	5	27	2,171	18
Balasore	7,598	920	17	3	527	24	198,820	35,645	2,218	195	6,725	137	27,038	4,982	10,344	333	15,436	325	912	101	295	16	2,058	16
Angul ...	594	345	2	...	93	5	44,061	2,229	62	7	2,968	68	8,877	37,743	14	19	1,513	766	29	14	5	...	14	1
Puri	55,171	1,687	1,135	155	4,601	56	100,244	8,760	1,673	157	9,724	131	43,371	10,180	6,252	2,778	15,448	908	710	42	177	0	382	38
Sambalpur	6,496	717	1,121	227	482	8	111,714	9,850	3,743	5,194	7,149	1,121	67,038	43,754	26,681	20,428	2,308	2,054	94	88	6	8	51	...
Chota Nagpur Division	**55,627**	**6,408**	**946**	**1,215**	**4,387**	**342**	**880,596**	**270,768**	**41,893**	**63,495**	**41,929**	**5,714**	**190,218**	**247,337**	**20,946**	**29,681**	**25,674**	**8,150**	**800**	**143**	**39**	**5**	**404**	**62**
Hazaribagh ...	3,382	721	43	47	388	59	278,977	116,337	1,164	1,686	4,104	1,495	30,572	50,005	37	69	3,680	2,317	79	25	...	...	98	35
Ranchi ...	18,236	1,940	626	859	488	34	152,942	94,045	36,829	58,919	11,125	1,990	10,376	13,646	10,194	18,778	1,909	452	170	97	35	5	158	25
Palamau	5,106	568	12	6	617	26	109,733	19,180	826	115	2,797	206	63,542	92,667	7,938	7,246	3,379	1,378	59	...	...	...	6	...
Manbhum	25,961	2,880	559	214	3,094	214	226,655	36,555	3,849	2,328	11,568	1,032	62,839	40,757	865	587	11,573	2,209	219	2	...	...	36	1
Singhbhum ...	2,360	399	6	59	200	9	114,291	14,743	725	447	12,335	991	22,889	41,262	1,932	3,006	5,423	1,734	273	19	4	...	106	1
Feudatory States ...	**34,142**	**3,560**	**424**	**96**	**1,746**	**91**	**676,369**	**90,402**	**3,980**	**3,832**	**33,148**	**12,357**	**310,065**	**252,098**	**48,977**	**98,912**	**52,450**	**13,393**	**563**	**226**	**3**	**1**	**9**	**1**
Orissa States ...	33,769	3,528	423	96	1,723	89	640,333	70,120	3,766	3,436	32,255	11,888	305,139	241,428	48,554	96,914	46,023	10,233	563	226	3	1	9	1
Chota Nagpur States ...	373	32	1	...	23	2	36,037	20,282	214	396	888	469	4,866	10,660	422	1,998	6,427	3,160	...	...	...	...	...	...
Cities	**260**	**35**	**55**	...	**58**	..	**15,287**	**1,495**	**247**	**30**	**1,388**	**34**	**4,367**	**657**	**114**	**3**	**250**	**49**	**415**	**69**	...	...	**105**	**1**
Patna City	41	23	...	...	22	...	5,668	968	40	3	609	2	263	192	1	1	20	...	118	38	...	...	...	...
Gaya City	156	...	55	...	36	...	6,023	288	165	6	194	...	3,761	276	96	...	192	...	71	20	...	...	5	...
Bhagalpur City ...	63	12	...	...	...	...	2,762	153	19	...	377	6	548	97	15	2	...	...	12	...	...	...	...	1
Jamshedpur City ...	...	...	...	...	...	...	834	86	23	31	208	26	295	92	1	...	48	49	214	11	...	...	100	...

TABLE X—*continued.*

OCCUPATION OR MEANS OF LIVELIHOOD. PART II—DETAILS FOR DISTRICTS AND CITIES.

DISTRICT, STATE OR CITY.	*Sub-order 1(b)—Cultivation of special crops, fruit, etc.—concluded.* Group 16.—Market gardeners, flower and fruit growers. *Earners (principal occupation).* Males.	Females.	*Working dependants.* Males.	Females.	*Earners (subsidiary occupation).* Males.	Females.	*Sub-order 1(c)—Forestry.* *Earners (principal occupation).* Males.	Females.	*Working dependants.* Males.	Females.	*Earners (subsidiary occupation).* Males.	Females.
1	71	72	73	74	75	76	77	78	79	80	81	82
BIHAR AND ORISSA	**8,187**	**3,671**	**392**	**107**	**4,901**	**252**	**6,841**	**3,661**	**151**	**795**	**4,039**	**1,456**
British Territory ...	**7,640**	**3,446**	**390**	**106**	**4,897**	**251**	**4,756**	**2,803**	**124**	**442**	**3,226**	**1,016**
PATNA DIVISION ...	**3,031**	**1,561**	**6**	**1**	**175**	**58**	**33**	**197**	...	...	**8**	**4**
Patna ...	956	360	...	...	47	11	15	21	...	...	8	1
Gaya ...	1,089	494	6	1	78	23	2	57	...	...	...	3
Shahabad ...	986	708	..	...	50	25	16	119	...	...	...	...
TIRHUT DIVISION ...	**867**	**490**	**36**	**36**	**576**	**96**	**721**	**202**	**5**	...	**196**	**1**
Saran ...	200	207	...	24	145	43	58	33	...	...	32	...
Champaran ...	39	10	...	...	68	12	253	65	...	...	70	...
Muzaffarpur ...	377	119	1	3	217	20	288	13	4	...	77	1
Darbhanga ...	251	154	35	9	146	11	122	91	1	...	8	...
BHAGALPUR DIVISION ...	**1,158**	**907**	**4**	**20**	**301**	**29**	**1,534**	**833**	**15**	**20**	**1,016**	**740**
Monghyr ...	571	568	3	20	20	7	844	313	6	20	196	139
Bhagalpur ...	324	307	1	...	75	20	253	336	1	...	81	8
Purnea ...	179	5	...	...	155	...	350	74	8	...	49	2
Santal Parganas ...	84	27	...	...	51	2	87	110	...	...	690	591
ORISSA DIVISION ...	**1,846**	**414**	**307**	**46**	**3,494**	**32**	**1,127**	**1,069**	**58**	**263**	**1,038**	**161**
Cuttack ...	892	266	4	27	1,306	16	349	795	58	254	537	103
Balasore ...	905	101	294	16	2,058	16	28	...	...	...	11	...
Angul ...	7	...	5	...	5	...	303	107	...	1	230	19
Puri ...	19	1	1	...	4	...	271	167	...	8	213	39
Sambalpur ...	23	46	3	3	31	...	176	...	...	...	47	...
CHOTA NAGPUR DIVISION	**738**	**74**	**37**	**3**	**351**	**37**	**1,341**	**502**	**46**	**159**	**968**	**110**
Hazaribagh ...	78	19	...	...	98	34	354	171	2	...	164	13
Ranchi ...	116	34	33	3	105	1	92	37	5	6	16	6
Palamau ...	54	...	...	...	6	...	321	82	4	33	216	8
Manbhum ...	219	2	...	...	36	1	227	108	35	118	373	75
Singhbhum ...	271	19	4	...	106	1	347	14	...	2	199	9
Feudatory States ...	**547**	**225**	**2**	**1**	**4**	**1**	**2,085**	**858**	**27**	**353**	**813**	**440**
Orissa States ...	547	225	2	1	4	1	2,044	858	25	353	784	440
Chota Nagpur States ...	...	...	...	...	...	...	41	...	2	...	29	...
Cities ...	**415**	**68**	...	...	**105**	**1**	**166**	**46**	...	**2**	**48**	**3**
Patna City ...	118	38	...	...	...	...	14	5	...	...	8	...
Gaya City ...	71	20	...	...	5	...	...	30	...	...	...	3
Bhagalpur City ...	12	...	...	...	...	1	52	1	...	...	26	...
Jamshedpur City ...	214	11	...	...	100	...	100	10	...	2	14	...

DISTRICT, STATE OR CITY.	*Sub-order 1(d)—Stock raising.* TOTAL OF SUB-ORDER 1(d). *Earners (principal occupation).* Males.	Females.	*Working dependants.* Males.	Females.	*Earners (subsidiary occupation).* Males.	Females.	Group 21.—Cattle and buffalo breeders and keepers. *Earners (principal occupation).* Males.	Females.	*Working dependants.* Males.	Females.	*Earners (subsidiary occupation).* Males.	Females.
1	83	84	85	86	87	88	89	90	91	92	93	94
BIHAR AND ORISSA	**181,064**	**31,642**	**60,546**	**11,065**	**29,420**	**2,103**	**47,166**	**18,397**	**11,127**	**4,400**	**11,038**	**907**
British Territory ...	**129,451**	**18,218**	**34,915**	**5,495**	**23,640**	**1,892**	**43,523**	**8,069**	**8,529**	**2,878**	**10,433**	**877**
PATNA DIVISION ...	**12,471**	**3,360**	**26**	**20**	**1,178**	**245**	**4,088**	**1,102**	**14**	**3**	**639**	**167**
Patna ...	1,282	373	13	3	197	85	389	146	12	3	147	72
Gaya ...	6,077	1,525	13	11	399	39	1,443	284	2	...	131	15
Shahabad ...	5,112	1,462	...	6	682	121	2,256	672	...	...	361	80
TIRHUT DIVISION ...	**8,961**	**1,955**	**816**	**554**	**2,777**	**328**	**7,879**	**1,907**	**760**	**508**	**2,165**	**290**
Saran ...	500	101	17	10	577	106	378	83	10	6	328	82
Champaran ...	2,565	111	5	...	414	48	2,435	111	5	...	335	48
Muzaffarpur ...	3,413	1,494	700	448	1,352	163	3,222	1,478	700	445	1,201	150
Darbhanga ...	2,483	240	94	96	434	11	1,844	235	45	57	291	10
BHAGALPUR DIVISION ...	**35,123**	**1,842**	**8,461**	**2,475**	**7,003**	**664**	**12,958**	**656**	**5,604**	**2,032**	**4,090**	**286**
Monghyr ...	2,790	182	31	14	182	13	1,966	65	21	12	107	3
Bhagalpur ...	5,049	80	41	1	455	9	1,476	29	22	...	134	8
Purnea ...	19,354	213	144	2	235	1	4,972	91	5	...	119	...
Santal Parganas ...	7,930	1,307	8,245	2,458	6,131	641	4,539	471	5,556	2,020	3,730	275
ORISSA DIVISION ...	**42,568**	**8,638**	**8,643**	**947**	**7,312**	**270**	**18,495**	**4,340**	**2,134**	**331**	**3,494**	**127**
Cuttack ...	19,306	4,313	1,970	257	3,633	91	10,046	3,137	479	69	1,270	32
Balasore ...	4,076	1,726	1,179	174	789	43	1,946	279	182	100	544	17
Angul ...	3,807	775	1,191	80	434	5	80	37	2	23	22	1
Puri ...	8,725	954	2,211	266	2,069	111	3,700	340	302	82	744	65
Sambalpur ...	6,564	870	2,092	170	1,307	20	2,633	547	669	57	914	12
CHOTA NAGPUR DIVISION	**30,328**	**2,423**	**16,969**	**1,499**	**5,370**	**385**	**108**	**64**	**17**	**4**	**55**	**7**
Hazaribagh ...	3,059	373	58	8	1,070	33	18	5	...	...	6	3
Ranchi ...	3,026	596	2,842	560	1,078	223	16	3	...	...	5	...
Palamau ...	6,638	519	930	137	1,303	58	62	51	1	3	30	4
Manbhum ...	13,199	521	10,633	462	1,430	48	2	...	10	...	2	...
Singhbhum ...	4,406	414	2,506	312	529	23	10	5	6	1	13	...
Feudatory States ...	**51,613**	**13,424**	**25,631**	**5,570**	**5,780**	**211**	**3,643**	**10,328**	**2,598**	**1,522**	**605**	**30**
Orissa States ...	48,257	12,593	24,777	5,503	5,514	196	3,607	10,295	2,537	1,514	591	29
Chota Nagpur States ...	3,356	831	854	67	266	15	36	33	61	8	14	1
Cities ...	**459**	**51**	**4**	...	**41**	...	**288**	**16**	**4**	...	**39**	...
Patna City ...	55	2	...	...	...	...	33	2	...	...	...	...
Gaya City ...	177	18	2	...	19	...	162	...	2	...	18	...
Bhagalpur City ...	171	23	2	...	21	...	93	14	2	...	21	...
Jamshedpur City ...	50	14	...	...	1	...	...	...	...	...	...	...

TABLE X—*continued.*

OCCUPATION OR MEANS OF LIVELIHOOD.

PART II—DETAILS FOR DISTRICTS AND CITIES.

Sub-order 1(d)—Stock raising—concluded.

Group 26.—Herdsmen, shepherds and breeders of other animals.

District, State or City.	Earners (principal occupation). Males.	Earners (principal occupation). Females.	Working dependants. Males.	Working dependants. Females.	Earners (subsidiary occupation). Males.	Earners (subsidiary occupation). Females.
1	95	96	97	98	99	100
BIHAR AND ORISSA	**133,834**	**13,245**	**49,419**	**6,665**	**18,323**	**1,196**
British Territory ..	**85,865**	**10,149**	**26,386**	**2,617**	**13,149**	**1,015**
PATNA DIVISION ...	**8,365**	**2,258**	**12**	**17**	**539**	**78**
Patna	893	227	1	..	60	13
Gaya	4,616	1,241	11	11	188	24
Shahabad	2,856	790	.	6	321	41
TIRHUT DIVISION ...	**1,066**	**48**	**56**	**46**	**591**	**38**
Saran	118	18	7	4	240	24
Champaran... ..	120	...			77	...
Muzaffarpur ..	191	16	..	3	123	13
Darbhanga .	637	14	49	30	143	1
BHAGALPUR DIVISION ..	**22,164**	**1,186**	**2,857**	**443**	**2,913**	**378**
Monghyr	823	117	10	3	76	10
Bhagalpur ..	3,569	61	19	1	331	1
Purnea .	14,382	173	139	2	116	1
Santal Parganas	3,390	836	2,689	438	2,401	366
ORISSA DIVISION ...	**24,052**	**4,298**	**6,569**	**616**	**3,792**	**143**
Cuttack	9,341	1,178	1,491	188	1,337	59
Balasore	2,130	1,447	497	74	245	23
Angul	3,817	738	1,189	57	412	4
Puri	1,933	614	1,406	184	1,315	46
Sambalpur	3,931	323	1,423	113	453	8
CHOTA NAGPUR DIVISION	**30,218**	**2,359**	**16,952**	**1,495**	**5,314**	**378**
Hazaribagh.. ...	3,041	368	58	5	1,064	30
Ranchi	3,010	508	4,949	560	1,072	323
Palamau	6,374	458	920	134	1,338	54
Manbhum .. .	13,197	581	10,833	182	1,428	45
Singhbhum ...	4,396	409	9,500	211	577	23
Feudatory States ...	**47,969**	**3,096**	**23,033**	**4,048**	**5,174**	**181**
Orissa States	44,650	2,298	22,240	3,989	4,923	167
Chota Nagpur States..	3,319	798	793	59	251	14
Cities	**171**	**35**	...	...	**2**	.
Patna City	22	...	..	...	...	...
Gaya City	15	12		..	1	...
Bhagalpur City ...	78	9	...	..	...	...
Jamshedpur City ...	56	14	...	...	1	..

Sub-order 1(e)—Raising of small animals and insects.

District, State or City.	Total of Sub-order 1(e). Earners (principal occupation). Males.	Females.	Working dependants. Males.	Females.	Earners (subsidiary occupation). Males.	Females.	Group 28.—Lac cultivation. Earners (principal occupation). Males.	Females.	Working dependants. Males.	Females.	Earners (subsidiary occupation). Males.	Females.
1	101	102	103	104	105	106	107	108	109	110	111	112
BIHAR AND ORISSA	**946**	**338**	**29**	**65**	**14,488**	**354**	**911**	**224**	**25**	**10**	**14,028**	**271**
British Territory ..	**643**	**141**	**14**	**9**	**1,832**	**84**	**617**	**128**	**14**	**8**	**1,886**	**76**
PATNA DIVISION ...	...	...	...	...	..	...	...	..	...	..	...	..
Patna	...	..	...	...	...	...	...	..	...	.		...
Gaya	...	..	...	..	..	...	...	...	...	..	.	...
Shahabad	...	...	...	...	...	...	...	..	..	...	...	...
TIRHUT DIVISION ...		**2**	...	...	**4**	**1**	.	..	...	...	**4**	..
Saran	-			...	...	...	...	...	...	...	...	...
Champaran... ..		...	..	...	...	...	...	..	..	...	...	...
Muzaffarpur ..	..	..	...	...	...	...	...	..	...	...	...	...
Darbhanga .	..	2	..		4	1	..	...	...	...	4	...
BHAGALPUR DIVISION ..	**8**	...	...	...	**5**	...	...	...	...	...	...	...
Monghyr	...	..	...	..	...	...	..	..	...	...	..	...
Bhagalpur ..	8	..	...	.	5	...	..	...	...	...	.	...
Purnea .	..	...	...	...	.	...	...	...	..	..	...	...
Santal Parganas			...	...	..	...	...	..	.	..	...	...
ORISSA DIVISION ...	**18**	**1**		**1**	**35**	**10**	**3**	..	...	.	**1**	**3**
Cuttack	14	1	...	...	13	...	..	..	...	...	..	...
Balasore	...	...	...	.	3	...	...	.	...	...	...	...
Angul	1	...	...	...	1	...	.	..	..	.	1	...
Puri	...	...	..	1	1	7	...		.	...	...	..
Sambalpur	3	..		...	17	3	3	...	...	..		3
CHOTA NAGPUR DIVISION	**617**	**138**	**14**	**8**	**1,888**	**73**	**614**	**128**	**14**	**8**	**1,881**	**73**
Hazaribagh.. ...	46	9	...	...	33	2	45	3	...		26	2
Ranchi	305	96	14	6	1,378	51	305	91	14	6	1,378	51
Palamau	45	12	...	2	70	3	45	12	...	2	70	3
Manbhum .. .	210	17		.	404	17	219	17	..	..	404	17
Singhbhum ...	2	4	...	...	8		...	..	..	...	1	..
Feudatory States ...	**303**	**197**	**15**	**56**	**12,556**	**270**	**294**	**96**	**11**	**2**	**12,142**	**195**
Orissa States	292	196	15	55	11,760	235	289	96	11	3	11,662	177
Chota Nagpur States..	11	1	...	1	796	35	5	..	..	..	480	18
Cities	...	...	...	...	...	...	...	...	...	...	...	...
Patna City	...	..	..	...	...	...	...	...	...	...	...	...
Gaya City	..	...	...	...	...	...		...	...	...	..	...
Bhagalpur City ...	...	...	...	...	...	...	...	...	..	...	...	...
Jamshedpur City ...	...	...	...	...	...	...	...	..	...	...	...	...

ORDER 2.—FISHING AND HUNTING.

District, State or City.	Total of Order 2. Earners (principal occupation). Males.	Females.	Working dependants. Males.	Females.	Earners (subsidiary occupation). Males.	Females.
1	113	114	115	116	117	118
BIHAR AND ORISSA	**48,535**	**10,265**	**949**	**660**	**31,259**	**1,769**
British Territory ..	**43,329**	**9,254**	**864**	**489**	**27,654**	**1,608**
PATNA DIVISION ...	**1,350**	**668**	**5**	...	**332**	**62**
Patna	165	42		...	31	..
Gaya	152	225	5	...	27	25
Shahabad	1,033	461		..	274	37
TIRHUT DIVISION ...	**10,367**	**4,628**	**102**	**104**	**10,794**	**1,049**
Saran	739	398	8	7	685	204
Champaran... ..	1,403	364	34	...	2,407	213
Muzaffarpur ..	3,630	2,222	17	57	4,389	269
Darbhanga .	4,595	1,644	43	40	3,313	364
BHAGALPUR DIVISION ..	**10,700**	**1,608**	**39**	**18**	**2,073**	**200**
Monghyr	1,110	539	22	...	159	4
Bhagalpur ..	2,079	583	9	12	1,061	48
Purnea .	6,779	165	2	..	374	13
Santal Parganas	832	331	6	6	479	136
ORISSA DIVISION ...	**17,610**	**1,695**	**529**	**150**	**12,681**	**230**
Cuttack	5,261	157	53	19	5,088	20
Balasore	3,969	506	241	41	4,658	45
Angul	81	31	1	.	67	...
Puri	6,236	293	179	13	1,171	20
Sambalpur	2,063	708	55	77	1,502	145
CHOTA NAGPUR DIVISION	**3,302**	**655**	**189**	**217**	**1,774**	**67**
Hazaribagh.. ...	293	66		.	313	17
Ranchi	770	97	51	105	298	18
Palamau	109	22	.		70	2
Manbhum .. .	1,577	370	113	64	679	28
Singhbhum ...	553	100	36	45	164	2
Feudatory States ...	**5,206**	**1,011**	**85**	**171**	**3,605**	**161**
Orissa States	5,020	977	84	168	3,471	144
Chota Nagpur States..	186	34	1	3	134	17
Cities	**171**	**49**	**5**	**5**	**7**	**1**
Patna City	19	13	...	...	3	..
Gaya City	...	10	...	...	...	...
Bhagalpur City ...	122	13	...	...	3	...
Jamshedpur City ...	30	14	5	5	1	1

TABLE X—*continued.*

OCCUPATION OR MEANS OF LIVELIHOOD. PART II—DETAILS FOR DISTRICTS AND CITIES.

DISTRICT, STATE OR CITY.	ORDER 2.—FISHING AND HUNTING—*concluded.*						*SUB-CLASS II.—EXPLOITATION OF MINERALS.*						ORDER 3.—METALLIC MINERALS.											
	Group 27.—Fishing and Pearling.												TOTAL OF ORDER 3.						Group 30.—Iron.					
	Earners (principal occupation).		*Working dependants.*		*Earners (subsidiary occupation).*		*Earners (principal occupation).*		*Working dependants.*		*Earners (subsidiary occupation).*		*Earners (principal occupation).*		*Working dependants.*		*Earners (subsidiary occupation).*		*Earners (principal occupation).*		*Working dependants.*		*Earners (subsidiary occupation).*	
	Males.	Females.	Males.	Females.	Males.	Females.	Males.	Females.	Males.	Females.	Males.	Females.	Males.	Females.	Males.	Females	Males.	Females.	Males.	Females.	Males.	Females.	Males.	Females.
1	119	120	121	122	123	124	125	126	127	128	129	130	131	132	133	134	135	136	137	138	139	140	141	142
BIHAR AND ORISSA	**47,251**	**10,110**	**944**	**660**	**30,377**	**1,720**	**87,243**	**31,388**	**647**	**336**	**29,869**	**7,398**	**4,908**	**4,319**	**324**	**85**	**2,478**	**873**	**3,819**	**3,803**	**16**	**12**	**2,128**	**803**
British Territory ...	**42,108**	**9,100**	**859**	**489**	**26,856**	**1,559**	**79,910**	**25,790**	**482**	**238**	**27,072**	**6,350**	**836**	**289**	**218**	**36**	**311**	**43**	**108**	**38**	**10**	...	**5**	**11**
PATNA DIVISION ...	**1,000**	**599**	**5**	...	**257**	**41**	**70**	**223**	..	...	**5**	**3**	**2**	...	...	...	...	...	...	...	...	...	...	...
Patna ...	108	37	...	...	31	...	9	213	...	...	...	...	2	...	...	...	...	...	...	...	...	...	...	...
Gaya	110	214	5	...	27	4	16	...	..	..	...	...	...	...	...	...	...	...	...	...	...	...	...	...
Shahabad	782	348	...	...	190	37	45	10	..	...	5	3	...	...	...	...	...	...	...	...	...	...	...	...
TIRHUT DIVISION ...	**10,096**	**4,600**	**100**	**104**	**10,632**	**1,045**	**2,832**	**2,394**	**13**	**29**	**4,473**	**1,448**	**132**	**28**	**1**	...	**190**	**22**	**1**	...	**1**	...	**1**	...
Saran	662	370	8	7	641	303	404	287	3	10	675	403	...	...	...	...	...	...	...	...	...	...	...	...
Champaran ...	1,358	364	34	...	2,378	210	246	251	3	1	436	190	...	18	...	...	...	22	...	...	...	...	...	...
Muzaffarpur ...	3,536	2,232	17	57	4,290	368	1,702	1,742	2	14	3,241	847	131	...	..	...	172	...	...	...	...	...	...	...
Darbhanga ...	4,538	1,644	41	40	3,313	364	300	114	5	4	121	8	1	10	1	...	18	...	1	...	1	...	1	...
BHAGALPUR DIVISION ...	**10,360**	**1,590**	**37**	**18**	**1,870**	**193**	**335**	**190**	**1**	...	**536**	**101**	...	...	...	...	...	...	...	...	...	...	...	...
Monghyr	1,731	512	23	...	132	4	16	57	.	...	5	..	...	...	...	...	..	...	...	...	...	...	...	...
Bhagalpur	1,075	582	9	12	931	44	40	19	1	...	27	...	...	...	..	...	.	...	...	...	...	...	...	...
Purnea	5,723	165	...	...	329	9	25	36		...	1	.	...	...	...	...	...	...	...	...	...	...	...	...
Santal Parganas ...	931	331	6	6	478	136	245	76	..	...	505	101	...	...	...	...	..	...	...	...	...	...	...	...
ORISSA DIVISION ...	**17,540**	**1,694**	**529**	**150**	**12,660**	**229**	**257**	**109**	**1**	..	**45**	...	**3**	**19**	...	...	**5**	...	...	..	...	...	...	...
Cuttack	6,237	156	58	19	5,073	19	3	...	..	...	...	...	...	...	...	...	...	...	..	...	...	...	...	...
Balasore	3,962	506	241	41	4,858	45	1	.	...	..	...	...	...	...	...	...	...	...	...	...	...	...	...	...
Angul	81	31	1	...	67	...	1	..	1	...	12	...	...	...	...	...	...	...	...	...	...	...	...	...
Puri	6,216	298	179	13	1,167	20	3	1	...	...	3	...	3	...	..	...	...	...	...	...	...	...	...	...
Sambalpur ...	2,044	708	56	77	1,495	145	249	108		...	31	...	...	19	...	...	5	...	..	...	...	...	...	...
CHOTA NAGPUR DIVISION	**3,112**	**617**	**188**	**217**	**1,447**	**51**	**76,416**	**22,874**	**467**	**209**	**22,011**	**4,798**	**699**	**242**	**217**	**36**	**116**	**21**	**107**	**38**	**9**	...	**4**	**11**
Hazaribagh ...	173	39	...	...	104	3	14,195	7,038	38	5	8,896	1,760	...	...	...	...	...	...	...	...	...	...	...	...
Ranchi	750	97	51	108	293	18	11	...	..	18	5	1	...	...	...	...	...	...	...	...	...	...	...	...
Palamau	73	22	...	..	42	..	60	...	1	...	15	...	1	...	...	...	...	...	...	...	...	...	...	...
Manbhum	1,568	369	111	64	854	28	57,910	14,128	204	152	11,953	2,201	10	77	...	7	55	9	...	...	...	...	...	...
Singhbhum ...	548	100	26	46	154	2	4,240	1,708	224	34	1,142	836	688	165	217	29	61	12	107	38	9	...	4	11
Feudatory States ...	**5,143**	**1,019**	**85**	**171**	**3,521**	**161**	**7,333**	**5,598**	**165**	**98**	**2,797**	**1,048**	**4,072**	**4,030**	**106**	**49**	**2,167**	**830**	**3,711**	**3,765**	**6**	**12**	**2,123**	**792**
Orissa States ...	4,959	976	84	168	3,390	144	7,283	5,545	165	94	2,791	1,047	4,022	3,988	106	45	2,167	830	3,674	3,765	6	12	2,123	792
Chota Nagpur States	184	34	1	3	131	17	50	53	..	4	6	1	50	42	...	4	...	...	37	...	...	...	...	...
Cities	**165**	**49**	**5**	**5**	**7**	**1**	**248**	**12**	**1**	...	..	...	...	**4**	...	...	...	...	...	**4**	...	...	...	...
Patna City	19	13	...	...	3	...	...	...	...	...	...	...	...	...	...	...	...	...	...	...	...	...	...	...
Gaya City	...	10	...	...	...	...	...	...	...	...	...	...	...	...	...	...	...	...	...	...	...	...	...	...
Bhagalpur City ...	116	13	...	...	3	...	20	7	1	...	...	...	...	...	...	...	...	...	...	...	...	...	...	...
Jamshedpur City ...	30	14	5	5	1	1	228	5	...	...	...	...	...	4	...	...	...	...	...	4	...	...	...	...

TABLE X—*continued.*

Occupation or Means of Livelihood.

Part II.—Details for Districts and Cities.

District, State or City.	Order 4.—Non-metallic minerals. Total of Order 4. Earners (principal occupation). Males.	Females.	Working dependants. Males.	Females.	Earners (subsidiary occupation). Males.	Females.	Group 35.—Coal. Earners (principal occupation). Males.	Females.	Working dependants. Males.	Females.	Earners (subsidiary occupation). Males.	Females.	Group 38.—Mica. Earners (principal occupation). Males.	Females.	Working dependants. Males.	Females.	Earners (subsidiary occupation). Males.	Females.	Class B.—Preparation and supply of material substances. Earners (principal occupation). Males.	Females.	Working dependants. Males.	Females.	Earners (subsidiary occupation). Males.	Females.
1	143	144	145	146	147	148	149	150	151	152	153	154	155	156	157	158	159	160	161	162	163	164	165	166
BIHAR AND ORISSA	**82,335**	**27,069**	**323**	**251**	**27,391**	**6,525**	**75,946**	**22,773**	**307**	**194**	**18,757**	**4,327**	**2,987**	**1,570**	**1**	**4**	**3,979**	**600**	**1,179,660**	**736,171**	**16,128**	**71,507**	**549,327**	**100,248**
British Territory ...	**79,074**	**25,501**	**284**	**202**	**26,761**	**6,307**	**73,194**	**21,445**	**250**	**168**	**18,465**	**4,278**	**2,987**	**1,570**	**1**	**4**	**3,979**	**600**	**1,056,897**	**593,541**	**12,746**	**46,519**	**479,889**	**83,397**
Patna Division ...	**68**	**223**	...	...	**5**	**3**	**17**	**209**	...	...	...	...	...	...	...	...	...	...	**280,849**	**131,921**	**600**	**401**	**29,305**	**8,467**
Patna	7	213	...	...	...	...	...	209	...	...	...	...	...	...	...	...	...	...	90,102	34,795	70	60	7,977	2,460
Gaya	16	...	...	...	...	...	13	...	...	...	...	...	...	...	...	...	...	...	91,555	44,420	520	331	8,208	2,488
Shahabad	45	10	...	...	5	3	4	...	...	...	...	...	...	...	...	...	...	...	99,192	52,706	10	10	13,120	3,519
Tirhut Division ...	**2,700**	**2,366**	**12**	**29**	**4,283**	**1,426**	**7**	**2**	...	...	**2**	...	...	...	...	...	...	...	**172,215**	**88,561**	**1,838**	**2,627**	**133,562**	**23,474**
Saran	494	287	3	10	675	403	...	...	...	...	1	...	...	...	...	...	...	...	40,533	24,866	452	569	36,362	10,550
Champaran ...	246	233	3	1	436	168	...	...	...	...	...	...	...	...	...	...	...	...	25,293	11,699	71	154	27,810	4,360
Muzaffarpur ...	1,661	1,742	2	14	3,060	847	7	2	...	...	1	...	...	...	...	...	...	...	51,821	29,801	104	861	38,945	5,695
Darbhanga ..	299	104	4	4	103	8	...	...	...	...	...	...	...	...	...	...	...	...	54,568	23,145	1,211	1,043	30,455	2,869
Bhagalpur Division ...	**335**	**190**	**1**	...	**538**	**101**	**232**	**87**	**1**	...	**533**	**101**	...	...	...	...	...	...	**236,009**	**105,138**	**1,152**	**2,101**	**72,115**	**21,359**
Monghyr	16	57	...	...	5	...	1	...	...	...	1	...	...	...	...	...	...	...	81,480	39,831	390	1,016	9,533	2,178
Bhagalpur	40	19	1	...	27	...	2	...	1	...	27	...	...	...	...	...	...	...	58,872	23,988	323	531	13,733	2,461
Purnea	25	38	...	...	1	...	3	11	...	...	1	...	...	...	...	...	...	...	62,234	22,136	135	308	4,743	410
Santal Parganas ...	245	76	...	...	505	101	226	76	...	...	504	101	...	...	...	...	...	...	33,423	19,193	295	246	44,116	16,310
Orissa Division ...	**254**	**90**	**1**	...	**40**	...	**252**	**90**	**1**	...	**40**	...	...	...	...	...	...	...	**184,173**	**204,847**	**4,432**	**34,427**	**158,248**	**16,018**
Cuttack	3	...	...	...	...	...	3	...	...	...	...	...	...	...	...	...	...	...	80,532	81,680	400	14,423	78,502	5,376
Balasore	1	...	...	...	...	...	1	...	...	...	...	...	...	...	...	...	...	...	16,443	31,588	1,076	3,507	38,349	2,269
Angul	1	...	1	...	12	...	1	...	1	...	12	...	...	...	...	...	...	...	6,673	8,584	22	77	3,507	533
Puri	...	1	...	...	2	...	...	1	...	...	2	...	...	...	...	...	...	...	47,271	48,964	1,956	11,532	21,354	5,060
Sambalpur ...	249	89	...	...	26	...	247	89	...	...	26	...	...	...	...	...	...	...	33,254	34,022	978	4,888	16,536	2,791
Chota Nagpur Division ...	**75,717**	**22,632**	**250**	**173**	**21,895**	**4,777**	**72,686**	**21,047**	**248**	**168**	**17,890**	**4,177**	**2,987**	**1,570**	**1**	**4**	**3,979**	**600**	**183,651**	**63,134**	**4,724**	**6,963**	**86,659**	**14,079**
Hazaribagh ...	14,195	7,038	38	5	8,896	1,760	11,298	5,438	37	1	4,917	1,160	2,987	1,570	1	4	3,979	600	28,520	10,882	201	239	22,027	2,851
Ranchi	11	...	...	18	5	1	11	...	...	18	5	1	...	...	...	...	...	...	28,212	10,646	2,445	4,532	13,979	2,837
Palamau	59	...	1	...	15	...	59	...	1	...	15	...	...	...	...	...	...	...	23,172	11,817	338	288	17,408	4,257
Manbhum	57,900	14,061	204	145	11,898	2,192	57,808	14,051	204	145	11,897	2,192	...	...	...	...	...	...	55,794	20,534	1,170	1,305	24,588	2,486
Singhbhum ...	3,552	1,543	7	5	1,081	834	3,510	1,558	6	4	1,056	824	...	...	...	...	...	...	49,953	9,256	567	490	8,663	1,648
Feudatory States ...	**3,261**	**1,568**	**59**	**49**	**630**	**218**	**2,752**	**1,330**	**57**	**26**	**292**	**49**	...	...	...	...	...	...	**122,763**	**142,630**	**3,382**	**24,988**	**69,438**	**16,851**
Orissa States ...	3,261	1,557	59	49	624	217	2,752	1,319	57	26	286	48	...	...	...	...	...	...	118,114	139,225	3,268	24,786	66,532	16,297
Chota Nagpur States	...	11	...	...	6	1	...	11	...	...	6	1	...	...	...	...	...	...	4,649	3,405	114	202	2,906	554
Cities	**248**	**8**	**1**	...	...	...	**225**	**1**	**1**	...	...	...	...	...	...	...	...	...	**67,441**	**12,189**	**301**	**115**	**1,298**	**295**
Patna City	...	...	...	...	...	...	...	...	...	...	...	...	...	...	...	...	...	...	30,155	3,209	31	10	239	...
Gaya City	...	...	...	...	...	...	...	...	...	...	...	...	...	...	...	...	...	...	9,642	2,507	176	2	65	7
Bhagalpur City ...	20	7	1	...	...	...	...	...	1	...	...	...	...	...	...	...	...	...	9,949	2,633	55	91	597	37
Jamshedpur City ...	228	1	...	...	...	...	225	1	...	...	...	...	...	...	...	...	...	...	27,695	3,840	39	12	397	251

TABLE X—*continued.*

OCCUPATION OR MEANS OF LIVELIHOOD. PART II—DETAILS FOR DISTRICTS AND CITIES.

DISTRICT, STATE OR CITY.	SUB-CLASS III.—INDUSTRY. Earners (principal occupation).		Working dependants.		Earners (subsidiary occupation).		ORDER 5.—TEXTILES. Total of Order 5. Earners (principal occupation).		Working dependants.		Earners (subsidiary occupation).	
	Males.	Females.	Males.	Females.	Males.	Females.	Males.	Females.	Males.	Females.	Males.	Females.
1	167	168	169	170	171	172	173	174	175	176	177	178
BIHAR AND ORISSA	**709,271**	**455,066**	**10,586**	**51,946**	**332,121**	**52,637**	**123,207**	**69,022**	**2,527**	**14,239**	**56,918**	**8,087**
British Territory ..	**623,405**	**365,935**	**8,824**	**32,481**	**289,017**	**42,355**	**91,988**	**47,744**	**1,853**	**7,047**	**43,930**	**6,153**
PATNA DIVISION ..	**176,349**	**81,033**	**477**	**225**	**16,488**	**3,764**	**18,667**	**10,112**	**36**	**25**	**1,452**	**146**
Patna	49,974	19,875	50	48	4,061	1,038	4,609	2,199	3	...	257	37
Gaya	62,195	20,685	417	173	5,300	1,280	7,505	4,545	33	35	583	23
Shahabad	64,180	31,473	10	4	7,127	1,446	6,553	3,368	..	...	612	86
TIRHUT DIVISION ...	**102,270**	**50,072**	**1,282**	**1,636**	**77,110**	**13,191**	**10,281**	**6,003**	**295**	**478**	**7,786**	**1,501**
Saran	35,409	15,555	365	379	22,280	6,584	2,376	1,627	61	109	3,235	921
Champaran ..	14,928	6,372	30	65	15,832	3,328	770	216	...	10	538	83
Muzaffarpur	30,017	15,892	50	495	21,372	2,068	1,773	1,628	16	202	1,547	270
Darbhanga ..	31,916	12,253	837	699	17,630	1,313	5,363	2,532	215	157	3,476	327
BHAGALPUR DIVISION ..	**118,062**	**64,358**	**653**	**1,159**	**40,723**	**8,583**	**15,394**	**5,583**	**50**	**219**	**8,055**	**748**
Monghyr	41,614	24,273	244	390	4,917	1,344	4,317	1,714	26	63	523	106
Bhagalpur	31,097	14,513	160	290	6,725	1,013	4,678	2,157	3	112	376	61
Purnea ..	39,506	13,421	36	279	1,752	135	3,156	696	10	1	38	...
Santal Parganas	16,845	12,152	213	194	27,329	6,091	3,343	1,026	11	23	7,118	579
ORISSA DIVISION	**121,861**	**136,227**	**2,892**	**24,283**	**98,842**	**8,576**	**30,570**	**21,836**	**668**	**4,846**	**13,182**	**1,735**
Cuttack . ..	53,570	58,714	270	10,890	68,941	3,356	13,255	6,897	39	977	3,003	421
Balasore ...	8,597	16,320	647	2,330	10,298	1,088	1,844	2,022	167	505	4,174	52
Angul	5,980	7,050	18	73	2,153	413	2,280	2,068	5	43	822	68
Puri ..	29,847	29,911	1,143	7,147	11,815	2,003	3,969	3,551	213	1,722	1,302	797
Sambalpur	23,867	24,232	814	3,853	11,635	1,631	9,223	6,092	244	1,599	3,881	399
CHOTA NAGPUR DIVISION	**104,863**	**34,245**	**3,520**	**5,176**	**55,854**	**8,247**	**17,076**	**4,216**	**804**	**1,479**	**13,455**	**2,023**
Hazaribagh ...	13,483	5,849	167	138	15,650	1,897	1,468	672	71	43	2,204	271
Ranchi ...	10,920	6,069	1,901	3,600	10,029	1,495	5,324	1,457	540	1,129	3,843	276
Palamau	13,053	5,809	160	220	11,945	2,444	1,962	1,161	49	123	3,477	1,386
Manbhum ...	24,443	9,307	771	803	12,321	1,092	4,430	651	114	143	2,839	57
Singhbhum ...	35,004	6,821	431	346	5,300	1,319	3,802	255	30	41	1,003	33
Feudatory States ...	**85,866**	**89,131**	**1,762**	**19,465**	**43,104**	**10,292**	**31,219**	**21,278**	**674**	**7,192**	**12,988**	**1,934**
Orissa States ...	82,358	86,744	1,074	19,295	41,173	9,883	30,544	20,353	654	7,168	12,636	1,892
Chota Nagpur States	3,508	2,387	88	170	1,931	390	675	925	20	24	352	42
Cities	**41,865**	**8,239**	**234**	**66**	**417**	**256**	**2,522**	**1,058**	...	**38**	**11**	**4**
Patna City ...	9,074	1,578	16	5	129	...	458	78	...	...	...	...
Gaya City	4,820	1,595	176	2	14	...	367	412	...	...	...	...
Bhagalpur City ...	5,265	1,709	12	52	141	16	1,688	555	...	38	6	4
Jamshedpur City ..	22,206	3,357	30	7	133	240	19	8	...	...	5	...

DISTRICT, STATE OR CITY.	Group 43.—Cotton spinning, sizing and weaving. Earners (principal occupation).		Working dependants.		Earners (subsidiary occupation).		Group 44.—Jute pressing, spinning and weaving. Earners (principal occupation).		Working dependants.		Earners (subsidiary occupation).	
	Males.	Females.	Males.	Females.	Males.	Females.	Males.	Females.	Males.	Females.	Males.	Females.
1	179	180	181	182	183	184	185	186	187	188	189	190
BIHAR AND ORISSA	**111,728**	**57,599**	**2,250**	**12,630**	**50,441**	**5,080**	**1,447**	**1,530**	**8**	**335**	**2,784**	**1,047**
British Territory ..	**81,427**	**37,420**	**1,687**	**5,668**	**37,849**	**3,406**	**1,424**	**1,468**	**7**	**335**	**2,741**	**1,036**
PATNA DIVISION ..	**13,313**	**7,261**	**19**	**19**	**1,004**	**97**	**482**	**10**	...	...	**21**	...
Patna	3,157	1,645	8	...	208	29	174	...	...	...	3	...
Gaya	6,003	3,562	16	19	379	11	41	...	...	...	10	...
Shahabad	4,153	2,054	...	...	417	57	267	10	...	...	8	...
TIRHUT DIVISION ...	**7,858**	**4,608**	**262**	**452**	**5,759**	**1,078**	**628**	**60**	**6**	**6**	**363**	**28**
Saran	1,596	927	59	106	1,284	603	126	3	.	...	105	12
Champaran ..	403	125	.	10	303	46	2	7	...	..	29	...
Muzaffarpur	908	1,212	2	200	952	209	237	10	4	...	119	13
Darbhanga ..	4,861	2,344	201	136	3,270	220	263	40	2	6	30	3
BHAGALPUR DIVISION ..	**14,047**	**4,675**	**47**	**214**	**7,799**	**711**	**32**	...	...	...	...	...
Monghyr	3,711	1,482	34	88	480	91	1	...	...	...	.	...
Bhagalpur	4,238	1,590	3	107	257	42	4	...	...	...	...	...
Purnea ..	9,938	623	10	1	10	..	26	...	...	...	..	...
Santal Parganas	3,160	974	11	23	7,052	578	1	...	...	...	..	...
ORISSA DIVISION	**29,998**	**17,398**	**566**	**3,566**	**12,063**	**676**	**170**	**1,286**	**1**	**328**	**853**	**46**
Cuttack . ..	13,041	4,792	88	518	2,070	112	102	1,236	1	327	796	46
Balasore ...	1,828	2,606	165	505	4,117	50	19	...	...	...	24	...
Angul	3,281	2,337	...	36	786	44	.	.	...	...	...	...
Puri ..	3,755	1,700	120	908	1,230	71	49	33	...	1	31	...
Sambalpur	9,145	6,054	243	1,599	3,868	309	...	17	...	...	2	...
CHOTA NAGPUR DIVISION	**16,211**	**3,478**	**788**	**1,417**	**11,224**	**844**	**112**	**112**	..	**1**	**1,504**	**962**
Hazaribagh ...	1,317	519	71	42	1,972	271	6	4	...	1	189	...
Ranchi ...	5,196	1,356	582	1,105	3,777	273	...	...	...	...	...	...
Palamau	1,460	749	47	118	1,591	215	107	108	...	...	1,315	962
Manbhum ...	4,392	637	114	111	2,801	57	..	...	..	...	...	...
Singhbhum ...	3,846	217	39	41	1,063	28	..		..	...	...	...
Feudatory States ...	**30,301**	**20,179**	**563**	**6,962**	**12,592**	**1,674**	**23**	**62**	**1**	...	**43**	**11**
Orissa States ...	29,633	19,531	543	6,940	12,254	1,642	23	62	1	...	43	11
Chota Nagpur States	668	648	20	22	338	32	..	...	...	...	...	...
Cities	**2,251**	**494**	...	**38**	**11**	**3**	**8**	...	...	...	...	...
Patna City ...	426	47	...	...	...	...	8	...	...	...	...	...
Gaya City	285	150	...	...	...	...	...	...	..	...	...	...
Bhagalpur City ...	1,521	289	...	38	6	3	...	...	...	...	...	...
Jamshedpur City ..	19	8	...	...	5	...	...	...	...	...	...	...

TABLE X—*continued.*

OCCUPATION OR MEANS OF LIVELIHOOD. PART II—DETAILS FOR DISTRICTS AND CITIES.

DISTRICT, STATE OR CITY.	ORDER 5—TEXTILES—*concluded.* Group 47.—Silk spinning and weaving. Earners (principal occupation). Males.	Females.	Working dependants. Males.	Females.	Earners (subsidiary occupation). Males.	Females.	ORDER 6—HIDES, SKINS AND HARD MATERIALS FROM THE ANIMAL KINGDOM. Earners (principal occupation). Males.	Females.	Working dependants. Males.	Females.	Earners (subsidiary occupation). Males.	Females.	ORDER 7—WOOD. Total of Order 7. Earners (principal occupation). Males.	Females.	Working dependants. Males.	Females.	Earners (subsidiary occupation). Males.	Females.	Group 55—Carpenters, turners and joiners, etc. Earners (principal occupation). Males.	Females.	Working dependants. Males.	Females.	Earners (subsidiary occupation). Males.	Females.
1	101	102	103	104	105	106	107	106	199	200	201	202	203	204	205	206	207	208	209	210	211	212	213	214
BIHAR AND ORISSA	**1,583**	**1,424**	**110**	**163**	**361**	**259**	**3,528**	**1,178**	**39**	**75**	**1,460**	**344**	**82,080**	**51,335**	**1,358**	**5,976**	**38,616**	**7,962**	**41,600**	**2,604**	**558**	**81**	**22,626**	**379**
British Territory	**1,055**	**860**	...	...	**25**	**23**	**3,484**	**1,100**	**39**	**63**	**1,444**	**312**	**71,962**	**36,999**	**1,205**	**2,889**	**31,893**	**5,089**	**39,372**	**2,531**	**539**	**81**	**19,610**	**356**
PATNA DIVISION	**978**	**357**	...	...	**6**	**5**	**157**	**266**	**1**	...	**25**	**37**	**17,560**	**4,878**	**109**	**34**	**2,270**	**279**	**13,559**	**987**	**106**	**34**	**2,132**	**143**
Patna	739	45	...	...	1	...	222	15	1	...	14	2	4,632	1,037	4	...	538	16	3,760	291	2	...	505	14
Gaya	237	303	...	...	5	5	207	218	...	...	4	34	7,464	1,612	101	34	973	100	6,407	501	101	34	942	75
Shahabad	3	9	...	...	...	...	28	33	...	...	7	1	5,464	2,220	4	...	771	161	3,392	105	3	...	685	54
TIRHUT DIVISION	**13**	**1**	...	...	**6**	**5**	**1,359**	**554**	**4**	**45**	**883**	**236**	**12,652**	**5,200**	**130**	**89**	**6,849**	**448**	**5,485**	**339**	**33**	**15**	**5,355**	**64**
Saran	...	...	...	...	...	...	239	108	3	...	152	16	2,490	1,265	17	19	1,830	103	951	79	6	2	1,399	30
Champaran	1	...	...	...	...	5	226	12	...	...	161	6	2,625	1,287	4	2	1,093	94	705	58	...	...	813	9
Muzaffarpur	12	1	...	...	6	...	380	272	...	...	134	133	3,477	1,324	1	23	1,717	86	1,365	41	1	...	1,168	7
Darbhanga	...	...	...	...	...	...	514	162	1	45	436	83	4,060	1,324	108	45	2,210	73	2,464	161	26	13	1,975	9
BHAGALPUR DIVISION	**64**	**502**	...	...	**13**	**12**	**335**	**37**	...	...	**30**	**7**	**15,503**	**6,641**	**92**	**138**	**5,210**	**1,851**	**9,659**	**784**	**77**	**5**	**2,440**	**87**
Monghyr	26	15	...	...	...	...	224	...	...	...	8	...	4,874	1,710	51	24	561	60	3,430	419	50	4	502	37
Bhagalpur	30	478	...	...	...	11	10	21	...	...	...	7	4,279	1,314	31	18	1,031	78	2,657	165	26	1	885	30
Purnea	5	...	...	...	1	...	80	1	...	...	1	...	4,539	1,739	1	...	232	13	3,913	125	...	...	148	4
Santal Parganas	3	9	...	...	12	1	21	15	...	...	21	...	1,811	1,878	9	96	3,386	1,701	659	75	1	...	906	16
ORISSA DIVISION	...	...	...	...	...	**1**	**400**	**150**	**3**	**16**	**59**	**17**	**15,491**	**13,734**	**289**	**1,764**	**11,008**	**1,383**	**7,418**	**120**	**116**	**14**	**6,516**	**12**
Cuttack	...	...	...	...	...	...	340	133	3	10	40	5	7,110	5,387	30	482	5,000	611	1,133	53	12	1	2,944	3
Balasore	...	...	...	...	...	1	56	2	...	...	5	...	963	2,136	71	310	2,506	138	653	11	23	1	1,470	7
Angul	...	...	...	...	...	...	2	...	...	...	...	...	768	1,261	1	16	234	174	110	...	...	...	124	...
Puri	...	...	...	...	...	...	1	15	...	...	...	12	4,203	2,739	105	655	1,800	185	3,287	52	75	11	1,375	1
Sambalpur	...	...	...	...	...	...	1	...	...	...	5	...	2,44[illegible]	2,311	82	302	1,416	272	336	4	6	...	603	1
CHOTA NAGPUR DIVISION	...	...	...	...	...	...	**533**	**93**	**31**	**2**	**447**	**15**	**10,756**	**6,546**	**585**	**864**	**6,556**	**1,128**	**3,251**	**301**	**207**	**13**	**3,167**	**50**
Hazaribagh	...	...	...	...	...	...	122	33	1	...	34	9	1,937	1,256	7	8	2,979	302	798	21	5	...	1,972	28
Ranchi	...	...	...	...	...	...	106	26	6	2	10	3	2,409	1,250	284	597	818	256	403	30	20	13	168	15
Palamau	...	...	...	...	...	...	25	7	1	...	15	...	1,700	767	10	1	894	111	789	19	6	...	621	4
Manbhum	...	...	...	...	...	...	211	35	23	...	383	3	2,733	2,232	223	173	1,097	102	711	219	164	...	289	...
Singhbhum	...	...	...	...	...	...	69	2	...	...	5	...	1,909	1,041	61	80	838	357	550	12	12	...	117	3
Feudatory States	**528**	**564**	**110**	**163**	**336**	**236**	**44**	**78**	...	**12**	**16**	**32**	**10,118**	**14,336**	**153**	**3,087**	**8,723**	**2,873**	**2,228**	**73**	**19**	...	**3,016**	**23**
Orissa States	528	564	110	163	336	234	14	78	...	12	5	32	9,903	14,156	135	3,041	8,550	2,850	2,194	73	19	...	2,936	21
Chota Nagpur States	...	...	...	...	...	2	30	...	...	...	11	...	215	180	18	46	173	23	34	...	...	...	80	2
Cities	**23**	**441**	...	...	...	...	**136**	...	**1**	...	...	...	**2,251**	**254**	**34**	**1**	**25**	...	**2,035**	**28**	**31**	**1**	**21**	...
Patna City	7	...	...	...	...	...	133	...	1	...	...	...	623	44	4	...	2	...	601	15	3	...	2	...
Gaya City	16	209	...	...	...	...	...	...	...	...	...	...	1,031	105	19	...	4	...	934	1	19	...	...	...
Bhagalpur City	...	232	...	...	...	...	...	...	...	...	...	...	323	87	4	1	7	...	248	8	4	1	7	...
Jamshedpur City	...	...	...	...	...	...	3	...	...	...	...	...	274	18	7	...	12	...	252	4	6	...	12	...

TABLE X—*continued.*

OCCUPATION OR MEANS OF LIVELIHOOD.

PART II—DETAILS FOR DISTRICTS AND CITIES.

DISTRICT, STATE OR CITY.	ORDER 7. WOOD *concluded.* Group 56.—Basket makers and other industries of woody materials, including leaves, and thatchers and builders working with bamboo, reeds or similar materials. Earners (principal occupation). Males.	Females.	Working dependants. Males.	Females.	Earners (subsidiary occupation). Males.	Females.	ORDER 8—METALS. Total of Order 8. Earners (principal occupation). Males.	Females.	Working dependants. Males.	Females.	Earners (subsidiary occupation). Males.	Females.
1	215	216	217	218	219	220	221	222	223	224	225	226
BIHAR AND ORISSA	**39,768**	**46,687**	**796**	**5,894**	**15,089**	**7,581**	**77,114**	**12,436**	**1,461**	**2,018**	**23,717**	**1,897**
British Territory ...	**32,258**	**34,426**	**662**	**2,807**	**11,877**	**4,733**	**65,638**	**8,683**	**1,147**	**1,285**	**20,521**	**1,658**
PATNA DIVISION	**4,001**	**3,891**	**3**	...	**138**	**136**	**11,337**	**1,152**	**5**	...	**984**	**65**
Patna ...	872	746	2	...	18	4	2,370	238	...	...	136	8
Gaya ...	1,057	1,111	...	...	21	25	4,325	341	5	...	344	29
Shahabad ...	2,072	2,034	1	...	99	107	4,642	573	...	...	504	28
TIRHUT DIVISION	**7,065**	**4,858**	**97**	**74**	**1,406**	**383**	**6,011**	**466**	**27**	**40**	**6,352**	**152**
Saran ...	1,514	1,186	11	17	421	154	1,272	127	2	2	2,190	72
Champaran ...	1,855	1,326	4	2	220	84	1,021	51	11	2	1,494	60
Muzaffarpur ...	2,006	1,283	...	23	530	81	2,728	183	3	...	2,170	18
Darbhanga ...	1,690	1,063	82	32	235	64	990	105	11	36	498	2
BHAGALPUR DIVISION ...	**5,835**	**5,857**	**15**	**133**	**2,770**	**1,764**	**5,133**	**475**	**17**	**2**	**2,539**	**210**
Monghyr ...	1,441	1,291	1	20	59	22	694	45	1	2	93	3
Bhagalpur ...	1,622	1,140	5	17	146	48	866	30	5	...	140	8
Purnea ...	1,617	1,614	1	...	84	9	1,766	60	...	...	99	...
Santal Parganas ...	1,155	1,812	8	96	2,481	1,685	1,807	340	11	...	2,207	199
ORISSA DIVISION ...	**7,960**	**13,614**	**171**	**1,750**	**4,475**	**1,371**	**10,452**	**1,611**	**336**	**209**	**3,980**	**32**
Cuttack ...	2,867	5,234	16	481	2,080	608	4,293	57	10	1	1,763	3
Balasore ...	409	2,126	48	309	1,088	141	619	579	40	...	1,284	6
Angul ...	658	1,361	1	15	110	174	663	343	...	2	131	3
Puri ...	1,915	2,586	30	643	486	177	2,025	68	179	48	393	1
Sambalpur ...	2,111	2,307	76	302	711	271	2,852	564	107	158	409	19
CHOTA NAGPUR DIVISION	**7,397**	**6,206**	**376**	**850**	**3,088**	**1,078**	**32,705**	**4,979**	**762**	**1,034**	**6,666**	**1,199**
Hazaribagh ...	1,193	1,230	2	8	1,005	404	1,226	181	15	11	951	76
Ranchi ...	1,936	1,216	264	584	635	211	1,466	1,092	515	910	1,778	220
Palamau ...	980	748	4	1	203	107	1,357	174	26	16	1,209	44
Manbhum ...	1,990	1,985	57	171	777	102	4,613	239	35	23	1,289	29
Singhbhum ...	1,298	1,027	49	86	468	261	23,044	3,293	169	74	1,439	830
Feudatory States ...	**7,510**	**14,261**	**134**	**3,087**	**3,212**	**2,846**	**11,476**	**3,753**	**304**	**728**	**3,196**	**239**
Orissa States ...	7,337	14,061	116	3,041	3,144	2,825	10,873	3,170	296	725	2,976	199
Chota Nagpur States ...	173	190	18	46	68	21	603	583	8	3	220	40
Cities ...	**203**	**226**	**3**	...	**4**	...	**20,515**	**2,899**	**9**	...	**16**	**231**
Patna City ...	22	29	2	...	...	...	587	6	...	...	...	...
Gaya City ...	97	104	...	...	4	...	227	13	...	...	...	...
Bhagalpur City ...	75	79	...	...	...	...	106	3	2	...	1	...
Jamshedpur City ...	9	14	1	...	...	...	19,595	2,877	7	...	15	231

DISTRICT, STATE OR CITY.	Group 57.—Smelting, forging and rolling of iron and other metals. Earners (principal occupation). Males.	Females.	Working dependants. Males.	Females.	Earners (subsidiary occupation). Males.	Females.	Group 58.—Blacksmiths, other workers in iron, makers of implements. Earners (principal occupation). Males.	Females.	Working dependants. Males.	Females.	Earners (subsidiary occupation). Males.	Females.
1	227	228	229	230	231	232	233	234	235	236	237	238
BIHAR AND ORISSA	**20,082**	**2,959**	**7**	**1**	**124**	**228**	**43,854**	**7,656**	**1,185**	**1,864**	**21,088**	**1,585**
British Territory ...	**20,054**	**2,944**	**7**	**1**	**104**	**222**	**34,396**	**4,384**	**926**	**1,183**	**18,348**	**1,363**
PATNA DIVISION	...		...	...		...	**9,101**	**906**	**5**	...	**951**	**45**
Patna ...	...	...	...	...	...	...	1,580	175	...	...	144	8
Gaya ...	...	...	...	...	...	...	3,372	242	5	...	233	9
Shahabad ...	...	...	...	...	...	...	4,149	489	...	...	574	28
TIRHUT DIVISION	**17**	...	...	...	...	...	**4,874**	**306**	**24**	**4**	**5,990**	**144**
Saran ...	...	...	...	...	...	...	1,114	102	1	2	2,170	72
Champaran ...	...	...	...	...	...	...	866	36	11	2	1,417	54
Muzaffarpur ...	...	...	...	...	...	...	2,137	67	1	...	1,983	15
Darbhanga ...	17	...	...	...	...	...	757	101	11	...	420	3
BHAGALPUR DIVISION ...	**127**	**21**	...	...	**5**	...	**4,078**	**343**	**17**	**2**	**2,327**	**190**
Monghyr ...	9		...	...	2	...	472	34	1	2	87	3
Bhagalpur ...	...	...	...	...	3		505	23	5	...	115	1
Purnea ...	...	...	...	...		...	1,448	24	...	...	77	...
Santal Parganas ...	118	21	...	...	...	...	1,653	262	11	...	2,048	186
ORISSA DIVISION ...	**37**	...	...	...	**8**		**4,706**	**1,069**	**282**	**162**	**2,762**	**23**
Cuttack ...	36	...	...	...	8	...	1,779	10	10	...	1,356	1
Balasore ...	1	...	...	...	...	...	396	11	39	...	943	1
Angul ...	...		...	...		...	516	307	...	2	104	3
Puri ...	...	...	...	...	...		550	24	158	38	105	...
Sambalpur ...	...	...	...	...	...	...	1,465	717	75	122	254	18
CHOTA NAGPUR DIVISION	**19,873**	**2,923**	**7**	**1**	**91**	**222**	**11,637**	**1,760**	**598**	**1,015**	**6,318**	**961**
Hazaribagh ...	...	...	...	...	...	...	976	114	15	10	897	69
Ranchi ...	...	...		...	...	...	4,217	1,032	497	904	1,740	214
Palamau ...	...	...		...	1	...	1,206	102	24	16	1,187	43
Manbhum ...	461	48	...	...	75		2,847	183	33	19	998	29
Singhbhum ...	19,412	2,875	7	1	15	222	2,339	329	29	66	1,496	606
Feudatory States ...	**28**	**15**	...	...	**20**	**6**	**8,658**	**3,272**	**259**	**681**	**2,690**	**222**
Orissa States ...	...	...	...	...	...	...	8,135	2,711	256	678	2,528	188
Chota Nagpur States ...	28	15	...	...	20	6	523	561	3	3	162	34
Cities ...	**19,409**	**2,875**	**7**	...	**14**	**222**	**669**	**10**	**2**	...	...	**7**
Patna City ...	...	...	...	...	...	...	328	4	...	...	...	...
Gaya City ...	...	...	...	...	...	...	133	2	...	...	...	...
Bhagalpur City ...	...	...	...	...	...	...	71	3	2	...	...	...
Jamshedpur City ...	19,409	2,875	7	...	14	222	137	1	...	...	...	7

TABLE X—*continued.*

OCCUPATION OR MEANS OF LIVELIHOOD.

PART II—DETAILS FOR DISTRICTS AND CITIES.

DISTRICT, STATE OR CITY.	ORDER 8.—METALS—*concluded.* Group 60.—Workers in brass, copper and bell metal. Earners (principal occupation). Males.	Females.	Working dependants. Males.	Females.	Earners (subsidiary occupation). Males.	Females.	ORDER 9.—CERAMICS. TOTAL OF ORDER 9. Earners (principal occupation). Males.	Females.	Working dependants. Males.	Females.	Earners (subsidiary occupation). Males.	Females.
1	239	240	241	242	243	244	245	246	247	248	249	250
BIHAR AND ORISSA	**13,153**	**1,663**	**250**	**112**	**2,158**	**61**	**67,691**	**43,470**	**1,324**	**3,079**	**35,539**	**5,449**
British Territory ...	**10,366**	**1,199**	**205**	**65**	**1,672**	**50**	**59,477**	**36,924**	**1,111**	**2,227**	**30,170**	**5,186**
PATNA DIVISION ...	**2,227**	**240**	..	...	**33**	**20**	**18,528**	**10,700**	**94**	**23**	**1,790**	**461**
Patna ...	788	58	...	.	12	...	5,517	3,841	3	3	619	174
Gaya ...	958	99	..	...	11	20	7,105	3,319	91	13	514	137
Shahabad ...	483	83	...	...	10	...	5,906	3,540	.	2	657	150
TIRHUT DIVISION ...	**867**	**71**	**1**	..	**202**	...	**9,373**	**4,840**	**98**	**135**	**9,251**	**1,486**
Saran ...	158	...	1	..	20	.	1,173	1,416	38	39	2,266	709
Champaran ...	66	11	.	...	33	..	961	558	6	9	1,779	319
Muzaffarpur ...	462	30	..	...	94	...	3,857	1,701	3	35	3,077	360
Darbhanga ...	162	1		...	55	..	3,383	1,165	51	53	2,139	98
BHAGALPUR DIVISION ...	**581**	**53**	..		**36**	**7**	**13,191**	**9,228**	**93**	**90**	**4,852**	**1,625**
Monghyr ...	135	3	..	..	2		5,178	3,391	33	44	332	274
Bhagalpur ...	264	7	..	..	10	7	3,312	2,367	18	12	900	195
Purnea ...	168	33	...		13	...	2,737	1,233	...	1	74	12
Santal Parganas ...	30	10	...	...	2	.	1,964	2,307	42	33	3,337	1,144
ORISSA DIVISION ...	**5,594**	**541**	**47**	**47**	**1,149**	**9**	**9,954**	**8,124**	**272**	**1,286**	**6,710**	**558**
Cuttack ...	2,431	17	..	1	769	3	5,027	3,672	16	100	2,240	255
Balasore ...	416	268	11	...	380	5	711	1,360	57	270	2,067	90
Angul ...	143	36	..	...	17	...	601	443	1	...	71	3
Puri ...	1,453	43	4	10	271	1	2,158	954	120	883	1,226	112
Sambalpur ...	1,151	147	32	36	112	1	1,457	1,695	78	230	1,106	98
CHOTA NAGPUR DIVISION	**1,097**	**294**	**157**	**18**	**252**	**14**	**8,431**	**4,032**	**554**	**693**	**7,567**	**1,056**
Hazaribagh ...	350	67		1	54	7	1,394	1,016	10	11	2,659	374
Ranchi ...	226	62	18	6	38	6	2,233	947	333	479	1,160	270
Palamau ...	52	60	4	.	31	1	1,300	563	23	16	1,193	318
Manbhum ...	383	8	2	4	116	...	1,889	397	115	133	1,816	105
Singhbhum ...	384	88	133	7	28		1,693	557	73	53	719	41
Feudatory States ...	**2,787**	**464**	**45**	**47**	**486**	**11**	**8,214**	**6,546**	**213**	**852**	**5,369**	**263**
Orissa States ...	2,736	457	45	47	448	11	7,856	6,365	206	823	5,057	245
Chota Nagpur States ...	51	7	...	..	38		358	181	7	29	312	18
Cities ...	**398**	**13**	...	...	**1**	...	**1,518**	**522**	**62**		**42**	**6**
Patna City ...	260	2	...	..		...	430	159	..	...	25	.
Gaya City ...	94	11		..	..	...	721	133	63		7	
Bhagalpur City ...	35	...	...	...	1	...	258	143	...	..	1	.
Jamshedpur City ...	10	...		.	.	...	109	87	...	...	9	6

DISTRICT, STATE OR CITY.	ORDER 9.—CERAMICS. Group 63. Potters and makers of earthen-ware. Earners (principal occupation). Males.	Females.	Working dependants. Males.	Females.	Earners (subsidiary occupation). Males.	Females.	ORDER 10.—CHEMICAL PRODUCTS PROPERLY SO CALLED AND ANALOGOUS. TOTAL OF ORDER 10. Earners (principal occupation). Males.	Females.	Working dependants. Males.	Females.	Earners (subsidiary occupation). Males.	Females.
1	251	252	253	254	255	256	257	258	259	260	261	262
BIHAR AND ORISSA	**63,254**	**41,790**	**1,316**	**3,051**	**34,089**	**5,190**	**44,634**	**35,026**	**555**	**1,673**	**26,232**	**5,895**
British Territory ...	**55,338**	**35,381**	**1,106**	**2,220**	**28,782**	**4,931**	**41,840**	**30,975**	**507**	**1,009**	**22,747**	**5,546**
PATNA DIVISION ...	**17,023**	**10,116**	**94**	**21**	**1,589**	**391**	**15,861**	**10,928**	**43**	**14**	**1,316**	**430**
Patna ...	5,029	[illegible]	3	3	549	156	2,442	1,960	4	...	337	53
Gaya ...	6,607	3,304	91	16	482	136	7,662	4,895	39	14	465	137
Shahabad ...	5,387	3,580	...	..	558	99	5,757	4,073		..	614	237
TIRHUT DIVISION ...	**8,537**	**4,801**	**97**	**135**	**8,980**	**1,462**	**7,221**	**6,737**	**164**	**234**	**8,128**	**2,510**
Saran ...	1,987	1,395	36	39	2,191	600	2,200	2,005	96	63	2,965	1,130
Champaran ...	843	575	6	9	1,724	367	994	842		6	1,953	541
Muzaffarpur ...	2,732	1,700	3	35	2,980	313	1,849	2,302		35	1,837	705
Darbhanga ...	2,975	1,131	51	53	2,085	93	2,178	1,588	68	131	1,374	144
BHAGALPUR DIVISION ...	**12,533**	**8,370**	**93**	**89**	**4,661**	**1,561**	**11,181**	**8,557**	**51**	**70**	**4,902**	**1,581**
Monghyr ...	5,016	3,202	33	44	580	273	3,468	3,361	20	36	574	244
Bhagalpur ...	3,202	2,364	18	13	891	195	2,339	2,081	11	25	1,211	305
Purnea ...	2,467	1,237	.	1	71	12	3,536	1,448	7	1	406	49
Santal Parganas ...	1,848	[illegible]	42	32	3,119	1,061	1,818	1,667	13	4	2,711	983
ORISSA DIVISION ...	**9,626**	**8,048**	**268**	**1,285**	**6,266**	**513**	**3,104**	**2,085**	**122**	**467**	**4,244**	**179**
Cuttack ...	4,827	3,569	16	100	1,879	225	1,031	61	4	2	938	6
Balasore ...	687	1,357	57	270	2,042	80	201	176	21	30	1,394	51
Angul ...	601	443	1	..	71	2	243	132		3	255	5
Puri ...	2,120	951	116	686	1,201	112	944	185	63	56	730	6
Sambalpur ...	1,391	1,638	78	229	1,073	94	655	1,581	34	309	1,027	111
CHOTA NAGPUR DIVISION	**7,619**	**3,746**	**554**	**690**	**7,286**	**1,004**	**4,473**	**2,668**	**127**	**224**	**4,157**	**846**
Hazaribagh ...	1,170	947	10	11	2,561	341	465	775	29	15	1,100	389
Ranchi ...	2,240	941	333	479	1,165	278	520	354	53	131	490	132
Palamau ...	1,155	503	23	15	1,111	188	1,132	777	29	73	1,360	254
Manbhum ...	1,516	882	115	130	1,752	163	2,088	652	5	7	1,223	68
Singhbhum ...	1,538	455	73	53	607	34	268	110	12	8	76	3
Feudatory States ...	**7,916**	**3,409**	**210**	**831**	**5,307**	**259**	**2,794**	**4,051**	**48**	**664**	**3,486**	**349**
Orissa States ...	7,558	3,250	203	802	4,996	241	2,726	4,013	47	658	3,316	326
Chota Nagpur States ...	358	159	7	29	311	18	68	38	1	6	169	23
Cities ...	**1,012**	**429**	**62**		**31**	...	**784**	**187**	**27**		**5**	...
Patna City ...	345	145		..	25	...	104	55		...	...	...
Gaya City ...	411	133	62		5	...	470	70	27	.	...	...
Bhagalpur City ...	227	143	..	..	...	..	203	62		...	3	...
Jamshedpur City ...	29	8	...	..	1	..	7	.	...	...	2	...

TABLE X—*continued.*

OCCUPATION OR MEANS OF LIVELIHOOD. PART II—DETAILS FOR DISTRICTS AND CITIES.

DISTRICT, STATE OR CITY.	ORDER 10.—CHEMICAL PRODUCTS PROPERLY SO CALLED AND ANALOGOUS—*concluded.* Group 68.—Manufacture and refining of vegetable oils. *Earners (principal occupation).* Males.	Females.	*Working dependants.* Males.	Females.	*Earners (subsidiary occupation).* Males.	Females.	ORDER 11.—FOOD INDUSTRIES. TOTAL OF ORDER 11. *Earners (principal occupation).* Males.	Females.	*Working dependants.* Males.	Females.	*Earners (subsidiary occupation).* Males.	Females.
1	263	264	265	266	267	268	269	270	271	272	273	274
BIHAR AND ORISSA	**41,353**	**33,747**	**488**	**1,620**	**24,453**	**5,698**	**53,843**	**132,657**	**748**	**17,218**	**23,336**	**11,430**
British Territory	**38,570**	**29,732**	**440**	**957**	**20,976**	**5,358**	**48,743**	**105,731**	**628**	**12,163**	**20,337**	**7,474**
PATNA DIVISION ...	**15,797**	**10,918**	**43**	**14**	**1,315**	**430**	**19,213**	**11,845**	**13**	**20**	**1,641**	**445**
Patna	2,379	1,954	4	...	336	56	5,613	2,921	3	2	442	96
Gaya	7,662	4,891	39	14	405	137	5,666	2,306	10	18	430	58
Shahabad	5,756	4,073	...	...	614	237	7,934	6,718	...	...	769	291
TIRHUT DIVISION ...	**7,118**	**6,435**	**164**	**225**	**8,091**	**2,467**	**8,672**	**6,088**	**110**	**111**	**4,104**	**1,541**
Saran	2,240	1,955	96	62	2,985	1,117	2,789	2,796	33	43	1,697	1,140
Champaran ...	978	814	.	6	1,046	525	1,562	1,055	3	4	752	183
Muzaffarpur ..	1,834	2,299	...	35	1,825	705	1,355	1,053	11	19	908	120
Darbhanga ...	2,066	1,367	68	122	1,355	120	2,966	1,184	63	40	747	98
BHAGALPUR DIVISION ...	**11,110**	**8,537**	**51**	**70**	**4,896**	**1,581**	**8,263**	**15,796**	**126**	**338**	**4,890**	**1,377**
Monghyr	3,461	3,361	20	36	574	244	4,136	4,972	7	53	898	177
Bhagalpur	2,313	2,061	11	25	1,308	305	1,071	1,203	5	1	135	63
Purnea	3,519	1,447	7	1	406	40	1,266	6,290	13	268	35	35
Santal Parganas ...	1,817	1,668	13	5	2,708	983	1,190	3,401	98	16	4,322	1,102
ORISSA DIVISION ...	**2,928**	**2,051**	**113**	**456**	**4,217**	**179**	**9,055**	**67,635**	**211**	**11,207**	**7,903**	**3,317**
Cuttack	1,013	58	4	3	925	6	3,657	38,102	38	8,274	3,145	1,730
Balasore	199	176	21	39	1,294	51	475	6,598	40	586	1,837	585
Angul	243	132	...	2	255	5	365	1,164	10	10	237	133
Puri	925	185	63	55	723	6	2,249	18,015	101	1,495	1,314	319
Sambalpur ...	548	1,500	25	358	1,021	111	2,309	8,756	22	830	1,370	591
CHOTA NAGPUR DIVISION	**1,617**	**1,791**	**69**	**192**	**2,457**	**701**	**3,540**	**4,367**	**168**	**487**	**1,799**	**794**
Hazaribagh ...	357	706	3	15	1,104	389	851	219	..	2	152	30
Ranchi	383	348	36	121	390	132	897	497	68	192	520	168
Palamau	712	646	18	48	923	176	353	401	1	12	127	71
Manbhum	61	29	...	...	21	3	1,206	2,694	37	232	653	308
Singhbhum ...	74	62	12	5	10	1	733	406	62	40	347	127
Feudatory States ...	**2,783**	**4,015**	**48**	**663**	**3,477**	**335**	**5,100**	**26,926**	**120**	**5,055**	**2,999**	**3,956**
Orissa States ...	2,716	3,982	47	659	3,308	313	4,972	20,630	98	5,028	2,712	3,775
Chota Nagpur States ...	66	33	1	4	169	22	128	296	22	27	287	181
Cities	**774**	**187**	**27**	...	**3**	..	**1,487**	**776**	**7**	**5**	**31**	**5**
Patna City... ...	104	55	...	...	...	...	638	317	3	2	1	...
Gaya City	470	70	27	...	3	...	150	173	...	2	...	...
Bhagalpur City ...	200	62	..	...	...	...	544	283	4	1	30	5
Jamshedpur City ...	...	...	...	...	...	...	155	3	...	...	...	...

DISTRICT, STATE OR CITY.	ORDER 11.—FOOD INDUSTRIES. Group 71.—Rice pounders and huskers and flour grinders. *Earners (principal occupation).* Males.	Females.	*Working dependants.* Males.	Females.	*Earners (subsidiary occupation).* Males.	Females.	Group 72.—Grain parchers, etc. *Earners (principal occupation).* Males.	Females.	*Working dependants.* Males.	Females.	*Earners (subsidiary occupation).* Males.	Females.
1	275	276	277	278	279	280	281	282	283	284	285	286
BIHAR AND ORISSA	**3,198**	**63,683**	**198**	**12,267**	**6,209**	**6,749**	**19,801**	**63,167**	**337**	**4,826**	**12,027**	**4,368**
British Territory	**2,897**	**52,052**	**189**	**9,234**	**6,052**	**3,653**	**15,245**	**47,974**	**228**	**2,805**	**9,268**	**3,508**
PATNA DIVISION ...	**403**	**2,255**	...	**11**	**5**	**26**	**5,468**	**7,113**	..	**1**	**713**	**354**
Patna	203	512	...	...	4	2	637	1,415	...	...	89	65
Gaya	141	914	.	11	...	14	185	583	..	1	44	26
Shahabad	60	829	...	...	1	10	[illegible],646	5,115	...	...	580	263
TIRHUT DIVISION ...	**292**	**1,339**	**3**	**2**	**257**	**117**	**1,796**	**3,919**	**27**	**72**	**1,709**	**1,309**
Saran	11	30	..	1	32	9	1,223	3,563	16	43	1,287	1,114
Champaran ...	70	521	...	...	51	47	106	410	...	4	176	110
Muzaffarpur ..	41	430	...	...	160	46	100	376	4	19	139	48
Darbhanga ...	100	358	3	1	24	15	277	570	7	6	107	37
BHAGALPUR DIVISION ...	**897**	**9,263**	**101**	**282**	**4,130**	**1,031**	**1,600**	**5,171**	**6**	**29**	**146**	**254**
Monghyr	111	379	1	2	47	5	756	3,881	5	24	88	115
Bhagalpur	326	532	..	...	83	17	106	410	...	1	15	32
Purnea	103	5,830	3	208	2	35	60	161	...	...	4	...
Santal Parganas ...	357	2,522	37	12	4,048	974	78	719	1	4	39	107
ORISSA DIVISION ...	**1,135**	**37,438**	**67**	**8,809**	**1,542**	**2,245**	**5,968**	**29,459**	**136**	**2,381**	**5,481**	**1,054**
Cuttack	772	20,578	31	7,701	523	1,341	1,[illegible]3	12,229	4	474	2,363	396
Balasore	198	2,727	34	521	954	459	[illegible]1	3,841	1	65	435	76
Angul	...	255	...	2	...	22	343	909	10	8	109	111
Puri	138	12,723	2	420	61	198	2,045	5,286	99	1,078	1,240	121
Sambalpur ...	27	1,155	...	75	4	225	1,8[illegible]6	7,194	22	756	1,335	350
CHOTA NAGPUR DIVISION	**240**	**1,757**	**13**	**139**	**118**	**234**	**1,013**	**2,312**	**59**	**322**	**1,219**	**537**
Hazaribagh ...	11	79	...	...	9	6	55	92	...	2	99	23
Ranchi	21	85	..	1	..	2	359	868	42	166	415	165
Palamau	36	283	...	3	23	24	71	105		6	94	46
Manbhum	72	1,206	10	123	70	202	383	1,333	17	109	357	176
Singhbhum ...	108	15	4	3	16	..	145	414	...	30	254	127
Feudatory States ...	**301**	**11,631**	**9**	**3,033**	**157**	**3,096**	**4,556**	**15,193**	**109**	**2,021**	**2,759**	**860**
Orissa States ...	301	11,631	9	3,033	156	3,096	4,439	14,899	88	1,994	2,503	679
Chota Nagpur States ...	...	...	.	...	1	...	117	294	21	27	256	181
Cities	**217**	**248**	...	**2**	**18**	**5**	**35**	**236**	...	**1**	...	...
Patna City... ...	4	50	...	...	...	...	17	81	...	...	...	...
Gaya City	...	107	...	2	.	...	...	56	...	...	...	...
Bhagalpur City ...	142	91	...	...	18	5	18	99	...	1	...	...
Jamshedpur City ...	71	...	...	...	...	...	...	...	...	...	...	...

TABLE X—*continued.*

OCCUPATION OR MEANS OF LIVELIHOOD. PART II—DETAILS FOR DISTRICTS AND CITIES.

ORDER 11.—FOOD INDUSTRIES—*concluded.*

DISTRICT, STATE OR CITY.	Group 73.—Butchers.						Group 75.—Sweetmeat and condiment makers.					
	Earners (principal occupation).		*Working dependants.*		*Earners (subsidiary occupation).*		*Earners (principal occupation).*		*Working dependants.*		*Earners (subsidiary occupation).*	
	Males.	Females.	Males.	Females.	Males.	Females.	Males.	Females.	Males.	Females.	Males.	Females.
1	287	288	289	290	291	292	293	294	295	296	297	298
BIHAR AND ORISSA	**4,284**	**799**	**31**	**16**	**599**	**63**	**6,835**	**2,166**	**62**	**34**	**907**	**98**
British Territory ...	**4,274**	**799**	**31**	**16**	**596**	**63**	**6,807**	**2,143**	**62**	**33**	**896**	**98**
PATNA DIVISION ...	**1,592**	**220**	...	...	**37**	...	**3,689**	**1,528**	**12**	**6**	**258**	**23**
Patna	668	48	...	..	7	...	1,164	729	3	...	99	9
Gaya	456	100	...	...	8	...	1,205	383	9	6	78	13
Shahabad	468	72	...		22	...	1,260	417	..		81	1
TIRHUT DIVISION ...	**1,598**	**371**	**20**	**6**	**563**	**42**	**1,605**	**313**	**22**	**2**	**513**	**65**
Saran	395	109	3	3	112	10	343	52	5	1	70	7
Champaran ...	302	32	...		99	1	430	56	..	...	151	17
Muzaffarpur ...	481	112	...		226	24	236	113	3	...	145	2
Darbhanga ...	420	118	17	3	66	7	596	92	14	1	147	39
BHAGALPUR DIVISION ...	**328**	**53**	...	...	**26**	...	**1,033**	**177**	**14**	...	**62**	**7**
Monghyr	111	13	...	...	11	...	198	3	...	...	7	...
Bhagalpur	43	15	...	...	11	...	67	4	4	...	2	1
Purnea	136	16	...	...	4	...	617	113	10	...	6	...
Santal Parganas ...	38	9	...	...	...	...	151	57	..	...	47	6
ORISSA DIVISION ...	**21**	**2**	...	...	...	...	**116**	**42**	...	...	**24**	**2**
Cuttack	2	2	...	...	...	...	116	42	...	...	23	2
Balasore	...	...	...	...	...	...	...	...	...	...	1	
Angul	1	...	...	...	...	...	...	...	...	...	...	..
Puri	...	...	...	...	...	...	...	...	...		...	
Sambalpur	18	...	...	...	...	...	...	..	...	...	...	..
CHOTA NAGPUR DIVISION .	**735**	**153**	**11**	**10**	**30**	**21**	**354**	**83**	**14**	**25**	**39**	**1**
Hazaribagh ...	159	45	...	...	13	...	48	3	...	...	3	1
Ranchi	184	28	8	...	12	...	201	12	14	25	24	...
Palamau	100	42	...	3	5	1	96	61	...	...	4	...
Manbhum	138	32	...	...	1	20	3	1	...	...	5	...
Singhbhum ...	164	6	3	7	...	...	16	6	...	...	3	...
Feudatory States ...	**10**	...	...	...	**3**	...	**28**	**23**	...	**1**	**11**	...
Orissa States ...	10	...	...	...	3	...	28	23	...	1	11	...
Chota Nagpur States ...	...	...	...	...	...	...	...	...	...	...	...	...
Cities	**341**	**24**	...	...	...	...	**224**	**169**	**3**	...	...	...
Patna City	212	5	...	...	...	...	221	103	3	...	...	...
Gaya City	67	4	...	...	...	...	...	6	...	...	...	...
Bhagalpur City ...	3	14	...	...	...	...	...	...	...	...	...	...
Jamshedpur City ...	69	1	...	...	...	...	3	...	...	...	...	...

DISTRICT, STATE OR CITY.	Group 76.—Toddy drawers.						Group 78.—Manufacturers of tobacco.					
	Earners (principal occupation).		*Working dependants.*		*Earners (subsidiary occupation).*		*Earners (principal occupation).*		*Working dependants.*		*Earners (subsidiary occupation).*	
	Males.	Females.	Males.	Females.	Males.	Females.	Males.	Females.	Males.	Females.	Males.	Females.
1	299	300	301	302	303	304	305	306	307	308	309	310
BIHAR AND ORISSA	**13,997**	**1,176**	**47**	**36**	**2,607**	**53**	**4,422**	**1,491**	**67**	**39**	**764**	**87**
British Territory ...	**13,983**	**1,176**	**47**	**36**	**2,602**	**53**	**4,292**	**1,465**	**65**	**39**	**716**	**87**
PATNA DIVISION ...	**7,204**	**703**	**1**	**2**	**560**	**42**	**832**	**21**	...	...	**65**	...
Patna	2,532	210	..	2	315	30	408	6	...	...	28	...
Gaya	3,556	218	1	...	266	5	61	9	...	...	34	...
Shahabad	1,114	275	...	...	79	17	363	6	...	...	3	...
TIRHUT DIVISION ...	**2,564**	**58**	**34**	**29**	**986**	...	**96**	**85**	...	...	**17**	**2**
Saran	534	41	9	...	306	...	33	1	...	...	...	...
Champaran ...	417	...	3	...	180	...	12	36	...	...	...	2
Muzaffarpur ...	350	17	..	...	301	...	44	2	...	...	17	...
Darbhanga ...	1,263	...	22	29	399	...	8	46	...	...	...	...
BHAGALPUR DIVISION ...	**3,488**	**411**	**4**	**4**	**245**	**11**	**1,280**	**616**	**1**	**23**	**227**	**68**
Monghyr	2,294	177	...	4	127	...	648	513	1	23	118	57
Bhagalpur	883	210	4	...	51	11	193	22	...	...	22	...
Purnea	125	1	...	...	3	...	96	18	...	...	9	...
Santal Parganas ...	186	23	...	...	64	...	343	63	.	...	78	11
ORISSA DIVISION ...	**702**	**4**	**8**	**1**	**790**	...	**1,001**	**687**	...	**16**	**45**	**16**
Cuttack	541	2	3	1	312	..	496	246	...	8	6	...
Balasore	117	3	5	...	439	...	64	28	...	...	5	...
Angul	21	..	...	...	38	...	...	..	...	...	...	...
Puri	23	...	...	...	1	...	3	6	...	...	3	...
Sambalpur	...	...	...	...	...	...	438	407	...	8	31	16
CHOTA NAGPUR DIVISION .	**25**	...	...	...	**21**	...	**1,083**	**56**	**64**	...	**362**	**1**
Hazaribagh ...	25	...	...	..	21	...	39	...	...	...	3	...
Ranchi	..	...	...	...	...	...	80	...	4	...	64	1
Palamau	...	...	...	...	...	...	48	...	...	...	1	...
Manbhum	.	...	...	...	...	...	617	33	9	...	220	...
Singhbhum ...	...	...	...	...	...	...	399	23	51	...	74	...
Feudatory States ...	**14**	...	...	...	**5**	...	**130**	**26**	**2**	...	**48**	...
Orissa States ...	14	...	...	...	5	...	119	24	1	...	18	...
Chota Nagpur States ...	...	...	...	...	...	...	11	2	1	...	30	...
Cities	**548**	**83**	**4**	**2**	**2**	...	**112**	**16**	...	...	**11**	...
Patna City	184	18	...	2	1	...	...	...	...	...	...	...
Gaya City	93	...	...	...	...	..	...	...	...	...	...	...
Bhagalpur City ...	271	65	4	...	1	...	100	14	...	...	11	...
Jamshedpur City ...	...	...	...	...	...	...	12	2	...	...	...	...

TABLE X—*continued.*

Occupation or Means of Livelihood. Part II– Details for Districts and Cities.

Order 12.—Industries of Dress and the Toilet.

District, State or City.	Total of Order 12. Earners (principal occupation). Males.	Total of Order 12. Earners (principal occupation). Females.	Total of Order 12. Working dependants. Males.	Total of Order 12. Working dependants. Females.	Total of Order 12. Earners (subsidiary occupation). Males.	Total of Order 12. Earners (subsidiary occupation). Females.	Group 82.—Boot, shoe, sandal and clog makers. Earners (principal occupation). Males.	Group 82. Earners (principal occupation). Females.	Group 82. Working dependants. Males.	Group 82. Working dependants. Females.	Group 82. Earners (subsidiary occupation). Males.	Group 82. Earners (subsidiary occupation). Females.
1	311	312	313	314	315	316	317	318	319	320	321	322
BIHAR AND ORISSA	**172,918**	**87,969**	**1,906**	**6,419**	**76,490**	**9,092**	**36,071**	**6,292**	**281**	**142**	**9,292**	**578**
British Territory ...	**162,123**	**80,054**	**1,793**	**5,344**	**70,319**	**8,786**	**29,464**	**6,117**	**281**	**85**	**9,290**	**578**
Patna Division ..	**50,127**	**23,933**	**132**	**95**	**5,085**	**955**	**12,977**	**2,309**	**49**	**1**	**1,492**	**145**
Patna	14,556	6,098	10	38	1,162	220	3,030	305	...	1	284	27
Gaya	16,869	9,438	116	55	1,639	387	4,256	972	49	...	410	80
Shahabad	18,712	8,397	6	2	3,384	348	5,701	1,032	...	...	798	38
Tirhut Division ...	**31,695**	**17,218**	**341**	**398**	**26,301**	**4,811**	**3,728**	**1,300**	**59**	**17**	**2,145**	**156**
Saran	7,347	5,348	89	76	6,750	2,194	942	860	31	...	503	61
Champaran ..	5,138	2,024	...	32	6,440	914	523	85	...	...	162	4
Muzaffarpur ..	10,126	6,424	16	172	7,604	1,185	827	191	...	6	569	56
Darbhanga ...	9,044	3,422	236	128	5,507	518	1,436	254	38	11	911	35
Bhagalpur Division ...	**36,509**	**15,492**	**207**	**288**	**8,814**	**1,096**	**7,629**	**2,030**	**96**	**50**	**1,512**	**162**
Monghyr	14,404	8,328	106	153	1,950	467	3,183	1,249	40	5	273	87
Bhagalpur	10,568	4,623	69	109	2,603	283	2,210	473	34	35	494	35
Purnea	8,403	1,535	3	8	704	24	1,416	188	...	...	97	1
Santal Parganas ...	3,134	1,106	29	18	3,557	332	820	130	24	10	648	39
Orissa Division ...	**27,209**	**13,391**	**755**	**4,276**	**17,512**	**965**	**906**	**89**	**19**	...	**337**	**6**
Cuttack	11,850	9,045	102	942	7,190	232	192	24	...	...	1	...
Balasore	2,162	2,976	190	599	4,861	203	36	5	...	...	5	...
Angul	800	735	...	1	319	29	...	...	...	...	...	..
Puri	9,187	3,746	243	2,426	3,558	405	86	...	..	...	1	...
Sambalpur	3,361	1,900	220	308	1,584	98	588	60	19	...	330	6
Chota Nagpur Division	**16,542**	**5,020**	**358**	**287**	**12,607**	**959**	**4,244**	**299**	**56**	**17**	**3,304**	**109**
Hazaribagh ..	3,664	1,247	32	46	4,778	333	859	71	1	...	1,108	49
Ranchi	2,476	751	102	108	1,004	133	514	69	11	11	145	26
Palamau	3,403	1,621	17	47	3,653	334	1,214	92	3	...	1,954	28
Manbhum	4,818	1,065	187	55	2,737	148	1,269	40	36	2	450	4
Singhbhum ...	2,181	336	20	31	445	16	388	18	15	4	57	2
Feudatory States ...	**16,795**	**7,945**	**203**	**1,075**	**6,180**	**306**	**587**	**275**	...	**62**	**2**	...
Orissa States ..	10,592	7,822	190	1,058	5,985	258	583	174	...	62	...	...
Chota Nagpur States ..	203	123	13	17	195	48	4	1	...	...	2	...
Cities	**6,116**	**1,557**	**32**	**22**	**183**	**6**	**1,557**	**89**	**60**	**4**	**141**	...
Patna City	2,572	637	7	3	98	...	681	13	...	...	95	...
Gaya City	1,413	462	63	...	...	...	319	38	45	...	...	...
Bhagalpur City ...	1,281	409	2	12	45	4	356	37	...	...	31	...
Jamshedpur City ...	850	49	15	7	40	2	301	1	15	4	26	...

District, State or City.	Group 83.—Tailors, milliners, dress-makers and darners. Earners (principal occupation). Males.	Group 83. Earners (principal occupation). Females.	Group 83. Working dependants. Males.	Group 83. Working dependants. Females.	Group 83. Earners (subsidiary occupation). Males.	Group 83. Earners (subsidiary occupation). Females.	Group 85.—Washing and cleaning. Earners (principal occupation). Males.	Group 85. Earners (principal occupation). Females.	Group 85. Working dependants. Males.	Group 85. Working dependants. Females.	Group 85. Earners (subsidiary occupation). Males.	Group 85. Earners (subsidiary occupation). Females.
1	323	324	325	326	327	328	329	330	331	332	333	334
BIHAR AND ORISSA	**22,494**	**8,070**	**115**	**150**	**5,201**	**889**	**56,603**	**56,382**	**731**	**4,968**	**27,545**	**5,736**
British Territory ...	**22,102**	**8,009**	**114**	**132**	**5,182**	**889**	**45,019**	**43,085**	**629**	**4,010**	**24,356**	**5,463**
Patna Division ..	**6,427**	**2,849**	**7**	...	**333**	**53**	**10,914**	**9,863**	**10**	**47**	**1,038**	**464**
Patna	2,634	665	7		39	4	2,882	2,504	2	26	176	85
Gaya	1,461	1,008	.	.	66	16	3,631	3,203	8	21	412	163
Shahabad	2,342	1,176	...	.	328	33	4,401	4,006		.	450	216
Tirhut Division ...	**6,489**	**2,714**	**41**	**37**	**3,147**	**689**	**11,515**	**9,956**	**121**	**177**	**10,960**	**3,271**
Saran	1,337	894	1	11	803	343	2,872	2,886	47	56	2,774	1,524
Champaran ..	1,330	562	...	4	941	151	2,180	1,199	.	8	3,207	678
Muzaffarpur ..	2,043	956	2	11	872	114	3,858	3,786	10	66	3,133	782
Darbhanga ...	1,780	303	38	11	531	82	2,605	2,085	64	47	1,840	287
Bhagalpur Division ...	**4,627**	**1,283**	**12**	**20**	**455**	**48**	**8,799**	**6,528**	**38**	**97**	**1,435**	**503**
Monghyr	1,519	570	3	3	102	30	3,292	3,036	24	47	422	179
Bhagalpur	1,122	441	5	8	103	15	2,880	2,079	13	48	531	174
Purnea	1,515	131	3	8	113	1	1,947	855	..		114	19
Santal Parganas ...	471	141	1	1	137	12	680	558	1	2	368	131
Orissa Division ...	**902**	**200**	**14**	**24**	**269**	**10**	**11,072**	**14,352**	**391**	**3,541**	**8,854**	**722**
Cuttack	301	.	3	.	65	1	5,872	7,409	66	729	3,640	181
Balasore	353	28	5	..	140	2	841	2,230	86	582	2,597	193
Angul	.	5	...		3	.	482	706	...	1	159	27
Puri	252	104	4	19	41	2	2,516	3,285	134	1,926	1,749	237
Sambalpur	186	63	2	5	20	5	1,361	1,718	105	308	700	84
Chota Nagpur Division	**3,567**	**963**	**40**	**51**	**988**	**89**	**2,719**	**2,386**	**69**	**148**	**2,069**	**503**
Hazaribagh ..	854	270	5	14	541	35	577	538	15	27	573	146
Ranchi	683	169	30	23	83	19	303	299	15	43	167	49
Palamau	535	414	6	9	72	20	640	745	3	25	653	243
Manbhum	811	83	7	4	257	14	705	547	35	27	467	54
Singhbhum ...	684	27	2	1	35	1	485	267	1	26	209	12
Feudatory States ...	**392**	**61**	**1**	**18**	**19**		**5,584**	**7,297**	**102**	**958**	**3,189**	**273**
Orissa States ..	385	61	...	18	19	...	5,493	7,215	101	948	3,130	244
Chota Nagpur States ..	7	...	1	...	..	...	91	82	1	10	59	29
Cities	**1,979**	**336**	**7**	**1**	**26**	**1**	**1,979**	**791**	**5**	**9**	**7**	**5**
Patna City	843	98	7	...	1	...	484	330	...	3	...	...
Gaya City	399	106	...	...	..	...	255	241	3	...	...	...
Bhagalpur City ...	380	123	...	...	12	...	263	183	2	4	7	4
Jamshedpur City ...	357	9	...	1	13	1	77	37	...	2	...	1

TABLE X—continued.

OCCUPATION OR MEANS OF LIVELIHOOD. PART II—DETAILS FOR DISTRICTS AND CITIES.

DISTRICT, STATE OR CITY.	ORDER 12.—INDUSTRIES OF DRESS AND THE TOILET—concluded. Group 86.—Barbers, hair-dressers and wig-makers. Earners (principal occupation).		Working dependants.		Earners (subsidiary occupation).		ORDER 13.—FURNITURE INDUSTRIES. Earners (principal occupation).		Working dependants.		Earners (subsidiary occupation).		ORDER 14.—BUILDING INDUSTRIES. Earners (principal occupation).		Working dependants.		Earners (subsidiary occupation).		ORDER 16.—CONSTRUCTION OF MEANS OF TRANSPORT. Earners (principal occupation).		Working dependants.		Earners (subsidiary occupation).	
	Males.	Females.	Males.	Females.	Males.	Females.	Males.	Females.	Males.	Females.	Males.	Females.	Males.	Females.	Males.	Females.	Males.	Females.	Males.	Females.	Males.	Females.	Males.	Females.
1	335	336	337	338	339	340	341	342	343	344	345	346	347	348	349	350	351	352	353	354	355	356	357	358
BIHAR AND ORISSA	**68,970**	**21,778**	**856**	**1,104**	**34,115**	**1,799**	**61**	**165**	...	...	**11**	**18**	**22,727**	**7,274**	**85**	**584**	**6,660**	**1,179**	**577**	**5**	**2**	...	**212**	...
British Territory ...	**64,769**	**21,461**	**756**	**1,073**	**31,228**	**1,767**	**61**	**165**	...	...	**11**	**18**	**21,633**	**5,172**	**70**	**40**	**5,916**	**922**	**519**	**5**	**2**	...	**136**	...
PATNA DIVISION ...	**19,591**	**8,499**	**66**	**47**	**2,205**	**293**	...	...	...	...	...	...	**9,696**	**4,262**	**30**	**14**	**1,554**	**809**	**6**	...	...	...	...	...
Patna	6,017	2,585	1	11	673	104	...	...	...	...	...	...	3,313	1,520	10	5	550	411	4	...	...	...	...	...
Gaya	7,474	3,989	59	34	727	128	...	...	...	...	...	...	2,638	1,491	14	9	356	271	...	...	...	...	...	...
Shahabad	6,100	1,925	6	2	805	61	...	...	...	...	...	...	3,745	1,351	...	...	648	127	2	...	...	...	...	...
TIRHUT DIVISION ..	**9,884**	**2,813**	**120**	**140**	**10,025**	**655**	**19**	**159**	...	...	...	**18**	**1,965**	**134**	**8**	**3**	**1,305**	**33**	**21**	**4**	...	...	**18**	...
Saran	2,180	635	10	8	2,649	354	10	...	...	...	...	...	354	15	7	...	403	8	1	...	...	...	9	...
Champaran ...	1,104	154	...	10	2,130	76	...	16	...	...	...	1	209	16	...	...	273	4	4	...	...	...	...	...
Muzaffarpur ...	3,403	1,358	4	67	3,037	236	8	...	...	...	...	...	1,048	62	1	1	294	20	...	...	...	...	1	...
Darbhanga .	3,197	676	106	55	2,219	90	1	143	...	...	...	17	354	41	...	2	335	1	16	4	...	...	8	...
BHAGALPUR DIVISION ..	**15,275**	**5,441**	**59**	**119**	**5,342**	**377**	**11**	**6**	...	...	**7**	...	**3,955**	**385**	**11**	**12**	**619**	**34**	**78**	...	...	...	**26**	...
Monghyr	6,364	3,263	39	96	1,128	181	3	...	...	...	2	...	1,620	91	...	...	55	3	1	...	...	...	...	...
Bhagalpur	4,277	1,600	17	18	1,448	57	8	...	...	...	...	...	959	39	9	12	119		59	...	...	...	4	...
Purnea	3,488	331	...	...	379	3	...	...	...	...	5	...	689	103	2	...	82	...	18	...	...	...	...	...
Santal Parganas ..	1,146	247	3	5	2,387	136	...	6	...	...	...	...	687	152		...	363	31	...	...	...	...	22	...
ORISSA DIVISION ...	**14,276**	**3,626**	**330**	**711**	**8,000**	**223**	**5**	...	...	...	**1**	...	**2,025**	**62**	**10**	...	**1,506**	**14**	**263**	...	...	...	**30**	...
Cuttack	5,583	1,598	33	213	3,428	50	3	...	...	...	...	...	180	...	1	...	324	7	171	...	...	...	1	...
Balasore	950	698	99	17	2,119	8	2	...	...	...	1	...	112	23	1	...	181	3	7	...	...	...	4	...
Angul	312	2	...	...	156	1	...	...	...	...	...	...	32	7	...	...	58	1	3	...	...	...	2	...
Puri	6,331	1,318	105	481	1,767	164	...	...	...	...	...	...	1,382	31	4	...	715	2	13	...	...	...	3	...
Sambalpur	1,100	10	93	...	530	...	...	...	...	...	...	...	319	1	4	...	228	1	69	...	...	...	20	...
CHOTA NAGPUR DIVISION	**5,743**	**1,082**	**181**	**56**	**5,656**	**219**	**26**	...	...	...	**3**	...	**4,017**	**329**	**11**	**11**	**932**	**32**	**151**	**1**	**2**	...	**62**	...
Hazaribagh ...	1,389	297	11	5	2,451	91	1	...	...	...	...	...	673	199	2	...	287	3	24	...	...	...	14	...
Ranchi	854	141	46	21	553	23	...	...	...	...	3	...	456	15	9	11	88	1	10	...	1	...	1	...
Palamau	987	346	5	8	963	33	...	...	...	...	...	...	707	25	...		65	7	3	...	...	...	...	...
Manbhum	2,002	374	119	22	1,546	71	9	...	...	...	...	...	1,957	57	...	...	361	20	94	1	...	...	44	...
Singhbhum ...	611	34	...	...	144	1	16	...	...	...	...	...	224	33	...	...	111	1	20	...	1	...	3	...
Feudatory States ...	**4,201**	**317**	**100**	**31**	**2,887**	**32**	...	...	...	...	...	...	**1,089**	**2,102**	**15**	**544**	**744**	**257**	**58**	...	...	...	**76**	...
Orissa States ...	4,100	277	89	24	2,753	13	...	...		...	...	...	1,068	2,102	15	544	723	257	57	...	...	...	74	...
Chota Nagpur States ...	101	40	11	7	134	19	...	...	...	...	...	...	21	...	...	...	21	...	1	...	...	...	2	...
Cities	**1,488**	**336**	**20**	**3**	**7**	...	...	...	...	...	...	...	**2,000**	**125**	**1**	...	**82**	**1**	**16**	...	**1**	...	...	...
Patna City	564	196	...	...	2	...	...	...	...	...	...	...	753	19	1	...	3	...	2	...	...	...	...	...
Gaya City	440	72	20	...	...	...	...	...	...	...	...	...	325	70	...	...	...	...	...	...	...	...	...	...
Bhagalpur City ...	373	66	...	3	3	...	...	...	...	...	...	...	505	17	...	...	49	...	1	...	...	...	...	...
Jamshedpur City ...	311	2	...	...	2	...	...	...	...	...	...	...	517	19	...	...	30	1	13	...	1	...	...	...

TABLE X.—*continued.*

Occupation or Means of Livelihood. Part II—Details for Districts and Cities.

District, State or City.	Order 16.—Production and transmission of physical forces. Earners (principal occupation). Males.	Females.	Working dependants. Males.	Females.	Earners (subsidiary occupation). Males.	Females.	Order 17.—Miscellaneous and undefined industries. Total of Order 17. Earners (principal occupation). Males.	Females.	Working dependants. Males.	Females.	Earners (subsidiary occupation). Males.	Females.	Group 98.—Makers of jewellery and ornaments. Earners (principal occupation). Males.	Females.	Working dependants. Males.	Females.	Earners (subsidiary occupation). Males.	Females.	Group 100.—Scavenging. Earners (principal occupation). Males.	Females.	Working dependants. Males.	Females.	Earners (subsidiary occupation). Males.	Females.
1	359	360	361	362	363	364	365	366	367	368	369	370	371	372	373	374	375	376	377	378	370	380	381	382
BIHAR AND ORISSA	**395**	**6**	**2**	...	**33**	...	**60,896**	**14,493**	**499**	**670**	**42,888**	**1,284**	**44,321**	**2,076**	**409**	**132**	**40,585**	**317**	**9,563**	**9,922**	**28**	**450**	**787**	**720**
British Territory ...	**350**	**6**	**2**	...	**33**	...	**55,962**	**12,377**	**467**	**414**	**41,560**	**1,211**	**40,398**	**1,934**	**378**	**111**	**39,390**	**286**	**8,862**	**7,967**	**27**	**215**	**750**	**681**
Patna Division ...	**9**	...	...	...	...	...	**14,888**	**2,957**	**14**	...	**371**	**137**	**10,471**	**638**	**8**	...	**274**	**105**	**1,836**	**1,493**	...	...	**47**	**28**
Patna	4	...	...	...	...	...	6,592	845	6	...	101	16	3,749	171	...	...	88	9	1,057	567	...	...	6	7
Gaya	1	...	...	...	...	...	2,763	1,030	8	...	92	104	2,356	220	8	...	71	94	285	467	...	...	4	10
Shahabad	4	...	...	...	...	...	5,533	1,092	...	...	178	17	4,366	247	...	...	115	2	494	460	...	...	37	11
Tirhut Division ...	**24**	**1**	...	...	**5**	...	**13,007**	**2,868**	**105**	**105**	**6,128**	**455**	**10,256**	**588**	**77**	**71**	**5,470**	**153**	**1,322**	**1,242**	**2**	**15**	**278**	**167**
Saran	2	1	...	...	1	...	4,067	847	18	24	1,793	211	3,270	235	16	8	1,525	44	476	339	2	...	186	125
Champaran ...	1	...	...	...	1	...	1,417	205	6	10	1,340	74	1,362	61	6	9	1,273	56	97	85	...	1	35	10
Muzaffarpur ...	...	...	...	...	3	...	4,417	943	...	8	1,980	112	3,209	129	...	7	1,734	84	489	539	...	1	32	30
Darbhanga ...	21	...	...	...	...	...	3,106	873	81	63	1,015	58	2,515	173	55	47	938	19	260	279	...	13	25	2
Bhagalpur Division ...	**8**	...	...	...	...	...	**8,501**	**2,158**	**6**	**2**	**779**	**54**	**6,292**	**439**	**4**	**1**	**639**	**6**	**1,503**	**1,245**	**2**	**1**	**95**	**36**
Monghyr	2	...	...	...	...	...	2,833	760	...	1	121	9	2,169	183	...	1	97	4	433	306	...	...	7	1
Bhagalpur	4	...	...	...	...	...	2,344	698	6	1	197	13	1,677	148	4	...	135	...	386	403	2	1	30	7
Purnea	2	...	...	...	...	...	2,315	356	...	...	76	2	1,769	63	...	...	68	...	408	254	...	...	7	2
Santal Parganas ...	...	...	...	...	...	...	1,009	344	...	...	385	30	677	46	...	...	339	2	276	283	...	...	42	26
Orissa Division ...	**19**	...	...	...	...	...	**13,263**	**2,605**	**226**	**212**	**32,707**	**370**	**9,909**	**94**	**204**	**10**	**31,984**	**7**	**2,138**	**2,323**	**5**	**150**	**205**	**306**
Cuttack	18	...	...	...	...	...	6,875	460	27	96	30,288	66	5,737	36	27	1	29,993	...	546	417	...	95	29	19
Balasore	1	...	...	...	...	...	1,194	143	61	11	1,132	20	851	15	60	3	1,057	2	311	112	...	7	50	11
Angul	...	...	...	...	...	...	173	307	...	...	44	19	115	...	...	...	30	...	53	307	...	...	14	19
Puri	...	...	...	...	...	...	3,717	607	115	57	714	221	2,255	15	101	3	510	1	1,024	474	2	7	103	217
Sambalpur	...	...	...	...	...	...	1,504	1,088	23	48	529	44	951	28	16	3	394	4	204	1,013	3	41	10	40
Chota Nagpur Division	**290**	**5**	**2**	...	**28**	...	**6,323**	**1,989**	**116**	**95**	**1,575**	**195**	**3,470**	**175**	**85**	**29**	**1,023**	**15**	**2,063**	**1,664**	**18**	**49**	**125**	**144**
Hazaribagh ...	16	...	...	...	18	...	1,152	262	...	2	465	40	785	15	...	2	392	2	276	212	...	...	42	23
Ranchi	14	2	...	...	...	...	877	276	81	51	295	27	548	55	61	24	256	11	183	208	11	10	1	12
Palamau	...	...	...	...	...	...	1,043	271	2	...	102	19	837	51	1	...	60	2	114	161	...	...	10	16
Manbhum	7	...	...	...	9	...	2,204	654	32	38	581	107	966	30	22	2	237	...	904	679	7	36	61	92
Singhbhum ...	253	3	2	...	1	...	1,047	526	1	4	132	2	334	18	1	1	78	...	586	504	...	3	11	1
Feudatory States ...	**45**	...	...	...	...	...	**4,914**	**2,116**	**32**	**256**	**1,328**	**73**	**3,923**	**142**	**31**	**21**	**1,195**	**31**	**701**	**1,955**	**1**	**235**	**37**	**39**
Orissa States ...	43	...	...	...	...	...	3,710	2,035	28	237	1,139	49	2,804	131	27	8	1,024	18	662	1,885	1	229	26	28
Chota Nagpur States ...	2	...	...	...	...	...	1,204	81	4	19	189	24	1,119	11	4	13	171	13	39	70	...	6	11	11
Cities	**238**	**3**	...	...	**1**	...	**3,782**	**363**	...	...	**21**	**3**	**1,208**	**38**	...	...	**15**	...	**917**	**805**	...	...	**6**	**3**
Patna City	1	...	...	...	...	...	2,773	263	...	...	...	...	708	7	...	...	...	...	511	239	...	...	...	...
Gaya City	1	...	...	...	...	...	225	157	...	...	...	...	195	4	...	...	...	...	13	153	...	...	...	...
Bhagalpur City ...	3	...	...	...	...	...	353	150	...	...	...	3	214	25	...	...	...	...	91	122	...	...	...	3
Jamshedpur City ...	233	3	...	...	1	...	431	293	...	...	21	...	91	2	...	...	15	...	302	291	...	...	6	...

TABLE X—*continued.*

Occupation or Means of Livelihood. Part II.—Details for Districts and Cities.

District, State or City.	Sub-Class IV.—Transport.						Order 19.—Transport by Water.					
	Earners (principal occupation).		Working dependants.		Earners (subsidiary occupation).		Earners (principal occupation).		Working dependants.		Earners (subsidiary occupation).	
	Males.	Females.	Males.	Females.	Males.	Females.	Males.	Females.	Males.	Females.	Males.	Females.
1	383	384	385	386	387	388	389	390	391	392	393	394
BIHAR AND ORISSA	**110,257**	**20,215**	**1,239**	**1,949**	**46,407**	**2,545**	**11,157**	**493**	**110**	**92**	**3,857**	**52**
British Territory ...	**99,019**	**12,959**	**478**	**433**	**42,411**	**2,236**	**8,600**	**478**	**104**	**90**	**2,797**	**49**
Patna Division ...	**24,584**	**2,600**	**6**	**37**	**4,636**	**432**	**2,355**	**228**	..	**1**	**253**	**18**
Patna	9,656	1,075	2	2	1,232	124	601	51	...	...	45	2
Gaya	6,342	806	4	35	1,084	172	643	53	...	1	79	7
Shahabad	8,386	710	..	..	2,320	136	1,015	124	...	...	129	9
Tirhut Division ...	**9,678**	**98**	**48**	**7**	**10,173**	**41**	**602**	**2**	**1**	...	**507**	**5**
Saran ...	2,364	18	12	...	2,440	23	308	2	1	..	290	5
Champaran ...	1,660	48	...	6	1,488	16	85	...	.	...	41	..
Muzaffarpur ...	3,176	24	..	...	3,537	3	129	...	...	..	152	...
Darbhanga ...	2,578	8	36	1	2,708	1	81	...	..	..	94	..
Bhagalpur Division ...	**22,587**	**1,579**	**50**	**135**	**4,906**	**261**	**2,143**	**133**	**14**	**88**	**272**	**9**
Monghyr	9,760	481	29	130	1,281	56	901	96	.	84	91	3
Bhagalpur	3,554	146	16	1	1,024	16	563	28	14	..	56	7
Purnea	6,575	551	5	..	451	39	568	9	...	...	20	...
Santal Parganas ..	2,698	401	...	4	2,150	150	108	..	...	4	105	.
Orissa Division ...	**12,677**	**1,381**	**187**	**93**	**13,233**	**533**	**3,185**	**4**	**80**	**1**	**1,601**	**7**
Cuttack	5,185	7	33	1	5,442	.	2,620	4	23	1	977	...
Balasore	1,812	187	53	15	5,355	80	186	...	6		353	..
Angul	100	132	1	..	450	14	8	..	...	..	8	..
Puri	2,304	99	100	37	552	32	80	...	51	...	139	7
Sambalpur	3,276	1,456	11	40	1,684	417	241	...	...	..	224	.
Chota Nagpur Division	**29,493**	**6,801**	**187**	**171**	**9,463**	**969**	**339**	**111**	**9**		**164**	**10**
Hazaribagh ...	4,856	1,446	4	36	1,731	130	1	...	...	...	...	...
Ranchi	1,461	210	26	23	594	86	158	74	8	...	39	5
Palamau	2,258	719	15	11	1,905	395	71	16	1	..	10	1
Manbhum	14,846	3,954	116	68	3,427	293	45	19	...	..	45	1
Singhbhum ...	6,072	472	20	33	1,806	65	54	...	...	...	70	..
Feudatory States ...	**11,238**	**7,256**	**761**	**1,516**	**3,996**	**309**	**2,597**	**15**	**6**	**2**	**1,060**	**3**
Orissa States ..	10,731	6,946	754	1,514	3,628	305	2,568	12	6	2	1,060	3
Chota Nagpur States ...	507	310	7	2	368	4	29	3	...	...	...	...
Cities	**6,832**	**466**	**16**	...	**184**	**8**	**229**	**7**	**14**	...	...	...
Patna City ...	2,041	310	...	...	35	...	208	7	...	...	...	...
Gaya City	631	16	...	...	4	...	18	...	...	...	...	...
Bhagalpur City ...	453	2	14	...	78	...	3	...	14	...	...	...
Jamshedpur City ...	2,817	138	2	...	67	8	...	...	...	...	...	...

District, State or City.	Order 20.—Transport by Road.											
	Total of Order 20.						Group 106.—Labourers employed on roads and bridges.					
	Earners (principal occupation).		Working dependants.		Earners (subsidiary occupation).		Earners (principal occupation)		Working dependants.		Earners (subsidiary occupation).	
	Males.	Females.	Males.	Females.	Males.	Females.	Males.	Females.	Males.	Females.	Males.	Females.
1	395	396	397	398	399	400	401	402	403	404	405	406
BIHAR AND ORISSA	**64,468**	**18,547**	**952**	**1,797**	**35,712**	**2,409**	**18,202**	**14,966**	**718**	**1,689**	**9,948**	**2,201**
British Territory ...	**57,733**	**11,611**	**307**	**308**	**33,315**	**2,121**	**12,510**	**8,046**	**88**	**200**	**9,251**	**1,919**
Patna Division ...	**18,243**	**2,331**	**2**	**26**	**4,112**	**414**	**2,395**	**2,046**		**26**	**716**	**335**
Patna	7,114	1,013	2	2	1,152	122	964	913	..	2	273	108
Gaya	5,116	743		24	944	165	959	718		24	339	139
Shahabad	6,013	575	...		2,016	127	473	415		...	104	88
Tirhut Division ...	**6,842**	**79**	**45**	**7**	**8,764**	**28**	**412**	**56**	..	...	**200**	**7**
Saran ...	1,093	16	11	..	1,979	10					6	.
Champaran ...	1,263	46	...	6	1,334	15	154	45	...	.	19	7
Muzaffarpur ...	2,386	11	.	.	3,116	2	162	7	..	...	168	...
Darbhanga ...	2,100	7	34	1	2,335	1	96	4	...	..	7	..
Bhagalpur Division ...	**11,832**	**1,352**	**35**	**47**	**3,382**	**249**	**2,242**	**1,290**	**2**	**7**	**741**	**238**
Monghyr	3,043	355	27	46	704	54	502	321	.	6	161	52
Bhagalpur	2,438	116	3	1	387	6	258	100	1	1	72	3
Purnea	4,637	402	5	...	325	39	957	489	1	...	78	39
Santal Parganas ..	1,414	380	...		1,466	150	525	380		...	430	144
Orissa Division ...	**5,545**	**1,777**	**93**	**66**	**10,336**	**516**	**2,161**	**1,730**	**1**	**55**	**4,157**	**510**
Cuttack	1,569	1	...	...	4,101	...	241	..	...	..	95	...
Balasore	968	185	82	15	4,306	80	335	183	1	15	2,886	79
Angul	75	132	1	..	437	14	8	132	..	...	419	14
Puri	578	53	6	11	373	5	15	9	...	.	3	...
Sambalpur	2,365	1,406	4	40	1,230	417	1,562	1,406		40	754	417
Chota Nagpur Division	**15,371**	**6,072**	**132**	**162**	**6,221**	**914**	**5,300**	**2,924**	**85**	**112**	**3,437**	**829**
Hazaribagh ...	3,847	1,267	3	36	1,366	112	2,163	1,236	1	..	418	110
Ranchi	1,130	128	23	10	485	81	115	98	3	13	73	75
Palamau	1,753	701	13	11	1,843	394	552	674	7	11	1,358	393
Manbhum	7,109	3,718	83	65	1,877	270	2,177	690	69	63	1,422	201
Singhbhum ...	1,533	258	10	31	630	57	292	237	5	25	166	50
Feudatory States ...	**6,735**	**6,936**	**645**	**1,489**	**2,397**	**288**	**5,692**	**6,920**	**630**	**1,489**	**697**	**282**
Orissa States ..	6,374	6,681	639	1,489	2,208	286	5,688	6,669	629	1,489	652	282
Chota Nagpur States ...	61	255	6	.	189	2	4	251	1	...	45	...
Cities	**3,520**	**314**	**1**	...	**151**	.	**183**	**292**	...	...	...	...
Patna City ...	2,237	293	..	...	35	...	168	279	...	...	...	...
Gaya City	345	12	..	...	4	...	14	12	...	...	...	...
Bhagalpur City ...	381	2	..	...	78	...	...	...	...	...	...	...
Jamshedpur City ...	557	7	1	...	34	...	1	1	...	...	...	...

TABLE X—*continued.*

OCCUPATION OR MEANS OF LIVELIHOOD. PART II—DETAILS FOR DISTRICTS AND CITIES.

ORDER 20.—TRANSPORT BY ROAD—*continued.*

DISTRICT, STATE OR CITY.	Group 107.—Owners, managers and employees (excluding personal servants) connected with mechanically driven vehicles (including trams). Earners (principal occupation). Males.	Females.	Working dependants. Males.	Females.	Earners (subsidiary occupation). Males.	Females.	Group 108.—Owners, managers and employees (excluding personal servants) connected with other vehicles. Earners (principal occupation). Males.	Females.	Working dependants. Males.	Females.	Earners (subsidiary occupation). Males.	Females.
1	407	408	409	410	411	412	413	414	415	416	417	418
BIHAR AND ORISSA	**2,879**	**16**	**11**	**35**	**772**	**2**	**16,898**	**172**	**134**	**19**	**10,040**	**71**
British Territory ...	**2,819**	**15**	**11**	**35**	**763**	**2**	**15,977**	**159**	**119**	**19**	**8,406**	**65**
PATNA DIVISION ...	**900**	**4**	...	...	**313**	...	**4,835**	**29**	...	...	**987**	**32**
Patna	442	3	...	...	50	...	1,805	3	...	...	212	2
Gaya	31	...	...	...	...	...	1,391	16	...	...	205	6
Shahabad	427	1	...	...	263	...	1,639	10	...	...	570	24
TIRHUT DIVISION ...	**22**	...	...	...	**104**	...	**2,545**	**7**	**14**	**7**	**2,498**	**7**
Saran	12	...	...	...	103	...	494	3	10	...	768	6
Champaran ...	10	...	...	...	1	...	779	...	...	6	560	...
Muzaffarpur ...	...	...	...	...	...	...	788	4	...	...	787	1
Darbhanga ...	...	...	...	...	...	...	484	...	4	1	383	...
BHAGALPUR DIVISION ...	**18**	...	...	...	...	...	**4,240**	**17**	**23**	...	**1,354**	**11**
Monghyr	2	...	...	...	...	...	784	4	18	...	290	2
Bhagalpur	5	...	...	...	...	...	930	6	1	...	270	3
Purnea	10	...	...	...	...	...	1,945	1	4	...	140	...
Santal Parganas ...	1	...	...	...	...	...	572	6	...	...	654	6
ORISSA DIVISION ...	**474**	**2**	**8**	...	**203**	**1**	**1,933**	**45**	**59**	**11**	**2,225**	**4**
Cuttack	88	...	...	...	3	...	910	1	...	...	1,308	...
Balasore	183	2	8	...	99	...	214	...	9	...	350	...
Angul	9	...	...	...	8	...	...	...	...	...	...	...
Puri	124	...	...	...	10	1	208	44	46	11	166	4
Sambalpur ...	70	...	...	...	83	...	503	...	4	...	393	...
CHOTA NAGPUR DIVISION ...	**1,405**	**9**	**3**	**35**	**143**	**1**	**2,424**	**61**	**23**	**1**	**1,342**	**11**
Hazaribagh ...	387	1	...	34	47	...	559	24	1	...	430	2
Ranchi	129	1	1	1	23	...	404	7	4	1	399	1
Palamau	92	...	...	...	9	...	300	2	2	...	107	...
Manbhum	512	5	1	...	31	1	561	23	14	...	271	2
Singhbhum ...	385	2	1	...	33	...	420	5	3	...	245	6
Feudatory States ...	**60**	**1**	...	...	**9**	...	**921**	**13**	**15**	...	**1,634**	**6**
Orissa States ...	34	...	...	...	6	...	898	10	10	...	1,495	4
Chota Nagpur States ...	26	1	...	...	3	...	23	3	5	...	139	2
Cities	**563**	**3**	...	...	**41**	...	**1,304**	**3**	**1**	...	**91**	...
Patna City	317	3	...	...	35	...	712	...	...	...	...	...
Gaya City	13	...	...	...	...	...	281	...	...	...	4	...
Bhagalpur City ...	2	...	...	...	...	...	208	1	...	...	71	...
Jamshedpur City ...	231	...	...	...	6	...	103	2	1	...	16	...

DISTRICT, STATE OR CITY.	Group 109.—Palki, etc., bearers and owners. Earners (principal occupation). Males.	Females.	Working dependants. Males.	Females.	Earners (subsidiary occupation). Males.	Females.	Group 110.—Pack elephant, camel, mule, ass and bullock, owners and drivers. Earners (principal occupation). Males.	Females.	Working dependants. Males.	Females.	Earners (subsidiary occupation). Males.	Females.
1	419	420	421	422	423	424	425	426	427	428	429	430
BIHAR AND ORISSA	**9,454**	**70**	**61**	**36**	**12,154**	**17**	**7,761**	**182**	**10**	**6**	**1,754**	**32**
British Territory ...	**9,449**	**69**	**61**	**36**	**12,107**	**17**	**7,696**	**182**	**10**	**6**	**1,754**	**32**
PATNA DIVISION ...	**2,143**	**18**	**1**	...	**929**	**3**	**6,183**	**168**	**1**	...	**1,090**	**30**
Patna	930	6	1	...	349	1	1,897	22	1	...	338	1
Gaya	304	...	...	...	76	...	2,094	9	...	...	308	20
Shahabad	909	12	...	...	504	2	2,192	137	...	...	544	9
TIRHUT DIVISION ...	**3,621**	**16**	**31**	...	**5,712**	**12**	**114**	...	...	...	**164**	...
Saran	553	13	1	...	1,061	4	2	...	...	...	...	...
Champaran ...	199	...	...	...	614	7	57	...	...	...	22	...
Muzaffarpur ...	1,360	...	...	...	1,995	...	47	...	...	...	140	...
Darbhanga ...	1,509	3	30	...	2,042	1	8	...	...	...	2	...
BHAGALPUR DIVISION ...	**3,045**	**14**	**6**	**36**	**947**	...	**119**	**2**	...	**4**	**8**	...
Monghyr	1,776	2	6	36	223	...	55	2	...	4	3	...
Bhagalpur	776	10	...	...	333	...	...	...	...	...	...	...
Purnea	335	...	...	...	23	...	41	...	...	...	4	...
Santal Parganas ...	158	2	...	...	368	...	23	...	...	...	1	...
ORISSA DIVISION ...	**366**	...	**23**	...	**4,062**	...	**22**	...	**1**	...	...	...
Cuttack	157	...	...	...	2,740	...	...	...	...	...	...	...
Balasore	182	...	23	...	1,216	...	...	...	...	...	...	...
Angul	...	...	...	...	...	...	20	...	1	...	...	...
Puri	26	...	...	...	102	...	...	...	...	...	...	...
Sambalpur ...	1	...	...	...	4	...	1	...	...	...	...	...
CHOTA NAGPUR DIVISION ...	**274**	**21**	...	...	**457**	**2**	**1,213**	**12**	**8**	**2**	**492**	**2**
Hazaribagh ...	100	3	...	...	129	...	472	5	1	2	268	...
Ranchi	16	5	...	...	9	2	59	...	4	...	31	...
Palamau	95	12	...	...	202	...	518	3	2	...	159	1
Manbhum	33	1	...	...	88	...	...	...	...	...	...	...
Singhbhum ...	30	...	...	...	29	...	164	4	1	...	34	1
Feudatory States ...	**5**	**1**	...	...	**47**	...	**5**	...	...	...	...	...
Orissa States ...	5	1	...	...	47	...	5	...	...	...	...	...
Chota Nagpur States ...	...	...	...	...	...	...	...	...	...	...	...	...
Cities	**142**	**1**	...	...	...	...	**462**	**4**	...	...	**12**	...
Patna City	30	...	...	...	...	...	389	...	...	...	...	...
Gaya City	...	...	...	...	...	...	8	...	...	...	...	...
Bhagalpur City ...	103	1	...	...	...	...	...	...	...	...	...	...
Jamshedpur City ...	9	...	...	...	...	...	65	4	...	...	12	...

TABLE X—*continued.*

OCCUPATION OR MEANS OF LIVELIHOOD. PART II—DETAILS FOR DISTRICTS AND CITIES.

DISTRICT, STATE OR CITY.	ORDER 20.—TRANSPORT BY ROAD—*concluded.*						ORDER 21.—TRANSPORT BY RAIL.																	
	Group 111.—Porters and messengers.						TOTAL OF ORDER 21.						Group 112.—Railway employees of all kinds other than coolies.						Group 113.—Labourers employed on railway construction and maintenance and coolies and porters employed on railway premises.					
	Earners (principal occupation).		*Working dependants.*		*Earners (subsidiary occupation).*		*Earners (principal occupation).*		*Working dependants.*		*Earners (subsidiary occupation).*		*Earners (principal occupation).*		*Working dependants.*		*Earners (subsidiary occupation).*		*Earners (principal occupation).*		*Working dependants.*		*Earners (subsidiary occupation).*	
	Males.	Females.	Males.	Females.	Males.	Females.	Males.	Females.	Males.	Females.	Males.	Females.	Males.	Females.	Males.	Females.	Males.	Females.	Males.	Females.	Males.	Females.	Males.	Females.
1	431	432	433	434	435	436	437	438	439	440	441	442	443	444	445	446	447	448	449	450	451	452	453	454
BIHAR AND ORISSA	**9,107**	**3,087**	**18**	**12**	**1,004**	**72**	**32,367**	**1,155**	**71**	**60**	**6,283**	**79**	**19,800**	**197**	**46**	**14**	**2,873**	**20**	**12,567**	**958**	**25**	**46**	**3,410**	**59**
British Territory ...	**9,101**	**3,086**	**18**	**12**	**1,004**	**72**	**30,714**	**850**	**65**	**35**	**5,812**	**61**	**18,813**	**153**	**41**	**12**	**2,487**	**18**	**11,901**	**697**	**24**	**23**	**3,325**	**43**
PATNA DIVISION ...	**1,785**	**12**	...	...	**77**	...	**3,820**	**41**	**4**	...	**238**	...	**1,541**	**6**	...	...	**175**	...	**2,279**	**35**	**4**	...	**63**	...
Patna	1,076	12	...	...	30	...	2,009	11	...	..	31	..	275	3	..	...	...	...	1,734	8	...		31	...
Gaya	337	..	...	...	16	...	558	10	4	...	59	...	301	1	...	...	27	...	257	9	4	...	32	...
Shahabad	372	...	...	...	31	...	1,253	20	.	...	148	...	965	2	...	...	148	...	388	18	...		...	...
TIRHUT DIVISION ...	**68**	...	...	...	**79**	**2**	**1,882**	**16**	**2**	...	**744**	**3**	**1,255**	**3**	**2**	...	**494**	...	**627**	**13**		...	**250**	**3**
Saran	21	..	...	...	39	...	775	...	..	...	189	2	585	...	...	...	119		190	..		...	70	2
Champaran ...	18	...	...	...	14	1	279	2	...		193	1	68	2	...	...	69	...	211	...	...	..	127	1
Muzaffarpur ...	28	...	...	...	25	1	524	13	...	...	195	...	422	...	..	...	153	...	103	19	..	...	42	...
Darbhanga ...	1	...	...	...	1	...	304	1	2	...	164	...	160	1	2	...	153	...	124	...	...	...	11	...
BHAGALPUR DIVISION ...	**2,164**	**29**	**4**	...	**332**	...	**8,251**	**94**	**1**	..	**1,196**	**3**	**7,639**	**37**	**1**	...	**894**	**3**	**612**	**57**	...	..	**302**	...
Monghyr	844	26	4	...	27	...	4,894	30	1	...	477	...	4,810	27	1	...	471	.	75	3	...	...	6	...
Bhagalpur	460	...	...	...	192	...	385	2	...	...	92	3	355		...	...	87	3	30	2		...	5	...
Purnea	727	2	...	...	80	...	1,830	50	...	...	94	.	1,460	4	...	...	85	...	370	46	.		9	...
Santal Parganas ...	133	1	...	...	33	...	1,142	12	..	...	583	..	1,006	6	.	...	251	..	137	6	..	..	282	...
ORISSA DIVISION ...	**356**	...	**1**		**177**	**1**	**3,583**	**100**	**13**	**26**	**679**	**10**	**2,375**	**6**	**8**	**8**	**387**	**1**	**1,208**	**94**	**5**	**18**	**292**	**9**
Cuttack	102	...	...	...	43	.	760	2		..	130	...	405			...	30		365	3	..	...	100	...
Balasore	48	...	1	..	45	1	610	2	4	...	359	...	534	2	4	...	222	...	76	...	..	.	137	
Angul	...	..	...	...	...	...	6	...	...	..	6	.	2	.	...	...	...	...	4	...		...	6	...
Puri	187	...	...	...	80	...	1,560	46	3	36	17	10	981	4	3	8	15	1	579	42		18	2	9
Sambalpur	19	...	...	...	...	...	647	50	6	...	167	...	453	..	1	...	130	.	194	50	5	..	47	...
CHOTA NAGPUR DIVISION...	**4,728**	**3,045**	**13**	**12**	**339**	**69**	**13,178**	**599**	**45**	**9**	**2,955**	**45**	**6,003**	**101**	**30**	**4**	**537**	**14**	**7,175**	**498**	**15**	**5**	**2,418**	**31**
Hazaribagh ...	263	9	...	..	103	...	936	179	1	..	318	15	341	9	1	..	51	...	595	170	...	...	237	18
Ranchi	311	17	1	4	40	3	133	6	1	4	56	...	52	6	4	4	30	.	71	1	.	...	26	...
Palamau	95	10	2	...	6	...	340	...	1	...	35	...	152	...	1	...	8	.	198	..		..	27	...
Manbhum	3,826	2,999	9	2	165	66	7,482	200	33	3	1,368	19	3,301	77	10		198	6	4,181	133	13	3	1,170	13
Singhbhum ...	233	10	1	6	18	...	4,388	214	16	2	1,178	8	2,314	11	14	...	220	8	2,130	204	2	2	958	...
Feudatory States ...	**6**	**1**		...	...	...	**1,653**	**305**	**6**	**25**	**471**	**18**	**987**	**44**	**5**	**2**	**386**	**2**	**666**	**261**	**1**	**23**	**85**	**16**
Orissa States ...	5	1	...	...	...	...	1,253	253	5	23	297	16	877	32	5	...	297	1	376	221	...	23	..	15
Chota Nagpur States ...	1	...	...	...	...	...	400	52	1	2	174	2	110	12	...	2	89	1	300	40	1	...	85	1
Cities	**866**	**11**	...	...	**7**	...	**2,956**	**145**	**1**	...	**17**	**8**	**1,414**	**4**	...	...	**6**	**8**	**1,542**	**141**	**1**	...	**11**	...
Patna City ...	621	11	...	...	...	...	486	10	...	...	...	...	51	2	...	...	...	...	435	8	...	...	...	...
Gaya City ...	20	...	...	...	...	...	248	4	...	...	...	...	245	1	...	...	...	...	3	3	...	...	...	...
Bhagalpur City ...	68	...	...	...	7	...	43	...	...	...	...	...	30	...	...	...	...	...	3	...	...	...	...	...
Jamshedpur City ...	148	...	...	...	...	...	2,180	131	1	...	17	8	1,079	1	...	...	6	8	1,101	130	1	...	11	...

1

TABLE X—*continued.*

OCCUPATION OR MEANS OF LIVELIHOOD. PART II—DETAILS FOR DISTRICTS AND CITIES.

DISTRICT STATE OR CITY.	ORDER 22.—POST OFFICE, TELEGRAPH AND TELEPHONE SERVICES. Earners (principal occupation). Males.	Earners (principal occupation). Females.	Working dependants. Males.	Working dependants. Females.	Earners (subsidiary occupation). Males.	Earners (subsidiary occupation). Females.	SUB-CLASS V.—TRADE. Earners (principal occupation). Males.	Earners (principal occupation). Females.	Working dependants. Males.	Working dependants. Females.	Earners (subsidiary occupation). Males.	Earners (subsidiary occupation). Females.
1	455	456	457	458	459	460	461	462	463	464	465	466
BIHAR AND ORISSA	**2,225**	**20**	**106**	...	**555**	**5**	**360,132**	**260,890**	**4,303**	**17,612**	**170,799**	**45,066**
British Territory ...	**1,972**	**20**	**2**	...	**487**	**5**	**334,473**	**214,647**	**3,444**	**13,605**	**148,461**	**38,806**
PATNA DIVISION ...	**166**	...	...	..	**33**	...	**79,916**	**48,288**	**117**	**149**	**8,181**	**4,271**
Patna	41	...	...	..	4		30,272	13,845	18	10	2,684	1,298
Gaya ...	20	...	...	...	2	....	23,018	13,929	99	133	1,824	1,036
Shahabad ..	105	...	...	...	27	...	26,626	30,514	...	6	3,673	1,937
TIRHUT DIVISION ...	**351**	**1**	...	..	**158**	**5**	**60,267**	**38,331**	**508**	**982**	**46,279**	**10,292**
Saran ...	88	..		...	52	5	12,860	9,283	75	190	11,632	3,944
Champaran ...	33	1	...	...	17	...	8,705	5,279	41	83	10,500	2,016
Muzaffarpur ...	137	...	...	...	74	..	18,628	13,885	54	366	14,036	2,727
Darbhanga ...	93	...	...	...	15	..	20,074	9,884	338	343	10,111	1,555
BHAGALPUR DIVISION ...	**356**	...	...	...	**56**	...	**95,360**	**39,201**	**449**	**807**	**26,486**	**12,515**
Monghyr	19	...	...	...	9	...	30,106	15,068	126	400	8,325	778
Bhagalpur	163	...	...	...	9	...	24,221	9,329	147	240	5,984	1,432
Purnea	140			...	12	..	27,153	8,184	94	20	2,540	236
Santal Parganas	34	...	...	...	26	...	13,880	6,040	82	46	14,637	10,069
ORISSA DIVISION ...	**494**	...	**1**	...	**117**	..	**49,635**	**66,739**	**1,353**	**10,051**	**46,173**	**6,915**
Cuttack	196	..	...	...	44		21,727	22,968	107	3,532	19,219	2,019
Balasore ...	78	...	...	...	37	...	6,034	15,081	377	1,172	13,796	1,101
Angul	11	...	...	...	9	...	643	1,402	3	4	904	87
Puri	86	...	...	..	23	...	15,120	18,954	713	4,348	8,987	2,965
Sambalpur	123	...	1	..	4	...	6,111	8,334	153	995	3,267	743
CHOTA NAGPUR DIVISION	**605**	**19**	**1**	...	**123**		**49,295**	**22,088**	**1,017**	**1,616**	**21,342**	**4,863**
Hazaribagh ...	72	...	...	...	27	...	9,181	3,587	30	65	4,646	824
Ranchi	70	2	1	...	14	...	6,931	3,766	431	909	3,356	1,256
Palamau	85	...		...	17	...	7,861	5,199	163	87	3,553	1,418
Manbhum	210	17	...	...	37	...	16,505	7,372	283	434	8,240	1,101
Singhbhum ...	168	...	...		28		9,817	2,163	110	121	1,547	264
Feudatory States ...	**253**	...	**104**	...	**68**	...	**25,659**	**46,243**	**859**	**4,007**	**22,338**	**6,260**
Orissa States ...	236	...	104	...	63	...	25,025	45,535	840	3,977	21,731	6,109
Chota Nagpur States	17	...	..		5	...	634	708	19	30	607	151
Cities	**127**	...	...	...	**16**		**19,244**	**3,484**	**51**	**49**	**687**	**31**
Patna City	18	..	...	...	...	...	8,140	1,331	15	5	65	...
Gaya City	2	..	...	...		...	4,201	896	...	...	47	7
Bhagalpur City ..	27	...	...	...	...	...	4,231	922	29	39	378	2
Jamshedpur City ...	80	...	..	...	16	...	2,672	345	7	5	197	3

DISTRICT STATE OR CITY.	ORDER 23.—BANKS, ESTABLISHMENTS OF CREDIT, EXCHANGE AND INSURANCE. Earners (principal occupation). Males.	Earners (principal occupation). Females.	Working dependants. Males.	Working dependants. Females.	Earners (subsidiary occupation). Males.	Earners (subsidiary occupation). Females.	ORDER 24.—BROKERAGE COMMISSION AND EXPORT. Earners (principal occupation). Males.	Earners (principal occupation). Females.	Working dependants. Males.	Working dependants. Females.	Earners (subsidiary occupation). Males.	Earners (subsidiary occupation). Females.
1	467	468	469	470	471	472	473	474	475	476	477	478
BIHAR AND ORISSA	**7,054**	**667**	**122**	**75**	**11,696**	**373**	**682**	**236**	**15**	**7**	**267**	**1**
British Territory ...	**6,713**	**636**	**113**	**72**	**10,720**	**347**	**562**	**230**	**15**	**5**	**241**	...
PATNA DIVISION ...	**850**	**127**	...	...	**414**	**22**	**85**	**140**			**11**	
Patna	203	27	..	...	6	...	63	...			10	...
Gaya ...	205	18	..	...	73	3	5	131			1	...
Shahabad ..	443	82	..	...	335	20	17	9	...	...	...	
TIRHUT DIVISION ...	**896**	**56**	**1**	...	**3,472**	**148**	**184**	**2**	**6**		**127**	...
Saran ...	189	2	1	...	785	58	2	..		...	7	...
Champaran ...	330	10	...	...	1,677	77	7	1	..		13	
Muzaffarpur ...	221	14			510	12	38	1	...	...	41	..
Darbhanga ...	156	23		...	500	1	147		6	...	66	...
BHAGALPUR DIVISION ...	**2,274**	**189**	**33**	**15**	**2,437**	**60**	**124**	**7**	...	...	**26**	...
Monghyr	622	109	10	8	448	25	85	1	...	...	23	...
Bhagalpur	400	15	7	7	777	14	4	...	..	...	...	..
Purnea	481	12	...	..	466	5	33	...	...	...	1	...
Santal Parganas	771	53	16	...	751	16	3	6	...	...	3	...
ORISSA DIVISION ...	**496**	**32**	**2**	..	**2,668**	**47**	**91**	..	...	..	**66**	...
Cuttack	90	1	...		1,563	35	70	...	...	...	58	...
Balasore ...	114	14	1		784	7	6	...	...	...	8	...
Angul	11	1	..	..	20	...	...	...	..	...		...
Puri	114	2	1		305	1	...	...	...	...	...	...
Sambalpur	167	14	..	...	87	4	15	...	...	...	...	...
CHOTA NAGPUR DIVISION	**2,197**	**232**	**77**	**57**	**1,729**	**70**	**78**	**81**	**9**	**5**	**11**	...
Hazaribagh ...	436	26	2	4	653	28	5	2		..	...	...
Ranchi	788	115	62	45	663	32	11	1		...	3	..
Palamau	533	77	4	8	320	7	..	...	9	5	...	...
Manbhum	340	10	9	...	162	3	37	72		..	7	..
Singhbhum ...	150	4	..	..	31	...	25	6	...	...	1	...
Feudatory States ...	**341**	**31**	**9**	**3**	**976**	**26**	**120**	**6**	...	**2**	**26**	**1**
Orissa States ...	272	27	9	3	874	21	117	6		2	26	1
Chota Nagpur States	69	4	..	...	103	5	3			...		...
Cities	**327**	**30**	**2**	**3**	**85**	...	**12**	**6**		..	..	...
Patna City	38	25	...	...	..	...	...	..	...	..	...	...
Gaya City	86	2	...	...	7	...	1		...	...	...	...
Bhagalpur City ..	182	3	2	3	77	...	...	...	...	...	...	...
Jamshedpur City ...	21		...	...	1	...	11	6	...	...	...	

TABLE X—*continued*

Occupation or Means of Livelihood. Part II.—Details for Districts and Cities.

District, State or City.	Order 25.—Trade in Textiles. Earners (principal occupation). Males.	Females.	Working dependants. Males.	Females.	Earners (subsidiary occupation). Males.	Females.	Order 26.—Trade in Skins, Leather and Furs. Earners (principal occupation). Males.	Females.	Working dependants. Males.	Females.	Earners (subsidiary occupation). Males.	Females.
1	479	480	481	482	483	484	485	486	487	488	489	490
BIHAR AND ORISSA	**16,615**	**3,178**	**140**	**351**	**5,600**	**330**	**4,675**	**1,080**	**68**	**92**	**2,252**	**261**
British Territory ...	**13,682**	**2,687**	**93**	**324**	**4,278**	**264**	**4,468**	**1,057**	**36**	**84**	**2,246**	**261**
Patna Division ...	**3,618**	**584**	...	**3**	**255**	**6**	**748**	**72**	...	...	**41**	**3**
Patna	1,119	160	...	...	44	...	101	4	...	...	1	...
Gaya	900	135	...	3	48	1	582	5	...	...	19	...
Shahabad	1,599	289	...	...	163	5	60	63	...	...	21	3
Tirhut Division ...	**1,422**	**86**	**3**	..	**940**	**35**	**254**	**63**	**3**	...	**289**	**7**
Saran	338	38	...	...	244	10	43	1	...		56	4
Champaran ...	71	20	...	...	86	10	35	10		...	39	2
Muzaffarpur ...	695	17	.	..	517	14	95	47	3	..	58	1
Darbhanga	318	17	3	..	93	1	71	5		..	136	...
Bhagalpur Division ...	**2,608**	**214**	**11**	..	**389**	**28**	**2,006**	**787**	...	**69**	**1,045**	**190**
Monghyr	265	11	...	...	46	1	211	33		60	18	3
Bhagalpur	398	78	11	...	51	5	530	64	...	...	641	67
Purnea	1,363	88	...	...	133	3	1,022	70	...		113	..
Santal Parganas ...	583	37	...	...	159	20	243	620	..	...	273	120
Orissa Division ...	**3,151**	**1,378**	**80**	**238**	**1,585**	**35**	**606**	**103**	**20**	**14**	**335**	**54**
Cuttack	2,129	347	8	114	1,066	11	48	...	...	...	50	...
Balasore	143	6	1	...	148	1	94	7	1	3	95	52
Angul	97	4	...	..	135	3	16	...		...	1	...
Puri	650	18	14	5	225	4	47	..	..	...	40	..
Sambalpur	132	1,003	7	119	21	16	391	93	19	11	149	3
Chota Nagpur Division	**2,883**	**425**	**49**	**83**	**1,109**	**160**	**863**	**32**	**13**	**1**	**536**	**7**
Hazaribagh ...	383	90	3	3	197	13	356	15	4		445	1
Ranchi	404	65	22	48	182	15	35	4	2	...	21	3
Palamau	516	70	3	6	207	112	131	8	3	..	18	1
Manbhum	1,094	146	18	8	373	10	143	3	4	1	33	1
Singhbhum ...	486	54	3	18	151	10	115	2	..	...	20	1
Feudatory States ...	**2,933**	**491**	**47**	**33**	**1,322**	**66**	**207**	**23**	**32**	**8**	**6**	...
Orissa States ...	2,880	491	43	33	1,318	66	201	22	32	8	...	
Chota Nagpur States ...	53	...	4	...	4		0	1	...	...	6	...
Cities	**576**	**47**	**1**	...	**22**	...	**50**	**2**	...	...	**4**	...
Patna City	343	1	...	...	...	...	3	...	...	...	...	...
Gaya City	68	...	...	...	1	...	15	...	...	...	...	...
Bhagalpur City ...	25	46	...	...	...	...	19	...	...	...	4	...
Jamshedpur City ...	140	...	1	...	21	...	13	2	...	...	...	...

District, State or City.	Order 27.—Trade in Wood. Earners (principal occupation). Males.	Females.	Working dependants. Males.	Females.	Earners (subsidiary occupation). Males.	Females.	Order 28.—Trade in Metals. Earners (principal occupation). Males.	Females.	Working dependants. Males.	Females.	Earners (subsidiary occupation). Males.	Females.
1	491	492	493	494	495	496	497	498	499	500	501	502
BIHAR AND ORISSA	**5,562**	**5,918**	**542**	**616**	**11,397**	**9,873**	**578**	**223**	**38**		**189**	**17**
British Territory ...	**4,611**	**4,994**	**420**	**491**	**10,496**	**9,691**	**444**	**100**	**9**	...	**156**	**17**
Patna Division ...	**663**	**255**	..	...	**50**	**1**	**7**	...	...	...		...
Patna	18		...	...	..	..	..	..		..	...	...
Gaya	588	209		..	50	1		...	...	...	...	..
Shahabad	57	46	...	...	...	...	7	...				...
Tirhut Division ...	**443**	**88**	...	**49**	**232**	**48**	**35**	**2**	...	..	**35**	**2**
Saran	80	28	...	8	33	9	5	...	...	...	...	...
Champaran ...	33	5	.	...	49	30	22	...	...	...	6	2
Muzaffarpur ...	152	43	...	41	130	6	8	2	...	...	29	...
Darbhanga	176	13	...	...	30	3		...	...	...	...	...
Bhagalpur Division ...	**1,311**	**1,926**	**33**	**21**	**8,500**	**9,218**	**35**	**2**	...		**1**	
Monghyr	208	304	...	11	115	105	1	..	..	..	...	
Bhagalpur	365	74		5	56	31	33	2			...	...
Purnea	96	43	3		11		10		..	...	...	..
Santal Parganas ...	352	1,506	31	5	8,318	9,083	2	...	...	..	1	
Orissa Division ...	**1,397**	**1,184**	**320**	**315**	**974**	**64**	**132**	**82**	**4**		**33**	**2**
Cuttack	128	117		1	523	9	90	...	...	...	26	...
Balasore	7	79	...	6	6	9	5	1	...	...	7	
Angul	31	39			25	...	...	81	...			3
Puri	743	479	319	94	376	43	33	...	4	...		
Sambalpur	400	470	1	214	44	3	4	...	...		...	...
Chota Nagpur Division	**1,957**	**1,541**	**67**	**106**	**650**	**360**	**235**	**14**	**5**	...	**87**	**13**
Hazaribagh ...	217	239	...	..	159	79	30	...		...	1	...
Ranchi	273	150	50	54	236	84	88	5	5	..	8	6
Palamau	91	232	3	8	95	76	16	4		...	2	6
Manbhum	46	785	5	23	39	98	81	3		...	76	..
Singhbhum ...	430	136	9	19	121	23	20	2	..		...	1
Feudatory States ...	**751**	**924**	**132**	**125**	**901**	**182**	**134**	**123**	**29**	...	**33**	...
Orissa States ...	718	879	100	124	804	140	130	123	29	...	33	...
Chota Nagpur States ...	33	45	13	1	97	42	4	...	...		...	...
Cities	**200**	**20**	...	...	**25**	**2**	**14**	**1**	...	...	...	**1**
Patna City	...	..	...		...		...	...	...	...	...	...
Gaya City	20		...	...	...	...	..	...	...	...	...	...
Bhagalpur City ...	19	2	...	...	...	...	...	...	...	...	...	...
Jamshedpur City ...	161	18	...	...	25	2	14	1	...	...	...	1

TABLE X—*continued.*

OCCUPATION OR MEANS OF LIVELIHOOD. PART II—DETAILS FOR DISTRICTS AND CITIES.

DISTRICT, STATE OR CITY.	ORDER 29.—TRADE IN POTTERY, BRICKS AND TILES.						ORDER 30.—TRADE IN CHEMICAL PRODUCTS.					
	Earners (principal occupation).		*Working dependants.*		*Earners (subsidiary occupation).*		*Earners (principal occupation).*		*Working dependants.*		*Earners (subsidiary occupation).*	
	Males.	Females.	Males.	Females.	Males.	Females.	Males.	Females.	Males.	Females.	Males.	Females.
1	503	504	505	506	507	508	509	510	511	512	513	514
BIHAR AND ORISSA	**1,183**	**1,650**	**54**	**178**	**1,315**	**228**	**2,912**	**573**	**9**	**11**	**1,464**	**62**
British Territory ...	**1,169**	**1,536**	**52**	**164**	**1,149**	**217**	**2,715**	**394**	**9**	**11**	**1,203**	**56**
PATNA DIVISION ...	**136**	**33**	...	.	**2**	**1**	**99**	**4**	...	...	**5**	...
Patna	77	25	...	...	2		24	4	...	...	.	...
Gaya	50	8	...	...	..	1	55	...	...	...	1	..
Shahabad	...	...	...	...	...	...	20	...	..	...	4	..
TIRHUT DIVISION ...	**130**	**128**	...		**13**	**45**	**245**	**26**	...	...	**278**	**1**
Saran	...	...	...	...		...	29	5	...	...	14	...
Champaran ...	127	...	...	...	11	...	34	1	...	...	161	...
Muzaffarpur ...	3	128	...	...	2	45	104	13	...	...	14	1
Darbhanga ...	...	...	...	...	...	...	78	7	...	...	89	...
BHAGALPUR DIVISION ...	**11**	**18**	...	...	**1**	...	**320**	**104**	...	...	**39**	**20**
Monghyr	...	...	...	...	...	...	109	39	...	...	12	...
Bhagalpur	...	1	...	...	...	...	76	44	...	...	8	12
Purnea	8	15	...	...	...	...	64	12	...	...	5	...
Santal Parganas ...	3	2	...	...	1	...	71	9	...	...	14	8
ORISSA DIVISION ...	**153**	**849**	**1**	**126**	**627**	**48**	**255**	**28**	...	**5**	**109**	**5**
Cuttack	103	447	...	14	553	16	75	3	...	...	40	1
Balasore	20	20	1	6	45	...	25	...	...	...	35	...
Angul	...	137	...	...	23	4	8	...	...	...	6	...
Puri	30	240	...	106	7	28	70	6	...	5	11	...
Sambalpur	...	5	...	...	...	...	77	19	...	...	17	4
CHOTA NAGPUR DIVISION	**739**	**508**	**51**	**38**	**506**	**123**	**1,796**	**222**	**9**	**6**	**772**	**30**
Hazaribagh... ...	28	57	...	...	10	24	114	4	...	..	5	3
Ranchi	31	30	7	3	9	15	118	33	...	2	178	3
Palamau	33	37	...	...	4	18	274	74	6	...	59	20
Manbhum	604	375	19	35	453	62	588	46	...	2	335	2
Singhbhum ...	43	9	25	..	31	4	702	66	3	2	195	2
Feudatory States ...	**14**	**114**	**2**	**14**	**166**	**11**	**197**	**189**	...	...	**261**	**6**
Orissa States ...	10	76	...	..	156	...	188	189	...	...	148	6
Chota Nagpur States ...	4	38	2	14	10	11	9	...	...	...	113	...
Cities	**19**	**9**	...	...	**14**	...	**96**	**40**	...	...	**11**	...
Patna City	...	...	...	...	...	..	23	...	...	...	...	...
Gaya City	...	8	...	...	...	...	...	...	...	...	...	..
Bhagalpur City ...	...	1	...	...	...	...	...	1	...	...	...	...
Jamshedpur City ...	19	...	...	...	14	...	73	39	...	...	11	...

DISTRICT, STATE OR CITY.	ORDER 31.—HOTELS, CAFES, RESTAURANTS, ETC. — TOTAL OF ORDER 31.						GROUP 126.—Vendors of wine, liquors, aerated waters and ice.					
	Earners (principal occupation).		*Working dependants.*		*Earners (subsidiary occupation).*		*Earners (principal occupation).*		*Working dependants.*		*Earners (subsidiary occupation).*	
	Males.	Females.	Males.	Females.	Males.	Females.	Males.	Females.	Males.	Females.	Males.	Females.
1	515	516	517	518	519	520	521	522	523	524	525	526
BIHAR AND ORISSA	**15,737**	**10,848**	**110**	**172**	**4,582**	**881**	**14,493**	**9,831**	**102**	**109**	**4,196**	**715**
British Territory ...	**13,956**	**10,512**	**53**	**149**	**3,509**	**785**	**12,739**	**9,497**	**45**	**86**	**3,133**	**620**
PATNA DIVISION ...	**5,962**	**6,220**	**4**	**1**	**384**	**267**	**5,829**	**6,090**	**4**	**1**	**384**	**267**
Patna	2,981	2,896	..	1	193	89	2,969	2,894	.	1	193	89
Gaya	2,306	2,642	4	.	142	140	2,250	2,525	4	...	142	140
Shahabad	675	682	.	...	49	38	610	671	...	...	49	38
TIRHUT DIVISION ...	**4,010**	**2,084**	**12**	**64**	**1,706**	**250**	**3,911**	**2,045**	**12**	**63**	**1,550**	**249**
Saran	471	257	3	8	192	50	468	257	3	8	192	50
Champaran ...	129	78	...	1	94	20	121	68	...	...	94	19
Muzaffarpur ...	2,376	1,076	4	8	1,166	111	2,333	1,049	4	8	1,148	111
Darbhanga ...	1,034	673	5	47	254	69	989	671	5	47	116	69
BHAGALPUR DIVISION ...	**533**	**1,112**	...	**11**	**47**	**94**	**250**	**962**	...	**8**	**28**	**67**
Monghyr	141	888	...	10	13	65	68	875	...	8	7	65
Bhagalpur	86	67	...	1	11	3	58	54	...	...	3	2
Purnea	241	96	...	...	9	1	71	13	...	...	9	...
Santal Parganas ...	55	61	...	...	14	25	53	20	...	...	9	...
ORISSA DIVISION ...	**1,761**	**101**	**14**	**2**	**882**	**7**	**1,579**	**71**	**14**	**1**	**850**	**5**
Cuttack	1,015	58	4	1	559	4	954	34	4	...	548	4
Balasore	116	5	...	...	89	3	62	1	...	...	74	1
Angul	23	...	...	...	8	...	10	...	...	...	8	...
Puri	251	7	5	...	124	...	196	5	5	...	119	...
Sambalpur	356	31	5	1	102	...	349	31	5	1	101	...
CHOTA NAGPUR DIVISION	**1,700**	**995**	**23**	**71**	**490**	**167**	**1,170**	**329**	**15**	**13**	**321**	**32**
Hazaribagh... ...	444	155	7	8	200	38	354	109	3	8	180	20
Ranchi	205	50	2	13	56	8	111	7	2	5	19	4
Palamau	400	166	4	...	27	23	384	152	4	...	27	1
Manbhum	398	436	10	43	168	105	223	3	6	...	79	...
Singhbhum ...	253	188	...	7	39	9	98	58	...	...	16	7
Feudatory States ...	**1,781**	**336**	**57**	**23**	**1,073**	**96**	**1,754**	**334**	**57**	**23**	**1,063**	**95**
Orissa States ...	1,721	331	57	23	1,034	93	1,705	330	57	23	1,029	93
Chota Nagpur States ...	60	5	...	...	39	3	49	4	...	...	34	2
Cities	**487**	**182**	...	...	**12**	...	**367**	**162**	...	...	**1**	...
Patna City	338	72	...	...	...	...	335	72	...	...	...	...
Gaya City	37	72	...	...	...	...	8	72	...	...	...	...
Bhagalpur City ...	15	17	...	...	2	...	15	17	...	...	1	...
Jamshedpur City ...	97	21	...	...	10	...	9	1	...	...	...	...

TABLE X—continued.

OCCUPATION OR MEANS OF LIVELIHOOD. PART II—DETAILS FOR DISTRICTS AND CITIES.

ORDER 32.—OTHER TRADE IN FOOD-STUFFS.

Total of Order 32.

District, State or City.	Earners (principal occupation). Males.	Earners (principal occupation). Females.	Working dependants. Males.	Working dependants. Females.	Earners (subsidiary occupation). Males.	Earners (subsidiary occupation). Females.
1	527	528	529	530	531	532
BIHAR AND ORISSA	**162,447**	**170,593**	**1,739**	**11,474**	**94,106**	**23,231**
British Territory ...	**147,572**	**135,885**	**1,439**	**8,361**	**79,208**	**19,107**
PATNA DIVISION ...	**30,962**	**26,928**	**14**	**79**	**4,995**	**3,119**
Patna	10,762	6,541	3	6	1,944	1,086
Gaya	8,039	6,127	11	67	940	473
Shahabad	12,161	14,200	...	6	2,111	1,560
TIRHUT DIVISION ...	**24,785**	**26,338**	**268**	**738**	**24,514**	**7,396**
Saran	5,029	6,336	67	154	6,546	3,159
Champaran... ...	3,794	3,341	3	53	4,624	1,153
Muzaffarpur ...	9,757	10,592	42	286	8,796	2,035
Darbhanga... ...	6,205	6,070	156	245	4,548	1,049
BHAGALPUR DIVISION ...	**42,054**	**23,391**	**182**	**358**	**7,605**	**2,385**
Monghyr	10,547	8,523	58	205	1,284	413
Bhagalpur	7,198	5,048	38	95	2,374	1,124
Purnea	19,488	6,877	73	15	1,429	205
Santal Parganas ...	4,821	2,943	13	43	2,518	648
ORISSA DIVISION ...	**33,317**	**47,358**	**629**	**6,340**	**32,773**	**3,519**
Cuttack	14,429	15,340	65	1,589	12,887	1,188
Balasore	4,617	13,767	305	966	10,439	785
Angul	324	1,076	3	2	646	78
Puri	11,041	12,473	198	3,331	6,521	1,055
Sambalpur... ...	2,906	4,693	58	452	2,280	415
CHOTA NAGPUR DIVISION	**16,454**	**11,870**	**346**	**846**	**9,321**	**2,688**
Hazaribagh ...	3,355	1,883	7	22	1,505	414
Ranchi	2,053	2,002	127	504	1,105	599
Palamau	4,225	3,592	82	37	2,530	1,036
Manbhum	4,792	3,300	101	238	3,639	472
Singhbhum ...	2,029	1,093	29	45	552	167
Feudatory States ...	**14,875**	**34,708**	**300**	**3,113**	**14,900**	**4,124**
Orissa States ...	14,739	34,470	300	3,101	14,772	4,046
Chota Nagpur States ...	136	238	.	12	128	78
Cities	**5,704**	**1,538**	**5**	**17**	**179**	**19**
Patna City... ...	3,122	579	1	3	57	...
Gaya City	792	283	...	...	...	...
Bhagalpur City ...	1,159	551	...	10	59	10
Jamshedpur City ...	631	125	4	4	63	...

Group 129.—Grain and pulse dealers.

District, State or City.	Earners (principal occupation). Males.	Earners (principal occupation). Females.	Working dependants. Males.	Working dependants. Females.	Earners (subsidiary occupation). Males	Earners (subsidiary occupation). Females.
1	533	534	535	536	537	538
BIHAR AND ORISSA	**36,094**	**29,988**	**221**	**1,303**	**15,584**	**3,614**
British Territory ...	**33,049**	**15,773**	**155**	**1,005**	**12,118**	**1,727**
PATNA DIVISION ...	**6,689**	**826**	...	**3**	**429**	**38**
Patna	,444	66	...	...	63	4
Gaya	,585	323	...	3	103	23
Shahabad	3,660	437	...	...	264	11
TIRHUT DIVISION ...	**8,474**	**2,826**	**40**	**45**	**4,779**	**553**
Saran	,475	306	10	2	643	90
Champaran... ...	,663	813	..	27	1,266	127
Muzaffarpur ...	3,606	1,596	5	12	2,089	276
Darbhanga... ...	,730	111	25	4	781	60
BHAGALPUR DIVISION ...	**9,789**	**2,698**	**31**	**18**	**1,640**	**314**
Monghyr	,436	234	5	14	113	...
Bhagalpur	,722	224	..	2	186	9
Purnea	4,779	1,354	23	..	358	11
Santal Parganas ...	,852	886	3	2	983	294
ORISSA DIVISION ...	**3,996**	**7,507**	**18**	**794**	**3,651**	**578**
Cuttack	,069	1,660	1	60	1,067	254
Balasore	303	1,953	6	33	1,110	133
Angul	33	787	...	2	38	46
Puri	1,063	2,437	3	686	1,324	108
Sambalpur... ...	508	661	8	13	112	37
CHOTA NAGPUR DIVISION	**4,101**	**1,916**	**66**	**145**	**1,619**	**244**
Hazaribagh ...	,286	276	3	12	345	40
Ranchi	574	508	27	102	225	100
Palamau	924	262	7	...	339	16
Manbhum	975	356	29	8	638	57
Singhbhum ...	342	454	...	23	72	31
Feudatory States ...	**3,045**	**14,215**	**66**	**298**	**3,466**	**1,887**
Orissa States ...	3,024	14,121	66	295	3,439	1,834
Chota Nagpur States ...	21	94	...	3	27	53
Cities	**1,052**	**73**	...	...	**43**	...
Patna City... ...	389	7	...	...	4	...
Gaya City	158	...	...	...	...	...
Bhagalpur City ...	497	60	...	...	27	...
Jamshedpur City ...	8	6	...	...	12	...

Group 130.—Dealers in sweetmeats, sugar and spices.

District, State or City.	Earners (principal occupation). Males.	Earners (principal occupation). Females.	Working dependants. Males.	Working dependants. Females.	Earners (subsidiary occupation). Males.	Earners (subsidiary occupation). Females.
1	539	540	541	542	543	544
BIHAR AND ORISSA	**17,676**	**5,761**	**90**	**268**	**4,557**	**345**
British Territory ...	**17,027**	**5,476**	**81**	**243**	**4,244**	**337**
PATNA DIVISION ...	**6,039**	**2,519**	...	**21**	**253**	**75**
Patna	2,710	1,133	...	3	77	39
Gaya	2,356	786	.	18	106	19
Shahabad	971	600	..	...	70	17
TIRHUT DIVISION ...	**1,368**	**599**	..	**1**	**644**	**116**
Saran	291	308	...	...	212	79
Champaran... ...	57	57	...	...	33	1
Muzaffarpur ...	840	147	...	1	351	36
Darbhanga... ...	180	87	...	...	48	...
BHAGALPUR DIVISION ...	**3,945**	**999**	**30**	**20**	**427**	**18**
Monghyr	621	245	1	10	16	1
Bhagalpur	871	176	10	5	104	5
Purnea	1,624	431	19	5	115	1
Santal Parganas ...	829	147		...	191	11
ORISSA DIVISION ...	**3,715**	**903**	**33**	**159**	**2,616**	**90**
Cuttack	2,162	376	2	53	1,309	23
Balasore	525	280	8	50	974	52
Angul	17	2	..	...	3	...
Puri	757	67	14	5	257	4
Sambalpur... ...	254	178	9	51	73	11
CHOTA NAGPUR DIVISION	**1,960**	**456**	**18**	**42**	**304**	**38**
Hazaribagh ...	354	110	...	6	60	12
Ranchi	132	41	11	28	37	8
Palamau	545	112	3	3	35	4
Manbhum	596	174	2	5	122	14
Singhbhum ...	333	19	2	...	50	...
Feudatory States ...	**649**	**285**	**9**	**25**	**313**	**8**
Orissa States ...	603	194	9	25	302	8
Chota Nagpur States ...	46	91	...	...	11	...
Cities	**1,057**	**163**	...	**2**	**16**	...
Patna City... ...	753	129	...	2	10	...
Gaya City	103	10	...	...	...	...
Bhagalpur City ...	57	7	...	...	3	...
Jamshedpur City ...	144	17	...	...	3	...

Group 131.—Dealers in dairy product, eggs and poultry.

District, State or City.	Earners (principal occupation). Males.	Earners (principal occupation). Females.	Working dependants. Males.	Working dependants. Females.	Earners (subsidiary occupation). Males.	Earners (subsidiary occupation). Females.
1	545	546	547	548	549	550
BIHAR AND ORISSA	**25,552**	**55,035**	**274**	**4,370**	**21,739**	**9,460**
British Territory ...	**25,229**	**50,360**	**266**	**3,538**	**21,178**	**9,316**
PATNA DIVISION ...	**7,126**	**16,199**	**7**	**51**	**2,858**	**2,538**
Patna	2,497	3,704	...	1	1,072	806
Gaya	1,461	3,448	7	45	419	336
Shahabad	3,168	9,047	...	5	1,367	1,396
TIRHUT DIVISION ...	**5,627**	**9,731**	**84**	**279**	**9,939**	**3,964**
Saran	1,611	4,013	36	100	3,855	2,127
Champaran... ...	530	1,241	2	10	2,061	753
Muzaffarpur ...	1,347	3,069	...	70	2,268	645
Darbhanga... ...	2,139	1,408	46	99	1,755	439
BHAGALPUR DIVISION ...	**7,663**	**8,055**	**52**	**107**	**2,778**	**1,036**
Monghyr	3,157	3,083	12	35	512	224
Bhagalpur	1,828	2,191	20	50	1,080	558
Purnea	1,829	1,716	13	...	383	26
Santal Parganas ...	849	1,066	7	22	863	228
ORISSA DIVISION ...	**3,357**	**14,767**	**85**	**3,040**	**4,239**	**1,289**
Cuttack	1,630	5,255	2	626	1,861	206
Balasore	268	3,099	43	135	1,359	122
Angul	1	196	...	...	9	3
Puri	1,307	5,702	40	2,226	893	797
Sambalpur... ...	61	515	...	53	117	71
CHOTA NAGPUR DIVISION	**1,456**	**1,608**	**38**	**61**	**1,364**	**489**
Hazaribagh ...	327	430	1	...	304	105
Ranchi	173	64	9	26	26	18
Palamau	260	686	2	...	521	217
Manbhum	370	386	18	33	477	96
Singhbhum ...	320	43	8	2	36	54
Feudatory States ...	**323**	**4,675**	**8**	**832**	**561**	**144**
Orissa States ...	319	4,675	8	832	561	144
Chota Nagpur States ...	4	...	...	...	...	...
Cities	**1,307**	**585**	...	**3**	**58**	**13**
Patna City... ...	665	237	...	1	41	...
Gaya City	161	127	...	...	...	...
Bhagalpur City ...	324	208	...	...	11	13
Jamshedpur City ...	157	13	...	2	6	...

TABLE X—*continued.*

Occupation or Means of Livelihood. Part II—Details for Districts and Cities.

District, State or City.	Order 33.—Other trade in food-stuffs—*concld.* Group 136.—Dealers in tobacco. Earners (principal occupation). Males.	Females.	Working dependants. Males.	Females.	Earners (subsidiary occupation). Males.	Females.	Order 33.—Trade in clothing and toilet articles. Earners (principal occupation). Males.	Females.	Working dependants. Males.	Females.	Earners (subsidiary occupation). Males.	Females.	Order 34.—Trade in furniture. Earners (principal occupation). Males.	Females.	Working dependants. Males.	Females.	Earners (subsidiary occupation). Males.	Females.	Order 35.—Trade in building materials. Earners (principal occupation). Males.	Females.	Working dependants. Males.	Females.	Earners (subsidiary occupation). Males.	Females.
1	551	552	553	554	555	556	557	558	559	560	561	562	563	564	565	566	567	568	569	570	571	572	573	574
BIHAR AND ORISSA	**2,463**	**913**	**46**	**45**	**1,262**	**99**	**3,514**	**1,344**	**26**	**42**	**918**	**231**	**1,519**	**349**	**6**	**14**	**427**	**78**	**272**	**273**	**12**	**10**	**195**	**154**
British Territory ...	**2,350**	**841**	**44**	**39**	**1,194**	**98**	**2,656**	**1,077**	**20**	**9**	**565**	**219**	**1,448**	**264**	**6**	**13**	**407**	**50**	**267**	**262**	**12**	**10**	**193**	**154**
Patna Division ...	**680**	**196**	...	...	**76**	...	**1,220**	**460**	**1**	...	**70**	**3**	**39**	**5**	...	...	...	...	**2**	...	...	...	...	...
Patna	275	79	...	...	13	...	681	110	1	...	15	1	...	...	...	...	...	...	...	...	...	...	...	...
Gaya	126	51	...	...	46	...	91	92	...	...	...	...		5		...	...	...	...	...	...	...	...	...
Shahabad	279	66	...	...	17	...	448	364	...	...	55	2	39	...	...		...	...	2	...	...	...	...	...
Tirhut Division ...	**652**	**243**	**10**	...	**629**	**87**	**496**	**461**	**3**	**9**	**148**	**208**	**55**	**99**	...	...	**71**	**43**	**17**	**97**	...	...	...	**135**
Saran	76	73	10	...	87	44	40	6	...	...	4	1	4	2	...	...	...	1	...	...	...	...	...	...
Champaran... ...	116	9	...	...	87	...	166	304	...	9	90	201	1	8	...	...	53	3		2	...	...	...	...
Muzaffarpur ...	296	67	...	...	359	21	171	8	...	...	46	...	33	17		..	12	7	9	46	...	...	...	133
Darbhanga... ...	164	94	...	...	96	22	119	143	3	...	8	6	18	73	...	...	6	32	8	40	...	...	...	2
Bhagalpur Division ...	**206**	**65**	...	**3**	**16**	...	**336**	**50**	...	...	**50**	...	**418**	**58**	...		**25**	...	**112**	**65**	**11**	**6**	**22**	**10**
Monghyr	10	28	...	3	1	...	6	1	...	...	...	...	78	5	...	...	4	...	37	4	11	4	3	...
Bhagalpur	32	8	...	...	..	..	79	14	...	...	20	...	113	31	...	...	6	...	14	19	...	2	4	9
Purnea	150	31	..	...	8	...	167	32	...	...	2	...	54	14	..	...	...	...	60	43	...	..	16	...
Santal Parganas ...	16	8	...	...	7	...	84	3	...	...	28	...	173	8	...	..	15	..	1	...	...	...	...	1
Orissa Division ...	**273**	**98**	**4**	**1**	**356**	**1**	**370**	**68**	**9**	...	**78**	**1**	**254**	**14**	**3**	**5**	**114**	...	**109**	**52**	**1**	**2**	**145**	**3**
Cuttack	39	...	...	...	255	...	110	...	..	...	9	...	202	7	...		58	...	77	1	1	...	33	..
Balasore	19	...		...	13	...	9	..	2	...	1	...	14	7	1	5	27		13	34	...	2	77	3
Angul	23	10	...	...	50	...	13	..	...	...		...	...	...	...	...	...	...	..	...	...	...	...	
Puri	34	22	1	...	16	...	5	...	...	...	10	...	37	...	2	...	29	...	12	..	...	...	41	...
Sambalpur	158	66	3	1	22	1	233	68	7	...	58	1	1	..	...	...	...	...	7	17	..	..	5	
Chota Nagpur Division...	**537**	**239**	**30**	**35**	**117**	**10**	**234**	**32**	**7**	...	**219**	**7**	**682**	**88**	**3**	**8**	**197**	**7**	**27**	**48**	...	**2**	**26**	**6**
Hazaribagh ...	214	101	1	...	19	6	32	15	2	...	186	6	71	33	...	4	3	7	1	2	...	...	3	1
Ranchi	120	38	36	35	22	4	16	2	...	...	8	...	...			...	...	...	3	12		...	13	.
Palamau	7	...	...		...	...	33	10	...	...	6	...	155	37	...	3	38	...	2	...	..	...	1	1
Manbhum	77	41	1	...	19	...	123	3	...	...	8	...	379	15	3	1	137	..	17	33		1	9	3
Singhbhum ...	119	59	2	..	57	...	31	2	5	...	17	1	77	13	...	...	19	..	4	1	...	1	...	1
Feudatory States ...	**113**	**72**	**4**	**6**	**68**	**1**	**858**	**267**	**6**	**33**	**353**	**12**	**71**	**85**	...	**1**	**20**	**28**	**5**	**11**			**2**	...
Orissa States ...	102	69	4	1	63	1	857	265	6	33	353	12	39	75	..	..	9	32	5	8		..	2	...
Chota Nagpur States ...	11	3	...	5	5	...	1	2	...	...			33	10	...	1	11	6	...	3	...		...	..
Cities	**142**	**16**	**1**	...	**12**	...	**235**	**12**	**1**	...		...	**33**	**9**	...		...	...	**2**	**2**	...	..	...	...
Patna City	88	12	...	..	...	...	217	11	1	...	...	...	..	...	...	...	...	...	...	...	...	...	...	...
Gaya City	30	4	...	...	...	...	16	...	...	...	...	...	...	...	...	...	...	...	...	...	...	...	...	...
Bhagalpur City ...	...	...	...	...	...	...	...	...	...	...	...	..	...	1	...	..	...		...	2	...	...	...	...
Jamshedpur City ...	24	...	1	...	12	...	2	1	...	...	...	...	33	8			...	...	2	...	...	...	...	...

TABLE X—*continued.*

OCCUPATION OR MEANS OF LIVELIHOOD.

PART II—DETAILS FOR DISTRICTS AND CITIES.

DISTRICT, STATE OR CITY.	ORDER 36.—TRADE IN MEANS OF TRANSPORT.					
	Earners (principal occupation).		*Working dependants.*		*Earners (subsidiary occupation).*	
	Males.	Females.	Males.	Females.	Males.	Females.
1	575	576	577	578	579	580
BIHAR AND ORISSA	**3,000**	**218**	**6**	**2**	**1,804**	**42**
British Territory ...	**2,978**	**193**	**6**	**2**	**1,779**	**42**
PATNA DIVISION ...	**250**	**165**	...	...	**39**	**18**
Patna	89	...	...	...	11	...
Gaya	11	45	...	...	...	2
Shahabad	150	120	...	...	38	16
TIRHUT DIVISION ...	**289**	**7**	...	...	**162**	**20**
Saran	35	5	...	...	17	8
Champaran ...	23	2	...	...	6	...
Muzaffarpur ...	199	...	...	...	129	12
Darbhanga ...	42	...	...	...	10	...
BHAGALPUR DIVISION ...	**578**	**9**	...	...	**376**	...
Monghyr	100	1	...	...	44	...
Bhagalpur	187	1	...	...	17	...
Purnea	134	4	...	...	20	...
Santal Parganas ...	167	3	...	...	295	...
ORISSA DIVISION ...	**587**	**6**	**4**	**1**	**952**	**2**
Cuttack	380	2	3	1	569	...
Balasore	154	4	...	...	317	2
Angul	14	...	...	...	5	...
Puri	34	...	1	...	50	...
Sambalpur ...	5	...	...	...	2	...
CHOTA NAGPUR DIVISION	**1,274**	**6**	**2**	**1**	**250**	**2**
Hazaribagh ...	45	1	1	...	81	...
Ranchi	30	1	...	1	16	2
Palamau	43	3	...	...	48	...
Manbhum	110	...	1	...	91	...
Singhbhum ...	1,047	1	...	...	14	...
Feudatory States ...	**22**	**25**	...	...	**25**	...
Orissa States ...	7	25	...	...	4	...
Chota Nagpur States ...	15	...	...	...	21	...
Cities	**8**	...	...	...	...	...
Patna Cit	1	...	...	...	...	...
Gaya City	...	...	...	...	...	...
Bhagalpur City ...	5	...	...	...	...	...
Jamshedpur City ...	2	...	...	...	...	...

DISTRICT, STATE OR CITY.	ORDER 37.—TRADE IN FUEL.					
	Earners (principal occupation).		*Working dependants.*		*Earners (subsidiary occupation).*	
	Males.	Females.	Males.	Females.	Males.	Females.
1	581	583	583	584	585	586
BIHAR AND ORISSA	**8,831**	**29,749**	**233**	**3,618**	**5,956**	**5,930**
British Territory ...	**6,572**	**21,527**	**211**	**3,062**	**4,085**	**4,321**
PATNA DIVISION ...	**1,306**	**3,884**	**1**	**17**	**86**	**459**
Patna	604	344	...	...	31	43
Gaya	207	2,579	1	17	12	323
Shahabad	495	961	...	...	43	90
TIRHUT DIVISION ...	**85**	**486**	**10**	**3**	**29**	**79**
Saran	41	95	...	...	5	13
Champaran ...	20	27	...	...	5	3
Muzaffarpur ...	10	322	...	3	14	41
Darbhanga ...	14	42	10	...	5	22
BHAGALPUR DIVISION ...	**41**	**210**	...	...	**15**	**17**
Monghyr	10	54	...	...	...	5
Bhagalpur	7	81	...	...	4	7
Purnea	7	39	...	...	1	2
Santal Parganas ...	17	36	...	...	10	3
ORISSA DIVISION ...	**3,769**	**14,632**	**170**	**2,943**	**2,615**	**3,041**
Cuttack	1,701	6,536	25	1,806	1,004	750
Balasore	124	945	52	177	335	186
Angul	...	44	...	2	21	2
Puri	1,366	5,070	64	814	928	1,833
Sambalpur ...	578	1,437	29	144	327	270
CHOTA NAGPUR DIVISION	**1,281**	**2,315**	**30**	**99**	**1,340**	**725**
Hazaribagh ...	89	410	...	3	105	148
Ranchi	18	459	3	63	44	218
Palamau	58	390	6	6	103	79
Manbhum	1,069	964	18	14	1,044	273
Singhbhum ...	47	92	3	13	44	7
Feudatory States ...	**2,259**	**8,222**	**22**	**556**	**1,871**	**1,609**
Orissa States ...	2,249	8,218	22	556	1,859	1,609
Chota Nagpur States ...	10	4	...	...	12	...
Cities	**505**	**110**	**2**	**1**	**9**	**2**
Patna Cit	447	11	...	...	8	...
Gaya City	11	69	...	...	...	2
Bhagalpur City ...	1	9	...	...	...	...
Jamshedpur City ...	46	21	2	1	1	...

DISTRICT, STATE OR CITY.	ORDER 38.—TRADE IN ARTICLES OF LUXURY AND THOSE PERTAINING TO LETTERS AND THE ARTS AND SCIENCES. TOTAL OF ORDER 38.					
	Earners (principal occupation).		*Working dependants.*		*Earners (subsidiary occupation).*	
	Males.	Females.	Males.	Females.	Males.	Females.
1	587	588	589	590	591	592
BIHAR AND ORISSA	**9,008**	**4,946**	**216**	**240**	**2,332**	**531**
British Territory ...	**8,271**	**4,739**	**79**	**157**	**2,181**	**453**
PATNA DIVISION ...	**1,665**	**1,095**	**7**	**21**	**44**	**25**
Patna	673	267	7	...	6	6
Gaya	574	402	...	21	31	6
Shahabad	418	436	...	...	7	13
TIRHUT DIVISION ...	**2,014**	**1,773**	**41**	**26**	**1,224**	**309**
Saran	243	379	...	2	133	76
Champaran ...	213	338	3	13	232	126
Muzaffarpur ...	973	796	...	11	521	63
Darbhanga ...	585	260	38	...	338	44
BHAGALPUR DIVISION ...	**1,807**	**941**	**5**	...	**168**	**44**
Monghyr	502	321	...	...	42	8
Bhagalpur	514	277	5	...	47	13
Purnea	603	215	...	...	6	1
Santal Parganas ...	128	128	...	...	73	22
ORISSA DIVISION ...	**1,109**	**175**	**7**	**13**	**266**	**8**
Cuttack	551	47	...	5	106	4
Balasore	52	50	...	1	29	1
Angul	58	20	...	...	4	...
Puri	398	31	7	3	79	1
Sambalpur ...	50	37	...	4	48	2
CHOTA NAGPUR DIVISION	**1,676**	**755**	**19**	**97**	**479**	**67**
Hazaribagh ...	232	130	1	1	166	8
Ranchi	319	165	15	60	79	18
Palamau	407	265	...	12	56	26
Manbhum	286	142	...	14	124	7
Singhbhum ...	432	53	3	10	54	8
Feudatory States ...	**737**	**207**	**137**	**83**	**151**	**78**
Orissa States ...	736	193	137	83	149	76
Chota Nagpur States ...	1	14	...	...	2	2
Cities	**352**	**51**	**7**	...	**16**	**1**
Patna Cit	154	5	7	...	...	...
Gaya City	44	8	...	...	...	...
Bhagalpur City ...	28	33	...	...	2	1
Jamshedpur City ...	126	5	...	...	14	...

DISTRICT, STATE OR CITY.	ORDER 38 (contd.). Group 147.—Dealers in common bangles, bead necklaces, fans, small articles, toys, hunting and fishing tackle, flowers, etc.					
	Earners (principal occupation).		*Working dependants.*		*Earners (subsidiary occupation).*	
	Males.	Females.	Males.	Females.	Males.	Females.
1	593	594	595	596	597	598
BIHAR AND ORISSA	**6,300**	**4,595**	**152**	**208**	**1,938**	**503**
British Territory ...	**5,976**	**4,395**	**71**	**126**	**1,850**	**425**
PATNA DIVISION ...	**1,260**	**1,041**	**7**	**21**	**30**	**25**
Patna	588	263	7	...	6	6
Gaya	324	376	...	21	10	6
Shahabad	348	402	...	...	5	13
TIRHUT DIVISION ...	**1,950**	**1,729**	**41**	**26**	**1,202**	**297**
Saran	222	379	...	2	131	76
Champaran ...	208	323	3	13	323	114
Muzaffarpur ...	936	770	...	11	510	63
Darbhanga ...	584	257	38	...	338	44
BHAGALPUR DIVISION ...	**1,194**	**768**	**1**	...	**94**	**39**
Monghyr	424	291	...	...	16	8
Bhagalpur	311	219	1	...	37	10
Purnea	400	151	...	...	5	...
Santal Parganas ...	59	108	...	...	36	21
ORISSA DIVISION ...	**400**	**173**	**7**	**11**	**151**	**7**
Cuttack	13	47	...	6	50	4
Balasore	39	49	...	1	24	1
Angul	22	20	...	...	3	...
Puri	316	30	7	1	74	...
Sambalpur ...	10	27	...	4	...	2
CHOTA NAGPUR DIVISION	**1,172**	**684**	**15**	**68**	**373**	**57**
Hazaribagh ...	178	133	1	1	143	7
Ranchi	237	144	14	50	33	15
Palamau	295	233	...	3	49	26
Manbhum	238	135	...	14	121	7
Singhbhum ...	224	50	...	...	27	2
Feudatory States ...	**324**	**200**	**81**	**82**	**88**	**78**
Orissa States ...	323	186	81	82	87	76
Chota Nagpur States ...	1	14	...	...	1	2
Cities	**285**	**50**	**7**	...	**14**	**1**
Patna Cit	148	5	7	...	...	...
Gaya City	28	8	...	...	...	...
Bhagalpur City ...	9	33	...	...	...	1
Jamshedpur City ...	100	4	...	...	14	...

TABLE X—*continued*.

Occupation or Means of Livelihood. Part II.—Details for Districts and Cities.

District, State or City.	Order 39.—Trade of other sorts. Total of Order 39. Earners (principal occupation). Males.	Females.	Working dependants. Males.	Females.	Earners (subsidiary occupation). Males.	Females.	Group 150.—General store-keepers and shop-keepers otherwise unspecified. Earners (principal occupation). Males.	Females.	Working dependants. Males.	Females.	Earners (subsidiary occupation). Males.	Females.
1	599	600	601	602	603	604	605	606	607	608	609	610
BIHAR AND ORISSA	**116,543**	**29,045**	**967**	**704**	**26,387**	**2,843**	**112,634**	**27,909**	**931**	**662**	**25,003**	**2,723**
British Territory ...	**116,189**	**28,564**	**871**	**691**	**26,135**	**2,822**	**112,292**	**27,434**	**835**	**649**	**24,753**	**2,702**
Patna Division ...	**32,279**	**8,310**	**90**	**28**	**1,785**	**347**	**31,014**	**7,845**	**88**	**28**	**1,764**	**332**
Patna	12,788	3,467	7	3	421	70	12,577	3,279	7	3	417	70
Gaya	9,456	1,531	83	25	507	87	8,889	1,390	81	25	405	87
Shahabad	10,035	3,312	...	...	857	190	9,548	3,176	...	...	853	175
Tirhut Division ...	**24,911**	**6,535**	**161**	**93**	**13,039**	**1,516**	**24,159**	**6,294**	**156**	**88**	**12,283**	**1,467**
Saran	6,307	2,138	4	18	3,596	555	5,834	2,072	4	18	3,065	533
Champaran	3,706	1,123	35	7	3,354	389	3,595	1,072	35	7	3,254	377
Muzaffarpur ...	3,795	764	5	17	2,051	246	3,716	743	...	16	1,967	241
Darbhanga ...	11,103	2,510	117	51	4,038	326	11,034	2,407	117	47	3,997	316
Bhagalpur Division ...	**40,802**	**10,118**	**174**	**327**	**5,740**	**449**	**40,713**	**10,113**	**174**	**327**	**5,723**	**449**
Monghyr	17,034	4,774	47	183	1,380	153	17,028	4,774	47	183	1,279	153
Bhagalpur	14,328	3,513	86	130	1,968	147	14,309	3,513	86	130	1,935	147
Purnea	3,334	606	19	14	328	20	3,275	603	19	14	315	20
Santal Parganas ...	6,106	1,325	22	...	2,164	129	6,101	1,223	22	...	2,164	130
Orissa Division ...	**2,078**	**677**	**139**	**47**	**1,951**	**79**	**1,890**	**613**	**138**	**45**	**1,837**	**76**
Cuttack	519	53	1	1	136	1	385	...	1	...	92	...
Balasore	521	143	13	6	1,354	52	504	143	13	6	1,320	50
Angul	58	...	...	...	12	..	58	...	...	...	5	...
Puri	200	28	98	...	332	...	261	28	97	...	307	...
Sambalpur	690	454	27	40	127	26	683	443	27	39	104	36
Chota Nagpur Division	**16,119**	**2,924**	**307**	**196**	**3,690**	**431**	**14,516**	**2,569**	**279**	**161**	**3,146**	**378**
Hazaribagh ...	3,343	535	3	20	933	69	2,260	414	2	3	576	44
Ranchi	2,569	673	135	114	735	253	2,406	644	127	101	713	235
Palamau	886	234	43	2	139	14	858	228	39	2	138	13
Manbhum	6,395	1,040	95	54	1,565	65	6,250	922	92	40	1,502	61
Singhbhum ...	2,926	442	31	6	258	30	2,742	361	19	6	217	35
Feudatory States ...	**354**	**481**	**96**	**13**	**252**	**21**	**342**	**475**	**96**	**13**	**250**	**21**
Orissa States ...	156	137	96	11	190	17	150	137	96	11	188	17
Chota Nagpur States ...	198	344	...	2	63	4	192	338	...	2	63	4
Cities	**10,624**	**1,425**	**33**	**28**	**310**	**6**	**10,416**	**1,286**	**33**	**28**	**306**	**6**
Patna City	3,454	617	6	2	...	...	3,404	489	6	2	...	...
Gaya City	3,111	454	...	...	39	5	3,008	450	...	...	39	5
Bhagalpur City ...	2,778	256	27	26	234	1	2,772	256	27	26	232	1
Jamshedpur City ...	1,281	98	...	...	37	...	1,237	91	...	...	35	...

District, State or City.	Class C.—Public Administration and Liberal Arts. Earners (principal occupation). Males.	Females.	Working dependants. Males.	Females.	Earners (subsidiary occupation). Males.	Females.	Sub-Class VI.—Public Force. Earners (principal occupation). Males.	Females.	Working dependants. Males.	Females.	Earners (subsidiary occupation). Males.	Females.
1	611	612	613	614	615	616	617	618	619	620	621	622
BIHAR AND ORISSA	**187,991**	**24,313**	**2,636**	**1,224**	**113,156**	**3,929**	**36,683**	**1**	**128**	...	**21,126**	...
British Territory ...	**164,531**	**23,163**	**2,419**	**1,133**	**93,640**	**3,791**	**27,814**	**1**	**111**	...	**16,435**	...
Patna Division ...	**42,419**	**8,078**	**92**	**55**	**9,921**	**727**	**3,973**	**1**	**9**	...	**1,553**	...
Patna	16,500	1,932	15	8	1,955	189	1,708	1	...	...	279	...
Gaya	12,526	3,826	62	21	1,952	283	831	...	6	...	288	...
Shahabad	13,393	3,330	15	26	6,014	255	1,434	...	3	...	986	...
Tirhut Division ...	**26,335**	**5,137**	**351**	**180**	**26,188**	**1,324**	**3,623**	..	**2**	...	**5,325**	...
Saran	5,339	684	95	73	7,221	374	596	...	2	...	1,460	...
Champaran	3,359	531	25	8	4,645	138	532	...	...	...	813	...
Muzaffarpur ...	10,431	1,932	10	25	9,616	553	1,755	...	...	...	2,097	...
Darbhanga ...	7,206	1,990	221	74	4,706	260	740	...	...	...	955	...
Bhagalpur Division ...	**31,774**	**4,031**	**458**	**343**	**11,259**	**672**	**8,355**	...	**22**	...	**2,943**	...
Monghyr	10,270	2,016	359	210	2,106	151	1,202	...	18	...	389	...
Bhagalpur	8,124	912	83	130	2,432	169	2,023	...	3	...	659	...
Purnea	9,142	596	6	...	1,567	46	4,272	...	1	...	660	...
Santal Parganas ...	4,238	507	10	3	5,154	306	858	...	...	...	1,235	...
Orissa Division ...	**42,854**	**2,706**	**961**	**148**	**34,372**	**336**	**7,087**	...	**35**	...	**3,188**	...
Cuttack	17,107	1,018	120	34	14,459	122	2,337	...	1	...	1,057	...
Balasore	5,770	430	307	37	9,007	50	402	...	5	...	800	...
Angul	1,394	22	2	4	1,480	..	508	...	...	...	271	...
Puri	13,525	961	388	68	7,034	119	1,808	...	9	...	460	...
Sambalpur	5,058	275	144	5	2,392	45	1,042	...	20	...	600	...
Chota Nagpur Division	**21,149**	**3,211**	**557**	**407**	**11,900**	**732**	**4,776**	...	**43**	...	**3,426**	...
Hazaribagh ...	3,617	973	15	18	3,778	275	684	...	1	...	940	...
Ranchi	4,716	474	246	293	2,275	118	654	...	26	...	533	...
Palamau	2,470	404	23	14	1,583	232	622	...	5	...	450	...
Manbhum	6,650	1,196	107	73	2,820	86	1,539	...	6	...	869	...
Singhbhum ...	3,767	164	166	9	1,444	21	1,277	...	5	...	626	...
Feudatory States ...	**23,460**	**1,150**	**217**	**91**	**19,516**	**138**	**8,869**	...	**17**	...	**4,691**	...
Orissa States ...	23,002	1,089	215	88	18,869	124	8,771	...	17	...	4,592	...
Chota Nagpur States ...	458	61	2	3	647	14	98	...	...	...	99	...
Cities	**11,953**	**874**	**20**	**7**	**312**	**3**	**1,317**	...	...	...	**35**	...
Patna City	6,637	470	7	5	18	...	338	...	...	...	...	...
Gaya City	1,749	233	...	...	31	...	86	...	...	...	...	...
Bhagalpur City ...	1,645	117	5	1	132	2	642	...	...	...	35	...
Jamshedpur City ...	1,922	54	8	1	131	1	751	...	...	...	...	...

TABLE X—*continued.*

OCCUPATION OR MEANS OF LIVELIHOOD. PART II—DETAILS FOR DISTRICTS AND CITIES.

DISTRICT, STATE OR CITY.	ORDER 40.—ARMY.						ORDER 43.—POLICE. Total of Order 43.					
	Earners (principal occupation).		*Working dependants.*		*Earners (subsidiary occupation).*		*Earners (principal occupation).*		*Working dependants.*		*Earners (subsidiary occupation).*	
	Males.	Females.	Males.	Females.	Males.	Females.	Males.	Females.	Males.	Females.	Males.	Females.
1	623	624	625	626	627	628	629	630	631	632	633	634
BIHAR AND ORISSA	**1,025**	**1**	...	...	**8**	...	**35,658**	...	**128**	...	**21,118**	...
British Territory ...	**1,025**	**1**	...	...	**8**	...	**26,769**	...	**111**	...	**16,427**	...
PATNA DIVISION ...	**785**	**1**	...	...	...	...	**3,188**	...	**9**	...	**1,553**	...
Patna	774	1	...	...	...	...	934	...	...	...	379	...
Gaya	8	...	...	...	...	...	823	...	6	...	288	...
Shahabad	3	...	...	...	...	...	1,431	...	3	...	986	...
TIRHUT DIVISION ...	**225**	...	...	...	**4**	...	**3,398**	...	**2**	...	**5,321**	...
Saran	32	...	...	...	2	...	664	...	2	...	1,458	...
Champaran ...	44	...	...	...	2	...	488	...	...	...	811	...
Muzaffarpur ...	147	...	...	...	...	...	1,608	...	...	...	2,097	...
Darbhanga ...	2	...	...	...	...	...	738	...	...	...	955	...
BHAGALPUR DIVISION ...	**11**	...	...	...	**4**	...	**8,344**	...	**22**	...	**2,939**	...
Monghyr	6	...	...	...	...	...	1,196	...	18	...	389	...
Bhagalpur	2	...	...	...	4	...	2,021	...	3	...	655	...
Purnea	1	...	...	...	...	...	4,271	...	1	...	660	...
Santal Parganas ...	2	...	...	...	...	...	855	...	...	...	1,235	...
ORISSA DIVISION ...	...	...	...	...	...	...	**7,087**	...	**35**	...	**3,188**	...
Cuttack	...	...	...	...	...	...	2,337	...	1	...	1,057	...
Balasore	...	...	...	...	...	...	402	...	5	...	800	...
Angul	...	...	...	...	...	...	508	...	...	...	271	...
Puri	...	...	...	...	...	...	1,898	...	9	...	460	...
Sambalpur	...	...	...	...	...	...	1,942	...	30	...	600	...
CHOTA NAGPUR DIVISION	**4**	...	...	...	...	...	**4,722**	...	**43**	...	**3,426**	...
Hazaribagh ...	3	...	...	...	...	...	681	...	1	...	949	...
Ranchi	...	...	...	...	...	...	654	...	26	...	593	...
Palamau	1	...	...	...	...	...	621	...	5	...	450	...
Manbhum	...	...	...	...	...	...	1,539	...	6	...	869	...
Singhbhum ...	...	...	...	...	...	...	1,277	...	5	...	625	...
Feudatory States ...	...	...	...	...	...	...	**8,869**	...	**17**	...	**4,691**	...
Orissa States ...	...	...	...	...	...	...	8,771	...	17	...	4,592	...
Chota Nagpur States ...	...	...	...	...	...	...	98	...	...	...	99	...
Cities	**3**	...	...	...	...	...	**1,814**	...	...	...	**35**	...
Patna City	3	...	...	...	...	...	335	...	...	...	...	...
Gaya City	...	...	...	...	...	...	86	...	...	...	...	...
Bhagalpur City ...	...	...	...	...	...	...	642	...	...	...	35	...
Jamshedpur City ...	...	...	...	...	...	...	751	...	...	...	...	...

DISTRICT, STATE OR CITY.	ORDER 43.—POLICE—Group 157.—Police.						Group 158.—Village watchmen.					
	Earners (principal occupation).		*Working dependants.*		*Earners (subsidiary occupation).*		*Earners (principal occupation).*		*Working dependants.*		*Earners (subsidiary occupation).*	
	Males.	Females.	Males.	Females.	Males.	Females.	Males.	Females.	Males.	Females.	Males.	Females.
1	635	636	637	638	639	640	641	642	643	644	645	646
BIHAR AND ORISSA	**15,197**	...	**33**	...	**2,521**	...	**20,461**	...	**95**	...	**18,597**	...
British Territory ...	**11,332**	...	**32**	...	**2,207**	...	**15,457**	...	**79**	...	**14,220**	...
PATNA DIVISION ...	**1,428**	...	**9**	...	**262**	...	**1,760**	...	...	...	**1,291**	...
Patna	525	...	...	...	17	...	409	...	...	...	262	...
Gaya	200	...	3	...	24	...	638	...	...	...	264	...
Shahabad	703	...	3	...	221	...	728	...	...	...	765	...
TIRHUT DIVISION ...	**1,575**	...	...	...	**1,021**	...	**1,823**	...	**2**	...	**4,300**	...
Saran	324	...	...	...	396	...	340	...	2	...	1,062	...
Champaran ...	214	...	...	...	108	...	274	...	...	...	703	...
Muzaffarpur ...	794	...	...	...	431	...	814	...	...	...	1,666	...
Darbhanga ...	243	...	...	...	86	...	495	...	...	...	869	...
BHAGALPUR DIVISION ...	**3,752**	...	**18**	...	**427**	...	**4,592**	...	**4**	...	**2,512**	...
Monghyr	427	...	18	...	73	...	769	...	...	...	316	...
Bhagalpur	1,045	...	...	...	136	...	976	...	3	...	519	...
Purnea	1,903	...	...	...	86	...	2,368	...	1	...	574	...
Santal Parganas ...	377	...	...	...	132	...	470	...	...	...	1,103	...
ORISSA DIVISION ...	**2,192**	...	...	...	**126**	...	**4,895**	...	**35**	...	**3,062**	...
Cuttack	561	...	...	...	31	...	1,776	...	1	...	1,026	...
Balasore	85	...	...	...	58	...	317	...	5	...	742	...
Angul	159	...	...	...	12	...	349	...	...	...	259	...
Puri	902	...	...	...	3	...	996	...	9	...	457	...
Sambalpur	485	...	...	...	22	...	1,457	...	20	...	578	...
CHOTA NAGPUR DIVISION	**2,385**	...	**5**	...	**371**	...	**2,387**	...	**38**	...	**3,055**	...
Hazaribagh ...	285	...	...	...	107	...	396	...	1	...	842	...
Ranchi	403	...	2	...	76	...	251	...	24	...	457	...
Palamau	256	...	...	...	34	...	365	...	5	...	416	...
Manbhum	674	...	3	...	79	...	865	...	3	...	790	...
Singhbhum ...	767	...	...	...	75	...	510	...	5	...	550	...
Feudatory States ...	**3,865**	...	**1**	...	**314**	...	**5,004**	...	**16**	...	**4,377**	...
Orissa States ...	3,805	...	1	...	291	...	4,966	...	16	...	4,301	...
Chota Nagpur States ...	60	...	...	...	23	...	38	...	...	...	76	...
Cities	**1,589**	...	...	...	**35**	...	**225**	...	...	...	...	...
Patna City	313	...	...	...	...	...	32	...	...	...	...	...
Gaya City	72	...	...	...	...	...	14	...	...	...	...	...
Bhagalpur City ...	639	...	...	...	35	...	3	...	...	...	...	...
Jamshedpur City ...	565	...	...	...	...	...	186	...	...	...	...	...

TABLE X—*continued.*

OCCUPATION OR MEANS OF LIVELIHOOD. PART II.—DETAILS FOR DISTRICTS AND CITIES.

DISTRICT, STATE OR CITY.	*SUB-CLASS VII AND ORDER 44.—PUBLIC ADMINISTRATION.*						*SUB-CLASS VIII.—PROFESSIONS AND LIBERAL ARTS.*						ORDER 45.—RELIGION.						ORDER 46.—LAW. Total of Order 46.					
	Earners (principal occupation).		*Working dependants.*		*Earners (subsidiary occupation).*		*Earners (principal occupation).*		*Working dependants.*		*Earners (subsidiary occupation).*		*Earners (principal occupation).*		*Working dependants.*		*Earners (subsidiary occupation).*		*Earners (principal occupation).*		*Working dependants.*		*Earners (subsidiary occupation).*	
	Males.	Females.	Males.	Females.	Males.	Females.	Males.	Females.	Males.	Females.	Males.	Females.	Males.	Females.	Males.	Females.	Males.	Females.	Males.	Females.	Males.	Females.	Males.	Females.
1	647	648	649	650	651	652	653	654	655	656	657	658	659	660	661	662	663	664	665	666	667	668	669	670
BIHAR AND ORISSA	**16,483**	**382**	**346**	**174**	**9,066**	**51**	**134,825**	**23,930**	**2,163**	**1,050**	**82,964**	**3,878**	**71,634**	**8,289**	**1,257**	**631**	**52,435**	**1,787**	**8,074**	**33**	**22**	...	**1,592**	**13**
British Territory ...	**13,414**	**305**	**322**	**174**	**3,595**	**37**	**123,363**	**22,857**	**1,986**	**959**	**73,610**	**3,754**	**65,911**	**7,590**	**1,136**	**609**	**46,912**	**1,748**	**8,028**	**33**	**22**	...	**1,573**	**13**
PATNA DIVISION ...	**1,677**	**32**	...	...	**156**	...	**36,769**	**8,045**	**83**	**55**	**8,212**	**727**	**21,794**	**3,137**	**66**	**51**	**6,916**	**433**	**2,093**	**1**	**1**	...	**150**	...
Patna ...	542	7	...	...	29	...	14,250	1,924	15	8	1,647	189	5,930	738	10	4	1,154	110	765	1	1	...	29	...
Gaya ...	154	2	...	...	17	...	11,541	3,824	56	21	1,647	283	8,438	936	44	21	1,254	114	593	..	...	...	34	...
Shahabad ...	981	23	...	...	110	...	10,078	2,297	12	26	4,918	255	7,426	1,463	12	26	4,408	209	735	...	...	...	87	...
TIRHUT DIVISION ...	**2,569**	**28**	**35**	...	**1,387**	...	**20,148**	**5,109**	**314**	**180**	**19,476**	**1,324**	**11,202**	**1,368**	**249**	**79**	**13,719**	**635**	**1,568**	**28**	...	...	**498**	**13**
Saran ...	343	1	2	...	275	...	4,400	683	91	73	5,486	374	3,059	449	86	68	4,494	303	384	...	...	..	152	...
Champaran ...	244	...	...	...	364	...	2,583	531	25	8	3,468	138	1,277	223	25	4	2,413	103	184	...	...	...	120	...
Muzaffarpur ...	1,461	8	...	...	416	...	7,215	1,924	10	25	7,103	553	3,217	358	9	3	4,729	187	738	...	...	...	108	2
Darbhanga ...	521	19	33	...	332	...	5,945	1,071	188	74	3,419	259	3,649	340	120	4	2,083	42	262	28	...	...	109	11
BHAGALPUR DIVISION ...	**1,025**	**53**	**234**	...	**241**	**1**	**22,394**	**3,978**	**202**	**343**	**8,075**	**671**	**13,812**	**1,153**	**163**	**318**	**4,086**	**284**	**1,481**	**1**	**2**	...	**356**	...
Monghyr ...	159	34	234	...	38	1	8,909	1,982	107	210	1,679	150	6,726	785	91	196	1,348	90	490	...	...	...	32	...
Bhagalpur ...	313	...	...	...	97	...	5,788	912	80	130	1,676	169	3,690	168	62	122	1,141	16	438	1	2	...	69	...
Purnea ...	460	4	...	...	60	...	4,410	592	5	...	847	46	1,392	67	...	..	240	13	439	...	...	...	189	...
Santal Parganas ...	93	15	...	...	46	...	3,287	492	10	3	3,873	306	1,995	133	10	..	1,357	165	114	...	...	...	59	...
ORISSA DIVISION ...	**6,225**	**132**	**43**	...	**1,464**	**7**	**29,542**	**2,574**	**383**	**148**	**29,720**	**329**	**14,493**	**1,501**	**582**	**92**	**17,953**	**179**	**1,596**	...	**10**	...	**491**	...
Cuttack ...	2,689	17	2	...	586	6	12,081	1,001	117	34	12,816	116	5,236	481	73	23	7,748	70	916	..	...	...	161	...
Balasore ...	803	...	1	...	266	...	4,565	430	301	37	7,941	50	2,316	332	214	31	4,600	44	138	...	...	...	86	...
Angul ...	371	2	...	...	118	...	515	20	2	4	1,091	..	118	10	...	1	366	...	1	...	..	...	...	...
Puri ...	1,411	99	...	...	7	...	10,216	862	379	68	6,587	119	6,056	462	234	33	4,286	42	473	...	10	...	287	...
Sambalpur ...	951	14	40	...	487	1	2,165	261	84	5	1,305	44	767	216	61	4	753	23	68	...	...	...	5	...
CHOTA NAGPUR DIVISION ...	**1,918**	**60**	**10**	**174**	**347**	**29**	**14,455**	**3,151**	**504**	**233**	**8,127**	**703**	**4,610**	**431**	**78**	**69**	**4,238**	**217**	**1,290**	**3**	**9**	...	**83**	...
Hazaribagh ...	387	23	...	...	137	...	2,446	950	14	18	2,699	275	1,307	165	6	8	2,102	143	221	1	...	...	24	...
Ranchi ...	804	37	6	172	47	28	3,258	447	214	121	1,695	90	989	146	37	48	392	48	224	...	1	...	14	...
Palamau ...	364	...	3	1	26	...	1,594	404	15	13	1,107	233	755	68	11	11	895	15	163	.	...	...	7	...
Manbhum ...	174	4	...	...	3	...	4,946	1,192	101	73	1,948	86	916	42	21	...	618	9	608	2	...	...	36	...
Singhbhum ...	289	6	1	1	134	1	2,221	158	160	8	685	20	646	10	3	2	231	2	74	...	8	...	3	...
Feudatory States ...	**3,069**	**77**	**24**	...	**5,471**	**14**	**11,522**	**1,073**	**176**	**91**	**9,354**	**124**	**5,723**	**699**	**119**	**22**	**5,523**	**39**	**46**	...	...	...	**19**	...
Orissa States ...	2,953	77	24	...	5,165	14	11,278	1,012	174	88	9,112	110	5,638	675	117	19	5,448	32	43	...	...	...	14	...
Chota Nagpur States ...	116	...	...	...	306	...	244	61	2	3	242	14	85	24	2	3	75	7	3	...	...	...	5	...
Cities ...	**547**	**11**	...	...	**7**	...	**9,589**	**863**	**20**	**7**	**270**	**3**	**2,397**	**236**	**5**	**2**	**170**	...	**1,156**	**2**	**10**	...	**69**	...
Patna City ...	290	7	...	...	...	...	6,009	463	7	5	18	...	721	115	5	1	11	...	508	1	1	...	6	...
Gaya City ...	46	...	...	...	...	...	1,618	233	...	...	31	...	827	83	...	...	...	...	437	...	...	...	30	...
Bhagalpur City ...	27	...	...	...	7	...	976	117	5	1	90	2	463	35	...	1	33	...	191	1	1	...	33	...
Jamshedpur City ...	185	4	...	...	...	...	986	50	8	1	131	1	386	3	...	...	126	...	30	...	8	...	...	...

TABLE X—*continued*.

OCCUPATION OR MEANS OF LIVELIHOOD. PART II—DETAILS FOR DISTRICTS AND CITIES.

DISTRICT, STATE OR CITY.	ORDER 46.—LAW—*concluded*. Group 167.—Lawyers of all kinds, including Qazis, Law Agents and Mukhtars. *Earners (principal occupation).* Males.	Females.	*Working dependants.* Males.	Females.	*Earners (subsidiary occupation).* Males.	Females.	ORDER 47.—MEDICINE. TOTAL OF ORDER 47. *Earners (principal occupation).* Males.	Females.	*Working dependants.* Males.	Females.	*Earners (subsidiary occupation).* Males.	Females.
1	671	672	673	674	675	676	677	678	679	680	681	682
BIHAR AND ORISSA	**5,210**	**3**	**3**	...	**839**	...	**7,411**	**11,836**	**58**	**213**	**3,568**	**1,712**
British Territory ...	**5,170**	**3**	**3**	...	**826**	...	**6,647**	**11,739**	**41**	**212**	**2,904**	**1,699**
PATNA DIVISION ...	**2,007**	**1**	**1**	...	**139**	..	**2,106**	**3,941**	...	**1**	**194**	**286**
Patna	747	1	1	...	25	...	976	895	...	1	67	77
Gaya	582	.	...	...	34	...	604	3,579	...	...	54	168
Shahabad	675	...	...	...	80	..	536	467	...	.	73	41
TIRHUT DIVISION ...	**836**	...	...	.	**246**	...	**1,996**	**3,274**	**18**	**89**	**748**	**605**
Saran	220	...	...	...	98		171	137	...	5	136	39
Champaran ..	78	..	..	...	38	..	164	205	...	...	123	23
Muzaffarpur ...	364	...	...	...	38	...	608	1,459	...	20	250	356
Darbhanga ...	174	...	...	...	73	...	453	1,473	18	64	339	187
BHAGALPUR DIVISION ...	**1,446**	**1**	**2**	...	**349**	...	**1,273**	**2,236**	**2**	**17**	**325**	**334**
Monghyr	463	...	...	...	39	...	424	1,069	...	12	48	53
Bhagalpur	433	1	2	...	65	...	316	537	2	2	35	144
Purnea	439	...	...	...	187	...	361	406	...	...	106	32
Santal Parganas ...	111	...	...	...	58	...	172	224	...	3	136	105
ORISSA DIVISION ...	**284**	...	...	...	**44**	...	**1,607**	**224**	**11**	**28**	**1,257**	**59**
Cuttack	133	...	...	...	24	...	204	113	3	4	442	4
Balasore	54	...	...	...	14	...	147	5	2	...	243	...
Angul	...	...	...	..	...	...	26	1	..	...	18	..
Puri	62	...	...	...	2	...	409	101	2	24	267	34
Sambalpur	36	...	..	...	4	...	131	4	4	...	287	21
CHOTA NAGPUR DIVISION	**597**	**1**	...	...	**48**	...	**1,165**	**2,064**	**10**	**77**	**380**	**415**
Hazaribagh ...	107	1	...	...	8	...	197	692	...	9	58	119
Ranchi	122	...	...	...	12	...	151	52	8	7	48	1
Palamau	54	...	...	...	2	...	97	287	...	2	29	215
Manbhum	252	...	...	...	26	...	505	971	2	56	163	67
Singhbhum ...	62	...	...	...	...	...	215	62	...	3	87	13
Feudatory States ...	**40**	...	...	...	**13**	...	**564**	**97**	**17**	**1**	**664**	**13**
Orissa States ...	40	...	...	...	13	...	525	61	17	1	577	6
Chota Nagpur States ...	...	...	...	...	...	...	39	36	...	...	87	7
Cities	**1,152**	**2**	**2**	...	**69**	...	**743**	**272**	...	**2**	**10**	...
Patna City	508	1	1	...	6	...	412	159	...	1	...	...
Gaya City	437	...	...	...	30	...	158	42	...	...	1	...
Bhagalpur City ...	191	1	1	...	33	...	97	48	...	...	9	...
Jamshedpur City ...	16	...	...	...	...	...	76	23	...	1	...	...

DISTRICT, STATE OR CITY.	ORDER 47.—MEDICINE. Group 169.—Registered medical practitioners, including oculists. *Earners (principal occupation).* Males.	Females.	*Working dependants.* Males.	Females.	*Earners (subsidiary occupation).* Males.	Females.	Group 172.—Midwives, vaccinators, compounders, nurses, masseurs, etc. *Earners (principal occupation).* Males.	Females.	*Working dependants.* Males.	Females.	*Earners (subsidiary occupation).* Males.	Females.
1	683	684	685	686	687	688	689	690	691	692	693	694
BIHAR AND ORISSA	**3,312**	**214**	**14**	...	**733**	**20**	**1,311**	**11,453**	**22**	**204**	**486**	**1,659**
British Territory ...	**3,222**	**212**	**14**	...	**717**	**20**	**1,113**	**11,361**	**7**	**203**	**381**	**1,648**
PATNA DIVISION ...	**1,483**	**68**	...	...	**156**	**4**	**349**	**3,852**	...	**1**	**22**	**280**
Patna	765	18		...	57	1	188	877	...	1	5	76
Gaya	471	38	...	..	48	2	82	2,545	...	...	3	166
Shahabad	244	22	..	..	51	1	79	430	...	..	14	38
TIRHUT DIVISION ...	**461**	**78**	**12**	.	**237**	**9**	**227**	**3,129**	**6**	**89**	**242**	**569**
Saran	65	4	...	...	43	...	39	124	...	5	7	34
Champaran ..	76	6	...	...	66	...	49	191	...	...	37	17
Muzaffarpur ...	220	68	...	...	92	9	78	1,343	...	20	53	331
Darbhanga ...	120	...	12	...	36	...	61	1,471	6	64	145	187
BHAGALPUR DIVISION ...	**512**	**25**	...	...	**107**	**2**	**109**	**2,175**	...	**12**	**14**	**332**
Monghyr	137	9	...	...	20	1	49	1,051	...	8	1	52
Bhagalpur	89	3	...	...	10	...	10	518	...	1	1	144
Purnea	196	7	..	...	35	1	37	393	...	...	...	81
Santal Parganas ...	90	6	...	.	42	...	13	213	...	3	12	105
ORISSA DIVISION ...	**232**	**13**	**1**	...	**74**	**2**	**201**	**203**	...	**28**	**68**	**56**
Cuttack	70	3	...	...	10	...	72	110	...	4	17	3
Balasore	25	2	1	...	12	...	23	1	...	...	12	...
Angul	7	..	...	...	...	...	18	1	...	...	1	...
Puri	107	7	..	...	51	2	42	88	...	24	22	32
Sambalpur	23	1	...	...	1	...	46	3	...	...	16	21
CHOTA NAGPUR DIVISION	**514**	**28**	**1**	...	**143**	**3**	**227**	**2,002**	**1**	**73**	**35**	**411**
Hazaribagh ...	57	6	...	...	6	1	62	683	...	9	12	118
Ranchi	58	7	...	...	15	1	28	42	1	6	6	...
Palamau	24	1	...	...	17	...	22	285	...	2	1	215
Manbhum	327	10	1	...	101	1	49	987	...	53	14	66
Singhbhum ...	48	4	...	...	4	...	66	55	...	3	2	12
Feudatory States ...	**90**	**2**	...	...	**16**	...	**198**	**92**	**15**	**1**	**55**	**11**
Orissa States ...	80	2	...	...	6	...	189	56	15	1	52	4
Chota Nagpur States ...	10	...	...	...	10	...	9	36	...	...	3	7
Cities	**529**	**16**	...	...	**3**	...	**123**	**254**	...	**2**	...	...
Patna City	339	8	...	...	...	...	68	151	...	1	...	...
Gaya City	136	3	...	...	1	...	7	39	...	...	...	...
Bhagalpur City ...	34	2	...	...	2	...	2	45	...	...	...	...
Jamshedpur City ...	20	3	...	...	...	...	46	19	...	1	...	...

TABLE X—*continued.*

OCCUPATION OR MEANS OF LIVELIHOOD. PART II—DETAILS FOR DISTRICTS AND CITIES.

ORDER 48.—INSTRUCTION.

District, State or City.	Total of Order 48. Earners (principal occupation). Males.	Earners (principal occupation). Females.	Working dependants. Males.	Working dependants. Females.	Earners (subsidiary occupation). Males.	Earners (subsidiary occupation). Females.	Group 174.—Professors and teachers of all kinds. Earners (principal occupation). Males.	Earners (principal occupation). Females.	Working dependants. Males.	Working dependants. Females.	Earners (subsidiary occupation). Males.	Earners (subsidiary occupation). Females.
1	695	696	697	698	699	700	701	702	703	704	705	706
BIHAR AND ORISSA	**29,167**	**1,444**	**401**	**52**	**9,633**	**69**	**23,910**	**1,339**	**387**	**48**	**8,768**	**68**
British Territory ...	**25,681**	**1,310**	**380**	**52**	**8,216**	**65**	**20,522**	**1,227**	**376**	**48**	**7,975**	**65**
PATNA DIVISION ...	**8,236**	**276**	**4**	**3**	**673**	**1**	**3,332**	**256**	...	...	**455**	**1**
Patna	5,940	162	4	3	320	1	1,671	137	...	...	155	1
Gaya	1,186	58	...	...	127	...	767	58	...	...	80	...
Shahabad	1,110	56	...	...	226	...	894	55	...	...	220	...
TIRHUT DIVISION ...	**2,533**	**131**	**12**	**10**	**1,830**	**19**	**2,447**	**125**	**12**	**10**	**1,878**	**19**
Saran	423	8	3	...	444	8	401	8	3	...	444	8
Champaran	440	43	...	3	326	2	440	43	...	3	326	2
Muzaffarpur ...	1,083	63	...	1	776	6	1,080	63	...	1	776	6
Darbhanga ...	587	17	9	6	334	3	536	11	9	6	332	3
BHAGALPUR DIVISION ...	**3,527**	**213**	**29**	**8**	**1,323**	**22**	**3,527**	**213**	**29**	**8**	**1,322**	**22**
Monghyr	630	42	16	2	130	...	620	42	16	2	130	...
Bhagalpur	733	53	8	6	316	2	733	53	8	6	316	2
Purnea	1,742	26	5	...	264	1	1,742	26	5	...	264	1
Santal Parganas ...	432	92	...	...	613	10	432	92	...	...	612	19
ORISSA DIVISION ...	**8,389**	**358**	**111**	**8**	**3,351**	**13**	**8,235**	**315**	**111**	**7**	**3,338**	**13**
Cuttack	4,091	189	9	1	1,103	6	4,033	164	9	1	1,103	6
Balasore	1,263	88	41	4	1,213	5	1,262	85	41	4	1,212	5
Angul	338	5	...	...	78	...	332	4	...	...	72	...
Puri	1,856	41	46	2	745	3	1,790	39	46	1	740	3
Sambalpur	841	35	15	1	212	...	818	23	15	1	211	...
CHOTA NAGPUR DIVISION...	**2,996**	**332**	**224**	**23**	**989**	**10**	**2,981**	**324**	**224**	**23**	**982**	**10**
Hazaribagh ...	363	45	8	1	163	4	357	45	8	1	161	4
Ranchi	636	163	49	10	339	4	626	153	40	10	239	4
Palamau ...	396	20	3	...	96	...	387	18	3	...	95	...
Manbhum	970	50	19	1	312	...	969	50	19	1	310	...
Singhbhum ...	642	64	145	2	179	2	642	56	145	2	177	2
Feudatory States ...	**3,486**	**134**	**21**	...	**817**	**4**	**3,388**	**112**	**21**	...	**793**	**3**
Orissa States ...	3,437	134	21	...	813	4	3,340	112	21	...	789	3
Chota Nagpur States ...	49	...	...	...	4	...	48	...	...	...	4	...
Cities	**4,711**	**168**	**5**	**3**	**17**	**2**	**868**	**164**	**4**	...	**16**	**2**
Patna City	4,389	102	1	3	1	...	489	98	...	...	...	...
Gaya City	124	10	...	...	...	...	81	10	...	...	...	...
Bhagalpur City ...	131	33	4	...	14	2	131	33	4	...	14	2
Jamshedpur City ...	167	23	...	...	2	...	167	23	...	...	2	...

ORDER 49.—LETTERS, ARTS AND SCIENCES (OTHER THAN 44).

District, State or City.	Total of Order 49. Earners (principal occupation). Males.	Earners (principal occupation). Females.	Working dependants. Males.	Working dependants. Females.	Earners (subsidiary occupation). Males.	Earners (subsidiary occupation). Females.	Group 182.—Musicians (composers and performers other than military), actors, dancers, etc. Earners (principal occupation). Males.	Earners (principal occupation). Females.	Working dependants. Males.	Working dependants. Females.	Earners (subsidiary occupation). Males.	Earners (subsidiary occupation). Females.
1	707	708	709	710	711	712	713	714	715	716	717	718
BIHAR AND ORISSA	**18,539**	**2,328**	**424**	**154**	**16,836**	**297**	**14,651**	**2,059**	**383**	**143**	**14,468**	**273**
British Territory ...	**16,836**	**2,185**	**405**	**86**	**14,005**	**229**	**13,913**	**1,927**	**371**	**78**	**12,618**	**207**
PATNA DIVISION ...	**2,540**	**690**	**12**	...	**279**	**7**	**2,359**	**670**	**12**	...	**245**	**7**
Patna	639	128	...	...	77	1	608	127	...	...	77	1
Gaya	720	251	12	...	78	1	683	241	12	...	68	1
Shahabad	1,181	311	...	...	124	5	1,068	302	...	...	100	5
TIRHUT DIVISION ...	**3,544**	**398**	**35**	**2**	**2,636**	**52**	**3,350**	**288**	**34**	**2**	**2,569**	**52**
Saran	383	89	2	...	260	24	366	88	2	..	252	24
Champaran	518	60	...	1	477	10	477	60	...	1	467	10
Muzaffarpur ...	1,649	46	1	1	1,245	2	1,547	31	...	1	1,216	2
Darbhanga ...	994	113	32	...	654	16	960	109	32	...	634	16
BHAGALPUR DIVISION ...	**2,301**	**375**	**6**	...	**1,985**	**31**	**1,850**	**359**	**6**	...	**1,768**	**24**
Monghyr	649	86	...	...	114	7	524	77	...	...	112	2
Bhagalpur	602	153	6	...	115	7	526	150	6	...	112	6
Purnea	476	93	...	...	48	...	394	90	...	...	43	...
Santal Parganas ...	574	43	...	...	1,708	17	415	42	...	...	1,502	16
ORISSA DIVISION ...	**4,057**	**491**	**169**	**20**	**6,668**	**78**	**3,092**	**337**	**157**	**19**	**5,954**	**72**
Cuttack	1,544	218	32	6	3,362	36	1,294	145	32	6	3,008	30
Balasore	701	5	44	2	1,597	1	594	5	43	2	1,425	1
Angul	32	4	2	3	620	...	13	2	2	3	578	...
Puri	1,423	268	87	9	1,032	41	949	184	77	8	936	41
Sambalpur	358	6	4	...	48	...	243	1	3	...	7	...
CHOTA NAGPUR DIVISION...	**4,394**	**321**	**183**	**64**	**2,437**	**61**	**3,253**	**273**	**162**	**57**	**2,082**	**52**
Hazaribagh ...	361	47	...	...	350	9	379	38	...	...	266	6
Ranchi	1,368	96	119	47	1,002	37	876	85	90	40	797	33
Palamau ...	174	29	1	...	80	2	126	11	1	...	45	1
Manbhum	1,947	127	60	16	610	10	1,674	120	50	16	799	10
Singhbhum ...	644	22	4	1	136	3	206	10	3	1	175	2
Feudatory States ...	**1,763**	**143**	**19**	**68**	**2,331**	**68**	**738**	**132**	**12**	**65**	**1,850**	**66**
Orissa States ...	1,635	142	19	68	2,260	68	716	132	12	65	1,818	66
Chota Nagpur States ...	68	1	...	...	71	...	22	...	...	...	32	...
Cities	**592**	**185**	...	...	**4**	**1**	**230**	**178**	...	...	**1**	...
Patna City	79	86	...	...	...	...	78	86	...	...	...	...
Gaya City	72	98	...	...	...	...	62	92	...	...	...	...
Bhagalpur City ...	94	...	...	...	1	...	62	...	...	...	1	...
Jamshedpur City ...	337	1	...	...	3	1	28	...	...	...	...	...

TABLE X—*continued.*

Occupation or Means of Livelihood. Part II—Details for Districts and Cities.

District, State or City.	Class D.—Miscellaneous.						Sub-Class IX and Order 50.—Persons living on their income.						Sub-Class X and Order 51.—Domestic service.						Sub-Class XI and Order 52.—Insufficiently described occupations. Total of Sub-Class XI and Order 52.					
	Earners (principal occupation).		Working dependants.		Earners (subsidiary occupation).		Earners (principal occupation).		Working dependants.		Earners (subsidiary occupation).		Earners (principal occupation).		Working dependants.		Earners (subsidiary occupation).		Earners (principal occupation).		Working dependants.		Earners (subsidiary occupation).	
	Males.	Females.	Males.	Females.	Males.	Females.	Males.	Females.	Males.	Females.	Males.	Females.	Males.	Females.	Males.	Females.	Males.	Females.	Males.	Females.	Males.	Females.	Males.	Females.
1	719	720	721	723	723	724	725	726	727	728	729	730	731	732	733	734	735	736	737	738	739	740	741	742
BIHAR AND ORISSA	**891,284**	**610,559**	**25,759**	**40,970**	**166,059**	**46,194**	**1,460**	**415**	**25**	**22**	**897**	**37**	**94,093**	**78,155**	**5,272**	**29,368**	**25,092**	**9,286**	**747,990**	**499,472**	**8,099**	**10,414**	**132,252**	**35,861**
British Territory ...	**849,212**	**565,375**	**24,171**	**37,443**	**154,383**	**43,070**	**1,338**	**351**	**24**	**17**	**825**	**29**	**82,211**	**63,712**	**5,179**	**28,544**	**23,796**	**8,961**	**726,654**	**474,731**	**7,408**	**8,037**	**122,516**	**33,163**
Patna Division ...	**257,786**	**187,199**	**5,837**	**392**	**18,309**	**6,251**	**279**	**21**	...	...	**235**	**3**	**13,834**	**23,679**	**22**	**70**	**818**	**1,012**	**238,616**	**160,561**	**368**	**287**	**17,002**	**5,184**
Patna	105,863	67,513	2,902	77	6,808	1,567	49	12	...	..	1	1	5,278	6,794	4	7	145	218	88,757	59,760	44	54	6,583	1,340
Gaya	120,537	95,605	1,524	312	7,193	3,345	15	1		...	...	...	4,695	8,051	18	63	288	297	114,071	86,579	282	233	6,836	3,040
Shahabad	31,396	24,081	1,411	3	4,308	1,389	215	8	...	...	234	2	3,861	8,834	...	...	385	497	35,788	14,222	42	..	3,583	804
Tirhut Division ...	**155,929**	**96,137**	**4,924**	**29,216**	**51,977**	**17,243**	**68**	**84**	**1**	**2**	**131**	**5**	**34,374**	**21,156**	**1,924**	**26,929**	**15,430**	**5,760**	**113,509**	**70,400**	**1,884**	**2,140**	**34,088**	**11,060**
Saran	19,787	17,912	436	231	13,063	4,459	51	2	1	...	89	3	5,136	1,735	28	71	5,453	624	13,215	14,450	160	137	6,997	3,711
Champaran ...	25,852	16,772	353	358	13,571	5,500	1	69	...	2	3	...	7,468	3,195	17	322	3,644	657	15,889	12,996	33	6	9,403	4,712
Muzaffarpur ...	18,091	14,461	1,772	26,180	6,164	4,609	13	12	...	...	38	2	6,707	10,270	1,428	26,144	2,511	4,070	9,117	2,715	78	21	2,846	428
Darbhanga ...	92,249	46,992	2,361	2,438	19,179	2,675	3	1	...	...	1	...	16,063	5,956	451	392	3,832	409	75,288	40,239	1,613	1,976	14,842	2,209
Bhagalpur Division ...	**242,393**	**160,459**	**3,621**	**2,236**	**27,992**	**9,337**	**145**	**24**	**3**	..	**31**	...	**4,721**	**5,088**	**67**	**83**	**711**	**892**	**232,577**	**152,811**	**1,119**	**2,003**	**26,583**	**8,362**
Monghyr	144,836	104,431	656	1,031	10,814	3,516	32	15	...	...	9	...	1,154	3,437	3	18	133	67	142,318	100,345	415	996	10,559	3,445
Bhagalpur	61,005	34,979	2,379	977	5,632	1,190	49	...	3	...	14	...	831	527	...	22	112	69	59,058	33,988	522	843	5,405	1,115
Purnea	14,566	3,406	305	100	706	17	10	...	...	...	2	...	2,283	465	9	48	27	3	10,473	2,126	107	57	600	10
Santal Parganas ...	21,986	17,843	281	128	10,840	4,624	54	9	...	...	0	...	454	650	55	...	439	763	30,728	16,352	75	108	10,010	3,792
Orissa Division ...	**81,068**	**50,551**	**3,568**	**2,874**	**25,985**	**1,532**	**462**	**55**	..	**1**	**371**	**14**	**19,103**	**7,035**	**187**	**1,203**	**4,706**	**239**	**46,213**	**31,561**	**2,190**	**1,477**	**18,100**	**1,092**
Cuttack	32,771	14,253	290	231	7,649	350	340	40	..	1	167	6	7,763	1,422	16	140	1,093	41	16,864	6,632	29	28	4,735	275
Balasore	13,207	11,348	2,413	240	9,549	255	23	...	...	.	130	5	3,919	3,528	56	38	1,891	19	7,467	5,097	1,674	163	6,695	216
Angul	2,056	1,456	43	2	609	56	2	3	...	...	8	1	495	120	...	...	76	2	1,550	1,326	...	2	491	51
Puri	18,657	6,739	499	732	4,114	342	85	12	...	..	...	...	5,515	855	73	267	410	44	9,069	3,479	352	399	3,421	194
Sambalpur	14,377	16,755	823	1,669	4,064	499	3	...	...	..	60	2	1,411	1,110	42	763	330	133	11,264	16,027	135	885	2,758	356
Chota Nagpur Division...	**112,036**	**71,029**	**6,231**	**2,725**	**30,120**	**8,707**	**384**	**167**	**20**	**14**	**57**	**7**	**10,179**	**7,754**	**2,979**	**259**	**2,133**	**1,058**	**95,739**	**59,398**	**1,847**	**2,130**	**26,743**	**7,465**
Hazaribagh ...	24,372	21,697	632	138	7,474	2,767	201	138	1	...	17	5	1,062	1,112	12	12	618	173	22,497	20,060	39	78	6,677	2,534
Ranchi	16,972	10,040	1,308	1,439	6,158	2,491	51	6	19	14	7	...	823	894	108	85	151	45	15,588	8,891	928	1,263	5,885	2,420
Palamau	10,835	10,705	2,893	110	2,777	1,673	21	5	...	...	9	1	1,512	2,680	2,816	8	357	700	8,797	7,671	55	87	2,313	961
Manbhum	40,774	18,371	760	640	9,678	1,117	82	14	...	...	20	...	4,044	2,013	40	110	852	50	33,157	14,014	305	371	8,067	992
Singhbhum ...	19,183	10,216	628	398	4,033	659	20	4	...	...	4	1	2,738	1,055	4	44	155	90	15,700	8,772	520	331	3,801	558
Feudatory States ...	**42,072**	**45,184**	**1,588**	**3,527**	**11,676**	**3,124**	**122**	**64**	**1**	**5**	**72**	**8**	**11,882**	**14,443**	**93**	**824**	**1,294**	**325**	**21,336**	**24,741**	**691**	**2,377**	**9,736**	**2,698**
Orissa States ...	39,351	41,517	1,381	3,070	9,013	1,715	117	58	1	5	69	7	11,771	14,132	87	821	1,260	297	18,887	21,666	498	1,930	7,177	1,322
Chota Nagpur States ...	2,721	3,667	207	457	2,663	1,409	5	6	...	...	3	1	111	311	6	3	34	28	2,449	3,075	193	447	2,559	1,376
Cities	**45,281**	**13,859**	**3,540**	**155**	**1,817**	**209**	**64**	**11**	**3**	..	**8**	**2**	**5,128**	**2,962**	**3**	**7**	**46**	**11**	**39,681**	**10,495**	**108**	**6**	**1,755**	**196**
Patna City	20,169	6,305	363	23	290	37	13	7	...	..	...	1	2,848	1,874	3	4	27	9	17,173	4,272	38	3	263	27
Gaya City	11,438	3,424	1,218	11	79	...	...	...	...	..	...	..	427	664	...	...	2	...	10,882	2,669	...	...	75	...
Bhagalpur City ...	10,375	2,683	1,890	107	1,115	37	36	...	3	..	8	...	159	14	...	..	13	1	10,114	2,574	68	3	1,088	36
Jamshedpur City ...	3,299	1,447	69	14	333	135	15	4	...	...	...	1	1,694	410	...	3	4	1	1,513	980	3	...	329	133

TABLE X—*continued*.

OCCUPATION OR MEANS OF LIVELIHOOD. PART II—DETAILS FOR DISTRICTS AND CITIES.

SUB-CLASS XI AND ORDER 53.—INSUFFICIENTLY DESCRIBED OCCUPATIONS—concluded.

Group 188.—Manufacturers, businessmen and contractors otherwise unspecified.

DISTRICT, STATE OR CITY.	Earners (principal occupation). Males.	Earners (principal occupation). Females.	Working dependants. Males.	Working dependants. Females.	Earners (subsidiary occupation). Males.	Earners (subsidiary occupation). Females.
1	743	744	745	746	747	748
BIHAR AND ORISSA	**11,681**	**1,316**	**69**	**84**	**2,343**	**202**
British Territory ...	**11,201**	**1,302**	**32**	**83**	**2,164**	**142**
PATNA DIVISION ...	**8,316**	**1,196**	**16**	**69**	**828**	**51**
Patna	3,386	232	10	...	174	8
Gaya	3,625	599	6	69	284	11
Shahabad	2,305	365	...	...	370	32
TIRHUT DIVISION ...	**742**	**54**	...	...	**783**	**15**
Saran	66	...	...	...	230	...
Champaran ...	170	20	...	...	147	15
Muzaffarpur ...	263	34	...	...	206	...
Darbhanga ...	243	...	...	...	200	...
BHAGALPUR DIVISION ...	**216**	**6**	...	...	**19**	...
Monghyr	47	...	...	...	7	...
Bhagalpur	22	1	...	...	1	...
Purnea	93	4	...	...	4	...
Santal Parganas ...	61	1	...	...	7	...
ORISSA DIVISION ...	**249**	...	**1**	...	**167**	...
Cuttack	120	...	...	...	104	...
Balasore	17	...	...	...	22	...
Angul	15	...	...	...	3	...
Puri	68	...	1	...	25	...
Sambalpur	29	...	...	...	13	...
CHOTA NAGPUR DIVISION	**1,678**	**46**	**15**	**14**	**367**	**76**
Hazaribagh ...	262	16	1	12	123	3
Ranchi	183	8	4	1	49	...
Palamau	197	2	...	...	59	...
Manbhum	524	8	10	...	49	...
Singhbhum... ...	512	12	...	1	87	73
Feudatory States ...	**480**	**14**	**37**	**1**	**179**	**60**
Orissa States ...	449	8	2	1	114	...
Chota Nagpur States ...	31	6	35	...	65	60
Cities	**1,753**	**275**	**9**	...	**52**	**72**
Patna City	1,009	122	9	...	3	...
Gaya City	571	142	...	...	1	...
Bhagalpur City ...	8	1	...	...	...	...
Jamshedpur City ...	165	10	...	...	48	72

Group 189.—Cashiers, accountants, book-keepers, clerks and other employees in unspecified offices and ware-houses and shops.

DISTRICT, STATE OR CITY.	Earners (principal occupation). Males.	Earners (principal occupation). Females.	Working dependants. Males.	Working dependants. Females.	Earners (subsidiary occupation). Males.	Earners (subsidiary occupation). Females.
1	749	750	751	752	753	754
BIHAR AND ORISSA	**185,962**	**20,900**	**1,045**	**431**	**31,006**	**1,440**
British Territory ...	**185,609**	**20,819**	**1,033**	**416**	**30,836**	**1,410**
PATNA DIVISION ...	**71,687**	**7,291**	**37**	**2**	**7,187**	**279**
Patna	32,128	3,800	27	...	2,864	133
Gaya	30,077	2,076	10	2	2,463	100
Shahabad	9,483	515	...	...	1,860	46
TIRHUT DIVISION ...	**11,690**	**1,199**	**306**	**40**	**6,026**	**238**
Saran	500	30	...	...	328	102
Champaran ...	455	101	...	...	202	19
Muzaffarpur ...	2,630	522	42	10	1,427	81
Darbhanga ...	8,105	546	264	30	4,069	36
BHAGALPUR DIVISION ...	**67,871**	**7,499**	**310**	**186**	**10,216**	**498**
Monghyr	30,214	3,518	66	130	4,592	207
Bhagalpur	25,743	1,920	169	28	3,226	109
Purnea	4,668	181	57	...	420	5
Santal Parganas ...	7,246	1,880	18	28	1,978	177
ORISSA DIVISION ...	**595**	**22**	**8**	...	**410**	...
Cuttack	49	12	...	...	33	...
Balasore	185	...	7	...	206	...
Angul	2	...	...	...	...	...
Puri	286	10	1	...	148	...
Sambalpur	73	...	...	...	23	...
CHOTA NAGPUR DIVISION	**33,766**	**4,808**	**372**	**188**	**6,997**	**395**
Hazaribagh ...	7,876	1,062	12	...	1,675	108
Ranchi	7,777	1,034	227	146	1,965	120
Palamau	2,317	112	19	4	411	8
Manbhum	12,615	2,204	88	33	2,153	125
Singhbhum... ...	3,181	396	26	5	793	34
Feudatory States ...	**353**	**81**	**12**	**15**	**170**	**30**
Orissa States ...	2	...	...	...	...	...
Chota Nagpur States ...	351	81	12	15	170	30
Cities	**26,248**	**3,463**	**90**	...	**1,322**	**37**
Patna City	10,694	1,385	23	...	172	15
Gaya City	8,043	1,127	...	...	65	...
Bhagalpur City ...	7,266	961	67	...	866	21
Jamshedpur City ...	245	10	...	...	219	1

Group 191.—Labourers and workmen otherwise unspecified.

DISTRICT, STATE OR CITY.	Earners (principal occupation). Males.	Earners (principal occupation). Females.	Working dependants. Males.	Working dependants. Females.	Earners (subsidiary occupation). Males.	Earners (subsidiary occupation). Females.
1	755	756	757	758	759	760
BIHAR AND ORISSA	**547,488**	**477,219**	**6,981**	**9,892**	**98,595**	**34,215**
British Territory ...	**527,037**	**452,573**	**6,339**	**7,531**	**89,208**	**31,607**
PATNA DIVISION ...	**158,316**	**152,074**	**315**	**216**	**8,987**	**4,854**
Patna	62,950	55,728	7	54	3,545	1,199
Gaya	81,369	83,004	266	162	4,089	2,929
Shahabad	13,997	13,342	42	...	1,353	726
TIRHUT DIVISION ...	**101,076**	**69,140**	**1,578**	**2,096**	**27,275**	**10,806**
Saran	12,648	14,420	160	137	6,435	3,609
Champaran ...	15,264	12,875	33	6	9,054	4,678
Muzaffarpur ...	6,224	2,159	36	11	1,213	346
Darbhanga ...	66,940	39,686	1,349	1,942	10,573	2,173
BHAGALPUR DIVISION ...	**164,487**	**145,306**	**809**	**1,817**	**16,348**	**7,863**
Monghyr	112,062	96,827	349	865	5,960	3,238
Bhagalpur	33,293	32,067	353	815	2,178	1,005
Purnea	6,712	1,041	50	57	185	5
Santal Parganas ...	12,420	14,471	57	80	8,025	3,615
ORISSA DIVISION ...	**45,360**	**31,539**	**2,180**	**1,477**	**17,412**	**1,092**
Cuttack	16,692	6,620	29	28	4,598	275
Balasore	7,262	5,097	1,666	163	6,446	216
Angul	1,542	1,326	...	2	398	51
Puri	8,715	3,469	350	399	3,248	194
Sambalpur	11,149	15,027	135	885	2,722	356
CHOTA NAGPUR DIVISION	**57,798**	**54,514**	**1,457**	**1,925**	**19,186**	**6,992**
Hazaribagh ...	14,110	18,966	24	66	4,854	2,423
Ranchi	7,604	7,849	697	1,113	3,864	2,300
Palamau	6,254	7,557	36	83	1,843	953
Manbhum	18,373	11,788	207	338	5,775	967
Singhbhum... ...	11,457	8,354	493	325	2,850	449
Feudatory States ...	**20,451**	**24,646**	**642**	**2,361**	**9,387**	**2,608**
Orissa States ...	18,386	21,658	496	1,929	7,063	1,322
Chota Nagpur States ...	2,065	2,988	146	432	2,324	1,286
Cities	**11,305**	**6,736**	**10**	**6**	**364**	**84**
Patna City	5,185	2,765	6	3	88	12
Gaya City	2,268	1,400	...	...	9	...
Bhagalpur City ...	2,840	1,612	1	3	222	14
Jamshedpur City ...	1,012	959	3	...	45	58

SUB-CLASS XII.—UNPRODUCTIVE.

DISTRICT, STATE OR CITY.	Earners (principal occupation). Males.	Earners (principal occupation). Females.	Working dependants. Males.	Working dependants. Females.	Earners (subsidiary occupation). Males.	Earners (subsidiary occupation). Females.
1	761	762	763	764	765	766
BIHAR AND ORISSA	**47,741**	**32,617**	**12,363**	**1,166**	**7,818**	**1,010**
British Territory ...	**39,009**	**26,581**	**11,560**	**845**	**7,244**	**917**
PATNA DIVISION ...	**5,067**	**2,838**	**5,447**	**35**	**274**	**52**
Patna	1,769	947	2,854	16	79	8
Gaya	1,756	874	1,224	16	89	8
Shahabad	1,532	1,017	1,369	3	106	36
TIRHUT DIVISION ...	**7,978**	**4,497**	**1,115**	**145**	**2,328**	**418**
Saran	1,335	725	249	23	524	121
Champaran ...	2,494	1,512	303	28	821	131
Muzaffarpur ...	2,354	1,464	266	24	269	109
Darbhanga ...	1,805	796	297	70	514	57
BHAGALPUR DIVISION ...	**4,950**	**2,536**	**2,432**	**150**	**667**	**83**
Monghyr	1,332	634	238	18	113	4
Bhagalpur	1,067	464	1,854	112	101	6
Purnea	1,801	815	189	...	68	4
Santal Parganas ...	750	623	151	20	385	60
ORISSA DIVISION ...	**15,290**	**12,900**	**1,191**	**193**	**2,898**	**187**
Cuttack	7,705	6,159	245	62	754	58
Balasore	1,798	3,723	683	44	827	15
Angul	...	7	43	...	34	2
Puri	3,988	2,393	74	66	283	104
Sambalpur	1,709	618	146	21	910	8
CHOTA NAGPUR DIVISION	**5,734**	**3,710**	**1,375**	**322**	**1,187**	**127**
Hazaribagh ...	512	397	580	48	162	55
Ranchi	510	240	253	77	115	26
Palamau	505	349	23	15	98	11
Manbhum	3,491	2,330	415	159	739	75
Singhbhum... ...	716	385	104	23	73	10
Feudatory States ...	**8,732**	**5,936**	**803**	**321**	**574**	**93**
Orissa States ...	8,576	5,661	795	314	507	89
Chota Nagpur States ...	156	275	8	7	67	4
Cities	**408**	**391**	**3,425**	**142**	**8**	...
Patna City	135	152	322	16	...	...
Gaya City	129	91	1,218	11	2	...
Bhagalpur City ...	66	95	1,819	104	6	...
Jamshedpur City ...	78	53	66	11	...	...

TABLE X—*concluded.*

OCCUPATION OR MEANS OF LIVELIHOOD. PART II—DETAILS FOR DISTRICTS AND CITIES.

DISTRICT, STATE OR CITY.	ORDER 53.—INMATES OF JAILS, ASYLUMS AND ALMS HOUSES.*				ORDER 54.—BEGGARS, VAGRANTS AND PROSTITUTES.												ORDER 55.—OTHER UNCLASSIFIED NON-PRODUCTIVE INDUSTRIES.					
					TOTAL OF ORDER 54.						Group 193.—Beggars and vagrants.											
	Working dependants.		*Non-working dependants.*		*Earners (principal occupation).*		*Working dependants.*		*Earners (subsidiary occupation).*		*Earners (principal occupation).*		*Working dependants.*		*Earners (subsidiary occupation).*		*Earners (principal occupation).*		*Working dependants.*		*Earners (subsidiary occupation).*	
	Males.	Females.	Males.	Females.	Males.	Females.	Males.	Females.	Males.	Females.	Males.	Females.	Males.	Females.	Males.	Females.	Males.	Females.	Males.	Females.	Males.	Females.
1	767	768	769	770	771	772	773	774	775	776	777	778	779	780	781	782	783	784	785	786	787	788
BIHAR AND ORISSA	**11,235**	**303**	**4,439**	**1,018**	**47,451**	**32,563**	**1,126**	**863**	**7,569**	**1,008**	**47,368**	**30,636**	**1,126**	**853**	**7,534**	**796**	**290**	**14**	**2**	...	**249**	**2**
British Territory ...	**10,470**	**249**	**4,246**	**1,005**	**38,733**	**26,567**	**1,088**	**596**	**6,996**	**915**	**38,651**	**24,782**	**1,088**	**587**	**6,961**	**713**	**276**	**14**	**2**	...	**248**	**2**
PATNA DIVISION ...	**5,433**	**27**	**515**	**79**	**4,862**	**2,926**	**14**	**8**	**236**	**52**	**4,850**	**2,790**	**14**	**8**	**231**	**42**	**195**	**12**	...	...	**18**	...
Patna	2,840	16	132	5	1,747	947	14	...	79	8	1,747	942	14	...	79	8	22	...	...	...	...	...
Gaya	1,224	11	214	71	1,674	974	...	5	69	8	1,674	908	...	5	69	8	82	...	...	...	...	...
Shahabad	1,369	...	179	3	1,441	1,005	...	3	88	36	1,439	940	...	3	83	26	91	12	...	...	18	...
TIRHUT DIVISION ...	**968**	**30**	**492**	**17**	**7,978**	**4,497**	**147**	**115**	**2,328**	**418**	**7,940**	**4,191**	**147**	**114**	**2,312**	**393**	...	...	...	...	...	...
Saran	198	4	138	11	1,335	725	51	19	524	121	1,317	661	51	19	514	113	...	...	...	...	...	...
Champaran	303	13	146	...	2,404	1,512	...	15	521	131	2,493	1,501	...	15	521	128	...	...	...	...	...	...
Muzaffarpur ...	247	9	147	6	2,254	1,464	19	15	769	109	2,249	1,275	19	15	769	99	...	...	...	...	...	...
Darbhanga	220	4	61	...	1,895	796	77	66	514	57	1,882	754	77	65	508	53	...	...	...	...	...	...
BHAGALPUR DIVISION ...	**2,363**	**109**	**1,025**	**180**	**4,879**	**2,536**	**69**	**41**	**613**	**83**	**4,866**	**1,948**	**69**	**37**	**604**	**42**	**71**	...	...	...	**49**	...
Monghyr	206	...	139	...	1,273	634	32	18	111	4	1,273	593	32	16	111	4	59	...	...	...	2	...
Bhagalpur	1,839	104	292	39	1,063	464	15	8	100	6	1,060	366	15	8	89	5	4	...	...	...	1	...
Purnea	178	...	210	...	1,790	815	11	...	68	4	1,789	543	11	...	68	4	2	...	...	...	...	...
Santal Parganas ...	140	5	384	141	744	623	11	15	329	69	744	446	11	13	336	29	6	...	...	...	46	...
ORISSA DIVISION ...	**476**	**17**	**321**	**62**	**15,289**	**12,900**	**713**	**176**	**2,628**	**187**	**15,278**	**12,278**	**713**	**175**	**2,623**	**69**	**1**	...	**2**	...	**180**	...
Cuttack	216	7	139	40	7,794	6,150	29	55	754	58	7,793	5,833	29	55	754	45	1	...	...	...	...	...
Balasore	61	...	60	4	1,798	3,723	632	44	837	15	1,797	3,611	632	43	837	8	...	...	...	...	...	...
Angul	43	...	...	3	...	7	...	...	34	2	...	7	...	...	34	2	...	...	...	...	...	...
Puri	43	4	90	15	3,988	3,303	29	62	103	104	3,970	2,212	29	62	103	6	...	...	...	...	...	...
Sambalpur	113	6	33	...	1,709	618	33	15	910	8	1,709	615	33	15	910	8	...	...	2	...	180	...
CHOTA NAGPUR DIVISION...	**1,230**	**66**	**1,895**	**667**	**5,725**	**3,708**	**145**	**256**	**1,136**	**175**	**5,717**	**3,575**	**145**	**253**	**1,136**	**167**	**9**	**2**	...	...	**1**	**2**
Hazaribagh ...	570	25	96	11	512	307	10	23	131	55	507	386	10	21	161	55	...	...	...	...	1	...
Ranchi	211	7	1,179	313	503	247	42	70	115	24	502	243	42	70	115	23	7	2	...	...	...	...
Palamau	11	1	36	1	503	340	12	14	98	11	501	325	12	14	98	11	2	...	...	...	...	2
Manbhum	339	18	539	341	3,401	2,330	76	141	739	75	3,491	3,241	76	140	739	69	...	...	...	...	...	...
Singhbhum... ...	90	15	55	1	716	385	5	8	73	10	716	380	5	8	73	10	...	...	...	...	...	...
Feudatory States ...	**765**	**54**	**191**	**13**	**8,718**	**5,936**	**38**	**267**	**573**	**93**	**8,717**	**5,854**	**38**	**266**	**573**	**83**	**14**	...	...	...	**1**	...
Orissa States ...	757	52	189	13	8,562	5,661	38	262	506	89	8,561	5,591	38	261	506	80	14	...	...	...	1	...
Chota Nagpur States ...	8	2	2	...	156	275	...	5	67	4	156	263	...	5	67	3	...	...	...	...	...	...
Cities	**3,416**	**142**	**463**	**112**	**399**	**391**	**9**	...	**8**	...	**399**	**312**	**9**	...	**8**	...	**9**	...	...	...	...	...
Patna City	317	16	55	3	126	152	5	...	...	...	126	151	5	...	...	...	9	...	...	...	...	...
Gaya City	1,218	11	185	71	129	91	...	...	2	...	129	64	...	...	2	...	...	...	...	...	...	...
Bhagalpur City ...	1,815	104	222	38	66	95	4	...	6	...	66	45	4	...	6	...	...	...	...	...	...	...
Jamshedpur City ...	66	11	1	...	78	53	...	...	...	...	78	52	...	...	...	...	...	...	...	...	...	...

* Persons undergoing rigorous imprisonment in jails have been treated as "working dependants". All other inmates of jails, asylums, etc., have been treated as "non-working dependants".

TABLE XI.

OCCUPATIONS OF SELECTED CASTES, TRIBES OR RACES.

In this table, which corresponds with Table XXI (Part A) of 1921, the occupations of the selected castes, etc., are grouped together by "sub-classes" (*vide* scheme of classification of occupations in Table X). The more important sub-classes have been divided up into smaller units, but these units do not always coincide with the "orders" and "groups" of the main occupation table. Columns 17—66 record the principal occupation of all *earners* (as distinct from working dependants) who are not accounted for in columns 9 and 10.

2. As in Table VIII, complete figures for the whole province have been given for some of the selected castes, etc., while in the case of others the statistics are for representative localities only. The *natural* (as opposed to the *administrative*) division has been taken as the unit of locality. The districts and states falling within each natural division of the province are given on the title-page of Table VIII.

TABLE XI.

OCCUPATIONS OF SELECTED CASTES, TRIBES OR RACES.

CASTE, TRIBE OR RACE.	TRADITIONAL OCCUPATION.	LOCALITY. (Natural Division or District.)	POPULATION DEALT WITH. Earners. Males.	Earners. Females.	Working Dependants. Males.	Working Dependants. Females.	Non-working Dependants. Both sexes.	EARNERS WHOSE TRADITIONAL CASTE OCCUPATION WAS RETURNED AS THEIR— Principal means of livelihood. Males.	Principal means of livelihood. Females.	Subsidiary means of livelihood. Males.	Subsidiary means of livelihood. Females.	Working Dependants following the traditional occupation of their caste. Males.	Working Dependants following the traditional occupation of their caste. Females.	Earners returning their traditional occupation as their principal means of livelihood who had some subsidiary occupation. Males.	Earners returning their traditional occupation as their principal means of livelihood who had some subsidiary occupation. Females.
1	2	3	4	5	6	7	8	9	10	11	12	13	14	15	16
ANGLO-INDIAN	...	Whole province	*1,774*	*274*	*1*	*11*	*4,578*	...	...	...	...	...	...	...	...
BARHI [VISHVAKARMA BRAHMAN] *Hindu*	Carpenter	*Total*	*95,406*	*29,577*	*1,204*	*1,458*	*202,577*	*28,658*	*2,047*	*13,931*	*351*	*199*	*123*	*5,161*	*225*
		Bihar	72,460	23,443	778	930	150,456	22,330	1,955	7,539	305	109	113	3,503	209
		Orissa	14,258	941	402	504	31,589	5,524	48	4,347	14	86	10	1,527	5
		Hazaribagh	8,688	5,193	24	15	20,532	804	44	2,045	32	4	...	131	11
BRAHMAN *Hindu*	Priest	*Total*	*620,425*	*58,274*	*11,092*	*21,126*	*1,390,370*	*64,297*	*5,601*	*54,307*	*2,418*	*1,388*	*962*	*14,475*	*891*
		Bihar	395,168	37,693	3,070	7,081	868,467	42,243	4,509	30,002	1,649	510	742	9,237	742
		Orissa	111,774	9,432	2,488	7,089	257,728	11,146	391	13,831	122	518	40	2,665	63
		C. N. Plateau	113,483	11,149	5,534	6,956	264,175	10,908	701	10,474	647	360	180	2,573	86
CHAMAR *Hindu*	Hide-dresser	*Total*	*361,482*	*272,447*	*3,488*	*5,069*	*627,421*	*35,093*	*18,817*	*19,584*	*6,286*	*549*	*515*	*5,822*	*3,263*
		Bihar	310,212	236,160	1,903	3,528	534,215	29,111	16,894	13,024	4,475	337	292	4,445	2,998
		C. N. Plateau	51,270	36,287	1,585	1,541	93,206	5,982	1,923	6,560	1,811	212	223	1,377	265
DHOBI [DHOBA] *Hindu*	Washerman	*Total*	*121,628*	*69,718*	*3,197*	*8,034*	*211,644*	*47,212*	*44,996*	*24,760*	*4,435*	*641*	*3,165*	*9,727*	*2,447*
		Bihar	63,289	38,509	601	1,635	104,560	26,593	22,180	9,973	2,862	92	438	3,209	1,135
		Orissa	24,823	11,348	1,013	3,569	48,038	9,245	10,383	8,211	468	274	1,513	3,325	422
		C. N. Plateau	33,516	19,861	1,583	2,830	59,046	11,374	12,433	6,576	1,105	275	1,214	3,193	890
EUROPEAN AND ALLIED RACES	...	Whole province	*2,886*	*367*	*18*	*11*	*3,107*	...	...	...	...	...	...	...	...
HAJJAM [NAI, NAPIT, NAI BRAHMAN] *Hindu*	Barber	*Total*	*110,580*	*51,604*	*788*	*1,578*	*219,641*	*43,291*	*17,309*	*18,320*	*1,837*	*252*	*235*	*5,885*	*1,084*
		Bihar	101,724	46,926	761	1,541	200,098	41,908	16,993	16,057	1,627	244	233	5,562	1,052
		Hazaribagh	8,856	4,678	27	37	19,543	1,383	316	2,263	210	8	2	323	32
JOLAHA [SHEIKH MOMIN] *Muslim*	Weaver	*Total*	*260,621*	*128,522*	*3,575*	*6,975*	*583,311*	*38,034*	*12,531*	*22,831*	*2,845*	*657*	*934*	*7,369*	*1,026*
		Bihar	163,144	80,731	785	3,026	369,240	27,098	9,197	7,308	1,349	241	365	4,761	495
		C. N. Plateau*	97,477	47,791	2,790	3,949	214,071	10,936	3,334	15,523	1,496	416	569	2,608	531
KAMAR [LOHAR, VISHVAKARMA BRAHMAN] *Hindu*	Blacksmith	*Total*	*68,102*	*25,968*	*5,185*	*8,245*	*150,146*	*25,477*	*5,549*	*12,617*	*1,286*	*1,243*	*1,140*	*5,611*	*821*
		Orissa	9,691	703	451	942	21,854	2,942	60	2,842	8	102	3	975	6
		C. N. Plateau	58,411	25,265	4,734	7,303	128,292	22,535	5,489	9,775	1,278	1,141	1,137	4,636	815
KARAN *Hindu*	Writer	Orissa	*29,479*	*2,831*	*662*	*2,632*	*78,379*	*4,243*	*86*	*1,592*	*11*	*52*	*1*	*564*	*21*
KAYASTH *Hindu*	Writer	Bihar	*86,626*	*5,866*	*1,031*	*1,674*	*215,946*	*20,003*	*329*	*7,189*	*69*	*150*	*62*	*2,105*	*18*
KUMHAR *Hindu*	Potter	*Total*	*174,450*	*87,277*	*5,360*	*9,689*	*322,262*	*64,840*	*43,164*	*35,189*	*5,944*	*1,082*	*2,687*	*12,991*	*3,055*
		Bihar	89,548	47,064	560	1,400	150,758	35,885	21,627	12,765	2,502	153	198	4,434	1,252
		Orissa	16,720	6,748	512	2,288	27,662	8,011	5,747	5,261	267	195	878	2,687	299
		C. N. Plateau	68,182	33,465	4,288	5,941	143,842	20,944	15,790	17,163	3,175	734	1,611	5,870	1,504
TANTI [TANWA] *Hindu*	Weaver	*Total*	*181,216*	*89,940*	*2,500*	*8,459*	*333,534*	*30,418*	*12,403*	*11,828*	*1,092*	*372*	*2,366*	*4,736*	*709*
		Bihar	132,245	74,370	924	2,099	242,804	7,968	2,900	2,927	895	75	217	1,084	446
		Orissa	37,001	10,117	1,132	5,588	69,230	17,661	6,362	6,791	93	247	1,634	2,436	156
		Orissa States	11,970	5,453	444	772	21,500	4,789	3,141	2,110	104	50	515	1,216	107
TELI *Hindu*	Oil-presser	*Total*	*346,316*	*131,101*	*10,658*	*17,815*	*704,606*	*57,267*	*44,880*	*36,639*	*7,862*	*904*	*2,436*	*10,337*	*2,491*
		Bihar	196,833	79,937	1,670	3,325	378,638	40,460	28,710	15,871	4,261	243	859	5,366	1,200
		Orissa	42,661	7,258	1,730	4,926	93,788	4,367	2,936	4,554	161	211	264	1,409	103
		C. N. Plateau	106,822	43,906	7,258	9,564	232,180	12,440	13,234	16,214	3,440	450	1,313	3,562	1,188

* *Excluding* Angul, Sambalpur *and* Feudatory States.

TABLE XI—*continued.*

Occupations of Selected Castes, Tribes or Races.

PRINCIPAL OCCUPATION OF EARNERS, OTHER THAN TRADITIONAL CASTE OCCUPATION.

Caste, Tribe or Race.	Traditional occupation.	Locality. (Natural Division or District)	I.—Exploitation of animals and vegetation. Income from rent of land. Males.	Females.	Cultivators of all kinds. Males.	Females.	Agents and managers of landed estates, planters, forest officers and their clerks, rent collectors, etc. Males.	Females.	Field labourers and wood cutters, etc. Males.	Females.	Raisers of livestock, milkmen and herdsmen. Males.	Females.	Fishing and hunting. Males.	Females.	II.—Exploitation of minerals. Owners, managers, clerks, etc. Males.	Females.	Labourers. Males.	Females.	III.—Industries. Owners, managers, clerks, etc. Males.	Females.	Artisans and other workmen. Males.	Females.	IV.—Transport. Owners, managers, ship's officers, etc. Males.	Females.	Labourers, boatmen, carters, palki-bearers, etc. Males.	Females.
1	2	3	17	18	19	20	21	22	23	24	25	26	27	28	29	30	31	32	33	34	35	36	37	38	39	40
ANGLO-INDIAN ...	...	Whole province	***18***	***12***	***19***	***3***	***27***	***5***	...	...	..	.		..	***51***	***1***	***1***	...	***62***	***9***	***154***	***6***	***645***	***12***	***404***	***1***
BARHI [VISHVAKARMA BRAHMAN] *Hindu*	Carpenter	*Total*	***593***	***83***	***48,487***	***16,086***	***262***	***17***	***9,010***	***7,005***	***621***	***30***	***135***	***49***	***2***	...	***526***	***159***	***24***	***1***	***833***	***403***	***41***	...	***449***	***14***
		Bihar	485	34	34,328	11,929	250	17	7,772	5,094	496	18	135	40		..	419	123	19	1	400	172	38		371	13
		Orissa	86	28	7,023	358	8	.	985	63	100	10		...	.	.	21	5	5		306	224	1		12	1
		Hazaribagh	32	21	7,137	3,099	4	..	253	948	16	2	..		2		86	32			37	7	2	.	66	..
BRAHMAN *Hindu*	Priest	*Total*	***26,893***	***3,361***	***452,299***	***39,559***	***5,033***	***217***	***13,632***	***2,534***	***723***	***56***	***11***	***3***	***622***	***98***	***1,922***	***155***	***874***	***31***	***1,853***	***1,351***	***1,930***	***7***	***1,662***	***59***
		Bihar	18,196	1,371	299,301	27,651	2,390	141	8,584	1,679	201	20		1	73	33	358	37	258	10	267	487	530	2	388	9
		Orissa	2,571	892	82,851	5,407	653	5	2,590	169	269	34	4		100	2	48	1	190	4	156	730	165		217	20
		C. N. Plateau	6,236	1,096	70,147	6,501	1,990	71	2,478	686	253	2	7		440	3	1,516	117	426	17	1,430	134	635	5	1,057	23
CHAMAR *Hindu*	Hide-dresser	*Total*	***521***	***237***	***128,071***	***70,034***	***976***	***63***	***143,838***	***138,464***	***2,584***	***333***	***18***	***36***	***41***	***7***	***8,341***	***5,260***	***57***	***2***	***1,077***	***333***	***72***	***11***	***1,160***	***360***
		Bihar	323	218	104,645	57,758	935	60	132,747	123,073	1,932	292	7	36	1		2,768	1,834	28	2	507	249	49	10	721	207
		C. N. Plateau	198	19	23,426	12,276	41	3	11,091	15,391	652	41	11		40	7	5,573	3,426	29		570	84	23	1	439	153
DHOBI [DHOBA] *Hindu*	Washerman	*Total*	***307***	***116***	***52,331***	***13,290***	***194***	***24***	***14,743***	***8,248***	***1,164***	***51***	***37***	***34***	***3***		***1,061***	***531***	***30***	***5***	***303***	***137***	***33***	***2***	***291***	***8***
		Bihar	228	69	25,469	9,439	39	4	8,080	5,144	155	11	18	20	.	...	215	140	4	5	74	21	4	2	105	
		Orissa	76	28	11,776	561	45	2	2,851	136	356	16	2	12	1	...	9	4	1	.	46	40	10		66	.
		C. N. Plateau	203	19	15,086	3,290	110	18	3,812	2,968	653	24	17	2	2	.	837	378	25	...	183	76	19		120	8
EUROPEAN AND ALLIED RACES	..	Whole province	***9***	***3***	***17***	***2***	***91***	***6***		..	...	...	...	..	***227***	***7***	...	..	***178***	***7***	***237***	***6***	***425***	***6***	***138***	...
HAJJAM [NAI, NAPIT, NAI BRAHMAN] *Hindu*	Barber	*Total*	***372***	***103***	***51,808***	***19,572***	***70***	***1***	***9,647***	***10,151***	***278***	***23***	***1***	***3***	***1***	...	***387***	***273***	***8***	***4***	***166***	***40***	***21***	***2***	***164***	***24***
		Bihar	365	90	45,114	16,544	62	1	9,341	9,103	229	20	1	3	...	..	263	232	8	4	154	38	13	2	142	21
		Hazaribagh	7	13	6,694	3,028	8	..	306	1,048	49	3	...	.	1	...	124	41	...	...	12	2	8		22	3
JOLAHA [SHEIKH MOMIN] *Muslim*	Weaver	*Total*	***2,849***	***550***	***147,292***	***63,166***	***409***	***1,172***	***33,765***	***34,841***	***1,566***	***214***	***92***	***32***	***52***	***3***	***4,230***	***2,121***	***521***	***52***	***4,828***	***1,521***	***247***	.	***1,703***	***107***
		Bihar	2,174	489	80,465	34,144	158	975	27,487	23,636	693	172	45	32	5	...	290	591	460	52	4,033	1,320	180	..	1,163	100
		C. N. Plateau*	675	61	66,827	29,022	251	197	6,378	11,205	873	42	47		47	3	3,940	1,530	61		795	201	67	.	540	7
KAMAR [LOHAR, VISHVAKARMA BRAHMAN] *Hindu*	Blacksmith	*Total*	***478***	***68***	***28,603***	***8,384***	***219***	***31***	***6,666***	***7,978***	***930***	***108***	***51***	***4***	***19***	***3***	***1,257***	***765***	***29***	***4***	***1,500***	***613***	***5***	..	***289***	***30***
		Orissa	141	10	4,971	174	17	.	785	101	61	6	32	1	2	.	23	1	.	..	528	142	.	.	25	5
		C. N. Plateau	337	58	23,632	8,210	202	31	5,881	7,877	879	102	19	3	17	3	1,234	764	29	4	972	471	5	..	264	25
KARAN *Hindu*	Writer	Orissa	***1,481***	***378***	***16,970***	***1,343***	***644***	***1***	***1,360***	***64***	***68***	***1***	...	..	***59***		***3***	***1***	***70***	...	***225***	***304***	***21***	...	***121***	***7***
KAYASTH *Hindu*	Writer	Bihar	***5,781***	***696***	***41,225***	***3,800***	***1,396***	***96***	***1,419***	***337***	***94***	***1***	...	..	***74***	...	***81***	***38***	***242***	***4***	***278***	***132***	***316***	..	***127***	...
KUMHAR *Hindu*	Potter	*Total*	***758***	***167***	***88,073***	***26,240***	***354***	***71***	***13,064***	***12,181***	***1,060***	***85***	***31***	***11***	***67***	***18***	***687***	***326***	***42***	.	***541***	***477***	***43***	***16***	***184***	***69***
		Bihar	396	80	41,442	15,154	166	43	8,114	7,064	120	18	1	11	5	13	234	142	2	...	215	96	29	16	98	49
		Orissa	62	21	7,272	330	13		989	175	135	3	..			.	12	.			49	211		.	16	2
		C. N. Plateau	300	66	39,360	10,756	175	28	3,961	4,942	805	64	30	...	62	5	441	164	40	...	277	170	14	..	70	18
TANTI [TATWA] *Hindu*	Weaver	*Total*	***524***	***225***	***67,440***	***18,133***	***248***	***11***	***55,552***	***38,537***	***1,713***	***105***	***16***	***1***	***34***	***40***	***1,646***	***2,104***	***98***	***8***	***1,798***	***1,886***	***206***	***25***	***1,582***	***284***
		Bihar	405	139	48,468	16,818	210	9	50,631	37,209	1,115	36	13	...	34	40	1,464	1,927	96	8	1,531	497	201	25	1,445	224
		Orissa	66	43	13,961	836	24	1	3,594	477	441	43	2			..	50	4	2	...	227	1,287		.	55	23
		Orissa States	53	43	5,011	479	14	1	1,327	851	157	26	1	1	...	...	132	173	...	...	40	102	5	.	82	37
TELI *Hindu*	Oil-presser	*Total*	***2,939***	***612***	***206,938***	***50,492***	***1,052***	***130***	***32,657***	***17,940***	***1,931***	***136***	***27***	***5***	***29***	***24***	***2,187***	***972***	***141***	***12***	***2,296***	***1,875***	***103***	***1***	***4,081***	***271***
		Bihar	1,481	306	107,837	31,012	580	67	19,188	11,145	390	87	2	..	10	24	464	208	67	2	878	789	75	1	3,014	162
		Orissa	303	85	26,901	1,403	38	11	5,439	240	374	14	3	..	3	..	77	..	27	.	305	791	2	...	285	34
		C. N. Plateau	1,155	221	72,200	18,077	434	52	8,030	6,555	1,167	35	22	5	16	..	1,646	764	57	10	1,113	295	26	...	782	75

*Excluding Angul, Sambalpur and Feudatory States.

TABLE XI—concluded.

Occupations of Selected Castes, Tribes or Races.

PRINCIPAL OCCUPATION OF EARNERS OTHER THAN TRADITIONAL CASTE OCCUPATION—concluded.

Caste, Tribe or Race.	Traditional occupation.	Locality. (Natural Division or District.)	V.—Trade. Males.	V.—Trade. Females.	VI.—Public Force. Commissioned and Gazetted Officers. Males.	VI.—Public Force. Commissioned and Gazetted Officers. Females.	VI.—Public Force. Others. Males.	VI.—Public Force. Others. Females.	VII.—Public Administration. Gazetted Officers. Males.	VII.—Public Administration. Gazetted Officers. Females.	VII.—Public Administration. Others. Males.	VII.—Public Administration. Others. Females.
1	2	3	41	42	43	44	45	46	47	48	49	50
ANGLO-INDIAN	...	Whole-province	*10*	*1*	*5*	...	*22*	...	*29*	*1*	*43*	*11*
BARHI [VISHVAKARMA BRAHMAN] Hindu	Carpenter	*Total*	*724*	*253*	...	...	*32*	...	...	...	*28*	*1*
		Bihar	683	200	...	...	15	...	...	...	23	1
		Orissa	36	48	...	...	1	...	...	...	1	...
		Hazaribagh	5	5	...	...	16	...	...	...	4	...
BRAHMAN Hindu	Priest	*Total*	*6,817*	*849*	*15*	...	*2,004*	...	*167*	...	*2,637*	*31*
		Bihar	2,087	140	12	...	850	...	83	...	803	36
		Orissa	1,866	336	1	...	327	...	25	...	400	...
		C. N. Plateau	2,864	383	2	...	827	...	59	...	1,434	5
CHAMAR Hindu	Hide-dresser	*Total*	*795*	*177*	...	...	*70*	...	...	...	*102*	*8*
		Bihar	604	98	...	...	51	...	...	...	97	6
		C. N. Plateau	191	79	...	...	19	...	...	...	5	2
DHOBI [DHOBA] Hindu	Washerman	*Total*	*319*	*188*	*1*	...	*68*	...	...	...	*45*	*11*
		Bihar	109	10	...	...	17	...	...	...	29	...
		Orissa	35	30	...	...	24	...	...	...	2	...
		C. N. Plateau	175	148	1	...	27	...	...	...	14	11
EUROPEAN AND ALLIED RACES	...	Whole province	*57*	*5*	*50*	...	*925*	...	*108*	*1*	*24*	*15*
HAJJAM [NAI, NAPIT, NAI BRAHMAN] Hindu	Barber	*Total*	*250*	*56*	*1*	...	*33*	...	...	...	*81*	...
		Bihar	238	51	1	...	19	...	...	...	80	...
		Hazaribagh	12	5	...	...	14	...	...	...	1	...
JOLAHA [SHEIKH MOMIN] Muslim	Weaver	*Total*	*6,095*	*1,300*	*25*	...	*133*	...	*9*	...	*220*	*22*
		Bihar	4,677	882	25	...	82	...	2	...	88	13
		C. N. Plateau*	1,418	418	...	...	51	...	7	...	132	9
KAMAR [LOHAR, VISHVAKARMA BRAHMAN] Hindu	Blacksmith	*Total*	*520*	*519*	...	...	*124*	...	...	...	*38*	...
		Orissa	52	56	...	...	1	...	...	...	...	...
		C. N. Plateau	468	463	...	...	123	...	...	...	38	...
KARAN Hindu	Writer	Orissa	*612*	*67*	...	...	*355*	...	*21*	...	*543*	...
KAYASTH Hindu	Writer	Bihar	*1,113*	*71*	*16*	...	*390*	...	*125*	...	*932*	*4*
KUMHAR Hindu	Potter	*Total*	*907*	*642*	...	...	*21*	...	*3*	...	*51*	*8*
		Bihar	267	64	...	...	6	...	...	...	28	1
		Orissa	34	46	...	...	1	...	3	...	2	...
		C. N. Plateau	606	532	...	...	14	...	...	...	21	7
TANTI [TATWA] Hindu	Weaver	*Total*	*1,447*	*981*	...	...	*141*	...	*2*	...	*142*	...
		Bihar	970	277	...	...	114	...	2	...	107	...
		Orissa	344	381	...	...	12	...	...	...	18	...
		Orissa States	133	323	...	...	15	...	...	...	17	...
TELI Hindu	Oil-presser	*Total*	*23,184*	*6,698*	*3*	...	*121*	*1*	*4*	...	*175*	*8*
		Bihar	14,799	3,371	...	...	34	1	2	...	84	6
		Orissa	3,443	1,037	...	...	5	...	...	...	22	...
		C. N. Plateau	4,942	2,290	3	...	82	...	2	...	69	2

Caste, Tribe or Race.	Traditional occupation.	Locality.	VIII.—Arts and Professions. Religious. Males.	Religious. Females.	Lawyers, doctors and teachers. Males.	Lawyers, doctors and teachers. Females.	Others. Males.	Others. Females.	IX.—Persons living on their incomes. Males.	IX. Females.	X.—Domestic service. Males.	X. Females.	XI.—Insufficiently described occupations. Contractors, clerks cashiers, etc., otherwise unspecified. Males.	Contractors etc. Females.	Labourers unspecified. Males.	Labourers unspecified. Females.	XII.—Beggars and Prostitutes. Males.	XII. Females.
1	2	3	51	52	53	54	55	56	57	58	59	60	61	62	63	64	65	66
ANGLO-INDIAN	...	Whole-province	*9*	*4*	*39*	*80*	*4*	*771*	*47*	*13*	*6*	*19*	*163*	*20*	*15*	*7*	*1*	*1*
BARHI [VISHVAKARMA BRAHMAN] Hindu	Carpenter	*Total*	*35*	...	*53*	...	*99*	*55*	*27*	*91*	*375*	*125*	*768*	*35*	*3,532*	*3,079*	*92*	*44*
		Bihar	35	...	42	...	57	16	15	14	314	56	720	33	3,343	2,897	80	22
		Orissa	...	...	8	...	16	36	12	73	29	58	13	...	52	76	11	13
		Hazaribagh	...	...	3	...	26	3	...	4	32	11	35	2	137	106	1	9
BRAHMAN Hindu	Priest	*Total*	*1,044*	*172*	*8,952*	*113*	*2,081*	*261*	*906*	*450*	*10,533*	*1,023*	*7,101*	*129*	*2,824*	*996*	*4,193*	*1,295*
		Bihar	435	60	3,510	56	790	72	257	464	5,251	376	5,138	87	1,202	374	1,890	506
		Orissa	335	85	2,040	21	476	143	293	222	2,528	258	382	9	230	410	923	303
		C. N. Plateau	294	27	3,402	36	806	46	356	174	2,754	389	1,581	33	1,303	212	1,380	486
CHAMAR Hindu	Hide-dresser	*Total*	*41*	*1*	*23*	*128*	*1,599*	*1,959*	*147*	*133*	*2,342*	*685*	*11,819*	*290*	*32,233*	*34,816*	*462*	*299*
		Bihar	34	...	17	119	1,499	1,899	78	4	1,850	548	1,326	177	30,457	32,453	425	231
		C. N. Plateau	7	1	6	9	100	60	69	129	402	137	493	113	1,776	2,363	37	68
DHOBI [DHOBA] Hindu	Washerman	*Total*	*16*	*4*	*55*	*3*	*132*	*37*	*45*	*109*	*378*	*171*	*284*	*23*	*2,297*	*1,660*	*79*	*69*
		Bihar	12	...	14	...	34	12	6	...	186	126	206	11	1,671	1,296	21	21
		Orissa	3	...	4	...	1	12	13	99	78	7	7	1	140	6	23	12
		C. N. Plateau	1	4	37	3	97	13	26	10	114	38	71	11	477	359	35	36
EUROPEAN AND ALLIED RACES	...	Whole province	*132*	*108*	*77*	*149*	*26*	*13*	*32*	*12*	*3*	*8*	*129*	*17*	*1*	*1*	...	*1*
HAJJAM [NAI, NAPIT, NAI BRAHMAN] Hindu	Barber	*Total*	*25*	*27*	*101*	*2*	*80*	*31*	*4*	*3*	*860*	*564*	*500*	*29*	*2,393*	*3,331*	*38*	*51*
		Bihar	25	27	97	2	78	30	2	1	787	551	463	29	2,298	3,133	36	46
		Hazaribagh	...	...	4	...	2	1	2	2	73	13	37	...	95	198	2	5
JOLAHA [SHEIKH MOMIN] Muslim	Weaver	*Total*	*284*	*7*	*417*	*21*	*769*	*145*	*284*	*82*	*5,413*	*1,293*	*3,865*	*287*	*7,160*	*8,783*	*350*	*272*
		Bihar	265	7	332	15	622	76	75	17	3,913	1,097	3,177	224	5,426	7,488	200	204
		C. N. Plateau*	19	...	85	6	147	69	209	65	1,500	196	688	63	1,734	1,295	150	68
KAMAR [LOHAR, VISHVAKARMA BRAHMAN] Hindu	Blacksmith	*Total*	*2*	*25*	*44*	*1*	*116*	*86*	*34*	*76*	*312*	*159*	*219*	*25*	*1,110*	*1,419*	*60*	*120*
		Orissa	...	...	8	...	3	21	4	26	18	36	3	...	68	49	17	14
		C. N. Plateau	2	25	36	1	113	65	30	50	294	123	216	25	1,043	1,370	43	106
KARAN Hindu	Writer	Orissa	*69*	*4*	*379*	*9*	*368*	*109*	*82*	*65*	*720*	*176*	*232*	*1*	*216*	*167*	*117*	*48*
KAYASTH Hindu	Writer	Bihar	*28*	...	*3,285*	*112*	*415*	*14*	*259*	*21*	*1,704*	*48*	*6,650*	*70*	*661*	*88*	*89*	*5*
KUMHAR Hindu	Potter	*Total*	*46*	*66*	*76*	*5*	*72*	*66*	*56*	*186*	*388*	*198*	*254*	*61*	*2,767*	*3,104*	*66*	*116*
		Bihar	15	61	22	...	28	2	4	...	216	111	176	41	2,055	2,453	24	18
		Orissa	...	...	6	1	3	18	12	101	21	2	2	...	62	74	16	17
		C. N. Plateau	31	5	48	4	41	46	40	85	151	85	76	20	650	577	26	81
TANTI [TATWA] Hindu	Weaver	*Total*	*8*	*2*	*133*	*5*	*371*	*175*	*23*	*271*	*1,761*	*414*	*1,228*	*78*	*14,441*	*14,059*	*244*	*193*
		Bihar	5	...	41	2	335	55	9	64	1,542	263	1,208	78	14,108	13,719	133	96
		Orissa	...	1	72	...	30	115	11	94	165	116	16	...	170	260	80	68
		Orissa States	3	1	20	3	6	5	3	123	54	35	4	...	73	80	31	29
TELI Hindu	Oil-presser	*Total*	*62*	*24*	*396*	*3*	*584*	*244*	*351*	*363*	*1,990*	*585*	*1,873*	*118*	*5,708*	*5,392*	*228*	*315*
		Bihar	55	...	144	...	325	115	73	31	1,276	242	1,550	110	3,953	3,481	102	67
		Orissa	2	...	61	...	52	62	170	251	251	146	80	2	412	193	39	53
		C. N. Plateau	5	24	191	3	207	67	108	81	403	197	243	6	1,343	1,718	87	195

*Excluding Angul, Sambalpur and Feudatory States.

TABLE XIII.

LITERACY BY RELIGION AND AGE.

This table, which corresponds with Table VIII of 1921, deals with the literacy of the population classified by religions and age-periods. As in 1921, the test of literacy was the ability to write a letter to a friend and to read the answer to it. No person below the age of 5 years was treated as literate. Persons literate in English have been shown separately, but they are included also in the columns for ordinary literates.

2. In general arrangement the table closely follows Table VII, except that only five age-periods are shown.

3. Out of the total Christian population, 403,708 persons (199,910 males and 203,798 females) are Indians by race, and 13,018 persons (7,275 males and 5,743 females) are non-Indians, *viz.*, Europeans, Anglo-Indians, etc. The following statement shows separately for Indian Christians and other Christians the number of literate persons and of those who are literate in English :—

AGE	INDIAN CHRISTIANS						CHRISTIANS OTHER THAN INDIANS.					
	LITERATE			LITERATE IN ENGLISH			LITERATE			LITERATE IN ENGLISH		
	Persons	Males	Females	Persons.	Males	Females	Persons	Males	Females	Persons	Males	Females
1	2	3	4	5	6	7	8	9	10	11	12	13
All ages	*31,465*	*21,374*	*10,091*	*8,546*	*6,240*	*2,306*	*9,427*	*5,449*	*3,978*	*9,121*	*5,293*	*3,828*
5—10	**3,442**	2,045	1,397	**466**	314	152	**739**	349	390	**692**	318	374
10—15	**5,168**	3,152	2,016	**914**	643	271	**913**	436	477	**860**	401	459
15—20	**5,031**	3,296	1,735	**1,441**	1,046	395	**1,086**	633	453	**1,040**	606	434
20 and over	**17,824**	12,881	4,943	**5,725**	4,237	1,488	**6,689**	4,031	2,658	**6,529**	3,968	2,561

4. Statistics of literacy by revenue thanas will be found in Provincial Table II at the end of the volume.

TABLE XIII.

LITERACY BY RELIGION AND AGE. PART I—PROVINCIAL SUMMARY.

AGE.	POPULATION.									LITERATE IN ENGLISH.		
	TOTAL.			LITERATE.			ILLITERATE.					
	Persons.	Males.	Females.	Persons.	Males.	Females.	Persons.	Males.	Females.	Persons.	Males.	Females.
1	2	3	4	5	6	7	8	9	10	11	12	13
ALL RELIGIONS	*42,329,583*	*21,082,560*	*21,247,023*	*1,853,094*	*1,714,011*	*139,083*	*40,476,489*	*19,368,549*	*21,107,940*	*178,701*	*165,642*	*13,059*
0—5 ...	6,395,658	3,121,282	3,274,376	...	...	...	6,395,658	3,121,282	3,274,376	...	...	...
5—10 ...	5,712,201	2,967,590	2,744,611	120,805	105,585	15,220	5,591,396	2,862,005	2,729,391	7,480	6,323	1,157
10—15 ...	4,893,370	2,585,354	2,308,016	186,602	166,330	20,272	4,706,768	2,419,024	2,287,744	15,126	13,443	1,683
15—20 ...	3,592,040	1,758,533	1,833,507	227,878	206,939	20,939	3,364,162	1,551,594	1,812,568	27,151	25,216	1,935
20 and over ...	21,736,314	10,649,801	11,086,513	1,317,809	1,235,157	82,652	20,418,505	9,414,644	11,003,861	128,944	120,660	8,284
HINDUS BRAHMANIC ...	*35,199,144*	*17,552,329*	*17,646,815*	*1,594,294*	*1,491,344*	*102,950*	*33,604,850*	*16,060,985*	*17,543,865*	*135,199*	*129,168*	*6,031*
0—5 ...	5,220,351	2,547,971	2,672,380	...	...	...	5,220,351	2,547,971	2,672,380	...	...	...
5—10 ...	4,670,499	2,429,215	2,241,284	101,248	90,356	10,892	4,569,251	2,338,859	2,230,392	5,207	4,668	540
10—15 ...	4,022,320	2,130,304	1,892,016	157,776	143,159	14,617	3,864,544	1,987,145	1,877,399	11,037	10,186	851
15—20 ...	2,986,673	1,470,638	1,516,035	195,467	179,970	15,407	2,791,206	1,290,668	1,500,538	20,742	19,773	969
20 and over ...	18,299,301	8,974,201	9,325,100	1,139,803	1,077,669	61,014	17,159,498	7,896,342	9,263,156	98,213	94,551	3,662
HINDUS BRAHMO ...	*445*	*232*	*213*	*272*	*147*	*125*	*173*	*85*	*88*	*183*	*106*	*77*
0—5 ...	64	33	31	...	...	...	64	33	31	...	...	...
5—10 ...	53	26	27	32	17	15	21	9	12	17	10	7
10—15 ...	55	27	28	38	22	16	17	5	12	19	13	6
15—20 ...	46	23	23	32	17	15	14	6	8	24	12	12
20 and over ...	227	123	104	170	91	79	57	32	25	123	71	52
HINDUS ARYA ...	*6,763*	*3,704*	*3,059*	*1,296*	*1,098*	*108*	*5,467*	*2,606*	*2,861*	*218*	*197*	*21*
0—5 ...	979	492	487	...	...	...	979	492	487	...	...	...
5—10 ...	875	489	386	113	85	28	762	404	358	13	11	2
10—15 ...	775	441	334	165	127	38	610	314	296	19	15	4
15—20 ...	648	346	302	180	144	36	468	202	266	42	37	5
20 and over ...	3,486	1,936	1,550	838	742	96	2,648	1,194	1,454	144	134	10
SIKHS ...	*5,869*	*3,760*	*2,109*	*1,517*	*1,356*	*161*	*4,352*	*2,404*	*1,948*	*302*	*283*	*19*
0—5 ...	770	304	376	...	...	...	770	304	376	...	...	...
5—10 ...	560	321	239	76	60	16	484	261	223	10	10	...
10—15 ...	496	301	195	97	80	17	399	221	178	14	14	...
15—20 ...	626	373	253	183	153	30	443	220	223	48	43	5
20 and over ...	3,417	2,371	1,046	1,161	1,063	98	2,256	1,308	948	230	216	14
JAINS ...	*4,052*	*2,224*	*1,828*	*1,444*	*1,191*	*253*	*2,608*	*1,033*	*1,575*	*167*	*163*	*4*
0—5 ...	529	242	287	...	...	...	529	242	287	...	...	...
5—10 ...	478	256	222	94	78	16	384	178	206	9	9	...
10—15 ...	469	271	198	141	114	27	328	157	171	13	13	...
15—20 ...	425	245	180	189	152	37	236	93	143	26	26	...
20 and over ...	2,151	1,210	941	1,020	847	173	1,131	363	768	119	115	4
BUDDHISTS ...	*2,295*	*1,235*	*1,060*	*220*	*201*	*19*	*2,075*	*1,034*	*1,041*	*23*	*21*	*2*
0—5 ...	319	156	163	...	...	...	319	156	163	...	...	...
5—10 ...	245	124	121	12	11	1	233	113	120	1	1	...
10—15 ...	210	104	106	13	12	1	197	92	105	...	...	...
15—20 ...	222	111	111	24	21	3	198	90	108	3	2	1
20 and over ...	1,299	740	559	171	157	14	1,128	583	545	19	18	1
ZOROASTRIANS	*264*	*159*	*105*	*194*	*123*	*71*	*70*	*36*	*34*	*153*	*110*	*43*
0—5 ...	28	14	14	...	...	...	28	14	14	...	...	...
5—10 ...	23	11	12	13	4	9	10	7	3	8	3	5
10—15 ...	21	10	11	14	5	9	7	5	2	6	2	4
15—20 ...	24	15	9	18	11	7	6	4	2	16	11	5
20 and over ...	168	109	59	149	103	46	19	6	13	123	94	29
MUSLIMS ...	*4,284,306*	*2,123,112*	*2,161,194*	*200,321*	*180,402*	*19,919*	*4,083,985*	*1,942,710*	*2,141,275*	*24,013*	*23,327*	*686*
0—5 ...	666,927	325,519	341,408	...	...	...	666,927	325,519	341,408	...	...	...
5—10 ...	620,769	323,282	297,487	13,964	11,688	2,276	606,805	311,594	295,211	997	930	67
10—15 ...	516,168	273,031	243,137	20,704	17,827	2,877	495,464	255,204	240,260	2,150	2,064	86
15—20 ...	357,581	171,211	186,370	23,942	20,974	2,968	333,639	150,237	183,402	3,635	3,533	102
20 and over ...	2,122,861	1,030,069	1,092,792	141,711	129,913	11,798	1,981,150	900,156	1,080,994	17,231	16,800	431
CHRISTIANS ...	*416,726*	*207,185*	*209,541*	*40,892*	*26,823*	*14,069*	*375,834*	*180,362*	*195,472*	*17,667*	*11,533*	*6,134*
0—5 ...	75,399	37,213	38,186	...	...	...	75,399	37,213	38,186	...	...	...
5—10 ...	62,524	31,962	30,562	4,181	2,394	1,787	58,343	29,568	28,775	1,158	633	526
10—15 ...	54,597	27,859	26,738	6,081	3,588	2,493	48,516	24,271	24,245	1,774	1,044	730
15—20 ...	37,745	17,040	19,706	6,117	3,929	2,188	31,628	14,020	17,608	2,481	1,652	829
20 and over ...	186,461	92,203	94,250	24,513	16,912	7,601	161,948	75,290	86,658	12,254	8,205	4,049
TRIBAL ...	*2,409,409*	*1,188,440*	*1,220,969*	*12,599*	*11,292*	*1,307*	*2,396,810*	*1,177,148*	*1,219,662*	*745*	*714*	*31*
0—5 ...	430,252	209,228	221,024	...	...	...	430,252	209,228	221,024	...	...	...
5—10 ...	356,137	181,881	174,256	1,070	890	180	355,067	180,991	174,076	59	58	1
10—15 ...	298,220	152,980	145,240	1,572	1,395	177	296,657	151,594	145,063	93	91	2
15—20 ...	206,031	97,615	110,416	1,722	1,565	157	206,309	96,050	110,259	132	126	6
20 and over ...	1,116,760	546,727	570,033	8,235	7,442	793	1,108,525	539,285	569,240	461	439	32
JEWS ...	*24*	*15*	*9*	*22*	*13*	*9*	*2*	*2*	...	*21*	*12*	*9*
10—15 ...	1	1	...	1	1	...	...	...	...	1	1	...
15—20 ...	2	1	1	2	1	1	...	...	...	1	...	1
20 and over ...	21	13	8	19	11	8	2	2	...	19	11	8
KUMBHIPATIAS	*271*	*153*	*118*	*13*	*13*	...	*258*	*140*	*118*	...	...	...
0—5 ...	39	19	20	...	...	...	39	19	20	...	...	...
5—10 ...	37	22	15	1	1	...	36	21	15	...	...	...
10—15 ...	29	16	13	...	...	...	29	16	13	...	...	...
15—20 ...	16	5	11	1	1	...	15	4	11	...	...	...
20 and over ...	150	91	59	11	11	...	139	80	59	...	...	...
INDEFINITE BELIEFS	*15*	*12*	*3*	*10*	*8*	*2*	*5*	*4*	*1*	*10*	*8*	*2*
0—5 ...	1	1	...	...	...	...	1	1	...	...	...	...
5—10 ...	1	1	...	1	1	...	...	...	...	1	1	...
15—20 ...	1	1	...	1	1	...	...	...	...	1	1	...
20 and over ...	12	9	3	8	6	2	4	3	1	8	6	2

TABLE XIII—*continued*.

LITERACY BY RELIGION AND AGE. **PART II—DETAILS FOR DISTRICTS.**

AGE.	POPULATION. Total Persons	Total Males	Total Females	Literate Persons	Literate Males	Literate Females	Illiterate Persons	Illiterate Males	Illiterate Females	Literate in English Persons	Literate in English Males	Literate in English Females
1	2	3	4	5	6	7	8	9	10	11	12	13
PATNA.												
ALL RELIGIONS	*1,846 474*	*956,124*	*890,350*	*178 900*	*160,993*	*17,916*	*1,667 565*	*795 131*	*872,434*	*22,934*	*20,589*	*2,345*
0—5	256 036	124,738	131,298			..	256 036	124 738	131,298			...
5—10	228 938	120,487	108,511	13 496	11,479	2,015	215,502	109,009	106,193	1 051	763	288
10—15	199 381	106,407	92,074	19,848	17,211	2,637	179 533	89,196	90,337	2 026	1,638	388
15—20	158 161	83,465	75,696	23 400	20,813	2 587	134 761	61 652	73 109	3 931	3,570	361
20 and over	1,003 898	522,027	481,871	122 165	111,401	10,674	881 733	410,570	471,197	15 926	14,518	1,308
HINDUS	*1,639 829*	*852,682*	*787,147*	*147,796*	*135,506*	*12,290*	*1,492 033*	*717,176*	*774,857*	*14,059*	*12,869*	*1,190*
0—5	226 452	110,608	115,844				226 452	110,608	115,844		..	...
5—10	201 257	106,323	94,934	11 078	9,690	1,388	190 179	96,633	93 546	608	476	132
10—15	175 219	93,726	81,493	16 368	14,532	1,836	158,851	79,194	79,657	1 219	1,018	201
15—20	130 927	72,966	66 031	19 178	17 399	1,779	120 749	55,567	65,152	2 483	2,288	195
20 and over	896 974	459,029	437,945	101 172	93,885	7,287	795 002	375,144	430,658	9 749	9,087	662
MUSLIMS	*202,655*	*101,175*	*101,480*	*28,151*	*23,606*	*4,545*	*174,504*	*77 569*	*96 935*	*6,098*	*5,974*	*124*
0—5	29 199	13,945	15,254			..	29 199	13,945	15,254			..
5—10	27,332	13,989	13,343	2 149	1,674	475	25 183	12,315	12,868	188	180	8
10—15	23 743	14,495	11,248	3 134	2 519	615	20 609	9,976	10 633	483	471	12
15—20	17,714	9,139	8,575	3 758	3,100	658	13 956	6,039	7,017	1 013	989	24
20 and over	104 667	51,607	53,060	19,110	16,313	2,797	85 557	35,294	50,263	4 414	4,334	80
GAYA.												
ALL RELIGIONS	*2,388,462*	*1,193,643*	*1,194,819*	*120,104*	*112,075*	*8,029*	*2,268 358*	*1,081,568*	*1,186,790*	*6,747*	*6,408*	*339*
0—5	371,470	180,664	190,806				371 470	180,664	190,806		..	...
5—10	308 482	160,038	147,544	7,750	7,056	694	300 732	153,862	140,850	304	286	18
10—15	263 576	136,647	126,929	13 968	12,916	1,052	249 608	125,731	125 877	620	586	34
15—20	199 040	96,990	102,050	18,917	17,619	1,298	180,123	79,371	100,752	972	922	50
20 and over	1,245 894	616,404	629,490	79 469	74,484	4,985	1 166 425	541,920	624,505	4,851	4,614	237
HINDUS	*2,133,541*	*1,075,495*	*1,058,046*	*104,491*	*98,219*	*6,272*	*2,029,050*	*977,276*	*1,051,774*	*4,864*	*4,724*	*140*
0—5	331 293	161,158	170,135			..	331 293	161,158	170,135			..
5—10	273 704	143,188	130,516	6 674	6,164	510	267 030	137,024	130,006	215	210	5
10—15	234 122	123,790	110,332	12 366	11,558	808	221,756	112,232	109 524	453	439	14
15—20	178 216	87,828	90,388	17 128	16,087	1,041	161 088	71,741	89,347	740	715	25
20 and over	1 116 206	559,531	556,675	68 323	64,410	3,913	1,047,883	495 121	552,763	3 456	3,360	96
MUSLIMS	*253,560*	*117,436*	*136 124*	*14,914*	*13,403*	*1,511*	*238 646*	*104 033*	*134,613*	*1,519*	*1,481*	*31*
0—5	40 021	19,437	20,584		.		40 021	19,437	20,584		...	..
5—10	34 647	17 677	16,970	1,029	862	167	33 618	16,815	16,803	69	68	1
10—15	29 333	14 789	14,544	1 548	1,328	220	27 785	13 461	14,324	139	138	1
15—20	20 695	9,100	11,595	1 717	1,495	222	18,978	7,605	11,373	199	196	3
20 and over	128 864	56,433	72,431	10,620	9,718	902	118 244	46,715	71 529	1,105	1,079	26
SHAHABAD.												
ALL RELIGIONS	*1,993 489*	*999 099*	*994 390*	*105 921*	*99 089*	*6,832*	*1 887 568*	*900 010*	*987,558*	*9,155*	*8,668*	*487*
0—5	287,248	[illegible]	[illegible]		..		287 248	[illegible]	[illegible]			
5—10	258 364	136,028	[illegible]	7,861	[illegible]	[illegible]	250 503	[illegible]	[illegible]	381	350	31
10—15	227 513	122,886	104,637	12 233	11,351	882	215 280	111,535	103,745	896	847	49
15—20	179 346	91,279	88,067	13 790	12,822	968	165 556	78,457	87,099	1 498	1 429	69
20 and over	1,041 018	508,057	532,961	72,037	67,703	4,334	968 981	440,354	528,627	6,380	6,042	338
HINDUS	*1,838 862*	*924,282*	*914 580*	*93,290*	*88 054*	*5 236*	*1 745 572*	*836,228*	*909,344*	*7,437*	*7,058*	*379*
0—5	263 160	128,525	134,635		...	.	263 160	128 525	134,635			
5—10	236 719	125,313	111,406	6,953	6 467	486	229 766	118,846	110 920	311	287	24
10—15	208,671	112,951	95,720	10 862	10 194	668	197 809	102,757	95,052	762	719	43
15—20	165 339	84 592	80,747	12 206	11,470	736	153 133	73,122	80,011	1,283	1 227	56
20 and over	964 973	472,901	492,072	63 269	59,923	3,346	901,704	412,078	488,726	5 081	4,825	256
MUSLIMS	*151 368*	*73,260*	*78,108*	*11,946*	*10,581*	*1,365*	*139 422*	*62,679*	*76,743*	*1,350*	*1,330*	*20*
0—5	23 573	11,482	12,091		.	...	23,573	11,482	12,091	...	..	...
5—10	21 175	11,067	10,108	859	709	150	20,316	10,358	9,958	38	37	1
10—15	18 425	9,719	8 706	1 299	1,101	198	17 126	8,618	8 508	93	92	1
15—20	13 702	6,541	7,161	1 502	1 296	206	12 200	5,245	6,955	170	167	3
20 and over	74 493	34,451	40,042	8 286	7,475	811	66 207	26,976	39,231	1 049	1,034	15
SARAN.												
ALL RELIGIONS	*2,486 468*	*1,220,049*	*1,266 419*	*91,311*	*86,120*	*5,191*	*2,395,157*	*1,133,929*	*1 261,228*	*7,317*	*7,094*	*223*
0—5	338 465	166,042	172,423	..	...	...	338 465	166,042	172,423			...
5—10	343 022	181,148	161,874	6 281	5,765	516	336 741	175,383	161,358	265	248	17
10—15	296 885	161,529	135,356	10 020	9,349	671	286 865	152,180	134,685	649	628	21
15—20	202 717	102,[illegible]	99,984	11 527	10,834	693	191,190	91,899	99,291	1,207	1,181	26
20 and over	1 305 379	696,507	[illegible]	63 483	60,172	3 311	1 241 896	[illegible]	608,471	5,196	5,037	159
HINDUS	*2 176,984*	*1,072 048*	*1,104 936*	*79,208*	*75,669*	*3,539*	*2,097,776*	*996,379*	*1,101 397*	*5,969*	*5,872*	*97*
0—5	291 838	142,697	149,141		.		291,838	142 697	149,141	..	...	
5—10	296 917	156,904	140 014	5,318	4,977	341	291 599	151,927	139,673	216	210	6
10—15	257 510	140,541	116,969	8,541	8 099	442	248,969	132,442	116,527	542	534	8
15—20	177,002	90 612	86,390	9 917	9,463	454	167,085	81,149	85,936	991	979	12
20 and over	1 153 717	541,295	612 422	55 432	53,130	2,302	1,098,285	488,165	610,120	4,220	4,149	71
MUSLIMS	*309,005*	*147,703*	*161,302*	*11,774*	*10,235*	*1,539*	*297 231*	*137,468*	*159,763*	*1,103*	*1,067*	*36*
0—5	46 555	23,305	23,250		.		46,555	23,305	23,250		...	...
5—10	46 055	24,211	21,844	935	767	168	45,120	23,444	21,676	36	30	6
10—15	39 331	20,954	18,377	1 446	1,223	223	37 885	19,731	18,154	92	85	7
15—20	25 672	12,090	13,582	1,573	1,345	228	24 099	10,745	13,354	193	187	6
20 and over	151 392	67,143	84,249	7 829	6,909	920	143 572	60,243	83,329	782	765	17
CHAMPARAN.												
ALL RELIGIONS	*2,145 687*	*1,080,956*	*1,064,731*	*62,360*	*57,869*	*4,491*	*2,083 327*	*1,023,087*	*1,060,240*	*5,394*	*5,029*	*365*
0—5	312 356	148,982	163,374			...	312,356	148,982	163,374			...
5—10	293,046	151,774	141,272	4,397	3,866	531	288 649	147,908	140,741	274	214	60
10—15	247,738	132,745	114,993	6 444	5,785	659	241,294	126,960	114,334	469	394	75
15—20	170 008	86,856	83,152	7 184	6,533	651	162,824	80,323	82,501	703	656	47
20 and over	1,122,539	560,599	561,940	44,335	41,685	2,650	1,078 204	518,914	559,290	3 948	3,765	183
HINDUS	*1,787,374*	*903,010*	*884,364*	*51,575*	*48,859*	*2,716*	*1,735 699*	*854,151*	*881,548*	*4,319*	*4,258*	*61*
0—5	257,714	122,816	134,898		..	...	257,714	122,816	134,898	.	...	...
5—10	241 036	125,498	116,438	3,511	3,215	296	238,425	122,283	116,142	186	183	3
10—15	205,037	110,106	94,931	5,191	4,822	369	199,846	105,284	94,562	340	331	9
15—20	141 072	72,501	68,571	5,874	5,492	382	135 198	67,009	68,189	562	552	10
20 and over	941,515	472,089	469,426	36,999	35,330	1,669	904,516	436,759	467,757	3,229	3,192	37
MUSLIMS	*354,235*	*175,988*	*178,247*	*9,794*	*8,449*	*1,345*	*344 441*	*167,539*	*176,902*	*550*	*516*	*34*
0—5	53,988	25,856	28,132				53,988	25,856	28,132	...	...	...
5—10	50,471	25,979	24,492	761	596	165	49,710	25,383	24,327	26	19	7
10—15	42 101	22,354	19,747	1,074	876	198	41,027	21,478	19,549	48	40	8
15—20	28 553	14,174	14,379	1,167	964	203	27,386	13,210	14,176	71	68	3
20 and over	179,122	87,625	91,497	6,792	6,013	779	172,330	81,612	90,718	405	389	16

TABLE XIII—*continued.*

LITERACY BY RELIGION AND AGE. **PART II—DETAILS FOR DISTRICTS.**

AGE.	POPULATION									LITERATE IN ENGLISH.		
	TOTAL			LITERATE			ILLITERATE.					
	Persons	Males	Females	Persons	Males	Females	Persons	Males	Females	Persons	Males	Females.
1	2	3	4	5	6	7	8	9	10	11	12	13
MUZAFFARPUR.												
ALL RELIGIONS	*2,941,025*	*1,443,847*	*1,497,178*	*110,136*	*100,050*	*9,186*	*2,831,889*	*1,343,794*	*1,487,995*	*8,921*	*8,467*	*454*
0—5	402,649	195,099	207,550	...	...	...	402,649	195,099	207,550	...	...	...
5—10	403,824	211,268	192 556	8,246	7,398	848	395,578	203,870	191,708	345	300	45
10—15	341,461	183,089	158,372	12,140	11 032	1,108	329,321	172,057	157,264	777	714	63
15—20	225,506	112 136	113,370	13,544	12,306	1,238	211,962	99,830	112,132	1,447	1,372	75
20 and over	1,567,585	742,255	825,330	85,206	79,217	5,989	1,482,379	663,038	819,341	6,352	6,081	271
HINDUS	*2,549,006*	*1,258,489*	*1,290,517*	*105,577*	*98,060*	*7,517*	*2,443,429*	*1,160,429*	*1,283,000*	*7,276*	*7,016*	*260*
0—5	345,076	167 106	177 970	...	...	...	345,076	167,106	177,970	...	...	...
5—10	347,575	182,189	165 386	7,240	6 603	637	340,335	175,586	164 749	282	261	21
10—15	294,712	158 427	136 285	10,784	9,933	851	283,928	148,494	135 434	648	610	38
15—20	195,864	98 188	97,676	12,082	11 079	1,003	183,782	87,109	96,673	1,226	1,180	46
20 and over	1,365,779	652,579	713,200	75,471	70,445	5 026	1,290,308	582,134	708,174	5,120	4,965	155
MUSLIMS	*391,091*	*184,852*	*206,239*	*13,102*	*11,606*	*1,496*	*377,989*	*173,246*	*204,743*	*1,225*	*1,188*	*37*
0—5	57,481	27,954	29,527	...	...	...	57,481	27,954	29,527	...	...	...
5—10	56,156	29 035	27 121	976	789	187	55,180	28,246	26,934	40	36	4
10—15	46,666	24 633	22,043	1,323	1,001	232	45,343	23,532	21,811	102	98	4
15—20	29 554	13,906	15,648	1,411	1,202	209	28,143	12,704	15,439	172	168	4
20 and over	201,234	89,334	111,900	9,392	8,524	868	191,842	80,810	111,032	911	886	25
DARBHANGA.												
ALL RELIGIONS	*3,166,094*	*1,570,959*	*1,595,135*	*124,140*	*117,429*	*6,711*	*3,041,954*	*1,453,530*	*1,588,424*	*8,104*	*7,651*	*453*
0—5	436,021	214,539	221 482	...	...	...	436,021	214,539	221,483	...	...	...
5—10	446,737	233 332	213 405	8,778	7,998	780	437,959	225,334	212 625	358	324	34
10—15	377,234	200 080	177,154	12,673	11,725	948	364,561	188,355	176,206	708	663	45
15—20	246,660	119 588	127,072	13,496	12,594	902	233 164	106,994	126,170	1,196	1,131	65
20 and over	1,659,442	803,420	856 022	89,193	85,112	4 081	1,570,249	718,308	851,941	5,842	5,533	309
HINDUS	*2,725,427*	*1,354,928*	*1,370,499*	*109,393*	*104,340*	*5,053*	*2,616,034*	*1,250,588*	*1,365,446*	*6,555*	*6,397*	*158*
0—5	371,602	182 567	189 035	...	...	...	371,602	182 567	189,035	...	...	...
5—10	381,833	199,409	182,424	7,576	6,975	601	374,257	192,424	181 823	280	269	11
10—15	323 543	171,819	151,724	11,023	10 311	712	312 520	161,508	151,012	590	572	18
15—20	212,278	103 540	108 738	11,851	11,181	670	200,427	92 359	108,068	1,014	987	27
20 and over	1,436,171	697 593	738,578	78,943	75 873	3,070	1,357 228	621,720	735,508	4,671	4,569	102
MUSLIMS	*440,037*	*215,663*	*224,374*	*14,371*	*12,865*	*1,506*	*425,666*	*202,798*	*222,868*	*1,222*	*1,073*	*149*
0—5	64,336	31 921	32 415	...	...	...	64,336	31,921	32,415	...	...	...
5—10	64 845	33 886	30,959	1,175	1,006	169	63,670	32,880	30,790	54	41	13
10—15	53 648	28 234	25 414	1,626	1,399	227	52,022	26,835	25,187	97	79	18
15—20	34 335	16 022	18 313	1,610	1 394	216	32,725	14 628	18,097	152	128	24
20 and over	222,873	105 600	117,273	9,960	9,066	894	212 913	96,534	116,379	919	825	94
MONGHYR.												
ALL RELIGIONS	*2,287 154*	*1,145,797*	*1,141,357*	*78,976*	*71,696*	*7,280*	*2,208,178*	*1,074,101*	*1,134,077*	*8,886*	*8,128*	*758*
0—5	343,583	168,249	175 334	...	...	...	343,583	168,249	175,334	...	...	...
5—10	313,187	164 928	148,259	5,306	4 506	800	307,881	160 422	147,459	427	368	59
10—15	264,682	141 058	123 624	7,812	6 835	977	256 870	134,223	122 647	754	682	72
15—20	178,438	87 191	91 247	9,235	8 222	1,013	169 203	78 969	90,234	1,243	1,158	85
20 and over	1,187,264	584 371	602 893	56,623	52 133	4 490	1,130,641	532,238	598,403	6,462	5,920	542
HINDUS	*2,049 192*	*1,031,465*	*1,017,727*	*68,119*	*62,572*	*5,547*	*1,981,073*	*968,893*	*1,012,180*	*6,360*	*6,118*	*242*
0—5	304,848	149 573	155 275	...	...	...	304,848	149 573	155,275	...	...	...
5—10	278,288	146,723	131,565	4,543	3,914	629	273,745	142 809	130,936	289	272	17
10—15	236,046	126,097	109,949	6 806	6 037	769	229,240	120,060	109,180	563	538	25
15—20	160,005	78 790	81 215	8,080	7,374	806	151,925	71,516	80 409	960	920	40
20 and over	1,070,005	530 282	539 723	48,690	45 347	3 343	1,021,315	484,935	536,380	4,548	4,388	160
MUSLIMS	*228,497*	*109,408*	*119,089*	*9,490*	*8,300*	*1,190*	*219,007*	*101,108*	*117,899*	*1,306*	*1,281*	*25*
0—5	37,097	17,908	19 189	...	...	...	37,097	17,908	19 189	...	...	...
5—10	33,512	17,465	16 047	661	531	130	32 851	16 934	15 917	46	44	2
10—15	27 510	14 336	13 174	899	739	160	26,611	13,597	13,014	95	92	3
15—20	17,683	8 023	9 660	1,015	857	158	16,668	7,166	9 502	162	160	2
20 and over	112,695	51 676	61 019	6,915	6 173	742	105,780	45,503	60,277	1,003	985	18
BHAGALPUR.												
ALL RELIGIONS	*2,234,632*	*1,130,584*	*1,104,048*	*82,063*	*76,376*	*5,687*	*2,152,569*	*1,054,208*	*1,098,361*	*10,487*	*9,769*	*718*
0—5	332,757	163 043	169 714	...	...	...	332,757	163,043	169 714	...	...	...
5—10	320,396	168,799	151 597	5,781	5 015	766	314,615	163,784	150 831	569	485	84
10—15	265,198	141 432	123 766	8 411	7 508	903	256,787	133 924	122,863	1,006	903	103
15—20	179 452	87,234	92 218	10,016	9 198	818	169,436	78,036	91,400	1,576	1,487	89
20 and over	1,136,829	570,076	566,753	57,855	54 655	3,200	1,078 974	515,421	563,553	7,336	6,894	442
HINDUS	*1,980,262*	*1,002,664*	*977,598*	*71,799*	*67,438*	*4,361*	*1,908 463*	*935,226*	*973,237*	*8,035*	*8,118*	*517*
0—5	292,255	143 212	149 043	...	...	...	292,255	143 212	149 043	...	...	...
5—10	282,239	148 739	133 500	4,918	4 361	557	277,321	144 378	132 943	468	400	68
10—15	234,328	125,006	109 322	7 328	6 632	696	227,000	118 374	108 626	822	737	85
15—20	159,142	77 419	81 723	8,823	8 197	626	150 319	69,222	81,097	1,299	1,228	71
20 and over	1,012,298	508,288	504 010	50,730	48 248	2,482	961,568	460 040	501 528	6,046	5,753	293
MUSLIMS	*249 436*	*125,257*	*124,179*	*9,444*	*8,350*	*1,094*	*239,992*	*116,907*	*123,085*	*1,446*	*1,372*	*74*
0—5	39,762	19 474	20 288	...	...	...	39,762	19 474	20,288	...	...	...
5—10	37,331	19 609	17 722	764	577	187	36 567	19,032	17 535	65	52	13
10—15	30,155	16 012	14 143	961	776	185	29 194	15,236	13,958	133	119	14
15—20	19,867	9,578	10 289	1,086	920	166	18,781	8,658	10,123	222	213	9
20 and over	122 321	60 584	61,737	6,633	6,077	556	115,688	54,507	61,181	1,026	988	38
PURNEA.												
ALL RELIGIONS	*2,186,543*	*1,129,681*	*1,056,862*	*95,140*	*91,016*	*4,124*	*2,091,403*	*1,038,665*	*1,052,738*	*8,342*	*8,007*	*335*
0—5	329,757	158 663	171 094	...	...	...	329,757	158,663	171,094	...	...	...
5—10	320,666	167 412	153 254	6,463	5 925	538	314,203	161 487	152,716	448	425	23
10—15	261,294	139 940	121 354	9,776	9 087	689	251,518	130 853	120,665	864	822	42
15—20	182,291	87 582	94 709	10,947	10 299	648	171,344	77,283	94,061	1,293	1,237	56
20 and over	1,092,535	576 084	516 451	67,954	65,705	2,249	1,024,581	510,379	514,202	5,737	5,523	214
HINDUS	*1,285,314*	*665,451*	*619,863*	*55,551*	*52,943*	*2,608*	*1,229,763*	*612,508*	*617,255*	*5,500*	*5,339*	*161*
0—5	190,007	91 452	98 555	...	...	...	190,007	91,452	98,555	...	...	...
5—10	184,661	96 304	88 357	3,917	3 565	352	180,744	92,739	88,005	210	194	16
10—15	150,532	80,207	70 325	5,663	5 205	458	144,869	75,002	69 867	419	388	31
15—20	104,088	49 765	54 323	6,304	5,873	431	97,784	43,892	53,892	717	681	36
20 and over	656,026	347 723	308 303	39,667	38,300	1,367	616,359	309,423	306,936	4,154	4,076	78
MUSLIMS	*886,368*	*456,347*	*430,021*	*38,889*	*37,570*	*1,319*	*847,479*	*418,777*	*428,702*	*2,539*	*2,511*	*28*
0—5	136,940	65 858	71,082	...	...	...	136,940	65 858	71,082	...	...	...
5—10	133,645	69 864	63 781	2,501	2,329	172	131 144	67 535	63,609	227	226	1
10—15	108,951	58 766	50 185	4,046	3 833	213	104 905	54,933	49 972	427	426	1
15—20	76,981	37 203	39 778	4,556	4 362	194	72,425	32,841	39,584	547	541	6
20 and over	429,851	224 656	205,195	27,786	27,046	740	402,065	197,610	204,455	1,338	1,318	20

TABLE XIII—*continued.*

LITERACY BY RELIGION AND AGE. PART II—DETAILS FOR DISTRICTS.

AGE.	POPULATION.									LITERATE IN ENGLISH.		
	TOTAL.			LITERATE.			ILLITERATE.					
	Persons	Males	Females	Persons.	Males	Females.	Persons	Males.	Females	Persons	Males.	Females.
1	2	3	4	5	6	7	8	9	10	11	12	13
SANTAL PARGANAS.												
ALL RELIGIONS	*2,051,472*	*1,025,921*	*1,025,551*	*59,499*	*54,408*	*5,091*	*1,991,973*	*971,513*	*1,020,460*	*10,911*	*9,852*	*1,059*
0—5	343,482	168,452	175,030		..		343,482	168,452	175,030			
5—10	300,235	156,042	144,193	4,038	3,382	656	296,197	152,660	143,537	614	506	108
10—15	247,962	130,043	117,919	6,031	5,162	869	241,931	124,881	117,050	1,011	877	134
15—20 ...	172 519	82,581	89,938	7,022	6,281	741	165,497	76,300	89,197	1,350	1,254	96
20 and over	987,274	488,803	498,471	42,408	39,583	2,825	944,866	449,220	405,046	7,936	7,215	721
HINDUS ..	*949,198*	*475,601*	*473,597*	*45,130*	*42,280*	*2,850*	*904,068*	*433,321*	*470,747*	*8,211*	*7,485*	*726*
0—5	153,008	75,220	77,788	...	.		153,008	75,220	77,788			
5—10 ...	133,305	69,939	63,366	2,935	2,615	320	130,370	67,324	63,046	456	369	87
10—15	110,113	58,566	51,547	4,441	4,038	403	105,672	54,528	51,144	761	655	106
15—20 ..	78,433	37,929	40,504	5,360	4,974	386	73,073	32,055	40,118	1,037	972	65
20 and over .	474,339	233,947	240,392	32,394	30,653	1,741	441,945	203,294	238,651	5,957	5,489	468
MUSLIMS .	*223,702*	*119,839*	*110,863*	*7,651*	*7,159*	*492*	*216,051*	*105,680*	*110,371*	*1,648*	*1,592*	*56*
0—5 ...	40,217	20,101	20,116		.		40,217	20,101	20,116			
5—10	34 958	18,414	16,544	491	432	59	34 467	17,982	16,485	91	85	6
10—15	27,943	14,825	13,118	708	624	84	27,235	14,201	13,034	153	146	7
15—20 .	18,580	8,897	9,683	811	726	85	17,769	8,171	9,598	184	180	4
20 and over ...	102,004	50,602	51,402	5,641	5,377	264	96,363	45,225	51,138	1,220	1,161	39
TRIBAL	*865,128*	*430,935*	*434,193*	*3,490*	*3,176*	*314*	*861,638*	*427,759*	*433,879*	*209*	*185*	*24*
0—5	148,252	72,168	76,084				148,252	72,168	76,084			
5—10	129,982	66,716	63,266	214	181	33	129,768	66,535	63,233	18	17	1
10—15 .	108 127	55,821	52,306	322	270	43	107,805	55,542	52,263	18	12	1
15—20 .	74,297	35,215	39,082	412	363	49	73,885	34,853	39,033	25	21	4
20 and over .	404,470	201,015	203,455	2,542	2,353	189	401,928	198,662	203,266	153	135	18
CUTTACK.												
ALL RELIGIONS	*2,176,707*	*1,098,134*	*1,148,573*	*163,124*	*151,796*	*11,328*	*2,013,583*	*876,338*	*1,137,245*	*12,869*	*12,260*	*609*
0—5 ...	285,267	140,384	144,883				285,267	140,384	144,883	...		
5—10 ..	247,574	126,358	121,216	7,463	6,378	1,085	240,111	119,980	120,131	313	269	44
10—15 ...	237,641	122,309	115,332	12,740	11,072	1,668	224,901	111,237	113,664	810	717	93
15—20 ...	211,103	101 918	109,185	19,248	17,344	1,904	191,855	84,574	107,281	2,126	2,002	124
20 and over .	1,195,122	537,165	657,957	123,673	117,002	6,671	1,071,449	420,163	651,286	9,620	9,272	348
HINDUS ...	*2,106,830*	*996,424*	*1,110,406*	*155,342*	*145,590*	*9,752*	*1,951,488*	*850,834*	*1,100,654*	*11,146*	*10,914*	*232*
0—5 ...	276,284	135,917	140,367				276,284	135,917	140,367			
5—10 ..	239,036	121,990	117,046	7,025	6,101	924	232,011	115,889	116 122	247	231	16
10—15 ..	229,134	117,994	111,140	12,007	10,595	1,412	217,127	107,399	109,728	662	632	30
15—20 ..	203,846	98,724	105,122	18,268	16,626	1,642	185,578	82,098	103,480	1,865	1,819	46
20 and over ...	1,158,530	521,799	636,731	118,042	112,268	5,774	1,040,488	409,531	630,957	8,372	8,232	140
MUSLIMS ...	*66,104*	*29,965*	*36,139*	*5,841*	*5,313*	*528*	*60,263*	*24,652*	*35,611*	*877*	*866*	*11*
0—5 ..	8,570	4,274	4,296				8,570	4,274	4,296			
5—10 ...	8,065	4,178	3,887	249	210	39	7,816	3,968	3,848	19	17	2
10—15 ...	7,979	4,114	3,865	437	375	62	7,542	3,739	3,803	42	40	2
15—20 ..	6,759	2 970	3,789	669	586	83	6,090	2,384	3,706	108	106	2
20 and over ..	34,731	14,429	20,302	4,466	4,142	344	30,245	10,287	19,958	708	703	5
BALASORE.												
ALL RELIGIONS	*990,600*	*480,518*	*510,082*	*81,532*	*76,682*	*4,850*	*909,068*	*403,836*	*505,232*	*4,586*	*4,394*	*192*
0—5 ..	122,988	60,512	62,476				122,988	60,513	62,476			
5—10 ..	107,241	55,579	51,662	3,583	3,161	422	103,658	52,418	51,240	129	117	12
10—15 .	101,140	53,374	47,766	6,032	5,387	645	95,108	47,987	47 121	312	288	24
15—20	97,909	47,354	50,555	8,946	8,138	808	88,963	39,216	49,747	657	622	35
20 and over ...	561,322	263,699	297,623	62,971	60,896	2,075	498,351	203,703	294,648	3 488	3,367	121
HINDUS	*944,681*	*457,943*	*486,738*	*78,527*	*74,329*	*4,198*	*866,154*	*383,614*	*482,540*	*4,004*	*3,942*	*62*
0—5	116,074	57,201	58,873				116,074	57 201	58,873			
5—10 .	101,637	52,680	48,957	3,421	3,065	356	98,216	49,615	48,601	114	108	6
10—15 ...	96,174	50,777	45,397	5,774	5,212	562	90,400	45 565	44,835	268	261	7
15—20 ...	93,326	46,305	47,021	8,612	7,900	712	84,714	37,405	47,309	582	575	7
20 and over .	537,470	251,980	285,490	60,720	58,152	2,568	476,750	193,828	[illegible]	3,040	2,998	42
MUSLIMS	*31,735*	*15,661*	*16,074*	*2,239*	*1,959*	*280*	*29,496*	*13,702*	*15,794*	*289*	*285*	*4*
0—5	4,374	2,106	2,268				4,374	2,106	2 268			.
5—10	3,645	1,913	1,732	103	74	29	3,542	1,830	1,708	5	5	.
10—15	3,384	1,798	1,586	163	131	32	3,221	1,667	1,554	15	14	1
15—20 ..	3,285	1,479	1,806	222	177	45	3,063	1,302	1,761	26	25	1
20 and over .	17,047	8,365	8 682	1,751	1,577	174	15,296	6,788	8,508	243	241	2
ANGUL.												
ALL RELIGIONS	*222,736*	*108,925*	*113,811*	*7,622*	*7,027*	*595*	*215,114*	*101,898*	*113,216*	*483*	*457*	*26*
0—5 ...	37,758	18,443	19,315				37,758	18,443	19,315			
5—10	28,427	14 182	14,245	711	622	89	27,716	13,560	14,156	38	37	1
10—15 .	24,258	12,347	11,911	1,082	962	120	23,176	11,385	11 791	75	73	2
15—20 ..	18,317	8,958	9,359	1,057	969	88	17,260	7,989	9,271	98	94	4
20 and over .	113,976	54,995	58,981	4,772	4,474	298	109,204	50,521	58,683	272	253	19
HINDUS	*163,663*	*80,344*	*83,319*	*7,013*	*6,489*	*524*	*156,650*	*73,855*	*82,795*	*381*	*373*	*8*
0—5 ...	29,083	14,261	14,822				29,083	14,261	14,822			.
5—10	21,064	10,496	10 568	655	572	83	20,409	9,924	10,485	29	29	.
10—15	17,599	9,031	8,568	995	883	112	16,604	8,148	8,456	62	61	1
15—20 ..	13,325	6,623	6,702	974	897	77	12,351	5,726	6,625	85	84	1
20 and over	82,592	39,933	42,659	4,389	4,137	252	78,203	35,796	42,407	205	199	6
TRIBAL	*58,473*	*28,249*	*30,224*	*372*	*367*	*5*	*58,101*	*27,882*	*30,219*	*27*	*27*	...
0—5	8,588	4,143	4,445				8,588	4,143	4,445			...
5—10 .	7,295	3,647	3,648	43	40	3	7,252	3,607	3,645	8	8	...
10—15 ...	6,600	3,284	3,316	70	68	2	6,530	3,216	3,314	10	10	...
15—20 .	4,935	2,308	2,627	56	56	.	4,879	2,252	2,627	4	4	..
20 and over ...	31,055	14,867	16,188	203	203	.	30,852	14,664	16,188	5	5	..
PURI.												
ALL RELIGIONS	*1,035,154*	*500,214*	*534,940*	*67,472*	*62,229*	*5,243*	*967,682*	*437,985*	*529,697*	*4,756*	*4,475*	*281*
0—5	140,420	68,188	72,232				140,420	68 188	72 232			
5—10	121,056	60,989	60 067	3,010	2,527	483	118 046	58,462	50,584	141	125	16
10—15	111,591	57,099	54 492	4,906	4,222	684	106,685	52 877	53,808	340	317	23
15—20 ..	96,961	46,402	50,559	7,292	6,488	804	89,669	39,914	49 755	710	665	45
20 and over	565,126	267,536	297,590	52,264	48,992	3,272	512,862	218 544	294,318	3,565	3,368	197
HINDUS	*1,011,079*	*488,555*	*522,524*	*65,150*	*60,383*	*4,767*	*945,929*	*428,172*	*517,757*	*4,190*	*4,079*	*111*
0—5 .	136,742	66,365	70,377				136,742	66,365	70,377			..
5—10 ...	117,906	59,391	58,515	2,874	2,426	448	115,032	56,965	58 067	113	107	6
10—15 ..	108,850	55,692	53,158	4,702	4,068	634	104,148	51,624	52,524	294	283	11
15—20 .	94,701	45,350	49,351	7,001	6,275	726	87,700	39,075	48,625	631	610	21
20 and over ..	552,880	261,757	291,123	50,573	47,614	2,959	502,307	214,143	288,164	3,152	3,079	73
MUSLIMS ..	*22,518*	*10,875*	*11,643*	*1,549*	*1,419*	*130*	*20,969*	*9,456*	*11,513*	*157*	*155*	*2*
0—5	3,448	1,705	1,743		.		3,448	1,705	1,743			..
5—10 .	2,954	1,497	1,457	85	74	11	2,869	1,423	1,446	8	7	1
10—15 ...	2,564	1,318	1,251	132	115	17	2,432	1,198	1 234	17	16	1
15—20 ...	2,097	974	1,123	180	155	25	1,917	819	1,098	20	20	...
20 and over ...	11,455	5,386	6,069	1,152	1,075	77	10,303	4,311	5,992	112	112	...

TABLE XIII—*continued.*

LITERACY BY RELIGION AND AGE. **PART II—DETAILS FOR DISTRICTS.**

AGE.	POPULATION									LITERATE IN ENGLISH.		
	TOTAL			LITERATE.			ILLITERATE.					
	Persons	Males	Females.	Persons	Males.	Females	Persons	Males	Females	Persons.	Males.	Females.
1	2	3	4	5	6	7	8	9	10	11	12	13
SAMBALPUR.												
ALL RELIGIONS	*880,945*	*431,460*	*449,485*	*39,603*	*37,186*	*2,417*	*841,342*	*394,274*	*447,068*	*2,534*	*2,450*	*84*
0—5	124,056	60,440	63,616	.	...		124,056	60,440	63,616			
5—10	109,285	55,292	53,993	1,702	1 433	269	107,583	53,859	53,724	52	45	7
10—15	98,878	51,492	47,386	3,084	2,726	358	95,794	48,766	47,028	139	133	6
15—20	76,520	36,808	39,712	4,506	4,176	330	72,014	32,632	39,382	376	363	13
20 and over	472,206	227,428	244,778	30,311	28,851	1,460	441,895	198,577	243,318	1,967	1,909	58
HINDUS	*870,178*	*426,029*	*444,149*	*38,428*	*36,184*	*2,244*	*831,750*	*389,845*	*441,905*	*2,202*	*2,164*	*38*
0—5	122,461	59,651	62,810				122,461	59,651	62,810	.		..
5—10	107,851	54,557	53,294	1,637	1,387	250	106,214	53,170	53,044	41	39	2
10—15	97,589	50,843	46,746	2,997	2,661	336	94,592	48,182	46,410	125	122	3
15—20	75,590	36,338	39,252	4,366	4,060	306	71,224	32,278	38,946	339	330	9
20 and over	466,687	224,640	242,047	29,428	28,076	1,352	437,259	196,564	240,695	1,697	1,673	24
MUSLIMS	*3,813*	*2,008*	*1,805*	*680*	*614*	*66*	*3,133*	*1,394*	*1,739*	*150*	*147*	*3*
0—5	449	230	219				449	230	219		.	.
5—10	399	208	191	27	19	8	372	189	183	2	1	1
10—15	382	193	189	38	30	8	344	163	181	4	3	1
15—20	362	195	167	81	70	11	281	125	156	17	16	1
20 and over	2,221	1,182	1,039	534	495	39	1,687	687	1,000	127	127	...
HAZARIBAGH.												
ALL RELIGIONS	*1,517,357*	*751,956*	*765,401*	*38,009*	*35,218*	*2,791*	*1,479,348*	*716,738*	*762,610*	*5,812*	*5,211*	*601*
0—5	270,516	131,062	139,454	.			270,516	131,062	139,454			..
5—10	216,827	112,321	104,506	2,482	2,143	339	214,345	110,178	104,167	291	242	40
10—15	178,083	93,172	84,911	3,789	3,359	430	174,294	89,813	84,481	564	485	79
15—20	128,091	61,295	66,796	4,716	4,300	416	123,375	56,995	66,380	860	767	93
20 and over	723,840	354,106	369,734	27,022	25,416	1,606	696,818	328,690	368,128	4,097	3,717	380
HINDUS	*1,208,099*	*597,528*	*610,571*	*31,084*	*29,089*	*1,995*	*1,177,015*	*568,439*	*608,576*	*4,455*	*4,170*	*285*
0—5	211,275	102,479	108,796				211,275	102,479	108,796			
5—10	169,650	87,814	81,836	1,990	1,747	243	167,660	86,067	81,593	224	194	30
10—15	140,592	73,484	67,108	3,080	2,763	317	137,512	70,721	66,791	454	406	48
15—20	102,607	49,129	53,478	3,808	3,518	290	98,799	45,611	53,188	687	638	49
20 and over	583,975	284,622	299,353	22,206	21,061	1,145	561,769	263,561	298,208	3,090	2,932	158
MUSLIMS	*171,694*	*84,799*	*86,895*	*4,868*	*4,670*	*198*	*166,831*	*80,129*	*86,702*	*492*	*486*	*6*
0—5	32,528	15,828	16,700				32,528	15,828	16,700			
5—10	25,997	13,488	12,509	313	284	29	25,684	13,204	12,480	12	12	
10—15	20,688	10,702	9,986	478	449	29	20,210	10,253	9,957	36	36	..
15—20	14,286	6,673	7,613	632	601	31	13,654	6,072	7,582	67	66	1
20 and over	78,195	38,108	40,087	3,440	3,336	104	74,755	34,772	39,983	377	372	5
TRIBAL	*133,156*	*67,192*	*65,964*	*349*	*308*	*41*	*132,807*	*66,884*	*65,923*	*6*	*6*	
0—5	26,078	12,450	13,628				26,078	12,450	13,628	.		
5—10	20,650	10,722	9,928	37	32	5	20,613	10,690	9,923	.	.	
10—15	16,275	8,670	7,605	41	38	3	16,234	8,632	7,602	1	1	
15—20	10,718	5,241	5,477	38	35	3	10,680	5,206	5,474		..	
20 and over	59,435	30,109	29,326	233	203	30	59,202	29,906	29,296	5	5	
RANCHI.												
ALL RELIGIONS	*1,567,149*	*777,063*	*790,086*	*43,386*	*35,193*	*8,193*	*1,523,763*	*741,870*	*781,893*	*5,697*	*4,715*	*982*
0—5	286,095	139,906	146,189				286,095	139,906	146,189			
5—10	227,866	116,620	111,246	4,023	2,823	1,200	223,843	113,797	110,046	312	227	85
10—15	191,980	99,065	92,915	5,892	4,380	1,512	186,088	94,685	91,403	655	503	152
15—20	132,593	63,817	68,776	6,088	4,740	1,348	126,505	59,077	67,428	950	781	169
20 and over	728,615	357,655	370,960	27,383	23,250	4,133	701,232	334,405	366,827	3,780	3,204	576
HINDUS	*869,492*	*433,323*	*436,169*	*22,917*	*20,096*	*2,821*	*846,575*	*413,227*	*433,348*	*2,794*	*2,598*	*196*
0—5	156,393	76,365	80,028				156,393	76,365	80,028	...	..	
5—10	123,069	63,152	59,917	1,672	1,274	398	121,397	61,878	59,519	144	125	19
10—15	102,751	53,392	49,359	2,352	1,958	394	100,399	51,434	48,965	280	249	31
15—20	72,950	35,640	37,310	2,921	2,488	433	70,029	33,152	36,877	420	385	35
20 and over	414,329	204,774	209,555	15,972	14,376	1,596	398,357	190,398	207,959	1,950	1,839	111
MUSLIMS	*66,047*	*33,778*	*32,269*	*2,582*	*2,342*	*240*	*63,465*	*31,436*	*32,029*	*220*	*211*	*9*
0—5	11,991	5,962	6,029				11,991	5,962	6,029			.
5—10	9,665	5,101	4,564	224	188	36	9,441	4,913	4,528	5	4	1
10—15	7,989	4,267	3,722	319	286	33	7,670	3,981	3,689	12	11	1
15—20	5,802	2,807	2,995	320	286	34	5,482	2,521	2,961	19	17	2
20 and over	30,600	15,641	14,959	1,719	1,582	137	28,881	14,059	14,822	184	179	5
CHRISTIANS	*262,608*	*130,114*	*132,494*	*14,936*	*10,567*	*4,369*	*247,672*	*119,547*	*128,125*	*2,522*	*1,758*	*764*
0—5	48,727	23,966	24,761				48,727	23,966	24,761		.	
5—10	40,124	20,619	19,505	1,782	1,129	653	38,342	19,490	18,852	148	83	65
10—15	34,873	17,944	16,929	2,793	1,807	986	32,080	16,137	15,943	333	213	120
15—20	23,459	11,140	12,319	2,470	1,666	804	20,989	9,474	11,515	483	353	130
20 and over	115,425	56,445	58,980	7,891	5,965	1,926	107,534	50,480	57,054	1,558	1,109	449
TRIBAL	*368,247*	*179,477*	*188,770*	*2,839*	*2,091*	*748*	*365,408*	*177,386*	*188,022*	*197*	*196*	*1*
0—5	68,883	33,568	35,315		..		68,883	33,568	35,315	...		
5—10	54,925	27,707	27,218	338	226	112	54,587	27,481	27,106	14	14	
10—15	46,282	23,420	22,862	418	320	98	45,864	23,100	22,764	27	27	
15—20	30,310	14,194	16,116	365	289	76	29,945	13,905	16,040	24	23	1
20 and over	167,847	80,588	87,259	1,718	1,256	462	166,129	79,332	86,797	62	62	
PALAMAU.												
ALL RELIGIONS	*818,736*	*409,778*	*408,958*	*19,875*	*18,390*	*1,485*	*798,861*	*391,388*	*407,473*	*1,433*	*1,377*	*56*
0—5	149,573	72,882	76,691				149,573	72,882	76,691			
5—10	118,657	61,680	56,977	1,478	1,287	191	117,179	60,393	56,786	42	39	3
10—15	96,574	50,866	45,708	2,246	2,004	242	94,328	48,862	45,466	111	105	6
15—20	69,772	33,977	35,795	2,497	2,285	212	67,275	31,692	35,583	208	197	11
20 and over	384,160	190,373	193,787	13,654	12,814	840	370,506	177,559	192,947	1,072	1,036	36
HINDUS	*669,961*	*335,519*	*334,442*	*17,136*	*16,056*	*1,080*	*652,825*	*319,463*	*333,362*	*1,176*	*1,154*	*22*
0—5	120,607	58,519	62,088		...		120,607	58,519	62,088	..	..	
5—10	96,527	50,159	46,368	1,244	1,118	126	95,283	49,041	46,242	31	30	1
10—15	79,367	42,067	37,300	1,922	1,758	164	77,445	40,309	37,136	97	93	4
15—20	57,220	28,016	29,204	2,149	1,997	152	55,071	26,019	29,052	192	186	6
20 and over	316,240	156,758	159,482	11,821	11,183	638	304,419	145,575	158,844	856	845	11
MUSLIMS	*74,501*	*37,369*	*37,132*	*2,165*	*1,936*	*229*	*72,336*	*35,433*	*36,903*	*129*	*126*	*3*
0—5	13,814	7,041	6,773	.	...		13,814	7,041	6,773			
5—10	10,965	5,741	5,224	149	124	25	10,816	5,617	5,199	7	7	
10—15	8,563	4,304	4,259	215	183	32	8,348	4,121	4,227	10	10	
15—20	6,448	3,154	3,294	278	240	38	6,170	2,914	3,256	6	5	1
20 and over	34,711	17,129	17,582	1,523	1,389	134	33,188	15,740	17,448	106	104	2
TRIBAL	*65,647*	*32,632*	*33,015*	*65*	*60*	*5*	*65,582*	*32,572*	*33,010*	*3*	*3*	
0—5	13,336	6,431	6,905		...		13,336	6,431	6,905			
5—10	9,862	5,122	4,740	8	5	3	9,854	5,117	4,737			
10—15	7,557	3,959	3,598	7	5	2	7,550	3,954	3,596			
15—20	5,400	2,457	2,943	3	3	..	5,397	2,454	2,943	...		
20 and over	29,492	14,663	14,829	47	47	...	29,445	14,616	14,829	3	3	

TABLE XIII—*continued.*

LITERACY BY RELIGION AND AGE. PART II—DETAILS FOR DISTRICTS.

AGE.	POPULATION. Total. Persons.	Total. Males.	Total. Females.	Literate. Persons.	Literate. Males.	Literate. Females.	Illiterate. Persons.	Illiterate. Males.	Illiterate. Females.	Literate in English. Persons.	Literate in English. Males.	Literate in English. Females.
1	2	3	4	5	6	7	8	9	10	11	12	13
MANBHUM.												
ALL RELIGIONS	*1,810,890*	*940,009*	*870,881*	*84,548*	*77,469*	*7,079*	*1,726,342*	*862,540*	*863,802*	*13,545*	*12,330*	*1,215*
0—5 ...	276,704	136,848	139,856	...	...	...	276,704	136,848	139,856	...	...	...
5—10 ...	232,094	121,543	110,551	4,952	4,329	623	227,142	117,214	109,928	507	438	69
10—15 ...	203,028	107,701	95,327	7,849	6,971	878	195,179	100,730	94,449	1,005	880	125
15—20 ...	171,303	84,450	86,853	10,690	9,558	1,132	160,613	74,892	85,721	1,835	1,640	195
20 and over ...	927,761	489,467	438,294	61,057	56,611	4,446	866,704	432,856	433,848	10,198	9,372	826
HINDUS ...	*1,592,527*	*824,012*	*768,515*	*76,583*	*70,756*	*5,827*	*1,515,944*	*753,256*	*762,688*	*11,130*	*10,478*	*652*
0—5 ...	242,748	120,349	122,399	...	...	...	242,748	120,349	122,399	...	...	...
5—10 ...	203,669	106,775	96,894	4,517	3,982	535	199,152	102,793	96,359	412	367	45
10—15 ...	178,071	94,335	83,736	7,144	6,406	738	170,927	87,929	82,998	826	749	77
15—20 ...	151,018	74,036	76,982	9,624	8,694	930	141,394	65,342	76,052	1,499	1,392	107
20 and over ...	817,021	428,517	388,504	55,298	51,674	3,624	761,723	376,843	384,880	8,393	7,970	423
MUSLIMS ...	*111,377*	*61,712*	*49,665*	*5,342*	*4,922*	*420*	*106,035*	*56,790*	*49,245*	*855*	*831*	*24*
0—5 ...	16,360	8,049	8,311	...	...	...	16,360	8,049	8,311	...	...	...
5—10 ...	13,937	7,279	6,658	286	251	35	13,651	7,028	6,623	26	26	...
10—15 ...	12,328	6,761	5,567	472	419	53	11,856	6,342	5,514	61	58	3
15—20 ...	10,506	5,692	4,814	700	632	68	9,806	5,060	4,746	121	118	3
20 and over ...	58,246	33,931	24,315	3,884	3,620	264	54,362	30,311	24,051	647	629	18
TRIBAL ...	*99,160*	*50,253*	*48,907*	*273*	*257*	*16*	*98,887*	*49,996*	*48,891*	*5*	*5*	...
0—5 ...	16,488	7,883	8,605	...	...	...	16,488	7,883	8,605	...	...	...
5—10 ...	13,640	7,061	6,579	13	10	3	13,627	7,051	6,576	...	...	...
10—15 ...	11,884	6,240	5,644	20	19	1	11,864	6,221	5,643	1	1	...
15—20 ...	9,044	4,375	4,669	35	34	1	9,009	4,341	4,668	1	1	...
20 and over ...	48,104	24,694	23,410	205	194	11	47,899	24,500	23,399	3	3	...
SINGHBHUM.												
ALL RELIGIONS	*929,802*	*469,421*	*460,381*	*41,136*	*36,292*	*4,844*	*888,666*	*433,129*	*455,537*	*11,021*	*9,818*	*1,203*
0—5 ...	155,394	76,320	79,074	...	...	...	155,394	76,320	79,074	...	...	...
5—10 ...	127,216	65,601	61,615	2,718	2,224	494	124,498	63,377	61,121	448	354	94
10—15 ...	110,172	57,069	53,103	4,034	3,364	670	106,138	53,705	52,433	842	713	129
15—20 ...	88,201	42,356	45,845	5,627	4,756	871	82,574	37,600	44,974	1,578	1,391	187
20 and over ...	448,819	228,075	220,744	28,757	25,948	2,809	420,062	202,127	217,935	8,153	7,360	793
HINDUS ...	*460,075*	*237,465*	*222,610*	*28,021*	*25,017*	*3,004*	*432,054*	*212,448*	*219,606*	*6,903*	*6,460*	*443*
0—5 ...	74,821	36,707	38,114	...	...	...	74,821	36,707	38,114	...	...	...
5—10 ...	60,946	31,650	29,296	1,763	1,472	291	59,183	30,178	29,005	205	171	34
10—15 ...	52,402	27,555	24,847	2,628	2,209	419	49,774	25,346	24,428	429	372	57
15—20 ...	43,732	21,390	22,342	3,808	3,204	604	39,924	18,186	21,738	949	852	97
20 and over ...	228,174	120,163	108,011	19,822	18,132	1,690	208,352	102,031	106,321	5,320	5,065	255
MUSLIMS ...	*26,754*	*16,543*	*10,211*	*3,266*	*2,973*	*293*	*23,488*	*13,570*	*9,918*	*619*	*612*	*7*
0—5 ...	3,319	1,653	1,666	...	...	...	3,319	1,653	1,666	...	...	...
5—10 ...	2,601	1,420	1,184	137	111	26	2,467	1,309	1,158	30	30	...
10—15 ...	2,366	1,345	1,021	245	205	40	2,121	1,140	981	81	81	...
15—20 ...	2,881	1,689	1,192	401	340	61	2,480	1,349	1,131	137	136	1
20 and over ...	15,584	10,436	5,148	2,483	2,317	166	13,101	8,110	4,983	371	365	6
CHRISTIANS ...	*19,552*	*10,056*	*9,496*	*4,427*	*3,154*	*1,273*	*15,125*	*6,902*	*8,223*	*2,815*	*2,108*	*707*
0—5 ...	3,490	1,753	1,737	...	...	...	3,490	1,753	1,737	...	...	...
5—10 ...	2,668	1,371	1,297	426	278	148	2,242	1,093	1,149	179	122	57
10—15 ...	2,189	1,117	1,072	506	334	172	1,683	783	900	277	209	68
15—20 ...	1,733	822	911	614	449	165	1,119	373	746	378	297	81
20 and over ...	9,472	4,908	4,470	2,881	2,093	788	6,591	2,900	3,691	1,981	1,480	501
TRIBAL ...	*419,338*	*202,616*	*216,722*	*4,258*	*4,143*	*115*	*415,080*	*198,473*	*216,607*	*330*	*326*	*4*
0—5 ...	73,239	35,932	37,307	...	...	...	73,239	35,932	37,307	...	...	...
5—10 ...	60,653	30,956	29,697	336	322	14	60,317	30,634	29,683	18	18	...
10—15 ...	52,915	26,862	26,053	589	508	81	52,326	26,294	26,032	39	38	1
15—20 ...	39,385	18,169	21,216	674	655	19	38,711	17,514	21,197	66	65	1
20 and over ...	193,146	90,697	102,449	2,659	2,598	61	190,487	88,099	102,388	207	205	2
ORISSA STATES.												
ALL RELIGIONS	*4,465,385*	*2,196,691*	*2,268,694*	*143,538*	*134,398*	*9,140*	*4,321,847*	*2,062,293*	*2,259,554*	*8,095*	*7,847*	*248*
0—5 ...	761,489	372,282	389,207	...	...	...	761,489	372,282	389,207	...	...	...
5—10 ...	612,075	310,886	301,189	9,931	8,751	1,180	602,144	302,135	300,009	139	131	8
10—15 ...	524,072	271,036	253,036	15,056	13,446	1,610	509,016	257,590	251,426	437	419	18
15—20 ...	390,072	186,439	203,633	17,435	16,034	1,401	372,637	170,405	202,232	1,235	1,198	37
20 and over ...	2,177,677	1,056,048	1,121,629	101,116	96,167	4,949	2,076,561	959,881	1,116,680	6,284	6,099	185
HINDUS ...	*4,067,176*	*1,999,547*	*2,067,629*	*138,577*	*130,032*	*8,545*	*3,928,599*	*1,869,515*	*2,059,084*	*7,440*	*7,304*	*136*
0—5 ...	686,385	335,405	350,980	...	...	...	686,385	335,405	350,980	...	...	...
5—10 ...	553,473	281,190	272,283	9,596	8,478	1,118	543,877	272,712	271,165	125	119	6
10—15 ...	475,201	246,183	229,018	14,496	12,982	1,514	460,705	233,201	227,504	406	392	14
15—20 ...	356,071	170,700	185,371	16,719	15,415	1,304	339,352	155,285	184,067	1,160	1,136	24
20 and over ...	1,996,046	966,069	1,029,977	97,766	93,157	4,609	1,898,280	872,912	1,025,368	5,749	5,657	92
CHRISTIANS ...	*74,468*	*36,878*	*37,590*	*2,310*	*1,876*	*434*	*72,158*	*35,002*	*37,156*	*436*	*330*	*106*
0—5 ...	14,056	7,036	7,020	...	...	...	14,056	7,036	7,020	...	...	...
5—10 ...	11,622	5,927	5,695	193	145	48	11,429	5,782	5,647	9	7	2
10—15 ...	10,207	5,202	5,005	353	280	73	9,854	4,922	4,932	22	20	2
15—20 ...	6,850	3,206	3,644	407	340	67	6,443	2,866	3,577	49	38	11
20 and over ...	31,733	15,507	16,226	1,357	1,111	246	30,376	14,396	15,980	356	265	91
TRIBAL ...	*304,502*	*150,172*	*154,330*	*543*	*522*	*21*	*303,959*	*149,650*	*154,309*	*9*	*8*	*1*
0—5 ...	58,247	28,457	29,790	...	...	...	58,247	28,457	29,790	...	...	...
5—10 ...	44,649	22,558	22,091	55	52	3	44,594	22,506	22,088	...	...	...
10—15 ...	36,627	18,578	18,049	78	73	5	36,549	18,505	18,044	1	1	...
15—20 ...	25,415	11,685	13,730	75	72	3	25,340	11,613	13,727	1	1	...
20 and over ...	139,564	68,894	70,670	335	325	10	139,229	68,569	70,660	7	6	1
CHOTA NAGPUR STATES.												
ALL RELIGIONS	*186,622*	*91,731*	*94,891*	*5,690*	*5,107*	*583*	*180,932*	*86,624*	*94,308*	*672*	*646*	*26*
0—5 ...	31,574	15,295	16,279	...	...	...	31,574	15,295	16,279	...	...	...
5—10 ...	26,926	13,783	13,143	355	305	50	26,571	13,478	13,093	32	30	2
10—15 ...	23,029	11,968	11,061	536	476	60	22,493	11,492	11,001	56	56	...
15—20 ...	17,060	8,124	8,936	698	630	68	16,362	7,494	8,868	102	99	3
20 and over ...	88,033	42,561	45,472	4,101	3,696	405	83,932	38,865	45,067	482	461	21
HINDUS ...	*127,702*	*63,461*	*64,241*	*5,155*	*4,628*	*527*	*122,547*	*58,833*	*63,714*	*594*	*581*	*13*
0—5 ...	21,268	10,343	10,925	...	...	...	21,268	10,343	10,925	...	...	...
5—10 ...	18,165	9,348	8,817	336	290	46	17,829	9,058	8,771	29	28	1
10—15 ...	15,587	8,183	7,404	509	452	57	15,078	7,731	7,347	53	53	...
15—20 ...	11,615	5,596	6,019	626	568	58	10,989	5,028	5,961	87	86	1
20 and over ...	61,067	29,991	31,076	3,684	3,318	366	57,383	26,673	30,710	425	414	11
TRIBAL ...	*56,098*	*26,746*	*29,352*	*222*	*207*	*15*	*55,876*	*26,539*	*29,337*	*15*	*14*	*1*
0—5 ...	9,859	4,743	5,116	...	...	...	9,859	4,743	5,116	...	...	...
5—10 ...	8,406	4,250	4,156	5	5	...	8,401	4,245	4,156	1	1	...
10—15 ...	7,134	3,627	3,507	9	9	...	7,125	3,618	3,507	1	1	...
15—20 ...	5,170	2,391	2,779	33	31	2	5,137	2,360	2,777	4	4	...
20 and over ...	25,529	11,735	13,794	175	162	13	25,354	11,573	13,781	9	8	1

TABLE XIII—*concluded.*

LITERACY BY RELIGION AND AGE. | **PART III—DETAILS FOR CITIES.**

AGE.	POPULATION									LITERATE IN ENGLISH.		
	TOTAL.			LITERATE.			ILLITERATE.					
	Persons.	Males.	Females.	Persons	Males.	Females	Persons	Males	Females.	Persons.	Males.	Females.
1	2	3	4	5	6	7	8	9	10	11	12	13
PATNA CITY.												
ALL RELIGIONS	*159,690*	*92,238*	*67,452*	*33,921*	*28,138*	*5,783*	*125,769*	*64,100*	*61,669*	*13,230*	*11,285*	*1,945*
0—5	18,259	9,176	9,083		...		18,259	9,176	9,083	..	...	...
5—10	17,434	9,617	7,817	2,355	1,670	685	15,079	7,947	7,132	675	427	248
10—15	17,326	10,031	7,295	3,484	2,586	898	13,842	7,445	6,397	1,208	859	349
15—20	16,931	10,457	6,474	5,051	4,209	842	11,880	6,248	5,632	2,369	2,063	306
20 and over	89,740	52,957	36,783	23,031	19,673	3,358	66,709	33,284	33,425	8,978	7,936	1,042
HINDUS	*119,644*	*69,285*	*50,359*	*24,320*	*20,489*	*3,831*	*95,324*	*48,796*	*46,528*	*8,951*	*7,828*	*1,123*
0—5	13,384	6,993	6,391	..	.	.	13,384	6,993	6,391			..
5—10	12,997	7,233	5,764	1,651	1,211	440	11,346	6,022	5,324	418	288	130
10—15	12,897	7,577	5,320	2,454	1,865	589	10,443	5,712	4,731	767	572	195
15—20	12,600	7,865	4,735	3,631	3,069	562	8,969	4,796	4,173	1,640	1,457	183
20 and over	67,266	39,617	27,649	16,584	14,344	2,240	50,682	25,273	25,409	6,126	5,511	615
MUSLIMS	*38,238*	*22,241*	*15,997*	*8,248*	*7,083*	*1,165*	*29,990*	*15,158*	*14,832*	*3,034*	*2,964*	*70*
0—5	4,168	2,087	2,081				4,168	2,087	2,081	..		
5—10	4,219	2,329	1,890	560	431	129	3,659	1,898	1,761	122	115	7
10—15	4,206	2,408	1,798	842	685	157	3,364	1,723	1,641	263	254	9
15—20	4,123	2,525	1,598	1,238	1,076	162	2,885	1,449	1 436	564	553	11
20 and over	21,522	12,892	8,630	5,608	4,891	717	15,914	8,001	7,913	2,085	2,042	43
GAYA CITY.												
ALL RELIGIONS	*88,005*	*50,625*	*37,380*	*14,783*	*13,068*	*1,715*	*73,222*	*37,557*	*35,665*	*3,627*	*3,365*	*262*
0—5	10,126	5,203	4,923				10,126	5,203	4,923	...	..	
5—10	8,964	4,953	4,011	792	650	142	8,172	4,303	3,869	162	147	15
10—15	8,649	4,938	3,711	1,228	1,032	196	7,421	3,906	3,515	299	273	26
15—20	8,139	4,705	3,434	1,778	1,541	237	6,361	3,164	3,197	482	442	40
20 and over	52,127	30,826	21,301	10,985	9,845	1,140	41,142	20,981	20,161	2,684	2,503	181
HINDUS	*66,462*	*38,502*	*27,960*	*10,749*	*9,691*	*1,058*	*55,713*	*28,811*	*26,902*	*2,471*	*2,386*	*85*
0—5	7,620	3,912	3,708				7,620	3,912	3,708			
5—10	6,534	3,621	2,913	532	452	80	6,002	3,160	2,833	113	110	3
10—15	6,326	3,635	2,691	871	751	120	5,455	2,884	2,571	212	205	7
15—20	6,096	3,563	2,533	1,306	1,105	41	4,790	2,308	2,302	342	326	16
20 and over	39,886	23,771	16,115	8,040	7,323	717	31,846	16,448	15,398	1,804	1,745	59
MUSLIMS	*20,596*	*11,626*	*8,970*	*3,476*	*3,040*	*436*	*17,120*	*8,586*	*8,534*	*819*	*802*	*17*
0—5	2,389	1,236	1,153				2,389	1,236	1,153			..
5—10	2,338	1,281	1,057	221	176	45	2,117	1,105	1,012	30	30	
10—15	2,239	1,258	981	311	258	53	1,928	1,000	928	59	59	
15—20	1,959	1,103	856	415	350	65	1,544	753	791	110	108	2
20 and over	11,671	6,748	4 923	2,529	2,256	273	9,142	4,492	4 650	620	605	15
BHAGALPUR CITY.												
ALL RELIGIONS	*83,847*	*46,868*	*36,979*	*12,514*	*10,694*	*1,820*	*71,333*	*36,174*	*35,159*	*3,537*	*3,094*	*443*
0—5	10,803	5,466	5,337		...	..	10,803	5,466	5,337	...		
5—10	10,272	5,433	4,839	879	638	241	9,393	4,795	4,598	208	154	54
10—15	9 414	5,078	4,336	1,318	1,029	289	8,096	4,049	4,047	373	301	72
15—20	8,221	4,603	3,618	1,889	1,641	248	6,332	2,962	3,370	621	563	58
20 and over	45,137	26,288	18,849	8,428	7,386	1,042	36,709	18,902	17,807	2,335	2,076	259
HINDUS	*58,348*	*33,299*	*25,049*	*9,437*	*8,031*	*1,406*	*48,911*	*25,268*	*23,643*	*2,407*	*2,066*	*341*
0—5	7,008	3,545	3,463	.			7,008	3,545	3,463			..
5—10	6,672	3,472	3,200	627	424	203	6,045	3,048	2,997	138	90	48
10—15	6,315	3,382	2,933	956	714	242	5,359	2,668	2,691	238	174	64
15—20	5,828	3,379	2,449	1,453	1,261	192	4,375	2,118	2,257	425	378	47
20 and over	32,525	19,521	13,004	6,401	5,632	769	26,124	13,889	12,235	1,606	1,424	182
MUSLIMS	*24,555*	*12,946*	*11,609*	*2,747*	*2,456*	*291*	*21,808*	*10,490*	*11,318*	*907*	*872*	*35*
0—5	3,732	1,890	1,842			.	3,732	1,890	1,842		...	...
5—10	3,427	1,837	1,590	219	186	33	3,208	1,651	1,557	48	42	6
10—15	2,900	1,543	1,357	313	273	40	2,587	1,270	1,317	98	91	7
15—20	2,287	1,146	1,141	380	340	40	1,907	806	1,101	159	154	5
20 and over	12,209	6,530	5,679	1,835	1,657	178	10,374	4,873	5,501	602	585	17
JAMSHEDPUR CITY.												
ALL RELIGIONS	*83,738*	*51,137*	*32,601*	*16,155*	*13,116*	*3,039*	*67,583*	*38,021*	*29,562*	*7,235*	*6,376*	*859*
0—5	10,338	5,249	5,089	.		.	10,338	5,249	5,089	..	..	.
5—10	7,327	4,004	3,323	910	632	278	6,417	3,372	3,045	331	266	65
10—15	6,421	3,504	2,827	1,310	924	386	5,111	2,670	2,441	571	480	91
15—20	9,220	4,992	4,228	2,328	1,742	586	6,892	3,250	3,642	1,053	902	151
20 and over	50,432	33,298	17,134	11,607	9,818	1,789	38,825	23,480	15,345	5,290	4,728	562
HINDUS	*60,494*	*36,395*	*24,099*	*11,056*	*8,991*	*2,065*	*49,438*	*27,404*	*22,034*	*4,640*	*4,247*	*393*
0—5	7,577	3,907	3,670				7,577	3,907	3,670			..
5—10	5,338	2,910	2,428	547	355	192	4,791	2,555	2,236	157	128	29
10—15	4,623	2,557	2,066	839	555	284	3,784	2,002	1,782	271	219	52
15—20	6,543	3,469	3,074	1,619	1,189	430	4,924	2,280	2,644	615	525	90
20 and over	36,413	23,552	12,861	8,051	6,893	1,158	28,362	16,660	11,702	3,597	3,375	222
MUSLIMS	*13,797*	*9,126*	*4,671*	*1,847*	*1,643*	*204*	*11,950*	*7,483*	*4,467*	*437*	*431*	*6*
0—5	1,432	683	749	.	..	.	1,432	683	749			
5—10	1,107	608	499	77	60	17	1,030	548	482	24	24	...
10—15	1,082	631	451	157	130	27	925	501	424	68	68	.
15—20	1,590	965	625	235	189	46	1,355	776	579	107	107	..
20 and over	8,586	6,239	2,347	1,378	1,264	114	7,208	4,975	2,233	238	232	6

TABLE XIV.

LITERACY BY SELECTED CASTES AND TRIBES.

This table, which corresponds with Table IX of 1921, gives for certain selected castes and tribes statistics of "literacy" in the sense in which that term is used in Table XIII. The statistics exhibited in the present table are confined to persons aged 7 and over, both in the case of the literate and of the illiterate population.

2. Figures for the "depressed classes" are given first (the significance and scope of this term are discussed in a special appendix to the report volume), and these are followed by figures for various other castes and tribes representative of the different strata of society. In the case of certain castes, etc., complete statistics for the whole province have been shown (and this course has been followed as far as possible for all the depressed classes)—while in the case of certain other castes, etc., the statistics are for representative localities only. Throughout, the *natural* (as opposed to the *administrative*) division has been taken as the unit of locality. The districts and states falling within each natural division of the province are specified on the title page of Table VIII.

TABLE XIV.

LITERACY BY SELECTED CASTES AND TRIBES

CASTE OR TRIBE	LOCALITY (Natural Division or District)	POPULATION (aged 7 and over)									LITERATE IN ENGLISH (aged 7 and over)		
		TOTAL			LITERATE			ILLITERATE					
		Persons	Males	Females	Persons.	Males	Females	Persons	Males	Females	Persons	Males.	Females
1	2	3	4	5	6	7	8	9	10	11	12	13	14
(1) Depressed classes—													
BAURI *Hindu*	*Total*	*266,429*	*130,911*	*136,918*	*1,937*	*1,846*	*91*	*264,492*	*128,365*	*136,127*	*41*	*40*	*1*
	Orissa	141,192	67,501	73,691	778	751	27	140 414	66,750	73,664	7	7	
	C N Plateau	125,237	62,710	62,527	1,159	1,095	64	124 078	61,615	62,463	34	33	1
BHOGTA *Hindu*	C N Plateau and Gaya	*52,295*	*27,285*	*25,010*	*200*	*177*	*23*	*52,095*	*27,108*	*24,987*	*2*	*2*	
BHUIYA *Hindu*	*Total*	*499,587*	*246,433*	*253,154*	*3,288*	*3,166*	*122*	*496,299*	*243,267*	*253,032*	*78*	*75*	*3*
	North Bihar	23,707	10,762	12,945	141	137	4	23,566	10,625	12,941	11	10	1
	South Bihar	125,754	61,088	63,816	97	82	15	125,657	61,856	63,801	2	2	
	Orissa	220	100	120	1	1		219	99	120			
	C N Plateau	349,906	173,633	176,273	3,049	2,946	103	346 857	170,687	176,170	65	63	2
BHUMIJ *Hindu*	*Total*	*230,870*	*114,876*	*115,994*	*3,163*	*3,037*	*126*	*227,707*	*111,839*	*115,868*	*71*	*60*	*11*
	Orissa	7,460	3,870	3,590	61	48	13	7 399	3,822	3,577			
	C N Plateau	223,410	111,006	112,404	3 102	2,989	113	220 308	108,017	112,291	71	60	11
CHAMAR *Hindu*	*Total*	*1,019,100*	*484,658*	*534,449*	*5,460*	*5,075*	*385*	*1,013,640*	*479,583*	*534,057*	*113*	*109*	*4*
	North Bihar	562,407	265,854	296,553	2,352	2 211	141	560,055	263,643	296,412	65	63	2
	South Bihar	295,119	139,086	156,033	1,690	1,511	179	293,429	137,575	155,854	24	23	1
	Orissa	22,589	10,379	12,210	504	472	32	22 085	9,007	12,178	6	6	
	C N Plateau	138,985	69,339	69,646	914	881	33	138,071	68,458	69,613	18	17	1
CHAUPAL *Hindu*	Purnea	*2,110*	*1,061*	*1,049*	*57*	*57*		*2,053*	*1,004*	*1,049*	..	..	
DHOBI *Hindu*	*Total*	*344,330*	*172,575*	*171,755*	*5,336*	*5,036*	*300*	*338,994*	*167,539*	*171,455*	*87*	*85*	*2*
	North Bihar	110,683	56,904	53,779	961	876	85	109,722	56,028	53,694	29	20	
	South Bihar	58,106	28 793	29,313	683	617	66	57,423	28,176	29,247	11	9	2
	Orissa	76,897	36,486	40 411	1,424	1,380	44	75,473	35,106	40,367	2	2	
	C N Plateau	98,644	50,392	48,252	2,268	2,163	105	96,376	48,229	48 147	45	45	
DOM	*Combined Total*	*227,680*	*113,507*	*114,173*	*909*	*825*	*84*	*226,771*	*112,682*	*114,089*	*30*	*25*	*5*
Hindu	*Total*	227,675	113,502	114,173	909	825	84	226,766	112,677	114,089	30	25	5
	North Bihar	37,183	18,708	18 475	136	117	19	37,047	18,591	18,456	13	13	
	South Bihar	19,724	9,925	9,799	73	40	33	19,651	9,885	9,766	8	3	5
	Orissa	7,956	3,981	3,975	33	33		7,923	3,948	3,975	1	1	
	C N Plateau	162,812	80,888	81,924	667	635	32	162,145	80,253	81 892	8	8	
Muslim	North Bihar	5	5			..	.	5	5				
DOSADH [GAHLOT RAJPUT] *Hindu*	*Total*	*1,043,958*	*511,877*	*532,081*	*6,675*	*6,305*	*370*	*1,037,283*	*505,572*	*531,711*	*206*	*200*	*6*
	North Bihar	592,949	287,912	305,037	3,056	2,900	156	589,893	285,012	304,881	75	71	4
	South Bihar	380,608	188,683	191,925	2,884	2,697	187	377,724	185,986	191,738	85	83	2
	C N Plateau	70,401	35,282	35,119	735	708	27	69,666	34,574	35,092	46	46	
GHASI *Hindu*	C N Plateau	*66,556*	*32,970*	*33,586*	*587*	*514*	*73*	*65,969*	*32,456*	*33,513*	*39*	*36*	*3*
GHUSURIA *Hindu*	Orissa	*1,617*	*706*	*911*	*5*	*5*		*1,612*	*701*	*911*			
GODRA *Hindu*	C N Plateau	*1,371*	*669*	*702*	*6*	*6*		*1,365*	*663*	*702*			
GOKHA *Hindu*	Orissa	*41,727*	*20,738*	*20,989*	*869*	*860*	*9*	*40,858*	*19,878*	*20,980*	*3*	*3*	
HALALKHOR	*Combined Total*	*17,443*	*8,501*	*8,942*	*227*	*209*	*18*	*17,216*	*8,292*	*8,924*	*3*	*3*	
Hindu	*Total*	16,279	7,967	8,312	195	178	17	16,084	7,789	8,295	3	3	
	North Bihar	11,535	5,533	6 002	106	96	10	11,429	5,437	5,992	3	3	
	South Bihar	4,744	2,434	2,310	89	82	7	4,655	2,352	2,303			
Muslim	*Total*	1,164	534	630	32	31	1	1,132	503	629			
	North Bihar	54	47	7	2	2		52	45	7			
	South Bihar	1,110	487	623	30	29	1	1,080	458	622			
HARI *Hindu*	*Total*	*97 185*	*48,377*	*48,808*	*961*	*924*	*37*	*96,224*	*47,453*	*48,771*	*10*	*10*	
	North Bihar	28,008	14,640	13,368	239	226	13	27,769	14,414	13,355	3	3	
	South Bihar	1,180	583	597	10	10		1,170	573	597			
	Orissa	21,465	9,576	11,889	190	187	3	21,275	9,380	11,886	1	1	
	C N Plateau	46,532	23,578	22,954	522	501	21	46,010	23,077	22,933	6	6	
IRIKA *Hindu*	Puri	*275*	*131*	*144*	*1*	*1*	.	*274*	*130*	*144*			
KANDRA *Hindu*	*Total*	*133,261*	*64,054*	*69,207*	*1,949*	*1,889*	*60*	*131,312*	*62,165*	*69,147*	*10*	*10*	
	Orissa	124,881	60,040	64 841	1,837	1,778	59	123,044	58,262	64,782	10	10	
	C N Plateau	8,380	4,014	4,366	112	111	1	8,268	3,903	4 365			
KANJAR *Hindu*	*Total*	*2,064*	*1,058*	*1,006*	*277*	*274*	*3*	*1,787*	*784*	*1,003*	*29*	*28*	*1*
	North Bihar	2,044	1,040	1,004	276	273	3	1,768	767	1,001	29	28	1
	South Bihar	20	18	2	1	1		19	17	2			
KELA *Hindu*	*Total*	*8,163*	*3,986*	*4,177*	*111*	*95*	*16*	*8,052*	*3,891*	*4,161*	*2*	*2*	
	Orissa	6,455	3,122	3,333	81	68	13	6,374	3,054	3,320	2	2	
	C N Plateau	1,708	864	844	30	27	3	1,678	837	841			
KURARIAR *Hindu*	Purnea	*517*	*205*	*312*				*517*	*205*	*312*			
LALBEGI	*Combined Total*	*132*	*76*	*56*	*2*	*2*		*130*	*74*	*56*			
Hindu	*Total*	86	48	38	1	1		85	47	38			
	South Bihar	81	48	33	1	1		80	47	33			
	C N Plateau	5		5				5		5			
Muslim	*Total*	46	28	18	1	1		45	27	18			
	South Bihar	33	21	12	1	1		32	20	12			
	C N Plateau	13	7	6				13	7	6			
MAHURIA *Hindu*	Orissa	*1,827*	*913*	*914*	*20*	*20*	..	*1,807*	*893*	*914*			
MANGAN *Hindu*	Sambalpur	*149*	*66*	*83*	*4*	*4*		*145*	*62*	*83*	*1*	*1*	
MOCHI *Hindu*	Manbhum and Santal Parganas	*17,715*	*9,199*	*8,516*	*224*	*215*	*9*	*17,491*	*8,984*	*8,507*	*6*	*6*	
NAT [NETUA] *Hindu*	*Total*	*7,578*	*3,700*	*3,878*	*95*	*86*	*9*	*7,483*	*3,614*	*3,869*			
	North Bihar	4,318	2,074	2,244	69	66	3	4,249	2,008	2,241			
	South Bihar	3,260	1,626	1,634	26	20	6	3,234	1,606	1,628			
PAN [PANIKA] *Hindu*	*Total*	*354,214*	*173,640*	*180,574*	*4,027*	*3,940*	*87*	*350,187*	*169,700*	*180,487*	*15*	*15*	
	Orissa	156,895	75,340	81,555	1,289	1,268	21	155,606	74,072	81,534	7	7	
	C N Plateau	197,319	98,300	99,019	2,738	2,672	66	194,581	95,628	98,953	8	8	
PASI *Hindu*	*Total*	*136,106*	*69,287*	*66,819*	*1,922*	*1,766*	*156*	*134,184*	*67,521*	*66,663*	*75*	*74*	*1*
	North Bihar	30,830	15,554	15,276	514	466	48	30,316	15,088	15,228	17	17	
	South Bihar	95,349	48,167	47,182	1,243	1,153	90	94,106	47,014	47,092	44	43	1
	C N Plateau	9,927	5,566	4,361	165	147	18	9,762	5,419	4,343	14	14	

TABLE XIV—*concluded.*

Literacy by selected Castes and Tribes.

Caste or tribe.	Locality. (Natural Division or District.)	Population (aged 7 and over). Total. Persons.	Total. Males.	Total. Females.	Literate. Persons.	Literate. Males.	Literate. Females.	Illiterate. Persons.	Illiterate. Males.	Illiterate. Females.	Literate in English (aged 7 and over). Persons.	Males.	Females.
1	2	3	4	5	6	7	8	9	10	11	12	13	14
RAJWAR *Hindu*	*Total*	*105,780*	*52,160*	*53,620*	*934*	*869*	*65*	*104,846*	*51,291*	*53,555*	*74*	*72*	*2*
	South Bihar ...	**50,875**	24,840	26,035	**128**	112	16	**50,747**	24,728	26,019	...	...	...
	C. N. Plateau ...	**54,905**	27,320	27,585	**806**	757	49	**54,099**	26,563	27,536	**74**	72	2
SIYAL *Hindu*	*Total*	*8,188*	*3,975*	*4,213*	*223*	*217*	*6*	*7,965*	*3,758*	*4,207*	*4*	*4*	...
	Orissa ...	**4,606**	2,231	2,375	**79**	78	1	**4,527**	2,153	2,374	...	...	...
	C. N. Plateau ...	**3,582**	1,744	1,838	**144**	139	5	**3,438**	1,605	1,833	**4**	4	...
TURI *Hindu*	*Total*	*42,700*	*21,821*	*20,879*	*171*	*160*	*11*	*42,529*	*21,661*	*20,868*	*5*	*5*	...
	South Bihar and Purnea.	**4,050**	2,042	2,008	**10**	8	2	**4,040**	2,034	2,006	**1**	1	...
	C. N. Plateau ...	**38,650**	19,779	18,871	**161**	152	9	**38,489**	19,627	18,862	**4**	4	...
(2) Other selected castes and tribes—													
BABHAN [BHUMIHAR BRAHMAN]. *Hindu*	*Total*	*722,561*	*384,187*	*338,374*	*97,973*	*89,646*	*8,327*	*624,588*	*294,541*	*330,047*	*5,615*	*5,504*	*111*
	North Bihar ...	**324,272**	166,839	157,433	**43,424**	39,298	4,126	**280,848**	127,541	153,307	**3,233**	3,180	53
	South Bihar ...	**398,289**	217,348	180,941	**54,549**	50,348	4,201	**343,740**	167,000	176,740	**2,382**	2,324	58
BRAHMAN *Hindu*	*Total*	*1,760,182*	*899,285*	*860,897*	*343,686*	*319,863*	*23,823*	*1,416,496*	*579,422*	*837,074*	*34,691*	*33,327*	*1,364*
	North Bihar ...	**721,084**	371,238	349,846	**110,380**	103,434	6,946	**610,704**	267,804	342,900	**9,328**	8,993	335
	South Bihar ...	**373,970**	191,760	182,210	**61,563**	56,837	4,726	**312,407**	134,914	177,493	**5,692**	5,343	349
	Orissa ...	**336,830**	163,137	173,693	**80,639**	76,420	4,219	**256,191**	86,717	169,474	**6,350**	6,209	141
	C. N. Plateau ...	**328,298**	173,160	155,138	**91,104**	83,172	7,932	**237,194**	89,987	147,207	**13,321**	12,792	539
CHASA *Hindu*	*Total*	*615,411*	*296,812*	*318,599*	*29,219*	*28,206*	*1,013*	*586,192*	*268,606*	*317,586*	*552*	*549*	*3*
	Orissa ...	**337,269**	161,948	175,321	**13,646**	13,177	469	**323,623**	148,771	174,852	**234**	234	...
	Orissa States ...	**278,142**	134,864	143,278	**15,573**	15,029	544	**262,569**	119,835	142,734	**318**	315	3
GAURA *Hindu*	*Total*	*773,688*	*375,015*	*398,673*	*19,630*	*18,770*	*860*	*754,058*	*356,245*	*397,813*	*500*	*496*	*4*
	Orissa ...	**218,147**	101,701	116,446	**10,072**	9,678	394	**208,075**	92,023	116,052	**284**	283	1
	C. N. Plateau ..	**555,541**	273,314	282,227	**9,558**	9,092	466	**545,983**	264,222	281,761	**216**	213	3
GOALA [AHIR, GOPA, YADAVA]. *Hindu*	*Total*	*2,779,933*	*1,430,884*	*1,349,049*	*55,464*	*52,959*	*2,505*	*2,724,469*	*1,377,925*	*1,346,544*	*2,492*	*2,455*	*37*
	North Bihar ..	**1,465,034**	749,386	715,648	**29,665**	28,538	1,127	**1,435,369**	720,848	714,521	**1,251**	1,240	11
	South Bihar ..	**963,834**	502,430	461,395	**19,607**	18,568	1,039	**944,227**	483,871	460,356	**851**	836	15
	C. N. Plateau ...	**351,065**	179,059	172,006	**6,192**	5,853	339	**344,873**	173,206	171,667	**390**	379	11
HO	Singhbhum and Feudatory States.	*446,568*	*215,703*	*230,865*	*3,776*	*3,596*	*180*	*442,792*	*212,107*	*230,685*	*287*	*282*	*5*
Hindu	...	**114,453**	55,971	58,482	**741**	723	18	**113,712**	55,248	58,464	**22**	22	...
Christian	...	**1,784**	854	930	**686**	577	109	**1,098**	277	821	**159**	155	4
Tribal religion	...	**330,331**	158,878	171,453	**2,349**	2,296	53	**327,982**	156,582	171,400	**106**	105	1
JOLAHA [SHEIKH MOMIN]. *Muslim*	*Total*	*773,370*	*374,428*	*398,942*	*28,187*	*24,974*	*3,213*	*745,183*	*349,454*	*395,729*	*1,517*	*1,481*	*36*
	North Bihar ...	**320,865**	154,050	166,815	**9,769**	8,682	1,087	**311,096**	145,368	165,728	**563**	547	16
	South Bihar ...	**163,419**	73,691	89,728	**10,920**	9,379	1,541	**152,499**	64,312	88,187	**615**	602	13
	C. N. Plateau ...	**289,086**	140,687	148,399	**7,498**	6,913	585	**281,588**	139,774	141,814	**339**	332	7
KARAN *Hindu*	Orissa ...	*97,855*	*45,000*	*52,855*	*31,070*	*26,149*	*4,921*	*66,785*	*18,851*	*47,934*	*4,563*	*4,506*	*57*
KAYASTH *Hindu*	*Total*	*267,584*	*140,635*	*126,949*	*100,140*	*85,120*	*15,020*	*167,444*	*55,515*	*111,929*	*27,446*	*25,498*	*1,948*
	North Bihar ..	**147,316**	76,758	70,558	**51,330**	45,457	5,873	**95,986**	31,301	64,685	**11,253**	10,868	385
	South Bihar ..	**109,951**	58,683	51,268	**44,374**	36,403	7,971	**65,577**	22,280	43,297	**14,475**	12,988	1,487
	Orissa	**10,317**	5,194	5,123	**4,436**	3,260	1,176	**5,881**	1,934	3,947	**1,718**	1,642	76
KHANDAIT *Hindu*	*Total*	*848,777*	*397,737*	*451,040*	*82,547*	*78,512*	*4,035*	*766,230*	*319,225*	*447,005*	*3,281*	*3,253*	*28*
	Orissa ...	**725,180**	336,920	388,260	**70,144**	66,881	3,263	**655,036**	270,039	384,997	**2,781**	2,761	20
	Orissa States ...	**123,597**	60,817	62,780	**12,403**	11,631	772	**111,194**	49,186	62,008	**500**	492	8
KURMI [KURMI KSHATRIYA]. *Hindu*	*Total*	*1,208,884*	*604,001*	*604,883*	*58,912*	*56,329*	*2,583*	*1,149,972*	*547,672*	*602,300*	*2,377*	*2,347*	*30*
	North Bihar ..	**376,875**	184,050	192,825	**11,756**	11,104	652	**365,119**	173,446	191,673	**628**	615	13
	South Bihar ..	**280,162**	145,203	134,959	**32,951**	31,520	1,431	**247,211**	113,683	133,528	**1,108**	1,101	7
	C. N. Plateau ..	**551,847**	274,248	277,599	**14,205**	13,705	500	**537,642**	260,543	277,099	**641**	631	10
MALLAH *Hindu*	*Total*	*353,366*	*170,908*	*182,458*	*3,088*	*2,946*	*142*	*350,278*	*167,962*	*182,316*	*59*	*58*	*1*
	North Bihar .	**307,946**	149,224	158,722	**2,118**	2,029	89	**305,828**	147,195	158,633	**46**	46	...
	South Bihar ..	**45,420**	21,684	23,736	**970**	917	53	**44,450**	20,767	23,683	**13**	12	1
MUNDA	C. N. Plateau* ..	*353,616*	*173,607*	*180,009*	*9,877*	*7,924*	*1,953*	*343,739*	*165,683*	*178,056*	*1,408*	*1,266*	*142*
Hindu	...	**102,692**	50,404	52,288	**1,786**	1,652	134	**100,906**	48,752	52,154	**28**	28	...
Christian		**83,577**	41,797	41,780	**7,046**	5,398	1,648	**76,531**	36,399	40,132	**1,328**	1,187	141
Tribal religion	...	**167,347**	81,406	85,941	**1,045**	874	171	**166,302**	80,532	85,770	**52**	51	1
ORAON	C. N. Plateau* ..	*388,965*	*189,171*	*199,794*	*10,241*	*7,461*	*2,780*	*378,724*	*181,710*	*197,014*	*1,338*	*1,100*	*238*
Hindu	...	**132,565**	63,174	69,391	**1,352**	1,155	197	**131,213**	62,019	69,194	**29**	28	1
Christian	..	**92,255**	45,898	46,357	**7,217**	5,211	2,006	**85,038**	40,687	44,351	**1,208**	974	234
Tribal religion	.	**164,145**	80,099	84,046	**1,672**	1,095	577	**162,473**	79,004	83,469	**101**	98	3
RAJPUT [CHHATRI, KSHATRIYA]. *Hindu*	*Total*	*994,110*	*523,702*	*470,408*	*119,572*	*113,560*	*6,012*	*874,538*	*410,142*	*464,396*	*8,303*	*8,156*	*147*
	North Bihar .	**598,786**	316,329	282,457	**66,205**	63,072	3,133	**532,581**	253,257	279,324	**4,656**	4,608	48
	South Bihar ...	**395,324**	207,373	187,951	**53,367**	50,488	2,879	**341,957**	156,885	185,072	**3,647**	3,548	99
SAVAR *Hindu*	Sambalpur and Orissa States.	*164,025*	*79,520*	*84,505*	*1,482*	*1,442*	*40*	*162,543*	*78,078*	*84,465*	*6*	*6*	..
SANTAL	*Combined Total*	*1,304,034*	*657,539*	*646,495*	*8,899*	*7,568*	*1,331*	*1,295,135*	*649,971*	*645,164*	*623*	*547*	*76*
Hindu	*Total*	**448,494**	**226,701**	**221,793**	**2,878**	**2,702**	**176**	**445,616**	**223,999**	**221,617**	**94**	**90**	**4**
	Monghyr, Bhagalpur and Purnea.	**63,955**	32,883	31,072	**361**	334	27	**63,594**	32,549	31,045	**21**	21	...
	Santal Parganas	**351**	166	185	..	...	...	**351**	166	185	...	...	...
	C. N. Plateau† ...	**384,188**	193,652	190,536	**2,517**	2,368	149	**381,671**	191,284	190,387	**73**	69	4
Christian	C. N. Plateau ...	**9,514**	**4,725**	**4,789**	**2,346**	**1,433**	**913**	**7,168**	**3,292**	**3,876**	**438**	**371**	**67**
Tribal religion	*Total*	**846,026**	**426,113**	**419,913**	**3,675**	**3,433**	**242**	**842,351**	**422,680**	**419,671**	**91**	**86**	**5**
	Monghyr, Bhagalpur and Purnea.	**13,440**	7,434	6,006	**80**	61	19	**13,360**	7,373	5,987	**1**	1	...
	Santal Parganas	**575,297**	288,133	287,164	**2,655**	2,506	149	**572,642**	285,627	287,015	**75**	70	5
	C. N. Plateau†	**257,289**	130,546	126,743	**940**	866	74	**256,349**	129,680	126,669	**15**	15	...
TELI *Hindu*	*Total*	*977,135*	*489,125*	*488,010*	*58,050*	*55,905*	*2,145*	*919,085*	*433,220*	*485,865*	*1,789*	*1,748*	*41*
	North Bihar	**356,825**	180,117	176,708	**15,422**	14,880	542	**341,403**	165,237	176,166	**392**	386	6
	South Bihar ...	**177,015**	89,279	87,736	**13,810**	13,079	731	**163,205**	76,200	87,005	**437**	427	10
	Orissa	**129,522**	62,215	67,307	**12,227**	11,988	239	**117,295**	50,227	67,068	**315**	310	5
	C. N. Plateau ...	**313,773**	157,514	156,259	**16,591**	15,958	633	**297,182**	141,556	155,626	**645**	625	20

* *Excluding* Santal Parganas, Angul, Sambalpur *and* Feudatory States.

† *Excluding* Santal Parganas.

TABLE XV.

LANGUAGE.

This table, which corresponds with Table X of 1921, is divided into two parts. Part I shows the languages spoken as mother-tongue by the population enumerated in the province. These languages have been arranged under the following heads—

(1) Indo-Aryan languages.
(2) Munda languages.
(3) Dravidian languages.
(4) Other languages of India.
(5) Asiatic (non-Indian) languages.
(6) European languages.

2. Part II of the table, which deals with bi-lingualism, is new. It represents an attempt to show the extent to which subsidiary languages are used in common, everyday life in addition to (and sometimes largely in supersession of) the mother-tongue of the speakers concerned. Particular attention has been paid to the cultural zones in which important vernaculars are found side by side or overlapping one another, and in such areas the subdivision, instead of the district, has ordinarily been taken as the unit of bi-lingualism. In each unit those languages only have been treated as "subsidiary languages" which are really in common use in that particular locality.

3. Any individual using two (or more) subsidiary languages has been counted as two (or more) persons in the statistics of bi-lingualism. This accounts for the fact that in very rare cases the sum of the persons shown as using different languages subsidiary to a single mother-tongue may actually exceed the total number of persons speaking that mother-tongue

4. Languages which are spoken (as mother-tongue) by a comparatively small number of persons have been clubbed together in their respective classes in both parts of the table. The statement below gives details of these languages according to the grouping in Part I :—

Language	Locality where spoken	Persons	Males.	Females
Other Indo-Aryan Languages—		*6,483*	*3,224*	*3,259*
Assamese	Puri (18) and various other localities	31	22	9
Banjari	Orissa States (3 351) Sambalpur (1 050)	4,401	2,031	2 370
Marathi	Singhbhum (607) Orissa States (348) Cuttack (235), Manbhum (138) Sambalpur (107) Other localities (187)	1,712	937	775
Sindhi (*including* Kachchi)	Singhbhum (157) and various other localities	339	234	105
Other Munda Languages—		*5,671*	*2,990*	*2,681*
Agaria	Manbhum (?5) Orissa States (?)	31	13	18
Asuri	Ranchi (2 184) Palamau (583) Sambalpur (2)	2,769	1,088	1,081
Birhor	Orissa States (259) Hazaribagh (251), Palamau (132), Manbhum (68) Ranchi (21)	731	391	340
Birjia	Palamau (612) Orissa States (16)	628	295	333
Gadaba	Orissa States (252)	252	119	133
Savara	Puri (45)	45	38	7
Turi	Ranchi (690) Orissa States (329), Sambalpur (189), Palamau (7)	1,215	746	469
Other Dravidian Languages—		*765*	*532*	*233*
Kanarese	Singhbhum (38) and various other localities	57	35	22
Malhar	Orissa States (305)	305	159	146
Malayalam	Singhbhum (305) and various other localities	403	338	65
Gipsy Languages—		*657*	*327*	*360*
Domra	Singhbhum (571) Orissa States (59), Manbhum (3)	633	302	331
Gulgulia	Hazaribagh (18) Purnea (1)	19	8	11
Malar	Orissa States (25) Ranchi (5)	30	15	15
Nati	Cuttack (5)	5	2	3
Miscellaneous Languages of India		*70*	*38*	*32*
Bhotia	Gaya (14) Singhbhum (4) Muzaffarpur (1)	19	11	8
Burmese	Various localities	9	6	3
Kashmiri	Various localities	16	11	5
Kham	Purnea (10) Orissa States (2)	12	5	7
Murmi	Hazaribagh (3)	3	2	1
Thado	Purnea (8)	8		8
Magari	Purnea (3)	3	[illegible]	[illegible]
Asiatic Languages foreign to India—		*495*	*308*	*117*
Arabic	Manbhum (62) Orissa States (25), and various other localities	148	94	54
Armenian	Manbhum (81) and various other localities	91	55	36
Chinese	Singhbhum (55) and various other localities	78	59	19
Hebrew	Ranchi (3)	3	1	2
Persian	Various localities	105	99	6
Other European Languages—		*485*	*237*	*248*
Basque	Ranchi (1)	1	1	
Danish	Santal Parganas (27) Bhagalpur (3), Monghyr (1)	31	7	24
Dutch	Ranchi (6) Cuttack (1)	7	5	2
Flemish	Ranchi (31) Hazaribagh (2)	33	23	10
French	Ranchi (40) and various other localities	86	49	37
Gaelic (Scotch)	Monghyr (14) and various other localities	26	14	12
German	Patna (25) Champaran (20), Ranchi (14) and various other localities	70	10	60
Greek	Monghyr (6), Champaran (1)	7	7	
Irish	Monghyr (4)	4		4
Italian	Manbhum (78) Ranchi (3)	81	40	41
Norwegian	Santal Parganas (17) Angul (4)	21	8	13
Portuguese	Singhbhum (34) and various other localities	74	47	27
Spanish	Ranchi (5), Cuttack (2)	7	7	
Welsh	Singhbhum (32), Hazaribagh (5)	37	19	18

TABLE XV.

LANGUAGE. PART I—MOTHER TONGUES.

DISTRICT OR STATE.	POPULATION.			INDO-ARYAN LANGUAGES. Bengali.			Gujarati.			Hindustani (Hindi and Urdu).			Marwari.			Naipali (Khas-Kura).		
	Persons.	Males.	Females.	Persons.	Males.	Females.	Persons.	Males.	Females.	Persons.	Males.	Females.	Persons.	Males.	Females.	Persons.	Males.	Females.
1	2	3	4	5	6	7	8	9	10	11	12	13	14	15	16	17	18	19
BIHAR AND ORISSA ...	*49,399,583*	*21,082,560*	*21,247,023*	*1,937,587*	*980,246*	*957,341*	*6,204*	*3,982*	*2,222*	*27,921,455*	*14,012,372*	*13,909,083*	*17,883*	*10,153*	*7,730*	*7,493*	*5,040*	*2,453*
British Territory ...	*37,677,576*	*18,794,138*	*18,883,438*	*1,851,797*	*937,090*	*914,707*	*5,304*	*3,412*	*1,892*	*27,731,601*	*13,916,017*	*13,815,584*	*16,895*	*9,596*	*7,299*	*7,411*	*4,982*	*2,429*
PATNA DIVISION	6,228,425	3,148,866	3,079,559	8,396	4,747	3,649	136	78	58	6,214,055	3,140,349	3,073,706	431	246	185	343	248	95
Patna	1,846,474	956,124	890,350	6,938	4,009	2,920	62	40	22	1,835,377	949,404	885,973	202	120	82	289	207	82
Gaya	2,388,462	1,193,643	1,194,819	840	415	425	47	19	28	2,386,852	1,192,774	1,194,078	129	80	49	19	14	5
Shahabad...	1,993,489	999,099	994,390	618	323	295	27	19	8	1,991,826	998,171	993,655	100	46	54	35	27	8
TIRHUT DIVISION	10,739,274	5,315,811	5,423,463	4,182	2,430	1,752	79	45	34	10,721,660	5,306,054	5,415,606	3,279	1,842	1,437	2,504	1,578	926
Saran	2,486,468	1,220,049	1,266,419	857	498	359	39	24	15	2,484,830	1,219,034	1,265,796	196	109	87	169	122	47
Champaran	2,145,687	1,080,956	1,064,731	783	420	363	5	2	3	2,135,936	1,075,878	1,060,058	928	470	458	1,690	1,166	524
Muzaffarpur	2,941,025	1,443,847	1,497,178	1,732	954	778	12	7	5	2,937,062	1,441,561	1,495,501	1,616	889	727	157	106	51
Darbhanga	3,166,094	1,570,959	1,595,135	810	558	252	23	12	11	3,163,832	1,569,581	1,594,251	539	374	165	488	184	304
BHAGALPUR DIVISION ..	8,759,801	4,431,983	4,327,818	407,360	206,334	201,026	136	109	27	7,394,629	3,746,811	3,647,818	5,842	3,212	2,630	1,527	947	580
Monghyr	2,287,154	1,145,797	1,141,357	3,320	1,982	1,338	7	6	1	2,265,494	1,133,995	1,131,499	1,041	607	434	160	139	21
Bhagalpur	2,234,632	1,130,584	1,104,048	4,538	2,315	2,223	11	10	1	2,206,235	1,116,067	1,090,168	1,732	880	852	374	211	163
Purnea	2,186,543	1,129,681	1,056,862	147,299	76,045	71,254	94	84	10	1,990,123	1,033,498	956,625	1,128	766	362	911	561	350
Santal Parganas	2,051,472	1,025,921	1,025,551	252,203	125,992	126,211	24	9	15	942,777	473,251	469,526	1,941	959	982	82	36	46
ORISSA DIVISION	5,306,142	2,549,251	2,756,891	35,625	18,863	16,762	1,230	808	422	164,610	79,905	84,705	1,843	1,036	807	176	131	45
Cuttack	2,176,707	1,028,134	1,148,573	13,880	6,953	6,927	382	258	124	67,122	30,656	36,406	393	190	203	31	27	4
Balasore	990,600	480,518	510,082	16,949	9,372	7,577	293	187	106	32,917	16,435	16,482	61	61	..	28	22	6
Angul	222,736	108,925	113,811	176	101	75	25	12	13	492	289	203	125	66	59	...	...	...
Puri	1,035,154	500,214	534,940	3,749	1,957	1,792	74	46	28	24,976	12,581	12,397	31	25	6	68	48	20
Sambalpur	880,945	431,460	449,485	871	480	391	456	305	151	39,101	19,944	19,157	1,233	694	539	49	34	15
CHOTA NAGPUR DIVISION ...	6,643,934	3,348,227	3,295,707	1,396,234	704,716	691,518	3,723	2,372	1,351	3,236,647	1,642,898	1,593,749	5,500	3,260	2,240	2,861	2,078	783
Hazaribagh	1,517,357	751,956	765,401	11,271	5,788	5,483	276	161	115	1,372,641	678,207	694,334	1,514	854	660	448	329	119
Ranchi	1,567,149	777,063	790,086	14,171	7,318	6,853	51	27	24	714,020	361,758	352,262	1,082	643	439	317	170	147
Palamau	818,736	409,778	408,958	586	300	286	42	25	17	747,249	373,112	374,137	274	164	110	34	20	14
Manbhum	1,810,890	940,009	870,881	1,222,689	615,665	607,024	1,912	1,147	765	321,690	183,150	138,540	1,774	1,005	769	662	430	232
Singhbhum	929,802	469,421	460,381	147,517	75,585	71,932	1,442	1,012	430	81,047	46,571	34,476	856	534	322	1,400	1,129	271
Feudatory States ...	*4,652,007*	*2,288,422*	*2,363,585*	*85,790*	*43,156*	*42,634*	*900*	*570*	*330*	*189,854*	*96,355*	*93,499*	*988*	*557*	*431*	*82*	*58*	*24*
Orissa States	4,465,385	2,196,691	2,268,694	40,426	20,379	20,047	866	542	324	179,628	91,026	88,602	885	506	379	64	44	20
Chota Nagpur States ...	186,622	91,731	94,891	45,364	22,777	22,587	34	28	6	10,226	5,329	4,897	103	51	52	18	14	4

TABLE XV—*continued*.

LANGUAGE.

PART I—MOTHER TONGUES.

DISTRICT OR STATE.	Indo-Aryan Languages—concluded. Oriya. Persons.	Oriya. Males.	Oriya. Females.	Punjabi. Persons.	Punjabi. Males.	Punjabi. Females.	Other Indo-Aryan Languages. Persons.	Other Indo-Aryan Languages. Males.	Other Indo-Aryan Languages. Females.	Munda Languages. Bhumij. Persons.	Bhumij. Males.	Bhumij. Females.	Ho. Persons.	Ho. Males.	Ho. Females.	Juang. Persons.	Juang. Males.	Juang. Females.	Karmali. Persons.	Karmali. Males.	Karmali. Females.
1	20	21	22	23	24	25	26	27	28	29	30	31	32	33	34	35	36	37	38	39	40
BIHAR AND ORISSA ...	*8,535,805*	*4,135,577*	*4,400,228*	*8,765*	*5,986*	*2,779*	*6,483*	*3,224*	*3,259*	*117,356*	*58,078*	*59,278*	*526,443*	*256,088*	*270,355*	*14,583*	*7,066*	*7,517*	*10,047*	*4,662*	*5,385*
British Territory ...	*5,136,195*	*2,467,513*	*2,668,683*	*8,430*	*5,751*	*2,679*	*2,714*	*1,499*	*1,215*	*34,113*	*16,957*	*17,156*	*309,101*	*148,524*	*160,577*	*5*	*4*	*1*	*10,047*	*4,662*	*5,385*
PATNA DIVISION	535	432	103	360	195	165	59	37	22	...	...	...	...	...	...	...	...	...	...	...	...
Patna	478	386	90	265	121	144	39	25	14	...	...	...	...	...	...	...	...	...	...	...	...
Gaya	30	26	4	64	50	14	20	12	8	...	...	...	...	...	...	...	...	...	...	...	...
Shahabad	27	18	9	31	24	7	...	...	...	...	...	...	...	...	...	...	...	...	...	...	...
TIRHUT DIVISION	41	38	3	272	222	50	19	9	10	...	...	...	...	...	...	...	...	...	...	...	...
Saran	11	11	...	105	92	13	3	...	3	...	...	...	...	...	...	...	...	...	...	...	...
Champaran	15	15	...	53	46	7	6	3	3	...		...	...	...	...	...	...	...	...	...	...
Muzaffarpur	6	5	1	78	57	21	...	...	...	...	...	...	...	...	...	...	...	...	...	...	...
Darbhanga	9	7	2	36	27	9	10	6	4	...	...	...	...	...	...	...	...	...	...	...	...
BHAGALPUR DIVISION	325	213	112	759	529	230	22	17	5	...	...	...	...	...	...	5	4	1	8,476	4,200	4,276
Monghyr	31	19	12	114	82	32	2	2	...	...	...	...	...	...	...	...	...	...	...		...
Bhagalpur	179	119	60	30	28	2	...	...	...	...	...	...	...	...	...	...	...	...	181	106	75
Purnea	11	3	8	504	333	171	18	13	5	...	...	...	...	...	...	5	4	1	181	90	91
Santal Parganas	104	72	32	111	86	25	2	2	...	...	...	...	...	...	...	...	...	...	8,114	4,004	4,110
ORISSA DIVISION	4,953,597	2,375,556	2,578,041	142	115	27	1,505	778	727	1,016	491	525	3,740	1,976	1,764	...	...	...	...	...	...
Cuttack	2,086,269	985,442	1,100,827	67	50	3	260	128	132	...	...	...	2,543	1,339	1,204	...	...	...	...	...	...
Balasore	920,963	445,004	475,959	15	11	4	5	5	...	1,000	481	519	761	412	349	...	...	...	...	...	...
Angul	170,469	83,693	86,776	4	4	...	5	3	2	...		...	112	51	61	...	...	...	...	...	...
Puri	997,810	481,165	516,645	15	12	3	63	35	28	...	...	...	...	...	...	...	...	...	...	...	...
Sambalpur	778,086	380,252	397,834	41	30	11	1,172	607	565	16	10	6	324	174	150	...	...	...	...	...	...
CHOTA NAGPUR DIVISION ...	181,697	91,274	90,423	6,897	4,690	2,207	1,109	658	451	33,097	16,466	16,631	305,361	146,548	158,813	...	...	...	1,571	462	1,109
Hazaribagh	317	176	141	817	488	329	56	29	27	...	...	...	33	33	...	...	...	...	3	...	3
Ranchi	7,897	4,174	3,723	77	45	32	22	12	10	...	...	...	14	...	14	...	...	...	...	...	...
Palamau	33	18	15	58	48	10	20	13	7	...	...	...	...	...	...	...	...	...	...	...	...
Manbhum	1,563	834	729	661	438	223	157	86	71	2,918	1,469	1,449	57	31	26	...	...	...	1,568	462	1,106
Singhbhum	171,887	86,072	85,815	5,284	3,681	1,603	854	518	336	30,179	14,997	15,182	305,257	146,484	158,773	...	...	...	...	...	...
Feudatory States ...	*3,399,610*	*1,668,064*	*1,731,546*	*335*	*235*	*100*	*3,769*	*1,725*	*2,044*	*83,243*	*41,121*	*42,122*	*217,342*	*107,564*	*109,778*	*14,578*	*7,062*	*7,516*	...	...	...
Orissa States	3,348,404	1,642,643	1,705,761	224	160	64	3,702	1,687	2,015	77,205	38,155	39,050	182,935	91,181	91,754	14,578	7,062	7,516	...	...	...
Chota Nagpur States ...	51,206	25,421	25,785	111	75	36	67	38	29	6,038	2,966	3,072	34,407	16,383	18,024	...	...	...	...	...	...

TABLE XV—*continued*.

LANGUAGE.

PART I—MOTHER TONGUES.

DISTRICT OR STATE.	MUNDA LANGUAGES—*concluded*.																				
	KHARIA.			KORA (KODA).			KORWA.			MAHILI.			MUNDARI.			SANTALI.			OTHER MUNDA LANGUAGES.		
	Persons.	Males.	Females.	Persons.	Males.	Females.	Persons.	Males.	Females.	Persons.	Males.	Females.	Persons.	Males.	Females.	Persons.	Males.	Females.	Persons.	Males.	Females.
1	41	42	43	44	45	46	47	48	49	50	51	52	53	54	55	56	57	58	59	60	61
BIHAR AND ORISSA ...	*113,680*	*57,812*	*55,868*	*9,739*	*5,033*	*4,706*	*12,434*	*6,258*	*6,176*	*13,704*	*6,611*	*7,093*	*521,891*	*255,471*	*266,420*	*1,628,957*	*818,650*	*810,307*	*5,671*	*2,990*	*2,681*
British Territory ...	*75,695*	*39,269*	*36,426*	*6,595*	*3,483*	*3,112*	*11,868*	*5,954*	*5,914*	*11,710*	*5,549*	*6,161*	*453,904*	*221,599*	*232,305*	*1,322,999*	*668,575*	*654,424*	*4,813*	*2,559*	*2,254*
PATNA DIVISION ...	...	...	...	...	...	...	...	...	...	...	...	...	**34**	**26**	**8**	**48**	**41**	**7**	...	...	...
Patna ...	...	...	...	...	...	...	...	...	...	...	...	...	**33**	25	8	**2**	1	1	...	...	...
Gaya ...	...	...	...	...	...	...	...	...	...	...	...	...	...	...	...	**46**	40	6	...	...	...
Shahabad ...	...	...	...	...	...	...	...	...	...	...	...	...	**1**	1	...	...	...	...	...	...	...
TIRHUT DIVISION ...	...	...	...	...	...	...	...	...	...	...	...	...	**240**	**132**	**108**	**3**	**2**	**1**	...	...	...
Saran ...	...	...	...	...	...	...	...	...	...	...	...	...	...	...	...	...	...	...	...	...	...
Champaran ...	...	...	...	...	...	...	...	...	...	...	...	...	**240**	132	108	**2**	2	...	...	...	...
Muzaffarpur ...	...	...	...	...	...	...	...	...	...	...	...	...	...	...	...	...	...	...	...	...	...
Darbhanga ...	...	...	...	...	...	...	...	...	...	...	...	...	...	...	...	**1**	...	1	...	...	...
BHAGALPUR DIVISION ...	...	...	...	**1,585**	**803**	**782**	**71**	**39**	**32**	**9,248**	**4,308**	**4,940**	**1,980**	**1,028**	**952**	**837,384**	**418,336**	**419,048**	...	...	...
Monghyr ...	...	...	...	**276**	142	134	...	...	...	...	...	...	**140**	90	50	**15,150**	7,915	7,235	...	...	...
Bhagalpur ...	...	...	...	...	...	...	...	...	...	...	...	...	**123**	65	58	**20,388**	10,353	10,035	...	...	...
Purnea ...	...	...	...	...	...	...	**71**	39	32	...	...	...	**1,230**	636	594	**40,158**	20,207	19,951	...	...	...
Santal Parganas ...	...	...	...	**1,309**	661	648	...	...	...	**9,248**	4,308	4,940	**487**	237	250	**761,688**	379,861	381,827	...	...	...
ORISSA DIVISION ...	**6,049**	**2,965**	**3,084**	**387**	**166**	**221**	**1**	...	**1**	...	...	...	**11,771**	**5,659**	**6,112**	**15,348**	**7,322**	**8,026**	**236**	**148**	**88**
Cuttack ...	...	...	...	...	...	...	**1**	...	1	...	...	...	**29**	23	6	**218**	110	108	...	...	...
Balasore ...	...	...	...	**387**	166	221	...	...	...	...	...	...	**145**	94	51	**15,120**	7,208	7,912	...	...	...
Angul ...	...	...	...	...	...	...	...	...	...	...	...	...	**487**	213	274	...	...	...	...	...	...
Puri ...	...	...	...	...	...	...	...	...	...	...	...	...	...	...	...	...	...	...	**45**	38	7
Sambalpur ...	**6,049**	2,965	3,084	...	...	...	...	...	...	...	...	...	**11,110**	5,329	5,781	**10**	4	[illegible]	**191**	110	81
CHOTA NAGPUR DIVISION ...	**69,646**	**36,304**	**33,342**	**4,623**	**2,514**	**2,109**	**11,796**	**5,915**	**5,881**	**2,462**	**1,241**	**1,221**	**439,879**	**214,754**	**225,125**	**470,216**	**242,874**	**227,342**	**4,577**	**2,411**	**2,166**
Hazaribagh ...	...	...	...	...	...	...	**62**	38	24	**62**	49	13	**831**	430	401	**123,844**	62,548	61,296	**251**	143	108
Ranchi ...	**66,185**	34,552	31,633	...	...	...	**502**	191	311	**87**	62	25	**383,035**	186,354	196,681	**548**	295	253	**2,895**	1,570	1,325
Palamau ...	...	...	...	...	...	...	**11,221**	5,676	5,545	...	...	...	**816**	446	370	**30**	15	15	**1,334**	654	680
Manbhum ...	**1,995**	1,002	993	**4,623**	2,514	2,109	...	...	...	**312**	166	146	**789**	393	396	**242,091**	128,186	113,905	**97**	44	53
Singhbhum ...	**1,466**	750	716	...	...	...	[illegible]	10	1	**2,001**	964	1,037	**54,408**	27,131	27,277	**103,703**	51,830	51,873	...	...	...
Feudatory States ...	*37,985*	*18,543*	*19,442*	*3,144*	*1,550*	*1,594*	[illegible]	*304*	*262*	*1,994*	*1,062*	*932*	*67,987*	*33,872*	*34,115*	*305,958*	*150,075*	*155,883*	*858*	*431*	*427*
Orissa States ...	**37,985**	18,543	19,442	**3,144**	1,550	1,594	**566**	304	262	**1,235**	705	530	**61,710**	30,872	30,838	**275,191**	135,408	139,783	**858**	431	427
Chota Nagpur States ...	...	...	...	...	...	...	...	...	...	**759**	357	402	**6,277**	3,000	3,277	**30,767**	14,667	16,100	...	...	...

TABLE XV—*continued.*

LANGUAGE. PART I—MOTHER TONGUES.

DISTRICT OR STATE.	DRAVIDIAN LANGUAGES.																				
	GONDI.			KANDHI (KUI).			MALTO.			ORAON (KURUKH).			TAMIL.			TELUGU.			OTHER DRAVIDIAN LANGUAGES.		
	Persons.	Males.	Females.	Persons.	Males.	Females.	Persons.	Males.	Females.	Persons.	Males.	Females.	Persons.	Males.	Females.	Persons.	Males.	Females.	Persons.	Males.	Females.
1	62	63	64	65	66	67	68	69	70	71	72	73	74	75	76	77	78	79	80	81	82
BIHAR AND ORISSA ...	*6,270*	*3,058*	*3,212*	*133,682*	*64,850*	*68,832*	*67,451*	*33,505*	*33,946*	*656,188*	*318,478*	*337,710*	*3,269*	*1,952*	*1,317*	*29,512*	*15,360*	*14,152*	*765*	*532*	*233*
British Territory ...	*1,135*	*551*	*584*	*49,163*	*23,753*	*25,410*	*67,403*	*33,484*	*33,919*	*517,015*	*250,052*	*266,963*	*3,219*	*1,930*	*1,289*	*22,107*	*11,721*	*10,386*	*450*	*364*	*86*
PATNA DIVISION	...	...	...	2	1	1	...	...	...	611	343	268	50	41	9	32	16	16	3	2	1
Patna	...	...	...	...	...	...	...	...	...	23	15	8	38	29	9	16	11	5	...	...	...
Gaya	...	...	...	1	1	...	...	...	...	...	...	...	5	5	...	16	5	11	3	2	1
Shahabad	...	...	...	1	...	1	...	...	...	588	328	260	7	7	...	...	...	...	...	...	...
TIRHUT DIVISION	...	...	...	...	...	...	...	...	...	5,511	2,598	2,913	23	18	5	9	9	...	7	5	2
Saran	...	...	...	...	...	...	...	...	...	...	...	...	6	6	...	...	...	...	...	...	...
Champaran	...	...	...	...	...	...	...	...	...	5,511	2,598	2,913	1	...	1	3	3	...	...	...	...
Muzaffarpur	...	...	...	...	...	...	...	...	...	...	...	...	5	4	1	...	...	...	...	...	...
Darbhanga	...	...	...	...	...	...	...	...	...	...	...	...	11	8	3	6	6	...	7	5	2
BHAGALPUR DIVISION	...	...	...	...	...	...	67,403	33,484	33,919	20,090	9,813	10,277	12	7	5	25	17	8	2	2	...
Monghyr...	...	...	...	...	...	...	...	...	...	...	...	...	8	5	3	12	8	4	...	...	...
Bhagalpur	...	...	...	...	...	...	187	92	95	345	141	204	...	...	...	13	9	4	...	...	...
Purnea	...	...	...	...	...	...	164	73	91	13,983	6,834	7,140	3	1	2	...	...	...	2	2	...
Santal Parganas	...	...	...	...	...	...	67,052	33,319	33,733	5,762	2,838	2,924	1	1	...	...	...	...	...	...	...
ORISSA DIVISION ...	138	68	70	49,153	23,748	25,405	...	...	...	43,372	21,054	22,318	140	75	65	14,855	7,688	7,167	31	29	2
Cuttack	...	...	...	30	30	...	...	...	...	114	98	16	39	24	15	4,891	2,575	2,316	25	25	...
Balasore	...	...	...	...	...	...	...	...	...	484	255	229	...	...	...	1,356	727	629	...	...	...
Angul	138	68	70	49,114	23,711	25,403	...	...	...	1,402	640	762	...	...	...	162	63	99	...	...	...
Puri	...	...	...	...	...	...	...	...	...	...	...	...	63	35	28	7,806	4,014	3,792	3	1	2
Sambalpur	...	...	...	9	7	2	...	...	...	41,372	20,061	21,311	38	16	22	640	309	331	3	3	...
CHOTA NAGPUR DIVISION ...	997	483	514	8	4	4	...	...	...	447,431	216,244	231,187	2,994	1,789	1,205	7,186	3,991	3,195	407	326	81
Hazaribagh	1	1	...	...	...	...	...	...	...	4,108	2,092	2,016	329	206	123	39	27	12	9	4	5
Ranchi	...	...	...	...	...	...	...	...	...	375,318	179,449	195,869	29	11	18	44	32	12	3	1	2
Palamau	1	1	...	...	...	...	...	...	...	56,947	29,163	27,784	...	...	...	2	2	...	1	1	...
Manbhum	...	...	...	...	...	...	...	...	...	946	518	428	525	319	206	1,332	717	615	1	1	...
Singhbhum	995	481	514	8	4	4	...	...	...	10,112	5,022	5,090	2,111	1,253	858	5,769	3,213	2,556	393	319	74
Feudatory States ...	*5,135*	*2,507*	*2,628*	*84,519*	*41,097*	*43,422*	*48*	*21*	*27*	*139,173*	*68,426*	*70,747*	*50*	*22*	*28*	*7,405*	*3,639*	*3,766*	*315*	*168*	*147*
Orissa States	5,135	2,507	2,628	84,519	41,097	43,422	48	21	27	138,138	67,935	70,203	25	8	17	7,269	3,556	3,713	314	167	147
Chota Nagpur States ...	...	...	...	...	...	...	...	...	...	1,035	491	544	25	14	11	136	83	53	1	1	...

TABLE XV—*continued*.

LANGUAGE. PART I.—MOTHER TONGUES.

DISTRICT OR STATE.	OTHER LANGUAGES OF INDIA.									ASIATIC LANGUAGES FOREIGN TO INDIA.			EUROPEAN LANGUAGES.					
	PASHTO.			GIPSY LANGUAGES.			MISCELLANEOUS LANGUAGES.						ENGLISH.			OTHER EUROPEAN LANGUAGES.		
	Persons.	Males.	Females.	Persons.	Males.	Females.	Persons.	Males.	Females.	Persons.	Males.	Females.	Persons.	Males.	Females.	Persons.	Males.	Females.
1	83	84	85	86	87	88	89	90	91	92	93	94	95	96	97	98	99	100
BIHAR AND ORISSA ...	*1,579*	*1,385*	*194*	*687*	*327*	*360*	*70*	*38*	*32*	*425*	*308*	*117*	*13,020*	*7,231*	*5,789*	*485*	*237*	*248*
British Territory ...	*1,536*	*1,358*	*178*	*603*	*279*	*324*	*68*	*36*	*32*	*376*	*274*	*102*	*12,838*	*7,116*	*5,722*	*466*	*225*	*241*
PATNA DIVISION	139	127	12	...	...	...	16	10	6	9	8	1	3,128	1,911	1,217	38	8	30
Patna	67	67	...	...	...	...	2	2	...	6	5	1	2,600	1,648	953	37	7	30
Gaya	7	7	..	...	...	...	14	8	6	2	2	...	366	182	184	1	1	...
Shahabad	65	53	12	...	...	...	...	...	...	1	1	...	162	81	81	.	...	...
TIRHUT DIVISION	80	79	1	...	...	...	3	2	1	16	13	3	1,317	729	588	29	6	23
Saran	14	14	...	...	...	...	...	...	...	...	...	...	236	138	98	2	1	1
Champaran	26	26	...	...	...	...	2	1	1	1	1	...	461	189	272	24	4	20
Muzaffarpur	33	33	1	...	..	..	1	1	...	4	1	3	317	230	87	2	..	2
Darbhanga	7	7	...	...	...	...	...	...	...	11	11	...	303	172	131	1	1	...
BHAGALPUR DIVISION	426	423	3	1	1	...	22	7	15	65	58	7	2,318	1,249	1,069	88	32	56
Monghyr	32	32	...	...	...	...	...	...	...	11	10	1	1,316	744	572	40	19	21
Bhagalpur	39	37	2	...	...	...	1	1	...	25	25	...	228	123	105	3	2	1
Purnea	342	341	1	1	1	...	21	6	15	24	20	4	269	123	146	1	1	...
Santal Parganas	13	13	...	...	...	...	...	...	...	5	3	2	505	259	246	44	10	34
ORISSA DIVISION	175	164	11	5	2	3	8	4	4	50	39	11	913	450	463	26	11	15
Cuttack	61	61	...	5	2	3	4	...	4	4	4	...	327	128	199	12	2	10
Balasore	23	23	...	...	...	...	4	4	...	9	9	...	75	39	36	5	3	2
Angul	...	...	...	...	...	...	...	...	...	...	...	...	21	9	12	4	2	2
Puri	16	16	...	...	...	...	...	...	...	29	22	7	404	219	185	...	...	...
Sambalpur	75	64	11	...	...	...	...	...	...	8	4	4	86	55	31	5	4	1
CHOTA NAGPUR DIVISION ...	716	565	151	597	276	321	19	13	6	236	156	80	5,162	2,777	2,385	285	168	117
Hazaribagh	38	38	...	18	7	11	8	6	2	8	7	1	363	188	175	10	7	3
Ranchi	17	17	...	5	...	5	3	1	2	10	7	3	713	306	407	104	68	36
Palamau	22	32	...	...	...	...	...	...	...	1	1	...	63	35	28	2	2	...
Manbhum	176	120	56	3	1	2	...	...	...	148	87	61	2,100	1,124	976	101	50	51
Singhbhum	463	368	95	571	268	303	8	6	2	69	54	15	1,923	1,124	799	68	41	27
Feudatory States ...	*43*	*27*	*16*	*84*	*48*	*36*	*2*	*2*	...	*49*	*34*	*15*	*189*	*115*	*67*	*19*	*12*	*7*
Orissa States	41	25	16	84	48	36	2	2	...	39	24	15	146	91	55	19	12	7
Chota Nagpur States ..	2	2	..	...	..	..	...	...	...	10	10	..	36	24	12	...	...	...

TABLE XV—*continued*.

LANGUAGE. PART II—BI-LINGUALISM.

AREA OF BI-LINGUALISM (District Subdivision or State)	TOTAL POPULATION	SUBSIDIARY LANGUAGE	Total persons speaking language in column 3 as mother-tongue	Total persons using language in column 3 as subsidiary to some other mother-tongue	INDO-ARYAN LANGUAGES — BENGALI — *Persons speaking above language as mother-tongue* Males	Females	BENGALI — *Persons using subsidiary language in column 3* Males	Females	HINDUSTANI — *Persons speaking above language as mother tongue* Males	Females	HINDUSTANI — *Persons using subsidiary language in column 3* Males	Females	ORIYA — *Persons speaking above language as mother tongue* Males	Females	ORIYA — *Persons using subsidiary language in column 3* Males	Females	OTHER INDO-ARYAN LANGUAGES — *Persons speaking above language as mother tongue* Males	Females	OTHER INDO-ARYAN LANGUAGES — *Persons using subsidiary language in column 3* Males.	Females.
1	2	3	4	5	6	7	8	9	10	11	12	13	14	15	16	17	18	19	20	21
PATNA	1,846,474	Hindustani	1,835,377	3 469	4,009	2,929	1,248	936	949 404	885,973			388	90	93	9	513	344	228	116
GAYA	2,338,462	Hindustani	2,336,852	468	415	425	88	53	1,192,774	1 194,078			26	4	16	1	175	104	97	40
SHAHABAD	1,993,489	Hindustani	1,991,826	399	323	295	97	79	998 171	993 655			18	9			116	77	31	13
SARAN ...	2,486,468	Hindustani	2,424,830	1 411	498	369	441	321	1 219,034	1 265 796			11		11	.	347	165	338	162
CHAMPARAN	2,145,687	Hindustani	2,135,936	8,862	420	363	418	352	1,075 878	1,060,058			15		15		1,687	995	1,610	627
MUZAFFARPUR	2,941,625	Hindustani	2,937,062	3 682	964	778	939	766	1,441,561	1,495 501			5	1	5	1	1,059	804	1,053	794
DARBHANGA	3,166,094	Hindustani	3,163,832	1,961	558	262	553	236	1 569 581	1,594 251			7	2	7	2	603	493	579	481
MONGHYR	2,287,154	Hindustani	2,265,494	5 672	1,982	1,338	818	609	1,133 995	1,131,499			19	12	6	11	836	488	330	256
BHAGALPUR	2,234,632	Hindustani	2,206,235	17,189	2,315	2,223	248	380	1,116,067	1,090,168			119	60	0	4	1,129	1,018	526	439
PURNEA— Araria	514,167	Hindustani	511,624	574	583	627	68	26	261,907	249,717							235	75	73	16
Kishanganj	560,577	Bengali Hindustani	59,396 494,120	1,588 4,546	32,546	26,850	1,738	1,075	256 836	237,284	450	636		6			493	179	1 191	.. 99
Sadr	1,111,799	Bengali Hindustani	86,691 974,379	879 24,693	42,914	43,777	2,888	3 080	504,755	469,624	435	163	3	2	1	.	1,039	644	662	200
SANTAL PARGANAS— Deoghar	346,946	Bengali Hindustani	13,609 280,659	8,791 7,389	6,418	7,197	1,362	1,017	143,038	137 621	3,602	3,356	55	31	13 5	31	231	298	3 119	7 176
Dumka	466,157	Bengali Hindustani Santali	46,077 179 434 226,266	34 126 3 211 1 081	23,476	22,601	331 247	147 88	88,463	90,971	4,727 250	3 561 191	4	1	2		307	267	2 143	45
Godda	387,801	Hindustani	245 266	1 839	3,906	3 792	136	39	120,682	124,584							129	123	40	26
Jamtara	243,858	Bengali	73,091	50 974	36,940	36,151			35,946	34,416	9,167	9,071	6				76	74	15	24
Rajmahal	331,136	Bengali Hindustani Santali	42,937 122,601 130 644	6 967 10,160 2 062	21,516	21,421	454 49	443 14	62,065	60,536	2 376 649	2,337 531	3				312	311	187	.. 133 ..
Pakaur	275,574	Bengali Hindustani	68,792 44,455	1,713 1,019	33,743	35,049	120	152	23,057	21,298	616	453	4		1		27	5	8	1
CUTTACK	2,176,707	Hindustani Oriya	67 122 2 086 269	1,398 67,842	6 953	6,927	412 5,210	30 5 309	30,656	36,466	25 519	23 823	985,442	1,100,827	523	40	662	471	136 298	15 98
BALASORE	990,600	Bengali Oriya	16,949 920 963	1,096 40,773	9 372	7,577	6,016	5,006	16,455	16 282	74 8,713	122 7,638	445,004	475,969	870	60	286	116	65	37
ANGUL— Sadr	140,458	Oriya	137,508	2,660	96	72	55	40	256	295	220	165	67,275	70,298			82	70	67	48
Khondmals	82,278	Oriya Kandhi	32,961 49,068	11,754 4,196	5	3	4	3	33	8	19	7 ..	16,418	16 543	2,377	1,815	3	4	3	4
PURI	1,035,154	Hindustani Oriya	24,978 997 810	1,259 17,181	1,967	1,799	33 457	16 380	12,581	12,397	5,853	6,033	481,165	516,645	339	161 ...	166	86	67 25	24 10

SAMBALPUR—Sadr	342,539	Hindustani ...	15,579	2,198	*403*	*342*	99	49	*7,977*	*7,602*	...	...	*139,599*	*139,988*	1,044	63	*891*	*647*	467	252
		Oriya ...	272,517	48,742			91	34			1,668	1,556			...	...			323	309
Bargarh	537,406	Oriya ...	505,569	11,181	*77*	*49*	37	31	*11,967*	*11,555*	2,636	2,477	*247,723*	*257,846*	...	...	*778*	*635*	455	448
HAZARIBAGH—Sadr	720,196	Hindustani ...	644,847	20,805	*4,230*	*4,070*	1,223	925	*317,706*	*327,141*	...	...	*156*	*129*	59	38	*1,268*	*811*	435	259
Chatra	238,874	Hindustani ...	237,945	433	*50*	*41*	30	17	*118,012*	*119,983*	...	...	...	...	...	...	*21*	*11*	6	1
Giridih	558,287	Hindustani ...	489,849	30,362	*1,508*	*1,372*	383	314	*242,589*	*247,960*	...	...	*20*	*12*	10	10	*677*	*498*	252	244
		Santali ...	63,776	600			...	...			264	331			...	...			...	...
RANCHI—Sadr	581,639	Bengali ...	7,571	890	*4,099*	*3,472*	...	...	*171,887*	*169,101*	456	368	*241*	*90*	11	1	*803*	*568*	1	1
		Hindustani ...	340,488	149,994			2,054	1,372			...	...			172	48			643	391
		Mundari ...	68,366	5,931			...	...			790	705			2	4			...	...
		Oraon ...	161,638	3,925			...	...			974	2,215			...	...			...	...
Khunti	373,800	Hindustani ...	131,544	64,930	*3,086*	*3,279*	1,063	1,002	*65,692*	*65,852*	...	...	*1,583*	*1,269*	1,362	1,112	*38*	*21*	39	11
		Mundari ...	220,242	7,264			111	108			3,564	2,853			11	14			8	...
Gumla	375,476	Hindustani ...	146,707	182,317	*118*	*98*	117	91	*75,537*	*71,170*	...	...	*594*	*624*	583	599	*20*	*15*	20	16
Simdega	236,234	Hindustani ...	95,281	132,138	*15*	*4*	13	4	*49,142*	*46,139*	...	...	*1,806*	*1,740*	1,569	1,721	*36*	*47*	36	47
PALAMAU—Sadr	641,122	Hindustani ...	613,796	25,841	*318*	*197*	361	145	*306,827*	*306,981*	...	...	*11*	*9*	8	9	*201*	*135*	201	135
Latehar	177,614	Hindustani ...	133,451	42,450	*42*	*29*	35	10	*66,295*	*67,156*	...	...	*7*	*6*	7	3	*60*	*23*	60	17
MANBHUM—Sadr	1,289,798	Bengali ...	1,048,653	75,306	*521,403*	*525,250*	...	...	*39,384*	*39,885*	4,168	3,813	*726*	*610*	220	188	*698*	*487*	80	36
		Hindustani ...	62,269	7,040			3,338	2,104			...	...			159	165			149	76
		Santali ...	168,714	1,465			737	525			24	8			...	...			...	...
Dhanbad	521,092	Bengali ...	176,036	8,011	*94,262*	*81,774*	...	...	*150,766*	*108,655*	3,182	1,179	*108*	*119*	10	1	*2,458*	*1,523*	70	28
		Hindustani ...	259,421	13,157			4,532	1,880			...	...			17	7			714	224
		Santali ...	73,377	1,487			240	272			208	741			...	...			...	...
SINGHBHUM—Sadr	535,207	Bengali ...	6,412	1,794	*3,382*	*3,029*	...	...	*16,501*	*14,922*	362	144	*62,413*	*64,834*	376	638	*653*	*444*	4	1
		Hindustani ...	31,423	21,698			524	102			...	...			4,745	2,819			523	231
		Oriya ...	127,247	11,428			314	211			1,862	1,531			...	...			2	1
		Ho ...	295,790	63,205			231	329			1,628	1,433			23,616	29,850			4	4
		Mundari ...	47,151	2,736			49	71			682	705			508	347			...	...
Dhalbhum (*excluding Jamshedpur City*).	310,857	Bengali ...	123,337	82,797	*61,751*	*61,586*	...	...	*7,798*	*5,174*	992	965	*17,861*	*17,988*	9,034	7,102	*1,295*	*374*	7	3
		Hindustani ...	12,902	3,900			699	746			...	...			258	357			892	158
		Oriya ...	35,849	10,058			1,098	1,258			179	134			...	...			...	...
		Ho	6,851	609			2	3			...	...			8	10			...	...
Jamshedpur City ...	83,738	Bengali ...	17,768	1,797	*10,421*	*7,317*	...	...	*22,342*	*14,380*	270	135	*5,798*	*2,993*	517	334	*4,926*	*2,144*	23	2
		Hindustani ...	36,722	18,780			4,383	942			...	...			3,872	1,061			2,600	1,023
		Oriya ...	8,791	631			60	46			194	57			...	...			3	...
FEUDATORY STATES—Mayurbhanj	889,603	Oriya ...	377,706	333,711	*16,638*	*16,605*	11,558	11,029	*19,805*	*19,597*	13,707	11,672	*189,202*	*188,504*	...	...	*93*	*50*	24	15
Keonjhar	460,609	Oriya ...	396,592	68,971	*1,636*	*1,496*	984	1,039	*20,511*	*20,130*	5,988	6,199	*159,827*	*166,765*	...	...	*85*	*61*	25	21
Bamra	151,047	Oriya ...	113,397	35,006	*56*	*60*	21	10	*3,694*	*3,403*	3,808	3,180	*54,943*	*58,454*	...	...	*67*	*53*	19	27
Patna	566,924	Hindustani ...	22,160	957	*104*	*83*	32	...	*11,465*	*10,705*	...	...	*266,409*	*273,694*	363	394	*486*	*350*	154	35
		Oriya ...	540,063	22,721			47	48			9,887	9,227			...	...			225	174
Kalahandi	513,716	Oriya ...	427,701	46,029	*46*	*20*	22	5	*3,718*	*3,794*	2,466	2,631	*210,373*	*217,328*	...	...	*1,742*	*1,944*	1,124	1,380
		Kandhi ...	69,292	1,086			...	...			...	...			737	349			...	...
Gangpur	356,674	Hindustani ...	51,431	29,411	*970*	*903*	120	83	*25,891*	*25,540*	...	...	*68,969*	*70,031*	1,198	1,008	*213*	*145*	62	36
		Oriya ...	138,990	118,588			339	340			15,528	15,097			...	...			53	53
Bonai	80,186	Oriya ...	42,761	24,198	*580*	*594*	547	535	*1,451*	*1,540*	860	1,085	*21,224*	*21,537*	...	...	*9*	*10*	4	...
Saraikela	143,525	Bengali ...	43,117	4,146	*21,652*	*21,465*	...	...	*2,683*	*2,228*	214	125	*18,257*	*18,111*	566	393	*143*	*78*	9	...
		Hindustani ...	4,911	672			133	35			...	...			186	31			60	22
		Oriya ...	36,368	9,717			1,736	1,388			138	113			...	...			1	...
Kharsawan	43,097	Bengali ...	2,247	571	*1,135*	*1,129*	...	...	*2,646*	*2,669*	27	17	*7,164*	*7,674*	226	23	*63*	*49*	...	...
		Hindustani ...	5,315	554			28	1			...	...			301	26			11	12
		Oriya ...	14,838	9,004			518	433			862	874			...	...			1	...
All other states ...	1,446,626	Oriya ...	1,381,254	53,187	*339*	*286*	188	95	*4,571*	*5,833*	3,094	2,749	*671,706*	*709,548*	...	...	*244*	*169*	115	92

TABLE XV—*continued.*

LANGUAGE. PART II—BI-LINGUALISM.[1]

AREA OF BI-LINGUALISM (District, Subdivision or State).	SUBSIDIARY LANGUAGE.	MUNDA LANGUAGES.																			
		BHUMIJ.				HO.				KARMALI.				KHARIA.				KORA (KODA).			
		Persons speaking above language as mother-tongue.		Persons using subsidiary language in column 3.		Persons speaking above language as mother-tongue.		Persons using subsidiary language in column 3.		Persons speaking above language as mother-tongue.		Persons using subsidiary language in column 3.		Persons speaking above language as mother-tongue.		Persons using subsidiary language in column 3.		Persons speaking above language as mother-tongue.		Persons using subsidiary language in column 3.	
		Males.	Females.	Males.	Females.	Males.	Females.	Males.	Females.	Males.	Females.	Males.	Females.	Males.	Females.	Males.	Females.	Males.	Females.	Males.	Females.
1	3	22	23	24	25	26	27	28	29	30	31	32	33	34	35	36	37	38	39	40	41
PATNA	Hindustani ...	...	...	...	...	...	...	...	...	...	...	...	...	...	...	...	...	...	...	...	...
GAYA	Hindustani ...	...	...	...	...	...	...	...	...	...	...	...	...	...	...	...	...	...	...	...	...
SHAHABAD	Hindustani ...	...	...	...	...	...	...	...	...	...	...	...	...	...	...	...	...	...	...	...	...
SARAN	Hindustani ...	...	...	...	...	...	...	...	...	...	...	...	...	...	...	...	...	...	...	...	...
CHAMPARAN	Hindustani ...	...	...	...	...	...	...	...	...	...	...	...	...	...	...	...	...	...	...	...	...
MUZAFFARPUR	Hindustani ...	...	...	...	...	...	...	...	...	...	...	...	...	...	...	...	...	...	...	...	...
DARBHANGA	Hindustani ...	...	...	...	...	...	...	...	...	...	...	...	...	...	...	...	...	...	...	...	...
MONGHYR	Hindustani ...	...	...	...	...	...	...	...	...	...	...	...	...	...	...	...	...	142	134	142	134
BHAGALPUR	Hindustani ...	...	...	...	...	...	...	...	...	106	75	30	13	...	...	...	...	...	...	...	...
PURNEA— Araria	Hindustani ...	...	...	...	...	...	...	...	...	90	91	...	...	...	...	...	...	...	...	...	...
Kishanganj	Bengali ...	...	...	...	...	...	...	...	...	...	...	...	...	...	...	...	...	...	...	...	...
	Hindustani ...			...	...			...	...			...	...			...	...			...	...
Sadr	Bengali ...	...	...	...	...	...	...	...	...	...	...	...	...	...	...	...	...	...	...	...	...
	Hindustani ...			...	...			...	...			...	...			...	...			...	...
SANTAL PARGANAS— Deoghar	Bengali ...	...	...	...	...	...	...	...	...	2,897	2,665	3	...	...	...	...	...	24	19	8	3
	Hindustani ...			...	...			...	...			328	324			...	...			...	...
Dumka	Bengali ...	...	...	...	...	...	...	...	...	1,965	1,809	66	83	...	...	...	...	175	170	...	...
	Hindustani ...			...	...			...	...			39	39			...	...			...	...
	Santali ...			...	...			...	...			1	14			...	...			...	...
Godda	Hindustani ...	...	...	...	...	...	...	...	...	1	2	...	...	...	...	...	...	22	22	...	...
Jamtara	Bengali ...	...	...	...	...	...	...	...	...	2	2	...	...	...	...	...	...	143	98	4	5
Rajmahal	Bengali ...	...	...	...	...	...	...	...	...	114	107	29	25	...	...	...	...	...	...	...	...
	Hindustani ...			...	...			...	...			10	10			...	...			...	...
	Santali ...			...	...			...	...			...	...			...	...			...	...
Pakaur	Bengali ...	...	...	...	...	...	...	...	...	35	83	...	10	...	...	...	...	297	339	...	...
	Hindustani ...			...	...			...	...			...	...			...	...			...	...
CUTTACK	Hindustani ...	...	...	...	...	1,339	1,204	...	...	...	...	...	...	...	...	...	...	...	...	...	...
	Oriya ...			...	...			323	303			...	...			...	...			...	...
BALASORE	Bengali ...	481	519	10	29	412	349	...	...	...	...	...	...	...	...	...	...	166	221	...	...
	Oriya ...			338	373			337	346			...	...			...	...			155	187
ANGUL— Sadr	Oriya ...	...	...	...	...	27	43	27	43	...	...	...	...	...	...	...	...	...	...	...	...
Khondmals	Oriya ...	...	...	...	...	24	18	11	11	...	...	...	...	...	...	...	...	...	...	...	...
	Kandhi ...			...	...			4	...			...	...			...	...			...	...
PURI	Hindustani ...	...	...	...	...	...	...	...	...	...	...	...	...	...	...	...	...	...	...	...	...
	Oriya ...			...	...			...	...			...	...			...	...			...	...

District	Language																				
Sambalpur—																					
Sadr	Hindustani	*10*	*6*	...	...	*162*	*148*	17	...	...	...	...	...	*2,837*	*3,011*	...	...	...	...	...	...
	Oriya			10	6			96	97			...	...			2,386	2,454			...	...
Bargarh	Oriya	...	...	...	...	*12*	*2*	6	2	...	...	...	...	*128*	*79*	95	61	...	...	...	...
Hazaribagh—																					
Sadr	Hindustani	...	...	...	...	*24*	...	...	...	...	*3*	...	...	...	...	...	...	...	...	...	...
Chatra	Hindustani	...	...	...	...	*1*	...	...	...	...	...	...	...	...	...	...	...	...	...	...	...
Giridih	Hindustani	...	...	...	...	*8*	...	...	...	...	...	...	...	...	...	...	...	...	...	...	...
	Santali			...	...			...	...			...	...			...	...			...	...
Ranchi—																					
Sadr	Bengali	...	...	...	...	...	*12*	...	...	...	...	...	...	*14*	...	...	...	...	...	...	...
	Hindustani			...	...			...	12			...	...			14	...			...	...
	Mundari			...	...			...	...			...	...			...	...			...	...
	Oraon			...	...			...	...			...	...			...	...			...	...
Khunti	Hindustani	...	...	...	...	...	...	...	...	...	...	...	...	*8*	*2*	8	2	...	...	...	...
	Mundari			...	...			...	...			...	...			...	...			...	...
Gumla	Hindustani	...	...	...	...	...	...	...	...	...	...	...	...	*13,795*	*14,615*	13,591	12,654	...	...	...	...
Simdega	Hindustani	...	...	...	...	...	*2*	...	2	...	...	...	...	*20,735*	*17,016*	20,359	14,909	...	...	...	...
Palamau—																					
Sadr	Hindustani	...	...	...	...	...	...	...	...	...	...	...	...	...	...	...	...	...	...	...	...
Latehar	Hindustani	...	...	...	...	...	...	...	...	...	...	...	...	...	...	...	...	...	...	...	...
Manbhum—																					
Sadr	Bengali	*1,463*	*1,449*	1,081	1,085	*19*	*17*	6	...	*108*	*128*	2	1	*1,002*	*999*	364	387	*148*	*187*	101	72
	Hindustani			...	2			12	4			..	...			21	3			...	...
	Santali			2	...			...	...			35	23			37	81			...	...
Dhanbad	Bengali	*11*	...	...	...	*12*	*9*	2	...	*354*	*978*	9	...	...	*1*	...	...	*2,366*	*1,979*	438	136
	Hindustani			...	...			11	2			117	...			...	...			275	187
	Santali			...	...			...	...			13	12			...	...			...	...
Singhbhum—																					
Sadr	Bengali	*3,607*	*3,744*	44	71	*141,334*	*154,456*	6	2	...	...	...	...	*84*	*69*	...	...	...	...	...	...
	Hindustani			322	336			5,114	824			...	...			44	8			...	...
	Oriya			387	189			4,786	1,590			...	...			20	34			...	...
	Ho			1,387	1,526			...	...			...	...			1	1			...	...
	Mundari			92	106			12	1			...	...			...	...			...	...
Dhalbhum (*excluding Jamshedpur City*).	Bengali	*11,209*	*11,312*	8,899	9,287	*3,876*	*3,275*	450	375	...	...	...	...	*666*	*647*	364	199	...	...	...	...
	Hindustani			3	1			87	25			...	...			...	1			...	...
	Oriya			775	598			147	48			...	...			107	99			...	...
	Ho			...	...			...	...			...	...			12	11			...	...
Jamshedpur City	Bengali	*181*	*126*	17	13	*1,574*	*1,949*	91	61	...	...	...	...	...	...	...	...	...	...	...	...
	Hindustani			17	18			1,035	360			...	...			...	...			...	...
	Oriya			33	13			87	20			...	...			...	...			...	...
Feudatory States—																					
Mayurbhanj	Oriya	*33,899*	*34,575*	25,725	26,531	*53,789*	*55,307*	19,617	30,897	...	...	...	...	*594*	*451*	461	48	*123*	*121*	114	110
Keonjhar	Oriya	*600*	*555*	302	340	*28,768*	*28,690*	15,472	16,310	...	...	...	...	*13*	*8*	...	8	*272*	*316*	214	205
Bamra	Oriya	...	...	...	...	*1,408*	*1,511*	1,151	1,451	...	...	...	...	*984*	*1,095*	948	959	*1*	*2*	...	...
Patna	Hindustani	...	...	...	...	*119*	*128*	1	1	...	...	...	...	*104*	*8[illegible]*	2	...	*5*	*3*	...	...
	Oriya			...	...			104	117			...	...			80	65			5	2
Kalahandi	Oriya	*2*	...	...	...	*14*	*15*	12	15	...	...	...	...	*15*	*9*	9	7	...	...	...	...
	Kandhi			...	...			...	...			...	...			...	...			...	...
Gangpur	Hindustani	*554*	*616*	22	39	*91*	*85*	4	2	...	...	...	...	*16,692*	*17,729*	3,790	3,690	...	...	...	...
	Oriya			352	257			35	25			...	...			9,815	10,358			...	...
Bonai	Oriya	*451*	*530*	313	216	*2,983*	*2,442*	1,910	786	...	...	...	...	*118*	*108*	38	48	...	...	...	...
Saraikela	Bengali	*1,949*	*2,035*	367	276	*11,508*	*12,394*	193	179	...	...	...	...	...	...	...	...	...	...	...	...
	Hindustani			3	...			67	17			...	...			...	...			...	...
	Oriya			346	284			2,069	2,050			...	...			...	...			...	...
Kharsawan	Bengali	*1,017*	*1,037*	58	55	*4,875*	*5,680*	9	5	...	...	...	...	...	...	...	...	...	...	...	...
	Hindustani			7	6			24	4			...	...			...	...			...	...
	Oriya			414	394			2,175	2,224			...	...			...	...			...	...
All other States	Oriya	*2,749*	*2,774*	2,208	2,226	*4,009*	*3,776*	2,814	2,656	...	...	...	...	*24*	*27*	24	27	*1,149*	*1,153*	1,027	1,026

TABLE XV—*continued.*

LANGUAGE. PART II—BI-LINGUALISM.

MUNDA LANGUAGES—*concluded.*

AREA OF BI-LINGUALISM (District, Subdivision or State)	SUBSIDIARY LANGUAGE.	KORWA. Persons speaking above language as mother tongue: Males	Females	KORWA. Persons using subsidiary language in column 3: Males.	Females	MAHILI. Persons speaking above language as mother tongue: Males	Females.	MAHILI. Persons using subsidiary language in column 3: Males	Females
1	3	42	43	44	45	46	47	48	49
PATNA	Hindustani	...	...			...	...	...	...
GAYA	Hindustani	...	...	...	...			...	
SHAHABAD	Hindustani	...			...	...			
SARAN	Hindustani				...	...			
CHAMPARAN	Hindustani			...			...	...	
MUZAFFARPUR	Hindustani	...	...				...		
DARBHANGA	Hindustani	...	...				...	...	
MONGHYR	Hindustani		...	...	...	...	...	...	
BHAGALPUR	Hindustani	...	...		...			...	
PURNEA—Araria	Hindustani	1	1		...	...	...	...	
Kishanganj	Bengali Hindustani	20	15		...	...		...	...
Sadr	Bengali Hindustani	18	16		...			...	
SANTAL PARGANAS—Deoghar	Bengali Hindustani			...	...	672	1,136	24 191	38 201
Dumka	Bengali Hindustani Santali	...		...		1,719	1,774	72 9 77	134 5 108
Godda	Hindustani	...	...			340	391	...	
Jamtara	Bengali	...	...			23	17	...	...
Rajmahal	Bengali Hindustani Santali			...	...	1,262	1,262	117 16 7	46 11 4
Pakaur	Bengali Hindustani	...	...	...	...	310	361	1 ...	2 ...
CUTTACK	Hindustani Oriya	...	1	...	...	...	...		...
BALASORE	Bengali Oriya	...	...	...	...		...	...	...
ANGUL—Sadr	Oriya	...	...	...	...	...	...		
Khondmals	Oriya Kandhi	...	...	...	...	...	...	...	...
PURI	Hindustani Oriya	...	...	...	...	...	...	...	...

AREA OF BI-LINGUALISM (District, Subdivision or State)	SUBSIDIARY LANGUAGE.	MUNDARI. Persons speaking above language as mother tongue: Males.	Females.	MUNDARI. Persons using subsidiary language in column 3: Males	Females.	SANTALI. Persons speaking above language as mother-tongue: Males.	Females	SANTALI. Persons using subsidiary language in column 3: Males	Females.	OTHER MUNDA LANGUAGES. Persons speaking above language as mother tongue: Males	Females.	OTHER MUNDA LANGUAGES. Persons using subsidiary language in column 3: Males.	Females
1	3	50	51	52	53	54	55	56	57	58	59	60	61
PATNA	Hindustani	25	8	7	4	1	1	1		...	...		...
GAYA	Hindustani	...	...	...	...	40	6	4					...
SHAHABAD	Hindustani	1	...	1		...	...		...		...	...	...
SARAN	Hindustani	...	...	...	...	...	...	...	...		...	...	...
CHAMPARAN	Hindustani	132	108	132	58	2	...	2	...		...	...	...
MUZAFFARPUR	Hindustani	...		...		...	...		...	...			...
DARBHANGA	Hindustani	...	...	...		...	1	...	1	...	...	...	...
MONGHYR	Hindustani	90	50	60	38	7,916	7,236	1,464	1,335	...		...	...
BHAGALPUR	Hindustani	65	58	53	45	10,363	10,035	7,616	7,673	...	...	...	...
PURNEA—Araria	Hindustani	3	...	...	...	303	268	126	92	...		...	
Kishanganj	Bengali Hindustani	26	45	... 15	16	2,354	2,329	225 417	273 189	...	...		... ...
Sadr	Bengali Hindustani	607	549	57	92	17,550	17,354	142 5,153	110 5,390	4	1	... ...	...
SANTAL PARGANAS—Deoghar	Bengali Hindustani	202	203	8	3	22,675	21,780	1,008 1,744	715 1,908			...	... ...
Dumka	Bengali Hindustani Santali	...	4	... ...	1 3 ...	118,036	114,232	8,714 1,072 ...	6,150 826	...		... ...	... ...
Godda	Hindustani	...	...	...		57,485	58,093	926	645		...	...	...
Jamtara	Bengali	...	1	...	...	49,983	49,134	17,300	14,466	...		...	...
Rajmahal	Bengali Hindustani Santali	35	40	... ...	...	64,932	65,712	1,290 1,294	637 890 ...	...	...	... ...	... ...
Pakaur	Bengali Hindustani	...	2	...	... ...	72,750	72,876	329 391	174 322	...	...	... ...	... ...
CUTTACK	Hindustani Oriya	23	6	9 13	... 1	110	108	... ...	... ...	...	...	... ...	... ...
BALASORE	Bengali Oriya	94	51	85	49	7,208	7,912	7 4,662	4 5,577	...	...	... ...	... ...
ANGUL—Sadr	Oriya	210	274	208	255	...	...	...	...	...	...	...	...
Khondmals	Oriya Kandhi	8	...	... ...	... ...	...	...	... ...	... ...	...	...	... ...	... ...
PURI	Hindustani Oriya	...	...	... ...	... ...	...	...	... ...	... ...	38	7	... ...	... ...

District	Language	C1	C2	C3	C4	C5	C6	C7	C8	C9	C10	C11	C12	C13	C14	C15	C16	C17	C18	C19	C20
SAMBALPUR—																					
Sadr	Hindustani ...	...	...	...	...	...	...	...	...	*4,987*	*5,437*	28	4	*4*	*6*	...	...	25	*26*	...	...
	Oriya ...			...	...			...	...			3,925	4,511			4	6			25	22
Bargarh	Oriya ...	...	...	...	...	...	...	...	...	*373*	*344*	300	380	...	...	...	...	*85*	*63*	68	53
HAZARIBAGH—																					
Sadr	Hindustani ...	*38*	*93*	38	23	*1*	...	...	...	*227*	*320*	218	180	*30,607*	*29,491*	9,136	7,546	*60*	*48*	25	24
Chatra	Hindustani ...	...	...	...	...	...	...	...	...	*7*	*4*	3	1	*30*	*40*	19	30	*56*	*47*	1	1
Giridih	Hindustani ...	...	*1*	...	...	*48*	*13*	17	10	*96*	*77*	33	52	*32,011*	*31,766*	14,458	14,414	*97*	*19*	...	...
	Santali ...			...	...			...	...			...	...			...	...			...	...
RANCHI—																					
Sadr	Bengali ...	...	...	...	...	...	...	...	...	*88,108*	*96,758*	24	28	*239*	*189*	...	...	*47*	*45*	...	...
	Hindustani ...			...	...			...	...			27,408	33,040			239	186			11	18
	Mundari ...			...	...			...	...			...	...			...	...			...	...
	Oraon ...			...	...			...	...			394	343			...	...			...	...
Khunti	Hindustani ...	...	...	...	...	*59*	*23*	47	8	*108,722*	*111,520*	25,344	24,409	*56*	*64*	13	20	*14*	*7*	...	...
	Mundari ...			...	...			3	...			...	...			41	40			...	5
Gumla	Hindustani ...	*44*	*112*	13	39	*3*	*2*	3	2	*15,674*	*16,826*	15,564	16,548	...	...	...	...	*1,085*	*1,079*	875	889
Simdega	Hindustani ...	*147*	*199*	147	190	...	...	...	...	*29,850*	*31,578*	29,309	31,383	...	...	...	...	*494*	*194*	412	189
PALAMAU—																					
Sadr	Hindustani ...	*5,127*	*5,016*	5,029	4,965	...	...	...	...	*53*	*23*	46	22	*15*	*15*	15	15	*4*	*15*	4	15
Latehar	Hindustani ...	*549*	*539*	549	529	...	...	...	...	*398*	*348*	387	348	...	...	...	...	*660*	*665*	640	643
MANBHUM—																					
Sadr	Bengali ...	...	...	...	...	*68*	*54*	10	22	*317*	*319*	181	133	*88,848*	*79,866*	33,876	28,760	*44*	*53*	3	3
	Hindustani ...			...	...			...	...			5	4			444	97			...	...
	Santali ...			...	...			...	...			...	...			...	...			...	...
Dhanbad	Bengali ...	...	...	...	...	*98*	*92*	...	...	*76*	*77*	13	3	*39,338*	*34,089*	1,674	1,306	...	...	...	...
	Hindustani ...			...	...			...	...			8	5			2,909	1,621			...	...
	Santali ...			...	...			...	...			...	...			...	...			...	...
SINGHBHUM—																					
Sadr	Bengali ...	...	*1*	...	...	*155*	*197*	...	...	*22,481*	*23,670*	5	1	*3,228*	*3,356*	3	11	...	...	...	...
	Hindustani ...			...	...			...	1			2,358	1,069			134	69			...	...
	Oriya ...			...	...			17	45			152	87			73	41			...	...
	Ho ...			...	...			29	22			464	289			941	945			...	...
	Mundari ...			...	...			...	...			...	...			16	117			...	...
Dhalbhum (*excluding Jamshedpur City*).	Bengali ...	*2*	...	...	...	*809*	*840*	640	654	*3,348*	*3,408*	2,043	1,760	*48,397*	*48,258*	15,361	23,705	...	...	...	...
	Hindustani ...			2	...			...	8			4	63			38	26			...	...
	Oriya ...			...	...			110	80			356	344			2,244	2,476			...	...
	Ho ...			...	...			...	...			...	...			253	310			...	...
Jamshedpur City ...	Bengali ...	*8*	...	...	...	...	...	...	...	*302*	*199*	8	17	*305*	*259*	79	54	...	...	...	...
	Hindustani ...			2	...			...	...			146	130			96	35			...	...
	Oriya ...			...	...			...	...			5	18			10	7			...	...
FEUDATORY STATES—																					
Mayurbhanj	Oriya ...	*192*	*186*	90	57	*618*	*464*	347	2	*574*	*380*	155	40	*125,779*	*130,109*	89,631	90,374	...	...	...	...
Keonjhar	Oriya ...	...	...	...	...	...	...	...	...	*2,962*	*2,905*	2,075	2,150	*8,047*	*7,982*	4,432	5,696	*3,448*	*3,610*	2,926	3,144
Bamra	Oriya ...	...	...	...	...	...	...	...	...	*1,245*	*1,405*	1,032	1,210	...	...	...	...	*9*	*8*	9	8
Patna	Hindustani ...	...	...	...	...	...	...	...	...	*698*	*698*	5	2	...	...	...	...	...	...	...	...
	Oriya ...			...	...			...	...			634	614			...	...			...	...
Kalahandi	Oriya ...	...	...	...	...	...	...	...	...	*624*	*546*	460	365	...	...	...	...	*119*	*133*	102	104
	Kandhi ...			...	...			...	...			...	...			...	...			...	...
Gangpur	Hindustani ...	*108*	*76*	6	10	*32*	*11*	19	4	*18,184*	*18,275*	2,806	2,466	...	...	...	...	*186*	*182*	22	23
	Oriya ...			53	56			10	7			8,881	8,555			...	...			159	159
Bonai	Oriya ...	...	...	...	...	*55*	*55*	13	10	*5,668*	*5,708*	3,298	3,062	...	...	...	...	...	...	...	...
Saraikela	Bengali ...	...	...	...	...	*188*	*197*	...	...	*89*	*93*	...	...	*14,159*	*15,556*	1,500	343	...	...	...	...
	Hindustani ...			...	...			...	...			9	15			10	...			...	...
	Oriya ...			...	...			83	78			19	14			707	557			...	...
Kharsawan	Bengali ...	...	...	...	...	*169*	*203*	...	...	*9,011*	*8,184*	25	25	*508*	*544*	40	51	...	...	...	...
	Hindustani ...			...	...			...	...			95	39			...	...			...	...
	Oriya ...			...	...			90	113			136	89			252	226			...	...
All other states ...	Oriya ...	*4*	...	...	...	...	...	...	...	*917*	*951*	614	751	*1,582*	*1,692*	1,186	1,225	*3,731*	*4,010*	3,436	3,806

TABLE XV—*continued.*

LANGUAGE. PART II—BI-LINGUALISM.

AREA OF BI-LINGUALISM (District, Subdivision or State).	SUBSIDIARY LANGUAGE.	DRAVIDIAN LANGUAGES.																			
		GONDI.				KANDHI (KUI).				MALTO.				ORAON (KURUKH).				TAMIL.			
		Persons speaking above language as mother-tongue.		*Persons using subsidiary language in column 3.*		*Persons speaking above language as mother-tongue.*		*Persons using subsidiary language in column 3.*		*Persons speaking above language as mother-tongue.*		*Persons using subsidiary language in column 3.*		*Persons speaking above language as mother-tongue.*		*Persons using subsidiary language in column 3.*		*Persons speaking above language as mother-tongue.*		*Persons using subsidiary language in column 3.*	
		Males.	Females.	Males.	Females.	Males.	Females.	Males.	Females.	Males.	Females.	Males.	Females.	Males.	Females.	Males.	Females.	Males.	Females.	Males.	Females.
1	3	62	63	64	65	66	67	68	69	70	71	72	73	74	75	76	77	78	79	80	81
PATNA ...	Hindustani ...	...	...			...	...		...	...	...	...	...	15	8	5	1	29	9	...	4
GAYA ...	Hindustani ...	...	...	...	...	1	...	...	...	...	...	...	...	...	...	...	...	5	...	3	...
SHAHABAD ...	Hindustani ...		...	...	...	...	1	...	1	...	...	...	...	838	260	2	51	7	...	3	...
SARAN ...	Hindustani ...	...		...	...	...	...	...	...	...	...	...	...	...	...	...	...	6	...	6	...
CHAMPARAN ...	Hindustani ...	...	...	...	...	...	...	...	...	...	...	...	...	2,598	2,913	2,596	2,913	...	1	...	1
MUZAFFARPUR ...	Hindustani ...	...	...		...	...	...	...	...	...	...	...	...	...	...	...	...	4	1	4	1
DARBHANGA ...	Hindustani		...	...	...	...	...	...	...	...	...	...	...	...	...	...	...	8	3	8	1
MONGHYR ...	Hindustani ...	...	...	...	...	...	...	...	...	...	...	...	...	...	...	...	...	5	3	...	...
BHAGALPUR ...	Hindustani ...	...	...	...	...	...	...	...	...	92	95	6	5	141	204	31	37	...	...	...	...
PURNEA— Araria ...	Hindustani ...			...		...	...		...	...	...	...	...	89	89	55	56	...	...	...	...
Kishanganj ...	Bengali		...	...	...	...	...	...	...	2	21	...	...	609	795	...	...	...	1	...	...
	Hindustani ...			...	...			...	...			...	...			344	338			...	...
Sadr ...	Bengali ...	...	...	...	...	...	...	...	...	71	70	2	4	6,136	6,835	16	0	1	1	...	...
	Hindustani ...			...	...			...	...			1	4			3,201	3,189			1	1
SANTAL PARGANAS— Deoghar ...	Bengali ...	...	...	...	...	...	...	...	...	28	83	...	...	...	2	...	...	...	...	...	...
	Hindustani ...			...	...			...	...			8	4			...	...			...	...
Dumka ...	Bengali ...	...	...	...	...	...	...	...	...	3,477	3,535	309	291	1	9	...	...	...	...	...	...
	Hindustani ...			...	...			...	...			130	155			1	4			...	...
	Santali ...			...	...			...	...			14	43			1	...			...	...
Godda ...	Hindustani ...	...	...	...	...	...	...	...	...	8,049	7,988	13	10	1,079	1,090	2	...	...	...	...	...
Jamtara ...	Bengali ...	...	...	...	...	...	...	...	...	388	430	99	123	...	2	...	...	...	...	...	...
Rājmahal ...	Bengali ...	...	...	...	...	...	...	...	...	15,687	14,284	8	5	1,767	1,816	54	30	1	...	...	...
	Hindustani ...			...	...			...	...			3,043	2,098			362	289			...	...
	Santali ...			...	...			...	...			304	488			...	...			...	...
Pakaur ...	Bengali ...	...	...	...	...	...	...	...	...	7,797	7,463	67	60	1	5	...	...	...	...	...	...
	Hindustani ...			...	...			...	...			9	13			1	...			...	...
CUTTACK ...	Hindustani ...	...	...	...	...	30	...	...	...	...	...	...	...	98	16	3	...	34	15	15	...
	Oriya ...			...	...			...	...			...	...			3	...			5	...
BALASORE ...	Bengali ...	...	...	...	...	...	...	...	...	...	...	...	...	255	299	...	...	...	...	...	...
	Oriya ...			...	...			...	...			...	...			236	231			...	...
ANGUL— Sadr ...	Oriya ...	...	...	...	...	40	6	34	4	...	...	...	...	640	768	635	748	...	...	...	...
Khondmals ...	Oriya ...	63	70	66	70	29,671	25,397	6,660	4,890	...	...	...	...	...	...	...	...	...	...	...	...
	Kandhi ...			...	...			...	...			...	...			...	...			...	...
PURI ...	Hindustani ...	...	...	...	...	...	...	...	...	...	...	...	...	...	...	...	...	35	28	11	5
	Oriya ...			...	...			...	...			...	...			...	...			1	...

Sambalpur—																					
Sadr	Hindustani	...	...	...	...	7	2	4	...	...	...	...	...	17,382	18,624	14	7	16	23	11	9
	Oriya			...	...			7	2			...	...			15,133	16,036			1	2
Bargarh	Oriya	...	...	...	...	...	...	...	...	...	...	...	...	2,679	2,687	2,004	1,948	...	...	...	...
Hazaribagh—																					
Sadr	Hindustani	...	...	...	...	...	...	...	...	...	...	...	...	1,719	1,691	316	315	143	89	35	14
Chatra	Hindustani	1	...	1	...	...	...	...	...	...	...	...	...	290	293	161	156	7	5	2	3
Giridih	Hindustani	...	...	...	...	...	...	...	...	...	...	...	...	83	89	22	17	57	86	8	3
	Santali			...	...			...	...			...	...			...	1			...	...
Ranchi—																					
Sadr	Bengali	...	...	...	...	...	...	...	...	...	...	...	...	77,837	89,801	...	...	11	18	...	...
	Hindustani			...	...			...	...			...	...			48,556	46,143			6	11
	Mundari			...	...			...	...			...	...			1,900	2,530			...	...
	Oraon			...	...			...	...			...	...			...	...			...	...
Khunti	Hindustani	...	...	...	...	...	...	...	...	...	...	...	...	6,347	6,170	5,360	5,124	...	...	...	...
	Mundari			...	...			...	...			...	...			96	114			...	...
Gumla	Hindustani	...	...	...	...	...	...	...	...	...	...	...	...	79,891	84,709	68,670	51,821	...	...	...	...
Simdega	Hindustani	...	...	...	...	...	...	...	...	...	...	...	...	15,944	21,196	10,889	20,853	...	...	...	...
Palamau—																					
Sadr	Hindustani	1	...	1	...	...	...	...	...	...	...	...	...	7,909	8,208	7,402	7,546	...	...	...	...
Latehar	Hindustani	...	...	...	...	...	...	...	...	...	...	...	...	21,264	19,876	20,684	18,536	...	...	...	...
Manbhum—																					
Sadr	Bengali	...	...	...	...	...	...	...	...	...	...	...	...	471	436	317	321	198	113	40	...
	Hindustani			...	...			...	...			...	...			31	6			8	9
	Santali			...	...			...	...			...	...			2	1			...	...
Dhanbad	Bengali	...	...	...	...	...	...	...	...	...	...	...	...	47	2	...	...	121	93	...	...
	Hindustani			...	...			...	...			...	...			8	1			7	6
	Santali			...	...			...	...			...	...			1	...			...	...
Singhbhum—																					
Sadr	Bengali	465	506	...	...	4	5	...	...	...	...	...	...	4,401	4,370	49	38	58	41	...	...
	Hindustani			6	1			2	1			...	...			792	729			58	26
	Oriya			74	72			1	1			...	...			150	62			...	...
	Ho			112	83			...	...			...	...			114	197			...	...
	Mundari			...	...			...	...			...	...			13	12			5	...
Dhalbhum (*excluding Jamshedpur City*).	Bengali	...	...	...	...	...	1	...	...	...	...	...	...	71	66	53	45	478	237	...	60
	Hindustani			...	...			...	...			...	...			...	...			202	66
	Oriya			...	...			...	...			...	...			...	...			...	...
	Ho			...	...			...	...			...	...			...	...			...	...
Jamshedpur City	Bengali	16	9	1	...	...	...	...	...	...	...	...	...	550	654	101	63	729	580	1	2
	Hindustani			...	...			...	...			...	...			353	353			382	246
	Oriya			1	...			...	...			...	...			9	...			1	...
Feudatory States—																					
Mayurbhanj	Oriya	135	143	120	134	4	6	4	6	14	15	14	15	828	771	625	573	...	...	...	...
Keonjhar	Oriya	...	...	...	...	...	...	...	...	7	13	...	1	932	889	628	684	...	...	...	...
Bamra	Oriya	1	...	...	...	...	...	...	...	...	...	...	...	10,896	11,814	10,181	11,434	...	...	...	...
Patna	Hindustani	3	5	...	...	51	55	...	...	...	...	...	...	546	599	6	...	5	1	5	...
	Oriya			...	...			24	22			...	...			477	524			...	...
Kalahandi	Oriya	290	480	388	420	33,876	35,416	19,740	14,624	...	...	...	...	33	26	34	17	...	...	...	...
	Kandhi			...	...			...	...			...	...			...	...			...	...
Gangpur	Hindustani	17	19	...	...	8	6	...	...	...	...	...	...	44,830	45,895	7,038	6,802	...	...	...	...
	Oriya			3	2			3	2			...	...			23,475	24,883			...	...
Bonai	Oriya	307	179	160	88	...	...	...	...	...	...	...	...	7,276	7,453	6,266	4,955	...	...	...	...
Saraikela	Bengali	...	...	...	...	...	...	...	...	...	...	...	...	263	313	38	36	14	11	...	...
	Hindustani			...	...			...	...			...	...			7	4			7	4
	Oriya			...	...			...	...			...	...			45	83			...	...
Kharsawan	Bengali	...	...	...	...	...	...	...	...	...	...	...	...	238	231	...	10	...	...	...	...
	Hindustani			...	...			...	...			...	...			...	...			...	...
	Oriya			...	...			...	...			...	...			96	77			...	...
All other states	Oriya	1,764	1,869	1,464	1,550	7,158	7,329	6,729	7,163	...	...	...	...	2,594	2,763	2,123	2,089	3	18	...	16

TABLE XV—*concluded.*

LANGUAGE. PART II—BI-LINGUALISM.

AREA OF BI-LINGUALISM (District, Subdivision or State).	SUBSIDIARY LANGUAGE.	DRAVIDIAN LANGUAGES—*concluded.*								OTHER LANGUAGES OF INDIA.				ASIATIC LANGUAGES FOREIGN TO INDIA.				EUROPEAN LANGUAGES.			
		TELUGU.				OTHER DRAVIDIAN LANGUAGES.															
		Persons speaking above language as mother-tongue.		*Persons using subsidiary language in column 3.*		*Persons speaking above language as mother-tongue.*		*Persons using subsidiary language in column 3.*		*Persons speaking above language as mother-tongue.*		*Persons using subsidiary language in column 3.*		*Persons speaking above language as mother-tongue.*		*Persons using subsidiary language in column 3.*		*Persons speaking above language as mother-tongue.*		*Persons using subsidiary language in column 3.*	
		Males.	Females.	Males.	Females.	Males.	Females.	Males.	Females.	Males.	Females.	Males.	Females.	Males.	Females.	Males.	Females.	Males.	Females.	Males.	Females.
1	3	82	83	84	85	86	87	88	89	90	91	92	93	94	95	96	97	98	99	100	101
PATNA	Hindustani ...	11	5	...	...	...	...	...	...	69	...	10	...	5	1	2	...	1,655	982	368	388
GAYA	Hindustani ...	5	11	...	4	2	1	...	...	15	6	...	...	2	...	...	...	183	184	77	85
SHAHABAD	Hindustani ...	...	...	...	...	...	...	...	...	53	12	9	...	1	...	...	...	81	81	65	48
SARAN	Hindustani ...	...	...	...	...	...	...	...	...	14	...	14	...	...	...	...	...	139	99	67	51
CHAMPARAN	Hindustani ...	3	...	3	...	...	...	...	...	27	1	27	1	1	...	1	...	193	292	55	43
MUZAFFARPUR	Hindustani ...	...	...	...	...	...	...	...	...	33	1	33	1	1	2	1	3	230	89	43	38
DARBHANGA	Hindustani ...	6	...	6	...	5	2	1	...	7	...	7	...	11	...	11	...	173	131	52	16
MONGHYR	Hindustani ...	8	4	...	3	...	...	...	...	39	...	5	...	10	1	...	...	763	593	215	197
BHAGALPUR	Hindustani ...	9	4	1	...	...	...	...	...	88	2	20	...	25	...	2	...	195	106	35	23
PURNEA— Araria	Hindustani ...	...	...	...	...	...	...	...	...	98	...	58	...	...	...	...	...	2	3	2	2
Kishanganj	Bengali ... Hindustani ...	...	...	... ...	... ...	1	...	... 1	... ...	97	16	... 32	... ...	9	...	... 3	... ...	51	60	1 45	2 43
Sadr	Bengali ... Hindustani ...	...	...	... ...	... ...	1	...	... 1	... ...	158	...	... 75	... ...	11	4	... ...	... ...	71	83	... 45	1 40
SANTAL PARGANAS— Deoghar	Bengali ... Hindustani ...	...	...	... ...	... ...	...	...	... ...	... ...	2	...	... ...	... ...	3	2	... 1	... ...	9	12	... ...	... ...
Dumka	Bengali ... Hindustani ... Santali ...	...	...	... ...	... ...	...	...	... ...	... ...	4	...	... 4 ...	... ...	...	...	... ...	... ...	135	196	9 140 17	8 126 29
Godda	Hindustani ...	...	...	...	...	...	...	...	...	...	...	...	...	...	...	...	...	11	10	2	...
Jamtara	Bengali ...	...	...	...	...	...	...	...	...	...	...	...	...	...	...	...	...	14	15	...	...
Rajmahal	Bengali ... Hindustani ... Santali ...	...	...	... ...	... ...	...	...	... ...	... ...	7	...	... ...	... ...	...	...	... ...	... ...	38	98	3 9 7	2 2 9
Pakaur	Bengali ... Hindustani ...	...	...	... ...	... ...	...	...	... ...	... ...	...	...	... ...	... ...	...	...	... ...	... ...	19	21	... 2	... ...
CUTTACK	Hindustani ... Oriya ...	2,575	2,816	83 672	20 1,941	25	...	... ...	... ...	63	7	8 2	... ...	4	...	1 1	... ...	130	209	61 22	42 ...
BALASORE	Bengali ... Oriya ...	727	699	1 353	4 367	...	...	... ...	... ...	97	...	... ...	... ...	9	...	... ...	... ...	43	88	... 7	... 13
ANGUL— Sadr	Oriya ...	59	96	55	72	...	...	...	...	...	...	...	...	...	...	...	...	9	13	5	1
Khondmals	Oriya ... Kandhi ...	4	3	4 ...	... ...	...	...	... ...	... ...	...	...	... ...	... ...	...	...	... ...	... ...	2	1	... ...	... ...
PURI	Hindustani ... Oriya ...	4,014	3,792	250 2,253	108 2,145	1	2	... ...	... ...	16	...	12 3	... ...	23	7	13 1	... 1	219	186	118 11	107 8

SAMBALPUR—																					
Sadr	Hindustani ...	157	153	41	19	3	...	2	...	57	9	11	...	4	4	2	...	57	32	40	17
	Oriya ...			40	45			...	...			6	1			...	...			2	8
Bargarh	Oriya ...	162	278	111	160	...	...	...	...	7	2	...	1	...	...	...	...	3	...	...	...
HAZARIBAGH—																					
Sadr	Hindustani ...	17	11	6	3	2	4	1	...	15	19	7	11	5	1	3	...	84	69	33	32
Chatra	Hindustani ...	...	...	.	...	2	...	...	...	5	...	1	...	2	...	..	...	7	9	...	...
Giridih	Hindustani ...	10	1	2	1	...	1	...	...	31	1	...	1	...	...	...	...	104	100	54	57
	Santali ...			...	...			...	...			...	...	...	...	...	...			2	2
RANCHI—																					
Sadr	Bengali ...	31	12	...	...	1	2	...	...	6	1	...	...	6	3	...	...	334	403	...	...
	Hindustani ...			25	9			1	2			1	1			...	2			288	346
	Mundari ...			...	...			...	...			...	...			...	...			...	...
	Oraon ...			...	...			...	...			...	...			...	...			...	...
Khunti	Hindustani ...	1	...	1	...	...	...	...	...	8	...	...	...	1	...	...	...	10	18	7	8
	Mundari ...			...	...			...	...			...	...			...	...			...	1
Gumla	Hindustani ...	...	..	...	...	...	...	...	...	4	2	4	1	...	...	...	...	30	16	2	6
Simdega	Hindustani ...	...	...	...	...	...	...	...	...	..	4	...	4	...	...	...	...	10	6	3	2
PALAMAU—																					
Sadr	Hindustani ..	1	...	1	..	1	...	1	...	20	...	6	...	..	...	...	...	27	19	13	8
Latehar	Hindustani ..	1	...	1	...	..	..	...	...	2		1	...	1	...	1	...	10	9	...	...
MANBHUM—																					
Sadr	Bengali ...	596	511	21	13	1	..	...	.	37	2	..	...	66	48	19	1	479	378	9	6
	Hindustani ...			68	39			..	...			...	...			6	18			107	75
	Santali ...			...	...			...	...			...	...			...	...			...	...
Dhanbad	Bengali ...	122	101	...	3	...	..	...	...	84	66	30	...	21	13	...	...	695	649	16	11
	Hindustani ...			55	39			...	...			...	16			1	1			216	218
	Santali .			..	...			...	...			...	...			...	...			...	...
SINGHBHUM—																					
Sadr	Bengali ...	282	222	...	...	9	1	...	...	291	306	...	...	..	...	...	...	370	395	...	40
	Hindustani ...			218	88			...	1			14	4			...	...			330	306
	Oriya ...			1	6			.	...			...	...			...	...			...	...
	Ho ...			...	...			..	...			...	...			...	...			...	...
	Mundari ...			...	...			...	...			...	...			...	...			...	...
Dhalbhum (*excluding Jamshedpur City*).	Bengali ...	138	56	...	1	134	15	...	...	71	6	3	...	27	1	3	...	136	41	2	...
	Hindustani ...			94	12			78	4			20	...			3	...			24	20
	Oriya ...			3	...			...	...			...	...			3	...			...	...
	Ho ...			...	...				...			...	...			...	...			...	...
Jamshedpur City ...	Bengali ...	2,793	2,278	10	...	183	58	...	...	280	88	...	...	37	14	...	...	669	460	5	3
	Hindustani ...			1,477	397			104	24			115	31			7	6			254	301
	Oriya ...			56	11			...	...			...	...			...	...			...	1
FEUDATORY STATES—																					
Mayurbhanj	Oriya ...	40	39	22	21	...	...	..	...	36	26	20	26	...	...	...	...	15	6	7	2
Keonjhar	Oriya ...	60	20	12	20	58	54	30	35	3	...	...	...	...	...	...	...	15	13	1	...
Bamra	Oriya ...	16	10	9	5	7	6	7	6	12	10	12	10	...	...	...	...	6	3	...	...
Patna	Hindustani ...	302	298	37	15	2	...	...	...	...	...	...	...	...	...	...	...	16	10	11	4
	Oriya ...			316	218			2	...			...	...			...	...			3	6
Kalahandi	Oriya ...	1,474	1,615	1,038	1,053	...	...	...	...	...	...	...	...	12	12	12	11	...	...	...	...
	Kandhi ...			...	...			...	...			...	...			...	...			...	...
Gangpur	Hindustani ...	121	142	46	17	43	19	13	13	18	16	13	15	7	2	5	1	35	23	22	8
	Oriya ...			37	42			13	4			...	...			...	...			2	...
Bonai	Oriya ...	...	...	..	...	3	4	3	4	...	...	...	...	...	...	...	...	1	...	...	...
Saraikela	Bengali ...	65	43	5	3	1	...	...	...	1	...	...	...	10	...	...	...	18	11	1	...
	Hindustani ...			36	12			...	...			1	...			...	...			9	4
	Oriya ...			4	2			...	...			...	...			...	...			1	...
Kharsawan	Bengali ...	18	10	...	...	...	...	...	...	1	...	...	...	...	...	...	...	6	1	...	...
	Hindustani ...			...	...			...	...			...	...			...	...			...	...
	Oriya ...			1	...			...	...			...	...			...	...			...	...
All other states ...	Oriya ...	1,543	1,589	1,054	1,345	54	64	35	43	6	...	1	...	5	1	...	...	15	7	...	1

TABLE XVI.

RELIGION.

This table shows the distribution of the population by religions. It corresponds with Table VI of 1921, from which it differs in form in the following respects :—

(1) The term " Animist " has been replaced by " Tribal " (in this and in all the other tables where distribution by religion is shown) to denote the religion of the primitive tribes.

(2) Christians have been classified as Roman Catholics and other sects. Table XV of 1921 showed a detailed classification of Christians by sect and race ; but no such table has been prepared on the present occasion.

2. " Brahmanic " is a term used, for the sake of convenience, to denote Hindus who do not belong to the Brahmo Samaj or the Arya Samaj. It includes the following number of persons returned as Deo Samajists and Adi-Hindus.

Sect and locality.	Persons.	Males.	Females.	Sect and locality.	Persons.	Males.	Females.
Deo-Samaj	*16,624*	*8,749*	*7,875*	**Adi-Hindu**	*525*	*243*	*282*
Patna ...	16,372	8,591	7,781	Saran	525	243	[illegible]
Monghyr ...	252	158	94				

3. The following statement shows the number of Jains and Buddhists who returned themselves as Hindus in addition to returning themselves as Jains or Buddhists :—

Religion and locality.	Persons.	Males.	Females.	Religion and locality.	Persons.	Males.	Females.
Jains	*236*	*135*	*101*	Hazaribagh ...	50	29	21
Patna ..	90	44	46	Orissa States ...	27	14	13
Gaya	7	5	2				
Monghyr ...	7	6	1	**Buddhists**	*19*	*19*	.
Bhagalpur	43	25	18	Patna	10	10	
Cuttack	3	3		Gaya	7	7	
Sambalpur	9	9		Cuttack	2	2	

4. The following statement shows the distribution of " Others " in columns 47—49 of the main table :—

Religion and locality.	Persons.	Males.	Females.	Religion and locality.	Persons.	Males.	Females.
Jew	*24*	*15*	*9*	Sambalpur .	29	17	12
Cuttack	3	2	1	Orissa States ..	239	134	105
Hazaribagh	2	2					
Ranchi ...	18	11	7				
Manbhum ..	1	..	1	**Indefinite Beliefs***	*15*	*12*	*3*
				Patna .	2	2	
Kumbhipatia	*271*	*153*	*118*	Muzaffarpur	1	1	
Cuttack ...	2	1	1	Ranchi ..	3	2	1
Puri	1	1	...	Orissa States	9	7	2

* " Indefinite beliefs " denotes Agnostics, Atheists and the like.

5. The following statement shows the distribution of " Others " in columns 17—19 of the subsidiary table relating to the Feudatory States :

Religion and State.	Persons.	Males.	Females.	Religion and State.	Persons.	Males.	Females.
Sikh	*216*	*138*	*78*	**Buddhist**	*1,376*	*682*	*694*
Talcher	12	9	3	Talcher .. .	14	9	5
Mayurbhanj .	6	6	.	Dhenkanal .	1		1
Keonjhar ..	7	3	4	Athmallik	1	1	
Bamra	35	22	13	Baramba .	871	429	442
Sonpur . ..	7	5	2	Tigiria	487	241	246
				Gangpur	2	2	
Patna ...	32	25	7				
Kalahandi .	63	37	26	**Zoroastrian** ...	*23*	*14*	*9*
Gangpur ..	12	9	3	Mayurbhanj ..	18	11	7
Saraikela	21	15	6	Patna	3	1	2
Kharsawan	21	7	14	Gangpur .. .	2	2	...
				Kumbhipatia	*239*	*134*	*105*
				Patna ..	238	134	104
Jain	*318*	*166*	*152*	Kalahandi . .	1		1
Mayurbhanj	1	1					
Bamra	9	4	5	**Indefinite Beliefs** .	*9*	*7*	*2*
Patna	281	147	134	Patna	3	2	1
Kalahandi	27	14	13	Gangpur . ..	6	5	1

6. The 41 Brahmo Samajists found in the Feudatory States are distributed as follows :—

State.	Persons	Males.	Females.
Mayurbhanj	6		3
Dhenkanal ...	14	5	9
Gangpur	21	7	14

TABLE XVI.

RELIGION.

DISTRICT OR STATE	POPULATION			HINDU.															SIKH.			JAIN.			BUDDHIST.		
				BRAHMANIC.			BRAHMO.			ARYA.			TOTAL HINDU.														
	Persons	Males	Females	Persons.	Males.	Females	P.	M	F.	P.	M.	F.	Persons.	Males	Females.				Persons	Males	Females	Persons	Males.	Females	Persons	Males.	Females.
1	2	3	4	5	6	7	8	9	10	11	12	13	14	15	16				17	18	19	20	21	22	23	24	25
BIHAR AND ORISSA	*42,329,583*	*21,082,560*	*21,247,023*	*35,199,144*	*17,552,329*	*17,646,815*	*445*	*232*	*213*	*6,763*	*3,704*	*3,059*	*35,206,352*	*17,556,265*	*17,650,087*				*5,869*	*3,760*	*2,109*	*4,052*	*2,224*	*1,828*	*2,295*	*1,235*	*1,060*
British Territory	*37,677,576*	*18,794,138*	*18,883,438*	*31,004,307*	*15,489,336*	*15,514,971*	*404*	*217*	*187*	*6,763*	*3,704*	*3,059*	*31,011,474*	*15,493,257*	*15,518,217*				*5,653*	*3,622*	*2,031*	*3,734*	*2,058*	*1,676*	*919*	*553*	*366*
PATNA DIVISION	6,228,425	3,148,866	3,079,559	5,608,547	2,850,396	2,758,151	115	69	46	3,570	1,994	1,576	5,612,232	2,852,459	2,759,773				800	456	344	1,280	626	654	46	33	13
Patna	1,846,474	956,124	890,350	1,636,263	850,685	785,578	105	62	43	3,461	1,935	1,526	1,639,829	852,682	787,147				220	126	94	204	102	102	16	15	1
Gaya	2,388,462	1,193,643	1,194,819	2,133,439	1,075,442	1,057,997	9	6	3	93	47	46	2,133,541	1,075,495	1,058,046				183	107	76	564	280	284	19	13	6
Shahabad	1,993,489	999,009	994,380	1,838,845	924,269	914,576	1	1	..	16	12	4	1,838,862	924,282	914,580				397	223	174	512	244	268	11	5	6
TIRHUT DIVISION	10,739,274	5,315,811	5,423,463	9,237,177	4,587,671	4,649,506	4	4		1,510	800	710	9,238,691	4,588,475	4,650,216				106	87	19	75	49	26	1	1	.
Saran	2,486,469	1,220,040	1,266,419	2,176,691	1,071,850	1,104,841				293	198	95	2,176,984	1,072,048	1,104,936				12	9	3	6	6			...	.
Champaran	2,145,687	1,080,956	1,064,731	1,786,597	902,702	883,895	4	4		673	304	360	1,787,274	903,010	884,264				32	21	11	5	3	2		..	
Muzaffarpur	2,941,025	1,443,847	1,497,178	2,548,666	1,258,287	1,290,379		.		340	202	138	2,549,006	1,258,489	1,290,517				18	13	5	9	2	7	1	1	...
Darbhanga ...	3,166,094	1,570,959	1,595,135	2,725,223	1,354,832	1,370,391				204	96	108	2,725,427	1,354,928	1,370,499				44	44		55	38	17	.	.	
BHAGALPUR DIVISION	8,759,801	4,431,983	4,327,818	6,262,502	3,174,398	3,088,104	68	36	32	1,396	747	649	6,263,966	3,175,181	3,088,785				830	469	361	501	331	170	4	3	1
Monghyr	2,287,154	1,145,797	1,141,357	2,047,828	1,030,739	1,017,089	.			1,364	726	638	2,049,192	1,031,465	1,017,727				8	8		24	14	10	4	3	1
Bhagalpur	2,234,632	1,130,584	1,104 048	1,980,187	1,002,621	977,566	68	36	32	7	7		1,980,262	1,002,664	977,598				50	19	31	280	162	118	..	.	
Purnea	2,186,543	1,129,681	1,056,862	1,285,289	665,437	619,852		.	.	25	14	11	-1,285,314	665,451	619,863				699	382	317	172	133	39	...	..	
Santal Parganas	2,051,472	1,025,931	1,025,561	949,198	475,601	473,597	...	.					949,198	475,601	473,597				73	60	13	25	22	3	..	...	..
ORISSA DIVISION	5,306,142	2,549,251	2,756,891	5,096,243	2,449,206	2,647,037	173	82	91	15	7	8	5,096,431	2,449,295	2,647,136				89	59	30	108	64	44	396	212	184
Cuttack	2,176,707	1,028,134	1,148,573	2,106,708	996,368	1,110,340	114	52	62	8	4	4	2,106,830	996,424	1,110,406				25	16	9	36	21	15	392	209	183
Balasore ..	990,600	480,518	510,082	944,636	457,919	486,717	45	24	21	...	.	.	944,681	457,943	486,738				12	8	4	..	...		1	1	
Angul ...	222,736	108,925	113,811	163,663	80,344	83,319			.				163,663	80,344	83,319								.	.	.	...	...
Puri ...	1,035,154	500,214	534,940	1,011,067	488,550	522,517	10	3	7	2	2		1,011,079	488,555	522,524				2	2		10	9	1	3	2	1
Sambalpur ..	880,945	431,460	449,485	870,169	426,025	444,144	4	3	1	5	1	4	870,178	426,029	444,149				50	33	17	62	34	28	..	...	...
CHOTA NAGPUR DIVISION	6,643,934	3,348,227	3,295,707	4,799,838	2,427,665	2,372,173	44	26	18	272	156	116	4,800,154	2,427,847	2,372,307				3,828	2,551	1,277	1,770	988	782	472	304	168
Hazaribagh	1,517,357	751,956	765,401	1,208,070	597,508	610,562	11	8	3	18	12	6	1,208,099	597,528	610,571				221	129	92	794	464	330	221	135	86
Ranchi ...	1,567,149	777,063	790,086	869,237	433,242	436,095	11	5	6	144	76	68	869,492	433,323	436,169				19	12	7	698	336	362	13	9	4
Palamau	818,736	409,778	408,958	669,953	335,512	334,441	3	2	1	5	5		669,961	335,519	334,442				11	8	3	9	8	1	..	..	..
Manbhum	1,810,890	940,009	870,881	1,592,508	824,004	768,504				19	8	11	1,592,527	824,012	768,515				79	62	17	83	45	38	6	2	4
Singhbhum ...	929,802	469,421	460,381	459,970	237,309	222,571	19	11	8	86	56	31	460,075	237,465	222,610				3,498	2,340	1,158	186	135	51	232	158	74
Feudatory States	*4,652,007*	*2,288,422*	*2,363,585*	*4,194,837*	*2,062,993*	*2,131,844*	*41*	*15*	*26*				*4,194,878*	*2,063,008*	*2,131,870*				*216*	*138*	*78*	*318*	*166*	*152*	*1,376*	*682*	*694*
Orissa States ..	4,465,385	2,196,601	2,268,684	4,067,135	1,999,532	2,067,603	41	15	26			..	4,067,176	1,999,547	2,067,629				174	116	58	318	166	152	1,376	682	694
Chota Nagpur States	186,622	91,731	94,891	127,702	63,461	64,241		...			..		127,702	63,461	64,241				42	22	20	.	...		..	.	

TABLE XVI—*continued.*

Religion.

District or State.	Zoroastrian (Parsi). Persons.	M.	F.	Muslim. Persons.	Males.	Females.	Christian. Roman Catholic. Persons.	Males.	Females.	Other Sects. Persons.	Males.	Females.	Sect not Returned. Persons.	M.	F.	Total Christian. Persons	Males.	Females.	Tribal. Persons.	Males.	Females.	Others. Persons.	M.	F.
1	26	27	28	29	30	31	32	33	34	35	36	37	38	39	40	41	42	43	44	45	46	47	48	49
BIHAR AND ORISSA	*264*	*159*	*105*	*4,284,306*	*2,123,112*	*2,161,194*	*205,209*	*100,915*	*104,294*	*187,983*	*94,037*	*93,946*	*23,534*	*12,233*	*11,301*	*416,726*	*207,185*	*209,541*	*2,409,409*	*1,188,440*	*1,220,969*	*310*	*180*	*130*
British Territory ...	*241*	*145*	*96*	*4,264,790*	*2,112,814*	*2,151,976*	*163,902*	*80,127*	*83,775*	*154,458*	*77,768*	*76,690*	*23,534*	*12,233*	*11,301*	*341,894*	*170,128*	*171,766*	*2,048,809*	*1,011,522*	*1,037,287*	*62*	*39*	*23*
Patna Division	**37**	**19**	**18**	**607,583**	**291,871**	**315,712**	**846**	**307**	**539**	**2,181**	**1,361**	**820**	**3,387**	**1,703**	**1,684**	**6,414**	**3,371**	**3,043**	**31**	**29**	**2**	**2**	**2**	...
Patna	26	15	11	202,655	101,175	101,480	773	270	503	1,625	1,080	545	1,105	640	465	3,503	1,990	1,513	19	17	2	2	2	...
Gaya	7	2	5	253,560	117,436	136,124	27	13	14	60	26	34	489	209	280	576	298	278	12	12	...	...	...	...
Shahabad	4	2	2	151,368	73,260	78,108	46	24	22	496	255	241	1,793	904	889	2,335	1,083	1,252	...	...	...	...	...	...
Tirhut Division ...	**7**	**3**	**4**	**1,494,368**	**724,206**	**770,162**	**2,969**	**1,321**	**1,648**	**1,257**	**666**	**591**	**1,307**	**743**	**564**	**5,533**	**2,730**	**2,803**	**492**	**259**	**233**	**1**	**1**	...
Saran	..	...	...	309,005	147,703	161,302	84	48	36	338	219	119	38	15	23	460	282	178	1	1	...	...	...	...
Champaran...	1	1	..	354,235	175,988	178,247	2,741	1,187	1,554	293	107	186	621	387	234	3,655	1,681	1,974	485	252	233	...	...	...
Muzaffarpur	6	2	4	391,091	184,852	206,239	62	39	23	520	288	232	305	154	151	887	481	406	6	6	...	1	1	...
Darbhanga	..	...	...	440,037	215,663	224,374	82	47	35	106	52	54	343	187	156	531	286	245	...	...	..	...		...
Bhagalpur Division ...	**4**	**3**	**1**	**1,588,003**	**803,851**	**784,152**	**2,331**	**1,255**	**1,076**	**8,085**	**3,923**	**4,162**	**8,230**	**4,198**	**4,032**	**18,646**	**9,376**	**9,270**	**887,847**	**442,769**	**445,078**	..	...	...
Monghyr	4	3	1	228,497	109,408	119,089	222	126	96	349	107	173	1,355	765	590	1,917	1,058	859	7,508	3,838	3,670	...	...	...
Bhagalpur	...	...	...	249,436	125,257	124,179	92	44	48	54	37	17	1,414	800	614	1,560	881	679	3,044	1,601	1,443	...	.	...
Purnea	...	...	...	886,368	456,347	430,021	1,190	636	554	242	124	118	391	213	178	1,823	973	850	12,167	6,395	5,772	...	...	...
Santal Parganas ...	...	...	...	223,702	112,839	110,863	827	449	378	7,449	3,595	3,854	5,070	2,420	2,650	13,346	6,464	6,882	865,128	430,935	434,193	...	...	...
Orissa Division ...	**20**	**9**	**11**	**124,463**	**58,685**	**65,778**	**499**	**240**	**259**	**9,210**	**4,371**	**4,839**	...	...	...	**9,709**	**4,611**	**5,098**	**74,891**	**36,295**	**38,596**	**35**	**21**	**14**
Cuttack	4	2	2	66,104	29,965	36,139	187	72	115	2,686	1,150	1,536	...	...	...	2,873	1,222	1,651	438	332	106	5	3	2
Balasore	...	...	...	31,735	15,661	16,074	58	30	28	1,317	655	662	...	...	..	1,375	685	690	12,796	6,220	6,576	...	...	...
Angul	...	...	...	293	176	117	7	3	4	300	153	147	...	.	...	307	156	151	58,473	28,249	30,224	...	...	...
Puri	5	2	3	22,518	10,875	11,643	160	87	73	1,376	681	695	...	...	...	1,536	768	768	...	...	...	1	1	...
Sambalpur	11	5	6	3,613	2,008	1,605	87	48	39	3,531	1,732	1,799	...	...	...	3,618	1,780	1,838	3,184	1,554	1,630	29	17	12
Chota Nagpur Division ...	**173**	**111**	**62**	**450,373**	**234,201**	**216,172**	**157,257**	**77,004**	**80,253**	**133,725**	**67,447**	**66,278**	**10,610**	**5,589**	**5,021**	**301,592**	**150,040**	**151,552**	**1,085,548**	**532,170**	**553,378**	**24**	**15**	**9**
Hazaribagh	1	1	..	171,694	84,799	86,895	221	126	95	957	554	403	1,991	1,026	965	3,169	1,706	1,463	133,156	67,192	65,964	2	2	...
Ranchi	4	1	3	66,047	33,778	32,269	145,233	70,908	74,325	117,375	59,206	58,169	...	...	...	262,608	130,114	132,494	368,247	179,477	188,770	21	13	8
Palamau	...	...	...	74,501	37,369	37,132	7,585	3,658	3,927	369	191	178	653	393	260	8,607	4,242	4,365	65,647	32,632	33,015	...	...	...
Manbhum	1	1	...	111,377	61,712	49,665	231	134	97	2,055	958	1,097	5,370	2,830	2,540	7,656	3,922	3,734	99,160	50,253	48,907	1	...	1
Singhbhum ...	167	108	59	26,754	16,543	10,211	3,987	2,178	1,809	12,969	6,538	6,431	2,596	1,340	1,256	19,552	10,056	9,496	419,338	202,616	216,722	...	...	...
Feudatory States ...	*23*	*14*	*9*	*19,516*	*10,298*	*9,218*	*41,307*	*20,788*	*20,519*	*33,525*	*16,269*	*17,256*	...	...	...	*74,832*	*37,057*	*37,775*	*360,600*	*176,918*	*183,682*	*248*	*141*	*107*
Orissa States	23	14	9	17,100	8,975	8,125	41,146	20,710	20,436	33,322	16,168	17,154	...	...	...	74,468	36,878	37,590	304,502	150,172	154,330	248	141	107
Chota Nagpur States ...	...	...	...	2,416	1,323	1,093	161	78	83	203	101	102	...	...	...	364	179	185	56,098	26,746	29,352	...	...	...

TABLE XVI—*concluded.*

RELIGION—DETAILED FIGURES FOR THE FEUDATORY STATES.

STATES.	POPULATION.			HINDU.			MUSLIM.			CHRISTIAN.			TRIBAL.			OTHERS.		
	Persons.	Males.	Females.	Persons.	Males.	Females.	Persons.	Males.	Females.	Persons.	Males.	Females.	Persons.	Males.	Females.	Persons.	Males.	Females.
1	2	3	4	5	6	7	8	9	10	11	12	13	14	15	16	17	18	19
Feudatory States ...	*4,652,007*	*2,288,422*	*2,363,585*	*4,194,878*	*2,063,008*	*2,131,870*	*19,516*	*10,298*	*9,218*	*74,832*	*37,057*	*37,775*	*360,600*	*176,918*	*183,682*	*2,181*	*1,141*	*1,040*
ORISSA STATES	**4,465,385**	**2,196,691**	**2,268,694**	**4,067,176**	**1,999,547**	**2,067,629**	**17,100**	**8,975**	**8,125**	**74,468**	**36,878**	**37,590**	**304,502**	**150,172**	**154,330**	**2,139**	**1,119**	**1,020**
Athgarh	50,148	24,843	25,305	49,567	24,543	25,024	266	140	126	315	160	155	...	...	...	...	...	...
Talcher	69,702	34,674	35,028	69,129	34,341	34,788	186	129	57	113	68	45	248	118	130	26	18	8
Mayurbhanj	889,603	442,378	447,225	876,419	435,570	440,849	5,310	2,854	2,456	885	473	412	6,964	3,463	3,501	25	18	7
Nilgiri	68,594	34,117	34,477	68,451	34,033	34,418	51	35	16	92	49	43	...	...	...	...	...	...
Keonjhar	460,609	227,143	233,466	378,236	185,974	192,262	1,315	693	622	130	71	59	80,921	40,402	40,519	7	3	4
Pal Lahara	27,974	13,835	14,139	27,947	13,820	14,127	26	15	11	1	...	1	...	...	...	...	...	...
Dhenkanal	284,326	136,646	147,680	283,530	136,229	147,301	760	399	361	35	18	17	...	...	...	1	...	1
Athmallik	64,272	32,287	31,985	63,640	31,968	31,672	84	51	33	6	5	1	541	262	279	1	1	...
Hindol	48,896	23,419	25,477	48,627	23,298	25,329	104	45	59	2	2	...	163	74	89	...	...	...
Narsinghpur	40,878	19,925	20,953	40,735	19,854	20,881	139	69	70	4	2	2	...	...	...	...	...	...
Baramba	46,688	22,596	24,092	45,609	22,050	23,559	200	112	88	8	5	3	...	...	...	871	429	442
Tigiria	24,822	12,141	12,681	23,797	11,644	12,153	538	256	282	...	...	...	...	...	...	487	241	246
Khandpara	77,929	37,281	40,648	77,825	37,219	40,606	94	56	38	10	6	4	...	...	...	...	...	...
Nayagarh	142,406	67,221	75,185	141,296	66,681	74,615	623	299	324	12	8	4	475	233	242	...	...	...
Ranpur	47,711	22,412	25,299	47,307	22,217	25,090	404	195	209	...	...	...	...	...	...	...	...	...
Daspalla	43,402	20,896	22,506	43,322	20,843	22,479	70	45	25	10	8	2	...	...	...	...	...	...
Baud	135,248	67,070	68,178	135,008	66,956	68,052	219	106	113	21	8	13	...	...	...	...	...	...
Bamra	151,047	73,285	77,762	148,098	71,834	76,264	272	137	135	1,404	684	720	1,229	604	625	44	26	18
Bairakhol	35,710	17,727	17,983	33,262	16,519	16,743	36	16	20	5	2	3	2,407	1,190	1,217	...	...	...
Sonpur	237,920	117,067	120,853	237,105	116,623	120,482	553	287	266	8	4	4	247	148	99	7	5	2
Patna	566,924	280,305	286,619	533,085	263,861	269,224	1,009	552	457	7,109	3,491	3,618	25,164	12,092	13,072	557	309	248
Kalahandi	513,716	252,438	261,278	441,450	217,134	224,316	677	322	355	111	57	54	71,387	34,874	36,513	91	51	40
Gangpur	356,674	176,959	179,715	212,766	106,000	106,766	4,012	2,068	1,944	61,171	30,210	30,961	78,703	38,663	40,040	22	18	4
Bonai	80,186	40,026	40,160	40,965	20,336	20,629	152	94	58	3,016	1,547	1,469	36,053	18,049	18,004	...	...	...
CHOTA NAGPUR STATES	**186,622**	**91,731**	**94,891**	**127,702**	**63,461**	**64,241**	**2,416**	**1,323**	**1,093**	**364**	**179**	**185**	**56,098**	**26,746**	**29,352**	**42**	**22**	**20**
Seraikela	143,525	70,990	72,535	97,506	48,787	48,719	1,834	1,029	805	311	153	158	43,853	21,006	22,847	21	15	6
Kharsawan	43,097	20,741	22,356	30,196	14,674	15,522	582	294	288	53	26	27	12,245	5,740	6,505	21	7	14

TABLE XVII.

RACE, TRIBE OR CASTE.

This table corresponds with Table XIII of 1921, but is presented in a different form. It gives statistics of the more important and numerous castes and tribes found in the province. For reasons of economy the tabulation of caste was restricted at this census, and several of the communities for which figures were shown in 1921 do not appear in the present table. On the other hand certain new communities figure in it. For example, an attempt has been made to obtain more or less complete figures for all "depressed classes" in the province, and these statistics are discussed in an appendix of the report volume. Special attention was paid, too, to the primitive and "semi-primitive" tribes, and detailed figures have been presented in Table XVIII of the territorial distribution of some of these tribes and the variation in their numbers during the last forty years. Apart from the depressed and primitive communities, the present table gives statistics of all castes which numbered not less than 1 *per cent.* of the provincial population in 1921, as well as of some other castes which are of importance in limited areas.

2. The total figure shown against each caste or tribe in this table cannot always be regarded as absolutely complete, because in localities where a particular caste was believed to be more or less unknown no attempt was made to extract statistics for it. This, however, does not apply to those castes which are found in considerable numbers throughout the province.

3. Below the total figures for each caste, etc. (other than those dealt with in Table XVIII) detailed figures are given for the districts in which it is *chiefly* found. As a rule, a district is mentioned only when the caste contributes not less than one *per mille* to the total population of the district; but this rule has not been strictly followed in the case of the less numerous castes.

4. *Jolahas* are the only purely Muslim community shown in this table. But, in the case of *Doms, Halalkhors* and *Lalbegis*, some of whom were returned as Hindus and some as Muslims, separate totals are given for each religion.

5. Christian converts from Hinduism and Islam do not ordinarily make any return of "caste" other than a simple return of Indian Christian. But the figures shown in this table for the various primitive tribes include converts to Christianity and Hinduism as well as the adherents of the old tribal religions; and here again separate totals have been shown for each religious group. In parts of the Chota Nagpur plateau, such castes as *Gaura* and *Kamar* have been treated for this purpose in the same way as the primitive communities.

6. Religious communities such as Sikhs, Jains, Buddhists and Zoroastrians, who do not ordinarily recognize caste distinctions, have been excluded altogether from this table. The same applies to Europeans, Anglo-Indians, etc. No return of caste was ordinarily made by members of the Brahmo, Arya or Dev Samaj. Apart from these particular Hindu sects, there were 6,743 Hindus (3,146 males and 3,597 females) who declined, or omitted, to make any declaration of caste.

7. In all, 33,934,751 persons, or more than 80 *per cent.* of the total population of the province, have been accounted for in this table. The statement below gives separate figures for the four main religious groups. Brahmos, Aryas and Dev Samajists, and persons who made no return of caste at all, have been excluded from the total Hindu population in this statement.

Religious group.	Total Population.			Accounted for in this table.		
	Persons.	Males.	Females.	Persons.	Males.	Females.
1	2	3	4	5	6	7
Hindus ..	**35,175,777**	17,540,434	17,635,343	**30,185,757**	15,051,506	15,134,251
Muslims ..	**4,284,306**	2,123,112	2,161,194	**985,448**	480,500	504,948
Tribal Religions ...	**2,409,409**	1,188,440	1,220,969	**2,399,470**	1,183,306	1,216,164
Indian Christians ...	**403,708**	199,910	203,798	**364,076**	180,643	183,433

TABLE XVII.

RACE, TRIBE OR CASTE.

CASTE OR TRIBE. *Religion.* District or State.	PERSONS.	MALES.	FEMALES.
1	2	3	4
*ASUR	2,024	1,159	865
Hindu	1,077	599	478
Christian	308	242	66
Tribal religion	639	318	321
BABHAN [BHUMIHAR BRAHMAN] *Hindu*	895,602	472,639	422,963
Patna	106,743	58,503	48,240
Gaya	104,701	27,777	76,924
Shahabad	61,176	32,369	28,807
Saran	95,422	47,735	47,687
Champaran	53,161	27,563	25,598
Muzaffarpur	165,446	83,728	81,718
Darbhanga	49,065	25,711	23,354
Monghyr	138,742	75,920	62,822
Bhagalpur	16,857	9,585	7,272
Purnea	3,693	2,203	1,490
Santal Parganas	11,027	6,074	4,953
Hazaribagh	21,467	11,283	10,184
Palamau	2,503	1,270	1,233
Manbhum	4,624	2,466	2,158
BANIA *Hindu*	220,071	113,828	106,243
Patna	10,626	5,632	4,994
Gaya	15,303	7,646	7,657
Shahabad	11,255	5,409	5,846
Saran	3,734	1,833	1,901
Champaran	5,068	2,811	2,257
Muzaffarpur	9,852	5,299	4,553
Darbhanga	7,666	3,664	4,002
Monghyr	36,944	18,999	17,945
Bhagalpur	23,912	12,568	11,344
Purnea	20,675	10,726	9,949
Santal Parganas	14,990	7,889	7,101
Cuttack	8,051	3,969	4,082
Balasore	9,200	4,668	4,532
Puri	2,697	1,354	1,343
Sambalpur	1,123	629	494
Hazaribagh	12,218	6,284	5,934
Ranchi	4,101	2,117	1,984
Palamau	2,045	1,079	966
Manbhum	10,076	5,705	4,371
Singhbhum	4,543	2,482	2,061
Orissa States	5,666	2,897	2,769
Chota Nagpur States	323	168	155
BANJARA	5,878	2,721	3,157
Hindu	5,818	2,691	3,127
Tribal religion	60	30	30
Sambalpur	2,112	1,021	1,091
Orissa States	3,766	1,700	2,066
BARHI [VISHVAKARMA BRAHMAN] *Hindu*	363,794	182,992	180,802
Patna	28,879	14,939	13,940
Gaya	49,272	24,820	24,452
Shahabad	16,695	8,367	8,328
Saran	19,571	9,722	9,849
Champaran	9,231	5,193	4,038
Muzaffarpur	14,588	6,956	7,632
Darbhanga	44,413	22,338	22,075
Monghyr	35,389	18,346	17,043
Bhagalpur	7,588	4,015	3,573
Purnea	22,450	11,486	10,964
Santal Parganas	8,923	4,405	4,518
Cuttack	25,622	12,564	13,058
Balasore	8,435	3,936	4,499
Puri	13,637	6,810	6,827
Hazaribagh	34,452	16,647	17,805
Palamau	9,359	4,642	4,717
Manbhum	3,642	2,048	1,594
Singhbhum	1,323	566	757
Orissa States	8,787	4,425	4,362
BATHUDI *Hindu*	73,891	36,516	37,375
BAURI	315,038	154,731	160,307
Hindu	314,979	154,701	160,278
Christian	59	30	29
Santal Parganas	23,891	11,808	12,083
Cuttack	78,553	37,122	41,431
Puri	86,796	42,407	44,389
Manbhum	121,321	61,249	60,072
BENTKAR	775	418	357
Hindu	587	324	263
Tribal religion	188	94	94
Orissa States	775	418	357
BHANDARI *Hindu*	121,092	58,341	62,751
Cuttack	42,884	20,252	22,632
Balasore	15,500	7,305	8,195
Angul	1,685	842	843
Puri	23,603	11,415	12,188
Sambalpur	5,938	2,941	2,997
Orissa States	30,164	14,924	15,240
Chota Nagpur States	1,318	662	656
BHOGTA	66,209	33,401	32,808
Hindu	66,054	33,327	32,727
Christian	12	7	5
Tribal religion	143	67	76
Gaya	4,114	2,163	1,951
Hazaribagh	31,703	16,084	15,619
Ranchi	18,595	9,264	9,331
Palamau	7,486	3,701	3,785
*BHUIYA	625,824	306,133	319,691
Hindu	621,062	303,800	317,262
Christian	36	19	17
Tribal religion	4,726	2,314	2,412
*BHUMIJ	274,058	136,255	137,803
Hindu	266,464	132,549	133,915
Christian	151	76	75
Tribal religion	7,443	3,630	3,813
BINJHIA [BINJHWAR]	71,608	35,204	36,404
Hindu	71,503	35,162	36,341
Tribal religion	105	42	63
Sambalpur	40,684	20,056	20,628
Ranchi	5,330	2,611	2,719
Orissa States	25,594	12,537	13,057
*BIRHOR	2,350	1,217	1,133
Hindu	1,723	878	845
Christian	1	1	...
Tribal religion	626	338	288
*BIRJIA	1,550	796	754
Hindu	938	509	429
Tribal religion	612	287	325
BRAHMAN *Hindu*	2,101,287	1,069,759	1,031,528
Patna	58,566	31,694	26,872
Gaya	74,297	36,688	37,609
Shahabad	199,544	99,573	99,971
Saran	176,875	89,532	87,343
Champaran	91,941	48,258	43,683
Muzaffarpur	130,927	65,724	65,203
Darbhanga	321,382	164,487	156,895
Monghyr	113,285	59,027	54,258
Bhagalpur	109,722	57,130	52,592
Purnea	34,940	18,849	16,091
Santal Parganas	42,668	22,978	19,690
Cuttack	186,021	89,859	96,162
Balasore	110,658	54,655	56,003
Angul	4,545	2,359	2,186
Puri	91,832	44,749	47,083
Sambalpur	35,493	17,489	18,004
Hazaribagh	36,804	19,376	17,428
Ranchi	11,379	6,549	4,830
Palamau	35,121	17,552	17,569
Manbhum	83,019	44,823	38,196
Singhbhum	15,900	9,204	6,696
Orissa States	132,432	67,058	65,374
Chota Nagpur States	3,936	2,146	1,790
CHAMAR *Hindu*	1,296,001	617,264	678,737
Patna	70,245	35,094	35,151
Gaya	103,903	49,303	54,600
Shahabad	138,921	64,756	74,165
Saran	140,763	63,068	77,695
Champaran	155,444	75,411	80,033
Muzaffarpur	155,474	71,573	83,901
Darbhanga	122,213	58,234	63,979
Monghyr	65,348	30,297	35,051
Bhagalpur	107,534	52,852	54,682
Purnea	26,173	13,386	12,787
Santal Parganas	42,774	21,364	21,410
Cuttack	16,954	7,632	9,322
Balasore	7,792	3,753	4,039
Angul	335	166	169
Puri	1,348	636	712
Sambalpur	6,457	3,312	3,145
Hazaribagh	65,675	31,460	34,215
Ranchi	4,368	2,164	2,204
Palamau	43,072	21,425	21,647
Manbhum	9,170	5,474	3,696
Singhbhum	4,335	2,013	2,322
Orissa States	7,426	3,741	3,685
Chota Nagpur States	277	150	127
CHASA *Hindu*	778,313	374,885	403,428
Cuttack	153,663	74,261	79,402
Balasore	11,541	5,672	5,869
Angul	59,598	28,964	30,634
Puri	231,021	110,078	120,943
Sambalpur	1,863	927	936
Orissa States	320,268	154,679	165,589
CHAUPAL *Hindu*	2,737	1,360	1,377
Purnea	2,737	1,360	1,377
*CHERO *Hindu*	17,906	8,968	8,938
CHIK BARAIK	30,037	14,929	15,108
Hindu	29,662	14,761	14,901
Christian	278	128	150
Tribal religion	97	40	57
Ranchi	29,739	14,812	14,927
DARZI *Hindu*	2,442	1,232	1,210
Cuttack	1,191	569	622
Puri	422	216	206
Sambalpur	263	126	137
Orissa States	352	195	157
DHANUK *Hindu*	547,308	267,572	279,736
Patna	35,687	17,568	18,119
Gaya	3,245	1,522	1,723
Saran	19,686	9,736	9,950
Champaran	12,663	6,454	6,209
Muzaffarpur	56,422	27,322	29,100
Darbhanga	147,210	70,249	76,961
Monghyr	114,133	55,634	58,499
Bhagalpur	97,315	47,986	49,329
Purnea	42,255	21,645	20,610
Santal Parganas	12,228	6,117	6,111
Palamau	3,778	1,882	1,896
DHOBI [DHOBA] *Hindu*	414,221	203,899	210,322
Patna	13,375	6,690	6,685
Gaya	18,138	8,980	9,158
Shahabad	17,364	8,696	8,668
Saran	20,899	10,165	10,734
Champaran	23,301	11,531	11,770
Muzaffarpur	34,594	16,719	17,875
Darbhanga	25,798	12,726	13,072
Monghyr	23,277	11,459	11,818
Bhagalpur	22,588	11,401	11,097
Purnea	9,240	4,943	4,297
Santal Parganas	8,449	4,317	4,132
Cuttack	45,949	21,727	24,222
Balasore	24,066	11,239	12,827
Angul	2,752	1,333	1,419
Puri	18,776	9,170	9,606
Sambalpur	9,148	4,441	4,707
Hazaribagh	13,781	6,663	7,118
Ranchi	5,693	2,817	2,876
Palamau	8,503	4,209	4,294
Manbhum	14,245	7,818	6,427
Singhbhum	5,885	3,075	2,810
Orissa States	47,522	23,254	24,268
Chota Nagpur States	858	436	422

* For the territorial distribution of these tribes *see* Table XVIII.

TABLE XVII—*continued.*

RACE, TRIBE OR CASTE.

CASTE OR TRIBE. *Religion.* District or State.	PERSONS.	MALES.	FEMALES.
1	2	3	4
DOM ...	*269,346*	*133,808*	*135,538*
Hindu	*269,340*	*133,802*	*135,538*
Muslim	*6*	*6*	.
Patna ...	4,812	2,389	2,423
Gaya ...	4,835	2,449	2,386
Shahabad	4,492	2,256	2,236
Saran ...	7,450	3,817	3,633
Champaran	7,186	3,743	3,443
Muzaffarpur	6,812	3,463	3,349
Darbhanga	7,098	3,467	3,631
Monghyr	11,359	5,630	5,729
Bhagalpur	12,384	6,059	6,325
Purnea ...	4,446	2,237	2,209
Santal Parganas	39,248	19,375	19,873
Cuttack ...	4,442	2,170	2,272
Balasore .	1,959	1,016	943
Angul ..	416	199	217
Puri ..	2,932	1,495	1,437
Hazaribagh	4,484	2,174	2,310
Ranchi ...	4,200	2,055	2,145
Palamau	2,458	1,229	1,229
Manbhum	24,673	12,609	12,064
Singhbhum	4,444	2,407	2,037
Orissa States	107,879	53,882	54,997
Chota Nagpur States	1,240	640	600
DOSADH [GAHLOT RAJPUT] *Hindu* ...	*1,290,936*	*633,336*	*657,600*
Patna ...	117,296	59,689	57,607
Gaya ..	130,558	64,539	66,019
Shahabad	93,399	46,477	46,922
Saran ...	84,460	39,466	44,994
Champaran	94,242	46,221	48,021
Muzaffarpur	200,219	96,076	104,143
Darbhanga	225,276	109,967	115,309
Monghyr	130,485	63,533	66,952
Bhagalpur	76,054	37,532	38,522
Purnea	51,653	26,149	25,504
Santal Parganas	10,959	5,457	5,503
Hazaribagh	28,784	13,544	15,240
Ranchi	1,683	873	810
Palamau	38,157	18,006	10,251
Manbhum	7,173	4,620	2,553
*GADABA *Hindu*	*277*	*139*	*138*
GANDA *Hindu* ...	*245,799*	*121,144*	*124,655*
Sambalpur	98,953	48,755	50,198
Orissa States	146,682	72,297	74,385
GAURA ...	*890,702*	*432,062*	*458,640*
Hindu ...	*890,694*	*432,007*	*458,587*
Tribal religion	*108*	*55*	*53*
Cuttack ..	145,132	67,671	77,461
Balasore	69,157	32,214	36,943
Angul ...	14,187	6,953	7,305
Puri ...	49,981	24,418	25,563
Sambalpur	101,861	49,894	51,967
Singhbhum	46,846	22,918	23,928
Orissa States	450,699	221,737	228,962
Chota Nagpur States	12,839	6,228	6,611
GHASI ...	*76,320*	*38,244*	*38,076*
Hindu ...	*75,579*	*37,831*	*37,748*
Christian	*33*	*16*	*17*
Tribal religion	*708*	*397*	*311*
Sambalpur	8,462	4,134	4,328
Hazaribagh	4,903	2,431	2,482
Ranchi	20,909	10,455	10,454
Palamau	2,086	1,065	1,021
Manbhum	6,753	3,369	3,384
Singhbhum	7,582	4,187	3,395
Orissa States	22,116	10,866	11,250
Chota Nagpur States	3,509	1,747	1,762
GHATWAR ...	*72,588*	*35,627*	*36,961*
Hindu ...	*72,580*	*35,620*	*36,960*
Christian	*8*	*7*	*1*
Hazaribagh	54,744	25,698	29,046
Manbhum	17,824	9,918	7,906
GHUSURIA *Hindu* ...	*1,846*	*805*	*1,041*
Cuttack ...	745	255	490
Balasore ..	655	340	315
Puri .	446	210	236
GOALA [AHIR, GOPA, YADAVA] *Hindu* ...	*3,455,141*	*1,765,379*	*1,689,762*
Patna ..	277,263	145,951	131,312
Gaya ..	072,611	101,190	181,675
Shahabad	273,005	140,328	133,677
Saran ...	332,608	167,786	164,822
Champaran	209,875	107,210	102,665
Muzaffarpur	354,607	179,683	174,924
Darbhanga	400,312	202,902	197,410
Monghyr	279,407	142,689	136,718
Bhagalpur	374,677	191,310	183,367
Purnea ...	134,934	70,610	64,324
Santal Parganas	123,177	62,860	60,317
Hazaribagh	156,430	77,136	79,294
Ranchi ...	39,486	19,974	19,512
Palamau	50,268	25,655	24,613
Manbhum	40,996	22,064	18,932
Singhbhum	35,285	18,084	17,201
GODRA *Hindu*	*1,553*	*753*	*800*
Angul ...	712	350	362
Orissa States	791	377	414
GOKHA *Hindu*	*48,622*	*23,660*	*24,962*
Cuttack	14,172	6,884	7,288
Balasore	33,912	16,505	17,407
*GOND ...	*255,752*	*124,711*	*131,041*
Hindu ...	*255,029*	*124,284*	*130,745*
Christian	*15*	*9*	*6*
Tribal religion	*708*	*418*	*290*
GORAIT ...	*5,682*	*2,836*	*2,846*
Hindu ..	*5,655*	*2,823*	*2,832*
Tribal religion	*27*	*13*	*14*
Ranchi ...	5,682	2,836	2,846

CASTE OR TRIBE. *Religion.* District or State.	PERSONS.	MALES.	FEMALES.
1	2	3	4
GURIA *Hindu* ...	*153,961*	*73,597*	*80,364*
Cuttack	73,925	34,722	39,203
Balasore	21,341	10,382	10,959
Angul ...	1,526	740	786
Puri ...	24,023	11,684	12,339
Sambalpur	1,066	485	581
Orissa States	31,446	15,311	16,135
Chota Nagpur States	462	226	236
HAJJAM [NAI, NAPIT, NAI BRAHMAN] *Hindu.*	*456,779*	*227,586*	*229,193*
Patna ..	30,885	15,778	15,107
Gaya ..	44,788	21,413	23,375
Shahabad	28,246	13,725	14,521
Saran ...	35,794	17,434	18,360
Champaran	26,105	13,162	12,943
Muzaffarpur	45,474	21,667	23,807
Darbhanga	37,279	18,179	19,100
Monghyr	44,798	22,106	22,692
Bhagalpur	38,587	20,028	18,559
Purnea ...	19,084	10,064	9,020
Santal Parganas	23,497	12,097	11,400
Hazaribagh	33,141	16,582	16,559
Ranchi ..	9,781	4,934	4,847
Palamau	10,545	5,336	5,210
Manbhum	24,936	13,028	11,908
Singhbhum	3,829	2,063	1,766
HALALKHOR	*22,289*	*10,988*	*11,301*
Hindu	*20,742*	*10,251*	*10,491*
Muslim	*1,547*	*737*	*810*
Patna ...	2,314	1,224	1,090
Gaya .	1,825	945	880
Shahabad	2,525	1,247	1,278
Saran ...	2,898	1,456	1,442
Champaran	3,309	1,651	1,658
Muzaffarpur	3,964	1,929	2,035
Darbhanga	4,284	2,006	2,278
HARI *Hindu*	*115,613*	*57,481*	*58,132*
Bhagalpur	3,419	1,719	1,700
Purnea ...	30,650	15,870	14,780
Santal Parganas	3,424	1,666	1,758
Cuttack	8,209	3,629	4,580
Balasore	5,515	2,682	2,833
Angul ...	4,001	1,931	2,070
Puri ...	11,746	5,162	6,584
Hazaribagh	1,479	744	735
Manbhum	20,786	10,514	10,272
Singhbhum	2,647	1,982	665
Orissa States	21,921	10,628	11,293
Chota Nagpur States	251	138	113
*HO ...	*523,158*	*253,713*	*269,445*
Hindu	*129,654*	*64,010*	*65,644*
Christian	*2,078*	*992*	*1,086*
Tribal religion	*391,426*	*188,711*	*202,715*
IRIKA *Hindu*	*332*	*163*	*169*
Puri ...	332	163	169
JOLAHA [SHEIKH MOMIN] *Muslim* ...	*983,843*	*479,726*	*504,117*
Patna ...	36,372	17,367	19,005
Gaya ..	87,382	38,437	48,945
Shahabad	52,316	24,456	27,860
Saran ...	99,310	46,771	52,539
Champaran	97,598	48,491	49,107
Muzaffarpur	92,544	43,333	49,211
Darbhanga	67,333	33,005	34,328
Monghyr	34,815	16,960	17,855
Bhagalpur	32,470	16,228	16,242
Purnea .	16,786	8,107	8,679
Santal Parganas	125,499	63,568	61,931
Hazaribagh	110,418	54,891	55,527
Ranchi ..	27,679	15,279	12,400
Palamau .	44,525	22,559	21,966
Manbhum	56,477	29,069	27,408
Singhbhum	1,460	765	715
Chota Nagpur States	263	124	139
*JUANG ...	*15,024*	*7,332*	*7,692*
Hindu	*7,887*	*3,855*	*4,032*
Tribal religion	*7,137*	*3,477*	*3,660*
KAHAR *Hindu* ...	*524,030*	*255,269*	*268,761*
Patna ...	97,359	49,197	48,162
Gaya ..	117,444	54,219	63,225
Shahabad	67,574	32,871	34,703
Saran ...	11,212	4,938	6,274
Champaran	10,523	5,207	5,316
Muzaffarpur	25,844	12,260	13,584
Darbhanga	4,149	2,213	1,936
Monghyr	48,511	23,505	25,006
Bhagalpur	24,621	12,066	12,555
Purnea ...	9,277	4,904	4,373
Santal Parganas	19,115	9,587	9,528
Hazaribagh	31,501	15,195	16,306
Ranchi ...	5,705	2,872	2,833
Palamau	35,489	17,462	18,027
Manbhum	14,084	7,892	6,192
Singhbhum	1,622	881	741
KAMAR [LOHAR, VISHVAKARMA BRAHMAN].	*539,809*	*268,849*	*264,050*
Hindu ...	*527,100*	*265,930*	*261,170*
Christian	*947*	*423*	*524*
Tribal religion	*4,852*	*2,496*	*2,356*
Patna .	7,650	3,979	3,671
Gaya ...	21,829	11,216	10,613
Shahabad	31,789	15,929	15,860
Saran ...	50,110	24,686	25,424
Champaran	32,446	16,321	16,125
Muzaffarpur	42,842	21,145	21,697
Darbhanga	18,414	9,543	8,871
Monghyr	17,837	8,811	9,026
Bhagalpur	29,211	15,320	13,891
Purnea ...	17,326	8,911	8,415
Santal Parganas	26,412	13,693	12,719
Cuttack	15,781	7,648	8,133
Balasore	10,890	5,480	5,410

*For the territorial distribution of these tribes, *see* Table XVIII.

TABLE XVII—*continued.*

Race, Tribe or Caste.

CASTE OR TRIBE. *Religion.* District or State.	PERSONS.	MALES.	FEMALES.
1	2	3	4
KAMAR—*concld.*			
Angul ...	1,869	970	899
Puri ...	6,970	3,424	3,546
Sambalpur	6,697	3,340	3,357
Hazaribagh	13,253	6,742	6,511
Ranchi ...	54,497	27,776	26,721
Palamau ...	15,172	7,707	7,465
Manbhum	35,279	18,315	16,964
Singhbhum	17,401	8,418	8,983
Orissa States	55,773	27,742	28,031
Chota Nagpur States	3,451	1,733	1,718
KANDRA *Hindu*	*155,113*	*74,619*	*80,494*
Cuttack ...	97,356	46,219	51,137
Balasore ...	30,794	15,309	15,485
Puri ...	17,617	8,616	0,001
Orissa States	8,655	4,143	4,512
KANDU *Hindu*	*506,384*	*254,770*	*251,614*
Patna ...	31,734	16,436	15,298
Gaya ...	24,606	12,443	12,163
Shahabad	60,586	31,358	29,228
Saran ...	80,942	40,666	40,276
Champaran	76,199	37,704	38,495
Muzaffarpur	89,765	44,754	45,011
Darbhanga	28,493	15,031	13,462
Monghyr	66,479	32,649	33,830
Bhagalpur	20,666	10,199	10,467
Purnea ...	6,193	3,282	2,911
Santal Parganas	2,497	1,260	1,237
Hazaribagh	6,450	3,161	3,289
Palamau ...	8,951	4,404	4,547
KANJAR *Hindu*	*2,566*	*1,294*	*1,272*
Purnea ...	2,215	1,144	1,071
KARAN *Hindu*	*146,750*	*70,401*	*76,349*
Cuttack ...	56,859	25,479	31,380
Balasore ...	22,354	10,943	11,411
Angul ...	1,478	792	686
Puri ...	34,770	16,718	18,052
Sambalpur	2,443	1,214	1,229
Singhbhum	896	479	417
Orissa States	27,156	14,347	12,809
Chota Nagpur States	794	429	365
*KARMALI	*8,632*	*4,852*	*3,780*
Hindu ...	*8,297*	*4,698*	*3,599*
Christian	*32*	*7*	*25*
Tribal religion	*303*	*147*	*156*
KAYASTH *Hindu*	*383,435*	*201,648*	*181,787*
Patna ...	34,061	18,980	15,081
Gaya ...	38,112	19,429	18,683
Shahabad	36,446	18,653	17,793
Saran ...	39,487	19,849	19,638
Champaran	27,697	14,896	12,801
Muzaffarpur	39,775	20,127	19,648
Darbhanga	40,596	20,403	20,193
Monghyr	24,030	12,805	11,225
Bhagalpur	21,893	11,704	10,189
Purnea ...	9,046	5,142	3,904
Santal Parganas	10,769	5,855	4,914
Cuttack ...	6,454	3,224	3,230
Balasore ...	2,452	1,228	1,224
Puri ...	2,654	1,343	1,311
Hazaribagh	12,075	6,006	5,460
Ranchi ...	5,174	3,115	2,059
Palamau ...	4,633	2,487	2,146
Manbhum	14,487	8,091	6,396
Singhbhum	9,647	5,532	4,115
Chota Nagpur States	1,103	543	560
KELA *Hindu*	*9,493*	*4,637*	*4,856*
Cuttack ...	3,415	1,691	1,724
Balasore ...	2,736	1,284	1,452
Angul ...	214	106	108
Puri ...	1,334	655	679
Orissa States	1,756	881	875
KEWAT *Hindu*	*471,389*	*228,647*	*242,742*
Champaran	2,725	1,354	1,371
Muzaffarpur	7,566	3,506	4,060
Darbhanga	77,512	35,990	41,522
Monghyr	2,250	1,016	1,234
Bhagalpur	52,693	25,938	26,755
Purnea ...	36,854	18,878	17,976
Santal Parganas	6,008	2,976	3,032
Cuttack ...	78,498	37,740	40,740
Balasore ...	14,204	7,062	7,142
Angul ...	3,111	1,525	1,586
Puri ...	33,754	16,348	17,406
Sambalpur	36,965	17,837	19,128
Hazaribagh	3,349	1,094	1,655
Manbhum	9,002	4,523	4,479
Singhbhum	3,269	1,661	1,608
Orissa States	99,976	48,560	51,416
Chota Nagpur States	241	138	103
KHANDAIT *Hindu* ...	*1,010,146*	*475,636*	*534,510*
Cuttack ...	548,664	254,907	293,757
Balasore	199,750	94,214	105,536
Angul ...	848	427	421
Puri ...	112,571	53,510	59,061
Singhbhum	2,691	1,536	1,155
Orissa States	144,026	70,223	73,803
Chota Nagpur States	1,253	625	628
*KHARIA ...	*146,037*	*72,376*	*73,661*
Hindu ..	*51,566*	*25,460*	*26,106*
Christian	*63,725*	*31,350*	*32,375*
Tribal religion	*30,746*	*15,566*	*15,180*
*KHARWAR	*64,570*	*32,692*	*31,878*
Hindu	*64,558*	*32,685*	*31,873*
Christian	*9*	*5*	*4*
Tribal religion	*3*	*2*	*1*
*KHETAURI	*26,787*	*12,655*	*14,132*
Hindu ...	*26,773*	*12,653*	*14,120*
Tribal religion	*14*	*2*	*12*

CASTE OR TRIBE. *Religion.* District or State.	PERSONS.	MALES.	FEMALES.
1	2	3	4
*KHOND [KANDH] ...	*315,709*	*152,528*	*163,181*
Hindu ...	*167,521*	*80,706*	*86,815*
Tribal religion	*148,188*	*71,822*	*76,366*
KISAN [NAGESIA] ...	*98,585*	*48,077*	*50,508*
Hindu ...	*64,689*	*31,733*	*32,956*
Christian	*3,397*	*1,540*	*1,857*
Tribal religion	*30,499*	*14,804*	*15,695*
Sambalpur	22,396	10,802	11,594
Ranchi ...	6,305	3,218	3,087
Palamau ...	6,293	3,117	3,176
Orissa States	63,219	30,680	32,539
KOIRI [DANGI, KUSHWAHA KSHATRIYA] *Hindu*	*1,301,988*	*661,899*	*640,089*
Patna ...	71,239	37,015	34,224
Gaya ..	158,073	80,796	77,277
Shahabad	148,659	75,838	72,821
Saran ...	168,060	85,676	82,384
Champaran	116,546	60,549	55,997
Muzaffarpur	144,877	72,607	72,270
Darbhanga	147,787	74,404	73,383
Monghyr	102,030	51,666	50,364
Bhagalpur	90,238	45,635	44,603
Purnea ...	24,694	12,820	11,874
Santal Parganas	18,629	9,302	9,237
Hazaribagh	63,632	31,276	32,356
Ranchi ...	9,145	4,553	4,592
Palamau ...	28,124	14,033	14,091
Manbhum	9,740	5,289	4,451
KOLI [KULI] *Hindu*	*5,001*	*2,540*	*2,461*
Sambalpur	2,953	1,500	1,453
Orissa States	2,014	1,021	993
KOLTA *Hindu*	*163,757*	*81,487*	*82,270*
Sambalpur	111,510	55,231	56,279
Orissa States	52,179	26,231	25,958
KORA [KUDA]	*49,036*	*24,726*	*24,310*
Hindu ...	*46,685*	*23,478*	*23,207*
Christian	*13*	*7*	*6*
Tribal religion	*2,338*	*1,241*	*1,097*
Monghyr	2,312	1,459	853
Santal Parganas	3,304	1,656	1,648
Sambalpur	11,606	5,630	5,976
Manbhum	15,518	8,146	7,372
Orissa States	13,027	6,445	6,582
Chota Nagpur States	728	362	366
*KORWA	*13,021*	*6,519*	*6,502*
Hindu ...	*1,462*	*781*	*681*
Christian	*6*	*5*	*1*
Tribal religion	*11,553*	*5,733*	*5,820*
KUMHAR *Hindu*	*599,038*	*301,441*	*297,597*
Patna ...	26,252	13,512	12,740
Gaya ...	32,343	16,048	16,295
Shahabad	25,463	12,976	12,487
Saran ...	34,507	18,208	16,299
Champaran	21,914	10,933	10,981
Muzaffarpur	40,225	19,767	20,458
Darbhanga	32,198	16,600	15,598
Monghyr ...	33,253	16,780	16,473
Bhagalpur	29,880	14,886	14,994
Purnea ...	13,355	6,872	6,483
Santal Parganas	31,233	15,839	15,394
Cuttack ...	27,901	13,728	14,173
Balasore ...	13,177	6,413	6,764
Angul ...	2,677	1,271	1,406
Puri	12,852	6,418	6,434
Sambalpur	9,201	4,590	4,611
Hazaribagh	33,826	16,854	16,972
Ranchi ...	21,074	10,682	10,392
Palamau ...	11,403	5,554	5,849
Manbhum	56,968	28,793	28,175*
Singhbhum	13,855	7,226	6,629
Orissa States	71,052	35,300	35,752
Chota Nagpur States	4,429	2,191	2,238
KURARIAR *Hindu*	*631*	*251*	*380*
Purnea ...	631	251	380
KURMI [KURMI KSHATRIYA] *Hindu*	*1,452,724*	*725,078*	*727,646*
Patna ...	173,146	91,076	82,070
Gaya ...	42,459	22,029	20,430
Shahabad	59,040	29,718	29,322
Saran ..	108,512	52,683	55,829
Champaran	100,981	50,085	50,896
Muzaffarpur	130,682	62,163	68,520
Darbhanga	67,295	33,281	34,014
Monghyr	58,891	29,774	29,117
Bhagalpur	35,645	18,115	17,530
Purnea ...	12,774	7,192	5,582
Santal Parganas	22,630	11,101	11,529
Hazaribagh	105,725	52,229	53,496
Ranchi ...	62,198	29,904	32,294
Palamau ...	5,985	2,977	3,008
Manbhum	323,068	161,072	161,996
Singhbhum	22,463	11,486	10,977
Orissa States	95,422	47,178	48,244
Chota Nagpur States	25,807	13,015	12,792
LALBEGI	*157*	*86*	*71*
Hindu	*105*	*55*	*50*
Muslim	*52*	*31*	*21*
Patna ..	102	58	44
MAHLI ...	*59,834*	*30,292*	*29,542*
Hindu ...	*41,444*	*21,258*	*20,186*
Christian	*412*	*184*	*228*
Tribal religion	*17,978*	*8,850*	*9,128*
Santal Parganas	17,687	8,640	9,047
Hazaribagh	4,592	2,227	2,365
Ranchi ...	17,002	8,805	8,197
Manbhum	10,850	5,608	5,242
Singhbhum	4,406	2,477	1,929
Orissa States	3,709	1,795	1,914
Chota Nagpur States	713	365	348

* For the territorial distribution of these tribes, *see* Table XVIII.

TABLE XVII—*concluded.*

RACE, TRIBE OR CASTE.

CASTE OR TRIBE. *Religion.* District or State.	PERSONS.	MALES.	FEMALES.
1	2	3	4
MAHURIA *Hindu*	*2,389*	*1,168*	*1,221*
Cuttack	726	347	379
Balasore	1,226	618	608
*MAL PAHARIA	*37,437*	*18,729*	*18,708*
Hindu	*205*	*112*	*93*
Christian	*62*	*33*	*29*
Tribal religion	*37,170*	*18,584*	*18,586*
MALI [MALAKAR] *Hindu*	*167,148*	*83,917*	*83,231*
Patna	5,887	3,050	2,837
Gaya	7,193	3,509	3,684
Shahabad	5,182	2,668	2,514
Saran	6,030	2,920	3,110
Champaran	5,516	2,937	2,579
Muzaffarpur	11,110	5,430	5,680
Darbhanga	6,542	3,431	3,111
Monghyr	5,719	2,914	2,805
Bhagalpur	3,067	1,746	1,321
Purnea	5,590	2,888	2,702
Santal Parganas	2,919	1,263	1,656
Cuttack	6,918	3,374	3,544
Balasore	1,068	522	546
Angul	1,116	539	577
Puri	13,775	6,737	7,038
Sambalpur	15,403	7,402	8,001
Hazaribagh	1,501	801	700
Manbhum	1,751	1,169	582
Singhbhum	3,202	1,956	1,246
Orissa States	56,454	27,929	28,525
MALLAH *Hindu*	*459,560*	*224,173*	*235,387*
Patna	16,327	8,115	8,212
Gaya	13,166	6,387	6,779
Shahabad	15,942	7,451	8,491
Saran	22,657	10,273	12,384
Champaran	75,327	37,142	38,185
Muzaffarpur	128,416	63,398	65,018
Darbhanga	142,264	69,712	72,552
Monghyr	10,966	5,068	5,898
Bhagalpur	11,488	5,730	5,758
Purnea	2,402	1,231	1,181
Hazaribagh	1,618	790	828
Palamau	15,670	7,639	8,031
Singhbhum	1,380	1,117	263
MANGAN *Hindu*	*184*	*79*	*105*
Sambalpur	184	79	105
MOCHI *Hindu*	*22,863*	*11,733*	*11,130*
Santal Parganas	5,827	2,907	2,920
Manbhum	16,960	8,786	8,174
Singhbhum	76	40	36
*MUNDA	*549,764*	*270,150*	*279,614*
Hindu	*163,776*	*80,212*	*83,564*
Christian	*133,506*	*66,435*	*67,071*
Tribal religion	*252,482*	*123,503*	*128,979*
MUSAHAR *Hindu*	*720,051*	*361,825*	*358,226*
Patna	50,631	25,990	24,641
Gaya	64,611	32,505	32,106
Shahabad	20,950	10,951	9,999
Saran	7,702	3,753	3,950
Champaran	46,630	23,062	23,568
Muzaffarpur	46,310	22,314	23,996
Darbhanga	96,161	47,295	48,866
Monghyr	147,942	74,008	73,934
Bhagalpur	99,592	50,197	49,395
Purnea	113,554	57,877	55,677
Santal Parganas	15,739	7,454	8,285
Hazaribagh	4,142	2,036	2,106
Manbhum	5,571	3,513	2,058
NAT [NETUA] *Hindu*	*9,628*	*4,599*	*5,029*
Patna	1,039	522	517
Gaya	883	441	442
Shahabad	2,091	1,029	1,062
Saran	1,449	427	1,022
Purnea	2,974	1,537	1,437
*ORAON	*637,111*	*312,428*	*324,683*
Hindu	*222,152*	*108,358*	*113,794*
Christian	*145,129*	*72,123*	*73,006*
Tribal religion	*269,830*	*131,947*	*137,883*
PAHIRA *Hindu*	*140*	*74*	*66*
Manbhum	140	74	66
PAN [PANIKA]	*418,169*	*204,095*	*214,074*
Hindu	*411,770*	*200,954*	*210,816*
Christian	*105*	*54*	*51*
Tribal religion	*6,294*	*3,087*	*3,207*
Cuttack	116,105	55,692	60,413
Balasore	59,545	28,443	31,102
Angul	28,868	14,196	14,672
Puri	6,311	3,146	3,165
Sambalpur	3,453	1,669	1,784
Ranchi	11,105	5,590	5,515
Orissa States	192,093	94,999	97,094
PARHAIYA	*10,382*	*5,386*	*4,996*
Hindu	*10,145*	*5,243*	*4,902*
Tribal religion	*237*	*143*	*94*
Palamau	9,671	5,004	4,667
PASI *Hindu*	*172,061*	*87,340*	*84,721*
Patna	39,340	19,738	19,602
Gaya	50,979	25,631	25,348
Shahabad	12,872	6,414	6,458
Saran	5,338	2,799	2,539
Champaran	3,147	1,725	1,422
Muzaffarpur	10,159	5,174	4,985
Darbhanga	13,330	6,529	6,801
Monghyr	17,265	8,874	8,391
Bhagalpur	6,405	3,147	3,258
Santal Parganas	3,312	1,746	1,566
Hazaribagh	4,769	2,356	2,413
Palamau	1,918	923	995
Manbhum	2,507	1,899	608
RAJPUT [CHHATRI, KSHATRIYA] *Hindu*	*1,412,440*	*740,500*	*671,940*
Patna	81,077	43,204	37,873
Gaya	120,364	63,949	56,415
Shahabad	200,253	100,457	99,796
Saran	251,348	125,859	125,489
Champaran	83,625	44,578	39,047
Muzaffarpur	162,168	84,586	77,582
Darbhanga	89,352	48,084	41,268
Monghyr	71,915	40,243	31,672
Bhagalpur	69,052	39,895	29,157
Purnea	55,106	30,523	24,583
Santal Parganas	21,200	11,469	9,731
Cuttack	15,167	7,268	7,899
Balasore	3,055	1,510	1,545
Puri	5,290	2,617	2,673
Sambalpur	5,481	2,708	2,773
Hazaribagh	35,760	18,547	17,213
Ranchi	24,108	12,521	11,587
Palamau	33,065	17,185	15,880
Manbhum	30,776	17,175	13,601
Singhbhum	12,977	7,264	5,713
Orissa States	39,254	19,590	19,664
Chota Nagpur States	1,595	861	734
RAJWAR	*133,952*	*65,165*	*68,787*
Hindu	*133,935*	*65,157*	*68,778*
Christian	*17*	*8*	*9*
Patna	4,180	2,064	2,116
Gaya	50,487	24,181	26,306
Shahabad	9,884	4,931	4,953
Santal Parganas	10,866	4,930	5,936
Hazaribagh	9,480	4,712	4,768
Palamau	9,188	4,587	4,601
Manbhum	38,930	19,362	19,568
*SANTAL	*1,712,133*	*855,103*	*857,030*
Hindu	*586,499*	*293,807*	*292,692*
Christian	*13,279*	*6,754*	*6,525*
Tribal religion	*1,112,355*	*554,542*	*557,813*
*SAURIA PAHARIA [MALER]	*59,891*	*30,555*	*29,336*
Hindu	*112*	*54*	*58*
Christian	*449*	*182*	*267*
Tribal religion	*59,330*	*30,319*	*29,011*
*SAVAR [SAWARA]	*244,678*	*118,593*	*126,085*
Hindu	*244,656*	*118,576*	*126,080*
Tribal religion	*22*	*17*	*5*
SIYAL *Hindu*	*9,281*	*4,506*	*4,775*
Cuttack	2,136	967	1,169
Angul	318	140	178
Puri	3,141	1,590	1,551
Sambalpur	868	420	448
Orissa States	2,818	1,389	1,429
TANTI [TATWA] *Hindu*	*689,791*	*333,431*	*356,360*
Patna	13,731	6,862	6,869
Gaya	3,264	1,681	1,583
Shahabad	7,698	3,709	3,989
Saran	7,588	3,630	3,958
Champaran	33,576	16,559	17,017
Muzaffarpur	56,811	26,621	30,190
Darbhanga	83,941	40,067	43,874
Monghyr	94,506	44,632	49,874
Bhagalpur	88,745	43,472	45,273
Purnea	62,582	31,462	31,120
Santal Parganas	13,146	6,575	6,571
Cuttack	58,673	28,308	30,365
Balasore	47,570	22,804	24,766
Angul	1,639	794	845
Puri	16,825	8,142	8,683
Hazaribagh	1,857	1,003	854
Manbhum	11,713	5,639	6,074
Singhbhum	38,038	18,003	20,035
Orissa States	40,139	19,603	20,536
Chota Nagpur States	5,813	2,868	2,945
TELI *Hindu*	*1,210,496*	*603,484*	*607,012*
Patna	47,501	24,398	23,103
Gaya	63,663	31,838	31,825
Shahabad	48,514	24,320	24,194
Saran	70,415	35,162	35,253
Champaran	69,548	35,345	34,203
Muzaffarpur	100,280	49,914	50,366
Darbhanga	91,447	45,539	45,908
Monghyr	60,007	29,912	30,095
Bhagalpur	73,705	37,485	36,220
Purnea	35,323	17,965	17,358
Santal Parganas	54,679	28,101	26,578
Cuttack	68,142	31,390	36,752
Balasore	43,783	21,562	22,221
Angul	3,790	1,992	1,798
Puri	36,438	16,735	19,703
Sambalpur	37,197	18,426	18,771
Hazaribagh	65,835	32,772	33,063
Ranchi	35,602	17,902	17,700
Palamau	21,296	10,642	10,654
Manbhum	48,457	24,680	23,777
Singhbhum	12,188	5,859	6,329
Orissa States	117,556	58,005	59,551
Chota Nagpur States	3,070	1,540	1,530
*THARU *Hindu*	*37,338*	*19,154*	*18,184*
TURI	*54,573*	*27,190*	*27,383*
Hindu	*54,041*	*26,914*	*27,127*
Christian	*9*	*6*	*3*
Tribal religion	*523*	*270*	*253*
Gaya	2,047	1,059	988
Purnea	2,957	1,442	1,515
Santal Parganas	3,644	1,873	1,771
Sambalpur	1,194	566	628
Hazaribagh	30,634	14,976	15,658
Ranchi	7,524	3,772	3,752
Palamau	2,923	1,444	1,479
Manbhum	2,607	1,592	1,015

*For the territorial distribution of these tribes, *see* Table XVIII.

TABLE XVIII.

VARIATION OF POPULATION OF SELECTED TRIBES.

This is a new table, showing in detail the territorial distribution of the more important aboriginal and semi-aboriginal tribes of the province, and the variations in their numbers during the last forty years.

2. Where statistics are given for localities smaller than a district, the unit of locality adopted is the *revenue thana*, except in those cases where it is expressly stated to be the subdivision.

TABLE XVIII.

VARIATION OF POPULATION OF SELECTED TRIBES.

TRIBE, RELIGION AND LOCALITY.	PERSONS					VARIATION (Increase +, Decrease −)				Net variation 1891 to 1931	MALES					FEMALES					REMARKS.
	1931.	1921	1911	1901	1891	1921 to 1931	1911 to 1921.	1901 to 1911	1891 to 1901		1931.	1921.	1911	1901	1891.	1931	1921	1911.	1901	1891.	
1	2	3	4	5	6	7	8	9	10	11	12	13	14	15	16	17	18	19	20	21	22
Asur	**2,024**	(a)**2,245**	**3,716**	**2,784**	§**2,303**	**−221**	**−1,471**	**+932**	**+481**	**−279**	**1,159**	(a)**1,124**	**1,822**	**1,418**	§**1,170**	**365**	(a)**1,121**	**1,894**	**1,366**	§**1,133**	(a) Excludes *Palamau*, for which figures are not available.
Hindu	*1,077*	*611*	*383*	*457*	*	*+466*	*+278*	*−124*			*599*	*294*	*150*	*241*	*	*478*	*317*	*183*	*216*	*	
Christian	*308*	*559*	*284*	*21*	†	*−251*	*+275*	*+263*			*243*	*298*	*143*	*13*	†	*66*	*261*	*141*	*8*	†	
Tribal religion	*639*	*1,075*	*3,099*	*2,306*	*	*−436*	*−2,024*	*+793*			*318*	*539*	*1,529*	*1,164*	*	*321*	*548*	*1,570*	*1,142*	*	
RANCHI	**1,940**	2,245	3 867	2,722	§1,639	−305	−1,432	+945	+1,083	+301	**1,107**	1,124	1,794	1,300	§801	**833**	1,121	1,873	1,332	§838	
Hindu	*993*	*611*	*284*	*457*	*	*+382*	*+327*	*−173*			*547*	*294*	*122*	*241*	*	*446*	*317*	*162*	*216*	*	
Christian	*308*	*559*	*284*	*21*	†	*−251*	*+275*	*+263*			*242*	*298*	*143*	*13*	†	*66*	*261*	*141*	*8*	†	
Tribal religion	*639*	*1,075*	*3,099*	*2 344*	*	*−436*	*−2,024*	*+855*			*318*	*539*	*1,529*	*1,136*	*	*321*	*543*	*1,570*	*1,108*	*	
Lohardaga	**387**	401	*	‡265		−14			+265	+387	**202**	195	*	‡119		**185**	206	*	‡146		
Bishunpur	**275**	415	*	‡1,499		−140			+1,499	+719	**145**	204	*	‡779		**130**	211	*	‡720		
Ghaghra ..	**444**	582	*			−138					**218**	295	*			**226**	287	*			
Chainpur	**809**	707	*	‡910	§707	+102			+203	+102	**520**	364	*	‡463	§337	**289**	343	*	‡447	§370	
Elsewhere ..	**25**	140	*	‡27	§932	−115			−905	−907	**22**	66	*	‡16	§464	**3**	74	*	‡11	§468	
PALAMAU	**84**	†	49	62	664			−13	−602	−580	**52**	†	28	28	369	**32**	†	21	34	295	
Hindu ...	*84*	†	*49*		*			*+49*		.	*59*	†	*28*		*	*33*	†	*21*		*	
Tribal ..		†		*69*	*		.	*−69*	..			†	...	*28*	*		†		*34*	*	
Mahuadanr	**67**	†	*	*				..		+67	**36**	†	*	*		**31**	†	*	*		
Elsewhere ..	**17**	†	*	*	664					−647	**16**	†	*	*	369	**1**	†	*	*	295	
Bathudi	**73,891**	(a)**59,183**	**54,418**	**44,670**	**40,489**	**+14,708**	**+4,765**	**+9,748**	**+4,181**	**+33,402**	**36,516**	(b)**29,063**	**27,613**	**22,149**	**20,312**	**37,375**	(a)**30,120**	**26,805**	**22,521**	**20,177**	(a) Excludes *Singhbhum*, for which figures are not available
Hindu	*73,891*	*59,167*	*54,414*	*33 086*	*	*+14,724*	*+4,753*	*+21,328*			*36,516*	*29,056*	*27,611*	*16,368*	*	*37 375*	*30,111*	*26 803*	*16,718*	*	
Tribal religion		*16*	*4*	*11,584*	*	*−16*	*+12*	*−11,580*				*7*	*2*	*5,781*	*		*9*	*2*	*5,803*	*	
SINGHBHUM *Hindu*	**998**	†	994	944	682	.		+50	+262	+316	**519**	†	520	479	323	**479**	†	474	465	359	
Kolhan	**26**	†	*	*	*					...	**26**	†	*	*	*		†	*	*	*	
Ghatsila	**972**	†	*	*	*						**493**	†	*	*	*	**479**	†	*	*	*	
ORISSA STATES	**72,893**	59,183	53,424	43,726	39,807	+13,710	+5,759	+9 698	+3,919	+33,086	**35,997**	29 063	27 093	21,670	19,989	**36,896**	30,120	26,331	22 056	19,818	
Hindu	*72 893*	*59,167*	*53,420*	*32,142*	*	*+13 726*	*+5,747*	*+21,278*	.		*35,997*	*29,056*	*27,091*	*15,889*	*	*36,896*	*30,111*	*26,329*	*16 253*	*	
Tribal religion		*16*	*4*	*11,584*	*	*−16*	*+12*	*−11,580*				*7*	*2*	*5,781*	*		*9*	*2*	*5,803*	*	
Mayurbhanj	**45,049**	*	*	*	26,018					+19,031	**22,345**	*	*	*	13,989	**22,704**	*	*	*	13,029	
Nilgiri .	**4,202**	*	*	*	2,307					+1,895	**2,063**	*	*	*	1,123	**2,139**	*	*	*	1,184	
Keonjhar .	**23,637**	*	*	*	11 482					+12,155	**11,584**	*	*	*	5,877	**12,053**	*	*	*	5,605	
Elsewhere .	**5**	*	*	*			..			+5	**5**	*	*	*			*	*	*		
Bhuiya	**625,824**	**578,810**	**663,954**	**618,938**	**480,055**	**+47,014**	**−85,144**	**+45,016**	**+138,883**	**+145,769**	**306,133**	**283,075**	**322,807**	**296,862**	**232,027**	**319,691**	**295,735**	**341,147**	**322,076**	**248,028**	
Hindu .	*621,062*	*578 497*	*663 280*	*609 989*	*442,844*	*+42,635*	*−84 853*	*+53,291*	*+167,145*	*+178,218*	*303 800*	*282,888*	*322,472*	*292,485*	*212,539*	*317,262*	*295,539*	*340 808*	*317,504*	*230,305*	
Christian ...	*36*	*20*	*197*			*+16*	*−177*	*+197*		*+36*	*19*	*8*	*99*			*17*	*12*	*98*			
Tribal religion ..	*4,726*	*363*	*477*	*8,949*	*37,911*	*+4,363*	*−114*	*−8 472*	*−28,962*	*−32,485*	*2,314*	*179*	*236*	*4,377*	*19,488*	*2,412*	*184*	*241*	*4,572*	*17,723*	
PATNA	**216**			55	5	+216		−55	+50	+211	**106**			22	5	**110**			33		
GAYA ...	**168,382**	130,624	127,606	111,831	91,110	+29,758	+3,018	+15,775	+20,721	+69,272	**78 443**	64,586	61,865	54,778	44,460	**81,939**	66,038	65,741	57,053	46,650	
SHAHABAD ...	**712**	133	914	86		+579	−781	+828	+86	+712	**426**	67	513	43		**286**	66	401	43	..	
SARAN .	**1**		477			+1	−477	+477		+1	**1**		277					200			
CHAMPARAN	**654**	144	860	.		+510	−716	+860		+654	**392**	83	415			**262**	61	445	..		
MUZAFFARPUR ..		3				−3	+3					2					1				
DARBHANGA	**2**			212		+2		−212	+212	+2	**2**			103					100		
MONGHYR ..	**5,516**	1,671	3,219	4,745	4,946	+3,845	−1,548	−1,526	−201	+570	**2,853**	793	1,487	2,184	2,329	**2,663**	878	1,732	2,561	2,617	
BHAGALPUR ...	**28,436**	23,945	26,958	29,378	29,602	+4,491	−3,013	−2,420	−224	−1,166	**13,035**	11,527	12,336	13,451	13,646	**15,401**	12,418	14,622	15,927	15,956	
PURNEA	**835**	682	2,851	1,484	28	+153	−2,169	+1,367	+1,456	+807	**421**	374	1,408	876	13	**414**	308	1,443	608	15	

SANTAL PARGANAS ...	**70,759**	82,000	117,624	119,059	26,351	−11,241	−35,624	−1,435	+92,708	+44,408	**33,708**	38,401	54,785	55,136	12,525	**37,051**	43,599	62,839	63,923	13,823
CUTTACK ...	**80**	73	17	48	172	+8	+55	−26	−129	−92	**35**	29	16	23	94	**45**	43	1	30	78
BALASORE ...	**176**	137	96	424	3,274	+39	+41	−328	−2,850	−3,098	**81**	68	54	193	1,67[illegible]	**95**	69	42	231	1,603
ANGUL ...	**2**	26	1	359	...	−24	+25	−358	+350	+2	**2**	10	...	181	...	...	16	1	178	...
PURI ...	**14**	28	5	22	...	−14	+23	−17	+22	+14	**8**	6	1	10	...	**6**	22	4	12	...
SAMBALPUR ...	**9,606**	8,777	8,754	9,073	8,159	+831	+23	−319	+914	+1,449	**4,658**	4,275	4,203	4,416	4,207	**4,950**	4,502	4,551	4,657	3,952
HAZARIBAGH ...	**85,138**	76,321	89,683	98,783	99,031	+8,817	−13,362	−9,100	−248	−13,393	**40,087**	36,434	42,248	45,366	43,58[illegible]	**45,051**	39,887	47,435	53,417	55,442
RANCHI ...	**5,845**	5,469	17,115	14,084	58,706	+376	−11,646	+3,081	−44,672	−52,861	**3,168**	2,838	8,307	6,806	29,481	**2,677**	2,631	8,808	7,238	29,225
PALAMAU ...	**97,386**	85,653	81,586	72,591	19,330	+11,733	+4,065	+8,997	+53,361	+78,156	**48,521**	42,746	41,001	35,320	9,752	**48,865**	42,907	40,587	37,371	9,478
MANBHUM ...	**33,743**	38,395	50,792	36,703	33,851	−4,652	−12,397	+14,089	+2,852	−108	**17,633**	19,600	26,220	17,640	16,408	**16,110**	18,786	24,572	18,863	17,443
SINGHBHUM ...	**18,273**	13,922	19,609	15,489	12,546	+4,351	−5,687	+4,120	+3,943	+5,727	**9,631**	6,904	9,336	7,546	6,335	**8,642**	7,018	10,273	7,943	6,211
ORISSA STATES ...	**100,851**	104,377	108,807	97,682	87,327	−3,526	−4,430	+11,125	+10,355	+13,524	**49,476**	51,062	55,061	49,404	44,712	**51,375**	53,315	53,748	48,278	43,616
CHOTA NAGPUR STATES	**7,195**	6,431	6,978	6,885	5,717	+764	−547	+93	+1,168	+1,478	**3,446**	3,361	3,374	3,264	3,757	**3,749**	3,170	3,704	3,621	2,920
Bhumij ...	(a) **274,018**	(b) **240,229**	**272,667**	**244,586**	**238,455**	**+33,789**	**−32,438**	**+28,081**	**+6,131**	**+35,563**	**136,239**	(b) **118,125**	**130,357**	**119,099**	**117,099**	**137,779**	(b) **122,104**	**142,310**	**125,487**	**121,356**
Hindu ...	*266,424*	*237,187*	*266,021*	*233,522*	*162,960*	*+29,237*	*−28,834*	*+32,499*	*+70,662*	*+103,464*	*132,538*	*116,877*	*127,002*	*113,613*	*79,800*	*133,891*	*120,310*	*139,019*	*119,909*	*83,160*
Christian ...	*151*	...	...	...	...	*+151*	...	..	...	*+151*	*76*	...	...	...	..	*75*	...	...	...	...
Tribal religion ...	*7,443*	*3,042*	*6,646*	*11,064*	*75,495*	*+4,401*	*−3,604*	*−4,418*	*−64,431*	*−68,062*	*3,630*	*1,248*	*3,355*	*5,486*	*37,299*	*3,813*	*1,794*	*3,291*	*5,578*	*38,196*
CUTTACK *Hindu* ...	**3,210**	2,916	3,424	3,338	3,277	+294	−508	+56	+61	−67	**1,576**	1,413	1,369	1,667	1,640	**1,634**	1,504	1,755	1,671	1,637
Jajpur ...	**1**	9	*	...	...	−8	...	...	...	+1	**1**	8	*	...	.	...	1	*	...	...
Dharamsala ...	**3,209**	2,907	*	3,338	3,277	+302	..	..	+61	−68	**1,575**	1,404	*	1,667	1,640	**1,634**	1,503	*	1,671	1,637
BALASORE ...	**5,944**	4,704	5,266	4,279	3,274	+1,240	−552	+977	+1,005	+2,670	**3,015**	2,324	2,558	2,144	1,671	**2,929**	2,380	2,698	2,135	1,603
Hindu ...	*5,900*	*4,701*	*5,266*	*4,239*	*3,274*	*+1,199*	*−555*	*+1,017*	*+965*	*+2,626*	*2,972*	*2,324*	*2,558*	*2,125*	*1,671*	*2,928*	*2,377*	*2,698*	*2,114*	*1,603*
Tribal religion ...	*44*	3	...	*40*	...	*+41*	+3	−40	+40	+44	43	...	...	*19*	...	*1*	*3*	...	*21*	...
Bhadrakh subdivision	**645**	300	*	385	329	+345	...	...	+56	−316	**333**	132	*	191	164	**312**	168	*	194	165
Sadr subdivision ...	**5,299**	4,404	*	3,894	2,945	+895	...	...	+949	+2,354	**2,682**	2,192	*	1,953	1,607	**2,617**	2,212	*	1,941	1,438
HAZARIBAGH ...	**200**	†	56	...	...	...	...	+56	...	+200	**87**	†	40	...	...	**113**	†	16	...	...
Hindu ...	*181*	†	*56*	...	...	...	...	*+56*	...	*+181*	76	†	*40*	...	...	*105*	†	*16*	...	...
Christian ...	*19*	†	...	...	...	...	...	...	...	*+19*	*11*	†	...	...	...	8	†	...	...	...
Ramgarh ...	**179**	†	*	...	...	...	...	...	...	+179	**75**	†	*	...	...	**104**	†	*	...	...
Elsewhere ...	**21**	†	*	...	...	...	...	...	...	+21	**12**	†	*	...	...	**9**	†	*	...	...
RANCHI ...	**1,442**	†	396	213	29	...	...	+683	+184	+1,413	**707**	†	393	112	16	**735**	†	503	101	13
Hindu ...	*1,442*	†	383	*213*	29	...	..	*+670*	*+184*	*+1,413*	*707*	†	388	*112*	*16*	*735*	†	*495*	*101*	*13*
Tribal religion ...	...	†	13	...	...	...	...	*+13*	...	...	...	†	*5*	...	...	...	†	*8*	...	...
Silli ...	**1,156**	†	*	*	*	...	...	...	...	...	**586**	†	*	*	*	**570**	†	*	*	*
Elsewhere ...	**286**	†	*	*	*	...	...	...	...	...	**121**	†	*	*	*	**165**	†	*	*	*
MANBHUM ...	**163,901**	92,194	115,994	109,016	106,437	+11,707	−23,800	+6,978	+2,579	−2,536	**52,135**	45,959	54,380	52,229	51,746	**51,766**	46,235	61,614	56,787	54,691
Hindu ...	*103,858*	*92,194*	*115,987*	*109,015*	*106,437*	*+11,664*	*−23,793*	*+6,972*	*+2,578*	*−2,579*	*52,114*	*45,959*	*54,373*	*52,228*	*51,746*	*51,744*	*46,235*	*61,614*	*56,787*	*54,691*
Christian ...	*27*	...	...	...	...	*+27*	...	...	...	*+27*	*14*	...	...	...	...	*13*	...	...	...	...
Tribal religion ...	*16*	...	7	*1*	...	*+16*	−7	+6	*+1*	*+16*	7	...	7	*1*	..	9	...	...	...	...
Jhalda ...	**6,363**	5,383	*	6,772	7,442	+980	...	...	−670	−1,079	**3,084**	2,636	*	3,249	3,074	**3,279**	2,747	*	3,523	3,768
Purulia ...	**22,836**	20,622	*	25,501	18,956	+2,214	.	...	+6,545	+3,880	**11,254**	10,204	*	12,315	9,525	**11,582**	10,418	*	13,186	9,431
Baghmundi ...	**9,120**	7,563	*	10,569	10,508	+1,557	...	...	+61	−1,388	**4,587**	3,789	*	5,222	5,123	**4,533**	3,774	*	5,347	5,385
Chandil ...	**26,947**	24,459	*	26,460	4,640	+2,488	...	...	+21,820	+22,307	**13,634**	12,248	*	11,655	2,540	**13,313**	12,211	*	14,805	2,100
Barahabhum ...	**23,547**	22,345	*	24,951	5,540	+1,202	...	...	+19,411	+18,007	**11,885**	11,315	*	12,376	2,890	**11,662**	11,030	*	12,575	2,650
Manbazar ...	**9,534**	9,250	*	10,382	9,041	+284	...	...	+1,291	+493	**4,662**	4,539	*	5,192	4,396	**4,872**	4,711	*	5,140	4,645
Gaurandi ...	**1,730**	1,777	*	...	2,243	−47	...	...	−2,243	−513	**815**	779	*	.	1,075	**915**	998	*	..	1,168
Gobindpur ...	**9**	12	*	370		−3	...	...			...	12	*	176		**9**	...	*	194	
Jherria ...	**2,054**	314	*	464	30,003	+1,740	...	...	−28,963	−28,030	**1,191**	207	*	263	14,687	**863**	107	*	201	15,406
Tundi ...	...	...	*	297		...	...	...			...	...	*	134		...	...	*	168	
Elsewhere ...	**1,761**	469	*	3,300	17,974	+1,392	...	...	−14,674	−16,213	**1,023**	230	*	1,647	7,836	**738**	239	*	1,653	10,138
SINGHBHUM ...	**53,058**	51,335	52,190	46,500	51,050	+1,723	−855	+5,681	−4,541	−2,008	**26,266**	24,541	25,580	22,630	25,046	**26,792**	26,794	26,610	23,879	26,004
Hindu ...	*47,127*	*50,362*	*49,071*	*42,389*	...	*−3,235*	*+1,291*	*+6,832*	*+42,239*	*+47,127*	*23,412*	*24,313*	*23,997*	*20,561*	...	*23,715*	*26,049*	*25,074*	*21,678*	...
Christian ...	*6*	...	...	...	...	+6	...	...	...	+6	4	...	..	...	...	*2*	...	...	...	...
Tribal religion ...	*5,925*	*973*	*3,119*	*4,270*	*51,050*	*+4,952*	*−2,146*	*−1,151*	*−46,780*	*−45,125*	*2,850*	*228*	*1,583*	*2,069*	*25,046*	*3,075*	*745*	*1,536*	*2,201*	*26,004*
Chakradharpur ...	**1,707**	1,307	*	961	5,805	+400	...	...	−4,844	−4,098	**863**	634	*	485	2,915	**844**	673	*	476	2,890
Kolhan ...	**2,377**	1,960	*	2,405	1,725	+417	...	...	+680	+652	**1,232**	679	*	1,175	868	**1,145**	1,281	*	1,230	857
Manoharpur ...	**1,180**	853	*	713	1,248	+327	...	...	−535	−68	**590**	425	*	362	749	**590**	428	*	351	499
Ghatsila ...	**47,794**	47,216	*	42,480	42,272	+570	...	...	+158	+5,522	**23,581**	22,803	*	20,608	20,514	**24,213**	24,412	*	21,822	21,758

(a) This total is less by 40 than the total given in Table XVII, because the latter includes 16 males and 24 females, enumerated in *Sambalpur* and *Palamau*, who have not been shown in this table.

(b) Excludes *Hazaribagh* and *Ranchi*, for which figures are not available.

*Details not recorded. † Not known. ‡ Excludes Christians, for whom the district total only is available. § Excludes Christians, whose number is unknown.

TABLE XVIII—*continued.*

VARIATION OF POPULATION OF SELECTED TRIBES

Tribe, religion and locality	Persons 1931	Persons 1921	Persons 1911	Persons 1901	Persons 1891	Variation (Increase +, Decrease —) 1921 to 1931	1911 to 1921	1901 to 1911	1891 to 1901	Net variation 1891 to 1931	Males 1931	Males 1921	Males 1911	Males 1901	Males 1891	Females 1931	Females 1921	Females 1911	Females 1901	Females 1891	Remarks
1	2	3	4	5	6	7	8	9	10	11	12	13	14	15	16	17	18	19	20	21	22
ORISSA STATES	**92,475**	77,722	83,521	68,643	63,173	+14,753	−5,799	+14 878	+6,470	+30,302	**45,660**	38,217	39 964	34,332	30,950	**46,815**	39,505	43,567	34,421	31,223	
Hindu	*90 945*	*75,656*	*80,161*	*62,666*	*49,943*	*+15 292*	*−4 505*	*+17,495*	*+12,723*	*+41 005*	*44 900*	*37,197*	*38,375*	*31,339*	*24,727*	*46,048*	*38,459*	*41,886*	*31,427*	*25,216*	
Christian	*99*					*+99*				*+99*	*47*					*52*					
Tribal religion	*1,428*	*2,066*	*9,360*	*5 977*	*19,230*	*−638*	*−1 294*	*−2,617*	*−6,253*	*−10,802*	*713*	*1,080*	*1,679*	*2,983*	*6,223*	*715*	*1,046*	*1,681*	*2,994*	*6,007*	
Mayurbhanj	**74,634**	*	*	*	52,149					+22,485	**36,795**	*	*	*	25,912	**37,839**	*	*	*	26,237	
Nilgiri	**7,289**	*	*	*	3,858					+3,431	**3,626**	*	*	*	1,862	**3,663**	*	*	*	1,996	
Keonjhar	**5,045**	*	*	*	2,578					+2,467	**2,495**	*	*	*	1,332	**2,550**	*	*	*	1,246	
Dhenkanal	**1,549**	*	*	*						+1,549	**766**	*	*	*		**783**	*	*	*		
Gangpur	**2,834**	*	*	*	1,564					+1,270	**1,430**	*	*	*	803	**1,404**	*	*	*	761	
Bonai	**1,049**	*	*	*	251					+798	**500**	*	*	*	133	**549**	*	*	*	118	
Elsewhere	75	*	*	*	1,773					−1,698	**48**	*	*	*	908	**27**	*	*	*	865	
CHOTA NAGPUR STATES	**13,796**	11,358	11,330	12,588	12,215	+2 430	+28	−1,258	+373	+1,578	**6,798**	5,672	5,783	6,095	6,030	**6,995**	5,686	5,547	6,493	6,185	
Hindu	*13,758*	*11,358*	*11,183*	*11 812*		*+2 400*	*+175*	*−629*	*+11,812*	*+13,758*	*6,776*	*5,672*	*5,702*	*5,681*		*6,982*	*5,686*	*5,481*	*6,121*		
Tribal religion	30		*147*	*776*	*12 215*	*+30*	*−147*	*−629*	*−11,439*	*−12,185*	*17*		*81*	*414*	*6,030*	*13*		*66*	*369*	*6,185*	
Saraikela	**11 390**	*	*	*	9,853					+1,537	**5,604**	*	*	*	4 834	**5,786**	*	*	*	5,019	
Kharsawan	**2,396**	*	*	*	2,363					+36	**1,189**	*	*	*	1,196	**1,209**	*	*	*	1,166	
Birhor	**2,350**	(a)**1,510**	**2,299**	**969**	**1,429**	**+840**	**−789**	**+1,330**	**−460**	**+921**	**1,217**	(a) **749**	**1,084**	**485**	**743**	**1,133**	(a)**761**	**1,215**	**484**	**686**	(a) Excludes *Orissa States*, for which figures are not available.
Hindu	*1 723*	*1,251*	*1,387*	*	*	*+472*	*−136*				*878*	*641*	*644*	*	*	*845*	*610*	*743*	*	*	
Christian	*1*					*+1*				*+1*	*1*										
Tribal religion	*626*	*259*	*912*	*	*	*+367*	*−653*				*338*	*108*	*440*	*	*	*288*	*151*	*472*	*	*	
HAZARIBAGH	**1 143**	582	1,024	506	717	+561	−442	+518	−211	+426	**607**	297	523	252	365	**536**	285	501	254	352	
Hindu	*701*	*542*	*781*	*	*	*+159*	*−239*				*373*	*293*	*407*	*	*	*328*	*249*	*374*	*	*	
Tribal religion	*442*	*40*	*243*	*	*	*+402*	*−203*				*234*	*4*	*116*	*	*	*208*	*36*	*127*	*	*	
Sadr subdivision	**530**	248	*	*	*	+282					**277**	103	*	*	*	**253**	145	*	*	*	
Chatra subdivision	**545**	333	*	*	*	+212					**291**	194	*	*	*	**254**	139	*	*	*	
Giridih subdivision	**68**	1	*	*	*	+67					**39**		*	*	*	**29**	1	*	*	*	
RANCHI	**441**	374	927	342	504	+67	−553	+585	−162	−63	**222**	181	386	169	265	**219**	193	541	173	239	
Hindu	*372*	*207*	*427*	*	*	*+165*	*−220*				*185*	*104*	*151*	*	*	*187*	*103*	*276*	*	*	
Christian	*1*					*+1*				*+1*	*1*										
Tribal religion	*68*	*167*	*500*	*	*	*−99*	*−333*				*36*	*77*	*235*	*	*	*32*	*90*	*265*	*	*	
Sadr subdivision	**67**	151	*	*	*	−84					**33**	68	*	*	*	**34**	83	*	*	*	
Khunti subdivision	**189**	27	*	*	*	+162					**92**	21	*	*	*	**97**	6	*	*	*	
Gumla subdivision	**169**	145	*	*	*	+24					**86**	67	*	*	*	**83**	78	*	*	*	
Simdega subdivision	**16**	51	*	*	*	−35					**11**	25	*	*	*	**5**	26	*	*	*	
PALAMAU	**141**	46	27			+95	+19	+27		+141	**83**	23	12			**58**	23	15			
Hindu	*141*		*27*			*+141*	*−27*	*+27*		*+141*	83		*12*			*58*		*15*			
Tribal religion		*46*				*−46*	*+46*					*23*					*23*				
Latehar subdivision	**141**	46	*			+95				+141	**83**	23	*			**58**	23	*			
MANBHUM	**308**	128	104	56		+180	+24	+48	+56	+308	**134**	65	57	34		**174**	63	47	22		
Hindu	*308*	*122*		*		*+186*	*+122*			+308	*134*	*61*		*		*174*	*61*		*		
Tribal religion		*6*	*104*	*		*−6*	*−98*					*4*	*57*	*			*2*	*47*	*		
Sadr subdivision	**175**	93	*	*		+82				+175	**100**	48	*	*		**75**	45	*	*		
Dhanbad subdivision	**133**	35	*	*		+98				+133	**34**	17	*	*		**99**	18	*	*		

Singhbhum ...	12	380	48	...	13	−368	+333	+48	−13	−1	12	183	22	...	...	...	197	26	...	6	
Hindu ...	...	380	...	...	*	−380	+380	...	...	...	...	183	...	...	*	...	197	...	...	*	
Tribal religion ...	12	...	48	...	*	+12	−48	+48	...	...	12	...	22	...	*	...	...	26	...	*	
Sadr subdivision ...	12	380	*	...	*	−368	...	...	...	...	12	183	*	...	*	...	197	*	...	*	
Orissa States ...	305	†	160	85	105	...	...	+104	−130	+110	159	†	84	80	106	146	†	85	35	89	
Hindu ...	201	†	152	*	*	...	...	...	...	...	103	†	74	*	*	98	†	78	*	*	
Tribal religion ...	104	†	17	*	*	...	...	...	...	...	56	†	10	*	*	48	†	7	*	*	
Nilgiri ...	142	†	*	*	*	...	...	...	...	...	75	†	*	*	*	67	†	*	*	*	
Keonjhar ...	83	†	*	*	*	...	...	...	...	...	43	†	*	*	*	40	†	*	*	*	
Elsewhere ...	80	†	*	*	*	...	...	...	...	...	41	†	*	*	*	39	†	*	*	*	
Birjia(a) ...	1,550	†	1,414	1,170	†	...	...	+244	...	...	796	†	647	549	†	754	†	767	621	†	(a) There has always been a tendency to confuse *Birjia* with *Binjhia* (*Binjhwar*), and this probably accounts for the fact that the statistics available for this tribe are so meagre. Actually, *Birjias* are very closely allied to *Asurs*.
Hindu ...	938	†	298	348	†	...	...	−50	...	...	509	†	125	160	†	429	†	173	188	†	
Tribal religion ...	612	†	1,116	822	†	...	...	+294	...	...	287	†	522	389	†	325	†	594	433	†	
Ranchi *Hindu* ...	245	†	...	3	†	...	...	−2	...	...	159	†	...	3	†	86	†	...	...	†	
Lobardaga ...	77	†	...	*	†	...	...	...	...	...	41	†	...	*	†	36	†	...	...	†	
Ranchi ...	99	†	...	*	†	...	...	...	...	...	72	†	...	*	†	27	†	...	...	†	
Bishunpur ...	34	†	...	*	†	...	...	...	...	...	21	†	...	*	†	13	†	...	...	†	
Elsewhere ...	35	†	...	*	†	...	...	...	...	...	25	†	...	*	†	10	†	...	...	†	
Palamau ...	1,305	†	1,414	1,168	†	...	...	+246	...	...	637	†	647	547	†	668	†	767	621	†	
Hindu ...	693	†	298	346	†	...	...	−48	...	...	350	†	125	158	†	343	†	173	188	†	
Tribal religion ...	612	†	1,116	822	†	...	...	+294	...	...	287	†	522	389	†	325	†	594	433	†	
Mahuadanr ...	1,282	†	*	*	†	...	...	...	...	...	623	†	*	*	†	659	†	*	*	†	
Elsewhere ...	23	†	*	*	†	...	...	...	...	...	14	†	*	*	†	9	†	*	*	†	
Chero *Hindu* ...	17,906	†	16,602	15,293	14,065	...	...	+1,309	+1,228	+3,841	8,968	†	8,239	7,717	6,976	8,938	†	8,363	7,576	7,089	
Palamau ...	17,906	†	16,602	15,293	14,065	...	...	+1,309	+1,228	+3,841	8,968	†	8,239	7,717	6,976	8,938	†	8,363	7,576	7,089	
Daltonganj ...	7,892	†	*	7,501	6,525	...	...	...	+976	+1,367	3,962	†	*	3,743	3,178	3,930	†	*	3,758	3,347	
Patan ...	3,104	†	*	2,800	2,404	...	...	...	+306	+610	1,543	†	*	1,437	1,219	1,561	†	*	1,363	1,275	
Hussainabad ...	1,480	†	*	1,168	971	...	...	...	+197	+509	736	†	*	577	487	744	†	*	591	484	
Latehar ...	4,940	†	*	3,265	3,755	...	...	...	−490	+1,185	2,465	†	*	1,649	1,921	2,475	†	*	1,616	1,834	
Elsewhere ...	490	†	*	559	320	...	...	...	+239	+170	262	†	*	311	180	228	†	*	248	140	
Gadaba *Hindu* ...	277	†	†	†	177	...	...	...	...	+100	139	†	†	†	89	138	†	†	†	88	
Kalahandi State ...	277	†	†	†	177	...	...	...	...	+100	139	†	†	†	89	138	†	†	†	88	
Gond ...	(a) 255,745	234,187	233,696	211,937	169,140	+21,558	+491	+21,759	+42,797	+86,605	124,704	114,645	115,647	104,770	84,202	131,041	119,542	118,049	107,167	84,938	(a) This total is less by 7 than that given in Table XVII, because the latter includes 7 males, enumerated in the *Chota Nagpur States*, who have not been shown in this table.
Hindu ...	255,022	209,302	208,023	*	*	+45,720	+1,279	...	...	...	124,277	102,314	103,103	*	*	130,745	106,988	104,920	*	*	
Christian ...	15	32	...	...	...	−17	+32	...	...	+15	9	16	...	...	...	6	16	...	...	...	
Tribal religion ...	708	24,853	25,673	*	*	−24,145	−820	...	...	...	418	12,315	12,544	*	*	290	12,538	13,129	*	*	
Sambalpur ...	54,768	50,057	50,147	63,248	56,205	+4,711	−90	−13,101	+6,953	−1,437	26,460	24,235	24,056	30,564	27,371	28,308	25,822	25,492	32,684	28,834	
Hindu ...	54,768	50,055	50,141	*	49,670	+4,713	−86	...	...	+5,098	26,460	24,235	24,052	*	24,142	28,308	25,820	25,490	*	25,528	
Tribal religion ...	...	2	6	*	6,535	−2	−4	...	...	−6,535	...	...	4	*	3,229	...	2	2	*	3,306	
Sadr subdivision ...	38,932	34,921	*	*	*	+4,011	...	...	...	...	18,742	17,002	*	*	*	20,190	17,919	*	*	*	
Bargarh subdivision	15,836	15,136	*	*	*	+700	...	...	...	...	7,718	7,233	*	*	*	8,118	7,903	*	*	*	
Ranchi ...	11,262	9,220	8,517	7,007	1,211	+2,042	+703	+1,510	+5,796	+10,051	5,614	4,611	4,245	3,467	654	5,648	4,609	4,272	3,540	557	
Hindu ...	11,236	8,680	8,258	7,001	1,211	+2,556	+422	+1,257	+5,790	+10,025	5,601	4,334	4,144	3,465	654	5,635	4,346	4,114	3,536	557	
Christian ...	8	31	...	...	...	−23	+31	...	...	+8	5	15	...	...	...	3	16	...	...	...	
Tribal religion ...	18	509	259	6	...	−491	+250	+253	+6	+18	8	262	101	2	...	10	247	158	4	...	
Simdega subdivision ...	10,327	8,880	*	6,837	867	+1,447	...	...	+5,960	+9,460	5,126	4,414	*	3,389	487	5,201	4,466	*	3,448	380	
Elsewhere ...	935	340	*	180	344	+595	...	...	−164	+591	488	197	*	88	167	447	143	*	92	177	

* Details not recorded. † Not known.

TABLE XVIII—*continued.*

VARIATION OF POPULATION OF SELECTED TRIBES.

Tribe, religion and locality.	Persons					Variation. (Increase +, Decrease −)				Net variation 1891 to 1931	Males					Females.					Remarks
	1931	1921.	1911.	1901.	1891	1921 to 1931	1911 to 1921.	1901 to 1911.	1891 to 1901		1931.	1921.	1911	1901.	1891	1931.	1921	1911	1901	1891.	
1	2	3	4	5	6	7	8	9	10	11	12	13	14	15	16	17	18	19	20	21	23
SINGHBHUM	7,026	(b) 21,124	5,613	6,343	3,212	−14,098	+15,511	−729	+4,130	+4 814	3,715	(b) 10,081	3,765	3,200	1,083	3,311	(b) 11,043	2,848	3,142	1,129	(b) Apparently inaccurate May include a considerable number who really described themselves as *Gaur*—i.e., the Oriya equivalent of *Goala.*
Hindu ..	*7,023*	*21,121*	*5,613*	*6,342*	*2,212*	*−14,098*	*+15,508*	*−729*	*+4,130*	*+4,811*	*3,714*	*10,080*	*2 765*	*3,200*	*1,083*	*3,309*	*11,041*	*2,848*	*3,142*	*1,129*	
Christian ...	*3*	*1*		..		*+2*	*+1*			*+3*	*1*	*1*				*2*		.			
Tribal religion		*2*				*−2*	*+2*					...				...	*2*			...	
Sadr subdivision	5,591	10,988	*	6,342	1,271	−14,397			+5,071	+4,320	3,080	9,515	*	3,200	600	2,511	10,473	*	3,142	671	
Dhalbhum subdivision	1,435	1,136	*	.	941	+299			−941	+494	635	566	*		483	800	570	*	...	468	
ORISSA STATES ...	182,689	153,786	169,419	135,340	109,422	+28,903	−15,633	+34,079	+25,918	+73,267	88,915	75,718	83,982	67,539	55,093	93,774	78,068	85,437	67,801	54,329	
Hindu ...	*181,995*	*129,446*	*144,011*	*	*	*+52,549*	*−14 565*		...		*88,502*	*63,665*	*71,543*	*	*	*93,493*	*65,781*	*72,468*	*	*	
Christian ...	*4*					*+4*				*+4*	*3*					*1*					
Tribal religion	*690*	*24,340*	*25,408*	*	*	*−23 650*	*−1,068*				*410*	*12,053*	*12,439*	*	*	*280*	*12,287*	*12,969*	*	*	
Mayurbhanj ..	11,519	*	*	*	107	...	..	...	..	+11,412	5,679	*	*	*	55	5,840	*	*	*	52	
Nilgiri ...	2	*	*	*	4,687					−4,685	1	*	*	*	2,342	1	*	*	*	2,345	
Keonjhar ...	12,353	*	*	*	616					+11,737	5,802	*	*	*	301	6,551	*	*	*	315	
Pal Lahara	1,415	*	*	*	1,111					+304	684	*	*	*	562	731	*	*	*	549	
Dhenkanal	3,215	*	*	*	3,703					−488	1,499	*	*	*	1,879	1,716	*	*	*	1,824	
Athmallik	5,601	*	*	*	3,313		.			+2,288	2,804	*	*	*	1,696	2,797	*	*	*	1,617	
Baud ..	8,832	*	*	*	1,340	.			...	+7,492	4,344	*	*	*	669	4,488	*	*	*	671	
Bamra	16,536	*	*	13,944	11,602				+2,342	+4,934	7,848	*	*	6,793	5,700	8,688	*	*	7,151	5,902	
Bairakhol	3,464	*	*	2,653	2,036				+617	+1,428	1,697	*	*	1,345	1,023	1,767	*	*	1,308	1,013	
Sonpur .	5,121	*	*	3,967	5,700	.			1,733	−579	2,427	*	*	1,879	2,737	2 694	*	*	2,088	2,963	
Patna ...	60,491	*	*	20,637	28,406				−7,779	+32,085	29,596	*	*	10,067	14 105	30,895	*	*	10,560	14,301	
Kalahandi .	29,721	*	*	31,770	20,125				+11,645	+9,596	14,407	*	*	15,974	10,152	15,314	*	*	15,796	9,973	
Gangpur ...	17,002	*	*	*	20,560		.			−3,558	8,431	*	*	*	10,664	8,571	*	*	*	9,896	
Bonai ...	6,128	*	*	*	4,424			..	.	+1,704	3,052	*	*	*	2,316	3,076	*	*	*	2,108	
Elsewhere ...	1,289	*	*	*	1,692				.	−403	644	*	*	*	892	645	*	*	*	800	
Ho	523,158	441,424	420,179	(a) 383,206	(a) §329,973	+81,734	+21,245	+36,973	+53,233	+193,185	253,713	214,109	203,494	(a) 187,189	(a) §162,632	269 445	227,315	216,685	(a) 196,017	(a) §167,341	(a) Includes the following, who were returned under the generic term *Kol*— 1901 — Males. Females. Orissa States 4,770 4,265 1891. Singhbhum 38,322 39,067 Orissa States 56,484 55,995 Chota Nagpur States. 6,723 7,182 It seems almost certain that the great majority, if not all, of these were really *Hos*, and they have been classified accordingly. It is possible, however, that in the States a certain number of *Kharias* and *Santals* (and possibly other tribes also) were concealed under this designation. In addition to the above, the following persons also were returned as *Kols* in 1901 and 1891— 1901 — Males Females Sambalpur 4,757 4,923 1891 Gaya 8 2
Hindu	*129,654*	*49,530*	*60,197*	*42,349*	*	*+80,124*	*−10,667*	*+17,848*			*64,010*	*24,502*	*29,879*	*21,088*	*	*65 644*	*26,028*	*30,318*	*21,261*	*	
Christian ...	*2,078*	*1,250*	*1,197*	*901*	†	*+828*	*+53*	*+296*			*992*	*592*	*607*	*426*	†	*1,086*	*658*	*590*	*475*	†	
Tribal religion ...	*391,426*	*390,644*	*358,785*	*339,956*	*	*+782*	*+31,859*	*+18,829*			*188,711*	*189,015*	*173,008*	*165,675*	*	*202,715*	*201 629*	*185,777*	*174,281*	*	
SINGHBHUM	301,158	258,585	257,181	233,644	(a) §189,276	+42,573	1,404	+23,537	+44,368	+111,882	144,140	123,821	123,082	113,265	(a) §92,281	157,018	134,764	134,090	120 379	(a) §96,995	
Hindu ...	*5,252*	*5,089*	*144*	*482*		*+163*	*+4,945*	*−338*	*+482*	*+5,252*	*4,516*	*2,638*	*79*	*247*		*736*	*2,451*	*65*	*235*		
Christian	*1,846*	*1,112*	*1,197*	*901*	†	*+734*	*−85*	*+296*			*885*	*523*	*607*	*426*	†	*961*	*589*	*590*	*475*	†	
Tribal religion .	*294,060*	*252,384*	*255,840*	*232,261*	*189,276*	*+41,676*	*−3,456*	*+23,579*	*+42,985*	*+104,784*	*140,736*	*120,660*	*122 396*	*112,592*	*92,281*	*153 324*	*131,724*	*133,444*	*119,669*	*96,995*	
Chakradharpur ...	46,575	‡40,409	*	‡41,708	§14,998	+6,076			+26 710	+31,677	22,316	‡19 407	*	‡20,453	§7,016	24,259	‡21,093	*	‡21,255	§7,982	
Kolhan .	224,888	‡188,900	*	‡172,178	§158,732	+35,898			+13 456	+66 166	107,029	‡89,796	*	‡83,017	§77 261	117,859	‡99,104	*	‡89,161	§81,471	
Manoharpur ...	21,139	‡21,602	*	‡17,234	§14,556	−463			+2,678	+6,583	10 447	‡10,780	*	‡8,585	§7,516	10,692	‡10 822	*	‡8,649	§7,040	
Ghatsila	8,556	‡5,382	*	‡1,633	§1,000	+3,174			+623	+7 556	4,348	‡2,225	*	‡794	§498	4,208	‡3,157	*	‡839	§502	
ORISSA STATES ...	184,331	152,616	126,349	(a) 112,856	(a) 112,479	+31,715	+26,267	+13,493	+377	+71,852	91,689	75,831	62,852	(a) 56,661	(a) 56 484	92,642	76,785	63,497	(a) 56,195	(a) 55,995	
Hindu ...	*122,854*	*43,568*	*60,048*	*41,967*	*	*+79,286*	*−16,480*	*+18,081*			*60,757*	*21,406*	*29,798*	*20,941*	*	*62,097*	*22,162*	*30,250*	*21,026*	*	
Christian .	*92*	*84*				*+8*	*+84*			*+92*	*45*	*42*				*47*	*42*	...			
Tribal religion .	*61,385*	*108,964*	*66,301*	*70,989*	*	*−47,579*	*+42,663*	*−4,688*	.		*[illegible]*	*54,383*	*33,054*	*35,820*	*	*30,498*	*54,581*	*33 247*	*35,169*	*	
Mayurbhanj .	110,217	*	*	*	57,685					+52,532	54,344	*	*	*	28,879	55,873	*	*	*	28,806	
Nilgiri	5,463	*	*	*	2,656					+2,807	2,713	*	*	*	1,350	2,750	*	*	*	1,297	
Keonjhar	57,247	*	*	*	18,212					+39,035	28,729	*	*	*	9,274	28,518	*	*	*	8,938	
Pal Lahara	1,582	*	*	*	725		.		.	+857	904	*	*	*	348	678	*	*	*	377	
Dhenkanal ...	668	*	*	*	788	.		.		−120	321	*	*	*	412	347	*	*	*	376	
Athmallik	312	*	*	*	285					+27	150	*	*	*	140	162	*	*	*	136	
Bamra .	2,808	*	*	6,829	1,818	.	.	...	+5,011	+990	1,363	*	*	3,532	901	1,445	*	*	3,307	917	
Bairakhol ...	378	*	*	817	210	...		.	+607	+168	201	*	*	548	112	177	*	*	269	98	
Sonpur	326	*	*	616	875			..	−359	−549	164	*	*	297	455	162	*	*	319	423	
Patna	291	*	*	453	736		..		−253	−445	156	*	*	241	379	135	*	*	242	357	

angpur ...	388	*	*	*	11,308	...	...	...	...	−10,920	188	*	*	*	5,605	200	*	*	*	5,613
Bonai ...	4,522	*	*	*	6,742	...	...	...	...	−2,220	2,385	*	*	*	3,370	2,137	*	*	*	3,372
Elsewhere ...	129	*	*	*	10,439	...	...	...	...	−10,310	71	*	*	*	5,163	58	*	*	*	5,280
CHOTA NAGPUR STATES	37,669	30,221	36,644	36,706	(a) 28,218	+7,448	6,423	−57	+8,488	+9,451	17,884	14,457	17,560	17,363	(a) 13,967	19,785	15,766	19,089	19,443	(a) 14,351
Hindu ...	*1,548*	*873*	*5*		...	*675*	*+868*	+5	..	*+1,548*	*737*	*458*	*2*	...	..	*811*	*415*	3	..	
Christian ..	*140*	*54*	.		...	*86*	*+54*		...	*+140*	*59*	*27*			.	*81*	*27*	.	...	...
Tribal religion ...	*35,981*	*29,296*	*36,644*	*36,706*	*28,218*	*+6,685*	*−7,348*	−62	+8,488	*+7,763*	*17,088*	*13,978*	*17,558*	*17,263*	*13,567*	*18,893*	*15,324*	*19,086*	*19,443*	*14,351*
Saraikela ...	25,963	*	*	*	7,402	...	−	...	..	+18,561	12,412	*	*	*	3,671	13,551	*	*	*	3,771
Kharsawan ...	11,706	*	*	*	20,816	...	...	...	..	−9,110	5,472	*	*	*	10,236	6,234	*	*	*	10,580
Juang	**15,024**	**10,454**	**12,823**	**11,159**	**9,173**	**+4,570**	**−2,369**	**+1,664**	**+1,986**	**+5,851**	**7,332**	**5,044**	**6,477**	**5,677**	**4,697**	**7,692**	**5,410**	**6,346**	**5,482**	**4,476**
Hindu ..	*7,887*	*2,542*	*1,306*	*1,848*	*	*+5,345*	*+1,236*	*−542*	.	...	*3,855*	*1,221*	*616*	*952*	*	*4,032*	*1,321*	*690*	*896*	*
Tribal religion ..	*7,137*	*7,912*	*11,517*	*9,311*	*	*−775*	*−3,606*	*+2,206*	...	...	*3,477*	*3,823*	*5,861*	*4,725*	*	*3,660*	*4,089*	*5,656*	*4,586*	*
ORISSA STATES ..	15,024	10,454	12,823	11,159	9,173	+4,570	−2,369	+1,664	+1,986	+5,851	7,332	5,044	6,477	5,677	4,697	7,692	5,410	6,346	5,482	4,476
Athgarh ...	280	*	*	*	97			.	...	+183	137	*	*	*	46	143	*	*	*	51
Talcher	2	*	*	*	..	..	...	..	...	+2	1	*	*	*	.	1	*	*	*	..
Mayurbhanj ...		*	*	*	528				...	−528		*	*	*	232		*	*	*	296
Keonjhar ..	7,029	*	*	*	5,676		...	..	...	+1,353	3,428	*	*	*	2,574	3,601	*	*	*	3,722
Pal Lahara	365	*	*	*		..			..	+365	190	*	*	*		175	*	*	*	
Dhenkanal ...	6,760	*	*	*	2,872	.	...	..	...	+3,888	3,296	*	*	*	1,465	3,464	*	*	*	1,407
Hindol ...	588	*	*	*		..	.		..	+588	280	*	*	*		308	*	*	*	..
Karmali(a) ...	**8,632**	†	**21,114**	†	†		..	...	...	...	**4,852**	†	**10,680**	†	†	**3,780**	†	**10,434**	†	†
Hindu ...	*8,297*	†	*16,330*	†	†	.	...	...	..	..	*4,698*	†	*8,349*	†	†	*3,599*	†	*7,981*	†	†
Christian ...	*32*	†	...	†	†	..	..	...	..	..	*7*	†		†	†	*25*	†		†	†
Tribal religion ..	*303*	†	*4,784*	†	†	.	..	..	..	...	*147*	†	*2,331*	†	†	*156*	†	*2,453*	†	†
SANTAL PARGANAS	361		13,085	†	†	.	..	...		...	173	†	6,542	†	†	188	†	6,547	†	†
Hindu	*35*	†	*10,205*	†	†		..	...	...	..	*25*	†	*5,150*	†	†	*10*	†	*5,055*	†	†
Christian	*32*	†		†	†	...	...	..			*7*	†	.	†	†	*26*	†	..	†	†
Tribal religion	*294*	†	*2,883*	†	†				...	...	*141*	†	*1,391*	†	†	*153*	†	*1,492*	†	†
Jamtara ...	274	†	*	†	†	...	...	...	...	...	133	†	*	†	†	141	†	*	†	†
Elsewhere ...	87	†	*	†	†	...	...	...	...	...	40	†	*	†	†	47	†	*	†	†
HAZARIBAGH ...	6,939	†	8,007	†	†	...	...		...	...	3,582	†	4,123	†	†	3,357	†	3,885	†	†
Hindu ...	*6,939*	†	*6,116*	†	†	.	...	...	...	...	*3,582*	†	*3,192*	†	†	*3,357*	†	*2,924*	†	†
Tribal religion ..	.	†	*1,891*	†	†	..	...	...	...	...	...	†	*930*	†	†		†	*961*	†	†
Ramgurh ..	4,124	†	*	†	†	..	...	...	...	...	2,145	†	*	†	†	1,979	†	*	†	†
Gumia ...	514	†	*	†	†	...	...	...	..	...	264	†	*	†	†	250	†	*	†	†
Mandu ..	1,340	†	*	†	†	..	...	...	...	...	674	†	*	†	†	666	†	*	†	†
Petarbar	723	†	*	†	†	...	...	...	...	...	364	†	*	†	†	359	†	*	†	†
Elsewhere ..	238	†	*	†	†	..	..	...	...	...	135	†	*	†	†	103	†	*	†	†
MANBHUM	73	†	10	†	†	...	...	..	...	...	42	†	10	†	†	31	†	...	†	†
Hindu ..	*73*	†	.	†	†	...	...	...	...	...	*42*	†	...	†	†	*31*	†	...	†	†
Tribal religion ...	..	†	*10*	†	†	...	...	...	...	...	...	†	*10*	†	†	..	†	..	†	†
Sadr subdivision ..	38	†	*	†	†	...	..	...	...	...	24	†	*	†	†	14	†	*	†	†
Dhanbad subdivision	35	†	*	†	†	...	...	..	...	...	18	†	*	†	†	17	†	*	†	†
SINGHBHUM ..	1,259	†	9	†	†	...	...	...	...	...	1,055	†	7	†	†	204	†	2	†	†
Hindu ..	*1,250*	†	*9*	†	†	.	...	...	...	...	*1,049*	†	*7*	†	†	*201*	†	*2*	†	†
Tribal religion ...	*9*	†	..	†	†	..	...	..	...	...	*6*	†	...	†	†	*3*	†	...	†	†
Sadr subdivision ..	243	†	*	†	†	.	...	...	...	...	42	†	*	†	†	201	†	*	†	†
Dhalbhum subdivision.	1,016	†	*	†	†	...	..	...	...	...	1,013	†	*	†	†	3	†	*	†	†
Kharia ...	**146,037**	**124,531**	**133,657**	**102,071**	(b) **§31,455**	**+21,506**	**−9,126**	**+31,586**	**+70,616**	**+114,582**	**72,376**	**61,614**	**65,792**	**50,357**	(b) **§15,740**	**73,661**	**62,917**	**67,865**	**51,714**	(b) **§15,715**
Hindu ...	*51,566*	*45,256*	*37,764*	*(a)28,642*	*4,526*	*+6,260*	*+7,522*	*+13,122*	*+20,116*	*+47,040*	*25,460*	*22,172*	*18,973*	*(a)12,397*	*2,235*	*26,106*	*23,114*	*18,791*	*(a)12,245*	*2,291*
Christian	*63,725*	*34,094*	*23,400*	*10,367*	†	*+29,631*	*+10,694*	*+18,033*	...	...	*31,360*	*17,050*	*13,998*	*5,132*	†	*32,365*	*17,044*	*14,418*	*5,235*	†
Tribal religion	*30,746*	*45,151*	*67,493*	*(a)62,033*	*26,929*	*−14,405*	*−22,342*	*+5,460*	*+35,104*	*+3,817*	*15,566*	*22,392*	*32,834*	*(a)30,390*	*13,505*	*15,180*	*22,759*	*34,659*	*(a)31,643*	*13,424*
SAMBALPUR ..	7,310	7,212	6,361	5,029	5,774	+98	+851	+1,332	−745	+1,536	3,521	3,538	3,053	3,436	2,812	3,789	3,674	3,308	2,591	2,962
Hindu	*7,310*	*5,322*	*1,168*	*	*2,677*	*+1,988*	*+4,154*	...	...	*+4,633*	*3,521*	*2,632*	*580*	*	*1,303*	*3,789*	*2,690*	*588*	*	*1,374*
Tribal religion ...		*1,890*	*6,193*	*	*3,097*	*−1,890*	*−3,303*	...	...	*−3,097*	...	*906*	*2,473*	*	*1,509*	...	*984*	*2,720*	*	*1,588*

Shahabad	69	145
Monghyr	303	310
Bhagalpur	6,420	6,546
Purnea	1,528	1,463
Santal Parganas	7,328	7,221
Cuttack	179	169
Balasore	2	...
Puri	3	
Sambalpur	4,352	4,388
Hazaribagh	5,063	5,170
Ranchi	437	373

There seems to be little doubt that the persons so returned in *Sambalpur* in 1901 were all, or nearly all, *Oraons*, and they have been shown accordingly in this table. No attempt has been made to classify the other persons returned as *Kols*, as there is not sufficient material to do so with any approach to accuracy. But the majority of them appear to be either *Oraons* or *Mundas*.

(a) The *Karmalis* are practically a branch of the Santal tribe, and are not always distinguished from the parent community.

(a) Excludes *Sambalpur*, where separate figures for *Hindu* and *Tribal religion* are not available.

(b) The 1891 figures appear to be incomplete, particularly in *Ranchi* district and the *Orissa States*.

* Details not recorded. † Not known. ‡ Excludes Christians, for whom the district total only is available. § Excludes Christians, whose number is unknown.

TABLE XVIII—*continued.*

Variation of Population of selected Tribes.

Tribe, religion and locality.	Persons. 1931.	Persons. 1921.	Persons. 1911.	Persons. 1901.	Persons. 1891.	Variation (Increase +, Decrease —.) 1921 to 1931.	Variation 1911 to 1921.	Variation 1901 to 1911.	Variation 1891 to 1901.	Net variation 1891 to 1931.	Males. 1931.	Males. 1921.	Males. 1911.	Males. 1901.	Males. 1891.	Females. 1931.	Females. 1921.	Females. 1911.	Females. 1901.	Females. 1891.	Remarks.
1	2	3	4	5	6	7	8	9	10	11	12	13	14	15	16	17	18	19	20	21	22
Sambalpur ...	**1,884**	1,685	*	*	*	+199	...	...	...	...	**894**	803	*	*	*	**990**	882	*	*	*	
Jharsugra ...	**1,436**	1,191	*	*	*	+245	...	...	...	...	**691**	565	*	*	*	**745**	626	*	*	*	
Laikera ..	**855**	710	*	*	*	+145	...	..	...	...	**402**	344	*	*	*	**453**	366	*	*	*	
Mura ...	**507**	432	*	*	*	+75	...	...	...	...	**241**	205	*	*	*	**266**	227	*	*	*	
Rampella ...	**173**	211	*	*	*	—38	...	..	...	...	**85**	109	*	*	*	**88**	102	*	*	*	
Katarbagha ...	**318**	672	*	*	*	—354	...	...	...	...	**153**	325	*	*	*	**165**	347	*	*	*	
Sason ...	**890**	777	*	*	*	+113	...	...	...	...	**426**	366	*	*	*	**464**	411	*	*	*	
Dhama ...	**351**	510	*	*	*	—159	...	...	...	...	**167**	262	*	*	*	**184**	248	*	*	*	
Mundher ...	**206**	125	*	*	*	+81	...	..	...	...	**121**	74	*	*	*	**85**	51	*	*	*	
Attabira ...	**189**	201	*	*	*	—12		...	...	...	**92**	114	*	*	*	**97**	87	*	*	*	
Ambabhona ...	**352**	421	*	*	*	—69	...	...	..	...	**179**	235	*	*	*	**173**	196	*	*	*	
Bhatli ...	**106**	113	*	*	*	—7	...		...	...	**46**	61	*	*	*	**60**	52	*	*	*	
Elsewhere ...	**43**	164	*	*	*	—121	...	...	...	...	**24**	85	*	*	*	**19**	79	*	*	*	
Ranchi ...	**75,083**	64,499	60,710	51,104	(c) §16,703	+10,584	+3,789	+9,606	+34,401	+58,380	**37,200**	32,094	29,598	24,806	(c) §8,261	**37,883**	32,405	31,112	26,298	(c) §8,442	(c) Apparently inaccurate. But in 1891 22,659 *Kharias* were enumerated in the adjoining district of *Palamau*. Since then few or none have been found in that district.
Hindu ...	*8,205*	*3,093*	*1,052*	*4,968*	...	*+5,112*	*+2,041*	*—3,906*	*+4,958*	*+8,205*	*3,864*	*1,497*	*592*	*2,493*	...	*4,341*	*1,596*	*460*	*2,465*	...	
Christian ...	*46,891*	*25,635*	*19,273*	*10,367*	†	*+21,256*	*+6,362*	*+8,906*			*23,103*	*12,883*	*9,536*	*5,132*	†	*23,788*	*12,752*	*9,737*	*5,235*	†	
Tribal religion ...	*19,987*	*35,771*	*40,385*	*35,779*	*16,703*	*—15,784*	*—4,614*	*+4,606*	*+19,076*	*+3,284*	*10,883*	*17,714*	*19,470*	*17,181*	*8,261*	*9,754*	*18,057*	*20,915*	*18,598*	*8,442*	
Sadr and Khunti subdivisions.	**130**	237	*	‡141	§130	—107	..	...	+11	...	**90**	116	*	‡77	§75	**40**	121	*	‡64	§55	
Bishunpur ...	...	...	*			...					...		*			...	...	*			
Ghagra ...	**506**	385	*			+121	..				**244**	189	*			**262**	196	*			
Gumla ...	**4,207**	3,610	*	‡12,151	§821	+597	...	...	+11,230	+15,536	**2,085**	1,758	*	‡5,774	§408	**2,122**	1,852	*	‡6,377	§413	
Raidih ...	**2,741**	2,402	*			+339	...				**1,359**	1,103	*			**1,382**	1,299	*			
Palkot ...	**8,903**	7,529	*			+1,374	..				**4,368**	3,624	*			**4,535**	3,905	*			
Sesai ...	**2,611**	2,292	*	‡2,011	...	+319	...	...	+2,011	+2,611	**1,260**	1,134	*	‡977	...	**1,351**	1,158	*	‡1,034	...	
Basia ...	**11,039**	9,706	*	‡7,861	...	+1,333	...	...	+7,861	+11,039	**5,325**	4,800	*	3,741	...	**5,714**	4,816	*	‡4,120	...	
Bano ...	**1,085**	736	*	‡636	...	+349	...		+636	+1,085	**567**	420	*	‡297	..	**518**	316	*	‡339	...	
Chainpur ...	**127**	86	*	‡140	§537	+41	...	...	+5,286	+8,870	**70**	39	*	‡75	§381	**57**	47	*	‡65	§256	
Kolebira ...	**9,280**	7,409	*	‡5,683		+1,871	...	...			**5,034**	3,738	*	‡2,763		**4,246**	3,671	*	‡2,920		
Simdega ...	**24,727**	21,747	*	‡8,680	§15,215	+2,980	...	...	—3,101	+19,239	**12,119**	10,890	*	‡4,218	§7,497	**12,608**	10,857	*	‡4,412	§7,718	
Kurdeg ...	**9,727**	8,360	*	‡3,484		+1,367	...	..			**4,679**	4,193	*	‡1,752		**5,048**	4,167	*	‡1,732		
Manbhum ...	**4,398**	3,666	6,747	3,945	644	+732	—3,081	+2,802	+3,301	+3,754	**2,310**	1,843	3,299	2,085	318	**2,088**	1,823	3,448	1,860	326	
Hindu ...	*4,334*	*3,662*	*1,999*	*2,256*	*644*	*+672*	*+1,663*	*—257*	*+1,612*	*+3,690*	*2,279*	*1,849*	*976*	*1,248*	*318*	*2,055*	*1,820*	*1,024*	*1,008*	*326*	
Tribal religion ...	*64*	*4*	*4,748*	*1,689*	...	*+60*	*—4,744*	*+3,059*	*+1,689*	*+64*	*31*	*1*	*2,324*	*837*		*33*	*3*	*2,424*	*852*	...	
Purulia ...	**558**	386	*	160	*	+172	...	..	...	...	**272**	203	*	88	*	**286**	183	*	72	*	
Chandil ...	**539**	376	*	282	*	+163	...	...	...	...	**273**	190	*	182	*	**266**	186	*	100	*	
Barabhum ...	**2,251**	2,091	*	2,420	*	+160	...	...	...	...	**1,193**	1,070	*	1,235	*	**1,058**	1,021	*	1,195	*	
Manbazar ...	**741**	705	*	138	*	+36	...	...	...	...	**361**	335	*	65	*	**380**	370	*	73	*	
Raghunathpur ...	**77**	...	*	893	*	+77	...	...	...	...	**73**	...	*	492	*	**4**	..	*	401	*	
Elsewhere ...	**232**	108	*	52	*	-124	...	...	...	...	**138**	45	*	33	*	**94**	63	*	19	*	
Singhbhum ...	**5,879**	5,657	6,106	3,183	3,865	+222	—449	+2,923	—682	+2,014	**3,144**	2,824	3,042	1,526	1,936	**2,735**	2,833	3,064	1,657	1,929	
Hindu ...	*4,590*	*4,136*	*3,374*	*2,630*	...	*+454*	*+762*	*+744*	*+2,630*	*+4,590*	*2,504*	*2,072*	*1,697*	*1,364*	..	*2,086*	*2,064*	*1,677*	*1,366*	...	
Christian ...	*10*	*8*	*3*	..	...	*+2*	*+5*	*+3*	...	*+10*	*6*	*4*	*2*	...	...	*4*	*4*	*1*	...	...	
Tribal religion ...	*1,279*	*1,513*	*2,729*	*553*	*3,865*	*—234*	*—1,216*	*+2,176*	*—3,312*	*—2,586*	*634*	*748*	*1,343*	*262*	*1,936*	*645*	*765*	*1,386*	*291*	*1,929*	
Sadr subdivision ...	**423**	‡45	*	194	376	+378	...	...	—182	+47	**169**	‡20	*	86	187	**254**	‡25	*	108	189	
Dhalbhum subdivision	**5,456**	‡5,604	*	2,989	3,480	—148	...	...	—500	+1,967	**2,975**	‡2,800	*	1,440	1,740	**2,481**	‡2,804	*	1,549	1,740	
Orissa States ...	**53,367**	43,497	58,733	38,810	(d) 4,169	+9,870	—10,236	+14,923	+34,641	+49,198	**26,201**	21,315	26,800	19,502	(d) 2,113	**27,166**	22,182	26,933	19,308	(d) 2,056	(d) Apparently inaccurate. But see also note (a) under *Ho* ante.
Hindu ...	*27,127*	*29,073*	*30,171*	*14,798*	*1,205*	*—1,946*	*—1,098*	*+15,373*	*+13,593*	*+25,922*	*13,292*	*14,129*	*15,129*	*7,392*	*614*	*13,835*	*14,944*	*15,042*	*7,406*	*591*	
Christian ...	*16,824*	*8,451*	*9,124*	...	...	*+8,373*	*—673*	*+9,124*	...	*+16,824*	*8,241*	*4,163*	*4,447*	...	...	*8,583*	*4,288*	*4,677*	..	...	
Tribal religion ...	*9,416*	*5,973*	*14,438*	*24,012*	*2,964*	*+3,443*	*—8,465*	*—9,574*	*-21,048*	*+6,452*	*4,668*	*3,023*	*7,224*	*12,110*	*1,499*	*4,748*	*2,950*	*7,214*	*11,902*	*1,465*	

Mayurbhanj ...	**11,573**	*	*	*	327	...	...	...	...	+11,246	**5,732**	*	*	*	163	**5,841**	*	*	*	164
Dhenkanal ...	**1,349**	*	*	*	...	...	...	...	...	+1,349	**601**	*	*	*	...	**748**	*	*	*	...
Bamra ...	**1,996**	*	*	319	904	...	...	...	−585	+1,092	**978**	*	*	151	443	**1,018**	*	*	168	450
Gangpur ...	**36,656**	*	*	*	1,863	...	...	...	...	+34,793	**17,966**	*	*	*	958	**18,690**	*	*	*	905
Elsewhere ...	**1,793**	*	*	*	1,075	...	...	...	...	+718	**924**	*	*	*	544	**869**	*	*	*	531
Kharwar ...	**(a) 63,124**	**58,772**	**53,331**	**41,925**	**41,787**	**+4,352**	**+5,441**	**+11,406**	**+138**	**+21,337**	**31,701**	**29,747**	**26,100**	**20,917**	**20,394**	**31,423**	**29,025**	**27,231**	**21,008**	**21,393**
Hindu ...	*63,124*	*58,772*	*53,330*	*41,915*	*38,826*	*+4,352*	*+5,442*	*+11,415*	*+3,089*	*+24,298*	*31,701*	*29,747*	*26,099*	*20,908*	*18,996*	*31,423*	*29,025*	*27,231*	*21,007*	*19,830*
Tribal religion ...	...	..	*1*	*10*	*2,961*	...	*−1*	*−9*	*−2,951*	*−2,961*	..	..	*1*	*9*	*1,398*	...	..	...	*1*	*1,563*
PALAMAU ...	**63,124**	58,772	53,331	41,925	41,787	+4,352	+5,441	+11,406	+138	+21,337	**31,701**	29,747	26,100	20,917	20,394	**31,423**	29,025	27,231	21,008	21,393
Daltonganj ...	**4,168**	4,501	*	4,443	357	−333	...	...	+4,086	+2,811	**2,110**	2,345	*	2,264	195	**2,058**	2,176	*	2,178	162
Garhwa ...	**7,785**	7,511	*	6,207	4,159	+274		...	+2,048	+2,626	**3,914**	3,884	*	3,148	2,086	**3,871**	3,677	*	3,059	2,073
Banka ...	**10,844**	11,445	*	8,628	1,995	−601		...	+6,633	+3,849	**5,400**	5,900	*	4,399	1,041	**5,444**	5,545	*	4,229	954
Chhatarpur ...	**4,782**	4,328	*	3,182	10,834	+454	...	...	−7,652	−6,052	**2,421**	2,173	*	1,578	5,122	**2,361**	2,155	*	1,604	5,712
Patan ...	**2,972**	2,718	*	2,780	...	+254	...	...	+2,780	+2,972	**1,508**	1,366	*	1,308	...	**1,464**	1,352	*	1,412	...
Hussainabad ..	**2,304**	1,825	*	2,095	12	+479	...	...	+2,083	+2,292	**1,191**	919	*	1,049	5	**1,113**	906	*	1,046	7
Balumath ...	**14,392**	11,877	*	2,240	9,572	+2,515	...	...	−7,332	+4,820	**7,152**	5,982	*	1,070	4,719	**7,240**	5,895	*	1,170	4,853
Latehar ...	**12,881**	11,843	*	9,316	12,345	+1,039	...	...	−2,529	+536	**6,518**	5,900	*	4,345	5,987	**6,363**	5,943	*	4,971	6,358
Mahuadanr ...	**2,996**	2,725	*	2,636	2,613	+271	...	...	+22	+483	**1,487**	1,348	*	1,196	1,239	**1,509**	1,377	*	1,339	1,374
Khetauri ...	**26,787**	**20,946**	**27,024**	**1,431**	†	**+5,841**	**−6,078**	**+25,593**	...		**12,655**	**9,399**	**12,968**	**732**	†	**14,132**	**11,547**	**14,056**	**699**	†
Hindu ...	*26,773*	*20,946*	*27,024*	*1,431*	†	*+5,827*	*−6,078*	*+25,593*	...	...	*12,653*	*9,399*	*12,968*	*732*	†	*14,120*	*11,547*	*14,056*	*699*	†
Tribal religion ...	*14*	...	..	...	†	*+14*	...	...	...	...	*2*	...	...		†	*12*	...	...	...	†
SANTAL PARGANAS ...	**26,787**	20,946	27,024	1,431	†	+5,841	−6,078	+25,593	...	...	**12,655**	9,399	12,968	732	†	**14,132**	11,547	14,056	699	†
Dumka ...	**20,037**	14,904	*	246	†	+5,133	...	...	.	..	**9,546**	6,352	*	122	†	**10,491**	8,552	*	124	†
Godda ...	**4,349**	3,209	*	134	†	+1,140		...		...	**1,999**	1,532	*	75	†	**2,350**	1,677	*	59	†
Godda Damin ...	**818**	1,254	*	123	†	−436	...	...	...	...	**375**	570	*	72	†	**443**	684	*	51	†
Rajmahal Damin ...	**1,324**	1,017	*	468	†	+307	...	...	...	...	**602**	485	*	243	†	**722**	532	*	236	†
Elsewhere ...	**259**	562	*	460	†	−303	...	...	...	...	**133**	460	*	231	†	**126**	102	*	229	†
Khond (Kandh) ...	**315,709**	**287,255**	**302,329**	**288,027**	**294,800**	**+28,454**	**−15,574**	**+14,302**	**−6,773**	**+20,909**	**152,528**	**139,304**	**143,048**	**142,488**	**146,526**	**163,181**	**147,951**	**154,781**	**145,539**	**148,274**
Hindu ...	*167,521*	*130,037*	*135,780*	*	*	*+37,484*	*−5,743*	...		...	*80,706*	*62,723*	*61,129*	*	*	*86,815*	*67,314*	*69,651*	*	*
Tribal religion ...	*148,188*	*157,218*	*167,049*	*	*	*−9,030*	*−9,831*	...		...	*71,822*	*76,581*	*81,919*	*	*	*76,366*	*80,637*	*85,130*	*	*
ANGUL ...	**57,811**	49,916	52,934	47,807	48,362	+7,895	−3,018	+5,127	−555	+9,440	**27,933**	24,185	25,796	23,474	24,150	**29,878**	25,731	27,138	24,333	24,212
Hindu ...	*6,635*	*5,037*	*8,278*	*11,713*	*	*+1,598*	*−3,241*	*−3,435*	.	...	*3,204*	*2,411*	*4,023*	*5,751*	*	*3,431*	*2,626*	*4,255*	*5,962*	*
Tribal religion ...	*51,176*	*44,879*	*44,656*	*36,094*	*	*+6,297*	*+223*	*+8,562*	...	..	*24,729*	*21,774*	*21,773*	*17,723*	*	*26,447*	*23,105*	*22,883*	*18,371*	*
Angul ...	**6,607**	5,011	*	7,756	*	+1,596		...		...	**3,188**	3,395	*	3,826	*	**3,419**	3,616	*	3,930	*
Phulbani ...	**51,204**	44,905	*	40,051	*	+6,299	...	...	...		**24,745**	21,790	*	19,648	*	**26,459**	23,115	*	20,403	*
PURI ...	**1,896**	1,609	1,861	2,560	2,229	+287	−252	−699	+331	−333	**911**	759	919	1,283	1,132	**985**	850	942	1,277	1,007
Hindu ...	*1,896*	*1,598*	*1,861*	*2,560*	*	*+304*	*−263*	*−699*	..	...	*911*	*752*	*919*	*1,283*	*	*985*	*846*	*942*	*1,277*	*
Tribal religion ...	...	*17*	...	...	*	*−17*	*+17*	...	..	...	..	*7*	.	.	*	..	*10*	..	...	*
Banpur ...	**1,866**	1,577	*	2,532	2,219	+289	...	..	+313	−353	**895**	743	*	1,267	1,127	**971**	834	*	1,265	1,092
Elsewhere ...	**30**	33	*	28	10	−2	..	...	+18	+20	**16**	16	*	16	5	**14**	16	*	12	5
SAMBALPUR ...	**14,915**	19,531	13,519	15,026	17,111	−4,616	+6,012	−1,507	−2,085	−2,196	**7,067**	9,632	6,505	7,166	8,208	**7,848**	9,899	7,014	7,860	8,903
Hindu ...	*14,915*	*19,531*	*13,519*	*	*14,984*	*−4,616*	*+6,012*	...	.	*69*	*7,067*	*9,632*	*6,505*	*	*7,198*	*7,848*	*9,899*	*7,014*	*	*7,786*
Tribal religion ...	...	...	...	*	*2,127*	...	..	...	...	*−2,127*	...	...	...	*	*1,010*	..	...	...	*	*1,117*
Sambalpur ...	**971**	988	*	*	*	−17	...	...	...	...	**421**	453	*	*	*	**550**	535	*	*	*
Jharsugra ...	**785**	262	*	*	*	+523	...	...	..	..	**351**	118	*	*	*	**434**	144	*	*	*
Laikera ..	**194**	155	*	*	*	+39	...	...	...	.	**92**	70	*	*	*	**102**	85	*	*	*
Mura ..	**551**	313	*	*	*	+238		..	...	..	**254**	145	*	*	*	**297**	168	*	*	*
Rampella ...	**1,034**	717	*	*	*	+317	..	...	...	...	**491**	340	*	*	*	**543**	377	*	*	*
Katarbagha ...	**220**	178	*	*	*	+42	...	...	...	...	**99**	83	*	*	*	**121**	95	*	*	*
Sason ...	**545**	564	*	*	*	−19	..	...	...	...	**255**	370	*	*	*	**290**	204	*	*	*
Dhama ...	**761**	774	*	*	*	−13	...	...	...	...	**348**	381	*	*	*	**413**	393	*	*	*
Mundher ...	**861**	853	*	*	*	+8	...	...	...	...	**411**	394	*	*	*	**450**	459	*	*	*
Bargarh ..	**263**	278	*	*	*	−15	...	...	...	...	**126**	142	*	*	*	**137**	136	*	*	*
Attabira ...	**528**	546	*	*	*	−20	...	...	...	...	**259**	265	*	*	*	**269**	283	*	*	*
Sobela ...	**1,161**	1,151	*	*	*	+10	..	...	...	...	**561**	550	*	*	*	**600**	601	*	*	*

(a) This total is less by 1,443 than the total given in Table XVII. The latter includes 991 male and 455 female *Kharwars* enumerated in *Singhbhum*, but it is doubtful whether they belong to the same tribe as the *Kharwars* of *Palamau*, and they have not been shown in this table.

* Details not recorded. † Not known. ‡ Excludes Christians, for whom the district total only is available. § Excludes Christians, whose number is unknown.

TABLE XVIII—*continued.*

Variation of Population of selected Tribes.

Tribe, religion and locality.	Persons. 1931.	1921.	1911.	1901.	1891.	Variation (Increase +, Decrease −.) 1921 to 1931.	1911 to 1921.	1901 to 1911.	1891 to 1901.	Net variation 1891 to 1931.	Males. 1931.	1921.	1911.	1901.	1891.	Females. 1931.	1921.	1911.	1901.	1891.	Remarks.
1	2	3	4	5	6	7	8	9	10	11	12	13	14	15	16	17	18	19	20	21	22
Ambabhona ...	**635**	611	*	*	*	+24	...	...	...	...	**292**	294	*	*	*	**343**	317	*	*	*	
Padampur ...	**1,187**	3,153	*	*	*	−1,966	...	...	...	...	**559**	1,564	*	*	*	**628**	1,589	*	*	*	
Bheran ...	**184**	179	*	*	*	+5	...	...	...	...	**84**	84	*	*	*	**100**	95	*	*	*	
Bijepur ...	**295**	337	*	*	*	−42	...	...	...	...	**146**	165	*	*	*	**149**	172	*	*	*	
Melchhamunda ...	**525**	4,361	*	*	*	−3,836	...	...	...	...	**265**	2,264	*	*	*	**260**	2,097	*	*	*	
Gaisilat ...	**312**	354	*	*	*	−42	...	...	...	...	**158**	181	*	*	*	**154**	173	*	*	*	
Jagdalpur ...	**768**	613	*	*	*	+155	...	...	...	...	**368**	297	*	*	*	**400**	316	*	*	*	
Barpali ...	**155**	164	*	*	*	−9	...	...	...	...	**75**	78	*	*	*	**80**	86	*	*	*	
Bhatli ...	**1,135**	1,217	*	*	*	−82	...	...	...	...	**530**	600	*	*	*	**605**	617	*	*	*	
Paikmal ...	**1,845**	1,761	*	*	*	+84	...	...	...	...	**922**	893	*	*	*	**923**	868	*	*	*	
Orissa States ...	**241,087**	216,199	234,515	222,634	227,098	+24,888	−18,316	+11,881	−4,464	+13,989	**116,617**	104,728	114,828	110,565	113,036	**124,470**	111,471	119,087	113,069	114,062	
Hindu ...	*144,075*	*103,877*	*112,122*	*	*	*+40,198*	*−8,245*	...	...	...	*69,524*	*49,928*	*54,682*	*	*	*74,551*	*53,949*	*57,440*	*	*	
Tribal religion ...	*97,012*	*d112,322*	*122,393*	*	*	*−15,310*	*−10,071*	...	...	...	*47,093*	*54,800*	*60,146*	*	*	*49,919*	*57,522*	*62,247*	*	*	
Talcher ...	**811**	*	*	*	1,336	...	...	...	...	−525	**384**	*	*	*	681	**427**	*	*	*	655	
Keonjhar ...	**595**	*	*	*	405	...	...	...	...	+190	**290**	*	*	*	220	**305**	*	*	*	185	
Dhenkanal ...	**1,864**	*	*	*	3,137	...	...	...	...	−1,273	**870**	*	*	*	1,538	**994**	*	*	*	1,509	
Athmallik ...	**3,139**	*	*	*	1,986	...	...	...	...	+1,153	**1,552**	*	*	*	1,004	**1,587**	*	*	*	982	
Hindol ...	**2,088**	*	*	*	1,939	...	...	...	...	+149	**970**	*	*	*	951	**1,118**	*	*	*	968	
Narsinghpur ...	**1,545**	*	*	*	1,448	...	...	...	...	+97	**794**	*	*	*	725	**751**	*	*	*	723	
Baramba ...	**1,973**	*	*	*	780	...	...	...	...	+1,184	**987**	*	*	*	406	**986**	*	*	*	383	
Khandpara ...	**1,590**	*	*	*	1,545	...	...	...	...	+45	**734**	*	*	*	766	**856**	*	*	*	779	
Nayagarh ...	**7,121**	*	*	*	8,519	...	...	...	...	−1,398	**3,423**	*	*	*	4,269	**3,698**	*	*	*	4,250	
Ranpur ...	**1,331**	*	*	*	1,343	...	...	...	...	−12	**641**	*	*	*	669	**690**	*	*	*	674	
Daspalla ...	**8,427**	*	*	*	11,532	...	...	...	...	−3,105	**3,993**	*	*	*	5,697	**4,434**	*	*	*	5,835	
Baud ...	**19,550**	*	*	*	17,851	...	...	...	...	+1,699	**9,603**	*	*	*	8,991	**9,947**	*	*	*	8,860	
Bamra ...	**6,806**	*	*	6,399	7,368	...	...	...	−969	−562	**3,248**	*	*	3,219	3,698	**3,558**	*	*	3,180	3,670	
Rairakhol ...	**2,426**	*	*	1,757	1,419	...	...	...	+338	+1,007	**1,188**	*	*	888	711	**1,238**	*	*	869	708	
Sonpur ...	**6,097**	*	*	5,659	7,914	...	...	...	−2,255	−1,817	**2,885**	*	*	2,689	3,807	**3,212**	*	*	2,970	4,107	
Patna ...	**56,201**	*	*	33,400	52,798	...	...	...	−19,398	+3,403	**27,003**	*	*	15,929	25,243	**29,198**	*	*	17,471	27,555	
Kalahandi ...	**117,393**	*	*	103,086	104,709	...	...	...	−1,623	+12,684	**56,969**	*	*	52,124	53,144	**60,424**	*	*	50,962	51,565	
Gangpur ...	**883**	*	*	*	...	...	...	...	...	+883	**449**	*	*	*	...	**434**	*	*	*	...	
Bonai ...	**1,098**	*	*	*	...	...	...	...	...	+1,098	**552**	*	*	*	...	**546**	*	*	*	...	
Elsewhere ...	**149**	*	*	*	1,060	...	...	...	...	−911	**82**	*	*	*	516	**67**	*	*	*	544	
Korwa ...	**13,021**	†	**13,720**	**11,105**	**9,710**	...	...	**+2,615**	**+1,395**	**+3,311**	**6,519**	†	**6,800**	**5,498**	**4,912**	**6,502**	†	**6,920**	**5,607**	**4,798**	
Hindu ...	*1,462*	†	*6,795*	*2,476*	*	...	...	*+4,319*	...	...	*781*	†	*3,309*	*1,204*	*	*681*	†	*3,486*	*1,272*	*	
Christian ...	*6*	†	...	...	...	...	...	...	...	+6	*5*	†	...	...	...	*1*	†	...	...	...	
Tribal religion ...	*11,553*	†	*6,925*	*8,629*	*	...	...	*−1,704*	...	...	*5,733*	†	*3,491*	*4,294*	*	*5,820*	†	*3,434*	*4,335*	*	
Ranchi ...	**1,495**	†	1,807	1,551	3,341	...	...	+256	−1,790	−1,846	**719**	†	961	779	1,899	**776**	†	846	772	1,643	
Hindu ...	*1,191*	†	*178*	*806*	*	...	...	*−628*	...	...	*593*	†	*111*	*414*	*	*598*	†	*67*	*392*	*	
Christian ...	*6*	†	...	...	...	...	...	...	...	+6	*5*	†	...	...	...	*1*	†	...	...	...	
Tribal religion ...	*298*	†	*1,629*	*745*	*	...	...	*+884*	...	...	*121*	†	*850*	*365*	*	*177*	†	*779*	*380*	*	
Chainpur ...	**831**	†	*	929	1,976	...	...	...	−1,047	−1,145	**423**	†	*	458	1,029	**408**	†	*	471	947	
Ghaghra ...	**96**	†	*	45	404	...	...	...	−359	−308	**44**	†	*	22	187	**52**	†	*	23	217	
Raidih ...	**159**	†	*	249	...	...	...	...	+249	+159	**66**	†	*	122	...	**93**	†	*	127	...	
Kurdeg ...	**368**	†	*	302	8	...	...	...	+294	+360	**168**	†	*	156	2	**200**	†	*	146	6	
Elsewhere ...	**41**	†	*	26	953	...	...	...	−927	−912	**18**	†	*	21	481	**23**	†	*	5	472	
Palamau ...	**11,303**	†	11,863	9,394	6,369	...	...	+2,469	+3,025	+4,934	**5,641**	†	5,813	4,636	3,213	**5,662**	†	6,050	4,758	3,150	
Hindu ...	*48*	†	*6,567*	*1,510*	*	...	...	*+5,057*	...	...	*29*	†	*3,172*	*707*	*	*19*	†	*3,395*	*803*	*	
Tribal religion ...	*11,255*	†	*5,296*	*7,884*	*	...	...	*−9,588*	...	...	*5,612*	†	*2,641*	*3,929*	*	*5,643*	†	*2,655*	*3,955*	*	

Daltonganj ...	**1,758**	†	*	1,344	903	...	...	...	+441	+855	**998**	†	*	628	480	**760**	†	*	716	423	
Garhwa ...	**2,575**	†	*	2,603	87	...	...	...	+2,516	+2,488	**1,228**	†	*	1,310	45	**1,347**	†	*	1,293	42	
Banka ...	**5,522**	†	*	4,497	...	...	...	...	+4,497	+5,522	**2,705**	†	*	2,245	...	**2,817**	†	*	2,252	...	
Hussainabad ...	**314**	†	*	234	4,324	...	...	...	−4,090	−4,010	**153**	†	*	117	2,174	**161**	†	*	117	2,150	
Latehar ...	**719**	†	*	344	414	...	...	...	−70	+305	**368**	†	*	167	104	**351**	†	*	177	220	
Mahuadanr ...	**411**	†	*	372	3	...	...	...	+369	+408	**189**	†	*	169	3	**222**	†	*	203	...	
Elsewhere ...	**4**	†	*	...	638	...	...	...	−638	−634	...	†	*	...	317	**4**	†	*	...	321	
SINGHBHUM *Hindu* ...	**223**	†	50	160	...	...	...	−110	+160	+223	**159**	†	26	83	...	**64**	†	24	77	...	
Kolhan ...	**49**	†	*	*	...	...	...	...	...	+49	**39**	†	*	*	...	**10**	†	*	*	...	
Ghatsila ...	**174**	†	*	*	...	...	...	...	...	+174	**120**	†	*	*	...	**54**	†	*	*	...	
Mal Paharia ...	**37,437**	**39,972**	**38,553**	**25,628**	**17,068**	**−2,535**	**+1,419**	**+12,925**	**+8,560**	**+20,369**	**18,729**	**20,214**	**19,068**	**12,266**	**8,349**	**18,708**	**19,758**	**19,485**	**13,362**	**8,719**	
Hindu ...	*205*	*5,257*	*36,962*	*24,353*	*	*−5,052*	*−31,705*	*+12,609*	...	...	*112*	*2,921*	*18,303*	*11,610*	*	*93*	*2,336*	*18,659*	*12,743*	*	
Christian ...	*69*	...	...	...	...	*+69*	...	...	...	*+62*	*33*	...	...	...	...	*29*	...	...	...	...	
Tribal religion ...	*37,170*	*34,716*	*1,591*	*1,275*	*	*+2,455*	*+33,124*	*+316*	...	...	*18,584*	*17,293*	*765*	*656*	*	*18,586*	*17,422*	*826*	*619*	*	
SANTAL PARGANAS ...	**37,437**	39,972	38,553	25,628	17,068	−2,535	+1,419	+12,925	+8,560	+20,309	**18,729**	20,214	19,068	12,266	8,340	**18,708**	19,758	19,485	13,362	8,719	
Deoghar ...	**571**	2,485	*	...	535	−1,914	...	...	−535	+36	**305**	1,554	*	...	200	**266**	931	*	...	275	
Madhupur ...	**963**	2,864	*	978	960	−1,901	...	...	+18	+3	**306**	1,485	*	457	466	**657**	1,379	*	521	494	
Dumka ...	**13,736**	12,095	*	17,110	905	+1,641	...	...	+16,205	+12,831	**6,777**	5,610	*	8,167	424	**6,959**	6,485	*	8,943	481	
Dumka Damin ...	**4,445**	3,882	*	145	1,440	+563	...	...	−1,295	+3,005	**2,214**	1,907	*	63	690	**2,231**	1,975	*	82	750	
Godda ...	**851**	856	*	892	2,260	−5	...	...	−1,368	−1,409	**466**	460	*	437	1,106	**385**	396	*	455	1,154	
Godda Damin ...	**2,878**	1,517	*	3,186	1,790	+1,361	...	...	+396	−1,088	**1,478**	376	*	1,078	894	**1,400**	1,141	*	1,108	896	
Jamtara ...	**1,484**	2,854	*	683	1,328	−1,370	...	...	−646	+156	**720**	1,366	*	330	659	**764**	1,588	*	352	669	
Rajmahal ...	**146**	602	*	32	2,321	−456	...	...	−2,289	−2,175	**50**	323	*	15	1,160	**96**	279	*	17	1,161	
Rajmahal Damin ...	**982**	1,389	*	316	1,695	−407	...	...	−1,379	−713	**531**	1,076	*	135	826	**451**	913	*	181	869	
Pakaur ...	**3,588**	9,260	*	2,608	2,604	−5,672	...	...	+64	+984	**1,979**	4,911	*	1,289	1,254	**1,609**	4,349	*	1,379	1,350	
Pakaur Damin ...	**7,793**	2,168	*	619	1,230	+5,625	...	...	−611	+6,563	**3,903**	1,246	*	295	610	**3,890**	922	*	324	620	
Munda ...	**549,764**	**460,319**	**490,946**	**367,730**	**§322,310**	**+89,445**	**−30,629**	**+123,216**	**+45,420**	**+227,454**	**270,150**	**230,422**	**240,985**	**180,447**	**§155,634**	**279,614**	**229,897**	**249,963**	**187,283**	**§163,676**	
Hindu ...	*163,776*	*126,115*	*88,840*	*(a)36,222*	*4,864*	*+37,661*	*+37,275*	*+52,618*	*+31,358*	*+158,912*	*80,212*	*66,078*	*42,937*	*(a)18,191*	*3,422*	*83,564*	*60,037*	*45,903*	*(a)18,031*	*2,442*	(a) Excludes *Sambalpur*, where separate figures for *Hindu* and *Tribal religion* are not available.
Christian ...	*133,506*	*93,814*	*80,508*	*56,447*	†	*+39,692*	*+13,306*	*+24,061*	...	...	*66,435*	*46,679*	*39,898*	*28,001*	†	*67,071*	*47,135*	*40,610*	*28,446*	†	
Tribal religion ...	*252,482*	*240,390*	*321,600*	*(a)272,703*	*317,446*	*+12,092*	*−81,210*	*+48,897*	*−44,743*	*−64,964*	*123,503*	*117,665*	*158,150*	*(a)133,002*	*152,212*	*128,979*	*122,725*	*163,450*	*(a)139,701*	*161,234*	
PATNA DIVISION ...	**221**	155	138	30	23	+66	+17	+108	+7	+198	**218**	131	53	21	13	**3**	24	85	9	10	
Hindu ...	*215*	*155*	*138*	*26*	*23*	*+60*	*+17*	*+112*	*+3*	*+192*	*214*	*131*	*53*	*18*	*13*	*1*	*24*	*85*	*8*	*10*	
Christian ...	*6*	...	...	...	...	*+6*	...	...	...	*+6*	*4*	...	...	...	...	*2*	...	...	...	...	
Tribal religion ...	...	...	...	*4*	...	...	...	*−4*	*+4*	...	...	...	...	*3*	...	...	...	...	*1*	...	
TIRHUT DIVISION *Hindu* ...	**436**	1,179	297	264	...	−743	+882	+33	+264	+436	**210**	639	137	160	...	**226**	540	160	104	...	
MONGHYR ...	**3**	75	3	152	...	−72	+72	−149	+152	+3	**3**	59	3	65	...	...	16	...	87	...	
Hindu ...	*3*	*75*	*3*	...	...	*−72*	*+72*	*+3*	...	*+3*	*3*	*59*	*3*	...	...	...	*16*	...	...	...	
Tribal religion ...	...	...	...	*152*	...	...	...	*−152*	*+152*	...	...	...	...	*65*	...	...	...	...	*87*	...	
BHAGALPUR ...	**41**	2	1,404	1,190	(b)43	+39	−1,402	+214	+1,147	−2	**35**	2	645	631	(b)22	**6**	...	759	559	(b)21	(a) See note (b) under *Ho* ante.
Hindu ...	*34*	*1*	*1,311*	*1,157*	*43*	*+33*	*−1,310*	*+144*	*+1,124*	*−9*	*28*	*1*	*617*	*618*	*22*	*6*	...	*694*	*549*	*21*	
Christian ...	*4*	*1*	...	...	...	*+3*	*+1*	...	...	*+4*	*4*	*1*	...	...	...	...	...	...	...	...	
Tribal religion ...	*3*	...	*93*	*28*	...	*+3*	*−93*	*+70*	*+28*	*+3*	*3*	...	*28*	*13*	...	...	...	*65*	*10*	...	
PURNEA ...	**4,818**	5,661	5,662	1,537	(b)...	−843	−1	+4,125	+1,537	+4,818	**2,367**	2,847	2,790	801	(b)...	**2,451**	2,814	2,872	736	(b)...	
Hindu ...	*4,491*	*3,442*	*1,401*	*1,445*	...	*+1,049*	*+2,041*	*−44*	*+1,445*	*+4,491*	*2,204*	*1,831*	*696*	*748*	...	*2,287*	*1,611*	*705*	*697*	...	
Christian ...	...	*7*	...	...	...	*−7*	*+7*	...	...	...	...	*6*	...	...	...	...	*1*	...	...	...	
Tribal religion ...	*327*	*2,212*	*4,261*	*92*	...	*−1,885*	*−2,049*	*+4,169*	*+92*	*+327*	*163*	*1,010*	*2,094*	*53*	...	*164*	*1,202*	*2,167*	*39*	...	
Araria subdivision ...	**79**	‡1,085	*	662	...	−1,006	...	...	+662	+79	**35**	‡533	*	314	...	**44**	‡552	*	348	...	
Kishanganj subdivision.	**278**	‡633	*	100	...	−355	...	...	+100	+278	**137**	‡186	*	56	...	**141**	‡447	*	44	...	
Sadr subdivision ...	**4,461**	‡3,936	*	775	...	+525	...	...	+775	+4,461	**2,195**	‡3,122	*	431	...	**2,266**	‡1,814	*	344	...	
SANTAL PARGANAS ...	**230**	1,290	1,194	1,213	(b)2	−1,060	+96	−19	+1,211	+228	**114**	612	650	588	(b)2	**116**	678	544	625	(b)...	
Hindu ...	*2*	*2*	*73*	*96*	*2*	...	*−71*	*−23*	*+94*	...	*2*	...	*44*	*55*	*2*	...	*2*	*29*	*41*	...	
Christian ...	*10*	...	...	...	...	*+10*	...	...	...	*+10*	...	...	...	...	...	*10*	...	...	...	...	
Tribal religion ...	*218*	*1,288*	*1,121*	*1,117*	...	*−1,070*	*+167*	*+4*	*+1,117*	*+218*	*112*	*612*	*606*	*533*	...	*106*	*676*	*515*	*584*	...	

*Details not recorded. †Not known. ‡Excludes Christians, for whom the district total only is available. §Excludes Christians, whose number is unknown.

TABLE XVIII—*continued.*

VARIATION OF POPULATION OF SELECTED TRIBES.

TRIBE, RELIGION AND LOCALITY.	PERSONS.					VARIATION (Increase +, Decrease −)				Net variation 1891 to 1931	MALES					FEMALES					REMARKS
	1931	1921	1911.	1901	1891.	1921 to 1931	1911 to 1921	1901 to 1911	1891 to 1901		1931	1921	1911	1901	1891	1931	1921	1911	1901	1891	
1	2	3	4	5	6	7	8	9	10	11	12	13	14	15	16	17	18	19	20	21	22
ORISSA DIVISION (excluding Sambalpur).	**804**	308	701	714	73	+496	−393	−13	+641	+731	**402**	161	327	357	39	**402**	157	374	357	34	
Hindu	*719*	*303*	*247*	*147*	*14*	+*416*	+*56*	+*100*	+*138*	+*705*	*357*	*149*	*115*	*84*	*9*	*362*	*154*	*132*	*63*	*5*	
Christian	*13*					+*13*				+*13*	*12*					*1*					
Tribal religion	*72*	*5*	*454*	*587*	*59*	+*67*	−*449*	−*113*	+*508*	+*13*	*33*	*2*	*212*	*273*	*30*	*39*	*3*	*242*	*294*	*29*	
SAMBALPUR	**10,619**	8,643	7,478	2,358	1,679	+1 777	+1 364	+5,120	+679	+8 940	**5 160**	4 309	3,674	1 253	822	**5,459**	4 533	3 904	1,105	857	
Hindu	*8,111*	*4,765*	*1,335*	*	*1,307*	+*3 346*	+*3,430*			+*6 804*	*3,963*	*2,366*	*670*	*	*641*	*4 148*	*2 400*	*666*	*	*666*	
Christian	*1 433*	*1,096*				+*337*	+*1,096*			+*1 433*	*686*	*543*			†	*747*	*553*				
Tribal religion	*1,075*	*2,981*	*6,143*	*	*372*	−*1,906*	−*3,163*			+*703*	*511*	*1 401*	*2 904*	*	*181*	*564*	*1,580*	*3,289*	*	*191*	
Sambalpur	**3,178**	‡2 743	*	*	*	+435					**1,538**	‡1 264	*	*	*	**1,640**	‡1 479	*	*	*	
Jharsugra	**1,460**	‡657	*	*	*	+803					**694**	‡313	*	*	*	**766**	‡344	*	*	*	
Laikera	**903**	‡673	*	*	*	+230					**471**	‡341	*	*	*	**432**	‡333	*	*	*	
Mura	**841**	‡397	*	*	*	+444					**439**	‡195	*	*	*	**411**	‡202	*	*	*	
Rampella	**288**	‡294	*	*	*	−6					**123**	‡146	*	*	*	**165**	‡148	*	*	*	
Katarbagha	**1,416**	‡1,011	*	*	*	+405					**655**	‡473	*	*	*	**761**	‡539	*	*	*	
Sason	**1,331**	‡831	*	*	*	+500					**630**	‡405	*	*	*	**701**	‡426	*	*	*	
Dhama	**96**	‡162	*	*	*	−66					**63**	‡97	*	*	*	**33**	‡65	*	*	*	
Mundher	**699**	‡412	*	*	*	+287					**338**	‡207	*	*	*	**361**	‡205	*	*	*	
Bargarh subdivision	**407**	‡566	*	*	*	−159					**218**	‡326	*	*	*	**189**	‡240	*	*	*	
HAZARIBAGH	**18,695**	17,846	16,694	15,067	§13,654	+849	+1,152	+1,627	+1,413	+5 041	**9,150**	8,838	7 065	7,404	§6,596	**9,545**	9 008	8,709	7 663	§7 058	
Hindu	*8,707*	*15 001*	*12,021*	*631*	*2 284*	−*6,294*	+*2,980*	+*11 390*	−*1,653*	+*6,423*	*4 153*	*7 287*	*5 725*	*280*	*1 108*	*4,555*	*7 714*	*6 296*	*351*	*1 176*	
Christian	*424*	*790*	*126*	*45*	†	−*366*	+*664*	+*81*			*259*	*498*	*58*	*34*	†	*165*	*299*	*68*	*11*	†	
Tribal religion	*9 564*	*2 055*	*4 547*	*14,391*	*11 370*	+*7 509*	−*2,492*	−*9,844*	+*3,021*	−*1,806*	*4,739*	*1,053*	*2 202*	*7,090*	*5,488*	*4,825*	*1 002*	*2 345*	*7 301*	*5,882*	
Barkagaon	**1,231**	‡1,114	*	‡903	§731	+117			+172	+500	**595**	‡571	*	‡437	§310	**636**	‡543	*	‡486	§421	
Ramgarh	**11,089**	‡8 966	*	‡10,831	§1,121	+2 123			+8,710	+9,968	**5,229**	‡4,325	*	‡4 706	§511	**5,860**	‡4 641	*	‡5 125	§610	
Gumia	**1,014**	‡558	*	‡330 }	§1,481	+456			−251	+1 074	**502**	‡276	*	‡220 }	§712	**512**	‡292	*	‡110 }	§769	
Mandu	**1,541**	‡1,036	*	‡900 }		+505					**775**	‡524	*	‡423 }		**766**	‡512	*	‡477 }		
Petarbar	**1,079**	‡1,055	*	‡1 633	§1,909	+24			−276	−830	**529**	‡590	*	‡810	§910	**550**	‡465	*	‡823	§999	
Giridih	**164**	‡2,438	*	‡829	§1 045	−2 274			−1 116	−1,781	**83**	‡1 107	*	‡428	§950	**81**	‡1 331	*	‡401	§995	
Dumri	**1,875**	‡866	*	‡168	§922	+1,009			−754	+953	**1,058**	‡586	*	‡84	§450	**817**	‡280	*	‡84	§472	
Elsewhere	**702**	‡1,023	*	‡428	§5,545	−321			−5,117	−4,843	**379**	‡361	*	‡263	§2,753	**323**	‡662	*	‡166	§2,792	
RANCHI	**386,420**	328,596	343,721	287,105	§167,273	+57,832	−15,133	+56,616	+119,832	+219,147	**189,445**	164,801	168 383	140 525	§81 364	**196,975**	163 797	175 338	146 580	§85 909	
Hindu	*110 556*	*65,486*	*56,720*	*12 278*	*369*	+*45 070*	+*8 766*	+*44 442*	+*11,909*	+*110,187*	*54,173*	*35 675*	*27 727*	*6,320*	*178*	*56 383*	*29 811*	*28 993*	*6 958*	*191*	
Christian	*97 241*	*74,264*	*66,992*	*51,505*	†	+*22,977*	+*7 272*	+*15 487*			*48,282*	*36,931*	*33 174*	*25 542*	†	*48 959*	*37 333*	*33 818*	*25 963*	†	
Tribal religion	*178 623*	*188,848*	*220,009*	*223,329*	*166,904*	−*10 225*	−*31,161*	−*3,313*	+*56 418*	+*11,719*	*86,990*	*92,196*	*107,482*	*108 663*	*81,186*	*91 633*	*96 653*	*112,527*	*114,659*	*85,718*	
Loherdaga	**1,566**	1 519	* }	‡2,210	§2,995	+47 }			−785	−207	**776**	738	* }	‡1,157	§1,381	**790**	781	* }	‡1 053	§1,614	
Kuru	**1,222**	1,139	* }			+83 }					**565**	629	* }			**657**	610	* }			
Burmu	**5,851**	5,014	* }	‡6,827	§7,264	+837 }			−437	+586	**2,911**	2,462	* }	‡3 284	§3,354	**2,940**	2,552	* }	‡3 543	§3,910	
Mandar	**1,999**	1,804	* }			+195 }					**948**	892	* }			**1 051**	917	* }			
Ranchi	**27,192**	23,591	* }	‡27,992	§29,456	+3 601 }			−1,464	+9,855	**13,241**	11,867	* }	‡13,979	§14,699	**13,951**	11,724	* }	‡14,018	§14,757	
Ormanjhi	**4,272**	3,571	* }			+701 }					**2,106**	1,759	* }			**2,166**	1 812	* }			
Angara	**7,847**	6,702	* }			+1,145 }					**3,923**	3 234	* }			**3,924**	3,468	* }			
Silli	**5,110**	5,358	* }	‡16,763	§6,589	−248 }			+8,173	+4 936	**2,549**	2 731	* }	‡8,582	§4,273	**2,561**	2 637	* }	‡8,180	§4 316	
Sonahatu	**8,415**	7,676	* }			+739 }					**4,172**	3,646	* }			**4 243**	4 090	* }			
Bero	**2,346**	2 268	* }	‡19,387	§23,630	+78 }			−4,143	+11,240	**1,057**	1 030	* }	‡9,216	§10 640	**1,289**	1 238	* }	‡10,171	§12,890	
Lapung	**10,235**	9,204	* }			+1,031 }					**4,770**	4,426	* }			**5 465**	4 778	* }			
Karra	**22,198**	19,557	* }			+2,641 }					**10,713**	9,487	* }			**11,485**	10 070	* }			
Torpa	**42,872**	39,205	* }	‡69,400	§49,109	+3 667 }			+10,201	+57,718	**20,826**	18,867	* }	‡28,907	§24,267	**22,046**	20 338	* }	‡30 403	§24 933	
Khunti	**64,045**	57,304	* }			+6,741 }					**31,561**	28,321	* }			**32,484**	28,263	* }			
Bundu	**14,800**	13,206	* }	‡57,360	(c)	+1,594 }					**7,407**	6,363	* }	‡37,509	(c)	**7,393**	6,844	* }	‡29,800	(c)	(c) There must really have been many *Mundas* in Bundu and Tamar in 1891 Some of them appear to have been incorrectly returned as *Oraons*—*q. v.*
Tamar	**65,349**	47,121	* }			+18,228 }					**32,778**	26,877	* }			**32,571**	20 244	* }			
Bishunpur	**1,643**	1,051	* }	‡2,910	§5,072	+592 }		...	−2,163	+1,461	**855**	629	* }	‡1,554	§2,497	**788**	432	* }	‡1,356	§2,575	
Ghaghra	**1,546**	1,199	* }			+347 }					**758**	530	* }			**788**	669	* }			
Gumla	**827**	721	* }			+106 }					**375**	332	* }			**452**	389	* }			
Raidih	**1,335**	1,142	* }			+193 }					**669**	514	* }			**666**	628	* }			
Palkot	**1,182**	836	* }			+346 }					**581**	412	* }			**601**	424	* }			

Sesai ...	**3,934**	3,366	*	‡2,894		+568	...	...			**1,849**	1,634	*	‡1,370		**2,085**	1,735	*	‡1,464	
Basia ...	**26,608**	23,623	*	‡12,362	§35,579	+2,986	...	...	−8,235	+17,194	**12,833**	11,277	*	‡5,963	§17,491	**13,775**	13,346	*	‡6,399	§18,086
Bano ...	**22,231**	17,946	*	‡12,146		+4,285	...	...			**10,879**	8,914	*	‡5,890		**11,352**	9,033	*	‡6,258	
Chaimpur ...	**2,396**	2,329	*	‡1,809	§3,520	+67	...	...	+8,752	+25,453	**1,259**	1,330	*	‡821	§1,725	**1,137**	990	*	‡988	§1,795
Kolebira ...	**26,577**	21,222	*	‡10,463		+5,355	...	...			**12,626**	10,491	*	‡5,130		**13,951**	10,734	*	‡5,333	
Simdega ...	**11,777**	9,577	*	‡2,774	§3,069	+2,200	...	...	+1,058	+10,763	**5,892**	4,824	*	‡1,341	§1,037	**5,885**	4,753	*	‡1,433	§1,032
Kurdeg ...	**1,045**	1,347	*	‡353		−302	...	...			**566**	696	*	‡190		**479**	651	*	‡163	
PALAMAU ...	**3,729**	3,231	3,968	9,607	§54,279	+498	−727	−5,649	−44,672	−50,556	**1,791**	1,612	2,098	4,591	§27,002	**1,938**	1,619	1,800	5,016	§27,277
Hindu ...	*115*	*2,714*	*881*	*9,013*	*87*	*−2,599*	*+1,883*	*−8,162*	*+8,926*	*+23*	*34*	*1,350*	*509*	*4,320*	*42*	*81*	*1,364*	*322*	*4,693*	*45*
Christian ...	*33*	*374*	*234*	...	†	*−341*	*+140*	*+234*	...	...	*16*	*196*	*126*	...	†	*17*	*178*	*108*	...	†
Tribal religion ...	*3,581*	*143*	*2,893*	*594*	*54,192*	*+3,438*	*−3,750*	*−2,299*	*−53,598*	*−50,611*	*1,741*	*66*	*1,463*	*271*	*26,960*	*1,840*	*77*	*1,430*	*323*	*27,232*
Palan ...	**15**	‡48	*	1	§47,115	−33	...	...	−47,114	−47,100	**8**	‡30	*	1	§23,473	**7**	‡28	*	...	§23,642
Balumath ...	**3,047**	‡3,739	*	9,001	§4,843	+308	...	...	+4,158	−1,796	**1,453**	‡1,370	*	4,315	§2,372	**1,594**	‡1,369	*	4,686	§2,471
Elsewhere ...	**667**	‡70	*	605	§2,321	+597	...	...	−1,716	−1,654	**330**	‡26	*	275	§1,157	**337**	‡44	*	330	§1,164
MANBHUM ...	**2,164**	2,312	7,361	3,832	§505	−148	−4,949	+3,429	+3,327	+1,659	**1,130**	1,218	2,983	1,792	§286	**1,034**	1,004	4,278	2,040	§219
Hindu ...	*1,910*	*2,218*	*4,504*	*2,366*	*505*	*−308*	*−2,286*	*+1,938*	*+2,061*	*+1,405*	*992*	*1,148*	*1,663*	*1,228*	*286*	*918*	*1,070*	*2,901*	*1,338*	*219*
Christian ...	*150*	*29*	*114*	*79*	†	*+121*	*−85*	*+35*	...	...	*72*	*22*	*50*	*41*	†	*78*	*7*	*64*	*38*	†
Tribal religion ...	*104*	*65*	*2,643*	*1,187*	...	*+39*	*−2,578*	*+1,456*	*+1,187*	*+104*	*66*	*48*	*1,330*	*523*	...	*38*	*17*	*1,313*	*664*	...
Sadr subdivision ...	**1,816**	‡1,650	*	‡2,107	*	+166	...	...	...	...	**911**	‡819	*	‡999	*	**905**	‡831	*	‡1,108	*
Dhanbad subdivision	**348**	‡633	*	‡1,646	*	−285	...	...	...	...	**219**	‡377	*	‡752	*	**129**	‡256	*	‡894	*
SINGHBHUM ...	**50,963**	39,268	31,612	28,807	§21,365	+11,695	+7,656	+2,805	+7,442	+29,598	**25,143**	19,518	15,803	14,255	§10,718	**25,820**	19,750	15,809	14,552	§10,647
Hindu ...	*19,085*	*6,812*	*173*	*2,076*	...	*+6,273*	*+6,639*	*−1,902*	*+2,075*	*+12,985*	*5,878*	*3,472*	*98*	*1,067*	...	*6,207*	*3,340*	*75*	*1,008*	...
Christian ...	*11,122*	*5,965*	*4,852*	*4,174*	†	*+5,167*	*+1,108*	*+678*	...	...	*5,631*	*2,909*	*2,455*	*2,058*	†	*5,491*	*3,053*	*2,397*	*2,116*	†
Tribal religion ...	*27,756*	*26,601*	*26,687*	*22,558*	*21,365*	*+1,955*	*−86*	*+4,029*	*+1,193*	*+6,391*	*13,634*	*13,144*	*13,260*	*11,130*	*10,718*	*14,122*	*13,357*	*13,337*	*11,428*	*10,647*
Chakradharpur ...	**32,278**	‡22,420	*	‡18,356	§1,420	+9,858	...	...	+16,936	+30,858	**15,319**	‡11,048	*	‡9,063	§740	**16,459**	‡11,372	*	‡9,293	§680
Kolhan ...	**962**	‡389	*	‡274	§11,305	+573	...	...	−11,001	−10,403	**459**	‡224	*	‡105	§5,718	**503**	‡165	*	‡169	§5,647
Manoharpur ...	**12,145**	‡4,383	*	‡1,984	§2,530	+7,762	...	...	−546	+9,615	**6,277**	‡2,195	*	‡1,007	§1,210	**5,868**	‡2,188	*	‡977	§1,320
Ghatsila ...	**5,578**	‡6,121	*	‡4,019	§6,050	−543	...	...	−2,031	−472	**2,588**	‡3,149	*	‡2,022	§3,050	**2,990**	‡2,972	*	‡1,997	§3,000
ORISSA STATES ...	**64,134**	46,369	66,323	(d)11,849	§56,702	+17,765	−19,954	+54,474	−44,943	+7,343	**31,837**	23,209	33,382	(d) 5,994	§28,443	**32,297**	23,160	32,941	(d)5,855	§28,349
Hindu ...	*11,875*	*22,293*	*9,751*	*4,803*	*230*	*−10,418*	*+12,542*	*+4,948*	*+4,573*	*+11,645*	*5,822*	*11,151*	*4,927*	*2,430*	*121*	*6,053*	*11,142*	*4,824*	*2,373*	*109*
Christian ...	*22,951*	*11,331*	*8,190*	*644*	†	*+11,720*	*+3,041*	*+7,546*	...	...	*11,417*	*5,645*	*4,035*	*326*	†	*11,534*	*5,686*	*4,155*	*318*	†
Tribal religion ...	*29,308*	*19,845*	*48,382*	*6,408*	*56,562*	*+16,463*	*−35,537*	*+41,980*	*−50,160*	*−27,254*	*14,598*	*6,518*	*24,420*	*3,238*	*28,322*	*14,710*	*6,332*	*23,962*	*3,164*	*28,240*
Mayurbhanj ...	**1,446**	*	*	*	§12,215	...	...	...	...	−10,767	**782**	*	*	*	§5,410	**686**	*	*	*	§6,805
Keonjhar ...	**6,239**	*	*	*	§20,841	...	...	...	...	−11,602	**3,089**	*	*	*	§10,333	**3,150**	*	*	*	§10,008
Athmallik ...	**791**	*	*	*	§173	...	...	...	...	+618	**397**	*	*	*	§90	**394**	*	*	*	§83
Bamra ...	**3,183**	*	*	*	§1,733	...	...	...	...	+1,450	**1,493**	*	*	*	§812	**1,690**	*	*	*	§921
Patna ...	**1,579**	*	*	*	§191	...	...	...	...	+1,388	**787**	*	*	*	§94	**792**	*	*	*	§97
Kalahandi ...	**1,310**	*	*	*	§123	...	...	...	...	+1,187	**699**	*	*	*	§66	**611**	*	*	*	§57
Gangpur ...	**36,251**	*	*	*	§9,788	...	...	...	...	+26,463	**17,962**	*	*	*	§5,070	**18,289**	*	*	*	§4,718
Bonai ...	**12,419**	*	*	*	§6,271	...	...	...	...	+6,148	**6,149**	*	*	*	§3,147	**6,270**	*	*	*	§3,124
Elsewhere ...	**914**	*	*	*	§5,457	...	...	...	...	−4,543	**479**	*	*	*	§2,921	**435**	*	*	*	§2,536
CHOTA NAGPUR STATES	**6,487**	5,183	4,502	4,005	6,622	+1,304	+681	+497	−2,617	−135	**3,145**	3,476	3,172	3,010	3,327	**3,342**	2,707	2,330	1,995	3,295
Hindu ...	*4,617*	*1,669*	*35*	*1,711*	...	*+2,948*	*+1,634*	*−1,676*	*+1,711*	*−4,517*	*2,180*	*820*	*13*	*868*	...	*2,337*	*849*	*22*	*848*	...
Christian ...	*119*	*67*	...	...	...	*+52*	*+67*	...	...	*+119*	*52*	*35*	...	...	...	*67*	*32*	...	...	...
Tribal religion ...	*1,851*	*3,447*	*4,467*	*2,294*	*6,622*	*−1,596*	*−1,020*	*+2,173*	*−4,328*	*−4,771*	*913*	*1,621*	*3,159*	*1,147*	*3,327*	*938*	*1,826*	*3,308*	*1,147*	*3,295*
Saraikela ...	**885**	*	*	*	2,216	...	...	...	...	−1,331	**463**	*	*	*	1,118	**422**	*	*	*	1,098
Kharsawan ...	**5,602**	*	*	*	4,406	...	...	...	...	+1,196	**2,682**	*	*	*	2,209	**2,920**	*	*	*	2,197
Oraon ...	**687,111**	**566,383**	**587,411**	**449,116**	(a) **§404,618**	**+70,728**	**−21,028**	**+138,295**	**+44,498**	**+232,493**	**312,428**	**277,340**	**232,867**	**214,194**	(a) §193,328	**324,633**	**289,043**	**304,544**	**234,922**	(a) §211,290
Hindu ...	*222,152*	*96,148*	*52,482*	*(b)49,218*	*(c)5,812*	*+126,004*	*+43,666*	*+10,264*	*+36,406*	*+216,340*	*108,358*	*48,660*	*36,309*	*(b)22,147*	*(c)2,924*	*113,794*	*47,488*	*26,173*	*(b)20,071*	*(c)3,888*
Christian ...	*145,129*	*119,481*	*112,238*	*91,477*	†	*+25,698*	*+6,693*	*+51,261*	...	...	*72,123*	*59,204*	*55,594*	*30,280*	†	*73,006*	*60,927*	*57,144*	*31,197*	†
Tribal religion ...	*269,830*	*360,804*	*422,191*	*(b)335,741*	*(c)396,586*	*−80,974*	*−71,387*	*+86,460*	*−59,846*	*−126,756*	*131,947*	*169,476*	*200,964*	*(b)157,010*	*(c)188,820*	*137,883*	*181,328*	*221,227*	*(b)178,731*	*(c)206,766*
PATNA ...	**39**	23	...	79	2	+ 16	+ 23	− 79	+ 77	+ 37	**31**	3	...	40	2	**8**	20	...	39	...
Hindu ...	*12*	*3*	...	*79*	*2*	*+ 9*	*+ 3*	*− 79*	*+ 77*	*+ 10*	*9*	...	...	*40*	*2*	*3*	*3*	...	*39*	...
Christian ...	*12*	*20*	...	...	...	*−8*	*+ 20*	...	...	*+ 12*	*7*	*3*	...	...	...	*5*	*17*	...	...	...
Tribal religion ...	*15*	...	...	...	...	*+ 15*	...	...	...	*+ 15*	*15*	...	...	...	...	...	...	...	...	...
GAYA ...	**191**	84	57	150	10	+107	+ 27	− 93	+140	+181	**80**	62	33	83	10	**111**	22	24	67	...
Hindu ...	*191*	*84*	*15*	*150*	*10*	*+107*	*+ 69*	*−135*	*+140*	*+181*	*80*	*62*	*14*	*83*	*10*	*111*	*22*	*1*	*67*	...
Tribal religion ...	...	...	*42*	...	...	...	*− 42*	*+ 42*	...	...	...	...	*19*	...	...	...	...	*23*	...	...

(d) Apparently inaccurate.

(a) Excludes *Cuttack*, *Balasore*, *Angul* and *Puri*, for which figures are not available.

(b) Excludes *Sambalpur*, where separate figures for *Hindu* and *Tribal religion* are not available.

(c) Excludes *Singhbhum*, where separate figures for *Hindu* and *Tribal religion* are not available.

* Details not recorded. † Not known. ‡ Excludes Christians, for whom the district total only is available. § Excludes Christians, whose number is unknown.

TABLE XVIII—*continued.*

VARIATION OF POPULATION OF SELECTED TRIBES.

Tribe, religion and locality.	Persons. 1931.	1921.	1911.	1901.	1891	Variation. (Increase +, Decrease −.) 1921 to 1931.	1911 to 1921.	1901 to 1911.	1891 to 1901.	Net variation 1891 to 1931.
1	2	3	4	5	6	7	8	9	10	11
Shahabad	**1,710**	1,874	1,599	1,604	7	−164	+275	−5	+1,597	+1,703
Hindu	*1,710*	*1,874*		*1,604*	*7*	*−164*	*+1,874*	*−1,604*	*+1,597*	*+1,703*
Tribal religion	.	.	*1,599*	..			*−1,599*	*+1,599*	...	..
Saran *Hindu*	...	1	2	.		−1	−1	+2		.
Champaran	**6,947**	9,586	3,103	791		−2,639	+6,483	+2,312	+791	+6,947
Hindu	*6,462*	*9,586*	*3,103*	*791*		*−3,124*	*+6,483*	*+2,312*	*+791*	*+6,462*
Tribal religion	*485*			.		*+485*	..	..		*+485*
Bagaha	**5,283**	5,301	*	*		−18		...	.	+5,283
Shikarpur	**1,664**	1,793	*	*		−129	..		..	+1,664
Elsewhere		2,492	*	*	..	−2,492	..	.	..	
Muzaffarpur	...	726	16	339	2	−726	+710	−323	+337	−2
Hindu	.	*552*	*16*	*339*	*2*	*−552*	*+536*	*−323*	*+337*	*−2*
Christian		*174*	..	..		*−174*	*+174*	.		
Darbhanga *Hindu*		1,024	900	587		−1,024	+124	+313	+587	
Monghyr *Hindu*	1	1	126				−125	+126	.	+1
Bhagalpur	**1,031**	973	2,164	4,804	(d)44	+58	−1,191	−2,640	+4,760	+987
Hindu	*890*	*628*	*1,730*	*4,790*	*44*	*+192*	*−1,102*	*−3,060*	*+4,746*	*+776*
Christian	*2*	*6*	...			*−4*	*+6*			*+2*
Tribal religion	*209*	*339*	*434*	*14*		*−130*	*−95*	*+420*	*+14*	*+209*
Colgong	**623**	‡616	*	1,954	*	+7	...			.
Supaul	**393**	‡296	*	91	*	+97				
Madhipura	**4**	..	*	704	*	+4				
Katoria	**2**		*	942	*	+2				
Elsewhere	**9**	‡55	*	1,023	*	−46			...	
Purnea	**18,115**	16,348	15,192	12,046	(d)1	+1,767	+1,156	+3,146	+12,045	+18,114
Hindu	*15,451*	*12,503*	*6,388*	*11,845*	*1*	*+2,948*	*+7,115*	*−6,457*	*+11,844*	*+15,450*
Christian		*151*				*−151*	*+151*			.
Tribal religion	*2,664*	*3,694*	*9,804*	*201*		*−1,030*	*−6,110*	*+9,603*	*+201*	*+2,664*
Araria subdivision	**203**	‡1,571	*	1,456	*	−1,368				
Kishanganj subdivision	**1,474**	‡633	*	15	*	+841				
Sadr subdivision	**16,438**	‡13,993	*	10,575	*	+2,445				
Santal Parganas	**5,816**	4,056	5,323	2,697	(d)236	+1,760	−1,167	+2,626	+2,461	+5,580
Hindu	*239*	*240*	*515*	*2,572*	*236*	*−1*	*−275*	*−2,057*	*+2,336*	*+3*
Christian	*31*	*1*	*5*			*+30*	*−4*	*+5*		*+31*
Tribal religion	*5,546*	*3,815*	*4,703*	*125*		*+1,731*	*−888*	*+4,578*	*+125*	*+5,546*
Godda subdivision	**2,021**	‡1,463	*		*	+558		.		
Rajmahal subdivision	**3,765**	‡2,418	*	2,687	*	+1,347				
Elsewhere	**30**	‡174	*	10	*	−144			...	
Cuttack	**2,069**	20			†	+2,049	+20	.	.	
Hindu	*1,892*	20			†	*+1,872*	+20	.	...	
Christian	*2*				†	*+2*		...	...	...
Tribal religion	*175*			.	†	*+175*	..		...	...

Tribe, religion and locality.	Males. 1931.	1921.	1911	1901.	1891	Females. 1931.	1921.	1911.	1901.	1891	Remarks
1	12	13	14	15	16	17	18	19	20	21	22
Shahabad	**890**	918	803	763	7	**820**	956	797	841		
Hindu	*890*	*918*		*763*	*7*	*820*	*956*		*841*		
Tribal religion		.	*803*	.	..			*797*			
Saran *Hindu*	.	1	1	.		...	.	1	.		
Champaran	**3,342**	4,965	1,621	526	.	**3,605**	4,621	1,482	265		
Hindu	*3,090*	*4,965*	*1,621*	*526*		*3,372*	*4,621*	*1,482*	*265*		
Tribal religion	*252*					*233*	.				
Bagaha	**2,506**	2,715	*	*		**2,777**	2,586	*	*		
Shikarpur	**836**	961	*	*		**828**	832	*	*		
Elsewhere		1,289	*	*			1,203	*	*		
Muzaffarpur		378	8	145	2		348	8	194	...	
Hindu		*282*	*8*	*145*	*2*		*270*	*8*	*194*		
Christian	...	*96*				..	*78*	.			
Darbhanga *Hindu*	..	550	464	289		...	474	436	298		
Monghyr *Hindu*	**1**		51	.	..	..	1	75	.		
Bhagalpur	**472**	531	1,099	2,486	(d)30	**559**	442	1,065	2,318	(d)14	(d) See note (a) under *Ho* ante
Hindu	*363*	*347*	*894*	*2,479*	*30*	*457*	*281*	*836*	*2,311*	*14*	
Christian	*2*	*4*			..		*2*			..	
Tribal religion	*107*	*180*	*205*	*7*		*102*	*159*	*229*	*7*		
Colgong	**281**	‡355	*	965	*	**342**	‡261	*	989	*	
Supaul	**181**	‡143	*	45	*	**212**	‡153	*	46	*	
Madhipura			*	439	*	**4**		*	365	*	
Katoria	**2**		*	513	*			*	429	*	
Elsewhere	**8**	‡29	*	534	*	**1**	‡26	*	489	*	
Purnea	**9,242**	8,170	7,661	6,607	(d)1	**8,873**	8,178	7,531	5,439	(d)	
Hindu	*7,865*	*6,317*	*3,704*	*6,505*	*1*	*7,586*	*6,186*	*2,684*	*5,340*		
Christian		*77*				.	*74*			..	
Tribal religion	*1,377*	*1,776*	*4,957*	*102*		*1,287*	*1,918*	*4,847*	*99*		
Araria subdivision	**104**	‡699	*	877	*	**99**	‡872	*	579		
Kishanganj subdivision	**696**	‡266	*	5	*	**778**	‡367	*	10	..	
Sadr subdivision	**8,442**	‡7,128	*	5,725	*	**7,996**	‡6,865	*	4,850		
Santal Parganas	**2,800**	2,091	2,578	1,384	(d)114	**3,016**	1,965	2,645	1,313	(d)122	
Hindu	*78*	*118*	*256*	*1,320*	*114*	*161*	*122*	*259*	*1,252*	*122*	
Christian	*4*	*1*	*2*			*27*		*3*			
Tribal religion	*2,718*	*1,972*	*2,320*	*64*		*2,828*	*1,843*	*2,383*	*61*		
Godda subdivision	**1,009**	‡818	*		*	**1,012**	645	*		*	
Rajmahal subdivision	**1,788**	‡1,183	*	1,374	*	**1,977**	1,235	*	1,313	*	
Elsewhere	**3**	‡89	*	10	*	**27**	85	*		*	
Cuttack	**1,146**	20	.	.	†	**923**	...			†	
Hindu	*1,018*	20		.	†	*874*	.		.	†	
Christian	*2*		..		†					†	
Tribal religion	*126*		...	..	†	*49*	.	.	..	†	

BALASORE ...	545	407	383	306	†	+138	+34	+77	...	...	247	186	173	156	†	298	221	211	151	†	
Hindu ...	544	304	11	161	†	+240	+293	−150	...	...	247	148	3	82	†	297	156	8	79	†	
Tribal religion ..	1	103	372	145	†	−102	−269	+237		...		44	169	73	†	1	59	203	72	†	
ANGUL ...	994	556	996	1,182	†	+438	−440	−186		..	420	274	478	609	†	574	282	518	573	†	
Hindu ...	903	556		96	†	+347	+556	−96		...	375	274	..	53	†	528	282	..	43	†	
Tribal religion ...	91	.	996	1,086	†	+91	−996	−90		...	45		478	556	†	46	..	518	530	†	
PURI *Hindu*	12		...		†	+12		...	...	..	11	..			†	1	..	..	...	†	
SAMBALPUR ..	6,686	4,967	10,369	(e)9,660	8,068	+1,719	−5,402	+689	+1,612	−1,382	3,269	2,436	5,100	(e) 4,757	3,982	3,417	2,531	5,269	(e) 4,973	4,086	(e) Returned as *Kol*. See note (a) under *Ho* ante.
Hindu .	5,593	3,266	6,272	*	4,044	+2,257	−3,006			+1,479	2,677	1,587	3,036	*	2,002	2,846	1,379	3,236	*	2,042	
Christian .	34	20			.	+14	+20	..	..	+34	17	8	...			17	12			...	
Tribal religion ..	1,129	1,681	4,097	*	4,024	−552	−2,416			−2,395	575	841	2,064	*	1,939	554	840	2,033	*	2,044	
Sambalpur .	2,856	‡2,318	*	*	*	+518					1,352	‡1,131	*	*	*	1,504	‡1,197	*	*	*	
Jharsugra ..	704	‡431	*	*	*	+223					358	‡247	*	*	*	346	‡234	*	*	*	
Laikera ...	328	‡186	*	*	*	+142					177	‡90	*	*	*	151	‡96	*	*	*	
Mura .	29	‡21	*	*	*	+8					12	‡9	*	*	*	17	‡12	*	*	*	
Rampella ...	454	‡386	*	*	*	+68					219	‡201	*	*	*	235	‡185	*	*	*	
Katarbagha	1,282	‡943	*	*	*	+339					622	‡466	*	*	*	660	‡477	*	*	*	
Sason	526	‡330	*	*	*	+196					243	‡163	*	*	*	283	‡168	*	*	*	
Dhama .	50	‡12	*	*	*	+38					34		*	*	*	16	‡12	*	*	*	
Mundher	343	‡137	*	*	*	+206					178	‡65	*	*	*	165	‡60	*	*	*	
Bargarh subdivision	114	‡133	*	*	*	−19					74	‡64	*	*	*	40	‡69	*	*	*	
HAZARIBAGH .	7,014	6,444	4,638	6,395	§984(f)	+570	+1,616	−1,567	+5,411	6,030	3,661	3,343	2,458	3,095	§485(f)	3,353	3,101	2,370	3,300	§499(f)	(f) Probably inaccurate. See note (a) under *Ho* ante.
Hindu .	4,323	4,630	2,143	427	464	+1,694	+487	+1,716	−37	+2,859	2,272	1,519	1,112	224	223	2,051	1,111	1,031	203	241	
Christian ..	387	504	14	45	†	−117	+490	−31			198	251	8	36	†	189	253	6	9	†	
Tribal religion ..	2,304	3,310	2,671	5,928	520	−1,006	+639	−3,257	+5,403	+1,784	1,191	1,573	1,338	2,836	262	1,113	1,737	1,333	3,088	258	
Hazaribagh	785	‡362	*	‡399	*	+423					379	‡178	*	‡137	*	406	‡184	*	‡262	*	
Barkagaon ...	3,012	‡2,602	*	‡1,967	*	+410					1,477	‡1,287	*	‡907	*	1,535	‡1,315	*	‡1,060	*	
Ramgarh	1,087	‡1,018	*	‡375	*	+69					586	‡508	*	‡178	*	501	‡510	*	‡197	*	
Simaria	1,083	‡634	*	‡806	*	+449					560	‡337	*	‡398	*	523	‡347	*	‡408	*	
Giridih	122	‡176	*	‡1,321	*	−54					74	‡154	*	‡634	*	48	‡22	*	‡697	*	
Dumri .	404	‡690	*	‡812	*	286					289	‡408	*	‡422	*	115	‡282	*	‡390	*	
Elsewhere . .	521	‡408	*	‡650	*	+113					296	‡240	*	‡393	*	225	‡168	*	‡257	*	
RANCHI	440,100	381,889	396,768	340,124	§301,549	+58,211	−16,879	+56,645	+36,574	+138,651	214,513	184,852	188,171	158,728	§141,271	225,587	197,037	210,597	181,395	§160,278	
Hindu . ..	163,764	7,511	7,343	1,354	284	+156,253	+168	+5,989	+1,070	+153,480	79,412	3,880	3,583	677	124	84,352	3,631	3,760	677	160	
Christian .	113,322	94,828	88,647	60,888	†	+18,494	+6,181	+27,759			56,226	47,009	43,438	29,934	†	57,096	47,819	45,209	30,954	†	
Tribal religion ...	163,014	279,550	302,778	277,881	301,265	−116,536	−23,228	+24,897	−23,384	−138,261	78,876	133,964	141,150	128,117	141,147	84,139	145,587	161,628	149,764	160,118	
Lohardaga ...	56,109	50,704	*	‡60,551	§27,459	+5,405	..		+33,092	+46,129	26,702	23,866	*	‡27,333	§12,294	29,407	26,838	*	‡33,218	§15,165	
Kuru .. .	17,479	15,727	*			+1,752	.				8,098	7,209	*			9,381	8,518	*			
Burmu .. .	2,570	2,170	*	‡32,044	§34,196	+400	..		−2,752	+3,442	1,312	1,075	*	‡13,433	§14,743	1,258	1,095	*	‡18,611	§19,448	
Mandar ..	35,068	33,041	*			+2,027	..				15,315	14,706	*			19,753	18,335	*			
Ranchi . .	67,598	56,300	*			+11,298	.				34,964	27,583	*			32,635	28,617	*			
Ormanjhi .	2,190	1,748	*	‡45,707	§53,991	+442	..	.	6,294	+19,736	1,141	859	*	‡31,550	§22,850	1,049	889	*	‡24,157	§28,141	
Angara . .	3,938	3,284	*			+654	...				2,015	1,715	*			1,923	1,569	*			
Silli	357	355	*	‡1,063	§2,992	+2	...		−1,910	−2,194	186	238	*	‡543	§1,533	171	117	*	‡539	§1,459	
Sonahatu ...	441	143	*			+299	.				241	73	*			200	64	*			
Bero .	25,966	21,647	*			+4,319	..				11,843	9,765	*			14,123	11,882	*			
Lapung ..	9,000	7,758	*	‡33,419	§53,613	+1,242	.	.	−20,194	−9,263	4,343	3,794	*	‡14,843	§27,573	4,657	4,024	*	‡18,576	§26,040	
Karra .	9,384	6,246	*			+1,138					4,572	3,994	*			4,812	4,254	*			
Torpa .. .	1,060	963	*	‡2,308	§1,857	+97	..		+451	+1,398	490	476	*	‡1,147	§964	570	484	*	‡1,161	§893	
Khunti . .	2,195	1,777	*			+418	..				1,135	887	*			1,060	890	*			
Bundu	2,270	1,751	*	‡2,340	§23,123(g)	+519	.		−20,083	−19,055	1,164	900	*	‡1,174	§10,818(g)	1,106	851	*	‡1,166	§12,305(g)	(g) Most of these should almost certainly have been returned as *Mundas*.
Tamar . .	1,098	719	*			+379	...				513	283	*			585	436	*			
Bishunpur ...	10,401	9,922	*			+479	.				5,258	5,139	*			5,143	4,783	*			
Ghaghra .. .	24,649	22,057	*			+2,592	.				12,370	10,866	*			12,279	11,191	*			
Gumla	29,145	23,380	*	‡54,804	§68,424	+5,765	.		−13,620	+15,451	14,448	11,737	*	‡26,474	§30,041	14,697	11,623	*	‡28,330	§38,383	
Baidih	13,592	11,374	*			+2,218	—				6,804	5,926	*			6,788	5,448	*			
Palkot . ..	6,088	5,051	*			+1,037					3,018	2,565	*			3,070	2,486	*			
Sesai ...	40,331	34,795	*	‡31,251		+5,536	..	...			19,289	16,753	*	‡14,474		21,042	18,043	*	‡16,777		
Basia	7,975	6,854	*	‡3,658	§4,089	+1,121	.		+30,994	+44,376	3,841	3,461	*	‡1,803	§2,037	4,134	3,393	*	‡1,855	§2,052	
Bano	159	168	*	‡174		−9	..				88	81	*	‡98		71	87	*	‡76		
Chainpur	37,120	32,866	*	‡3,473	§19,017	+4,254	.		14,844	+19,450	18,222	16,373	*	‡1,753	§9,576	18,898	16,493	*	‡1,720	§9,441	
Kolebira	1,347	1,246	*	‡700		+101					671	583	*	‡362		676	663	*	‡338		
Simdega	17,483	15,207	*	‡4,190	§13,488	+2,276		...	−5,764	+19,061	8,708	7,623	*	‡2,055	§6,437	8,775	7,585	*	‡2,135	§7,051	
Kurdeg .. .	15,086	12,756	*	‡3,534		+2,330					7,762	6,374	*	‡1,752		7,324	6,382	*	‡1,782		

* Details not recorded. † Not known ‡ Excludes Christians, for whom the district total only is available. § Excludes Christians, whose number is unknown.

TABLE XVIII—*continued.*

VARIATION OF POPULATION OF SELECTED TRIBES.

Tribe, religion and locality.	Persons 1931	Persons 1921	Persons 1911.	Persons 1901.	Persons 1891	Variation (Increase+, Decrease—) 1921 to 1931	1911 to 1921	1901 to 1911	1891 to 1901	Net variation 1891 to 1931	Males 1931.	Males 1921.	Males 1911.	Males 1901.	Males 1891.	Females 1931.	Females 1921.	Females 1911.	Females 1901.	Females 1891.	Remarks.
1	2	3	4	5	6	7	8	9	10	11	12	13	14	15	16	17	18	19	20	21	23
PALAMAU	**57,877**	48,599	43,951	21,930	§43,546	+9,278	+4,648	+22,021	—26,616	+9,331	**28,776**	24,262	21,085	10,802	§23,799	**29,101**	24,337	21,966	11,128	§24,747	
Hindu	*364*	*7,718*	*11 226*	*12,017*	*44*	*—7,454*	*—3,608*	*—791*	*+11,973*	*+220*	*149*	*3 784*	*5,588*	*6,959*	*20*	*115*	*3,934*	*5,638*	*5,058*	*24*	
Christian	*7,870*	*6 436*	*7 340*		†	*+1 434*	*—904*	*+7 340*			*3,865*	*3,157*	*3,680*		†	*4,005*	*3,279*	*3,660*		†	
Tribal religion	*49,743*	*34,445*	*25,385*	*9,913*	*48,502*	*+15,298*	*+9,060*	*+15,472*	*—38,589*	*+1,241*	*24,762*	*17,321*	*12,717*	*4,843*	*23,779*	*24,981*	*17,124*	*12,668*	*5,070*	*24,723*	
Daltonganj	**5,363**	‡5,825	*	3,686	§4,293	+38			—1,607	+1,070	**2 612**	‡2,754	*	1,333	§2,277	**2,751**	‡2,571	*	1,353	§2,016	
Garhwa	**4,236**	‡3,367	*	2,780	§2,189	+869			+591	+2,047	**2,221**	‡1 709	*	1,341	§1,066	**2,015**	‡1,658	*	1,439	§1,123	
Ranka	**2,620**	‡2,104	*	1,564	§3,640	+516			—2 085	—1,029	**1,298**	‡1,044	*	765	§1,811	**1,322**	‡1,060	*	799	§1,838	
Chhatarpur	**995**	‡876	*	672	§4,404	+119			—3,732	—3,409	**506**	‡432	*	330	§2,210	**489**	‡444	*	342	§2,194	
Patan	**1,825**	‡1,561	*	1,726	§3,406	+264			—1,680	—1,581	**909**	‡754	*	911	§1,695	**916**	‡807	*	815	§1,711	
Hussainabad	**1,696**	‡1,086	*	823	§2,233	+610			—1,410	—537	**845**	‡527	*	419	§1,113	**851**	‡559	*	404	§1,121	
Balumath	**17,454**	‡13,790	*	3,976	§18,450	+3,664			—14,474	—996	**8,567**	‡6 773	*	1,918	§8,280	**8,887**	‡7,017	*	2,058	§10,170	
Latehar	**9,262**	‡7,373	*	4,935	§4,829	+1,889			+106	+4,483	**4,642**	‡3,738	*	2,438	§2,359	**4,620**	‡3,635	*	2,497	§2,470	
Mahuadanr	**14,426**	‡6,681	*	2,768	§5,093	+7,745			—2,335	+9,333	**7,176**	‡3,374	*	1,347	§2,989	**7,250**	‡3,307	*	1,431	§2,104	
MANBHUM	**3,724**	3,214	4,611	2,775	§659	+510	—1,397	+1,836	+2,116	+3,065	**1,871**	1,752	2,361	1,672	§380	**1,853**	1,462	2,250	1,103	§270	
Hindu	*3 400*	*2,946*	*2,475*	*2,278*	*659*	*+454*	*+471*	*+197*	*+1,619*	*+2,741*	*1,738*	*1,577*	*1,319*	*1,423*	*380*	*1,662*	*1,369*	*1,156*	*855*	*279*	
Christian	*46*	*49*	*38*		†	*—3*	*+11*	*+38*			*31*	*31*	*22*		†	*15*	*18*	*16*		†	
Tribal religion	*278*	*219*	*2,098*	*497*		*+59*	*—1,879*	*+1,001*	*+497*	*+278*	*102*	*144*	*1,020*	*249*		*176*	*75*	*1,078*	*248*	..	
Sadr subdivision	**3,240**	‡3,475	*	2,121	*	+765				...	**1,642**	‡1,349	*	1,338	*	**1,598**	‡1,126	*	783	*	
Dhanbad subdivision	**484**	‡690	*	654	*	—206					**229**	‡372	*	334	*	**255**	‡318	*	320	*	
SINGHBHUM	**10,111**	8 471	7 424	5,530	§3,220	+1 640	+1,047	+1,894	+2,310	+6,891	**4,828**	4,096	3,675	2,664	§1,584	**5,283**	4,375	3,749	2,866	§1,636	
Hindu	*6 069*	*1,359*	*7*	*522*	*	*+4,700*	*+1,352*	*—515*			*2,835*	*725*	*6*	*254*	*	*3,234*	*634*	*1*	*268*	*	
Christian	*1 435*	*567*	*443*	*198*	†	*+868*	*+124*	*+245*			*713*	*263*	*212*	*119*	†	*722*	*304*	*231*	*79*	†	
Tribal religion	*2 617*	*6,545*	*6,974*	*4,810*	*	*—3,928*	*—429*	*+2,164*			*1,290*	*3,108*	*3,457*	*2,291*	*	*1,327*	*3,437*	*3,517*	*2,519*	*	
Chakradharpur	**1,698**	‡1 214	*	‡851	§261	+484			+590	+1,437	**881**	‡556	*	‡387	§100	**817**	‡658	*	‡464	§161	
Kolhan	**3,734**	‡2,273	*	‡2 096	§1,584	+1,461			+512	+2,150	**1,672**	‡1,095	*	‡918	§649	**2,062**	‡1,178	*	‡1,178	§935	
Manoharpur	**3,262**	‡3 563	*	‡1,207	§937	—301			+1,270	+2,325	**1,583**	‡1,707	*	‡1 139	§597	**1,679**	‡1,856	*	‡1,068	§340	
Ghatsila	**1,417**	‡854	*	‡178	§438	+563			—260	+979	**692**	‡475	*	‡111	§238	**725**	‡379	*	‡67	§200	
ORISSA STATES	**73,020**	76,236	87,064	36 783	§40,438	—3,216	—10,828	+50,281	—3,655	+32,582	**36,294**	38,022	43,828	18,741	§21,253	**36,726**	38,214	43,236	18,042	§19,185	
Hindu	*9,608*	*42,786*	*11,210*	*2,606*	*15*	*—33,178*	*+31,576*	*+8,604*	*+2,591*	*+9,593*	*4,794*	*21,316*	*5 649*	*1,325*	*9*	*4,814*	*21,470*	*5,561*	*1,281*	*6*	
Christian	*21,964*	*16,669*	*16 251*	*346*	†	*+5,295*	*+418*	*+15,905*			*11,038*	*8,302*	*8,232*	*191*	†	*10,926*	*8,367*	*8 019*	*155*	†	
Tribal religion	*41,448*	*16,781*	*59,603*	*33,831*	*40,423*	*+24,667*	*—42,822*	*+25,772*	*—6,592*	*+1,025*	*20,462*	*8,404*	*29,947*	*17,225*	*21,244*	*20,986*	*8,377*	*29,656*	*16,606*	*19,179*	
Athgarh		*	*	*	§1 625					—1,625		*	*	*	§982		*	*	*	§643	
Mayurbhanj	**1,471**	*	*	*	§2,410				..	—939	**732**	*	*	*	§1,454	**739**	*	*	*	§956	
Keonjhar	**958**	*	*	*	§97					+861	**500**	*	*	*	§47	**458**	*	*	*	§50	
Athmallik	**562**	*	*	*						+562	**279**	*	*	*		**283**	*	*	*		
Khandpara	**2**	*	*	*	§3,489					—3,457	**1**	*	*	*	§2,292	**1**	*	*	*	§1,197	
Bamra	**582**	*	*	*	§9,403					—8,821	**299**	*	*	*	§4,821	**283**	*	*	*	§4,582	
Gangpur	**63,471**	*	*	*	§21,533					+41,938	**31,500**	*	*	*	§10,678	**31,971**	*	*	*	§10,855	
Bonai	**5,403**	*	*	*	§577					+4,826	**2,683**	*	*	*	§293	**2,720**	*	*	*	§284	
Elsewhere	**571**	*	*	*	§1,304					—733	**300**	*	*	*	§686	**271**	*	*	*	§618	
CHOTA NAGPUR STATES	**1,109**	884	635	1,315	862	+225	+249	—680	+463	+257	**534**	438	331	648	408	**575**	456	314	667	444	
Hindu	*974*	*556*	.			*+418*	*+556*		...	*+974*	*464*	*276*	.		.	*510*	*280*	...	.	...	
Christian	*24*	*6*				*+18*	*+6*			*+24*	*20*	*2*	.	.		*4*	*4*	.			
Tribal religion	*111*	*322*	*635*	*1,315*	*852*	*—911*	*—313*	*—680*	*+463*	*—741*	*50*	*150*	*331*	*648*	*408*	*61*	*172*	*314*	*667*	*444*	
Seraikela	**558**	*	*	*	304	...	...			+254	**253**	*	*	*	155	**305**	*	*	*	149	
Kharsawan	**551**	*	*	*	548		..			+3	**281**	*	*	*	253	**270**	*	*	*	295	

Santal	**1,712,133**	**1,477,471**	**1,407,346**	**1,298,347**	**§1,114,861**	**+234,662**	**+70,125**	**+108,999**	**+153,486**	**+567,272**	**855,103**	**734,414**	**695,917**	**641,898**	**§571,491**	**857,030**	**743,057**	**711,429**	**656,449**	**§573,370**
Hindu	*686,489*	*557,341*	*271,280*	*390,229*	(a)*154,529*	*+29,158*	*+286,061*	*−118,959*	*+235,710*	*+431,970*	*293,807*	*276,289*	*131,245*	*193,078*	(a)*75,980*	*292,682*	*281,052*	*140,037*	*197,161*	(a)*78,549*
Christian	*13,879*	*8,367*	*7,896*	*7,928*	†	*+4,912*	*+471*	*−32*	...	...	*6,754*	*4,185*	*3,860*	*3,814*	†	*6,525*	*4,132*	*4,046*	*4,114*	†
Tribal religion ...	*1,112,355*	*911,763*	*1,128,170*	*900,180*	(a)*986,739*	*+200,592*	*−216,407*	*+227,990*	*−85,559*	*+126,626*	*554,542*	*453,940*	*560,824*	*445,006*	(a)*493,258*	*557,813*	*457,823*	*567,346*	*455,174*	(a)*492,481*
PATNA DIVISION ...	**475**	159	121	23	130	+316	+38	+98	107	+345	**346**	140	72	11	76	**129**	10	50	12	54
Hindu	*471*	*159*	*121*	*20*	*130*	*+312*	*+38*	*+101*	*−110*	*+341*	*342*	*140*	*72*	*10*	*76*	*129*	*19*	*50*	*10*	*54*
Christian ...	*1*	...	...	.	...	*+1*	...	...	...	*+1*	*1*	...	...	...	...	...	...	...	...	...
Tribal religion	*3*		...	*3*	...	*+3*	...	*−3*	*+3*	*+3*	*3*	...	...	*1*	...	...	...	...	*2*	...
TIRHUT DIVISION .	**3**	4	24	61	...	1	−20	−37	+61	−3	**3**	4	15	27	...	...	...	9	34	...
Hindu ...	...	..	*24*	*41*	...	..	*−24*	*−17*	*+41*	.	...	...	*15*	*18*	...	...	...	*9*	*23*	...
Christian ...	...	*4*	...	...	...	*−4*	*+4*	...	...	...	...	*4*	...	...	...	...	...	...	...	...
Tribal religion ...	*3*	...	..	*20*	...	*+3*	...	*−20*	*+20*	*+3*	*3*	...	...	*9*	...	...	...	...	*11*	...
MONGHYR ...	**26,742**	23,080	20,479	19,758	18,827	+3,662	+2,601	+721	+931	+7,915	**13,494**	9,947	9,088	9,534	9,232	**13,248**	13,133	10,551	10,224	9,595
Hindu ...	*20,545*	*15,107*	*13,632*	*17,333*	...	*+5,438*	*+1,476*	*−3,702*	*+17,333*	*+20,545*	*10,294*	*5,976*	*6,552*	*8,328*	...	*10,251*	*9,131*	*7,079*	*9,005*	...
Christian ...	*204*	*3*	..	.	...	*+201*	*+3*	...	...	*+204*	*95*	*1*		...	..	*109*	*2*	...	...	...
Tribal religion	*5,993*	*7,970*	*6,848*	*2,425*	*18,827*	*−1,977*	*+1,122*	*+4,423*	*−16,402*	*−12,834*	*3,105*	*3,970*	*3,576*	*1,206*	*9,232*	*2,888*	*4,000*	*3,472*	*1,219*	*9,595*
Kharagpur ...	**‡3,853**	*	*	3,766	3,013	...	...	...	+773	+840	**‡1,935**	*	*	1,830	1,487	**‡1,918**	*	*	1,956	1,526
Jamui ...	**‡4,240**	*	*	4,006	3,607	...	...	...	+399	+633	**‡2,104**	*	*	1,806	1,743	**‡2,136**	*	*	2,200	1,864
Chakai ...	**‡16,849**	*	*	11,816	9,317	...	...	...	+2,499	+7,532	**‡8,534**	*	*	5,837	4,643	**‡8,315**	*	*	5,089	4,669
Elsewhere ..	**‡1,596**	*	*	150	2,890	...	...	...	−2,740	−1,294	**‡826**	*	*	71	1,354	**‡770**	*	*	79	1,536
BHAGALPUR ...	**30,799**	33,503	25,249	26,632	50,063	−2,704	+8,254	−1,383	−23,431	−19,264	**15,967**	17,577	12,847	13,122	24,875	**14,832**	15,926	12,702	13,510	25,187
Hindu ...	*27,722*	*28,734*	*4,826*	*24,506*	*38,287*	*−1,012*	*+23,908*	*−19,680*	*−13,781*	*−10,565*	*14,304*	*15,148*	*2,420*	*12,055*	*19,025*	*13,418*	*12,586*	*2,406*	*12,451*	*19,262*
Christian ...	*293*	*36*	...	...	..	*+257*	*+36*	.	...	*+293*	*211*	*11*	...	...	...	*82*	*25*	...	...	...
Tribal religion ..	*2,784*	*4,733*	*20,423*	*2,126*	*11,776*	*−1,949*	*−15,690*	*+18,297*	*−9,650*	*−8,992*	*1,452*	*2,418*	*10,327*	*1,067*	*5,851*	*1,332*	*2,315*	*10,296*	*1,059*	*5,925*
Sadr subdivision	**4,974**	‡7,575	*	6,062	17,479	−2,601	...	...	−10,517	−12,505	**2,760**	‡3,954	*	3,357	5,741	**2,214**	‡3,621	*	3,605	8,738
Supaul subdivision	**220**	‡974	*	209	1,611	−754	...	...	−1,402	−1,391	**218**	‡537	*	95	731	**2**	‡447	*	111	880
Madhipura subdivision ..	**2,028**	‡2,282	*	887	22	−254	...	...	+865	+2,006	**1,106**	‡1,416	*	460	12	**922**	‡866	*	427	10
Banka subdivision ...	**23,577**	‡22,636	*	18,574	30,051	+941	...	...	−12,377	−7,374	**11,883**	‡11,669	*	9,207	15,403	**11,694**	‡10,967	*	9,367	15,549
PURNEA	**46,985**	34,985	21,012	6,643	215	+12,000	+13,973	+14,179	+6,628	+46,760	**24,345**	18,425	10,513	3,710	112	**22,650**	16,570	10,209	3,133	103
Hindu	*37,009*	*19,241*	*5,630*	*6,843*	*215*	*+17,768*	*+13,611*	*−1,213*	*+6,628*	*+36,794*	*19,055*	*9,785*	*2,869*	*3,710*	*112*	*17,954*	*9,456*	*2,761*	*3,133*	*103*
Christian .	*810*	*378*	...	...	...	*+432*	*+378*	..	...	*+810*	*435*	*194*		...	...	*375*	*184*	...	...	...
Tribal religion ...	*9,176*	*15,376*	*15,392*	...	...	*−6,200*	*−16*	*+15,392*	...	*+9,176*	*4,855*	*8,446*	*7,944*	...	...	*4,321*	*6,930*	*7,448*	...	...
Purnea	**‡1,100**	‡638	*	79	*	+463	..	...	..	...	**‡567**	‡330	*	47	*	**‡533**	‡200	*	32	*
Amaur	**‡489**	‡14	*	...	*	+475	...	...	...	...	**‡249**	‡14	*	..	*	**‡240**	.	*	..	*
Dhamdaha ..	**‡14,254**	‡13,572	*	4,431	*	+682	...	...	...	..	**‡7,414**	‡7,202	*	2,401	*	**‡6,840**	‡6,370	*	2,030	*
Korha .. .	**‡5,775**	‡3,140	*	550	*	+2,635	...	...	...	...	**‡2,998**	‡1,898	*	300	*	**‡2,777**	‡1,442	*	250	*
Gopalpur	**‡5,239**	‡3,559	*	442	*	+1,680	...	...	...	...	**‡2,765**	‡1,610	*	227	*	**‡2,474**	‡1,749	*	215	*
Kadwa .	**‡3,472**	‡2,263	*	292	*	+1,209	..	...	...		**‡1,781**	‡1,011	*	180	*	**‡1,691**	‡1,252	*	112	*
Katihar ..	**‡10,002**	‡7,782	*	469	*	+2,220	..	...	...	...	**‡5,113**	‡4,339	*	248	*	**‡4,889**	‡3,452	*	221	*
Araria subdivision	**‡1,132**	‡498	*	5	*	+624	...	...	..	...	**‡500**	‡245	*	5	*	**‡632**	‡253	*	3	*
Kishanganj subdivision ...	**‡4,722**	‡3,151	*	573	*	+1,571	...	...	...	...	**‡2,523**	‡1,562	*	303	*	**‡2,199**	‡1,560	*	270	*
SANTAL PARGANAS ...	**754,804**	676,459	668,149	670,535	§617,158	+78,345	+8,310	−2,386	+53,377	+137,646	**375,109**	386,103	331,610	330,805	§307,382	**379,695**	340,356	336,539	329,730	§309,876
Hindu ...	*423*	*498*	*365*	*73,881*	*67,188*	*−75*	*+133*	*−73,516*	*+6,693*	*−66,765*	*197*	*379*	*138*	*36,671*	*32,554*	*226*	*129*	*127*	*37,210*	*34,634*
Christian ...	*9,963*	*7,120*	*7,037*	*7,064*	†	*+2,843*	*+83*	*−27*	[illegible]	[illegible]	*4,998*	*3,540*	*3,408*	*3,378*	†	*4,965*	*3,580*	*3,629*	*3,691*	†
Tribal religion ...	*744,418*	*668,841*	*660,847*	*589,590*	*549,970*	*+75,577*	*+7,994*	*+71,257*	*+39,620*	*+194,448*	*369,914*	*382,194*	*328,064*	*290,761*	*274,828*	*374,504*	*336,647*	*332,783*	*298,829*	*275,342*
Deoghar	**11,153**	‡8,768	*	‡4,904	§6,431	+2,385		..	−1,527	−4,722	**5,524**	‡4,518	*	‡2,400	§3,222	**5,629**	‡4,250	*	‡2,495	§3,209
Madhupur ...	**39,714**	‡32,865	*	‡32,139	§30,098	+6,849	.	...	+2,041	−9,616	**19,994**	‡16,635	*	‡16,281	§15,064	**19,720**	‡16,230	*	‡15,858	§15,034
Dumka ..	**195,181**	‡168,461	*	‡168,409	§201,677	+26,720	...	...	−33,268	−6,496	**96,263**	‡83,041	*	‡84,220	§100,543	**98,918**	‡85,420	*	‡84,189	§101,134
Dumka Damin ...	**29,816**	‡25,507	*	‡15,409	§19,598	+4,309	...	...	−3,599	+10,218	**15,055**	‡12,957	*	‡7,911	§9,797	**14,761**	‡12,550	*	‡8,088	§9,801
Godda	**62,914**	‡55,289	*	‡61,165	§58,348	+7,625	...	...	+2,817	+4,566	**31,296**	‡27,067	*	‡29,246	§28,733	**31,618**	‡28,222	*	‡31,919	§29,615
Godda Damin ..	**51,122**	‡61,454	*	‡71,218	§63,886	−10,332	..	..	+7,330	−12,766	**25,485**	‡30,606	*	‡34,379	§31,899	**25,637**	‡30,848	*	‡36,839	§31,989
Jamtara	**96,482**	‡81,230	*	‡73,203	§45,813	+15,252	..	...	+27,390	+50,669	**48,647**	‡41,408	*	‡36,293	§23,113	**47,835**	‡39,822	*	‡36,910	§22,700
Rajmahal .	**10,861**	‡10,619	*	‡12,784	§45,460	+242	...	...	32,726	−34,599	**5,308**	‡5,320	*	‡6,341	§22,673	**5,553**	‡5,299	*	‡6,393	§22,767
Rajmahal Damin ...	**116,538**	‡92,191	*	‡97,468	§17,392	+24,347	...	...	+80,076	+99,146	**57,202**	‡45,341	*	‡47,779	§8,612	**59,336**	‡46,850	*	‡49,689	§8,780
Pakaur ..	**95,852**	‡86,727	*	‡84,377	§122,729	+9,125	...	...	−36,352	−26,877	**47,572**	‡42,765	*	‡42,071	§60,789	**48,280**	‡43,962	*	‡42,306	§61,940
Pakaur Damin	**45,171**	‡46,228	*	‡42,635	§5,724	−1,057	...	...	+36,131	+39,447	**22,763**	‡23,005	*	‡20,502	§2,837	**22,408**	‡23,223	*	‡21,353	§2,887
CUTTACK	**1,073**	491	...	52	...	+582	+401	−52	+52	+1,073	**535**	228	...	23	...	**538**	263	...	29	...
Hindu	*855*	*488*	...	*52*	...	*+367*	*+488*	*−52*	*+52*	*+855*	*425*	*225*	...	*23*	...	*430*	*263*	...	*29*	...
Tribal religion ...	*218*	*3*	...	...	...	*+215*	*+3*	...	...	*+218*	*110*	*3*	...	...	...	*108*	...	...	...	...

(a) Excludes *Balasore*, where separate figures for *Hindu* and *Tribal religion* are not available.

* Details not recorded. † Not known. ‡ Excludes Christians, for whom the district total only is available. § Excludes Christians, whose number is unknown.

TABLE XVIII—*continued.*

VARIATION OF POPULATION OF SELECTED TRIBES.

TRIBE, RELIGION AND LOCALITY.	PERSONS. 1931.	PERSONS. 1921.	PERSONS. 1911.	PERSONS. 1901.	PERSONS. 1891.	VARIATION (Increase +, Decrease —.) 1921 to 1931.	VARIATION 1911 to 1921.	VARIATION 1901 to 1911.	VARIATION 1891 to 1901.	Net variation 1891 to 1931.	MALES. 1931.	MALES. 1921.	MALES. 1911.	MALES. 1901.	MALES. 1891.	FEMALES. 1931.	FEMALES. 1921.	FEMALES. 1911.	FEMALES. 1901.	FEMALES. 1891.	REMARKS.
1	2	3	4	5	6	7	8	9	10	11	12	13	14	15	16	17	18	19	20	21	22
BALASORE	**15,444**	9,536	10,524	8,864	4,593	+5,909	—989	+1,660	+4,271	+10,851	**7,338**	4,743	5,204	4,428	2,253	**8,106**	4,793	5,320	4,436	2,340	
Hindu	*3,179*	*2,156*	*2,269*	*1,374*	*	*+1,017*	*—114*	*+895*	...	...	*1,446*	*1,121*	*1,129*	*641*	*	*1,726*	*1,034*	*1,140*	*733*	*	
Christian ...	...	...	...	*8*	...	...	...	*—8*	*+8*	...	...	...	...	*3*	...	...	...	...	*5*	...	
Tribal religion ...	*12,273*	*7,380*	*8,255*	*7,482*	*	*+4,893*	*—875*	*+773*	...	...	*5,893*	*3,622*	*4,075*	*3,784*	*	*6,380*	*3,758*	*4,180*	*3,698*	*	
Bhadrakh subdivision	**37**	30	*	...	8	+17	...	...	—8	+29	**29**	13	*	...	8	**8**	7	*	...	...	
Sadr subdivision ...	**15,407**	9,516	*	8,864	4,585	+5,892	...	...	+4,279	+10,822	**7,309**	4,730	*	4,438	2,245	**8,098**	4,785	*	4,436	2,340	
ANGUL	**1**	...	1	...	...	+1	—1	+1	...	+1	...	...	1	...	...	**1**	...	...	...	...	
Hindu	...	...	*1*	...	...	...	*—1*	*+1*	...	...	...	...	*1*	...	...	...	...	...	...	...	
Tribal religion ...	*1*	...	...	...	...	*+1*	...	...	...	*+1*	...	...	...	...	...	*1*	...	...	...	...	
PURI	**311**	286	...	3	...	+25	+286	—3	+3	+311	**142**	137	...	3	†	**169**	149	...	...	...	
Hindu ...	*311*	*173*	...	*3*	...	*+138*	*+173*	*—3*	*+3*	*+311*	*142*	*72*	...	*3*	...	*169*	*101*	...	...	...	
Tribal religion ...	...	*113*	...	...	...	*—113*	*+113*	...	...	...	...	*65*	...	...	...	...	*48*	...	...	...	
SAMBALPUR ...	**5,070**	4,500	...	...	...	+570	+4,500	...	...	+5,070	**2,498**	2,264	...	...	...	**2,572**	2,236	...	...	...	
Hindu ...	*5,070*	*4,480*	...	...	...	*+590*	*+4,480*	...	...	*+5,070*	*2,498*	*2,254*	...	...	...	*2,572*	*2,226*	...	...	...	
Tribal religion ...	...	*20*	...	...	...	*—20*	*+20*	...	...	...	...	*10*	...	...	...	...	*10*	...	...	...	
Sadr subdivision ...	**125**	88	...	...	...	+37	+88	...	...	+125	**66**	46	...	...	...	**59**	42	...	...	...	
Bargarh subdivision	**4,945**	4,412	...	...	...	+533	+4,412	...	...	+4,945	**2,432**	2,218	...	...	...	**2,513**	2,194	...	...	...	
HAZARIBAGH ...	**129,103**	96,738	93,269	78,379	§69,245	+30,365	+5,469	+14,890	+9,134	+59,858	**65,334**	50,355	46,428	38,792	§34,497	**63,769**	48,383	46,841	39,587	§34,748	
Hindu ...	*7,837*	*38,238*	*15,771*	*148*	...	*—30,401*	*+22,467*	*+15,623*	*+148*	*+7,837*	*4,079*	*20,396*	*7,866*	*89*	...	*3,758*	*17,842*	*7,905*	*59*	...	
Christian ...	*751*	*472*	*210*	*170*	†	*+279*	*+262*	*+40*	...	...	*391*	*197*	*110*	*104*	†	*360*	*275*	*100*	*66*	†	
Tribal religion ...	*120,515*	*60,028*	*77,288*	*78,061*	*69,245*	*+60,487*	*—17,260*	*—773*	*+8,815*	*+51,270*	*60,864*	*29,762*	*38,452*	*38,599*	*34,497*	*59,651*	*30,266*	*38,836*	*39,462*	*34,748*	
Barhi	**1,836**	‡1,055	*	‡1,417	§1,175	+781	...	...	+242	+661	**957**	‡328	*	‡695	§579	**879**	‡727	*	‡722	§596	
Hazaribagh ...	**1,057**	‡769	*	‡592	§6,328	+288	...	...	—5,736	—5,271	**545**	‡367	*	‡290	§3,118	**512**	‡402	*	‡302	§3,210	
Bagodar ...	**4,247**	‡3,351	*	‡2,775	§2,090	+896	...	...	+685	+2,157	**2,173**	‡1,726	*	‡1,363	§1,037	**2,074**	‡1,625	*	‡1,412	§1,053	
Barkagaon ...	**1,999**	‡872	*	‡1,346	§945	+1,127	...	...	+401	+1,054	**1,004**	‡694	*	‡692	§480	**995**	‡178	*	‡654	§465	
Ramgarh ...	**5,500**	‡4,546	*	‡4,129	§4,251	+954	...	...	—122	+1,240	**2,774**	‡2,290	*	‡2,023	§2,095	**2,726**	‡2,256	*	‡2,106	§2,156	
Gumia	**10,237**	‡8,362	*	‡7,171	§12,083	+1,875	...	...	+377	+7,087	**5,246**	‡4,211	*	‡3,441	§5,978	**4,991**	‡4,151	*	‡3,730	§6,105	
Mandu	**8,933**	‡6,967	*	‡5,280		+1,966	...	...			**4,526**	‡3,614	*	‡2,613		**4,407**	‡3,353	*	‡2,676		
Petarbar	**25,879**	‡19,800	*	‡16,114	§4,360	+6,079	...	...	+11,754	+21,519	**13,076**	‡9,916	*	‡8,003	§2,150	**12,803**	‡9,884	*	‡8,111	§2,210	
Kodarma	**807**	‡878	*	‡285	§276	—71	...	...	+9	+531	**418**	‡396	*	‡153	§142	**389**	‡482	*	‡132	§134	
Gawan	**7,413**	‡4,055	*	‡4,744	§3,062	+3,358	...	...	+1,682	+4,351	**3,917**	‡3,071	*	‡2,347	§1,994	**3,496**	‡984	*	‡2,397	§1,068	
Kharagdiha ...	**5,492**	‡4,227	*	‡3,611	§4,414	+1,265	...	...	—43	+1,969	**2,663**	‡2,020	*	‡1,830	§2,232	**2,829**	‡2,207	*	‡1,772	§2,182	
Dhanwar... ...	**891**	‡791	*	‡760		+100	...	...			**437**	‡413	*	‡373		**454**	‡378	*	‡387		
Giridih	**26,266**	‡20,831	*	‡15,661	§62	+5,435	...	...	+15,599	+26,204	**13,083**	‡10,364	*	‡7,782	§30	**13,183**	‡10,467	*	‡7,879	§32	
Dumri	**28,507**	‡21,640	*	‡14,310	§5,025	+6,867	...	...	+9,285	+23,482	**14,495**	‡10,712	*	‡7,069	§2,550	**14,012**	‡10,928	*	‡7,241	§2,475	
Chatra subdivision...	**39**	‡122	*	‡5	§25,174	—83	...	...	—25,169	—25,135	**20**	‡36	*	‡5	§12,112	**19**	‡86	*	...	§13,062	
RANCHI	**601**	802	706	544	§361	—201	+96	+162	+183	+240	**312**	392	350	260	§193	**289**	410	356	375	§168	
Hindu ...	*545*	*385*	*179*	*137*	*17*	*+160*	*+206*	*+42*	*+120*	*+528*	*267*	*190*	*93*	*72*	*8*	*278*	*195*	*86*	*65*	*9*	
Christian ...	*35*	*23*	*9*	*16*	†	*+12*	*+ 14*	*—7*	...	...	*24*	*9*	*3*	*9*	†	*11*	*14*	*6*	*7*	†	
Tribal religion ...	*21*	*394*	*518*	*391*	*344*	*—373*	*—124*	*+127*	*+47*	*—323*	*21*	*193*	*254*	*188*	*185*	...	*201*	*264*	*203*	*159*	
PALAMAU	**3**	...	1	1,953	...	+3	—1	—1,962	+1,953	+3	**2**	...	...	965	...	1	...	1	988	...	
Hindu ...	...	...	*1*	*109*	...	...	*—1*	*—108*	*+109*	...	...	...	...	*74*	...	...	...	*1*	*35*	...	
Tribal religion ...	*3*	...	...	*1,844*	...	*+3*	...	*—1,844*	*+1,844*	*+3*	*2*	...	...	*891*	...	*1*	...	...	*953*	...	
MANBHUM	**282,315**	238,747	232,206	195,400	§181,374	+43,568	+6,451	+36,806	+14,026	+100,941	**143,540**	119,207	116,646	97,697	§89,935	**138,775**	119,540	115,650	97,703	§91,439	
Hindu ...	*182,748*	*209,545*	*35,545*	*95,606*	*40,275*	*—26,797*	*+174,000*	*—60,061*	*+55,331*	*+142,473*	*93,098*	*104,274*	*17,883*	*48,019*	*19,840*	*89,650*	*105,271*	*17,662*	*47,587*	*20,435*	
Christian ...	*1,055*	*213*	*624*	*670*	†	*+842*	*—411*	*—46*	...	...	*512*	*166*	*323*	*325*	†	*543*	*47*	*301*	*345*	†	
Tribal religion ...	*98,512*	*28,989*	*196,127*	*99,124*	*141,099*	*+69,523*	*—167,138*	*+97,003*	*—41,975*	*—42,587*	*49,930*	*14,767*	*98,440*	*49,353*	*70,095*	*48,582*	*14,222*	*97,687*	*49,771*	*71,004*	
Jhalda	**8,648**	‡5,866	*	‡6,597	§7,099	+2,782	...	...	—502	+1,549	**4,317**	‡2,501	*	‡3,240	§3,504	**4,331**	‡3,365	*	‡3,357	§3,595	
Purulia	**39,310**	‡31,769	*	‡28,253	§23,491	+7,541	...	...	+4,762	+15,819	**19,639**	‡15,905	*	‡14,046	§11,562	**19,671**	‡15,864	*	‡14,207	§11,929	
Baghmundi ...	**4,592**	‡3,532	*	‡3,408	§3,523	+1,060	...	...	—115	+1,069	**2,318**	‡1,797	*	‡1,918	§1,859	**2,274**	‡1,735	*	‡1,490	§1,664	
Chandil	**19,470**	‡15,210	*	‡12,943	§11,347	+4,260	...	...	+1,596	+8,123	**9,612**	‡7,610	*	‡6,483	§5,456	**9,858**	‡7,600	*	‡6,460	§5,891	
Barahabhum ...	**36,159**	‡30,148	*	‡26,155	§11,627	+6,011	...	...	+14,528	+24,532	**17,962**	‡15,148	*	‡13,321	§6,084	**18,197**	‡15,000	*	‡12,934	§5,543	

Manbazar ...	**31,559**	‡27,638	*	‡22,994	§21,660	+3,921	...	...	+1,334	+9,899	**15,578**	‡13,615	*	‡11,171	§10,589	**15,981**	‡14,023	*	‡11,823	§11,071
Bagbunathpur ...	**27,112**	‡25,087	*	‡21,415	§18,253	+2,025	...	...	+3,162	+8,859	**13,529**	‡12,297	*	‡10,517	§8,183	**13,583**	‡12,790	*	‡10,898	§10,070
Gaurandi ...	**17,884**	‡15,611	*	‡14,306	§14,547	+2,273	...	...	−241	+3,337	**8,925**	‡7,730	*	‡7,117	§7,269	**8,959**	‡7,881	*	‡7,189	§7,278
Para ...	**2,776**	‡2,330	*	‡1,891	§1,616	+556	...	...	+275	+1,160	**1,346**	‡1,060	*	‡914	§791	**1,430**	‡1,260	*	‡977	§825
Chas ...	**9,507**	‡8,855	*	‡6,204	§7,189	+652	...	...	−985	+2,318	**4,734**	‡3,996	*	‡3,037	§3,603	**4,773**	‡4,859	*	‡3,167	§3,586
Gobindpur ...	**10,586**	‡9,392	*	‡7,243		+1,194	...	...			**5,264**	‡4,478	*	‡3,661		**5,322**	‡4,914	*	‡3,592	
Jherria ...	**21,546**	‡18,047	*	‡10,658	§34,068	+3,499	...	...	−2,850	+20,730	**12,700**	‡9,303	*	‡5,596	§17,680	**8,946**	‡8,144	*	‡5,003	§16,388
Tundi ...	**22,666**	‡17,885	*	‡13,317		+5,281	...	...			**11,612**	‡8,961	*	‡6,681		**11,054**	‡8,434	*	‡6,636	
Topchanchi ...	**10,769**	‡10,060	*	‡6,119	§4,593	+700	...	...	+1,526	+6,176	**5,963**	‡5,413	*	‡3,116	§2,215	**4,806**	‡4,647	*	‡3,003	§2,378
Nirsa ...	**19,731**	‡17,714	*	‡13,227	§23,361	+2,017	...	...	−9,134	−3,630	**10,041**	‡9,227	*	‡6,664	§11,140	**9,690**	‡8,487	*	‡6,563	§11,221
SINGHBHUM ...	**108,890**	94,381	88,241	77,363	81,808	+14,509	+6,140	+10,878	−4,445	+27,082	**53,669**	46,372	43,498	37,994	42,084	**55,221**	48,009	44,743	39,369	39,724
Hindu ...	*34,765*	*63,935*	*28*	*19,891*	*8,417*	*−29,170*	*+53,897*	*−19,863*	*+3,874*	*+16,538*	*11,992*	*26,147*	*12*	*5,969*	*4,866*	*12,763*	*37,778*	*16*	*6,322*	*4,159*
Christian ...	*165*	*7*	*14*	...	...	*+158*	*−7*	*+14*	...	*+165*	*87*	*5*	*5*	...	...	*78*	*2*	*9*	...	...
Tribal religion ...	*83,970*	*40,449*	*88,199*	*65,072*	*73,391*	*+43,521*	*−47,750*	*+23,127*	*−8,319*	*+10,379*	*41,590*	*20,220*	*43,431*	*32,025*	*37,519*	*42,380*	*20,229*	*44,718*	*33,047*	*35,672*
Chakradharpur ...	**2,061**	‡1,631	*	1,693	4,211	+430	...	...	−2,519	−2,150	**971**	‡746	*	785	2,080	**1,090**	‡885	*	907	2,131
Kolhan ...	**2,509**	‡2,292	*	2,113	15,208	+217	...	...	−13,095	−12,699	**1,141**	‡1,083	*	1,028	9,234	**1,368**	‡1,209	*	1,085	5,974
Manoharpur ...	**1,297**	‡1,211	*	1,168	4,975	+86	...	...	−3,807	−3,678	**684**	‡611	*	609	2,536	**613**	‡600	*	559	2,439
Ghatsila ...	**103,023**	‡89,240	*	72,390	57,414	+13,763	...	...	+14,976	+45,609	**50,873**	‡43,927	*	35,572	28,234	**52,150**	‡45,313	*	36,818	29,180
ORISSA STATES ...	**278,284**	235,347	227,784	197,164	99,922	+42,937	+7,563	+30,620	+97,242	+178,362	**137,488**	116,247	109,509	97,001	50,569	**140,796**	119,100	118,275	100,163	49,353
Hindu ...	*261,715*	*178,345*	*193,986*	*157,895*	...	*+83,370*	*−14,641*	*+35,091*	*+157,895*	*+261,715*	*129,259*	*87,815*	*99,191*	*77,396*	...	*132,463*	*90,530*	*100,795*	*80,499*	...
Christian ...	*2*	*109*	*2*	...	...	*−107*	*+107*	*+2*	...	*+2*	...	*56*	*1*	...	...	*2*	*53*	*1*	...	...
Tribal religion ...	*16,667*	*56,893*	*34,796*	*39,269*	*99,922*	*−40,226*	*+22,097*	*−4,473*	*−60,653*	*−83,255*	*8,236*	*28,376*	*17,317*	*19,605*	*50,569*	*8,331*	*28,517*	*17,479*	*19,664*	*49,353*
Mayurbhanj ...	**258,848**	*	*	*	91,490	...	...	...	...	+167,358	**127,732**	*	*	*	46,236	**131,116**	*	*	*	45,254
Nilgiri ...	**3,235**	*	*	*	334	...	...	...	...	+2,901	**1,561**	*	*	*	167	**1,674**	*	*	*	167
Keonjhar ...	**16,172**	*	*	*	1,726	...	...	...	...	+14,446	**8,178**	*	*	*	900	**7,994**	*	*	*	826
Elsewhere ...	**29**	*	*	*	6,372	...	...	...	...	−6,343	**17**	*	*	*	3,266	**12**	*	*	*	3,106
CHOTA NAGPUR STATES	**31,220**	26,444	19,480	14,773	21,165	+4,776	+6,964	+4,707	−6,392	+10,055	**14,981**	12,273	9,297	7,517	10,382	**16,239**	14,171	10,183	7,256	10,783
Hindu ...	*13,321*	*5,868*	*3*	...	...	*+7,453*	*+5,865*	*+3*	...	*+13,321*	*6,416*	*2,377*	*3*	...	...	*6,905*	*3,491*	...	...	...
Christian ...	...	*2*	...	...	...	*−2*	*+2*	...	...	...	...	*2*	...	...	...	...	...	...	...	...
Tribal religion ...	*17,899*	*20,574*	*19,477*	*14,773*	*21,165*	*−2,675*	*+1,097*	*+4,704*	*−6,392*	*−3,266*	*8,565*	*9,894*	*9,294*	*7,517*	*10,382*	*9,334*	*10,680*	*10,183*	*7,256*	*10,783*
Saraikela ...	**30,006**	*	*	*	17,974	...	...	...	...	+12,032	**14,401**	*	*	*	8,815	**15,605**	*	*	*	9,159
Kharsawan ...	**1,214**	*	*	*	3,191	...	...	...	...	−1,977	**580**	*	*	*	1,547	**634**	*	*	*	1,634
Sauria Paharia ...	**59,891**	**55,600**	**62,734**	**47,066**	†	**+4,291**	**−7,134**	**+15,668**	...	...	**30,555**	**28,336**	**31,158**	**24,170**	†	**29,336**	**27,264**	**31,576**	**22,896**	†
Hindu ...	*119*	*148*	*6,424*	*11,377*	†	*−33*	*−5,279*	*−5,953*	...	...	*54*	*58*	*2,742*	*5,538*	†	*58*	*87*	*2,682*	*5,839*	†
Christian ...	*449*	*482*	*407*	...	†	*−33*	*+75*	*+407*	...	...	*182*	*217*	*191*	...	†	*267*	*265*	*216*	...	†
Tribal religion ...	*59,330*	*54,973*	*56,903*	*35,689*	†	*+4,357*	*−1,930*	*+21,214*	...	...	*30,319*	*28,061*	*28,225*	*18,639*	†	*29,011*	*26,912*	*28,678*	*17,057*	†
SANTAL PARGANAS ...	**59,891**	55,600	62,734	47,066	†	+4,291	−7,134	+15,668	...	...	**30,555**	28,336	31,158	24,170	†	**29,336**	27,264	31,576	22,896	†
Deoghar ...	**1**	‡22	*	3,253	†	−21	...	...	...	...	**1**	‡22	*	1,693	†	...	...	*	1,660	†
Madhupur ...	**343**	‡18	*	550	†	+336	...	...	...	...	**343**	...	*	212	†	...	‡18	*	338	†
Dumka ...	**104**	‡92	*	5,459	†	+12	...	...	...	...	**41**	‡38	*	2,748	†	**63**	‡54	*	2,711	†
Dumka Damin ...	**2**	‡5	*	...	†	−3	...	...	...	...	**1**	...	*	...	†	**1**	‡5	*	...	†
Godda ...	**209**	‡252	*	10,982	†	−43	...	...	...	...	**98**	‡84	*	6,161	†	**111**	‡168	*	4,821	†
Godda Damin ...	**14,684**	‡16,918	*	...	†	−2,234	...	...	...	...	**7,325**	‡8,802	*	...	†	**7,359**	‡8,116	*	...	†
Jamtara ...	**11**	‡3	*	770	†	+8	...	...	...	...	**11**	...	*	377	†	...	‡3	*	303	†
Rajmahal ...	**167**	‡289	*	178	†	−122	...	...	...	...	**91**	‡174	*	106	†	**76**	‡115	*	72	†
Rajmahal Damin ...	**29,760**	‡24,892	*	23,739	†	+4,868	...	...	...	...	**15,317**	‡12,755	*	11,862	†	**14,443**	‡12,137	*	11,877	†
Pakaur ...	**1,944**	‡3,677	*	1,648	†	−1,733	...	...	...	...	**761**	‡1,451	*	861	†	**1,183**	‡2,226	*	787	†
Pakaur Damin ...	**12,666**	‡8,950	*	487	†	+3,716	...	...	...	...	**6,566**	‡4,793	*	250	†	**6,100**	‡4,157	*	237	†
Savar ...	(a) **244,670**	(b) **202,635**	**217,948**	**212,138**	**208,115**	**+42,035**	**−15,313**	**+5,810**	+9,023	**+[illegible]1,555**	**118,585**	(b) **96,971**	**105,987**	**104,069**	**100,179**	**126,085**	(b) **105,664**	**111,961**	**108,069**	**102,936**
Hindu ...	*244,648*	*189,897*	*204,458*	*	*	*+54,751*	*−14,561*	...	...	...	*118,568*	*90,690*	*99,222*	*	*	*126,080*	*99,207*	*105,236*	*	*
Tribal religion ...	*22*	*12,738*	*13,490*	*	*	*−12,716*	*−752*	...	...	...	*17*	*6,281*	*6,765*	*	*	*5*	*6,457*	*6,725*	*	*
CUTTACK *Hindu*	**33,368**	24,991	26,88[illegible]	27,934	25,332	+8,397	−1,891	−1,052	+2,612	+8,066	**16,485**	12,058	13,155	18,943	12,463	**16,903**	13,933	13,737	13,991	12,859
Sadr subdivision ...	**13,958**	11,486	*	13,590	12,604	+2,473	...	...	−14	+1,354	**6,738**	5,561	*	6,233	6,222	**7,220**	5,924	*	6,357	6,382
Kendrapara subdn....	**421**	213	*	367	2	+208	...	...	+365	+419	**214**	111	*	174	2	**207**	102	*	193	...
Jajpur subdivision	**19,009**	13,293	*	14,977	12,716	+5,716	...	...	+2,261	+6,293	**9,533**	6,386	*	7,536	6,330	**9,476**	6,907	*	7,441	6,477
BALASORE *Hindu*	**1,305**	†	1,011	1,378	915	...	...	−367	+463	+390	**652**	†	504	606	470	**653**	†	507	683	445
Bhadrakh subdn. ...	**642**	†	*	448	*	...	...	...	...	...	**318**	†	*	228	*	**324**	†	*	221	*
Sadr subdivision ...	**663**	†	*	929	*	...	...	...	...	...	**334**	†	*	468	*	**329**	†	*	461	*

(a) This total is less by 8 than the total given in Table XVII, because the latter includes 8 males, enumerated in *Ranchi* and the *Chota Nagpur States*, who have not been shown in this table.

(b) Excludes *Balasore*, *Angul* and *Singhbhum*, for which figures are not available.

* Details not recorded.

† Not known.

‡ Excludes Christians, for whom the district total only is available.

§ Excludes Christians, whose number is unknown.

TABLE XVIII—*concluded.*

VARIATION OF POPULATION OF SELECTED TRIBES.

TRIBE, RELIGION AND LOCALITY.	PERSONS 1931.	1921.	1911.	1901	1891	VARIATION. (Increase +, Decrease —) 1921 to 1931	1911 to 1921.	1901 to 1911	1891 to 1901	Net variation 1891 to 1931	MALES 1931	1921	1911	1901	1891	FEMALES 1931	1921	1911	1901	1891	REMARKS
1	2	3	4	5	6	7	8	9	10	11	12	13	14	15	16	17	18	19	20	21	23
ANGUL	**1,221**	†	1,328	831	805			+507	+16	+416	**586**	†	644	422	423	**635**	†	684	[illegible]	382	
Hindu	*1,221*	†	*1,320*	*726*	*			+584			*586*	†	*638*	*374*	*	*635*	†	*682*	[illegible]	*	
Tribal religion		†	*8*	*85*	*			−77				†	*6*	*48*	*		†	*2*	*37*	*	
Sadr subdivision	**622**	†	*	*	*				...		**309**	†	*	*	*	**313**	†	*	*	*	
Khondmals sub-division	**599**	†	*	*	*						**277**	†	*	*	*	**322**	†	*	*	*	
PURI *Hindu*	**23,755**	18,461	23 038	21,355	18,887	+5,294	−4 567	+1,673	+2,468	+4 868	**11,185**	8,372	10,856	10 391	9,297	**12,570**	10,089	12,172	10,944	9,590	
Sadr subdivision	**548**	553	*	453	10 245	−5			−9 792	−9,697	**268**	248	*	235	5,080	**280**	305	*	2[illegible]8	5,165	
Khurda subdivision	**23,207**	17,908	*	20,902	8,642	+5,299			+12,260	+14,565	**10,917**	8 124	*	10,166	4 217	**12,290**	9,784	*	10,746	4,425	
SAMBALPUR	**79,106**	69 039	70,706	76,841	76,165	+10,067	−1,666	−6,136	+686	+2,951	**38 198**	33,227	34,184	37,271	37,227	**40,908**	35,812	36,521	39,570	38,928	
Hindu	*79,106*	*69,039*	70,705	*76,841*	*75,248*	+10,067	−1,666	−6,136	+1,593	+3,858	*38,198*	*33,227*	*34,184*	*37,271*	*36,789*	*40,908*	*35,812*	*36,521*	*39,570*	*38,459*	
Tribal religion					*907*				−907	−907					*438*					*469*	
Sadr subdivision	**19,974**	18,890	*	*	*	+1,584	..				**9 544**	8,745	*	*	*	**10,430**	9,045	*	*	*	
Bargarh subdivision	**59,132**	50,049	*	*	*	+8,483		...	..		**28 654**	24,482	*	*	*	**30,478**	26,167	*	*	*	
SINGHBHUM	**762**	†	1,617	2,986	241	..		−1,369	+2,745	+521	**418**	†	785	1,400	120	**344**	†	832	1,586	121	
Hindu	*762*	†	*1,614*	*2,786*	*			−1,172	...		*418*	†	782	*1,354*	*	*344*	†	832	*1,432*	*	
Tribal religion		†	*3*	*200*	*			−197	..	...	...	†	3	*106*	*		†		94	*	
Sadr subdivision	**11**	†	*	14	*			...			**7**	†	*	3	*	**4**	†	*	1[illegible]	*	
Dhalbhum subdivision	**751**	†	*	2,972	*						**411**	†	*	1,457	*	**340**	†	*	1,515	*	
ORISSA STATES	**105,133**	90,144	93 377	80,823	80,790	+14,989	−3,233	+12,554	+33	+24,343	**51,061**	43,314	45 859	39,886	40,179	**54,072**	46,830	47,518	40,937	40 611	
Hindu	*105,111*	77 406	79,898	*	*	+27,705	−2,492	...			*51,044*	*37,033*	*39,103*	*	*	*54,067*	*40,373*	*40,795*	*	*	
Tribal religion	22	*12,738*	*13,479*	*	*	−12,716	−741				*17*	*6,281*	*6,756*	*	*	*5*	*6,457*	*6,723*	*	*	
Athgarh	**6,257**	*	*	*	5,169					+1,088	**3,166**	*	*	*	2,644	**3,091**	*	*	*	2,525	
Mayurbhanj	**4,855**	*	*	*	2,870		...		...	+1 985	**2,362**	*	*	*	1,412	**2,493**	*	*	*	1,458	
Keonjhar	**9,748**	*	*	*	6,060					+3 688	**4,664**	*	*	*	3,103	**5,084**	*	*	*	2,957	
Dhenkanal	**20,402**	*	*	*	21,166		...			−764	**9,471**	*	*	*	10,512	**10,931**	*	*	*	10 654	
Sonpur	**8,217**	*	*	5,669	9,046		...		−3,377	−829	**3,983**	*	*	2,615	4,375	**4,234**	*	*	3,054	4 671	
Patna	**26 950**	*	*	13,065	15 358				−2,373	+11 592	**13,390**	*	*	6,280	7 553	**13,560**	*	*	6 805	7,805	
Kalahandi	**15,697**	*	*	9,053	8,410				+643	+7,287	**7,758**	*	*	4 623	4 224	**7,939**	*	*	4,430	4,186	
Elsewhere	**13,007**	*	*	*	12,711		...			+296	**6,267**	*	*	*	6,356	**6,740**	*	*	*	6,355	
Tharu *Hindu*	**37,338**	**32,817**	**34,602**	**26,687**	**27,620**	**+4,521**	**−1,785**	**+7,915**	**−933**	**+9,718**	**19,154**	**16,848**	**17,609**	**13,591**	**13,810**	**18,184**	**15,969**	**16,993**	**13,096**	**13,810**	
CHAMPARAN	**37,338**	32,817	34,602	26,687	27,620	+4,521	−1,785	+7,915	−933	+9,718	**19,154**	16,848	17,609	13,591	13 810	**18,184**	16,969	16,993	13,096	13,810	
Bagaha	**13,042**	11,771	*	7,987	9,724	+1,271			−1,737	+3,318	**6,702**	6,154	*	3,968	4 810	**6,340**	5,617	*	4 019	4,914	
Shikarpur	**24,236**	21,028	*	16,551	15,913	+3,208	..		+2,638	+8,323	**12,398**	10,676	*	9,488	8 165	**11,838**	10,352	*	9,063	7,748	
Elsewhere	**60**	16	*	149	1,983	+42			−1,834	−1,923	**54**	16	*	135	835	**6**		*	14	1,148	

* Details not recorded

† Not known

TABLE XIX.

EUROPEAN AND ALLIED RACES AND ANGLO-INDIANS

BY RACE AND AGE.

This table, which corresponds with table XVI of 1921, is divided into two parts. The first part relates to European and allied races, and distinguishes between British subjects and others; while the second part relates to Anglo-Indians, *i.e.*, persons of mixed race. Statistics for cities have been shown separately, but these statistics are also included in those of the districts to which the cities belong.

2. Armenians have been included among "European and allied races", and separate figures for persons who described themselves as Armenians by race have not been extracted. But 91 persons (55 males and 36 females) returned Armenian as their mother-tongue, mostly from Manbhum district.

3. All the persons shown in this table returned themselves as Christians except 9 (7 males and 2 females), who returned "indefinite" religious beliefs, viz., agnostic or atheist.

TABLE XIX.

EUROPEAN AND ALLIED RACES AND ANGLO-INDIANS BY RACE AND AGE.

(a) EUROPEAN AND ALLIED RACES (INCLUDING ARMENIANS).

District, State or City.	Total.			British Subjects.																	Others.																
				All Ages.			0–13.		14–16.		17–23.		24–33.		34–43.		44–53.		54 and over.		All Ages.			0–13.		14–16.		17–23.		24–33.		34–43.		44–53.		54 and over.	
	Persons.	M.	F.	Persons.	M.	F.	M.	F.	M.	F.	M.	F.	M.	F.	M.	F.	M.	F.	M.	F.	Persons.	M.	F.	M.	F.	M.	F.	M.	F.	M.	F.	M.	F.	M.	F.	M.	F.
1	2	3	4	5	6	7	8	9	10	11	12	13	14	15	16	17	18	19	20	21	22	23	24	25	26	27	28	29	30	31	32	33	34	35	36	37	38
BIHAR AND ORISSA	*6,389*	*3,823*	*2,566*	*5,675*	*3,443*	*2,232*	*507*	*496*	*97*	*122*	*522*	*218*	*988*	*453*	*592*	*438*	*489*	*271*	*248*	*239*	*714*	*380*	*334*	*50*	*68*	*6*	*5*	*23*	*20*	*85*	*68*	*106*	*93*	*68*	*41*	*42*	*39*
British Territory ...	*6,255*	*3,745*	*2,510*	*5,572*	*3,386*	*2,186*	*496*	*491*	*97*	*122*	*520*	*212*	*977*	*441*	*580*	*421*	*474*	*266*	*242*	*233*	*683*	*359*	*324*	*47*	*67*	*6*	*5*	*20*	*18*	*77*	*67*	*104*	*90*	*65*	*40*	*40*	*37*
Patna Division ...	**1,260**	**992**	**268**	**1,219**	**982**	**237**	**44**	**36**	**18**	**16**	**320**	**18**	**438**	**46**	**73**	**60**	**68**	**41**	**21**	**18**	**41**	**10**	**31**	...	**1**	...	...	**2**	...	**3**	**7**	**1**	**6**	**2**	**5**	**2**	**12**
Patna	1,176	945	231	1,139	938	201	35	33	18	13	310	14	429	43	63	52	57	33	17	13	37	7	30	...	1	...	...	2	...	1	7	1	6	1	4	2	12
Gaya	65	36	29	62	34	28	6	3	...	2	1	4	6	4	8	5	10	7	3	3	3	2	1	...	...	...	...	...	...	1	...	...	...	1	1	...	...
Shahabad	19	11	8	18	10	8	3	...	...	1	...	...	3	1	2	3	1	1	1	2	1	1	...	...	...	...	...	...	...	1	...	...	...	...	...	...	...
Tirhut Division ...	**701**	**431**	**270**	**678**	**421**	**257**	**53**	**40**	...	**14**	**41**	**24**	**154**	**63**	**69**	**54**	**56**	**32**	**48**	**30**	**23**	**10**	**13**	**1**	**1**	...	...	**1**	...	**4**	**1**	**4**	**4**	...	**1**	...	**6**
Saran	137	74	63	137	74	63	15	12	...	3	4	6	16	17	16	10	11	10	12	5	...	...	...	...	...	...	...	...	...	...	...	...	...	...	...	...	...
Champaran	170	89	81	153	80	73	13	7	...	7	6	5	15	17	15	16	13	7	18	14	17	9	8	...	...	...	...	1	...	4	1	4	1	...	...	...	6
Muzaffarpur	253	189	64	249	188	61	11	13	...	3	26	8	109	17	24	12	11	4	7	4	4	1	3	1	1	...	...	...	...	...	...	...	2	...	...	...	...
Darbhanga	141	79	62	139	79	60	14	8	...	1	5	5	14	12	14	16	21	11	11	7	2	...	2	...	...	...	...	...	...	...	...	...	1	...	1	...	...
Bhagalpur Division ...	**1,016**	**522**	**494**	**888**	**467**	**421**	**88**	**93**	**7**	**12**	**33**	**26**	**92**	**78**	**96**	**79**	**93**	**50**	**56**	**83**	**128**	**55**	**73**	**15**	**14**	**1**	...	**2**	**4**	**11**	**14**	**16**	**25**	**8**	**13**	**2**	**3**
Monghyr	502	275	227	473	257	216	57	43	4	7	27	18	41	43	58	46	50	22	20	37	29	18	11	5	4	1	...	2	...	3	1	2	4	4	1	1	1
Bhagalpur	86	56	30	75	51	24	7	1	...	...	4	...	14	8	13	8	7	3	6	4	11	5	6	...	1	...	...	...	...	1	1	3	4	1	...	...	...
Purnea	99	46	53	93	45	48	5	15	3	...	2	...	10	9	9	5	9	6	7	13	6	1	5	...	2	...	...	...	...	...	1	...	2	...	...	1	...
Santal Parganas ...	329	145	184	247	114	133	19	34	...	5	...	8	27	18	18	20	37	19	23	20	82	31	51	10	7	...	...	...	4	7	11	11	15	3	12	...	2
Orissa Division ...	**221**	**115**	**106**	**182**	**98**	**84**	**17**	**17**	**2**	**4**	**4**	**11**	**19**	**21**	**23**	**17**	**22**	**7**	**11**	**7**	**39**	**17**	**22**	**2**	**4**	**1**	...	...	...	**2**	**8**	**9**	**5**	**3**	**3**	...	**2**
Cuttack	74	37	37	58	32	26	4	1	...	...	...	3	6	9	10	8	10	4	2	1	16	5	11	...	...	...	...	...	...	...	6	3	1	2	2	...	2
Balasore	45	27	18	32	21	11	2	7	1	1	2	1	4	1	3	...	7	...	2	1	13	6	7	1	1	1	...	...	...	1	2	3	3	...	1	...	...
Angul	23	9	14	19	8	11	2	3	...	...	1	2	1	2	3	3	1	1	...	...	4	1	3	...	3	...	...	...	...	...	...	1	...	...	...	...	...
Puri	49	23	26	43	18	25	7	5	...	2	...	5	4	4	2	5	3	1	2	3	6	5	1	1	...	...	...	...	...	1	...	2	1	1	...	...	...
Sambalpur	30	19	11	30	19	11	2	1	1	1	1	...	4	5	5	1	1	1	5	2	...	...	...	...	...	...	...	...	...	...	...	...	...	...	...	...	...
Chota Nagpur Division ...	**3,057**	**1,685**	**1,372**	**2,605**	**1,418**	**1,187**	**294**	**305**	**70**	**76**	**122**	**133**	**274**	**231**	**317**	**211**	**235**	**136**	**106**	**95**	**452**	**267**	**185**	**29**	**47**	**4**	**5**	**15**	**14**	**57**	**37**	**74**	**50**	**52**	**18**	**36**	**14**
Hazaribagh	259	135	124	253	132	121	16	24	6	...	6	7	23	29	43	37	28	19	11	15	6	3	3	1	...	...	...	...	...	...	...	...	1	1	1	1	1
Ranchi	630	287	343	494	199	295	61	80	30	27	8	25	24	41	34	45	17	33	25	35	136	88	48	1	2	2	2	...	4	23	6	27	22	9	9	26	3
Palamau	42	24	18	40	22	18	2	4	...	...	2	4	7	3	5	4	5	2	1	1	2	2	...	...	...	...	...	...	...	...	...	...	...	2	...	...	...
Manbhum	1,159	637	522	997	549	448	116	117	23	35	50	49	91	86	127	82	97	50	45	29	162	88	74	14	23	...	2	9	5	25	24	10	10	16	1	5	9
Singhbhum	967	602	365	821	516	306	100	71	11	14	56	48	129	72	108	53	88	32	24	15	146	86	60	13	22	2	1	6	5	9	7	28	17	24	7	4	1
Feudatory States ...	**134**	**78**	**56**	**103**	**57**	**46**	**11**	**5**	...	...	**2**	**6**	**11**	**12**	**12**	**12**	**15**	**5**	**6**	**6**	**31**	**21**	**10**	**3**	**1**	...	...	**3**	**2**	**8**	**1**	**2**	**3**	**3**	**1**	**2**	**2**
Orissa States ...	114	69	45	85	49	36	10	2	...	...	1	5	9	9	11	10	13	4	5	6	29	20	9	2	1	...	...	3	2	8	1	2	2	3	1	2	2
Chota Nagpur States ...	20	9	11	18	8	10	1	3	...	...	1	1	2	3	1	2	2	1	1	...	2	1	1	1	...	...	...	...	...	...	...	...	1	...	...	...	...
Cities	*984*	*529*	*455*	*839*	*466*	*373*	*80*	*74*	*7*	*20*	*26*	*42*	*92*	*70*	*116*	*85*	*115*	*59*	*30*	*23*	*145*	*63*	*82*	*12*	*21*	*2*	*1*	*2*	*5*	*9*	*9*	*17*	*21*	*16*	*12*	*5*	*13*
Patna City	246	103	143	217	100	117	18	16	3	9	1	9	13	16	25	31	38	28	7	8	29	3	26	...	...	...	...	...	...	1	4	...	6	1	4	1	12
Gaya City	63	34	29	60	32	28	6	3	...	2	1	4	4	4	8	5	10	7	3	3	3	2	1	...	...	...	...	...	...	1	...	...	...	1	1	...	...
Bhagalpur City ...	41	24	17	41	24	17	6	1	...	...	2	...	4	4	4	6	4	3	4	3	...	...	...	...	...	...	...	...	...	...	...	...	...	...	...	...	...
Jamshedpur City ...	634	368	266	521	310	211	55	54	4	9	22	20	71	46	79	43	63	21	16	9	113	58	55	12	21	2	1	2	5	7	5	17	15	14	7	4	1

TABLE XIX—*concluded.*

European and Allied Races and Anglo-Indians by Race and Age.

(*b*) ANGLO-INDIANS

District, State or City.	All Ages. Persons.	All Ages. Males	All Ages. Females	0—3. Males.	0—3. Females.	4—6. Males.	4—6. Females	7—13. Males.	7—13. Females	14—16. Males.	14—16. Females	17—19 Males.	17—19 Females	20—29. Males	20—29. Females	30—39. Males	30—39. Females	40—49. Males	40—49. Females	50—59. Males.	50—59. Females.	60—69. Males.	60—69. Females.	70 and over. Males.	70 and over. Females
1	39	40	41	42	43	44	45	46	47	48	49	50	51	52	53	54	55	56	57	58	59	60	61	62	63
BIHAR AND ORISSA	*6,638*	*3,459*	*3,179*	*327*	*335*	*263*	*276*	*485*	*530*	*227*	*200*	*243*	*216*	*602*	*531*	*549*	*481*	*445*	*276*	*202*	*171*	*80*	*109*	*36*	*34*
British Territory	*6,527*	*3,395*	*3,132*	*323*	*330*	*262*	*272*	*484*	*519*	*213*	*198*	*236*	*212*	*591*	*544*	*536*	*473*	*439*	*274*	*198*	*168*	*77*	*108*	*36*	*34*
PATNA DIVISION ..	**1,801**	**921**	**880**	**81**	**78**	**72**	**77**	**199**	**167**	**91**	**70**	**57**	**60**	**105**	**150**	**115**	**120**	**107**	**70**	**58**	**43**	**23**	**36**	**12**	**9**
Patna	**1,337**	691	646	54	52	48	58	157	135	81	53	46	43	82	103	83	90	76	41	37	32	19	31	8	8
Gaya	**305**	149	156	33	19	18	10	30	25	3	14	6	12	13	31	22	18	15	19	14	5	3	3	1	1
Shahabad	**159**	81	78	5	7	8	9	12	7	7	3	5	5	10	16	10	12	12	10	8	6	1	3	3	...
TIRHUT DIVISION ...	**307**	**176**	**131**	**19**	**10**	**15**	**8**	**22**	**12**	**6**	**16**	**13**	**12**	**31**	**28**	**26**	**18**	**22**	**21**	**14**	**8**	**6**	**4**	**2**	...
Saran	**110**	66	44	9	3	3	4	7	7	1	6	7	2	12	7	12	2	6	10	6	1	1	3	1	
Champaran	**34**	16	18			.	1	3	..	..	.	3	3	4	5	3	5	3	3	1	1	2	1	...	...
Muzaffarpur	**60**	36	24	4	3	4	1	3	4	3	3		2	3	5	7	3	6	3	3	3	3	1	...	..
Darbhanga ...	**103**	58	45	6	4	8	3	10	3	2	3	3	6	11	11	5	8	8	6	4	3	...	...	1	...
BHAGALPUR DIVISION ...	**1,333**	**705**	**628**	**53**	**62**	**48**	**47**	**70**	**81**	**41**	**30**	**61**	**40**	**145**	**101**	**106**	**111**	**102**	**69**	**49**	**50**	**18**	**24**	**12**	**13**
Monghyr	**823**	455	368	37	32	27	24	53	56	30	19	45	21	107	65	74	66	50	40	24	30	5	10	4	5
Bhagalpur ...	**143**	67	76	5	10	4	10	11	6	4	2	5	4	13	8	8	15	7	3	5	7	2	5	3	4
Purnea	**163**	78	85	3	9	5	5	1	6	2	4	6	7	16	14	14	11	14	16	11	7	4	4	...	...
Santal Parganas ...	**204**	106	99	8	11	12	8	5	9	15	5	3	9	9	14	10	19	33	10	9	6	7	5	5	4
ORISSA DIVISION ...	**635**	**307**	**328**	**22**	**23**	**23**	**19**	**54**	**102**	**29**	**30**	**24**	**22**	**58**	**49**	**38**	**40**	**35**	**20**	**9**	**14**	**12**	**5**	**4**	**4**
Cuttack ...	**283**	106	177	2	5	5	9	34	83	18	28	7	7	13	10	7	11	6	5	2	6	11	2	1	3
Balasore ..	**36**	24	12	2		2		.	1	1	1	2	1	3	3	7	5	6	1	.	...	...	..	1	...
Angul ...	**3**	2	1			1	...					.	1	.			...			1	...	...	...	.	...
Puri ...	**254**	138	116	17	15	13	6	20	15	8	1	13	12	20	25	17	18	16	13	4	7	.	3	2	1
Sambalpur ...	**59**	47	22	1	3	2	4	..	3	2		3	1	11	4	8	6	7	1	2	1	1	...	...	1
CHOTA NAGPUR DIVISION ...	**2,451**	**1,286**	**1,165**	**148**	**157**	**104**	**121**	**139**	**157**	**46**	**58**	**81**	**78**	**254**	**216**	**250**	**184**	**173**	**94**	**67**	**53**	**18**	**39**	**6**	**8**
Hazaribagh ...	**108**	55	53	7	9	6	5	3	6	3	3	3	4	10	5	11	10	10	4	3	2		1	1	1
Ranchi	**205**	99	106	3	3	5	6	4	13	4	1	6	4	13	19	27	28	25	15	8	13	4	5	1	...
Palamau ...	**20**	12	8	1	2	1	1	1			2	1		2	1	1	1	5	1			...	...		...
Manbhum	**1,110**	579	531	71	74	45	58	31	64	15	31	35	38	129	99	108	74	67	41	35	28	7	10	3	5
Singhbhum	**1,008**	541	467	66	70	47	51	71	74	21	21	38	32	100	90	103	71	66	33	21	10	7	14	1	2
Feudatory States ...	*111*	*64*	*47*	*4*	*5*	*1*	*4*	*1*	*11*	*14*	*2*	*7*	*4*	*11*	*7*	*13*	*8*	*6*	*2*	*4*	*3*	*3*	*1*	...	...
Orissa States ...	**95**	49	46	2	5	...	4	1	11	14	2	4	1	9	6	7	8	5	2	4	3	3	1	.	...
Chota Nagpur States ...	**16**	15	1	2	..	1		...	..			3	.	2	1	6	...	1	..	...	...	..	...	...	..
Cities ..	*1,315*	*637*	*678*	*75*	*68*	*56*	*54*	*96*	*147*	*22*	*59*	*39*	*52*	*97*	*197*	*129*	*87*	*85*	*46*	*38*	*17*	*14*	*17*	*3*	*4*
Patna City ...	**482**	173	309	25	30	13	19	17	92	7	38	9	26	19	54	45	31	29	13	13	7	6	7	...	3
Gaya City ...	**290**	142	148	22	18	15	10	30	24	3	14	5	11	12	30	23	17	18	17	11	4	3	3	1	1
Bhagalpur City ...	**16**	8	8	.	...		1	1			.	1		4	1	..	1	1	1	...	3	2	1	1	.
Jamshedpur City ...	**527**	314	213	48	30	38	24	48	31	12	7	24	15	64	44	55	39	87	15	14	3	3	7	1	1

PROVINCIAL TABLE I.

AREA AND POPULATION OF DISTRICTS, SUBDIVISIONS AND REVENUE THANAS.

THE population figures of the previous census have been adjusted, where necessary, so as to allow for transfers of area during the decade.

PROVINCIAL TABLE I.

Area and Population of Districts, Subdivisions and Revenue Thanas.

District, Subdivision and Thana.	Area in square miles.	Number of: Towns.	Number of: Villages.	Number of: Occupied houses.	Population 1931: Persons.	Population 1931: Males.	Population 1931: Females.	Population 1921 (Both sexes.)	Percentage of variation: 1921 to 1931.	Percentage of variation: 1911 to 1921.	Persons per square mile: 1931.	Persons per square mile: 1921.
1	2	3	4	5	6	7	8	9	10	11	12	13
BIHAR AND ORISSA	*111,702*	*85*	*102,780*	*8,174,899*	*42,329,583*	*21,082,560*	*21,247,023*	*37,955,087*	*+11·53*	*−1·23*	*379*	*340*
British Territory ...	*83,054*	*78*	*83,409*	*7,222,758*	*37,677,576*	*18,794,138*	*18,883,438*	*33,995,415*	*+10·83*	*−1·41*	*454*	*409*
PATNA DIVISION ...	*11,154*	*21*	*13,108*	*1,169,180*	*6,228,425*	*3,148,866*	*3,079,559*	*5,544,038*	*+12·34*	*−1·57*	*558*	*497*
PATNA	*2,068*	*8*	*2,315*	*334,653*	*1,846,474*	*956,124*	*890,350*	*1,576,879*	*+17·10*	*−1·98*	*893*	*763*
Patna City*	15	1	...	32,548	**159,690**	92,238	67,452	**119,976**	+33·10	−11·88	10,646	7,998
City Subdivision	**42**	**1**	**24**	**31,368**	**153,294**	**85,730**	**67,564**	**119,578**	**+28·20**	**−18·57**	**3,650**	**2,847**
Pirbahor Ward	...	...	...	5,248	**30,050**	18,774	11,276	**21,335**	+40·85	−36·19	...	...
Sultanganj Ward	...	...	...	2,415	**11,144**	5,854	5,290	**8,347**	+35·06	...	...	...
Alamganj Ward	...	...	...	4,703	**19,890**	10,527	9,363	**17,138**	+16·06	−15·72	...	...
North Khajekalan Ward ...	...	...	...	1,636	**8,108**	4,423	3,685				...	...
South Khajekalan Ward ...	...	...	...	4,200	**19,915**	10,772	9,143	**23,515**	+19·17	−20·40	...	...
Bakarganj Ward	...	...	...	1,777	**10,535**	6,868	4,167	**6,809**	+54·72	+0·25	...	...
Chauk Kalan Ward ...	...	...	...	3,074	**17,254**	9,255	7,999	**13,717**	+25·79	−31·00	...	...
Malsalami Ward	...	...	...	3,753	**16,562**	9,846	6,716	**11,423**	+44·99	−22·31	...	...
Rural area	33	...	24	3,633	**19,836**	9,911	9,925	**16,794**	+18·11	−8·84	601	509
Sadr Subdivision ...	**291**	...	**414**	**43,959**	**250,628**	**132,511**	**118,117**	**203,911**	**+22·91**	**+4·89**	**861**	**701**
Phulwari	93	...	124	20,083	**113,275**	62,407	50,862	**88,339**	+28·23	+7·38	1,218	950
New Capital ...	*6*	...	...	*2,578*	*14,258*	*8,701*	*5,557*	*9,453*	*+50·83*	...	*2,376*	*1,576*
Bankipore Ward ...	...	...	...	*2,264*	*11,974*	*7,718*	*4,256*	*7,739*	*+54·72*	*+0·25*	...	..
Masaurhi Buzurg	198	...	290	23,876	**137,353**	70,104	67,249	**115,572**	+18·85	+3·06	691	584
Dinapore Subdivision ...	**430**	**3**	**491**	**68,131**	**376,075**	**196,312**	**179,763**	**328,922**	**+14·34**	**+3·69**	**875**	**765**
Maner	124	...	98	16,171	**91,477**	47,043	43,834	**82,878**	+10·38	+0·30	738	668
Dinapore	26	3	43	15,435	**81,367**	43,123	38,244	**64,451**	+26·25	+2·79	3,130	2,479
Bikram	280	...	350	36,535	**203,231**	105,546	97,685	**181,598**	+11·91	+5·60	726	649
Barh Subdivision ...	**519**	**3**	**469**	**73,263**	**414,444**	**210,883**	**203,561**	**354,833**	**+16·80**	**−5·38**	**799**	**684**
Fatwa	98	1	133	16,780	**85,544**	43,001	42,543	**70,199**	+21·86	−0·10	873	716
Barh	368	1	253	37,150	**221,984**	112,953	109,031	**193,517**	+14·71	−2·17	828	722
Mokameh	153	1	83	10,833	**106,916**	54,920	51,987	**91,117**	+17·34	−11·05	699	596
Bihar Subdivision ...	**786**	**1**	**917**	**117,932**	**652,033**	**330,688**	**321,345**	**569,635**	**+14·47**	**−0·95**	**830**	**725**
Bihar	437	1	468	60,323	**382,956**	194,002	188,954	**335,619**	+14·10	−0·10	876	768
Hilsa	231	...	307	33,851	**185,096**	94,460	90,636	**158,493**	+16·78	−1·90	801	686
Islampur	118	...	142	14,858	**83,981**	42,226	41,755	**75,523**	+11·20	−2·60	712	640
GAYA	*4,714*	*7*	*6,058*	*452,362*	*2,388,462*	*1,193,643*	*1,194,819*	*2,152,930*	*+10·94*	*−0·37*	*507*	*457*
Sadr Subdivision	**1,877**	**2**	**2,514**	**175,444**	**891,393**	**449,355**	**442,038**	**792,321**	**+12·50**	**+0·90**	**475**	**422**
Gaya Town	8	1	...	21,686	**88,005**	50,625	37,380	**67,562**	+30·26	+35·34	11,001	8,445
Gaya Mufassal	425	...	504	40,720	**205,417**	101,973	103,444	**183,549**	+11·91	−4·14	483	432
Atri	225	...	238	18,827	**100,885**	50,514	50,371	**92,130**	+9·50	−2·36	448	410
Tikari	382	1	390	31,973	**166,340**	83,114	83,226	**155,431**	+7·02	−6·15	590	551
Barachatti	420	..	546	24,723	**131,458**	65,094	66,364	**117,597**	+11·79	+3·18	313	280
Sherghati	517	...	746	37,565	**199,288**	98,035	101,253	**176,052**	+13·20	+3·63	385	341
Nawada Subdivision ...	**954**	**2**	**955**	**94,333**	**489,260**	**241,007**	**248,253**	**447,708**	**+9·28**	**−3·20**	**513**	**469**
Nawada	466	2	584	61,108	**313,517**	164,196	159,321	**287,583**	+9·02	−3·54	673	617
Rajauli	273	...	242	15,172	**84,070**	41,260	42,810	**77,357**	+8·68	+0·09	308	283
Pakribarwan	215	...	129	17,903	**91,673**	45,551	46,122	**82,768**	+10·76	−8·19	426	385
Jahanabad Subdivision ...	**609**	**1**	**855**	**83,263**	**461,938**	**234,066**	**227,872**	**412,096**	**+12·09**	**−2·41**	**759**	**677**
Jahanabad	406	1	626	57,700	**319,208**	161,467	157,741	**283,725**	+12·51	−1·80	786	699
Arwal	203	...	229	25,563	**142,730**	72,599	70,131	**128,371**	+11·10	−3·55	703	632
Aurangabad Subdivision ...	**1,274**	**2**	**1,734**	**99,322**	**545,871**	**269,215**	**276,656**	**500,805**	**+9·00**	**+2·00**	**428**	**393**
Daudnagar	243	1	288	24,901	**137,385**	68,723	68,662	**125,201**	+8·73	+2·29	558	509
Nabinagar	300	...	530	19,366	**115,335**	57,252	58,083	**109,897**	+4·95	+8·36	373	356
Aurangabad	719	1	916	55,055	**293,151**	143,240	149,911	**265,707**	+10·33	−0·54	408	370
SHAHABAD	*4,372*	*6*	*4,735*	*375,165*	*1,993,489*	*999,099*	*994,390*	*1,814,229*	*+9·88*	*−9·62*	*456*	*415*
Sadr Subdivision	**908**	**2**	**952**	**130,781**	**696,033**	**345,951**	**350,082**	**625,203**	**+11·33**	**−0·55**	**767**	**689**
Arrah	353	1	346	57,347	**307,885**	152,430	155,455	**272,774**	+12·87	+0·49	875	775
Shahpur	248	1	227	32,958	**169,971**	84,218	85,753	**153,623**	+10·64	−5·00	685	618
Piro	308	...	379	40,476	**218,177**	109,303	108,874	**198,806**	+9·74	+1·79	708	645
Buxar Subdivision ...	**673**	**2**	**772**	**73,164**	**383,050**	**194,919**	**188,131**	**352,137**	**+8·78**	**−8·05**	**569**	**523**
Buxar	315	1	427	27,292	**141,179**	72,432	68,747	**131,274**	+7·55	−11·80	448	412
Dumraon	358	1	345	45,872	**241,871**	122,487	119,384	**220,863**	+9·51	−5·67	676	617
Sasaram Subdivision ...	**1,490**	**1**	**1,707**	**110,014**	**589,565**	**294,355**	**295,210**	**538,903**	**+9·40**	**−1·01**	**396**	**362**
Bikramganj	367	...	553	37,731	**208,190**	103,470	104,711	**189,737**	+9·73	−1·45	567	517
Karghar	265	...	304	19,071	**100,188**	49,723	50,465	**95,512**	+4·90	−4·07	378	360
Sasaram	690	1	581	34,377	**176,583**	88,664	87,919	**158,116**	+11·68	−1·54	256	229
Dehri	168	...	179	18,835	**104,604**	52,489	52,115	**95,538**	+9·49	+4·19	623	569
Bhabua Subdivision ...	**1,301**	**1**	**1,304**	**61,206**	**324,841**	**163,874**	**160,967**	**297,986**	**+9·01**	**−2·96**	**250**	**229**
Mohania	387	...	497	25,579	**139,723**	70,574	69,149	**132,322**	+5·59	−3·11	361	342
Bhabua	914	1	807	35,627	**185,118**	93,300	91,818	**165,664**	+11·74	−2·85	203	181
TIRHUT DIVISION ...	*12,598*	*15*	*14,047*	*2,007,595*	*10,739,274*	*5,315,811*	*5,423,463*	*9,949,268*	*+7·94*	*−0·24*	*852*	*790*
SARAN	*2,683*	*3*	*4,305*	*463,745*	*2,486,468*	*1,220,049*	*1,266,419*	*2,339,953*	*+6·26*	*+2·21*	*927*	*872*
Sadr Subdivision	**1,057**	**2**	**1,502**	**184,426**	**973,116**	**469,305**	**503,811**	**914,028**	**+6·46**	**+2·21**	**921**	**864**
Chapra...	354	2	455	71,534	**366,953**	178,252	188,701	**342,948**	+7·00	+3·15	1,037	969
Manjhi...	149	...	197	23,162	**130,863**	62,954	67,909	**128,029**	+3·21	+5·59	878	859
Parsa	265	...	478	44,608	**233,687**	112,327	121,360	**214,239**	+9·08	+0·54	883	808
Mashrak	173	...	241	26,922	**144,334**	69,931	74,403	**134,892**	+7·00	+0·94	834	780
Sonpur	116	...	131	16,210	**97,279**	45,841	51,438	**93,920**	+3·58	+0·11	839	810
Siwan Subdivision ...	**838**	**1**	**1,385**	**153,905**	**824,853**	**408,272**	**416,581**	**775,536**	**+6·36**	**+2·27**	**984**	**925**
Basantpur	246	...	379	46,512	**253,620**	123,955	129,665	**232,252**	+9·20	+1·85	1,031	944
Siwan	332	1	532	65,173	**343,035**	170,754	172,281	**328,254**	+4·50	+3·12	1,033	989
Darauli	260	...	474	40,220	**228,198**	113,563	114,635	**215,030**	+6·12	+1·43	878	827
Gopalganj Subdivision ...	**788**	...	**1,418**	**125,414**	**688,499**	**342,472**	**346,027**	**650,389**	**+5·86**	**+2·13**	**874**	**825**
Mirganj	437	...	986	72,960	**405,039**	201,588	203,451	**380,617**	+6·42	+2·63	927	871
Gopalganj	351	...	432	52,454	**283,460**	140,884	142,576	**269,772**	+5·07	+1·43	808	769
CHAMPARAN	*3,531*	*2*	*2,548*	*385,702*	*2,145,687*	*1,080,956*	*1,064,731*	*1,940,841*	*+10·55*	*+1·70*	*608*	*550*
Sadr Subdivision	**1,518**	**1**	**1,262**	**221,362**	**1,238,789**	**617,102**	**621,687**	**1,123,614**	**+10·25**	**+2·01**	**816**	**740**
Motihari	285	1	198	36,216	**213,890**	109,142	104,748	**188,656**	+13·37	+2·93	750	662
Adapur	227	...	191	37,888	**202,722**	104,037	98,695	**185,039**	+9·56	+4·22	893	815
Dhaka (Ram Chandra) ...	336	...	239	58,078	**323,224**	158,969	164,255	**299,060**	+8·08	+4·24	962	890
Kesariya	269	...	237	37,332	**200,870**	98,133	102,737	**179,645**	+11·81	−3·08	747	668
Madhuban	129	...	197	20,705	**111,212**	53,865	57,347	**103,432**	+7·52	−0·47	862	802
Gobindganj	272	...	200	31,163	**186,871**	93,966	93,905	**167,780**	+11·38	+2·00	687	617

*Patna City includes (1) the whole of the City Subdivision, except the Rural Area; and (2) the New Capital and Bankipore Ward, which for administrative purposes fall within the Phulwari thana of the Sadr Subdivision.

Correction slip no. 2.

CENSUS REPORT OF BIHAR AND ORISSA, 1931.

PART II.—BIHAR AND ORISSA TABLE VOLUME.

Figures revised with reference to Government notification no. 2093—11J—15-32-R., dated the 25th February 1932, transferring 16 villages from thana Korha and one village from thana Katihar, district Purnea, to thana Colgong, district Bhagalpur.

PROVINCIAL TABLE I.

District, subdivision and thana.	Area in square miles.	Towns.	Villages.	Occupied houses.	Population. 1931. Persons.	Population. 1931. Males.	Population. 1931. Females.	Population. 1921. (Both sexes).	Percentage of variation. 1921 to 1931.	Percentage of variation. 1911 to 1921.	Persons per square mile. 1931.	Persons per square mile. 1921.
1	2	3	4	5	6	7	8	9	10	11	12	13
To be substituted for the figures under district Bhagalpur, Sadr Subdivision (Bhagalpur) and thana Colgong and for figures also under district Purnea, Sadr Subdivision (Purnea) and thanas Korha and Katihar, at page 167.												
Bhagalpur	4,280	...	3,097	...	**2,241,699**	1,134,324	1,107,375	...	+10·22	...	524	...
Sadr Subdivision (district Bhagalpur).	988	...	904	...	**648,473**	329,422	319,051	...	+12·96	...	656	...
Colgong	467	...	359	...	**218,519**	109,683	108,836	...	+10·15	...	468	...
Purnea	4,918	...	4,143	...	**2,179,476**	1,125,941	1,053,535	...	+7·81	...	443	...
Sadr Subdivision (district Purnea).	2,495	...	2,310	...	**1,104,732**	569,599	530,133	...	+9·93	...	443	...
Korha	371	...	176	...	**147,272**	75,490	71,782	...	+21·39	...	397	...
Katihar	208	...	303	...	**160,546**	82,422	78,124	...	+16·09	...	772	...

NOTE.—(1) Revised figures for column 5 are not available.

(2) The figures in columns 9, 11 and 13 remain unchanged.

Correction slip no. 1.

CENSUS REPORT OF BIHAR AND ORISSA, 1931.

PART II.—BIHAR AND ORISSA TABLE VOLUME.

Figures revised with reference to Government notification no. 5886—11J—15-R., dated the 15th July 1931, transferring 91 villages from thana Gopalpur to thana Kadwa, district Purnea.

PROVINCIAL TABLE I.

District, subdivision and thana.	Area in square miles.	Towns.	Villages.	Occupied houses.	Population. 1931. Persons.	Population. 1931. Males.	Population. 1931. Females.	Population. 1921. (Both sexes.)	Percentage of variation. 1921 to 1931.	Percentage of variation. 1911 to 1921.	Persons per square mile. 1931.	Persons per square mile. 1921.
1	2	3	4	5	6	7	8	9	10	11	12	13
To be substituted for the figures under thanas Gopalpur and Kadwa, district Purnea, at page 167.												
Gopalpur	**284**	...	307	13,003	**61,011**	31,540	29,471	...	−18·76	...	214	...
Kadwa	**405**	...	585	32,037	**174,841**	90,145	84,696	...	+12·82	...	431	...

NOTE.—The figures in columns 9, 11 and 13 remain unchanged.

[Price 9 pies.]

PROVINCIAL TABLE I—*continued*.

AREA AND POPULATION OF DISTRICTS, SUBDIVISIONS AND REVENUE THANAS.

DISTRICT, SUBDIVISION AND THANA.	Area in square miles.	Number of: Towns.	Villages.	Occupied houses.	Population. 1931. Persons.	Males.	Females.	1921. (Both sexes.)	Percentage of variation. 1921 to 1931.	1911 to 1921.	Persons per square mile. 1931.	1921.
1	2	3	4	5	6	7	8	9	10	11	12	13
Bettiah Subdivision	**2,013**	**1**	**1,286**	**164,340**	**906,898**	**463,854**	**443,044**	**817,227**	**+10·97**	**+1·28**	**451**	**406**
Bettiah	550	1	381	71,943	418,589	214,330	204,259	371,827	+13·58	+3·03	761	676
Bagaha	690	...	318	43,366	234,758	120,803	113,955	215,027	+9·18	+3·15	340	312
Shikarpur	773	...	587	49,033	253,551	128,721	124,830	230,373	+10·06	−3·00	328	298
MUZAFFARPUR	*3,036*	*5*	*4,059*	*555,681*	*2,941,025*	*1,443,847*	*1,497,178*	*2,754,945*	*+6·75*	*−3·18*	*969*	*907*
Sitamarhi Subdivision ...	**1,016**	**1**	**995**	**211,192**	**1,124,302**	**559,588**	**564,714**	**1,051,897**	**+6·88**	**−0·17**	**1,107**	**1,035**
Sitamarhi	359	1	347	75,738	397,960	198,881	199,079	368,708	+7·93	−0·29	1,100	1,027
Sheohar	202	...	204	40,602	217,648	108,513	109,135	207,063	+5·11	−3·50	1,077	1,025
Belsand	206	...	224	42,040	225,494	112,191	113,303	216,182	+4·31	+0·85	1,096	1,049
Pupri	240	...	230	52,732	283,200	140,003	143,197	259,944	+8·95	+1·06	1,137	1,044
Sadr Subdivision	**1,222**	**2**	**1,712**	**215,480**	**1,121,033**	**547,105**	**573,928**	**1,047,046**	**+7·07**	**−3·18**	**917**	**857**
Paru	414	...	555	63,371	318,297	151,982	166,315	295,070	+7·87	−6·83	769	713
Muzaffarpur	578	1	899	108,882	568,449	279,069	288,779	526,118	+8·05	−3·67	983	910
Katra	230	...	258	44,227	234,288	116,454	118,634	225,858	+3·73	+3·85	1,019	983
Hajipur Subdivision ...	**798**	**2**	**1,352**	**129,009**	**695,690**	**337,154**	**358,536**	**656,002**	**+6·05**	**−7·64**	**872**	**822**
Mahuwa	316	...	600	58,629	293,330	141,592	151,738	275,272	+6·56	−8·11	928	871
Lalganj	168	1	295	29,432	144,595	68,447	76,148	137,641	+5·05	−10·67	861	819
Hajipur	314	1	457	40,948	257,765	127,115	130,650	243,089	+6·04	−5·29	821	774
DARBHANGA	*3,348*	*5*	*3,135*	*602,467*	*3,166,094*	*1,570,959*	*1,595,135*	*2,913,529*	*+8·67*	*−0·55*	*946*	*870*
Madhubani Subdivision ...	**1,346**	**2**	**1,027**	**238,304**	**1,272,148**	**627,219**	**644,929**	**1,166,430**	**+9·06**	**+2·70**	**945**	**867**
Benipatti	270	...	230	53,148	292,183	144,168	148,015	266,803	+9·51	+0·69	1,082	988
Khajauli	323	1	188	55,708	303,097	150,511	152,586	278,239	+8·93	+2·58	938	861
Madhubani	298	1	278	62,920	320,643	158,508	162,136	297,498	+7·78	+5·25	1,076	998
Phulparas	455	...	331	60,518	356,225	174,033	182,193	323,890	+9·98	+2·31	783	712
Sadr Subdivision ...	**876**	**1**	**928**	**165,201**	**877,578**	**435,167**	**442,411**	**801,960**	**+9·43**	**−0·17**	**1,002**	**915**
Darbhanga	428	1	550	93,030	485,040	240,793	244,247	447,774	+8·32	−1·77	1,133	1,046
Bahera	440	...	378	72,181	392,538	194,374	198,164	354,186	+10·83	+1·92	870	791
Samastipur Subdivision ...	**1,126**	**2**	**1,180**	**198,962**	**1,016,368**	**508,573**	**507,795**	**945,139**	**+7·54**	**−4·58**	**903**	**839**
Samastipur	296	1	364	59,609	296,647	148,363	148,285	280,401	+5·77	−7·50	1,003	948
Rosera	348	1	349	52,055	294,441	148,034	146,407	268,131	+9·81	+2·95	846	770
Warisnagar	196	...	242	35,356	171,925	85,762	86,163	164,037	+4·81	−1·32	877	837
Dalsingh Sarai	286	...	225	52,042	253,355	130,415	126,940	232,510	+8·97	−10·72	886	813
BHAGALPUR DIVISION...	*18,583*	*17*	*20,010*	*1,626,036*	*8,759,801*	*4,431,983*	*4,327,818*	*7,880,211*	*+11·16*	*−3·19*	*471*	*424*
MONGHYR	*3,027*	*6*	*2,610*	*426,591*	*2,287,154*	*1,145,797*	*1,141,357*	*2,029,965*	*+12·67*	*−4·92*	*582*	*517*
Sadr Subdivision	**1,905**	**5**	**1,414**	**218,911**	**1,205,113**	**610,568**	**594,545**	**1,073,181**	**+12·29**	**−2·15**	**633**	**563**
Gogri	752	1	379	73,566	464,258	236,039	228,219	412,798	+12·47	−2·38	617	549
Monghyr	158	1	157	32,715	179,396	92,285	87,111	159,701	+12·33	+3·32	1,136	1,011
Jamalpur	4	1	...	6,265	30,346	16,278	13,068	24,827	+22·23	+20·95	7,587	6,207
Surajgarha	174	...	120	15,264	75,898	37,340	38,558	74,213	+2·27	−0·49	436	437
Lakhisarai	223	1	153	25,390	133,824	68,329	65,495	119,537	+11·95	−7·80	600	536
Kharagpur	359	...	326	29,647	161,405	79,864	81,541	139,612	+15·61	−6·56	450	389
Shaikhpura	235	1	279	30,144	159,986	80,333	79,653	142,493	+12·28	−2·02	681	606
Begusarai Subdivision ...	**746**	**1**	**684**	**125,026**	**644,245**	**315,697**	**328,548**	**586,089**	**+9·92**	**−10·06**	**864**	**786**
Teghra	240	...	250	47,200	232,639	114,454	118,185	215,550	+7·93	−10·83	980	898
Begusarai	506	1	434	77,826	411,606	201,343	210,363	370,539	+11·08	−12·01	813	732
Jamui Subdivision ...	**1,276**	...	**512**	**82,654**	**437,796**	**219,532**	**218,264**	**370,695**	**+18·10**	**−4·11**	**343**	**291**
Sikandra	243	...	218	22,636	117,621	58,116	59,505	101,446	+15·94	−5·56	484	417
Jamui	445	...	246	31,110	162,461	81,259	81,202	135,378	+20·01	−5·53	365	304
Chakai	588	...	48	28,908	157,714	80,157	77,557	133,871	+17·81	−1·46	268	328
BHAGALPUR	*4,226*	*3*	*3,080*	*406,446*	*2,234,632*	*1,130,584*	*1,104,048*	*2,033,770*	*+9·88*	*−4·93*	*529*	*481*
Sadr Subdivision ...	**934**	**2**	**887**	**111,240**	**641,466**	**325,682**	**315,724**	**574,081**	**+11·73**	**−4·06**	**687**	**615**
Sultanganj	165	...	203	20,021	110,107	54,767	55,340	96,612	+13·97	+1·48	667	586
Bhagalpur	181	1	263	35,498	204,741	107,054	97,687	173,518	+17·90	−6·30	1,131	959
Colgong	413	1	342	36,453	211,452	105,943	105,509	198,382	+6·59	−4·61	512	480
Bihpur	175	...	79	19,268	115,106	57,918	57,188	105,569	+9·03	−4·06	658	603
Supaul Subdivision ...	**934**	...	**484**	**89,330**	**508,989**	**256,227**	**252,762**	**488,557**	**+4·18**	**−1·04**	**545**	**523**
Supaul	593	...	294	67,476	384,789	192,769	192,020	353,837	+8·75	−0·62	649	597
Partapganj	341	...	190	21,854	124,200	63,458	60,742	134,720	−7·81	−2·11	364	396
Madhipura Subdivision ...	**1,176**	...	**641**	**113,035**	**611,679**	**313,852**	**297,827**	**578,568**	**+5·72**	**−5·09**	**520**	**492**
Bangaon	263	...	180	29,046	164,595	81,304	83,291	145,398	+13·20	−5·40	626	553
Madhipura	547	...	264	50,120	274,262	141,825	132,437	258,740	+6·00	−11·67	501	473
Kishanganj	366	...	197	32,079	172,822	90,723	82,099	174,430	−0·92	+7·01	472	477
Banka Subdivision ...	**1,182**	...	**1,068**	**92,841**	**472,558**	**234,823**	**237,735**	**392,564**	**+20·38**	**−10·30**	**400**	**332**
Amarpur	294	...	435	32,148	159,013	78,833	80,180	127,362	+24·85	−17·78	541	433
Katoria	534	...	178	25,045	100,019	66,461	66,558	113,641	+17·67	−3·78	240	212
Banka	354	...	455	35,649	180,526	89,529	90,007	152,161	+18·64	−7·04	510	430
PURNEA	*4,972*	*4*	*4,160*	*401,874*	*2,186,543*	*1,129,681*	*1,056,862*	*2,021,568*	*+8·16*	*+1·76*	*440*	*407*
Araria Subdivision ...	**1,077**	**1**	**668**	**93,653**	**514,167**	**263,296**	**250,871**	**455,974**	**+12·76**	**+3·58**	**477**	**423**
Araria	431	...	314	41,237	228,676	116,251	112,425	209,691	+9·05	−0·94	531	487
Forbesganj	376	1	233	33,240	177,791	91,638	86,153	152,586	+16·53	+9·73	473	406
Raniganj	270	...	121	19,176	107,700	55,407	52,293	93,697	+14·94	+4·68	399	347
Kishanganj Subdivision ...	**1,346**	**1**	**1,165**	**107,337**	**560,577**	**293,046**	**267,531**	**560,738**	**−0·03**	**−7·57**	**416**	**417**
Kishanganj	337	1	334	25,338	129,260	68,362	60,898	129,130	+0·10	−11·33	395	395
Bahadurganj	393	...	387	38,029	198,200	101,943	96,257	192,141	+3·15	−6·85	504	490
Islampur	626	...	444	43,970	233,117	122,741	110,376	239,467	−2·65	−6·03	373	383
Sadr Subdivision	**2,549**	**2**	**2,327**	**200,884**	**1,111,799**	**573,339**	**538,460**	**1,004,856**	**+10·64**	**+6·91**	**436**	**394**
Purnea	424	1	326	30,461	157,110	82,454	74,656	149,045	+5·41	−6·71	371	352
Amaur	279	...	350	24,622	137,369	60,463	67,906	122,014	+12·58	−3·32	492	437
Dhamdaha	524	...	263	45,304	266,583	138,085	128,498	244,122	+9·20	+38·42	509	466
Korha	421	...	192	26,630	153,409	78,709	74,700	121,316	+26·45	+2·74	364	288
Gopalpur	323	...	398	15,243	73,257	37,940	35,317	75,097	−2·45	−7·07	227	232
Kadwa	366	...	494	29,707	162,595	83,745	78,850	154,975	+4·92	+3·24	444	423
Katihar	212	1	304	28,837	161,476	82,943	78,533	138,287	+16·77	+7·54	762	653
SANTAL PARGANAS ...	*5,458*	*5*	*10,160*	*391,195*	*2,051,479*	*1,025,991*	*1,025,551*	*1,794,908*	*+14·29*	*−4·46*	*376*	*329*
Deoghar Subdivision ...	**952**	**2**	**2,384**	**66,215**	**346,946**	**175,948**	**170,998**	**290,758**	**+19·32**	**−5·13**	**364**	**305**
Deoghar	424	1	1,161	31,743	161,422	82,268	79,154	135,330	+19·28	−6·83	381	319
Madhupur	528	1	1,223	34,472	185,524	93,680	91,844	155,428	+19·36	−3·50	351	294
Dumka Subdivision ...	**1,463**	**1**	**2,681**	**89,891**	**466,157**	**231,105**	**235,052**	**395,135**	**+17·97**	**−4·89**	**319**	**270**
Dumka	1,222	1	2,359	81,805	421,735	208,830	212,905	356,480	+18·31	−5·49	345	292
Dumka Damin	241	...	322	8,086	44,422	22,275	22,147	38,655	+14·93	+0·95	184	160
Godda Subdivision ...	**850**	...	**1,622**	**71,829**	**387,801**	**191,706**	**196,095**	**340,082**	**+14·03**	**−6·76**	**456**	**400**
Godda	555	...	1,095	54,159	298,217	146,979	151,238	258,102	+15·54	−6·04	537	465
Godda Damin	295	...	527	17,670	89,584	44,727	44,857	81,980	+9·28	−6·21	304	278

PROVINCIAL TABLE I—*continued.*

AREA AND POPULATION OF DISTRICTS, SUBDIVISIONS AND REVENUE THANAS.

DISTRICT, SUBDIVISION AND THANA	Area in square miles	Number of			Population				Percentage of variation.		Persons per square mile.	
		Towns	Villages	Occupied houses	1931			1921	1921 to 1931	1911 to 1921	1931	1921.
					Persons	Males	Females	(Both sexes)				
1	2	3	4	5	6	7	8	9	10	11	12	13
JAMTARA SUBDIVISION	**692**		**1,070**	**46,170**	**243,858**	**123,520**	**120,338**	**207,876**	**+17·31**	**+0·91**	**352**	**300**
Jamtara	692		1,070	46,170	243,858	123,520	120,338	207,876	+17·31	+0·91	352	300
RAJMAHAL SUBDIVISION	**801**	**2**	**1,291**	**63,126**	**331,136**	**165,619**	**165,517**	**305,295**	**+8·46**	**—6·93**	**413**	**381**
Rajmahal	211	2	336	25,719	131,862	66,778	65,084	122,133	+7·97	—7·01	625	579
Rajmahal Damin	590		955	37,407	199,274	98,841	100,433	183,162	+8·80	—6·88	338	310
PAKAUR SUBDIVISION	**700**		**1,112**	**53,894**	**275,574**	**138,023**	**137,551**	**255,762**	**+7·75**	**—0·73**	**394**	**365**
Pakaur	433		728	39,177	197,177	97,873	99,304	186,872	+5·51	—2·4	455	433
Pakaur Damin	267		384	14,717	78,397	40,150	38,247	68,890	+13·80	+4·2	294	258
ORISSA DIVISION	***13,706***	***9***	***15,523***	***1,134,679***	***5,306,142***	***2,549,251***	***2,756,891***	***4,968,873***	***+6·79***	***—3·17***	***387***	***362***
CUTTACK	***3,654***	***3***	***5,506***	***456,507***	***2,176,707***	***1,028,134***	***1,148,573***	***2,064,678***	***+5·43***	***—2·11***	***596***	***565***
SADR SUBDIVISION	**1,562**	**1**	**2,526**	**230,511**	**1,087,991**	**518,671**	**569,320**	**1,043,301**	**+4·28**	**—2·38**	**697**	**668**
Cuttack	298	1	362	49,326	237,148	117,897	119,251	214,872	+10·37	—5·84	796	731
Banki	198		140	17,451	84,406	40,984	43,422	70,110	+20·39	—10·81	426	354
Salipur	303		605	60,467	266,449	124,106	142,343	289,245	—7·88	—0·89	879	955
Tirtol	391		716	39,818	193,491	91,901	101,590	181,549	+6·58	—1·19	495	464
Jagatsinghpur	372		694	63,340	306,497	143,783	162,714	287,525	+6·60	+0·40	824	773
KENDRAPARA SUBDIVISION	**977**	**1**	**1,353**	**98,625**	**496,498**	**231,998**	**264,500**	**478,773**	**+3·70**	**—1·47**	**508**	**490**
Kendrapara	301	1	597	49,882	248,069	117,312	130,757	249,369	—0·53	—0·41	824	826
Patamundi	302		284	25,312	127,112	58,446	68,666	120,707	+5·31	+0·29	421	400
Aul or Rajabari	374		472	23,431	121,317	56,240	65,077	108,697	+11·61	—5·61	324	291
JAJPUR SUBDIVISION	**1,115**	**1**	**1,627**	**127,371**	**592,218**	**277,465**	**314,753**	**542,604**	**+9·14**	**—2·14**	**531**	**487**
Jajpur	320	1	610	60,632	281,789	129,596	152,193	259,377	+8·64	—3·96	881	811
Dharamshala	795		1,017	66,739	310,429	147,860	162,560	283,227	+9·60	—0·40	390	356
BALASORE	***2,055***	***2***	***3,479***	***214,945***	***990,600***	***480,518***	***510,082***	***980,504***	***+1·03***	***—7·11***	***482***	***470***
BHADRAKH SUBDIVISION	**907**	**1**	**1,238**	**97,399**	**446,771**	**207,288**	**239,483**	**438,601**	**+1·86**	**—4·78**	**493**	**472**
Bhadrakh	288	1	439	39,426	171,884	78,880	92,005	181,841	—5·48	—2·42	597	623
Basudebpur	190		219	15,973	78,757	36,549	42,208	71,026	+10·88	—0·20	415	370
Dhamnagar	230		325	28,842	133,711	61,758	71,953	129,056	+3·61	—4·14	581	554
Chandbali	199		255	13,158	62,419	30,092	32,327	56,678	+10·13	—7·74	314	266
SADR SUBDIVISION	**1,148**	**1**	**2,241**	**117,546**	**543,829**	**273,230**	**270,599**	**541,903**	**+0·36**	**—8·91**	**474**	**469**
Soro	400		817	43,462	191,755	91,974	99,781	218,633	—12·29	—3·52	479	544
Balasore	226	1	395	24,883	111,759	58,230	53,529	102,384	+9·18	—15·84	495	451
Jaleswar	134		179	12,011	56,899	28,684	28,215	53,027	+7·30	—14·39	425	396
Baliapal	206		470	21,398	108,107	55,552	52,555	100,106	+7·99	—4·22	525	484
Basta	182		380	15,792	75,309	38,790	36,519	67,773	+11·12	—15·60	414	366
ANGUL	***1,681***		***1,608***	***49,177***	***222,736***	***108,925***	***113,811***	***182,574***	***+22·00***	***—8·46***	***133***	***109***
SADR SUBDIVISION	**881**		**467**	**30,087**	**140,458**	**68,694**	**71,764**	**108,315**	**+29·68**	**—13·51**	**159**	**123**
Angul	881		467	30,087	140,458	68,694	71,764	108,315	+29·68	—13·51	159	123
KHONDMALS SUBDIVISION	**800**		**1,141**	**19,090**	**82,278**	**40,231**	**42,047**	**74,259**	**+10·80**	**+0·06**	**103**	**93**
Phulbani	800		1,141	19,090	82,278	40,231	43,047	74,259	+10·80	+0·06	103	93
PURI	***2,492***	***1***	***2,987***	***213,167***	***1,035,154***	***500,214***	***534,940***	***951,651***	***+8·77***	***—7·01***	***415***	***382***
SADR SUBDIVISION	**1,521**	**1**	**1,830**	**131,529**	**657,625**	**321,429**	**336,196**	**614,754**	**+6·97**	**—6·26**	**432**	**404**
Puri	858	1	653	51,024	255,821	127,152	128,660	242,190	+5·63	—7·70	298	282
Gop	288		439	22,958	128,914	63,396	65,518	110,337	+16·84	—4·04	448	383
Pipli	375		738	57,547	272,890	130,881	142,009	262,227	+4·07	—5·72	728	699
KHURDA SUBDIVISION	**971**		**1,157**	**81,638**	**377,529**	**178,785**	**198,744**	**336,897**	**+12·06**	**—8·35**	**389**	**347**
Khurda	605		712	58,055	262,560	124,790	137,770	237,727	—10·45	—8·08	434	393
Banpur	366		445	23,583	114,969	53,995	60,974	99,170	+15·93	—6·82	314	271
SAMBALPUR	***3,824***	***3***	***1,943***	***200,883***	***880,945***	***431,460***	***449,485***	***789,460***	***+11·59***	***+6·08***	***230***	***206***
SADR SUBDIVISION	**1,612**	**2**	**752**	**79,428**	**343,539**	**167,478**	**176,061**	**303,719**	**+13·11**	**+0·56**	**213**	**188**
Sambalpur	144	1	93	14,045	57,553	28,231	29,322	51,709	+11·30	+2·25	400	359
Jharsugra	208	1	107	11,139	51,125	25,284	25,841	41,944	+21·89	+0·25	246	202
Laikera	273		118	10,748	51,043	24,940	26,103	42,951	+18·84	+4·45	187	157
Mura	158		77	7,080	30,089	14,805	15,284	27,310	+10·18	—2·41	190	173
Rampella	110		44	7,698	32,385	15,715	16,670	30,148	+7·42	—3·82	294	274
Katarbagha	220		72	9,840	39,711	19,272	20,439	35,407	+12·16	+2·61	181	161
Sason	123		78	7,067	32,388	15,502	16,886	29,731	+8·94	+2·90	263	242
Dhama	166		84	7,872	30,934	14,711	16,223	28,975	+6·76	—3·82	186	175
Mundher	210		80	4,480	18,311	9,018	9,293	15,544	+17·80	—0·74	87	74
BARGARH SUBDIVISION	**2,212**	**1**	**1,191**	**121,455**	**537,406**	**263,982**	**273,424**	**485,747**	**+10·63**	**+9·86**	**243**	**220**
Bargarh	150	1	64	14,107	60,956	29,831	31,125	55,834	+9·17	+8·40	406	372
Attabira	258		86	13,115	53,985	26,253	27,732	49,091	+9·97	+0·44	209	190
Sohela	164		93	10,404	44,660	21,954	22,706	39,757	+12·33	+11·62	272	242
Ambabhona	204		110	7,468	31,041	15,200	15,841	28,616	+8·47	+9·14	152	140
Padampur	191		125	9,306	41,974	20,814	21,160	38,496	+9·03	+22·17	220	202
Bheran	153		93	12,332	50,386	24,344	26,042	47,855	+5·29	+12·81	329	313
Bijepur	125		107	9,368	43,455	21,432	22,023	38,541	+12·75	+15·49	348	308
Melchhamunda	125		74	5,578	26,640	13,245	13,395	23,714	+12·34	+11·90	213	190
Gaisilat	116		82	5,631	29,251	14,559	14,692	25,791	+13·42	+11·06	252	222
Jagdalpur	243		101	6,987	34,705	17,303	17,402	28,728	+20·81	+14·56	143	119
Barpali	100		74	10,564	47,434	23,127	24,307	43,457	+9·15	+9·88	435	399
Bhatli	184		84	10,878	43,947	21,430	22,517	41,218	+6·62	+4·12	239	224
Paikmal	191		98	5,768	28,972	14,490	14,482	24,649	+17·54	+25·53	152	129
CHOTA NAGPUR DIVISION	***27,013***	***16***	***20,714***	***1,292,268***	***6,643,934***	***3,348,227***	***3,295,707***	***5,653,028***	***+17·53***	***+0·85***	***246***	***209***
HAZARIBAGH	***7,021***	***3***	***6,087***	***297,372***	***1,517,357***	***751,956***	***765,401***	***1,276,946***	***+18·83***	***—0·91***	***216***	***182***
SADR SUBDIVISION	**3,460**	**1**	**2,173**	**137,759**	**720,196**	**356,296**	**363,900**	**590,487**	**+21·97**	**—3·60**	**208**	**171**
Barhi	358		228	12,684	59,110	28,392	30,718	50,881	+16·17	—3·33	165	142
Hazaribagh	456	1	306	21,843	110,873	53,460	57,414	92,671	+19·64	—8·35	243	203
Bagodar	426		245	16,696	84,049	41,261	42,788	69,742	+20·51	—3·36	197	164
Barkagaon	486		320	13,080	73,370	36,243	37,127	60,510	+21·25	—1·57	151	125
Ramgarh	369		246	19,029	110,441	55,522	54,910	83,774	+31·83	—11·93	299	227
Gumia	258		131	8,580	44,580	22,728	21,852	33,287	+33·93	—6·58	173	129
Mandu	344		165	8,595	47,078	23,668	23,410	34,530	+36·34	—5·19	137	100
Petarbar	320		197	15,061	83,643	42,617	41,026	66,578	+25·63	—4·89	261	208
Kodarma	443		434	20,686	107,052	52,406	54,646	98,514	+8·67	+11·98	242	222
CHATRA SUBDIVISION	**1,559**	**1**	**1,384**	**47,844**	**238,874**	**118,491**	**120,383**	**218,567**	**+9·29**	**—2·17**	**153**	**140**
Chauparan	354		437	13,952	73,640	36,330	37,310	61,066	+20·59	—2·81	208	173
Hunterganj	477		448	14,339	70,958	35,479	35,479	71,085	—0·18	+4·88	149	149
Chatra	347	1	306	12,158	57,942	28,704	29,238	53,347	+8·61	—3·34	167	154
Simaria	381		193	7,395	36,334	17,078	18,356	33,069	+9·87	—12·06	95	87
GIRIDIH SUBDIVISION	**2,002**	**1**	**2,530**	**111,769**	**558,287**	**277,169**	**281,118**	**467,892**	**+19·32**	**+3·87**	**279**	**234**
Gawan	438		402	13,946	72,561	35,919	36,642	63,664	+13·97	—0·71	166	145
Kharagdiha	340		533	19,143	99,110	47,767	51,343	86,783	+14·20	—3·97	292	255
Dhanwar	249		445	17,270	87,165	41,208	45,957	75,707	+15·13	+2·95	350	304
Giridih	461	1	681	31,726	155,494	78,064	77,430	129,659	+19·93	—0·13	337	281
Dumri	514		469	29,684	143,957	74,211	69,746	112,079	+28·44	+18·22	280	218

PROVINCIAL TABLE I—*concluded.*

Area and Population of Districts, Subdivisions and Revenue Thanas.

District, Subdivision and Thana.	Area in square miles.	Number of			Population.				Percentage of variation.		Persons per square mile.	
		Towns.	Villages.	Occupied houses.	1931. Persons.	1931. Males.	1931. Females.	1921 (Both sexes.)	1921 to 1931.	1911 to 1921.	1931.	1921.
1	2	3	4	5	6	7	8	9	10	11	12	13
RANCHI	*7,102*	*3*	*3,838*	*228,594*	*1,567,149*	*777,063*	*790,086*	*1,334,473*	*+17·44*	*—3·79*	*221*	*188*
Sadr Subdivision	**2,052**	**2**	**1,369**	**109,490**	**581,639**	**287,164**	**294,475**	**495,043**	**+17·49**	**—5·84**	**283**	**241**
Lohardaga	474	1	273	18,590	99,298	48,305	50,993	87,712	+13·21	—9·95	209	185
Kuru	98	...	75	6,715	32,405	15,533	16,882	28,304	+14·49	—9·60	331	289
Burmu	176	...	96	5,074	27,475	13,818	13,657	23,176	+18·55	+0·52	156	132
Mandar	200	...	133	11,855	58,133	27,166	30,967	52,311	+11·13	—7·10	291	262
Bero	152	...	115	8,364	43,010	19,943	23,067	36,194	+18·83	—9·02	283	238
Lapung	117	...	78	4,704	27,264	13,165	14,099	23,875	+14·19	+2·60	233	204
Ranchi	450	1	331	35,969	194,007	99,031	94,976	161,009	+20·49	—3·45	431	358
Ormanjhi	88	...	89	4,332	22,261	11,241	11,020	18,157	+22·60	—9·82	253	206
Silli	123	...	107	8,701	43,349	21,614	21,735	36,308	+19·39	—8·82	352	295
Angara...	174	...	92	5,883	34,437	17,358	17,079	27,997	+23·00	—5·45	198	161
Khunti Subdivision ...	**1,545**	**1**	**1,073**	**71,574**	**373,800**	**185,575**	**188,225**	**317,843**	**+17·61**	**—9·09**	**242**	**206**
Karra	190	...	176	7,988	40,100	21,087	22,083	38,431	+13·33	—0·98	217	193
Torpa	276	...	152	10,650	60,468	29,509	30,959	54,090	+10·08	—0·69	219	199
Khunti...	330	...	296	15,935	86,840	43,314	43,526	76,255	+13·88	—1·07	260	225
Bundu	103	1	83	6,604	32,882	16,454	16,428	27,348	+20·24	—17·18	310	266
Sonahatu	146	...	99	9,027	43,417	21,557	21,860	35,208	+23·32	—17·93	297	241
Tamar	482	...	267	21,163	107,024	53,654	53,370	85,672	+24·92	—16·42	222	178
Gumla Subdivision ...	**2,057**	...	**932**	**67,703**	**375,476**	**186,215**	**189,261**	**322,327**	**+16·49**	**—1·90**	**183**	**157**
Bishunpur	237	...	88	2,995	18,370	9,331	9,039	16,165	+13·64	—10·00	78	68
Chainpur	407	...	192	10,085	56,272	28,153	28,119	51,755	+8·73	—4·37	138	127
Ghaghra	207	...	118	7,014	38,637	19,164	19,473	33,148	+16·50	—0·05	187	160
Sesai	261	...	156	14,169	70,192	34,276	35,916	59,539	+17·89	—3·14	260	212
Gumla	208	...	111	9,627	56,891	28,815	28,076	46,322	+22·82	—0·40	274	223
Raidih	198	...	61	5,551	31,519	15,751	15,768	26,767	+17·75	+2·24	159	135
Palkot	223	...	67	6,047	33,081	16,419	16,662	27,183	+21·70	+1·50	148	122
Basia	296	...	161	12,225	70,514	34,306	36,208	61,448	+14·75	+3·22	238	208
Simdega Subdivision ...	**1,448**	...	**444**	**39,827**	**236,234**	**118,109**	**118,125**	**199,260**	**+18·56**	**+8·80**	**163**	**138**
Bano	212	...	93	6,269	40,349	19,970	20,379	32,988	+22·31	+3·36	190	156
Kolebira	397	...	126	10,860	61,721	30,808	30,913	50,892	+21·28	+11·22	155	128
Simdega	530	...	155	14,906	87,689	44,000	43,790	75,569	+16·04	+9·37	165	142
Kurdeg	309	...	70	7,763	46,475	23,432	23,043	39,811	+16·74	+11·24	150	129
PALAMAU	*4,916*	*2*	*3,134*	*154,873*	*818,736*	*409,778*	*408,958*	*733,394*	*+11·64*	*+6·64*	*167*	*149*
Sadr Subdivision ...	**3,271**	**2**	**2,404**	**121,281**	**641,122**	**320,505**	**320,617**	**585,837**	**+9·44**	**+10·43**	**196**	**179**
Daltonganj	566	1	491	38,832	149,760	74,656	75,104	135,448	+10·57	+8·47	265	239
Garhwa...	567	1	378	24,552	130,286	64,541	65,745	121,988	+6·80	+13·29	230	215
Ranka	611	...	195	7,732	47,262	23,892	23,370	44,591	+5·99	—5·64	77	73
Chhatarpur	338	...	331	12,304	62,809	31,810	30,999	56,747	+10·68	+16·67	186	168
Patan	506	...	497	21,313	107,528	53,446	54,082	98,784	+8·85	+7·98	213	195
Husainabad ...	683	...	512	26,458	143,477	72,160	71,317	128,279	+11·85	+16·00	210	188
Latehar Subdivision ...	**1,645**	...	**730**	**33,592**	**177,614**	**89,273**	**88,341**	**147,557**	**+20·37**	**—6·14**	**108**	**89**
Balumath	666	...	306	15,006	80,851	40,177	40,674	67,459	+19·85	—7·47	121	101
Latehar	479	...	271	12,592	63,804	32,588	31,216	52,378	+21·81	+0·63	133	109
Mahuadanr	500	...	153	5,994	32,959	16,508	16,451	27,720	+18·90	—14·04	66	55
MANBHUM	*4,095*	*4*	*4,642*	*357,180*	*1,810,890*	*940,009*	*870,881*	*1,548,777*	*+16·92*	*+0·08*	*442*	*378*
Sadr Subdivision	**3,308**	**3**	**3,255**	**251,056**	**1,289,798**	**649,070**	**640,728**	**1,094,831**	**+17·81**	**—5·90**	**390**	**331**
Jhalda	309	1	359	26,207	130,369	65,443	64,926	104,961	+24·21	—12·59	422	340
Purulia	772	1	612	61,554	313,433	157,742	155,691	265,596	+18·01	—7·50	406	344
Baghmundi	164	...	137	9,164	47,344	24,044	23,300	37,565	+26·03	—17·75	289	229
Chandil	384	...	307	23,352	123,115	61,904	61,211	100,715	+22·24	—8·28	331	262
Barahabhum	509	...	497	30,624	162,502	81,546	80,956	141,829	+14·58	—1·51	319	279
Manbazar	257	...	357	21,009	109,590	54,782	54,808	97,504	+12·40	—3·40	426	379
Raghunathpur	300	1	395	29,198	152,080	77,579	74,501	132,982	+14·40	+0·24	507	443
Gaurangdih	173	...	199	13,959	63,441	31,612	31,829	56,652	+11·98	—3·38	367	327
Para	119	...	132	11,024	53,446	26,512	26,934	45,023	+18·71	—5·54	449	378
Chas	321	...	270	24,995	134,478	67,906	66,572	112,054	+20·01	—4·99	419	349
Dhanbad Subdivision ...	**787**	**1**	**1,387**	**106,124**	**521,092**	**290,939**	**230,153**	**453,946**	**+14·79**	**+18·18**	**662**	**577**
Gobindpur	119	...	211	9,106	50,823	26,564	25,259	45,497	+11·71	—0·07	427	382
Jherria...	158	1	*247*	*45,957*	*211,906*	*127,489*	*84,537*	*180,072*	*+17·72*	*+39·07*	*1,342*	*1,140*
Topchanchi	187	...	412	28,180	128,921	71,629	57,292	114,466	+12·63	+22·17	680	612
Nirsa	171	...	255	16,863	84,443	43,455	40,988	77,315	+9·22	+12·11	494	452
Tundi	152	...	262	7,028	44,939	22,862	22,077	36,596	+22·80	+0·51	296	241
SINGHBHUM	*3,879*	*4*	*3,013*	*194,249*	*929,802*	*469,421*	*460,381*	*759,438*	*+22·43*	*+9·37*	*240*	*196*
Sadr Subdivision	**2,719**	**2**	**1,582**	**108,306**	**535,207**	**260,712**	**274,495**	**443,012**	**+20·81**	**+0·99**	**197**	**163**
Chakradharpur	506	1	482	26,766	133,335	65,397	67,938	110,531	+20·63	—2·38	224	186
Kolhan	1,811	1	790	68,784	335,644	162,056	173,588	278,263	+20·62	+2·38	256	212
Manoharpur	812	...	310	13,756	66,228	33,359	33,969	54,218	+22·15	+1·31	82	67
Dhalbhum Subdivision ...	**1,160**	**2**	**1,431**	**85,943**	**394,595**	**208,709**	**185,886**	**316,426**	**+24·70**	**+23·73**	**340**	**273**
Ghatsila	1,160	2	1,431	85,943	394,595	208,709	185,886	316,426	+24·70	+23·73	340	273
Feudatory States ...	*28,648*	*7*	*19,378*	*952,141*	*4,652,007*	*2,288,422*	*2,363,585*	*3,959,669*	*+17·48*	*+0·37*	*162*	*138*
ORISSA STATES... ...	*28,046*	*7*	*18,706*	*914,652*	*4,465,385*	*2,196,691*	*2,268,694*	*3,807,172*	*+17·29*	*+0·28*	*159*	*136*
Athgarh	168	...	187	11,009	50,148	24,843	25,305	42,351	+18·41	—9·58	290	252
Talcher	399	...	281	14,288	69,702	34,674	35,028	51,015	+36·63	—22·94	175	128
Mayurbhanj	4,240	1	3,708	100,674	889,603	442,378	447,225	754,314	+17·94	+3·44	210	178
Nilgiri	278	...	291	16,862	68,594	34,117	34,477	65,222	+5·17	—5·08	247	235
Keonjhar	3,096	...	1,956	90,417	460,609	227,143	233,466	379,496	+21·37	+4·06	149	123
Pal Lahara	452	...	236	6,217	27,974	13,835	14,139	23,789	+17·59	—7·36	62	53
Dhenkanal	1,463	2	820	63,666	284,326	136,646	147,680	233,691	+21·67	—13·50	194	160
Athmallik	730	...	513	13,816	64,272	32,287	31,985	59,749	+7·57	+11·13	88	82
Hindol	312	...	149	10,418	48,896	23,419	25,477	38,617	+26·62	—21·52	157	124
Narsinghpur	199	...	188	8,808	40,878	19,925	20,953	33,002	+23·87	—17·42	205	166
Baramba	184	...	127	10,186	46,688	22,596	24,092	38,630	+20·86	—6·76	248	298
Tigiria...	46	...	46	5,570	24,822	12,141	12,681	19,534	+27·07	—16·95	540	425
Khandpara	244	...	274	16,364	77,929	37,281	40,648	64,289	+21·22	—13·91	319	263
Nayagarh	586	...	565	31,892	142,406	67,221	75,185	122,842	+15·93	—18·81	242	209
Ranpur	203	...	265	10,207	47,711	22,412	25,299	41,282	+15·57	—10·17	235	203
Daspalla	568	...	391	10,041	43,402	20,896	22,506	34,509	+25·77	—39·51	76	61
Baud	1,264	...	1,029	29,936	135,248	67,070	68,178	124,411	+8·71	+9·67	107	98
Bamra...	1,988	...	1,045	34,313	151,047	73,285	77,762	134,721	+12·12	—2·39	76	68
Bairakhol	833	...	812	7,932	35,710	17,727	17,983	31,225	+14·36	—1·59	43	37
Sonpur	906	2	827	52,333	237,920	117,007	120,863	226,751	+4·93	+5·12	263	250
Patna	2,390	1	1,766	111,229	566,924	280,305	286,619	494,456	+14·66	+20·97	236	206
Kalahandi	3,745	1	2,245	106,434	513,716	252,438	261,278	415,827	+23·54	—0·75	137	111
Gangpur	2,492	...	1,118	68,332	356,674	176,959	179,715	309,271	+15·33	+1·79	143	124
Bonai	1,296	...	867	16,468	80,186	40,026	40,160	68,178	+17·61	+16·93	62	53
CHOTA NAGPUR STATES ...	*602*	...	*672*	*37,489*	*186,622*	*91,731*	*94,891*	*152,497*	*+22·38*	*+2·59*	*310*	*253*
Saraikela	449	...	475	28,015	143,525	70,990	72,535	115,192	+24·60	+4·92	320	257
Kharsawan	153	...	197	9,474	43,097	20,741	22,356	37,305	+15·53	—3·98	282	244

PROVINCIAL TABLE II.

POPULATION OF REVENUE THANAS AND POLICE-STATIONS BY RELIGION AND LITERACY.

This table shows the total population of each revenue thana and police-station jurisdiction, and the distribution of that population between the five main religious groups. For each revenue thana the following additional information is given :—

(*i*) The distribution of the Hindu population between (*a*) Brahmans, (*b*) Depressed classes and (*c*) Other Hindus.

(*ii*) The number of literate persons in each religious group or sub-group.

(*iii*) The total number of literate persons in the revenue thana, and their distribution between certain age-groups.

(*iv*) The total number of persons in the revenue thana who are literate in English.

2. The literacy figures in this table differ slightly from those in Imperial Table XIII, as the latter table shows all persons aged 5 and over who were returned as literate, whereas no person below the age of 7 is shown as literate in this table.

3. The following castes and tribes have been treated as " Depressed classes " :—

Bauri	Ghusuria	Mahuria
Bhogta	Godra	Mangan
Bhuiya	Gokha	Mochi
Bhumij	Halalkhor	Musahar
Chamar	Hari	Nat
Chaupal	Irika	Pan
Dhobi	Kandra	Pasi
Dom	Kanjar	Rajwar
Dosadh	Kela	Siyal
Ghasi	Kurariar	Turi
	Lalbegi	

PROVINCIAL TABLE II.

POPULATION OF REVENUE THANAS AND POLICE-STATIONS BY RELIGION AND LITERACY.

REVENUE THANA	POLICE-STATION	POPULATION.			HINDUS — TOTAL HINDUS		HINDUS — BRAHMANS. Number of persons		BRAHMANS. Number literate.		DEPRESSED CLASSES Number of persons.		DEPRESSED CLASSES Number literate		OTHER HINDUS Number of persons		OTHER HINDUS Number literate		MUSLIMS Number of persons		MUSLIMS Number literate.	
		Persons	Males	Females	Males	Females.	Males	Females	Males	Females	Males	Females	Males	Females	Males	Females	Males	Females	Males	Females.	Males	Females.
1	2	3	4	5	6	7	8	9	10	11	12	13	14	15	16	17	18	19	20	21	22	23
PATNA		1 846 474	956,124	890,350	852,682	787,147	31,694	26,872	13,214	1,860	153,422	149,888	2 689	227	667,566	610,387	117,642	9,744	101,175	101,480	23,454	4,452
Patna City		(a) 159 690	92,338	67,452	60,285	50,359	5,167	2,671	2,875	649	6,905	5,830	308	31	57,213	41,858	17,221	3 101	22,241	15,907	7,041	1,120
Pirbahor Ward		30,050	18,774	11,276	13,380	8,259													5,323	2,903		
Sultanganj Ward		11,144	5,854	5,290	3,970	3,548													1,877	1,740		
Alamganj Ward		19,890	10,527	9,363	7,989	7,160													2,451	3,067		
North Khajekalan Ward ...		8,108	4,423	3,685	2,841	2,380													1,561	1,304		
South Khajekalan Ward		19 915	10,772	9,143	6,356	5,363													4,413	3,780		
Bakarganj Ward		10 535	6,368	4,167	4 806	3,073													1,417	783		
Chauk Kalan Ward		17 254	9,255	7,999	7,477	6,436													1,695	1 503		
Malsalami Ward		16 562	9,846	6,716	9,058	6,092													788	624		
Rural area		(a) 19 836	9,911	9,925	9,318	9,303	56	70	26	2	1,676	1,625	47		7,586	7,607	1,096	48	593	623	94	31
Phulwari		113 275	63,407	50,868	54,041	44,254	2,369	1,284	1,361	457	9,355	8,939	337	24	43,317	34,031	9 814	1,537	7,729	6,116	2,321	386
	New Capital	(a) 14 258	8,701	5,557	7,086	4,676	1,030	640	587	344	929	700	57		5,137	3,318	3,379	854	1,331	637	638	108
	Bankipore Ward	(a) 11 974	7,718	4,256	6,232	3,372	491	168	350	76	507	365	80	9	5,234	2,839	1,496	375	1,366	650	439	66
	Phulwari	65 331	32,777	32,554	20,281	28,791													3,491	3 761		
	Digha	14 116	7 793	6,323	6,384	5,501													1,195	806		
	Patna	7 596	5,418	2,178	5,058	1,914													346	263		
Masaurhi Buzurg		(b) 137 353	70,104	67,249	63,795	60,380	1,548	1,535	532	80	14,490	14,212	163	15	47,757	44,643	6,992	350	6 280	6,848	1,074	303
	Masaurhi	(f) 103 451	52,692	50,759	48,151	45,712													4 513	5,026		
	Punpun	33,847	17,311	16,536	15,588	14,754													1,724	1,782		
Maner		(c) 91,477	47,643	43,834	43,901	39,489	1,660	1,540	686	122	5,757	5,740	127	14	36,484	32,200	6 732	606	3,731	4,333	969	329
	Maner	(d) 94 512	49,263	45,249	45,521	40,904													3 731	4,333		
Dinapore		81,367	43,123	38,244	36,302	32,722	1,170	940	575	97	5,601	5,549	202	8	29,531	36,233	4,407	216	5,673	5,112	1 333	241
	Dinapore	(c) 71 272	37,361	33,921	31,998	29,528													4,457	4,221		
	Khagaul	10 840	6,160	4,680	4,692	3,551													1,216	891		
Bikram		(d) 203 231	105,546	97,685	98,500	90,062	5,534	5,333	1 676	146	16,945	15,921	122	30	76,021	68 808	9 730	1,086	7,031	7,618	928	313
	Bikram	97,691	50,801	46,890	46,849	42,706													3 950	4,184		
	Paliganj	52 006	27,201	24,805	25,435	22,860													1,759	1,944		
	Naubatpur	52 892	27,222	25,670	25,894	24,176													1 322	1,490		
Fatwa		85 544	43,001	42,543	30,249	38,255	1,122	1,153	592	64	7,901	7,044	183	3	30,236	29,158	6,126	465	3 747	4,287	760	114
	Fatwa	(b) 86 489	43,516	42,973	30,710	38,636													3,801	4,336		
Barh		221,984	112,953	109,031	106,596	102,027	3,910	3,545	1,399	186	19,480	19 613	439	72	83,206	78,870	14,458	1,110	6,353	6 994	1,130	163
	Barh	136 588	69,115	67,473	64 725	62,534													4 386	4,929		
	Bakhtiyarpur	85,396	43,838	41,558	41,871	39,493													1,967	2 065		
Mokameh		106 916	54,929	51,987	51,794	48,601	2,123	1,735	607	90	11,400	11,010	249	22	38 271	35,867	5,910	349	3,087	3 353	518	56
	Mokameh	80 400	41,395	39,005	38,733	36,146													2 614	2,826		
	Sarmera	26,516	13,534	12,982	13,061	12,455													473	527		
Bihar		382,956	194,002	188,954	167,386	159,819	5,136	4,632	2,204	310	34,188	33,988	429	6	128,062	121,109	21 477	1,281	26,581	29 098	6 868	1,621
	Bihar	178,622	91,540	87,082	76,284	72,154													15,269	14,917		
	Asthanwan	71,927	35,628	36,299	30,415	29,114													5,311	7,183		
	Giriak	(e) 39 698	19,897	19,801	18,341	18,009													1,543	1,780		
	Silao	92,918	47,038	45,880	42,467	40,650													4 558	5,218		
Hilsa		(f) 185,096	94,460	90,636	87,705	82,985	2,350	2,303	1,039	129	15 009	14,424	180	8	70,346	66,308	12,040	681	6,754	7,701	942	141
	Chandi	80,139	41,072	39,067	37,860	35,496													3,213	3,571		
	Hilsa	67,310	34,313	33,097	31,670	30,191													2,542	2,906		
	Ekangar Sarai	36,757	18,761	17,996	17,770	16,781													991	1,215		
Islampur	Islampur	83,981	42,226	41,755	38,128	36,990	1,060	1,068	498	30	6,151	6,150	51	3	30,017	29,772	5,524	143	4,072	4,896	564	.

PROVINCIAL TABLE II—*continued.*

POPULATION OF REVENUE THANAS AND POLICE-STATIONS BY RELIGION AND LITERACY.

REVENUE THANA.	POLICE-STATION.	CHRISTIANS. *No. of persons.* Males.	Females.	*No. literate.* Males.	Females.	TRIBAL. *No. of persons.* M.	F.	*No. literate.* M.	F.	OTHERS. *No. of persons.* Males.	Females.	*No. literate.* Males.	Females.	NUMBER LITERATE (AGED 7 AND OVER). TOTAL. Persons.	Males.	Females.	AGED 7—13. Males.	Females.	AGED 14—23. Males.	Females.	AGED 24 AND OVER. Males.	Females.	LITERATE IN ENGLISH. Males.	Females.
1	2	24	25	26	27	28	29	30	31	32	33	34	35	36	37	38	39	40	41	42	43	44	45	46
PATNA ...	...	**1,990**	**1,513**	**1,704**	**1,020**	**17**	**2**	**15**	...	**260**	**208**	**146**	**37**	**176,204**	**158,864**	**17,340**	**21,147**	**3,392**	**41,122**	**5,111**	**96,595**	**8,837**	**20,575**	**2,309**
Patna City ...		548	1,032	467	754	15	...	15	...	140	71	78	21	**33,680**	27,996	5,685	3,049	1,200	8,417	1,670	16,529	2,915	11,366	1,919
Pirbahor Ward ...	...	50	103	...	...	...	...	...	...	23	12	...	...	...	...	...	...	...	...	...	...	...	...	...
Sultanganj Ward ...	...	...	...	...	...	...	...	...	...	7	3	...	...	...	...	...	...	...	...	...	...	...	...	...
Alamganj Ward ...	...	80	133	...	...	...	...	...	...	7	4	...	...	...	...	...	...	...	...	...	...	...	...	...
North Khajekalan Ward ...	...	1	1	...	...	...	...	...	...	...	...	...	...	...	...	...	...	...	...	...	...	...	...	...
South Khajekalan Ward ...	...	...	...	...	...	...	...	...	...	3	...	...	...	...	...	...	...	...	...	...	...	...	...	...
Bakarganj Ward ...	...	54	312	...	...	...	...	...	...	1	...	...	...	...	...	...	...	...	...	...	...	...	...	...
Chauk Kalan Ward ...	...	12	10	...	...	...	...	...	...	71	51	...	...	...	...	...	...	...	...	...	...	...	...	...
Malsalami Ward ...	...	...	...	...	...	...	...	...	...	...	...	...	...	...	...	...	...	...	...	...	...	...	...	...
Rural area ...	...	...	...	...	...	...	...	...	...	...	...	...	...	**1,344**	1,263	81	181	16	316	34	764	30	113	...
Phulwari ...	...	579	401	444	348	15	...	15	...	43	7	38	8	**17,115**	14,360	2,756	1,713	564	3,778	774	8,869	1,307	4,166	712
	New Capital ..	251	241	185	158	15	...	15	...	18	9	13	2	**5,343**	3,877	1,466	568	318	976	380	2,323	759	2,317	394
	Bankipore Ward.	100	233	86	174	...	...	...	...	20	2	13	1	**3,174**	2,473	701	235	145	650	300	1,508	366	1,106	298
	Phulwari ...	...	...	...	...	...	...	...	...	5	2	...	...	...	...	...	...	...	...	...	...	...	...	...
	Digha ...	214	16	...	...	...	...	...	...	...	...	...	...	...	...	...	...	...	...	...	...	...	...	...
	Patna ...	14	11	...	...	...	...	...	...	...	...	...	...	...	...	...	...	...	...	...	...	...	...	...
Masaurhi Buzurg ...	...	5	4	3	3	...	...	...	...	24	17	...	...	**9,424**	8,794	630	1,366	109	3,166	181	5,333	370	408	11
	Masaurhi ...	4	4	...	...	...	...	...	...	24	17	...	...	...	...	...	...	...	...	...	...	...	...	...
	Punpun ...	1	...	...	...	...	...	...	...	...	...	...	...	...	...	...	...	...	...	...	...	...	...	...
Maner ...	...	...	1	...	1	...	...	...	...	11	11	6	3	**9,495**	8,520	975	1,201	157	2,010	273	5,309	545	1,028	10
	Maner ...	...	1	...	...	...	...	...	...	11	11	...	...	...	...	...	...	...	...	...	...	...	...	...
Dinapore ...	...	1,147	410	475	213	...	...	...	...	1	...	1	...	**8,257**	7,483	774	784	144	1,749	396	4,950	334	2,464	247
	Dinapore ...	895	172	...	...	...	...	...	...	1	...	...	...	...	...	...	...	...	...	...	...	...	...	...
	Khagaul ...	252	238	...	...	...	...	...	...	...	...	...	...	...	...	...	...	...	...	...	...	...	...	...
Bikram ...	...	7	1	4	...	...	...	...	...	8	4	5	...	**14,029**	12,455	1,574	1,806	347	3,152	385	7,467	939	630	9
	Bikram ...	...	...	...	...	...	...	...	...	2	...	...	...	...	...	...	...	...	...	...	...	...	...	...
	Paliganj ...	7	1	...	...	...	...	...	...	...	...	...	...	...	...	...	...	...	...	...	...	...	...	...
	Naubatpur ...	...	...	...	...	...	...	...	...	6	4	...	...	...	...	...	...	...	...	...	...	...	...	...
Fatwa ...	...	1	1	1	...	...	...	...	...	4	...	4	...	**8,311**	7,665	646	1,164	148	1,884	219	4,597	279	330	11
	Fatwa ...	1	1	...	...	...	...	...	...	4	...	...	...	...	...	...	...	...	...	...	...	...	...	...
Barh ...	...	4	10	1	8	...	...	...	...	...	...	...	...	**18,956**	17,417	1,539	2,452	327	4,417	405	10,545	807	987	22
	Barh ...	4	10	...	...	...	...	...	...	...	...	...	...	...	...	...	...	...	...	...	...	...	...	...
	Bakhtiyarpur	...	...	...	...	...	...	...	...	...	...	...	...	...	...	...	...	...	...	...	...	...	...	...
Mokameh ...	...	48	33	42	23	...	...	...	...	...	...	...	...	**7,875**	7,326	549	830	84	1,806	184	4,606	381	633	38
	Mokameh	48	33	...	...	...	...	...	...	...	...	...	...	...	...	...	...	...	...	...	...	...	...	...
	Sarmera ...	...	...	...	...	...	...	...	...	...	...	...	...	...	...	...	...	...	...	...	...	...	...	...
Bihar ...	...	2	4	1	3	2	2	...	...	31	31	30	12	**34,232**	31,099	3,133	4,380	501	7,846	943	18,874	1,599	1,598	20
	Bihar ...	...	4	...	...	...	...	...	...	7	7	...	...	...	...	...	...	...	...	...	...	...	...	...
	Asthanwan ...	...	...	...	...	2	2	...	...	...	...	...	...	...	...	...	...	...	...	...	...	...	...	...
	Giriak ...	...	...	...	...	...	...	...	...	13	12	...	...	...	...	...	...	...	...	...	...	...	...	...
	Silao ...	2	...	...	...	...	...	...	...	11	12	...	...	...	...	...	...	...	...	...	...	...	...	...
Hilsa ...	...	...	...	...	...	...	...	...	...	1	...	...	...	**15,169**	14,310	959	3,012	304	3,547	234	8,651	471	321	3
	Chandi ...	...	...	...	...	...	...	...	...	...	...	...	...	...	...	...	...	...	...	...	...	...	...	...
	Hilsa ...	...	...	...	...	...	...	...	...	1	...	...	...	...	...	...	...	...	...	...	...	...	...	...
	Ekangar Sarai	...	...	...	...	...	...	...	...	...	...	...	...	...	...	...	...	...	...	...	...	...	...	...
Islampur ...	Islampur ...	...	...	...	...	...	...	...	...	36	69	30	1	**6,834**	6,657	177	1,092	82	1,627	59	3,938	86	75	...

REMARKS. (47)

(*a*) *Patna City* includes the *New Capital* and *Bankipore Ward* (which for administrative purposes fall within *Phulwari* thana), and excludes the *Rural Area.*

(*b*) *Masaurhi Buzurg* includes one mauza (*Kansari*) which belongs to police-station *Fatwa.*

(*c*) *Maner* thana includes one mauza (*Dariapur*) which belongs to police-station *Dinapore.*

(*d*) *Bikram* thana includes one mauza (*Banwaripur*) which belongs to police-station *Maner.* In police-station *Maner* there are also seven mauzas which are included in the population of *Arrah* thana in Shahabad district.

(*e*) In police-station *Giriak* there is one mauza (*Murghichak*) which is included in the population of *Nawada* thana in Gaya district.

(*f*) *Hilsa* thana includes two mauzas (*Mohiuddinpur* and *Naneuri*) which belong to police-station *Masaurhi.*

PROVINCIAL TABLE II—*continued*.

POPULATION OF REVENUE THANAS AND POLICE-STATIONS BY RELIGION AND LITERACY.

GAYA.]

REVENUE THANA.	POLICE-STATION.	POPULATION.			HINDUS. TOTAL HINDUS.		HINDUS. BRAHMANS. Number of persons.		HINDUS. BRAHMANS. Number literate.		HINDUS. DEPRESSED CLASSES. Number of persons.		HINDUS. DEPRESSED CLASSES. Number literate.		HINDUS. OTHER HINDUS. Number of persons.		HINDUS. OTHER HINDUS. Number literate.		MUSLIMS. Number of persons.		MUSLIMS. Number literate.	
		Persons.	Males.	Females.	Males.	Females.	Males.	Females.	Males.	Females.	Males.	Females.	Males.	Females.	Males.	Females.	Males.	Females.	Males.	Females.	Males.	Females.
1	2	3	4	5	6	7	8	9	10	11	12	13	14	15	16	17	18	19	20	21	22	23
GAYA ...	...	**2,388,462**	**1,193,643**	**1,194,819**	**1,075,495**	**1,058,046**	**36,686**	**37,609**	**11,675**	**756**	**290,396**	**301,790**	**1,246**	**133**	**748,411**	**718,647**	**84,954**	**5,307**	**117,436**	**136,124**	**13,940**	**1,498**
Gaya Town ...	Gaya Town ...	88,005	50,625	37,380	38,502	37,960	3,865	1,155	1,538	139	4,913	4,262	138	31	30,724	33,543	7,985	898	11,636	8,970	3,023	430
Gaya Mufassal ...	...	205,417	101,973	103,444	93,321	93,304	1,427	1,613	483	16	33,726	35,463	70	10	58,168	56,319	5,655	353	8,631	10,023	602	45
	Gaya Mufassal	57,017	28,071	28,946	24,024	25,456	...	...	...	...	...	...	...	...	...	...	...	...	3,139	3,475	...	...
	Bodh Gaya ...	40,254	20,404	19,850	18,826	18,053	...	...	...	...	...	...	...	...	...	...	...	...	1,565	1,792	...	...
	Wazirganj ...	63,026	31,256	31,770	29,264	29,425	...	...	...	...	...	...	...	...	...	...	...	...	1,092	2,341	...	...
	Paraia ...	45,120	22,242	22,878	20,307	20,461	...	...	...	...	...	...	...	...	...	...	...	...	1,935	2,414	...	...
Atri ...	...	100,885	50,514	50,371	40,285	45,247	1,006	1,065	371	23	14,001	13,977	33	1	31,278	30,205	3,082	109	4,229	5,122	290	51
	Atri ...	59,259	29,721	29,538	27,171	26,594	...	...	...	...	...	...	...	...	...	...	...	...	2,550	2,944	...	...
	Khizer Sarai ...	41,626	20,793	20,833	19,114	18,653	...	...	...	...	...	...	...	...	...	...	...	...	1,679	2,178	...	...
Tikari ...	...	166,340	83,114	83,226	75,766	74,428	3,018	3,639	850	78	16,553	17,066	68	10	56,196	53,833	9,155	531	7,331	8,785	685	70
	Tikari ...	121,254	60,767	60,487	56,167	54,813	...	...	...	...	...	...	...	...	...	...	...	...	4,592	5,665	...	...
	Belaganj ...	45,086	22,347	22,739	19,599	19,615	...	...	...	...	...	...	...	...	...	...	...	...	2,739	3,120	...	...
Barachatti ...	...	131,458	65,004	66,364	59,701	59,831	1,004	930	268	6	23,874	25,104	20	1	34,833	33,707	1,208	41	5,389	6,532	282	29
	Barachatti ...	76,620	38,007	38,613	34,739	34,611	...	...	...	...	...	...	...	...	...	...	...	...	3,268	4,002	...	...
	Fatehpur ...	54,838	27,087	27,751	24,962	25,220	...	...	...	...	...	...	...	...		...	...	...	2,121	2,530	...	...
Sherghati ...	...	199,288	98,035	101,253	86,187	87,115	1,785	1,806	407	9	37,742	38,770	43	3	40,660	40,533	4,265	291	11,845	14,125	537	23
	Sherghati ...	81,322	39,985	41,337	35,368	35,647	...	...	...	...	...	...	...	...	...	...	...	...	4,616	5,790	...	...
	Gurua ...	36,010	17,457	18,553	15,494	15,888	...	...	...	...	...	...	...	...	...	...	...	...	1,063	2,665	...	...
	Imamganj ...	54,449	26,845	27,604	23,221	23,700	...	...	...	...	...	...	...	...	...	...	...	...	3,622	3,891	...	...
	Dumaria ...	27,507	13,748	13,759	12,104	11,080	...	...	...	...	...	...	...	...	...	...	...	...	1,644	1,779	...	...
Nawada ...	...	(a)313,517	154,196	159,321	130,283	140,478	4,887	5,052	1,361	73	38,694	41,202	227	23	95,701	94,324	12,120	580	14,790	18,729	1,338	133
	Nawada ...	116,064	57,338	58,726	51,567	51,693	...	...	...	...	...	...	...	...	...	...	...	...	5,709	7,002	...	...
	Haswa ...	89,804	43,335	46,469	39,462	41,165	...	...	...	...	...	...	...	...	...	...	...	...	3,847	5,280	...	...
	Gobindpur ...	51,420	24,756	26,664	21,632	22,591	...	...	...	...	...	...	...		...	...	...	...	3,116	4,064	...	...
	Worsleyganj ...	55,014	28,083	26,931	26,122	24,663	...	...	...	...	...	...	...	...	...	...	...	...	1,913	2,219	...	...
Rajauli ...	Rajauli ...	84,070	41,260	42,810	37,316	38,103	820	909	208	8	12,981	14,043	37	1	23,506	23,152	2,035	115	3,943	4,705	209	5
Pakribarwan ...	...	91,673	45,551	46,122	40,573	40,260	889	948	330	17	11,781	12,230	34	10	27,903	27,087	3,460	128	4,978	5,862	389	81
	Pakribarwan ...	(a)67,173	33,493	33,680	29,638	29,176	...	...	...	...	...	.	...	...	...	...	...	...	3,855	4,504	...	...
	Kauakol ...	25,506	12,641	12,865	11,313	11,343	...	...	...	...	...	...	...	...	...	...	...	...	1,328	1,523	...	...
Jahanabad ...	...	319,208	161,467	157,741	147,559	141,481	5,527	5,702	1,282	93	37,280	37,113	100	3	114,752	108,666	15,775	302	13,908	16,260	1,638	177
	Jahanabad ...	93,975	47,575	46,400	41,956	40,114	...	...	...	...	...	.	...	...	...	...	...	...	5,619	6,286	...	...
	Kurtha ...	74,641	37,804	36,837	34,179	32,569	..	...	...	...	...	...	...	...	...	..	...	...	3,625	4,278	...	...
	Ghosi ...	82,814	41,869	40,945	40,066	38,673	...	...	...	...	...	...	...	...	...	..	...	...	1,803	2,272	...	...
	Makhdumpur	67,778	34,219	33,559	31,358	30,135	...	.	...	...	...	...	...	...	...	...	...	...	2,861	3,424	...	...
Arwal ...	Arwal ...	142,730	72,599	70,131	67,434	64,511	2,471	3,651	899	86	12,934	12,039	132	17	53,029	48,931	6,333	219	5,161	5,614	709	103
Daudnagar ...	...	137,385	68,723	68,662	62,514	62,200	3,488	3,495	807	61	13,295	13,786	113	30	46,731	45,919	4,560	270	6,209	6,462	740	101
	Daudnagar ...	84,426	42,616	41,810	38,080	37,328	...	...	...	...	...	...	...	...	...	...	...	...	4,536	4,482	...	...
	Goh ...	52,959	26,107	26,852	24,434	24,872	...	...	...	...	...	...	...	...	...	...	...	...	1,673	1,980	...	...
Nabinagar ...	...	115,385	57,252	58,083	53,208	53,619	3,960	3,883	1,007	46	12,397	13,554	53	...	37,851	36,182	2,743	152	4,043	4,464	439	39
	Nabinagar ...	65,475	32,915	32,560	31,090	30,633	..	...	...	...	...	...	...	...	...	...	...	...	1,825	1,927	...	...
	Kutumba ...	49,860	24,337	25,523	22,118	22,986	...		.	...	...	...	...	..	...	...	...	...	2,218	2,537	...	...
Aurangabad ...	...	293,151	143,240	149,911	127,847	129,419	5,532	5,877	1,764	111	30,226	33,196	188	4	92,089	91,346	7,579	328	15,353	20,472	3,360	307
	Aurangabad ...	89,474	43,951	45,523	39,491	39,739	...	...	...	...	...	...	...	..	...	...	...	...	4,440	5,778	...	...
	Rafiganj ...	68,706	33,507	35,199	27,899	27,551	...	...	...	...	...	..	...	...	...	..	...	...	5,586	7,634	...	...
	Obra ...	47,789	23,086	24,703	21,084	21,900	...	...	...	...	...	...	..	...	...	...	...	...	2,003	2,803	...	...
	Madanpur ...	50,343	24,148	26,195	22,157	23,508	...	...	...	...	...	...	...	...	...	...	...	...	1,991	2,687	...	...
	Barun ...	36,839	18,548	18,291	17,216	16,721	...	...	...	...	...	...	...	...	...	...	...	...	1,326	1,570	...	...

PROVINCIAL TABLE II—*continued.*

POPULATION OF REVENUE THANAS AND POLICE-STATIONS BY RELIGION AND LITERACY.

REVENUE THANA.	POLICE-STATION.	CHRISTIANS. No. of persons. Males.	CHRISTIANS. No. of persons. Females.	CHRISTIANS. No. literate. Males.	CHRISTIANS. No. literate. Females.	TRIBAL. No. of persons. M.	TRIBAL. No. of persons. F.	TRIBAL. No. literate. M.	TRIBAL. No. literate. F.	OTHERS. No. of persons. Males.	OTHERS. No. of persons. Females.	OTHERS. No. literate. Males.	OTHERS. No. literate. Females.	NUMBER LITERATE (AGED 7 AND OVER). TOTAL. Persons.	TOTAL. Males.	TOTAL. Females.	AGED 7—13. Males.	AGED 7—13. Females.	AGED 14—23. Males.	AGED 14—23. Females.	AGED 24 AND OVER. Males.	AGED 24 AND OVER. Females.	LITERATE IN ENGLISH. Males.	LITERATE IN ENGLISH. Females.	REMARKS.
1	2	24	25	26	27	28	29	30	31	32	33	34	35	36	37	38	39	40	41	42	43	44	45	46	47
GAYA ...	...	298	278	219	184	12	...	...	...	402	371	230	59	119,596	111,664	7,932	13,285	1,191	35,238	2,596	63,141	4,145	6,395	333	(a) *Nawada* thana includes three mauzas (*Bauri, Kashichak* and *Dulachak*) which belong to police-station *Pakribarawan*, and one mauza (*Murghichak*) which belongs to police-station *Giriak* in Patna district.
Gaya Town ...	Gaya Town ...	262	246	263	174	12	...	...	...	223	204	130	44	14,713	13,017	1,696	1,199	240	3,061	476	8,737	980	3,359	262	
Gaya Mufassal ...	...	6	11	2	2	...	...	...	...	15	17	5	...	7,342	6,907	435	831	28	1,791	166	4,285	241	284	5	
	Gaya Mufassal	6	10	...	...	...	...	...	...	2	5	...	...	...	...	...	...	...	...	...	...	...	...	...	
	Bodh Gaya ...	...	...	...	...	...	...	...	...	13	6	...	...	...	...	...	...	...	...	...	...	...	...	...	
	Wasirganj ...	...	1	...	...	...	...	...	...	...	3	...	...	...	...	...	...	...	...	...	...	...	...	...	
	Paraia ...	...	...	...	...	...	...	...	...	...	3	...	...	...	...	...	...	...	...	...	...	...	...	...	
Atri ...	...	...	...	...	...	...	...	...	...	...	3	...	...	3,960	3,776	184	394	38	973	47	2,409	99	29	...	
	Atri ...	...	...	...	...	...	...	...	...	...	...	...	...	...	...	...	...	...	...	...	...	...	...	...	
	Khizer Sarai ...	...	...	...	...	...	...	...	...	...	2	...	...	...	...	...	...	...	...	...	...	...	...	...	
Tikari ...	...	1	...	1	...	...	...	...	...	16	13	9	...	11,457	10,768	689	2,226	47	4,280	323	4,262	319	221	4	
	Tikari ...	1	...	...	...	...	...	...	...	7	9	...	...	...	...	...	...	...	...	...	...	...	...	...	
	Belaganj ...	...	...	...	...	...	...	...	...	9	4	...	...	...	...	...	...	...	...	...	...	...	...	...	
Barachatti ...	...	4	1	2	1	...	...	...	...	...	...	...	...	1,858	1,780	78	156	12	400	18	1,224	48	58	2	
	Barachatti ...	...	...	...	...	...	...	...	...	...	...	...	...	...	...	...	...	...	...	...	...	...	...	...	
	Fatehpur ...	4	1	...	...	...	...	...	...	...	...	...	...	...	...	...	...	...	...	...	...	...	...	...	
Sherghati ...	...	3	2	1	...	...	...	...	...	...	11	...	...	5,579	5,253	326	229	13	2,265	109	2,759	206	135	1	
	Sherghati ...	1	...	...	...	...	...	...	...	...	...	...	...	...	...	...	...	...	...	...	...	...	...	...	
	Gurua ...	...	...	...	...	...	...	...	...	...	...	...	...	...	...	...	...	...	...	...	...	...	...	...	
	Imamganj ...	2	2	...	...	...	...	...	...	...	11	...	...	...	...	...	...	...	...	...	...	...	...	...	
	Dumaria ...	...	...	...	...	...	...	...	...	...	...	...	...	...	...	...	...	...	...	...	...	...	...	...	
Nawada ...	...	...	...	...	...	...	...	...	...	124	114	76	15	15,945	15,122	823	1,886	126	4,424	247	8,812	450	364	9	
	Nawada ...	...	...	...	...	...	...	...	...	42	32	...	...	...	...	...	...	...	...	...	...	...	...	...	
	Haswa ...	...	...	...	...	...	...	...	...	26	24	...	...	...	...	...	...	...	...	...	...	...	...	...	
	Gobindpur ...	...	...	...	...	...	...	...	...	8	9	...	...	...	...	...	...	...	...	...	...	...	...	...	
	Worsleyganj ...	...	...	...	...	...	...	...	...	48	40	...	...	...	...	...	...	...	...	...	...	...	...	...	
Rajauli ...	Rajauli ...	1	2	1	1	...	...	...	...	...	...	...	...	2,610	2,480	130	235	5	1,303	68	942	57	28	3	
Pakribarawan ...	...	...	...	...	...	...	...	...	...	...	...	...	...	3,458	3,222	236	319	96	1,344	81	1,559	59	100	5	
	Pakribarawan	...	...	...	...	...	...	...	...	...	...	...	...	...	...	...	...	...	...	...	...	...	...	...	
	Kanakol ...	...	...	...	...	...	...	...	...	...	...	...	...	...	...	...	...	...	...	...	...	...	...	...	
Jahanabad ...	...	...	...	...	...	...	...	...	...	...	...	...	...	20,070	18,895	1,175	2,146	191	8,005	453	8,744	531	485	12	
	Jahanabad ...	...	...	...	...	...	...	...	...	...	...	...	...	...	...	...	...	...	...	...	...	...	...	...	
	Kurtha ...	...	...	...	...	...	...	...	...	...	...	...	...	...	...	...	...	...	...	...	...	...	...	...	
	Ghosi ...	...	...	...	...	...	...	...	...	...	...	...	...	...	...	...	...	...	...	...	...	...	...	...	
	Makhdumpur	...	...	...	...	...	...	...	...	...	...	...	...	...	...	...	...	...	...	...	...	...	...	...	
Arwal ...	Arwal ...	4	6	1	...	...	...	...	...	...	...	...	...	8,599	8,064	535	1,012	89	1,890	129	5,162	307	400	6	
Daudnagar ...	...	...	...	...	...	...	...	...	...	...	...	...	...	6,972	6,220	752	908	157	1,657	191	3,655	404	150	2	
	Daudnagar ...	...	...	...	...	...	...	...	...	...	...	...	...	...	...	...	...	...	...	...	...	...	...	...	
	Goh ...	...	...	...	...	...	...	...	...	...	...	...	...	...	...	...	...	...	...	...	...	...	...	...	
Nabinagar ...	...	...	...	...	...	...	...	...	...	1	...	1	...	4,480	4,243	237	456	69	1,036	98	2,751	70	161	1	
	Nabinagar ...	...	...	...	...	...	...	...	...	...	...	...	...	...	...	...	...	...	...	...	...	...	...	...	
	Kutumba ...	...	...	...	...	...	...	...	...	1	...	...	...	...	...	...	...	...	...	...	...	...	...	...	
Aurangabad ...	...	17	10	8	6	...	...	...	...	23	10	9	...	12,563	11,917	646	1,288	91	2,799	180	7,830	375	631	26	
	Aurangabad ...	11	6	...	...	...	...	...	...	...	...	...	...	...	...	...	...	...	...	...	...	...	...	...	
	Rafiganj ...	5	4	...	...	...	...	...	...	17	10	...	...	...	...	...	...	...	...	...	...	...	...	...	
	Obra ...	...	...	...	...	...	...	...	...	...	...	...	...	...	...	...	...	...	...	...	...	...	...	...	
	Madanpur ...	...	...	...	...	...	...	...	...	...	...	...	...	...	...	...	...	...	...	...	...	...	...	...	
	Barun ...	1	...	...	...	...	...	...	...	6	...	...	...	...	...	...	...	...	...	...	...	...	...	...	

PROVINCIAL TABLE II—*continued.*

POPULATION OF REVENUE THANAS AND POLICE-STATIONS BY RELIGION AND LITERACY.

REVENUE THANA.	POLICE-STATION.	POPULATION.			HINDUS. TOTAL HINDUS.		HINDUS. BRAHMANS. Number of persons.		BRAHMANS. Number literate.		DEPRESSED CLASSES. Number of persons.		DEPRESSED CLASSES. Number literate.		OTHER HINDUS. Number of persons.		OTHER HINDUS. Number literate.		MUSLIMS. Number of persons.		MUSLIMS. Number literate.	
		Persons.	Males.	Females.	Males.	Females.	Males.	Females.	Males.	Females.	Males.	Females.	Males.	Females.	Males.	Females.	Males.	Females.	Males.	Females.	Males.	Females.
1	2	3	4	5	6	7	8	9	10	11	12	13	14	15	16	17	18	19	20	21	22	23
SHAHABAD	...	**1,993,489**	**999,099**	**994,390**	**924,282**	**914,580**	**99,573**	**99,971**	**21,183**	**1,689**	**147,184**	**156,685**	**1,536**	**125**	**677,525**	**656,524**	**64,971**	**3,945**	**73,260**	**78,108**	**10,526**	**1,343**
Arrah	...	(a) 307,885	152,430	155,455	139,241	141,109	12,184	12,548	4,293	248	10,684	20,889	479	34	107,373	107,672	17,663	1,318	12,856	13,978	3,013	632
	Arrah Town...	48,922	26,635	22,287	19,860	15,927	...	...	...	...	...	...	...	...	...	...	...	...	6,439	5,903	...	...
	Arrah Mufassal	131,467	63,905	67,582	60,071	62,725	...	...	...	...	...	...	...	...	...	...	...	...	3,834	4,857	...	...
	Sandes ...	56,414	28,212	28,202	26,845	26,580	...	...	...	...	...	...	...	...	...	...	...	...	1,364	1,621	...	...
	Barahra ...	67,924	31,992	35,932	30,773	34,425	...	...	...	...	...	...	...	...	...	...	...	...	1,219	1,507	...	...
Shahpur	...	169,971	84,218	85,753	79,453	80,314	9,833	10,626	2,148	66	10,407	11,228	119	7	59,133	58,460	5,630	297	4,631	5,275	570	31
	Shahpur ...	92,011	45,707	46,304	43,480	43,542	...	...	...	...	...	...	...	...	...	...	...	...	2,120	2,630	...	...
	Jagdispur ...	77,960	38,511	39,449	35,973	36,772	...	...	...	...	...	...	...	...	...	...	...	...	2,511	2,645	...	...
Piro	...	218,177	109,303	108,874	102,892	102,003	8,057	8,341	1,690	143	17,595	18,706	198	15	77,240	74,866	8,690	303	6,406	6,866	623	30
	Piro ...	154,854	77,795	77,059	73,448	72,560	...	...	...	...	...	...	...	...	...	...	...	...	4,342	4,494	...	...
	Sahar ...	63,323	31,508	31,815	29,444	29,443	...	...	...	...	...	...	...	...	...	...	...	...	2,064	2,372	...	...
Buxar	...	141,179	72,432	68,747	67,210	63,811	9,431	9,282	2,035	107	9,717	9,942	130	8	48,062	44,587	3,937	247	4,975	4,714	663	35
	Buxar ...	91,410	47,429	43,981	43,667	40,625	...	...	...	...	...	...	...	...	...	...	...	...	3,621	3,257	...	...
	Rajpur ...	49,769	25,003	24,766	23,543	23,186	...	...	...	...	...	...	...	...	...	...	...	...	1,354	1,457	...	...
Dumraon	...	241,871	122,487	119,384	115,328	111,698	18,373	18,705	3,987	179	11,797	12,467	97	1	85,158	80,506	7,363	582	6,634	7,104	845	31
	Dumraon ...	133,740	68,022	65,718	63,464	60,990	...	...	...	...	...	...	...	...	...	...	...	...	4,232	4,370	...	...
	Nawanagar ...	46,113	23,277	22,836	22,204	21,712	...	...	...	...	...	...	...	...	...	...	...	...	1,026	1,078	...	...
	Barhampur ...	62,018	31,188	30,830	29,660	28,996	...	...	...	...	...	...	...	...	...	...	...	...	1,376	1,656	...	...
Bikramganj	...	208,190	103,479	104,711	96,644	97,298	9,718	9,467	1,796	77	14,608	16,608	178	32	72,318	71,223	6,339	328	6,795	7,364	1,071	221
	Bikramganj ...	156,441	77,652	78,789	71,724	72,347	...	...	...	...	...	...	...	...	...	...	...	...	5,888	6,393	...	...
	Dinara ...	51,749	25,827	25,922	24,920	24,951	...	...	...	...	...	...	...	...	...	...	...	...	907	971	...	...
Karghar	...	100,188	49,723	50,465	47,071	47,725	5,532	5,625	923	59	8,126	8,642	48	3	33,413	33,358	2,156	145	2,638	2,695	173	17
	Karghar ...	56,412	28,173	28,239	26,735	26,769	...	...	...	...	...	...	...	...	...	...	...	...	1,438	1,470	...	...
	Nokha ...	43,776	21,550	22,226	20,336	20,956	...	...	...	...	...	...	...	...	...	...	...	...	1,200	1,225	...	...
Sasaram	...	176,583	88,664	87,919	77,865	76,342	6,948	6,889	997	40	15,664	16,018	62	2	55,253	53,435	3,481	238	10,646	11,419	1,851	164
	Sasaram ...	111,386	55,648	55,738	48,168	47,640	...	...	...	...	...	...	...	...	...	...	...	...	7,336	7,947	...	...
	Rohtas ...	40,312	20,565	19,747	18,137	17,243	...	...	...	...	...	...	...	...	...	...	...	...	2,419	2,497	...	...
	Chenari ...	24,885	12,451	12,434	11,560	11,459	...	...	...	...	...	...	...	...	...	...	...	...	891	975	...	...
Dehri	...	104,604	52,489	52,115	47,185	46,578	3,426	3,419	750	49	8,035	8,547	110	20	35,734	34,612	3,327	34	5,238	5,467	482	37
	Dehri ...	53,881	27,462	26,419	25,081	24,091	...	...	...	...	...	...	...	...	...	...	...	...	3,220	2,259	...	...
	Nasriganj ...	50,723	25,027	25,696	22,104	22,487	...	...	...	...	...	...	...	...	...	...	...	...	2,018	3,208	...	...
Mohania	...	139,723	70,574	69,149	65,396	63,397	7,298	6,928	1,353	88	13,736	13,900	78	...	44,362	43,569	3,430	218	5,168	5,750	580	60
	Mohania ...	38,034	19,150	18,884	17,501	17,127	...	...	...	...	...	...	...	...	...	...	...	...	1,649	1,757	...	...
	Ramgarh ...	49,332	25,058	24,274	23,500	22,447	...	...	...	...	...	...	...	...	...	...	...	...	1,557	1,827	...	...
	Durgauti ...	27,600	13,896	13,704	12,850	12,503	...	...	...	...	...	...	...	...	...	...	...	...	1,041	1,199	...	...
	Kudra ...	(b) 27,297	13,735	13,562	12,766	12,552	...	...	...	...	...	...	...	...	...	...	...	...	965	1,010	...	...
Bhabua	...	(b) 185,118	93,300	91,818	85,997	84,305	8,783	8,141	1,211	83	17,735	18,828	54	3	59,470	57,336	3,065	235	7,273	7,476	655	85
	Bhabua ...	98,800	49,616	49,184	46,381	45,746	...	...	...	...	...	...	...	...	...	...	...	...	3,321	3,406	...	...
	Chainpur ...	39,787	19,946	19,841	17,435	17,179	...	...	...	...	...	...	...	...	...	...	...	...	2,605	2,657	...	...
	Adhaura ...	14,015	7,163	6,852	6,954	6,646	...	...	...	...	...	...	...	...	...	...	...	...	209	206	...	...
	Chand ...	29,976	15,310	14,666	14,116	13,502	...	...	...	...	...	...	...	...	...	...	...	...	1,194	1,184	...	...

PROVINCIAL TABLE II—*continued.*

POPULATION OF REVENUE THANAS AND POLICE-STATIONS BY RELIGION AND LITERACY.

REVENUE THANA.	POLICE-STATION.	CHRISTIANS. No. of persons. Males.	CHRISTIANS. No. of persons. Females.	CHRISTIANS. No. literate. Males.	CHRISTIANS. No. literate. Females.	TRIBAL. No. of persons. Males.	TRIBAL. No. of persons. Females.	TRIBAL. No. literate. Males.	TRIBAL. No. literate. Females.	OTHERS. No. of persons. Males.	OTHERS. No. of persons. Females.	OTHERS. No. literate. Males.	OTHERS. No. literate. Females.	NUMBER LITERATE (AGED 7 AND OVER). Total. Persons.	Total. Males.	Total. Females.	Aged 7—13. Males.	Aged 7—13. Females.	Aged 14—33. Males.	Aged 14—33. Females.	Aged 34 and over. Males.	Aged 34 and over. Females.	Literate in English. Males.	Literate in English. Females.
1	2	24	25	26	27	28	30	30	31	33	33	34	35	36	37	38	39	40	41	42	43	44	45	46
SHAHABAD	...	**1,083**	**1,252**	**195**	**117**	...	...	...	...	**474**	**450**	**256**	**114**	**1,05,400**	**98,667**	**6,733**	**13,577**	**1,093**	**25,841**	**1,931**	**59,449**	**3,709**	**8,662**	**484**
Arrah	...	54	101	74	20	...	...	...	...	239	267	104	108	28,055	25,686	2,369	3,704	434	7,001	648	14,831	1,287	3,585	346
	Arrah Town ...	54	101	...	...	...	...	...	...	236	266	...	...	...	...	...	...	...	...	...	...	...	...	...
	Arrah Mufassal	...	...	...	...	...	...	...	...	...	...	...	...	...	...	...	...	...	...	...	...	...	...	...
	Sandes ...	...	...	...	...	...	...	...	...	3	1	...	...	...	...	...	...	...	...	...	...	...	...	...
	Barahara ...	...	...	...	...	...	...	...	...	...	...	...	...	...	...	...	...	...	...	...	...	...	...	...
Shahpur	...	134	164	7	3	...	...	...	...	...	...	...	...	8,768	8,364	404	1,036	56	2,016	117	5,252	231	341	11
	Shahpur ...	107	132	...	...	...	...	...	...	...	...	...	...	...	...	...	...	...	...	...	...	...	...	...
	Jagdispur ..	27	32	...	...	...	...	...	...	...	...	...	...	...	...	...	...	...	...	...	...	...	...	...
Piro	...	5	5	4	...	...	...	...	...	...	...	...	...	11,696	11,205	491	1,027	83	2,813	135	6,775	274	346	5
	Piro ...	5	5	...	...	...	...	...	...	...	...	...	...	...	...	...	...	...	...	...	...	...	...	...
	Sahar ...	...	...	...	...	...	...	...	...	...	...	...	...	...	...	...	...	...	...	...	...	...	...	...
Buxar	...	204	210	33	50	...	...	...	...	43	12	12	3	7,259	6,810	449	536	46	1,744	131	4,340	370	767	53
	Buxar ...	98	87	...	...	...	...	...	...	43	12	...	...	...	...	...	...	...	...	...	...	...	...	...
	Rajpur ..	106	123	...	...	...	...	...	...	...	...	...	...	...	...	...	...	...	...	...	...	...	...	...
Dumraon	...	490	576	33	15	...	...	...	...	26	6	8	1	13,142	12,333	809	1,016	113	3,148	333	7,560	474	1,100	21
	Dumraon ...	312	358	...	...	...	...	...	...	14	...	...	...	...	...	...	...	...	...	...	...	...	...	...
	Nawanagar ...	35	40	...	...	...	...	...	...	12	6	...	...	...	...	...	...	...	...	...	...	...	...	...
	Barhampur ...	153	178	...	...	...	...	...	...	...	...	...	...	...	...	...	...	...	...	...	...	...	...	...
Bikramganj	...	40	49	3	...	...	...	...	...	...	...	...	...	10,045	9,387	658	1,530	102	2,558	201	5,299	355	628	6
	Bikramganj ...	40	49	...	...	...	...	...	...	...	...	...	...	...	...	...	...	...	...	...	...	...	...	...
	Dinara ...	...	...	...	...	...	...	...	...	...	...	...	...	...	...	...	...	...	...	...	...	...	...	...
Karghar	...	14	45	...	...	...	...	...	...	...	...	...	...	3,522	3,298	224	367	14	774	64	2,157	146	85	1
	Karghar ...	...	...	...	...	...	...	...	...	...	...	...	...	...	...	...	...	...	...	...	...	...	...	...
	Nokha ...	14	45	...	...	...	...	...	...	...	...	...	...	...	...	...	...	...	...	...	...	...	...	...
Sasaram	...	9	18	4	10	...	...	...	...	144	140	65	1	6,905	6,450	455	702	77	1,517	158	4,231	320	745	13
	Sasaram ...	8	18	...	...	...	...	...	...	136	133	...	...	...	...	...	...	...	...	...	...	...	...	...
	Rohtas ...	1	...	...	...	...	...	...	...	8	7	...	...	...	...	...	...	...	...	...	...	...	...	...
	Chenari ...	...	...	...	...	...	...	...	...	...	...	...	...	...	...	...	...	...	...	...	...	...	...	...
Dehri	...	60	67	27	8	...	...	...	...	6	3	4	2	4,850	4,700	150	731	34	1,301	34	2,668	82	554	8
	Dehri ...	60	67	...	...	...	...	...	...	1	2	...	...	...	...	...	...	...	...	...	...	...	...	...
	Nasriganj ...	...	...	...	...	...	...	...	...	5	1	...	...	...	...	...	...	...	...	...	...	...	...	...
Mohania	...	10	3	3	2	...	...	...	...	...	...	...	...	5,757	5,439	318	731	65	1,391	100	3,317	153	186	13
	Mohania ...	...	...	...	...	...	...	...	...	...	...	...	...	...	...	...	...	...	...	...	...	...	...	...
	Ramgarh ...	1	...	...	...	...	...	...	...	...	...	...	...	...	...	...	...	...	...	...	...	...	...	...
	Durgauti ...	5	2	...	...	...	...	...	...	...	...	...	...	...	...	...	...	...	...	...	...	...	...	...
	Kudra ..	4	...	...	...	...	...	...	...	...	...	...	...	...	...	...	...	...	...	...	...	...	...	...
Bhabua	...	14	15	7	...	...	...	...	...	16	22	3	...	5,401	4,995	406	597	69	1,388	121	3,110	217	325	7
	Bhabua ...	11	13	...	...	...	...	...	...	3	19	...	...	...	...	...	...	...	...	...	...	...	...	...
	Chainpur ...	3	2	...	...	...	...	...	...	13	3	...	...	...	...	...	...	...	...	...	...	...	...	...
	Adhaura ...	...	...	...	...	...	...	...	...	...	...	...	...	...	...	...	...	...	...	...	...	...	...	...
	Chand ...	...	...	...	...	...	...	...	...	...	...	...	...	...	...	...	...	...	...	...	...	...	...	...

(a) *Arrah* thana includes seven mauzas which belong to police-station *Maner* in Patna district.

(b) *Bhabua* thana includes 22 mauzas which belong to police-station *Kudra*.

PROVINCIAL TABLE II—*continued.*

POPULATION OF REVENUE THANAS AND POLICE-STATIONS BY RELIGION AND LITERACY.

Revenue Thana.	Police-station.	Population. Persons.	Population. Males.	Population. Females.	Hindus. Total Hindus. Males.	Hindus. Total Hindus. Females.	Hindus. Brahmans. Number of persons. Males.	Hindus. Brahmans. Number of persons. Females.	Hindus. Brahmans. Number literate. Males.	Hindus. Brahmans. Number literate. Females.	Hindus. Depressed classes. Number of persons. Males.	Hindus. Depressed classes. Number of persons. Females.	Hindus. Depressed classes. Number literate. Males.	Hindus. Depressed classes. Number literate. Females.	Hindus. Other Hindus. Number of persons. Males.	Hindus. Other Hindus. Number of persons. Females.	Hindus. Other Hindus. Number literate. Males.	Hindus. Other Hindus. Number literate. Females.	Muslims. Number of persons. Males.	Muslims. Number of persons. Females.	Muslims. Number literate. Males.	Muslims. Number literate. Females.
1	2	3	4	5	6	7	8	9	10	11	12	13	14	15	16	17	18	19	20	21	22	23
SARAN	...	2,486,468	1,220,049	1,266,419	1,072,048	1,104,936	89,532	87,343	14,960	962	124,953	146,075	850	50	857,563	871,518	60,276	2,516	147,763	161,302	10,142	1,515
Chapra	...	366,953	178,252	188,701	158,701	166,963	11,200	10,412	2,526	104	16,815	20,550	181	14	130,686	135,901	15,153	581	19,510	21,806	2,360	431
	Chapra town ...	47,448	25,934	21,514	19,888	15,985	...	...	...	...	...	...	...	...	...	...	...	...	6,006	5,499	...	...
	Revelganj ...	33,144	15,558	17,586	14,233	16,002	...	...	...	...	...	...	...	...	...	...	...	...	1,335	1,584	...	...
	Chapra Mufassal.	130,694	62,308	68,386	57,341	62,552	...	...	...	...	...	...	...	...	...	...	...	...	4,967	5,834	...	...
	Baniapur ...	93,233	44,586	48,647	39,464	42,460	...	...	...	...	...	...	...	...	...	...	...	...	5,128	6,187	...	...
	Garakha ...	62,434	29,866	32,568	27,775	29,864	...	...	...	...	...	...	...	...	...	...	...	...	2,090	2,702	...	...
Manjhi	...	130,863	62,954	67,909	57,876	62,162	5,772	6,176	1,595	46	5,634	6,855	57	1	46,270	49,131	5,606	313	5,076	5,745	420	11
	Manjhi ...	69,512	33,247	36,265	29,847	32,415	...	...	...	...	...	...	...	...	...	...	...	...	3,400	3,850	...	...
	Ekma ...	61,351	29,707	31,644	28,029	29,747	...	...	...	...	...	...	...	...	...	...	...	...	1,676	1,895	...	...
Parsa	...	233,687	112,327	121,360	102,650	109,423	4,998	5,265	1,053	51	11,065	13,065	145	3	86,587	91,093	6,250	446	9,645	11,917	878	128
	Parsa ...	119,209	57,152	62,057	51,968	55,447	...	...	...	...	...	...	...	...	...	...	...	...	5,183	6,609	...	...
	Mirzapur ...	114,478	55,175	59,303	50,682	53,976	...	...	...	...	...	...	...	...	...	...	...	...	4,462	5,308	...	...
Mashrak	Mashrak ...	144,334	69,931	74,403	63,014	66,224	3,765	3,740	476	36	6,246	7,533	14	...	53,003	54,951	1,572	160	6,916	8,179	230	19
Sonpur	...	97,279	45,841	51,438	43,124	47,998	1,599	1,733	599	66	4,200	5,137	80	6	37,325	41,128	4,825	31	2,621	3,381	315	64
	Sonpur ...	62,242	29,608	32,634	28,260	31,136	...	...	...	...	...	...	...	...	...	...	...	...	1,252	1,439	...	...
	Dighwara ...	35,037	16,233	18,804	14,864	16,862	...	...	...	...	...	...	...	...	...	...	...	...	1,369	1,942	...	...
Basantpur	...	253,620	123,955	129,665	109,135	113,170	9,234	9,460	1,413	72	11,326	12,953	34	2	88,575	90,758	5,383	269	14,816	16,489	964	141
	Basantpur ...	167,732	81,327	86,405	70,859	74,543	...	...	...	...	...	...	...	...	...	...	...	...	10,464	11,856	...	...
	Maharajganj	(a)107,251	53,494	53,757	47,782	47,781	...	...	...	...	...	...	...	...	...	...	...	...	5,708	5,971	...	...
Siwan	...	(a)343,035	170,754	172,281	137,315	136,934	9,410	9,306	1,342	179	16,117	19,443	122	2	111,788	108,185	6,962	161	33,348	35,320	2,039	509
	Siwan ...	180,096	89,835	90,263	70,403	69,715	...	...	...	...	...	...	...	...	...	...	...	...	19,348	20,527	...	...
	Mairwa ...	68,534	34,529	34,005	31,547	31,092	...	...	...	...	...	...	...	...	...	...	...	...	2,982	2,913	...	...
	Barharia ...	71,730	34,859	36,871	25,240	26,392	...	...	...	...	...	...	...	...	...	...	...	...	9,616	10,478	...	...
Darauli	...	228,198	113,563	114,635	104,113	104,312	13,657	12,970	2,261	217	12,857	14,062	79	7	77,699	77,180	4,007	231	9,446	10,418	716	77
	Darauli ...	100,277	50,408	49,869	46,879	46,082	...	...	...	...	...	...	...	...	...	...	...	...	3,528	3,783	...	...
	Guthni ...	35,460	17,784	17,676	16,681	16,567	...	...	...	...	...	...	...	...	...	...	...	...	1,100	1,108	...	...
	Raghunathpur	51,987	25,551	26,436	22,841	23,262	...	...	...	...	...	...	...	...	...	...	...	...	2,710	3,174	...	...
	Siswan ...	40,474	19,820	20,654	17,712	18,301	...	...	...	...	...	...	...	...	...	...	...	...	2,108	2,353	...	...
Mirganj	...	405,039	201,588	203,451	175,770	176,689	21,675	20,796	1,859	41	25,067	28,300	67	3	129,028	127,584	5,695	150	25,797	26,742	788	51
	Mirganj ...	(a)150,212	74,395	75,817	61,616	62,286	...	...	...	...	...	...	...	...	...	...	...	...	12,763	13,514	...	...
	Bhore ...	94,721	47,849	46,872	43,791	42,721	...	...	...	...	...	...	...	...	...	...	...	...	4,055	4,149	...	...
	Katea ...	74,215	37,408	36,807	33,708	33,201	...	...	...	...	...	...	...	...	...	...	...	...	3,700	3,606	...	...
	Kuchaikot ...	87,201	43,601	44,600	37,274	39,062	...	...	...	...	...	...	...	...	...	...	...	...	5,325	5,537	...	...
Gopalganj	...	283,460	140,884	142,576	120,250	121,261	8,322	7,485	1,206	90	15,426	18,169	71	12	96,602	95,607	4,823	154	20,528	21,305	843	84
	Gopalganj ...	130,105	65,410	64,695	53,312	52,294	...	...	...	...	...	...	...	...	...	...	...	...	12,095	12,394	...	...
	Barauli ...	77,487	38,591	38,896	33,306	33,437	...	...	...	...	...	...	...	...	...	...	...	...	5,282	5,456	...	...
	Baikunthpur	75,868	36,863	38,985	33,732	35,530	...	...	...	...	...	...	...	...	...	...	...	...	3,161	3,455	...	...

PROVINCIAL TABLE II—*continued.*

POPULATION OF REVENUE THANAS AND POLICE-STATIONS BY RELIGION AND LITERACY.

REVENUE THANA.	POLICE-STATION.	CHRISTIANS. No. of persons. Males.	CHRISTIANS. No. of persons. Females.	CHRISTIANS. No. literate. Males.	CHRISTIANS. No. literate. Females.	TRIBAL. No. of persons. Males.	TRIBAL. No. of persons. Females.	TRIBAL. No. literate. Males.	TRIBAL. No. literate. Females.	OTHERS. No. of persons. Males.	OTHERS. No. of persons. Females.	OTHERS. No. literate. Males.	OTHERS. No. literate. Females.	NUMBER LITERATE (AGED 7 AND OVER). Total. Persons.	Total. Males.	Total. Females.	Aged 7—13. Males.	Aged 7—13. Females.	Aged 14—23. Males.	Aged 14—23. Females.	Aged 24 and over. Males.	Aged 24 and over. Females.	Literate in English. Males.	Literate in English. Females.
1	3	24	25	26	27	28	29	30	31	32	33	34	35	36	37	38	39	40	41	42	43	44	45	46
SARAN	...	**282**	**178**	**199**	**110**	**1**	...	...	...	**15**	**3**	**15**	**1**	**90,836**	**85,742**	**5,094**	**10,772**	**836**	**21,668**	**1,385**	**53,302**	**2,873**	**7,085**	**221**
Chapra	...	36	32	19	18	...	...	...	...	6	...	6	...	**21,393**	20,245	1,148	2,500	189	5,331	331	13,414	636	2,397	45
	Chapra Town	34	30	...	...	...	...	...	...	6	...	...	...	...	...	...	...	...	...	...	...	...	...	...
	Revelganj	...	...	...	...	...	...	...	...	...	...	...	...	...	...	...	...	...	...	...	...	...	...	...
	Chapra Mufassal.	...	...	...	...	...	...	...	...	...	...	...	...	...	...	...	...	...	...	...	...	...	...	...
	Baniapur	...	...	...	...	...	...	...	...	...	...	...	...	...	...	...	...	...	...	...	...	...	...	...
	Garakha	1	2	...	...	...	...	...	...	...	...	...	...	...	...	...	...	...	...	...	...	...	...	...
Manjhi	...	2	2	1	2	...	...	...	...	...	...	...	...	**7,982**	7,609	373	1,011	52	1,033	97	4,665	224	455	8
	Manjhi	...	...	...	...	...	...	...	...	...	...	...	...	...	...	...	...	...	...	...	...	...	...	...
	Ekma	2	2	...	...	...	...	...	...	...	...	...	...	...	...	...	...	...	...	...	...	...	...	...
Parsa	...	30	17	26	13	1	...	...	...	1	3	1	1	**5,997**	5,355	642	1,133	71	1,095	150	5,227	421	552	16
	Parsa	...	1	...	...	1	...	...	...	...	...	...	...	...	...	...	...	...	...	...	...	...	...	...
	Mirzapur	30	16	...	...	...	...	...	...	1	3	...	...	...	...	...	...	...	...	...	...	...	...	...
Mashrakh	Mashrakh	1	...	1	...	...	...	...	...	...	...	...	...	**2,508**	2,293	215	333	35	636	63	1,335	117	116	...
Sonpur	...	68	50	62	43	...	...	...	...	8	...	8	...	**6,099**	5,889	210	679	40	1,470	59	3,732	111	603	47
	Sonpur	68	50	...	...	...	...	...	...	8	...	...	...	...	...	...	...	...	...	...	...	...	...	...
	Dighwara	...	...	...	...	...	...	...	...	...	...	...	...	...	...	...	...	...	...	...	...	...	...	...
Basantpur	...	4	6	3	1	...	...	...	...	...	...	...	...	**8,282**	7,797	485	1,040	96	1,816	116	4,941	273	606	8
	Basantpur	4	6	...	...	...	...	...	...	...	...	...	...	...	...	...	...	...	...	...	...	...	...	...
	Maharajganj	4	5	...	...	...	...	...	...	...	...	...	...	...	...	...	...	...	...	...	...	...	...	...
Siwan	...	91	27	69	16	...	...	...	...	...	...	...	...	**12,011**	11,124	887	1,383	136	2,575	273	7,216	478	1,133	67
	Siwan	84	21	...	...	...	...	...	...	...	...	...	...	...	...	...	...	...	...	...	...	...	...	...
	Mairwa	...	...	...	...	...	...	...	...	...	...	...	...	...	...	...	...	...	...	...	...	...	...	...
	Barharia	3	1	...	...	...	...	...	...	...	...	...	...	...	...	...	...	...	...	...	...	...	...	...
Darauli	...	4	5	4	3	...	...	...	...	...	...	...	...	**7,601**	7,066	535	943	107	1,013	146	4,211	280	268	7
	Darauli	1	4	...	...	...	...	...	...	...	...	...	...	...	...	...	...	...	...	...	...	...	...	...
	Guthni	3	1	...	...	...	...	...	...	...	...	...	...	...	...	...	...	...	...	...	...	...	...	...
	Raghunathpur	...	...	...	...	...	...	...	...	...	...	...	...	...	...	...	...	...	...	...	...	...	...	...
	Siswan	...	...	...	...	...	...	...	...	...	...	...	...	...	...	...	...	...	...	...	...	...	...	...
Mirganj	...	21	20	9	9	...	...	...	...	...	...	...	...	**8,672**	8,418	254	838	55	2,370	59	5,210	140	367	17
	Mirganj	16	17	...	...	...	...	...	...	...	...	...	...	...	...	...	...	...	...	...	...	...	...	...
	Bhore	3	2	...	...	...	...	...	...	...	...	...	...	...	...	...	...	...	...	...	...	...	...	...
	Katea	...	...	...	...	...	...	...	...	...	...	...	...	...	...	...	...	...	...	...	...	...	...	...
	Kuchaikot	2	1	...	...	...	...	...	...	...	...	...	...	...	...	...	...	...	...	...	...	...	...	...
Gopalganj	...	6	10	3	5	...	...	...	...	...	...	...	...	**7,291**	6,946	345	872	55	1,723	80	4,361	201	590	16
	Gopalganj	3	7	...	...	...	...	...	...	...	...	...	...	...	...	...	...	...	...	...	...	...	...	...
	Barauli	3	3	...	...	...	...	...	...	...	...	...	...	...	...	...	...	...	...	...	...	...	...	...
	Baikunthpur	...	...	...	...	...	...	...	...	...	...	...	...	...	...	...	...	...	...	...	...	...	...	...

(a) Siwan thana includes one mauza (*Siari*) which belongs to police-station *Mirganj*, and 34 mauzas which belong to police-station *Maharajganj*.

PROVINCIAL TABLE II—*continued.*

POPULATION OF REVENUE THANAS AND POLICE-STATIONS BY RELIGION AND LITERACY.

REVENUE THANA.	POLICE-STATION.	POPULATION.			HINDUS.														MUSLIMS.			
					TOTAL HINDUS.		BRAHMANS.				DEPRESSED CLASSES.				OTHER HINDUS.							
							Number of persons.		Number literate.		Number of persons.		Number literate.		Number of persons.		Number literate.		Number of persons.		Number literate.	
		Persons.	Males.	Females.	Males.	Females.	Males.	Females.	Males.	Females.	Males.	Females.	Males.	Females.	Males.	Females.	Males.	Females.	Males.	Females.	Males.	Females.
1	2	3	4	5	6	7	8	9	10	11	12	13	14	15	16	17	18	19	20	21	22	23
CHAMPARAN	...	**2,145,687**	**1,080,956**	**1,064,731**	**963,010**	**884,264**	**48,258**	**43,683**	**10,703**	**485**	**163,973**	**170,344**	**723**	**62**	**690,779**	**670,237**	**37,258**	**2,108**	**175,988**	**178,247**	**8,398**	**1,314**
Motihari	...	213,890	100,143	104,748	80,030	85,416	3,333	2,697	1,007	78	16,597	16,606	103	10	70,010	66,183	4,648	308	19,145	19,255	1,118	140
	Motihari	158,457	81,221	77,236	67,342	63,247	...	...	...	...	...	...	...	...	...	...	...	...	13,915	13,916	...	...
	Sugauli ...	55,433	27,921	27,512	22,688	22,169	...	...	...	...	...	...	...	...	...	...	...	...	5,230	5,339	...	...
Adapur	...	202,722	104,027	98,695	81,619	77,074	3,198	2,746	714	39	14,278	14,152	87	2	64,143	60,176	3,300	100	22,382	21,613	943	115
	Adapur ...	99,997	51,169	48,828	39,512	37,635	...	...	...	...	...	...	...	...	...	...	...	...	11,657	11,193	...	...
	Raxaul ...	102,725	52,858	49,867	42,107	39,439	...	...	...	...	...	...	...	...	...	...	...	...	10,725	10,420	...	...
Dhaka (Ramchandra) ...	...	323,224	158,969	164,255	131,070	133,789	5,587	5,387	1,353	60	19,560	21,296	108	1	105,914	107,106	6,854	404	27,897	30,464	1,674	220
	Dhaka Ramchandra.	245,881	120,011	125,870	97,058	100,476	...	...	...	...	...	...	...	...	...	...	...	...	22,951	25,392	...	...
	Ghorasahan ...	77,343	38,958	38,385	34,012	33,313	...	...	...	...	...	...	...	...	...	...	...	...	4,946	5,072	...	...
Kesariya	...	200,870	98,133	102,737	87,999	91,239	4,097	3,974	956	35	14,724	16,704	78	31	69,178	70,561	3,668	491	10,123	11,494	517	66
	Kesariya ...	142,373	68,994	73,379	61,330	64,678	...	...	...	...	...	...	...	...	...	...	...	...	7,661	8,701	...	...
	Pipra ...	58,497	29,139	29,358	26,669	26,561	...	...	...	...	...	...	...	...	...	...	...	...	2,462	2,793	...	...
Madhuban	Madhuban ...	111,212	53,865	57,347	48,388	50,856	1,560	1,260	472	12	8,330	9,726	70	...	38,480	39,861	2,317	80	5,474	6,490	318	24
Gobindganj	Gobindganj ...	186,871	92,966	93,905	81,875	82,674	9,450	9,432	1,496	81	12,468	13,072	60	3	59,957	60,180	2,567	177	11,089	11,231	439	90
Bettiah	...	418,589	214,330	204,259	174,160	164,575	9,862	8,390	3,002	108	33,144	32,955	87	4	131,154	123,230	7,509	300	38,950	38,058	1,671	220
	Bettiah ...	225,497	115,432	110,065	94,003	88,642	...	...	...	...	...	...	...	...	...	...	...	...	20,216	19,804	...	...
	Jogapatti ...	58,903	30,357	28,546	26,512	24,063	...	...	...	...	...	...	...	...	...	...	...	...	3,845	3,583	...	...
	Manjhaulia ...	76,198	39,033	37,165	31,238	29,483	...	...	...	...	...	...	...	...	...	...	...	...	7,792	7,680	...	...
	Sikta ...	57,991	29,508	28,483	23,407	21,487	...	...	...	...	...	...	...	...	...	...	...	...	7,097	6,991	...	...
Bagaha	...	234,758	120,803	113,955	106,656	100,804	5,007	4,356	1,175	56	21,263	20,881	63	5	80,306	75,667	2,808	30	13,897	12,983	408	55
	Bagaha ...	128,990	66,868	62,122	59,167	55,093	...	...	...	...	...	...	...	...	...	...	...	...	7,453	6,863	...	...
	Dhanaha ...	105,768	53,935	51,833	47,489	45,711	...	...	...	...	...	...	...	...	...	...	...	...	6,444	6,120	...	...
Shikarpur	...	253,551	128,721	124,830	101,313	97,837	6,084	5,612	1,438	16	23,001	24,952	67	6	71,628	67,273	3,507	140	27,031	26,659	1,320	375
	Shikarpur ...	116 380	59,053	57,327	46,867	45,473	...	...	...	...	...	...	...	...	...	...	...	...	12,150	11,831	...	...
	Ramnagar ...	42,125	21,603	20,522	17,351	16,411	...	...	...	...	...	...	...	...	...	...	...	...	4,246	4,107	...	...
	Mainatanr ...	37,725	19,013	18,712	14,436	14,076	...	...	...	...	...	...	...	...	...	...	...	...	4,256	4,345	...	...
	Lauriya ...	57,321	29,052	28,269	22,657	21,877	...	...	...	...	...	...	...	...	...	...	...	...	6,379	6,376	...	...

PROVINCIAL TABLE II—*continued.*

POPULATION OF REVENUE THANAS AND POLICE-STATIONS BY RELIGION AND LITERACY.

REVENUE THANA.	POLICE-STATION.	CHRISTIANS. No. of persons. Males.	CHRISTIANS. No. of persons. Females.	CHRISTIANS. No. literate. Males.	CHRISTIANS. No. literate. Females.	TRIBAL. No. of persons. Males.	TRIBAL. No. of persons. Females.	TRIBAL. No. literate. Males.	TRIBAL. No. literate. Females.	OTHERS. No. of persons. Males.	OTHERS. No. of persons. Females.	OTHERS. No. literate. Males.	OTHERS. No. literate. Females.	NUMBER LITERATE (AGED 7 AND OVER.) TOTAL. Persons.	TOTAL. Males.	TOTAL. Females.	AGED 7—13. Males.	AGED 7—13. Females.	AGED 14—23. Males.	AGED 14—23. Females.	AGED 24 AND OVER. Males.	AGED 24 AND OVER. Females.	LITERATE IN ENGLISH. Males.	LITERATE IN ENGLISH. Females.
1	2	24	25	26	27	28	29	30	31	32	33	34	35	36	37	38	39	40	41	42	43	44	45	46
CHAMPARAN	...	**1,681**	**1,974**	**546**	**416**	**252**	**233**	...	...	**25**	**13**	**13**	**4**	**62,030**	**57,641**	**4,389**	**7,273**	**855**	**13,068**	**1,304**	**37,300**	**2,230**	**5,024**	**362**
Motihari	...	64	77	30	18	...	...	...	...	3	...	3	...	**7,463**	6,909	554	878	96	1,717	162	4,314	296	1,206	47
	Motihari ...	61	73	...	...	...	...	...	...	3	...	...	...	...	...	...	...	...	...	...	...	...	...	...
	Sugauli ...	3	4	...	...	...	...	...	...	...	...	...	...	...	...	...	...	...	...	...	...	...	...	...
Adapur	...	36	8	10	4	...	...	...	...	...	...	...	...	**5,314**	5,054	260	506	48	1,096	81	3,363	131	229	7
	Adapur ...	...	...	...	...	...	...	...	...	...	...	...	...	...	...	...	...	...	...	...	...	...	...	...
	Raxaul ...	36	8	...	...	...	...	...	...	...	...	...	...	...	...	...	...	...	...	...	...	...	...	...
Dhaka (Ramchandra) ...	...	1	...	1	...	...	...	...	...	1	3	1	...	**10,576**	9,891	685	1,353	139	2,223	209	6,315	337	340	4
	Dhaka (Ram Chandra).	1	...	...	...	...	...	...	...	1	3	...	...	...	...	...	...	...	...	...	...	...	...	...
	Ghorasahan ...	...	...	...	...	...	...	...	...	...	...	...	...	...	...	...	...	...	...	...	...	...	...	...
Kesariya	...	11	4	9	1	...	...	...	...	...	...	...	...	**5,852**	5,238	624	761	86	1,185	138	3,282	400	193	1
	Kesariya ...	3	...	...	...	...	...	...	...	...	...	...	...	...	...	...	...	...	...	...	...	...	...	...
	Pipra ...	8	4	...	...	...	...	...	...	...	...	...	...	...	...	...	...	...	...	...	...	...	...	...
Madhuban	Madhuban ...	3	1	1	1	...	...	...	...	...	...	...	...	**3,304**	3,178	126	327	24	659	31	2,193	71	136	3
Gobindganj	Gobindganj ...	3	...	1	...	...	...	...	...	...	...	...	...	**4,904**	4,553	351	781	69	1,102	107	2,670	175	314	1
Bettiah	...	1,306	1,619	362	356	...	...	...	...	14	7	4	3	**12,784**	11,725	1,050	1,342	254	2,051	337	7,732	468	1,131	265
	Bettiah ...	1,302	1,617	...	...	...	...	...	...	11	2	...	...	...	...	...	...	...	...	...	...	...	...	...
	Jogapatti ...	...	...	...	...	...	...	...	...	...	...	...	...	...	...	...	...	...	...	...	...	...	...	...
	Manjhaulia ...	3	2	...	...	...	...	...	...	...	...	...	...	...	...	...	...	...	...	...	...	...	...	...
	Sikta ...	1	...	...	...	...	...	...	...	3	5	...	...	...	...	...	...	...	...	...	...	...	...	...
Bagaha	...	346	164	93	17	...	...	...	...	4	4	3	2	**4,894**	4,729	165	532	35	1,123	56	3,084	74	226	15
	Bagaha ...	344	162	...	...	...	...	...	...	4	4	...	...	...	...	...	...	...	...	...	...	...	...	...
	Dhanaha ...	2	2	...	...	...	...	...	...	...	...	...	...	...	...	...	...	...	...	...	...	...	...	...
Shikarpur	...	123	111	40	19	253	233	...	...	3	...	2	...	**6,939**	6,374	565	714	104	1,312	183	4,348	278	1,240	19
	Shikarpur ...	38	33	...	...	...	...	...	...	...	...	...	...	...	...	...	...	...	...	...	...	...	...	...
	Ramnagar ...	6	4	...	...	...	...	...	...	...	...	...	...	...	...	...	...	...	...	...	...	...	...	...
	Mainatanr ...	64	58	...	...	253	233	...	...	3	...	...	...	...	...	...	...	...	...	...	...	...	...	...
	Lauriya ...	16	16	...	...	...	...	...	...	...	...	...	...	...	...	...	...	...	...	...	...	...	...	...

PROVINCIAL TABLE II—*continued*.

MUZAFFARPUR.]

POPULATION OF REVENUE THANAS AND POLICE-STATIONS BY RELIGION AND LITERACY.

Revenue thana.	Police-station.	Population. Persons.	Population. Males.	Population. Females.	Hindus. Total Hindus. Males.	Hindus. Total Hindus. Females.	Hindus. Brahmans. Number of persons. Males.	Hindus. Brahmans. Number of persons. Females.	Hindus. Brahmans. Number literate. Males.	Hindus. Brahmans. Number literate. Females.	Hindus. Depressed classes. Number of persons. Males.	Hindus. Depressed classes. Number of persons. Females.	Hindus. Depressed classes. Number literate. Males.	Hindus. Depressed classes. Number literate. Females.	Hindus. Other Hindus. Number of persons. Males.	Hindus. Other Hindus. Number of persons. Females.	Hindus. Other Hindus. Number literate. Males.	Hindus. Other Hindus. Number literate. Females.	Muslims. Number of persons. Males.	Muslims. Number of persons. Females.	Muslims. Number literate. Males.	Muslims. Number literate. Females.
1	2	3	4	5	6	7	8	9	10	11	12	13	14	15	16	17	18	19	20	21	22	23
MUZAFFARPUR	...	**2,941,025**	**1,443,847**	**1,497,178**	**1,258,489**	**1,290,517**	**65,724**	**65,203**	**17,944**	**1,924**	**217,419**	**240,481**	**2,284**	**121**	**975,346**	**984,833**	**77,488**	**5,390**	**184,852**	**206,239**	**11,527**	**1,468**
Sitamarhi	...	**397,960**	196,881	199,079	169,411	169,246	3,694	2,929	1,121	51	26,601	27,305	146	4	139,116	139,012	8,768	416	29,447	29,802	1,100	99
	Sitamarhi ...	**232,762**	116,716	116,046	103,760	102,777	...	...	...	...	...	...	...	...	...	...	...	...	12,933	13,238	...	...
	Sonbarsa (Frontier).	**71,480**	35,685	35,795	29,953	30,264	...	...	...	...	...	...	...	...	...	...	...	...	5,733	5,531	...	...
	Belamuch Pakauni.	**93,718**	46,480	47,238	35,609	36,206	...	...	...	...	...	...	...	...	...	...	...	...	10,781	11,033	...	...
Sheohar	...	**217,648**	108,513	109,135	93,048	92,441	5,759	5,363	961	27	15,532	16,530	10	2	71,757	70,548	4,192	101	15,336	16,589	575	58
	Sheohar ...	**120,694**	60,214	60,480	51,973	51,394	...	...	...	...	...	...	...	...	...	...	...	...	8,233	9,073	...	...
	Bairagnia ...	**42,498**	20,981	21,517	16,464	16,553	...	...	...	...	...	...	...	...	...	...	...	...	4,415	4,877	...	...
	Majorganj ...	**54,456**	27,318	27,138	24,611	24,494	...	...	...	...	...	...	...	...	...	...	...	...	3,698	3,639	...	...
Belsand	Belsand ...	**225,494**	112,191	113,303	98,878	99,384	3,154	3,066	490	33	14,968	15,566	24	1	80,756	80,752	4,579	435	13,209	13,893	373	85
Pupri	...	**283,200**	140,003	143,197	108,454	109,402	6,046	5,866	1,370	62	14,802	15,504	75	1	87,606	88,092	7,326	207	31,545	33,735	1,479	182
	Pupri ...	**218,401**	107,549	110,852	81,566	82,804	...	...	...	...	...	...	...	...	...	...	...	...	25,979	28,048	...	...
	Sursand ...	**64,799**	32,454	32,345	26,888	26,658	...	...	...	...	...	...	...	...	...	...	...	...	5,566	5,687	...	...
Paru	...	**318,297**	151,982	166,315	137,207	148,606	9,998	10,266	2,653	346	21,493	25,091	211	3	105,716	113,241	7,541	578	14,771	17,616	706	74
	Paru ...	**164,685**	78,730	85,955	71,136	76,788	...	...	...	...	...	...	...	...	...	...	...	...	7,602	9,166	...	...
	Sahibganj ...	**60,920**	29,215	31,705	26,657	28,743	...	...	...	...	...	...	...	...	...	...	...	...	2,558	2,962	...	...
	Baruraj ...	**92,692**	44,037	48,655	39,424	43,167	...	...	...	...	...	...	...	...	...	...	...	...	4,611	5,488	...	...
Muzaffarpur ...	...	**568,448**	279,669	288,779	242,440	246,560	15,178	14,631	4,333	468	50,190	56,419	416	20	177,072	175,319	15,022	1,860	36,916	41,975	3,569	446
	Muzaffarpur ...	**311,716**	150,101	161,615	130,926	138,754	...	...	...	...	...	...	...	...	...	...	...	...	19,156	22,853	...	...
	Muzaffarpur Town.	**43,049**	25,050	17,990	18,375	12,313	...	...	...	...	...	...	...	...	...	...	...	...	6,384	5,463	...	...
	Minapur ...	**85,328**	41,911	43,417	38,365	39,228	...	...	...	...	...	...	...	...	...	...	...	...	3,546	4,189	...	...
	Shakra ...	**128,355**	62,607	65,748	54,774	56,274	...	...	...	...	...	...	...	...	...	...	...	...	7,830	9,470	...	...
Katra	Katra ...	**234,288**	115,454	118,834	100,019	101,530	9,462	9,928	2,623	230	14,651	15,260	255	7	75,906	76,331	4,742	708	15,427	17,286	697	86
Mahuwa	...	**293,330**	141,592	151,738	126,304	133,072	4,733	4,907	1,473	92	27,176	31,412	379	33	94,395	96,753	9,010	368	15,284	19,664	1,315	136
	Mahuwa ...	**216,973**	105,061	111,912	94,972	00,086	...	...	...	...	...	...	...	...	...	...	...	...	10,088	12,826	...	...
	Patepur ...	**76,357**	36,531	39,826	31,332	32,986	...	...	...	...	...	...	...	...	...	...	...	...	5,196	6,838	...	...
Lalganj	Lalganj ...	**144,595**	68,447	76,148	62,688	68,040	3,201	3,376	1,070	56	11,707	14,110	78	14	47,780	51,464	5,244	441	5,754	7,203	666	130
Hajipur	...	**257,765**	127,115	130,650	120,040	122,166	4,499	4,671	1,850	539	20,299	23,264	690	36	95,248	94,231	11,055	157	7,073	8,476	1,047	222
	Hajipur ...	**121,305**	59,837	61,468	55,845	56,701	...	...	...	...	...	...	...	...	...	...	...	...	3,990	4,759	...	...
	Mehnar ...	**94,009**	45,690	48,319	42,708	44,687	...	...	...	...	...	...	...	...	...	...	...	...	2,982	3,632	...	...
	Raghopur ...	**42,451**	21,588	20,863	21,487	20,778	...	...	...	...	...	...	...	...	...	...	...	...	101	85	...	...

PROVINCIAL TABLE II—*continued*.

POPULATION OF REVENUE THANAS AND POLICE-STATIONS BY RELIGION AND LITERACY.

REVENUE THANA.	POLICE-STATION.	CHRISTIANS.				TRIBAL.				OTHERS.				NUMBER LITERATE (AGED 7 AND OVER).										
		No. of persons.		*No. literate.*		*No. of persons.*		*No. literate.*		*No. of persons.*		*No. literate.*		Total.			Aged 7—13		Aged 14—23.		Aged 24 and over.		Literate in English.	
		Males.	Females.	Males.	Females.	Males.	Females.	Males.	Females.	Males.	Females.	Males.	Females.	Persons.	Males.	Females.	Males.	Females.	Males.	Females.	Males.	Females.	Males.	Females.
1	2	24	25	26	27	28	29	30	31	32	33	34	35	36	37	38	39	40	41	42	43	44	45	46
MUZAFFARPUR	...	**481**	**406**	**270**	**161**	**6**	...	**2**	...	**19**	**16**	**13**	**4**	**118,596**	**109,528**	**9,068**	**13,947**	**1,462**	**24,613**	**2,474**	**70,968**	**5,132**	**8,462**	**449**
Sitamarhi	...	21	24	8	1	...	...	...	...	3	7	3	2	11,719	11,146	573	1,193	125	2,556	131	7,397	317	750	15
	Sitamarhi ...	21	24	...	...	...	...	...	...	3	7	...	...	...	...	...	...	...	...	...	...	...	...	...
	Sonbarsa (Frontier).	...	...	...	...	...	...	...	...	...	...	...	...	...	...	...	...	...	...	...	...	...	...	...
	Belamuch Pakauni.	...	...	...	...	...	...	...	...	...	...	...	...	...	...	...	...	...	...	...	...	...	...	...
Sheohar	...	137	105	19	5	...	...	...	...	2	...	2	...	5,952	5,759	193	542	34	1,333	63	3,884	96	223	7
	Sheohar ...	18	13	...	...	...	...	...	...	...	...	...	...	...	...	...	...	...	...	...	...	...	...	...
	Bairagnia ...	102	87	...	...	...	...	...	...	...	...	...	...	...	...	...	...	...	...	...	...	...	...	...
	Majorganj ...	7	5	...	...	...	...	...	...	2	...	...	...	...	...	...	...	...	...	...	...	...	...	...
Belsand	Belsand ...	14	26	4	...	...	...	...	...	...	...	...	...	6,024	5,470	554	642	94	1,147	152	3,681	308	210	1
Pupri	...	...	...	...	...	...	...	...	...	4	...	4	...	10,746	10,254	492	1,372	124	2,378	128	6,504	240	548	13
	Pupri ...	...	...	...	...	...	...	...	...	4	...	...	...	...	...	...	...	...	...	...	...	...	...	...
	Sursand ...	...	...	...	...	...	...	...	...	...	...	...	...	...	...	...	...	...	...	...	...	...	...	...
Paru	...	4	1	3	...	...	...	...	...	...	...	...	...	12,115	11,114	1,001	1,524	133	2,406	272	7,187	596	711	29
	Paru ...	2	1	...	...	...	...	...	...	...	...	...	...	...	...	...	...	...	...	...	...	...	...	...
	Sahibganj ...	...	...	...	...	...	...	...	...	...	...	...	...	...	...	...	...	...	...	...	...	...	...	...
	Baruraj ...	2	...	...	...	...	...	...	...	...	...	...	...	...	...	...	...	...	...	...	...	...	...	...
Muzaffarpur	...	302	231	232	152	6	...	2	...	5	4	1	2	26,572	23,575	2,997	2,961	447	5,888	768	14,786	1,762	4,374	276
	Muzaffarpur ...	19	3	...	...	...	...	...	...	...	...	...	...	...	...	...	...	...	...	...	...	...	...	...
	Muzaffarpur Town.	280	219	...	...	6	...	...	...	5	4	...	...	...	...	...	...	...	...	...	...	...	...	...
	Minapur ...	...	...	...	...	...	...	...	...	...	...	...	...	...	...	...	...	...	...	...	...	...	...	...
	Shakra ...	3	4	...	...	...	...	...	...	...	...	...	...	...	...	...	...	...	...	...	...	...	...	...
Katra	Katra ...	8	9	...	...	...	...	...	...	...	...	...	...	9,348	8,317	1,031	1,183	124	1,857	302	5,277	605	262	68
Mahuwa	...	3	2	2	2	...	...	...	...	1	...	1	...	12,820	12,189	631	1,564	86	2,396	177	8,229	368	384	4
	Mahuwa ...	...	...	...	...	...	...	...	...	1	...	...	...	...	...	...	...	...	...	...	...	...	...	...
	Patepur ...	3	2	...	...	...	...	...	...	...	...	...	...	...	...	...	...	...	...	...	...	...	...	...
Lalganj	Lalganj ...	...	...	...	...	...	...	...	...	5	5	2	...	7,701	7,060	641	933	106	1,460	168	4,667	367	286	5
Hajipur	...	2	8	2	1	...	...	...	...	...	...	...	...	15,599	14,644	955	3,096	189	3,192	313	9,356	453	706	6
	Hajipur ...	2	8	...	...	...	...	...	...	...	...	...	...	...	...	...	...	...	...	...	...	...	...	...
	Mehnar ...	...	...	...	...	...	...	...	...	...	...	...	...	...	...	...	...	...	...	...	...	...	...	...
	Raghopur ...	...	...	...	...	...	...	...	...	...	...	...	...	...	...	...	...	...	...	...	...	...	...	...

PROVINCIAL TABLE II—*continued.*

POPULATION OF REVENUE THANAS AND POLICE-STATIONS BY RELIGION AND LITERACY.

DARBHANGA.]

REVENUE THANA.	POLICE-STATION.	POPULATION.			HINDUS.														MUSLIMS.			
					TOTAL HINDUS.		BRAHMANS.				DEPRESSED CLASSES.				OTHER HINDUS.							
							Number of persons.		*Number literate.*		*Number of persons.*		*Number literate.*		*Number of persons.*		*Number literate.*		*Number of persons.*		*Number literate.*	
		Persons.	Males.	Females.	Males.	Females.	Males.	Females.	Males.	Females.	Males.	Females.	Males.	Females.	Males.	Females.	Males.	Females.	Males.	Females.	Males.	Females.
1	2	3	4	5	6	7	8	9	10	11	12	13	14	15	16	17	18	19	20	21	22	23
DARBHANGA	...	**3,166,094**	**1,570,959**	**1,595,135**	**1,354,928**	**1,370,499**	**164,487**	**156,895**	**36,938**	**1,961**	**240,305**	**254,006**	**1,531**	**148**	**950,136**	**959,596**	**65,445**	**2,820**	**215,663**	**224,374**	**12,779**	**1,477**
Benipatti	...	**292,183**	144,168	148,015	116,639	119,667	19,805	19,482	4,088	137	18,718	19,756	93	8	78,116	80,429	5,607	144	27,496	26,345	1,495	177
	Benipatti ...	**192,707**	94,084	97,723	73,831	75,705	...	...	...	...	...	...	...	...	...	...	...	...	21,153	22,018	...	...
	Harlakhi ...	**57,086**	28,238	28,848	24,080	24,737	...	...	...	...	...	...	...	...	...	...	...	...	4,158	4,131	...	...
	Madhwapur ...	**42,390**	20,946	21,444	18,728	19,235	...	...	...	...	...	...	...	...	...	...	...	...	2,185	2,206	...	...
Khajauli	...	**303,097**	150,511	152,586	135,165	137,113	9,710	10,090	2,138	33	22,643	23,649	175	3	102,802	103,374	7,744	105	15,351	15,468	739	89
	Khajauli ...	**146,973**	72,748	74,225	64,650	65,045	...	...	...	...	...	...	...	...	...	...	...	...	8,093	8,275	...	...
	Ladania ...	**49,124**	24,289	24,835	22,891	23,478	...	...	...	...	...	...	...	...	...	...	...	...	1,398	1,357	...	...
	Jaynagar ...	**107,000**	53,474	53,526	47,614	47,600	...	...	...	...	...	...	...	...	...	...	...	...	5,860	5,836	...	...
Madhubani	...	**320,643**	158,508	162,135	134,488	137,821	24,339	24,296	5,416	286	23,530	24,718	116	17	86,619	88,805	5,770	161	24,004	24,307	1,311	89
	Madhubani ...	**225,416**	111,890	113,526	92,237	93,714	...	...	...	...	...	...	...	...	...	...	...	...	19,637	19,807	...	...
	Jhanjharpur ...	**95,227**	46,618	48,609	42,251	44,107	...	...	...	...	...	...	...	...	...	...	...	...	4,367	4,500	...	...
Phulparas	...	**356,225**	174,032	182,193	164,348	161,366	13,123	11,863	3,039	19	21,997	24,151	195	3	119,228	125,352	7,873	85	19,645	20,812	998	154
	Phulparas ...	**137,134**	67,126	70,008	61,908	64,757	...	...	...	...	...	...	...	...	...	...	...	...	5,095	5,238	...	...
	Laukahi ...	**100,104**	49,365	50,739	42,045	44,065	...	...	...	...	...	...	...	...	...	...	...	...	6,417	6,654	...	...
	Madhaipur ...	**118,987**	57,541	61,446	49,405	52,524	...	...	...	...	...	...	...	...	...	...	...	...	8,133	8,020	...	...
Darbhanga	...	**485,040**	240,793	244,247	182,362	182,508	24,002	23,010	5,514	355	33,708	35,433	244	32	123,752	124,065	8,835	838	58,354	61,656	3,804	584
	Darbhanga ...	**344,324**	169,269	175,055	131,398	134,362	...	...	...	...	...	...	...	...	...	...	...	...	37,867	40,688	...	...
	Darbhanga Town.	**60,676**	32,274	28,402	22,769	19,448	...	...	...	...	...	...	...	...	...	...	...	...	9,432	8,876	...	...
	Jale ...	**80,040**	39,250	40,790	28,195	28,698	...	...	...	...	...	...	...	...	...	...	...	...	11,055	12,092	...	...
Bahera	Bahera ...	**392,538**	194,374	198,164	163,995	166,451	30,543	29,135	5,106	295	27,675	28,674	67	10	105,777	108,642	4,315	261	30,378	31,709	1,215	44
Samastipur	...	**296,647**	148,362	148,285	133,636	133,281	13,907	12,878	4,059	447	26,423	28,477	300	42	93,316	91,926	7,567	800	14,505	14,886	1,039	236
	Samastipur ...	**186,894**	93,659	93,235	84,962	84,556	...	...	...	...	...	...	...	...	...	...	...	...	8,552	8,572	...	...
	Tajpur ...	**109,753**	54,703	55,050	48,674	48,725	...	...	...	...	...	...	...	...	...	...	...	...	6,013	6,314	...	...
Roserha	...	**294,441**	148,034	146,407	137,441	135,601	10,988	10,038	2,830	154	27,410	27,028	109	4	90,043	97,635	5,544	135	10,583	10,802	453	38
	Roserha ...	**185,218**	93,525	91,693	87,368	85,446	...	...	...	...	...	...	...	...	...	...	...	...	6,147	6,243	...	...
	Singia ...	**109,223**	54,509	54,714	50,073	50,155	...	...	...	...	...	...	...	...	...	...	...	...	4,436	4,559	...	...
Warisnagar	Warisnagar ...	**171,925**	85,762	86,163	77,003	77,513	6,040	6,902	1,929	80	16,378	17,103	94	4	54,285	53,448	4,026	126	8,157	8,648	615	60
Dalsingh Sarai... ...	...	**253,355**	126,415	126,940	119,261	119,178	10,140	9,139	2,770	147	21,823	24,117	178	25	87,298	85,922	8,164	165	7,130	7,741	511	33
	Dalsingh Sarai	**158,478**	78,571	79,907	73,754	74,826	...	...	...	...	...	...	...	...	...	...	...	...	4,797	5,067	...	...
	Mohiuddin-nagar.	**94,877**	47,844	47,033	45,507	44,352	...	...	...	...	...	...	...	...	...	...	...	...	2,333	2,674	...	...

PROVINCIAL TABLE II—*continued*.

POPULATION OF REVENUE THANAS AND POLICE-STATIONS BY RELIGION AND LITERACY.

REVENUE THANA.	POLICE-STATION.	CHRISTIANS. No. of persons. Males.	Females.	No. literate. Males.	Females.	TRIBAL. No. of persons. Males.	Females.	No. literate. Males.	Females.	OTHERS. No. of persons. Males.	Females.	No. literate. Males.	Females.	NUMBER LITERATE (AGED 7 AND OVER.) Total. Persons.	Males.	Females.	Aged 7–13. Males.	Females.	Aged 14–33. Males	Females.	Aged 34 and over. Males.	Females.	Literate in English. Males.	Females.
1	2	24	25	26	27	28	29	30	31	32	33	34	35	36	37	38	39	40	41	42	43	44	45	46
DARBHANGA	...	**286**	**245**	**181**	**149**	...	...	...	...	**82**	**17**	**37**	...	**123,466**	**116,911**	**6,555**	**14,960**	**1,247**	**25,188**	**1,802**	**76,763**	**3,506**	**7,641**	**445**
Benipatti		3	3	...	1	...	...	...	...	30	...	10	...	**11,760**	11,293	467	1,461	83	2,623	121	7,200	264	336	3
	Benipatti ...	...	...	...	...	...	...	...	...	...	...	...	...	...	...	...	...	...	...	...	...	...	...	...
	Harlakhi ...	...	...	...	...	...	...	...	...	...	...	...	...	...	...	...	...	...	...	...	...	...	...	...
	Madhwapur ...	3	3	...	...	...	...	...	...	30	...	...	...	...	...	...	...	...	...	...	...	...	...	...
Khajauli		5	5	5	5	...	...	...	...	...	...	...	...	**11,025**	10,791	234	1,418	40	2,460	63	6,004	122	351	7
	Khajauli ...	5	5	...	...	...	...	...	...	...	...	...	...	...	...	...	...	...	...	...	...	...	...	...
	Ladania ...	...	...	...	...	...	...	...	...	...	...	...	...	...	...	...	...	...	...	...	...	...	...	...
	Jaynagar ...	...	...	...	...	...	...	...	...	...	...	...	...	...	...	...	...	...	...	...	...	...	...	...
Madhubani		16	7	13	4	...	...	...	...	...	...	...	...	**13,176**	12,626	550	1,528	114	3,189	197	7,909	230	1,310	15
	Madhubani ...	16	5	...	...	...	...	...	...	...	...	...	...	...	...	...	...	...	...	...	...	...	...	...
	Jhanjharpur ...	...	2	...	...	...	...	...	...	...	...	...	...	...	...	...	...	...	...	...	...	...	...	...
Phulparas		6	2	1	1	...	...	...	...	33	13	24	...	**12,392**	12,130	262	1,432	38	2,661	78	8,037	146	930	165
	Phulparas ...	...	...	...	...	...	...	...	...	33	13	...	...	...	...	...	...	...	...	...	...	...	...	...
	Laukahi ...	3	...	...	...	...	...	...	...	...	...	...	...	...	...	...	...	...	...	...	...	...	...	...
	Madhaipur ...	3	2	...	...	...	...	...	...	...	...	...	...	...	...	...	...	...	...	...	...	...	...	...
Darbhanga		77	83	41	38	...	...	...	...	...	...	...	...	**20,285**	18,438	1,847	2,637	393	4,233	511	11,579	943	1,936	53
	Darbhanga ...	4	5	...	...	...	...	...	...	...	...	...	...	...	...	...	...	...	...	...	...	...	...	...
	Darbhanga Town.	73	78	...	...	...	...	...	...	...	...	...	...	...	...	...	...	...	...	...	...	...	...	...
	Jale ...	...	...	...	...	...	...	...	...	...	...	...	...	...	...	...	...	...	...	...	...	...	...	...
Bahera	Bahera ...	1	4	...	2	...	...	...	...	...	...	...	...	**11,375**	10,763	612	1,441	126	2,288	157	7,034	329	446	3
Samastipur		151	118	116	89	...	...	...	...	10	...	1	...	**15,246**	13,643	1,604	1,837	270	2,092	400	9,123	934	1,407	146
	Samastipur ...	135	107	...	...	...	...	...	...	10	...	...	...	...	...	...	...	...	...	...	...	...	...	...
	Tajpur ...	16	11	...	...	...	...	...	...	...	...	...	...	...	...	...	...	...	...	...	...	...	...	...
Roserha		1	...	1	...	...	...	...	...	9	4	2	...	**9,268**	8,937	331	1,184	59	1,881	102	5,873	170	366	1
	Roserha ...	1	...	...	...	...	...	...	...	9	4	...	...	...	...	...	...	...	...	...	...	...	...	...
	Singia ...	...	...	...	...	...	...	...	...	...	...	...	...	...	...	...	...	...	...	...	...	...	...	...
Warisnagar	Warisnagar ...	2	2	2	2	...	...	...	...	...	...	...	...	**6,937**	6,666	271	803	53	1,301	81	4,559	137	330	15
Dalsingh Sarai		34	21	2	7	...	...	...	...	...	...	...	...	**12,002**	11,625	377	1,236	64	1,851	91	8,538	222	327	7
	Dalsingh Sarai	20	14	...	...	...	...	...	...	...	...	...	...	...	...	...	...	...	...	...	...	...	...	...
	Mohiuddin-nagar.	4	7	...	...	...	...	...	...	...	...	...	...	...	...	...	...	...	...	...	...	...	...	...

PROVINCIAL TABLE II—*continued.*

POPULATION OF REVENUE THANAS AND POLICE-STATIONS BY RELIGION AND LITERACY.

REVENUE THANA.	POLICE-STATION.	POPULATION.			HINDUS.														MUSLIMS.			
					TOTAL HINDUS.		BRAHMANS.				DEPRESSED CLASSES.				OTHER HINDUS.							
							Number of persons.		*Number literate.*		*Number of persons.*		*Number literate.*		*Number of persons.*		*Number literate.*		*Number of persons.*		*Number literate.*	
		Persons.	Males.	Females.	Males.	Females.	Males.	Females.	Males.	Females.	Males.	Females.	Males.	Females.	Males.	Females.	Males.	Females.	Males.	Females.	Males.	Females.
1	2	3	4	5	6	7	8	9	10	11	12	13	14	15	16	17	18	19	20	21	22	23
MONGHYR	...	**2,287,154**	**1,145,797**	**1,141,357**	**1,031,465**	**1,017,727**	**59,827**	**54,258**	**10,765**	**1,021**	**198,318**	**204,985**	**1,215**	**180**	**774,120**	**758,484**	**50,272**	**4,210**	**109,408**	**119,089**	**8,230**	**1,168**
Gogri	...	464,258	236,039	228,219	213,877	205,437	8,836	7,813	1,130	69	42,508	41,771	150	70	162,443	155,853	7,272	700	22,134	22,760	1,351	294
	Gogri ...	118,263	58,968	59,295	52,573	52,587	...	...	...	...	...	...	...	...	...	...	...	...	6,395	6,708	...	...
	Khagaria ...	147,795	75,194	72,601	69,593	66,890	...	...	...	...	...	...	...	...	...	...	...	...	5,583	5,694	...	...
	Bakhtiyarpur ...	120,023	61,080	58,943	53,670	51,118	...	...	...	...	...	...	...	...	...	...	...	...	7,401	7,821	...	...
	Chautham ...	78,177	40,797	37,380	38,041	34,842	...	...	...	...	...	...	...	...	...	...	...	...	3,755	2,537	...	...
Monghyr	...	179,396	92,285	87,111	80,581	76,049	3,685	2,870	1,297	164	12,136	12,133	173	4	64,760	61,046	7,978	660	10,637	9,974	1,659	189
	Monghyr Town	52,863	27,843	25,020	21,691	19,235	...	...	...	...	...	...	...	...	...	...	...	...	6,102	5,710	...	...
	Monghyr Mufassal.	126,533	64,442	62,091	58,890	56,814	...	...	...	...	...	...	...	...	...	...	...	...	4,535	4,264	...	...
Jamalpur	Jamalpur ...	30,346	16,378	13,968	13,077	11,179	1,169	800	705	251	2,120	2,112	107	2	9,788	8,267	2,462	314	2,608	2,282	531	80
Surajgarha	Surajgarha ...	75,898	37,340	38,558	34,562	35,103	2,260	2,089	404	38	6,414	6,727	64	2	25,888	26,287	2,005	118	2,633	3,208	256	71
Lakhisarai	Lakhisarai ...	133,824	68,329	65,495	64,551	61,387	2,779	3,027	483	25	12,372	12,061	58	5	49,400	46,299	3,667	209	3,743	4,061	222	16
Kharagpur	...	161,405	79,864	81,541	73,916	74,643	4,237	3,996	897	84	14,512	14,702	61	8	55,167	55,855	4,145	234	5,063	6,034	243	8
	Kharagpur ...	85,132	42,321	42,811	39,681	40,132	...	...	...	...	...	...	...	...	...	...	...	...	1,557	1,815	...	...
	Tarapur ...	76,273	37,543	38,730	34,035	34,511	...	...	...	...	...	...	...	...	...	...	...	...	3,506	4,219	...	...
Sheikhpura	...	159,986	80,333	79,653	70,288	68,039	2,802	2,870	457	13	15,027	15,052	69	3	52,459	50,117	4,276	162	10,045	11,614	1,035	163
	Sheikhpura ...	106,401	53,413	52,988	46,237	44,714	...	...	...	...	...	...	...	...	...	...	...	...	7,176	8,274	...	...
	Barbigha ...	53,585	26,920	26,665	24,051	23,325	...	...	...	...	...	...	...	...	...	...	...	...	2,869	3,340	...	...
Teghra	Teghra ...	232,639	114,454	118,185	102,921	104,466	12,750	11,637	1,605	128	17,769	20,364	139	14	72,402	72,475	4,219	352	11,454	13,662	738	80
Begusarai	...	411,606	201,243	210,363	180,250	185,847	13,809	12,916	2,109	145	31,108	33,446	161	18	135,242	139,485	6,823	774	20,984	24,508	1,131	175
	Begusarai ...	191,311	94,727	96,584	85,978	86,705	...	...	...	...	...	...	...	...	...	...	...	...	8,743	9,871	...	...
	Balia ...	104,390	49,498	54,892	41,950	45,473	...	...	...	...	...	...	...	...	...	...	...	...	7,548	9,419	...	...
	Bariarpur ...	115,905	57,018	58,887	52,322	53,669	...	...	...	...	...	...	...	...	...	...	...	...	4,693	5,218	...	...
Sikandra	Sikandra ...	117,621	58,116	59,505	51,749	52,301	1,474	1,736	431	30	13,045	14,203	67	20	37,230	36,262	2,336	262	6,362	7,302	308	55
Jamui	Jamui ...	162,461	81,259	81,202	73,805	73,683	3,052	2,770	605	38	17,738	18,755	60	23	53,015	52,158	2,011	298	7,084	7,189	422	13
Chakai	...	157,714	80,157	77,557	71,888	69,693	2,084	1,744	382	36	13,479	13,569	88	2	56,326	54,380	2,178	107	6,663	6,385	334	24
	Chakai ...	57,618	28,660	28,958	26,490	26,749	...	...	...	...	...	...	...	...	...	...	...	...	1,248	1,284	...	...
	Jhajha ...	100,096	51,497	48,599	45,398	42,944	...	...	...	...	...	...	...	...	...	...	...	...	5,415	5,101	...	...

PROVINCIAL TABLE II—*continued.*

POPULATION OF REVENUE THANAS AND POLICE-STATIONS BY RELIGION AND LITERACY.

REVENUE THANA.	POLICE-STATION.	CHRISTIANS.				TRIBAL.				OTHERS.				NUMBER LITERATE (AGED 7 AND OVER).										
		No. of persons.		*No. literate.*		*No. of persons.*		*No. literate.*		*No. of persons.*		*No. literate.*		TOTAL.			AGED 7—13.		AGED 14—23.		AGED 24 AND OVER.		LITERATE IN ENGLISH.	
		Males.	Females.	Males.	Females.	Males.	Females.	Males.	Females.	Males.	Females.	Males.	Females.	Persons.	Males.	Females.	Males.	Females.	Males.	Females.	Males.	Females.	Males.	Females.
1	2	24	25	26	27	28	29	30	31	32	33	34	35	36	37	38	39	40	41	42	43	44	45	46
MONGHYR	...	**1,058**	**859**	**782**	**533**	**3,838**	**3,670**	**14**	...	**28**	**12**	**11**	**3**	**78,404**	**71,289**	**7,115**	**8,194**	**1,273**	**16,403**	**2,039**	**46,692**	**3,803**	**7,391**	**261**
Gogri	...	19	13	13	8	...	...	...	...	9	9	5	2	11,073	9,921	1,152	1,176	263	2,012	277	6,733	612	530	6
	Gogri ...	...	...	...	...	...	...	...	...	...	...	...	...	...	...	...	...	...	...	...	...	...	...	...
	Khagaria ...	9	8	...	...	...	...	...	...	9	9	...	...	...	...	...	...	...	...	...	...	...	...	...
	Bakhtiarpur ...	9	4	...	...	...	...	...	...	...	...	...	...	...	...	...	...	...	...	...	...	...	...	...
	Chautham ...	1	1	...	...	...	...	...	...	...	...	...	...	...	...	...	...	...	...	...	...	...	...	...
Monghyr	...	49	77	36	48	1,017	1,011	9	...	1	...	...	...	12,216	11,151	1,065	1,321	200	3,876	355	6,954	510	2,565	87
	Monghyr Town	49	75	...	...	...	...	...	...	1	...	...	...	...	...	...	...	...	...	...	...	...	...	...
	Monghyr Mufassal.	...	2	...	...	1,017	1,011	...	...	...	...	...	...	...	...	...	...	...	...	...	...	...	...	...
Jamalpur	Jamalpur ...	689	605	610	314	...	...	...	...	6	2	3	...	5,279	4,318	961	546	165	1,057	246	2,715	550	1,231	52
Surajgarha	Surajgarha ...	...	2	...	1	143	155	...	...	2	...	...	...	2,959	2,729	230	377	41	674	61	1,678	138	89	7
Lakhisarai	Lakhisarai ...	14	10	10	6	14	16	...	...	7	1	3	1	4,705	4,443	262	406	33	995	90	3,040	140	126	6
Kharagpur	...	3	1	2	...	880	863	5	...	2	...	...	...	5,677	5,343	334	677	67	1,259	99	3,407	168	338	4
	Kharagpur ...	3	1	...	...	880	863	...	...	...	...	...	...	...	...	...	...	...	...	...	...	...	...	...
	Tarapur ...	...	...	...	...	...	...	...	...	2	...	...	...	...	...	...	...	...	...	...	...	...	...	...
Sheikhpura	...	...	...	...	...	...	...	...	...	...	...	...	...	6,198	5,837	361	696	54	1,396	113	3,745	194	258	5
	Sheikhpura ...	...	...	...	...	...	...	...	...	...	...	...	...	...	...	...	...	...	...	...	...	...	...	...
	Barbigha ...	...	...	...	...	...	...	...	...	...	...	...	...	...	...	...	...	...	...	...	...	...	...	...
Teghra	Teghra ...	15	15	11	9	64	43	...	...	...	...	...	...	7,495	6,912	583	708	117	1,421	148	4,788	318	734	13
Begusarai	...	9	8	7	5	...	...	...	...	...	...	...	...	11,428	10,311	1,117	1,217	201	2,315	360	6,779	566	750	25
	Begusarai ...	6	8	...	...	...	...	...	...	...	...	...	...	...	...	...	...	...	...	...	...	...	...	...
	Balia ...	...	...	...	...	...	...	...	...	...	...	...	...	...	...	...	...	...	...	...	...	...	...	...
	Bariarpur ...	3	...	...	...	...	...	...	...	...	...	...	...	...	...	...	...	...	...	...	...	...	...	...
Sikandra	Sikandra ...	...	...	...	...	5	2	...	...	...	...	...	...	3,509	3,142	367	411	60	715	94	2,016	213	37	9
Jamui	Jamui ...	...	5	...	3	370	324	...	...	...	...	...	...	4,382	4,007	375	370	19	959	132	2,678	224	302	35
Chakai	...	260	223	193	139	1,345	1,256	...	...	1	...	...	...	3,483	3,175	308	292	54	724	74	2,159	180	431	12
	Chakai ...	123	134	...	...	799	79[illegible]	...	...	...	...	...	...	...	...	...	...	...	...	...	...	...	...	...
	Jhajha ...	137	89	...	...	546	465	...	...	1	...	...	...	...	...	...	...	...	...	...	...	...	...	...

PROVINCIAL TABLE II—*continued.*

POPULATION OF REVENUE THANAS AND POLICE-STATIONS BY RELIGION AND LITERACY.

REVENUE THANA.	POLICE-STATION.	POPULATION.			HINDUS. TOTAL HINDUS.		HINDUS. BRAHMANS. Number of persons.		BRAHMANS. Number literate.		DEPRESSED CLASSES. Number of persons.		DEPRESSED CLASSES. Number literate.		OTHER HINDUS. Number of persons.		OTHER HINDUS. Number literate.		MUSLIMS. Number of persons.		MUSLIMS. Number literate.	
		Persons.	Males.	Females.	Males.	Females.	Males.	Females.	Males.	Females.	Males.	Females.	Males.	Females.	Males.	Females.	Males.	Females.	Males.	Females.	Males.	Females.
1	2	3	4	5	6	7	8	9	10	11	12	13	14	15	16	17	18	19	20	21	22	23
BHAGALPUR	...	2,234,632	1,130,584	1,104,048	1,002,664	977,598	57,130	52,592	15,827	1,016	165,824	168,330	1,057	125	779,710	756,676	50,248	3,127	125,257	124,179	8,272	1,036
Sultanganj	...	(a)110,107	54,767	55,340	48,577	48,481	4,338	3,820	1,133	53	8,061	8,347	46	13	30,178	30,305	1,003	240	6,180	6,857	116	81
	Sultanganj ...	55,730	27,074	27,756	25,232	24,642	...	...	...	...	...	...	...	...	...	...	...	...	2,751	3,112	...	...
	Shahkund ...	49,302	24,201	25,101	20,865	21,465	...	...	...	...	...	...	...	...	...	...	...	...	3,330	3,636	...	...
Bhagalpur	...	204,741	107,054	97,687	82,793	74,885	7,408	5,553	3,516	441	13,227	13,371	100	28	62,098	55,961	7,587	1,045	23,033	23,477	4,040	657
	Bhagalpur Town.	83,847	46,868	36,979	33,200	25,040	3,932	2,166	2,225	368	4,174	3,880	150	28	26,193	19,003	5,617	977	12,040	11,609	3,441	283
	Bhagalpur Mufassal.	92,662	46,325	46,337	37,337	37,333	...	...	...	...	...	...	...	...	...	...	...	...	8,983	9,010	...	...
	Nathnagar ...	(a)33,937	16,778	17,159	14,970	15,190	...	...	...	...	...	...	...	...	...	...	...	...	1,808	1,969	...	...
Colgong	...	211,453	105,943	105,509	93,848	93,806	5,306	5,107	1,720	122	13,221	13,633	98	27	75,321	74,866	5,687	328	11,600	11,828	582	75
	Colgong ...	107,946	53,714	54,232	46,558	46,930	...	...	...	...	...	...	...	...	...	...	...	...	6,902	7,176	...	...
	Gopalpur ...	51,403	25,066	25,447	24,571	24,102	...	...	...	...	...	...	...	...	...	...	...	...	1,385	1,345	...	...
	Pirpainti ...	52,103	26,273	25,830	22,719	22,305	...	...	...	...	...	...	...	...	...	...	...	...	3,313	3,307	...	...
Bihpur	...	(a)115,106	57,918	57,188	52,366	51,444	6,001	6,408	1,305	66	4,679	4,626	36	...	40,606	40,410	2,123	100	5,402	5,711	219	21
	Bihpur ...	114,476	57,593	56,883	52,063	51,141	...	...	...	...	...	...	...	...	...	...	...	...	5,490	5,700	...	...
Supaul	...	384,789	192,769	192,020	170,171	169,448	6,402	5,990	1,103	49	26,368	27,332	176	10	137,401	136,186	5,288	200	22,312	22,311	803	35
	Supaul ...	258,177	128,078	130,099	111,243	113,110	...	...	...	...	...	...	...	...	...	...	...	...	16,757	16,952	...	...
	Dagmara ...	64,704	32,940	31,764	29,787	28,648	...	...	...	...	...	...	...	...	...	...	...	...	3,122	3,101	...	...
	Daparkha ...	61,908	31,751	30,157	29,141	27,690	...	...	...	...	...	...	...	...	...	...	...	...	2,433	2,258	...	...
Partapganj	...	124,200	63,458	60,742	55,249	52,970	2,079	2,006	576	15	10,788	11,000	45	7	41,783	39,364	2,056	144	8,172	7,735	204	31
	Partapganj ...	92,969	47,539	45,430	42,333	40,474	...	...	...	...	...	...	...	...	...	...	...	...	5,185	4,939	...	...
	Bhimnagar ...	31,231	15,919	15,312	12,916	12,496	...	...	...	...	...	...	...	...	...	...	...	...	2,987	2,796	...	...
Bangaon	Bangaon ...	164,595	81,304	83,291	71,801	73,014	7,388	7,778	1,101	32	12,307	13,256	70	8	51,611	51,981	2,630	153	9,882	10,199	308	20
Madhipura	...	274,262	141,825	132,437	131,106	122,547	3,715	2,347	963	26	25,680	24,781	70	9	102,703	95,519	7,093	103	10,694	9,877	624	28
	Madhipura ...	182,464	94,252	88,212	87,723	82,322	...	...	...	...	...	...	...	...	...	...	...	...	6,528	5,885	...	...
	Mirganj ...	91,798	47,573	44,225	43,383	40,225	...	...	...	...	...	...	...	...	...	...	...	...	4,166	3,992	...	...
Kishanganj	...	172,822	90,723	82,099	82,998	74,885	3,471	3,150	1,136	44	18,086	16,773	143	12	61,441	54,962	3,095	187	7,638	7,121	313	5
	Kishanganj ...	136,964	72,066	64,898	65,425	58,790	...	...	...	...	...	...	...	...	...	...	...	...	6,558	6,019	...	...
	Sonbarsa ...	35,858	18,657	17,201	17,573	16,095	...	...	...	...	...	...	...	...	...	...	...	...	1,080	1,102	...	...
Amarpur	...	159,013	78,833	80,180	73,045	74,012	4,890	4,946	1,668	71	13,035	14,628	46	1	54,220	54,438	4,984	238	5,785	6,161	406	30
	Amarpur ...	115,257	57,169	58,088	52,818	53,300	...	...	...	...	...	...	...	...	...	...	...	...	4,348	4,781	...	...
	Rajaun ...	43,756	21,664	22,092	20,227	20,712	...	...	...	...	...	...	...	...	...	...	...	...	1,437	1,380	...	...
Katoria	...	133,019	66,461	66,558	63,161	63,091	1,605	1,494	522	15	9,107	9,787	76	1	52,440	51,820	2,300	91	2,553	2,753	58	5
	Katoria ...	81,996	41,180	40,816	38,713	38,220	...	...	...	...	...	...	...	...	...	...	...	...	1,726	1,884	...	...
	Belhar ...	51,023	25,281	25,742	24,448	24,871	...	...	...	...	...	...	...	...	...	...	...	...	827	868	...	...
Banka	...	180,526	89,529	90,997	77,939	79,515	3,972	3,494	1,024	83	10,266	10,807	63	9	63,701	65,214	4,403	238	11,317	11,150	510	20
	Banka ...	136,923	68,098	68,825	61,503	62,466	...	...	...	...	...	...	...	...	...	...	...	...	6,227	6,039	...	...
	Dhuraia ...	43,603	21,431	22,172	16,436	17,049	...	...	...	...	...	...	...	...	...	...	...	...	4,090	5,121	...	...

PROVINCIAL TABLE II—*continued.*

POPULATION OF REVENUE THANAS AND POLICE-STATIONS BY RELIGION AND LITERACY.

REVENUE THANA.	POLICE-STATION.	CHRISTIANS. No. of persons. Males.	CHRISTIANS. No. of persons. Females.	CHRISTIANS. No. literate. Males.	CHRISTIANS. No. literate. Females.	TRIBAL. No. of persons. Males.	TRIBAL. No. of persons. Females.	TRIBAL. No. literate. Males.	TRIBAL. No. literate. Females.	OTHERS. No. of persons. Males.	OTHERS. No. of persons. Females.	OTHERS. No. literate. Males.	OTHERS. No. literate. Females.	NUMBER LITERATE (AGED 7 AND OVER). Total. Persons.	Total. Males.	Total. Females.	Aged 7—13. Males.	Aged 7—13. Females.	Aged 14—23. Males.	Aged 14—23. Females.	Aged 24 and over. Males.	Aged 24 and over. Females.	Literate in English. Males.	Literate in English. Females.
1	2	24	25	26	27	28	29	30	31	32	33	34	35	36	37	38	39	40	41	42	43	44	45	46
BHAGALPUR	...	**881**	**679**	**434**	**197**	**1,601**	**1,443**	**56**	**14**	**181**	**149**	**92**	**13**	**81,514**	**75,986**	**5,528**	**9,246**	**1,211**	**18,394**	**1,638**	**48,346**	**2,679**	**9,750**	**701**
Sultanganj	...	1	2	...	...	...	...	...	...	...	...	...	...	3,584	3,198	386	413	83	924	123	1,861	180	343	19
	Sultanganj ...	1	2	...	...	...	...	...	...	...	...	...	...	...	...	...	...	...	...	...	...	...	...	...
	Shahkund ...	...	...	...	...	...	...	...	...	...	...	...	...	...	...	...	...	...	...	...	...	...	...	...
Bhagalpur	...	408	380	196	124	93	3	12	...	37	32	...	...	17,834	15,541	2,293	1,682	530	4,385	654	9,474	1,109	4,189	511
	Bhagalpur Town	403	376	194	122	93	3	12	...	37	32	...	...	12,417	10,639	1,778	1,164	392	3,380	495	6,195	891	3,002	481
	Bhagalpur Mufassal.	5	4	...	...	...	...	...	...	...	...	...	...	...	...	...	...	...	...	...	...	...	...	...
	Nathnagar ...	...	...	...	...	...	...	...	...	...	...	...	...	...	...	...	...	...	...	...	...	...	...	...
Colgong	...	21	15	8	4	384	360	43	14	...	...	...	...	8,608	8,038	570	1,208	129	1,899	169	4,931	272	328	34
	Colgong ...	8	5	...	...	156	112	...	...	...	...	...	...	...	...	...	...	...	...	...	...	...	...	...
	Gopalpur ...	...	...	...	...	...	...	...	...	...	...	...	...	...	...	...	...	...	...	...	...	...	...	...
	Pirpainti ...	13	10	...	...	228	248	...	...	...	...	...	...	...	...	...	...	...	...	...	...	...	...	...
Bihpur	...	6	3	1	...	3	...	...	...	31	30	23	5	3,909	3,707	202	557	49	817	65	2,333	88	103	3
	Bihpur ...	6	3	...	...	3	...	...	...	31	30	...	...	...	...	...	...	...	...	...	...	...	...	...
Supaul	...	241	234	197	49	...	3	...	...	45	25	35	1	7,995	7,661	344	960	74	1,669	105	5,032	165	806	34
	Supaul ...	51	21	...	...	...	2	...	...	27	14	...	...	...	...	...	...	...	...	...	...	...	...	...
	Dagmara ...	13	4	...	...	...	...	...	...	18	11	...	...	...	...	...	...	...	...	...	...	...	...	...
	Daparkha ...	177	209	...	...	...	...	...	...	...	...	...	...	...	...	...	...	...	...	...	...	...	...	...
Partapganj	...	12	15	3	3	...	...	...	...	26	22	11	1	3,096	2,895	201	388	40	563	54	1,944	107	300	6
	Partapganj ...	1	1	...	...	...	...	...	...	20	16	...	...	...	...	...	...	...	...	...	...	...	...	...
	Bhimnagar ...	11	14	...	...	...	...	...	...	6	6	...	...	...	...	...	...	...	...	...	...	...	...	...
Bangaon	Bangaon ..	31	78	9	9	...	...	...	...	...	...	...	...	4,639	4,417	222	584	45	1,025	66	2,808	111	370	5
Madhipura	...	1	2	...	...	...	...	...	...	24	10	16	...	8,992	8,766	226	899	53	2,034	54	5,833	119	1,631	38
	Madhipura ...	1	2	...	...	...	...	...	...	...	2	...	...	...	...	...	...	...	...	...	...	...	...	...
	Mirganj ...	...	...	...	...	...	...	...	...	24	8	...	...	...	...	...	...	...	...	...	...	...	...	...
Kishanganj	...	...	...	...	...	87	93	1	...	...	...	...	...	5,835	5,587	248	316	48	1,447	85	3,524	115	433	52
	Kishanganj ...	...	...	...	...	83	89	...	...	...	...	...	...	...	...	...	...	...	...	...	...	...	...	...
	Sonbarsa ...	...	...	...	...	4	4	...	...	...	...	...	...	...	...	...	...	...	...	...	...	...	...	...
Amarpur	...	2	3	1	...	1	1	...	...	...	...	...	...	7,454	7,105	349	900	69	1,619	107	4,587	173	179	...
	Amarpur ...	2	3	...	...	1	1	...	...	...	...	...	...	...	...	...	...	...	...	...	...	...	...	...
	Rajaun ...	...	...	...	...	...	...	...	...	...	...	...	...	...	...	...	...	...	...	...	...	...	...	...
Katoria	...	24	23	10	5	723	692	...	...	...	...	...	...	3,083	2,966	117	357	24	707	45	1,902	48	428	5
	Katoria ...	18	20	...	...	723	692	...	...	...	...	...	...	...	...	...	...	...	...	...	...	...	...	...
	Belhar ...	6	3	...	...	...	...	...	...	...	...	...	...	...	...	...	...	...	...	...	...	...	...	...
Banka	...	44	20	9	5	310	282	...	...	19	30	17	6	6,485	6,115	370	743	67	1,305	111	4,067	192	651	5
	Banka ...	44	20	...	...	305	280	...	...	19	30	...	...	...	...	...	...	...	...	...	...	...	...	...
	Dhuraia ...	...	...	...	...	5	2	...	...	...	...	...	...	...	...	...	...	...	...	...	...	...	...	...

(a) *Sultanganj* thana includes eleven mauzas, and *Bihpur* thana includes two mauzas, which belong to police-station *Nathnagar*.

PROVINCIAL TABLE II—*continued.*

PURNEA.]

Population of Revenue Thanas and Police-stations by Religion and Literacy.

Revenue Thana.	Police-station.	Population.			Hindus. Total Hindus.		Hindus. Brahmans. Number of persons.		Brahmans. Number literate.		Depressed classes. Number of persons.		Depressed classes. Number literate.		Other Hindus. Number of persons.		Other Hindus. Number literate.		Muslims. Number of persons.		Muslims. Number literate.	
		Persons.	Males.	Females.	Males.	Females.	Males.	Females.	Males.	Females.	Males.	Females.	Males.	Females.	Males.	Females.	Males.	Females.	Males.	Females.	Males.	Females.
1	2	3	4	5	6	7	8	9	10	11	12	13	14	15	16	17	18	19	20	21	22	23
PURNEA	...	**2,186,543**	**1,129,681**	**1,056,862**	**665,451**	**619,863**	**18,849**	**16,091**	**7,762**	**658**	**128,972**	**121,815**	**1,361**	**67**	**519,630**	**481,957**	**43,575**	**1,855**	**456,347**	**430,021**	**37,402**	**1,298**
Araria	...	228,676	116,251	112,425	58,192	56,826	2,919	2,743	1,194	88	9,059	8,622	163	5	46,214	44,460	4,029	90	58,058	55,596	5,346	244
	Araria ...	141,183	71,887	69,206	29,063	27,603	...	...	...	...	...	...	...	...	...	...	...	...	43,834	41,601	...	...
	Palasi ...	53,336	26,972	26,366	16,662	16,241	...	...	...	...	...	...	...	...	...	...	...	...	10,320	10,126	...	...
	Sikti ...	34,155	17,392	16,763	12,487	11,981	...	...	...	...	...	...	...	...	...	...	...	...	4,005	4,783	...	...
Forbesganj	Forbesganj ...	177,791	91,638	86,153	70,857	66,849	2,446	2,194	900	34	16,016	15,818	336	7	52,396	48,837	5,261	161	20,738	19,271	1,466	64
Raniganj	Raniganj ...	107,700	55,407	52,293	45,012	42,130	2,142	2,013	674	12	11,510	11,060	98	4	31,364	29,057	2,680	189	10,368	10,043	686	38
Kishanganj	...	129,260	68,362	60,898	19,760	18,482	467	206	249	25	2,783	2,258	19	7	16,510	14,018	1,359	113	48,217	44,172	3,656	55
	Kishanganj ...	92,121	49,052	43,069	17,407	14,466	...	...	...	...	...	...	...	...	...	...	...	...	31,170	28,369	...	...
	Goalpokhar ...	37,139	19,310	17,829	2,283	2,016	...	...	...	...	...	...	...	...	...	...	...	...	17,047	15,818	...	...
Bahadurganj	...	198,290	101,043	96,257	34,922	32,551	339	293	137	14	5,154	4,778	87	2	29,429	27,482	2,318	36	67,000	63,700	6,942	210
	Bahadurganj ...	126,912	64,956	61,956	17,157	16,075	...	...	...	...	...	...	...	...	...	...	...	...	47,700	45,881	...	...
	Dighalbank ..	36,296	18,847	17,449	8,589	7,800	...	...	...	...	...	...	...	...	...	...	...	...	10,204	9,643	...	...
	Terhagach ...	34,992	18,140	16,852	9,243	8,676	...	...	...	...	...	...	...	...	...	...	...	...	8,807	8,176	...	...
Islampur	...	233,117	122,741	110,376	37,840	38,367	282	121	135	8	4,081	3,554	53	3	33,483	29,692	2,346	44	83,558	75,880	4,548	112
	Islampur ...	107,034	55,793	51,242	13,443	12,307	...	...	...	...	...	...	...	...	...	...	...	...	42,125	38,790	...	...
	Chopra ...	56,419	29,871	26,548	8,165	7,209	...	...	...	...	...	...	...	...	...	...	...	...	21,209	18,910	...	...
	Thakurganj ...	69,664	37,078	32,586	16,238	13,851	...	...	...	...	...	...	...	...	...	...	...	...	20,224	18,180	...	...
Purnea	...	157,110	82,454	74,656	67,011	51,355	2,124	1,643	1,073	202	13,866	12,566	93	4	41,021	37,148	5,625	383	24,926	22,835	2,657	
	Purnea ...	94,263	50,220	44,043	35,923	31,206	...	...	...	...	...	...	...	...	...	...	...	...	14,019	12,588	...	...
	Kasba ...	45,796	23,502	22,294	14,865	13,679	...	...	...	...	...	...	...	...	...	...	...	...	6,960	8,472	...	...
	Khasauchi Hat	17,046	8,726	8,320	6,723	6,470	...	...	...	...	...	...	...	...	...	...	...	...	1,921	1,775	...	...
Amaur	...	137,369	69,463	67,906	22,461	21,653	211	187	135	22	3,170	3,066	83	1	19,071	18,400	2,148	61	46,915	46,189	4,663	172
	Amaur ...	88,896	44,949	43,947	13,783	13,331	...	...	...	...	...	...	...	...	...	...	...	...	31,104	30,616	...	...
	Baisi ...	48,473	24,514	23,959	8,678	8,322	...	...	...	...	...	...	...	...	...	...	...	...	15,751	15,573	...	...
Dhamdaha	...	266,583	138,085	128,498	125,059	116,217	3,044	3,151	1,209	28	28,320	27,785	121	11	93,060	85,281	5,874	205	11,398	10,833	582	26
	Dhamdaha ...	110,379	57,269	53,110	51,681	47,762	...	...	...	...	...	...	...	...	...	...	...	...	4,626	4,392	...	...
	Rupauli ...	83,299	42,849	40,450	39,110	36,962	...	...	...	...	...	...	...	...	...	...	...	...	3,597	3,338	...	...
	Dharhara ...	72,905	37,967	34,938	34,379	31,493	...	...	...	...	...	...	...	...	...	...	...	...	3,173	3,103	...	...
Korha	...	153,409	78,709	74,700	64,379	61,318	1,068	1,879	805	110	14,349	13,936	153	4	48,362	46,013	3,872	165	13,074	12,764	799	86
	Korha ...	80,813	41,348	39,465	35,292	33,805	...	...	...	...	...	...	...	...	...	...	...	...	5,928	5,653	...	—
	Barari ...	72,596	37,361	35,235	29,087	27,513	...	...	...	...	...	...	...	...	...	...	...	...	7,746	7,211	...	...
Gopalpur	Karandighi ...	73,257	37,940	35,317	24,488	22,671	282	335	54	12	3,043	2,184	13	...	22,163	20,152	983	45	13,045	13,278	776	41
Kadwa	...	162,595	83,745	78,850	43,609	40,290	713	607	336	43	6,292	5,906	95	...	36,604	34,426	3,040	91	39,486	37,294	3,945	105
	Kadwa ...	77,820	40,238	37,582	23,670	22,073	...	...	...	...	...	...	...	...	...	...	...	...	16,210	15,196	...	...
	Barsoi ...	48,743	25,274	23,469	9,736	8,000	...	...	...	...	...	...	...	...	...	...	...	...	15,479	14,521	...	...
	Azamnagar ...	36,032	18,233	17,799	10,203	10,026	...	...	...	...	...	...	...	...	...	...	...	...	7,797	7,577	...	...
Katihar	...	161,476	82,943	78,533	61,865	58,446	1,612	1,319	782	63	10,306	10,234	110	19	49,937	46,993	3,660	202	19,050	18,155	1,242	63
	Katihar ...	86,610	45,123	41,487	34,298	31,334	...	...	...	...	...	...	...	...	...	...	...	...	8,933	8,325	...	...
	Manihari ...	74,866	37,820	37,046	27,567	27,112	...	...	...	...	...	...	...	...	...	...	...	...	10,117	9,830	...	...

Correction slip no. 1.

PROVINCIAL TABLE II—*continued*.

Revenue Thana.	Police-station.	Christians. No. of persons. Males.	Christians. No. of persons. Females.	Christians. No. literate. Males.	Christians. No. literate. Females.	Tribal. No. of persons. Males.	Tribal. No. of persons. Females.	Tribal. No. literate. Males.	Tribal. No. literate. Females.	Others. No. of persons. Males.	Others. No. of persons. Females.	Others. No. literate. Males.	Others. No. literate. Females.	Number literate (aged 7 and over). Total. Persons.	Total. Males.	Total. Females.	Aged 7—13. Males.	Aged 7—13. Females.	Aged 14—23. Males.	Aged 14—23. Females.	Aged 24 and over. Males.	Aged 24 and over. Females.	Literate in English. Males.	Literate in English. Females.
1	2	24	25	26	27	28	29	30	31	32	33	34	35	36	37	38	39	40	41	42	43	44	45	46
To be substituted, for the figures under thanas Gopalpur and Kadwa, district Purnea, at page 190.																								
Gopalpur	Karandighi ...	...	...	...	...	254	258	...	...	...	...	...	...	1,558	1,464	94	144	20	283	19	1,038	55	22	...
Kadwa	...	...	...	...	...	668	589	...	...	...	...	...	...	8,086	7,823	263	986	71	1,793	85	5,044	107	455	...
	Barsoi ...	...	...	...	...	391	367	...	...	...	...	...	...	...	...	...	...	...	...	...	...	...	...	...

NOTE.—The figures in columns 24 to 27 and 30 to 35 remain unchanged.

Correction slip no. 1.

PROVINCIAL TABLE II.

Revenue Thana.	Police-station.	Population. Persons.	Population. Males.	Population. Females.	Hindus. Total Hindus. Males.	Total Hindus. Females.	Brahmans. Number of persons. Males.	Brahmans. Number of persons. Females.	Brahmans. Number literate. Males.	Brahmans. Number literate. Females.	Depressed class. Number of persons. Males.	Depressed class. Number of persons. Females.	Depressed class. Number literate. Males.	Depressed class. Number literate. Females.	Other Hindus. Number of persons. Males.	Other Hindus. Number of persons. Females.	Other Hindus. Number literate. Males.	Other Hindus. Number literate. Females.	Muslims. Number of persons. Males.	Muslims. Number of persons. Females.	Muslims. Number literate. Males.	Muslims. Number literate. Females.
1	2	3	4	5	6	7	8	9	10	11	12	13	14	15	16	17	18	19	20	21	23	23
To be substituted for the figures under thanas Gopalpur and Kadwa, district Purnea, at page 190.																						
Gopalpur	Karandighi ...	61,011	31,540	29,471	21,098	19,720	...	...	...	...	...	...	...	...	...	...	...	...	10,040	9,378	474	34
Kadwa	...	174,841	90,145	84,696	46,909	43,060	...	...	...	...	...	...	...	...	...	...	...	...	42,491	40,194	4,246	112
	Barsa ...	60,989	31,674	29,315	13,126	11,851	...	...	...	...	...	...	...	...	...	...	...	...	18,484	17,421	...	...

NOTE.—Revised figures in columns 8 to 19 are not available.

PROVINCIAL TABLE II—*continued.*

POPULATION OF REVENUE THANAS AND POLICE-STATIONS BY RELIGION AND LITERACY.

REVENUE THANA.	POLICE-STATION.	CHRISTIANS. No. of persons. Males.	CHRISTIANS. No. of persons. Females.	CHRISTIANS. No. literate. Males.	CHRISTIANS. No. literate. Females.	TRIBAL. No. of persons. Males.	TRIBAL. No. of persons. Females.	TRIBAL. No. literate. Males.	TRIBAL. No. literate. Females.	OTHERS. No. of persons. Males.	OTHERS. No. of persons. Females.	OTHERS. No. literate. Males.	OTHERS. No. literate. Females.
1	3	24	25	26	27	28	29	30	31	32	33	34	35
PURNEA	...	**973**	**850**	**216**	**173**	**6,395**	**5,772**	**21**	**9**	**515**	**356**	**264**	**14**
Araria	...	...	2	...	...	...	...	...	...	...	...	...	...
	Araria ...	...	2	...	...	...	...	...	...	...	...	...	...
	Palasi ...	...	...	...	...	...	...	...	...	...	...	...	...
	Sikti ...	...	...	...	...	...	...	...	...	...	...	...	...
Forbesganj	Forbesganj ...	18	16	9	4	15	7	...	...	10	10	3	1
Raniganj	Raniganj ...	4	1	...	...	108	119	...	...	...	...	...	...
Kishanganj	...	261	206	59	42	41	26	...	...	83	12	13	3
	Kishanganj ...	261	206	...	...	41	26	...	...	83	12	...	...
	Goalpokhar ...	...	...	...	...	...	...	...	...	...	...	...	...
Bahadurganj	...	...	...	...	...	21	6	...	...	...	...	...	...
	Bahadurganj...	...	...	...	...	...	...	...	...	...	...	...	...
	Dighalbank ...	...	...	...	...	21	6	...	...	...	...	...	...
	Terhagach ...	...	...	...	...	...	...	...	...	...	...	...	...
Islampur	...	435	356	102	65	898	764	...	...	4	...	1	...
	Islampur ...	213	141	...	...	11	4	...	...	...	...	...	...
	Chopra ...	14	13	...	...	483	407	...	...	...	...	...	...
	Thakurganj ...	208	202	...	...	404	353	...	...	4	...	...	...
Purnea	...	57	48	16	13	425	411	3	...	35	7	21	...
	Purnea ...	57	48	...	...	192	193	...	...	35	7	...	...
	Kasba ...	...	...	...	...	151	143	...	...	.	...	...	...
	Khazanchi Hat	...	...	...	...	82	75	...	...	...	...	...	...
Amaur	...	...	...	...	...	77	64	...	...	10	...	2	...
	Amaur ...	...	...	...	...	...	...	...	...	2	...	...	...
	Baisi ...	...	...	...	...	77	64	...	...	8	...	...	...
Dhamdaha	...	3	4	1	1	1,614	1,442	...	...	13	2	2	...
	Dhamdaha ..	1	...	...	...	1,076	956	...	...	5	...	...	...
	Rupauli ...	...	...	...	...	129	148	...	...	4	2	...	...
	Dharhara ...	2	4	...	...	409	338	...	...	4	...	...	...
Korha	...	4	4	1	1	332	306	3	...	320	308	204	9
	Korha ...	4	4	...	...	50	47	...	...	74	56	...	...
	Barari ...	...	...	...	...	282	259	...	...	246	252	...	...
Gopalpur	Karandighi ...	93	63	13	10	314	305	11	7	1	...	1	...
Kadwa	...	3	...	1	...	608	542	4	2	39	15	18	1
	Kadwa ...	2	...	...	...	331	310	...	...	25	3	...	...
	Barsoi ...	1	...	...	...	44	36	...	...	14	12	...	...
	Azamnagar ...	...	...	...	...	233	196	...	...	...	...	...	...
Katihar	...	96	150	15	37	1,942	1,780	...	...	...	2	...	...
	Katihar ...	95	150	...	...	1,797	1,678	...	...	...	...	...	...
	Manihari ...	1	...	...	...	145	102	...	...	...	2	...	...

REVENUE THANA.	POLICE-STATION.	NUMBER LITERATE (AGED 7 AND OVER). TOTAL. Persons.	TOTAL. Males.	TOTAL. Females.	AGED 7—13. Males.	AGED 7—13. Females.	AGED 14—23. Males.	AGED 14—23. Females.	AGED 24 AND OVER. Males.	AGED 24 AND OVER. Females.	LITERATE IN ENGLISH. Males.	LITERATE IN ENGLISH. Females.
1	3	36	37	38	39	40	41	42	43	44	45	46
PURNEA	...	**94,695**	**90,621**	**4,074**	**11,056**	**974**	**20,598**	**1,296**	**58,967**	**1,804**	**7,953**	**335**
Araria	...	11,759	11,332	427	1,326	97	2,406	136	7,600	194	390	8
	Araria ...	...	...	...	...	...	...	...	...	...	...	...
	Palasi ...	...	...	...	...	...	...	...	...	...	...	...
	Sikti ...	...	...	...	...	...	...	...	...	...	...	...
Forbesganj	Forbesganj ...	8,235	7,974	261	1,087	59	1,789	87	5,098	115	531	8
Raniganj	Raniganj ...	4,361	4,118	243	568	60	943	59	2,607	124	133	1
Kishanganj	...	5,600	5,355	245	683	63	1,903	87	2,679	95	1,868	66
	Kishanganj ...	...	...	...	...	...	...	...	...	...	...	...
	Goalpokhar ...	...	...	...	...	...	...	...	...	...	...	...
Bahadurganj	...	9,745	9,484	261	1,089	58	1,903	65	6,402	138	137	6
	Bahadurganj...	...	...	...	...	...	...	...	...	...	...	...
	Dighalbank ...	...	...	...	...	...	...	...	...	...	...	...
	Terhagach ...	...	...	...	...	...	...	...	...	...	...	...
Islampur	...	7,412	7,180	232	643	49	1,251	58	5,286	125	1,134	68
	Islampur ...	...	...	...	...	...	...	...	...	...	...	...
	Chopra ...	...	...	...	...	...	...	...	...	...	...	...
	Thakurganj ...	...	...	...	...	...	...	...	...	...	...	...
Purnea	...	10,062	9,386	676	1,239	193	2,122	252	6,025	231	1,553	54
	Purnea ...	...	...	...	...	...	...	...	...	...	...	...
	Kasba ...	...	...	...	...	...	...	...	...	...	...	...
	Khazanchi Hat	...	...	...	...	...	...	...	...	...	...	...
Amaur	...	7,227	6,971	256	873	63	1,520	75	4,578	118	196	...
	Amaur ...	...	...	...	...	...	...	...	...	...	...	...
	Baisi ...	...	...	...	...	...	...	...	...	...	...	...
Dhamdaha	...	8,148	7,879	269	1,013	64	1,863	121	5,003	84	280	1
	Dhamdaha ..	...	...	...	...	...	...	...	...	...	...	...
	Rupauli ...	...	...	...	...	...	...	...	...	...	...	...
	Dharhara ...	...	...	...	...	...	...	...	...	...	...	...
Korha	...	6,212	5,837	375	687	66	1,431	119	3,719	190	261	3
	Korha ...	...	...	...	...	...	...	...	...	...	...	...
	Barari ...	...	...	...	...	...	...	...	...	...	...	...
Gopalpur	Karandighi ...	1,963	1,848	115	195	25	381	25	1,273	65	29	12
Kadwa	...	7,681	7,439	242	935	66	1,694	70	4,810	97	448	7
	Kadwa ...	...	...	...	...	...	...	...	...	...	...	...
	Barsoi ...	...	...	...	...	...	...	...	...	...	...	...
	Azamnagar ...	...	...	...	...	...	...	...	...	...	...	...
Katihar	...	6,290	5,818	472	708	111	1,302	133	3,808	228	984	71
	Katihar ...	...	...	...	...	...	...	...	...	...	...	...
	Manihari ...	...	...	...	...	...	...	...	...	...	...	...

PROVINCIAL TABLE II—*continued.*

POPULATION OF REVENUE THANAS AND POLICE-STATIONS BY RELIGION AND LITERACY.

REVENUE THANA.	POLICE-STATION, SADR ABI CIRCLE OR BUNGALOW.	POPULATION.			HINDUS. TOTAL HINDUS.		HINDUS. BRAHMANS. Number of persons.		BRAHMANS. Number literate.		DEPRESSED CLASSES. Number of persons.		DEPRESSED CLASSES. Number literate.		OTHER HINDUS. Number of persons.		OTHER HINDUS. Number literate.		MUSLIMS. Number of persons.		MUSLIMS. Number literate.	
		Persons.	Males.	Females.	Males.	Females.	Males.	Females.	Males.	Females.	Males.	Females.	Males.	Females.	Males.	Females.	Males.	Females.	Males.	Females.	Males.	Females.
1	2	3	4	5	6	7	8	9	10	11	12	13	14	15	16	17	18	19	20	21	22	23
SANTAL PARGANAS ...	...	2,051,472	1,025,921	1,025,551	475,601	473,597	22,978	19,696	9,418	901	117,369	123,049	1,494	72	335,254	330,858	31,200	1,835	112,839	110,963	7,118	485
Deoghar	...	161,422	82,268	79,154	69,992	67,120	6,323	5,517	2,748	230	15,369	15,613	122	28	48,300	45,990	3,188	492	6,165	5,786	249	12
	Deoghar ...	117,994	60,488	57,506	52,513	49,814	...	...	...	...	...	...	...	...	...	...	...	...	3,792	3,444	...	...
	Sarawan ...	43,428	21,780	21,648	17,479	17,306	...	...	...	...	...	...	...	...	...	...	...	...	2,373	2,342	...	...
Madhupur	...	185,524	93,680	91,844	56,998	55,709	3,718	3,584	1,388	130	15,312	15,298	311	13	37,968	36,827	3,672	190	14,869	14,524	405	83
	Madhupur ...	99,789	50,284	49,505	30,785	30,232	...	...	...	...	...	...	...	...	...	...	...	...	9,782	9,589	...	...
	Sarath ...	85,735	43,396	42,339	26,213	25,477	...	...	...	...	...	...	...	...	...	...	...	...	5,087	4,935	...	...
Dumka	...	421,735	205,830	212,905	94,997	96,487	2,672	2,190	1,341	204	27,590	28,448	318	...	64,730	65,789	8,012	358	8,231	7,902	540	42
	Dumka Thana	3,650	1,892	1,758	966	882	...	...	...	...	...	...	...	...	...	...	...	...	234	222	...	...
	Dumka Municipality	9,471	5,317	4,154	4,267	3,481	...	...	...	...	...	...	...	...	...	...	...	...	635	571	...	...
	Dumka extra Damin.	408,614	201,621	206,993	89,764	92,124	...	...	...	...	...	...	...	...	...	...	...	...	7,363	7,109	...	...
	Sardari Circles.																					
	Jhopa ...	9,048	4,408	4,640	3,124	3,374	...	...	...	...	...	...	...	...	...	...	...	...	4	5	...	...
	Kankati ...	7,360	3,701	3,659	2,376	2,345	...	...	...	...	...	...	...	...	...	...	...	...	353	369	...	...
	Sareya ...	5,967	2,932	3,035	2,451	2,527	...	...	...	...	...	...	...	...	...	...	...	...	106	110	...	...
	Sareya Bazar ...	1,349	653	696	543	578	...	...	...	...	...	...	...	...	...	...	...	...	110	118	...	...
	Siltha ...	9,152	4,563	4,589	2,711	2,773	...	...	...	...	...	...	...	...	...	...	...	...	112	83	...	...
	Ramgarh ...	7,205	3,547	3,658	1,638	1,727	...	...	...	...	...	...	...	...	...	...	...	...	9	8	...	...
	Bhalsuman ...	8,152	3,919	4,233	1,944	2,132	...	...	...	...	...	...	...	...	...	...	...	...	...	...	...	...
	Mohubuna ...	8,087	4,049	4,038	1,826	1,845	...	...	...	...	...	...	...	...	...	...	...	...	13	5	...	...
	Amrapahari ...	6,704	3,285	3,419	918	954	...	...	...	...	...	...	...	...	...	...	...	...	10	4	...	...
	Kamardiha ...	6,721	3,277	3,444	2,183	2,393	...	...	...	...	...	...	...	...	...	...	...	...	149	139	...	...
	Sahara Mahara	7,578	3,806	3,772	2,410	2,844	...	...	...	...	...	...	...	...	...	...	...	...	181	170	...	...
	Jorfal ...	6,374	3,179	3,195	1,384	1,420	...	...	...	...	...	...	...	...	...	...	...	...	31	24	...	...
	Sugnibad ...	8,452	4,091	4,361	1,897	2,003	...	...	...	...	...	...	...	...	...	...	...	...	1	...	...	...
	Jarmandi ...	6,917	3,308	3,609	2,095	2,378	...	...	...	...	...	...	...	...	...	...	...	...	166	162	...	...
	Jarmandi Bazar.	1,775	911	864	888	855	...	...	...	...	...	...	...	...	...	...	...	...	6	...	...	...
	Beldaha ...	8,250	4,017	4,233	3,500	3,685	...	...	...	...	...	...	...	...	...	...	...	...	23	20	...	...
	Baskinath ...	8,584	4,301	4,283	2,008	1,930	...	...	...	...	...	...	...	...	...	...	...	...	3	...	...	...
	Naudiha ...	6,890	3,391	3,499	2,919	2,982	...	...	...	...	...	...	...	...	...	...	...	...	73	71	...	...
	Sukjora ...	6,966	3,361	3,605	2,019	2,233	...	...	...	...	...	...	...	...	...	...	...	...	154	130	...	...
	Nunihat Bazar	2,870	1,429	1,441	1,335	1,350	...	...	...	...	...	...	...	...	...	...	...	...	88	90	...	...
	Kendua ...	7,506	3,654	3,852	2,165	2,393	...	...	...	...	...	...	...	...	...	...	...	...	76	70	...	...
	Amarpur ...	8,630	4,148	4,482	1,271	1,406	...	...	...	...	...	...	...	...	...	...	...	...	14	14	...	...
	Bara ...	9,253	4,493	4,760	2,476	2,035	...	...	...	...	...	...	...	...	...	...	...	...	8	3	...	...
	Danro ...	5,072	2,491	2,581	746	806	...	...	...	...	...	...	...	...	...	...	...	...	...	...	...	...
	Guhiajuri ...	5,881	2,939	2,942	1,053	1,077	...	...	...	...	...	...	...	...	...	...	...	...	75	70	...	...
	Lakrapahari ...	6,518	3,082	3,436	925	981	...	...	...	...	...	...	...	...	...	...	...	...	23	39	...	...
	Dhuria ...	5,428	2,717	2,711	870	851	...	...	...	...	...	...	...	...	...	...	...	...	3	2	...	...
	Choto ...	8,118	4,036	4,082	1,619	1,706	...	...	...	...	...	...	...	...	...	...	...	...	69	70	...	...
	Phuljhari ...	12,399	6,157	6,242	1,218	1,183	...	...	...	...	...	...	...	...	...	...	...	...	34	33	...	...
	Singro ...	8,166	4,075	4,091	1,066	962	...	...	...	...	...	...	...	...	...	...	...	...	17	13	...	...
	Haripur ...	6,583	3,201	3,382	2,129	2,268	...	...	...	...	...	...	...	...	...	...	...	...	42	40	...	...
	Gumro ...	9,502	4,718	4,784	2,388	2,461	...	...	...	...	...	...	...	...	...	...	...	...	479	480	...	...
	Kumrabad ...	10,009	5,015	4,994	3,022	2,959	...	...	...	...	...	...	...	...	...	...	...	...	61	51	...	...
	Lakhanpur ...	9,275	4,585	4,690	926	956	...	...	...	...	...	...	...	...	...	...	...	...	47	63	...	...
	Banskuli ...	6,814	3,350	3,464	1,196	1,249	...	...	...	...	...	...	...	...	...	...	...	...	122	124	...	...
	Masanjore ...	8,938	4,435	4,503	1,531	1,516	...	...	...	...	...	...	...	...	...	...	...	...	148	141	...	...

PROVINCIAL TABLE II—*continued.*

POPULATION OF REVENUE THANAS AND POLICE-STATIONS BY RELIGION AND LITERACY.

REVENUE THANA.	POLICE-STATION, SARDARI CIRCLE OR BUNGALOW.	CHRISTIANS. *No. of persons.* Males.	CHRISTIANS. *No. of persons.* Females.	CHRISTIANS. *No. literate.* Males.	CHRISTIANS. *No. literate.* Females.	TRIBAL. *No. of persons.* Males.	TRIBAL. *No. of persons.* Females.	TRIBAL. *No. literate.* Males.	TRIBAL. *No. literate.* Females.	OTHERS. *No. of persons.* Males.	OTHERS. *No. of persons.* Females.	OTHERS. *No. literate.* Males.	OTHERS. *No. literate.* Females.
1	2	24	25	26	27	28	29	30	31	32	33	34	35
SANTAL PARGANAS ...	...	**6,464**	**6,662**	**1,741**	**1,419**	**430,935**	**434,193**	**3,149**	**304**	**82**	**16**	**35**	**1**
Deoghar	...	40	168	40	68	6,008	6,072	28	13	63	8	27	1
	Deoghar	27	154	...	.	4,093	4,086	...	...	63	8	...	...
	Sarawan ...	13	14	...	...	1,915	1,986	...	...	...	...	...	...
Madhupur	..	353	361	84	88	21,458	21,248	176	33	2	2	...	...
	Madhupur ...	289	285	...	...	9,426	9,397	...	...	2	2	...	...
	Sarath ...	64	76	...	..	12,032	11,851	...	...	...	...	...	...
Dumka	...	1,414	1,710	451	416	104,185	106,864	902	114	3	2	1	...
	Dumka Thana	19	17	..	...	673	637	...	...	...	...	..	...
	Dumka Municipality.	104	83	...	...	311	79	...	...	...	...	...	..
	Dumka Extra Damin.	1,291	1,610	..	...	103,201	106,148	...	...	3	2	...	...
	Sardari Circles												
	Jhopa ...	...	...	...	...	1,380	1,361	...	...	...	...	...	...
	Kankni ..	...	...	...	...	972	945	...	..	..	...	...	...
	Sareya ..	...	...	...	.	375	398	...	...	...	...	...	...
	Sareya Bazar	..	...	...	...	...	...	...	...	...	...	...	...
	Siltha ...	6	5	...	..	1,734	1,758	...	.	...	...	..	...
	Ramgarh ...	2	1	...	...	1,898	1,912	...	...	..	...	...	...
	Bhalsumar ...	9	4	...	..	1,966	2,097	..	...	...	...	...	...
	Mohubura ...	...	...	...	...	2,210	2,138	...	...	..	...	...	...
	Amrapahari...	3	2	..	...	2,354	2,459	...	...	...	...	...	...
	Kamardiha ...	...	...	...	...	946	1,013	...	...	...	...	...	...
	Sahara Mahara	...	...	...	...	915	958	...	...	...	...	...	...
	Jortal ...	.	...	...	...	1,764	1,751	...	...	...	...	...	...
	Sugnibad ...	41	41	...	..	2,152	2,317	...	...	...	...	...	...
	Jarmandi ...	5	8	...	...	1,043	1,062	...	...	...	...	...	...
	Jarmandi Bazar.	...	...	...	...	23	9	...	..	...	...	...	...
	Beldaha ...	...	..	...	...	495	538	..	..	...	.	...	...
	Baskinath ...	...	...	...	...	2,290	2,353	..	...	...	...	...	...
	Naudiha ...	...	...	...	...	399	446	...	...	...	...	...	...
	Sukjora ...	...	...	...	...	1,188	1,242	...	...	...	...	...	...
	Nunihat Bazar	...	...	...	...	6	1	...	...	...	...	...	...
	Kendua ..	...	...	...	..	1,413	1,389	...	...	...	.	...	...
	Amarpur ...	12	13	...	...	2,851	3,049	...	..	...	..	...	...
	Bara ..	18	22	...	...	1,991	2,100	...	...	...	...	...	...
	Danro ...	7	13	...	...	1,738	1,762	...	...	...	...	...	..
	Gulijajuri ...	5	2	...	...	1,906	1,793	..	...	..	.	...	..
	Lakrapahari...	110	390	...	...	2,024	2,026	...	...	...	...	...	...
	Dhuria ..	39	53	...	...	1,806	1,805	...	..	...	...	...	...
	Choto ...	25	20	...	...	2,323	2,296	...	...	..	...	...	...
	Phuljhari ...	6	4	...	...	4,869	4,022	...	...	...	...	...	...
	Singro ...	16	20	...	...	2,076	2,096	...	...	...	...	...	...
	Haripur ...	14	8	...	...	1,016	1,066	...	...	...	...	...	...
	Gumro ..	..	..	...	...	1,861	1,843	...	...	...	...	...	...
	Kumrabad ...	3	1	...	...	1,922	1,983	...	..	...	...	...	...
	Lakhanpur ...	44	46	...	...	3,568	3,625	...	...	...	..	...	...
	Banskuli ...	...	...	...	...	2,032	2,091	...	...	..	...	...	...
	Masanjore ...	9	12	...	...	2,757	2,834	...	...	...	...	...	...

REVENUE THANA.	POLICE-STATION, SARDARI CIRCLE OR BUNGALOW.	NUMBER LITERATE (AGED 7 AND OVER). TOTAL. Persons.	TOTAL. Males.	TOTAL. Females.	AGED 7—13. Males.	AGED 7—13. Females.	AGED 14—23. Males.	AGED 14—23. Females.	AGED 24 AND OVER Males.	AGED 24 AND OVER Females.	LITERATE IN ENGLISH. Males.	LITERATE IN ENGLISH. Females.
1	2	36	37	38	39	40	41	42	43	44	45	46
SANTAL PARGANAS ...	...	**59,167**	**54,150**	**5,017**	**6,241**	**1,163**	**12,564**	**1,481**	**35,345**	**2,373**	**9,810**	**1,045**
Deoghar	...	7,236	6,402	834	774	159	1,506	156	4,123	519	2,906	541
	Deoghar	...	...	...	...	...	...	...	...	...	...	...
	Sarawan ...	...	.	.	..	...	...	...	..	...	...	.
Madhupur	..	6,562	6,036	526	793	104	1,277	123	3,966	290	620	158
	Madhupur ...	...	...	...	...	...	...	...	...	...	...	...
	Sarath ...	..	...	...	...	...	...	...	...	...	...	...
Dumka	...	12,713	11,579	1,134	1,388	355	2,848	345	7,343	434	1,243	99
	Dumka Thana	...	...	...	...	...	...	...	...	...	...	...
	Dumka Municipality.	...	...	...	...	...	...	...	...	...	...	...
	Dumka Extra Damin.	...	...	...	...	...	...	...	...	...	...	...
	Sardari Circles											
	Jhopa ...	...	...	...	...	...	...	...	...	...	...	...
	Kankni ..	...	...	...	...	...	...	...	...	...	...	...
	Sareya ..	...	...	...	...	...	...	...	...	...	...	...
	Sareya Bazar	...	...	...	...	...	...	...	...	...	...	...
	Siltha ...	...	...	...	...	...	...	...	...	...	...	...
	Ramgarh ...	..	...	...	...	...	...	...	...	...	...	...
	Bhalsumar ...	...	...	...	...	...	...	...	...	...	...	...
	Mohubura ...	...	...	...	...	...	...	...	...	...	...	...
	Amrapahari...	...	...	...	...	...	...	...	...	...	...	...
	Kamardiha ...	...	...	...	...	...	...	...	...	...	...	...
	Sahara Mahara	..	...	...	...	...	...	..	...	...	...	...
	Jortal ...	...	...	...	...	...	...	...	...	...	...	...
	Sugnibad ...	...	...	...	...	...	...	...	...	...	...	...
	Jarmandi ...	...	...	...	...	...	...	...	...	...	...	...
	Jarmandi Bazar.	...	...	...	...	...	...	...	...	...	...	...
	Beldaha ...	...	...	...	...	...	...	...	...	...	...	...
	Baskinath ...	...	...	...	...	...	...	...	...	...	...	...
	Naudiha ...	...	...	...	...	...	...	...	...	..	...	...
	Sukjora ...	...	...	...	...	...	...	...	...	...	...	...
	Nunihat Bazar	...	...	...	...	...	...	...	...	...	...	...
	Kendua ..	...	...	...	...	...	...	...	...	...	...	...
	Amarpur ...	...	...	...	...	...	...	...	...	...	...	...
	Bara ..	...	...	...	...	...	...	...	...	...	...	...
	Danro ...	...	...	...	...	...	...	...	...	...	...	...
	Gulijajuri ...	...	...	...	...	...	...	...	...	...	..	...
	Lakrapahari...	...	...	...	...	...	...	...	...	...	.	...
	Dhuria ..	...	...	...	...	...	...	...	...	...	...	...
	Choto ...	...	...	...	...	...	...	...	...	...	...	...
	Phuljhari ...	...	...	...	...	...	...	...	...	...	...	...
	Singro ...	...	...	...	...	...	...	...	...	...	...	...
	Haripur ...	...	...	...	...	...	...	...	...	...	...	...
	Gumro ..	...	...	...	...	...	...	...	...	...	...	...
	Kumrabad ...	...	...	...	...	...	...	...	...	...	...	...
	Lakhanpur ...	...	...	...	...	...	...	...	...	...	...	...
	Banskuli ...	...	...	...	...	...	...	...	...	...	...	...
	Masanjore ...	...	...	...	...	...	...	...	...	...	...	...

PROVINCIAL TABLE II—*continued.*

POPULATION OF REVENUE THANAS AND POLICE-STATIONS BY RELIGION AND LITERACY.

SANTAL PARGANAS.]

REVENUE THANA.	POLICE-STATION, SARDARI CIRCLE OR BUNGALOW.	POPULATION.			HINDUS. TOTAL HINDUS.		BRAHMANS. Number of persons.		BRAHMANS. Number literate.		DEPRESSED CLASSES. Number of persons.		DEPRESSED CLASSES. Number literate.		OTHER HINDUS. Number of persons.		OTHER HINDUS. Number literate.		MUSLIMS. Number of persons.		MUSLIMS. Number literate.	
		Persons.	Males.	Females.	Males.	Females.	Males.	Females.	Males.	Females.	Males.	Females.	Males.	Females.	Males.	Females.	Males.	Females.	Males.	Females.	Males.	Females.
1	2	3	4	5	6	7	8	9	10	11	12	13	14	15	16	17	18	19	20	21	22	23
SANTAL PARGANAS—continued.																						
	Kumirdaha ...	6,219	3,081	3,138	1,663	1,717	...	...	...	...	...	...	...	...	...	...	...	...	313	285	...	...
	Amjora ...	6,797	3,367	3,430	1,937	1,935	...	...	...	...	...	...	...	...	...	...	...	...	259	262	...	...
	Sukjora ...	5,163	2,588	2,575	1,875	1,880	...	...	...	...	...	...	...	...	...	...	...	...	288	287	...	...
	Patjore ...	6,493	3,153	3,340	1,658	1,741	...	...	...	...	...	...	...	...	...	...	...	...	46	33	...	...
	Dighi ...	6,752	3,372	3,380	813	806	...	...	...	...	...	...	...	...	...	...	...	...	83	92	...	...
	Gando ...	10,617	5,297	5,320	1,279	1,244	...	...	...	...	...	...	...	...	...	...	...	...	648	615	...	...
	Baromesia ...	9,384	4,635	4,749	1,324	1,284	...	...	...	...	...	...	...	...	...	...	...	...	10	3	...	...
	Dhaka ...	6,436	3,173	3,263	581	615	...	...	...	...	...	...	...	...	...	...	...	...	1,198	1,214	...	...
	Dhanbasa ...	8,456	4,213	4,243	1,023	939	...	...	...	...	...	...	...	...	...	...	...	...	210	216	...	...
	Jagatpur ...	4,290	2,089	2,201	409	399	...	...	...	...	...	...	...	...	...	...	...	...	52	57	...	...
	Banspahari ...	5,560	2,761	2,799	248	231	...	...	...	...	...	...	...	...	...	...	...	...	49	52	...	...
	Porghodih ...	7,647	3,813	3,834	2,306	2,357	...	...	...	...	...	...	...	...	...	...	...	...	133	108	...	...
	Sapchala ...	5,934	2,984	2,950	886	860	...	...	...	...	...	...	...	...	...	...	...	...	28	25	...	...
	Gormala ...	6,605	3,305	3,300	1,031	1,044	...	...	...	...	...	...	...	...	...	...	...	...	54	53	...	...
	Rangamoslia	6,024	2,946	3,078	717	756	...	...	...	...	...	...	...	...	...	...	...	...	...	...	...	...
	Tesria ...	7,633	3,827	3,806	951	983	...	...	...	...	...	...	...	...	...	...	...	...	22	20	...	...
	Dudhua ...	8,767	4,355	4,412	1,443	1,431	...	...	...	...	...	...	...	...	...	...	...	...	4	4	...	...
	Dhanghara ...	5,541	2,727	2,814	713	717	...	...	...	...	...	...	...	...	...	...	...	...	300	288	...	...
	Kasba ...	6,991	3,450	3,541	2,301	2,343	...	...	...	...	...	...	...	...	...	...	...	...	193	183	...	...
	Haripur ...	4,846	2,387	2,459	447	425	...	...	...	...	...	...	...	...	...	...	...	...	346	194	...	...
	Benagaria ...	5,003	2,456	2,547	470	454	...	...	...	...	...	...	...	...	...	...	...	...	217	200	...	...
	Rajbandh ...	4,963	2,418	2,545	627	627	...	...	...	...	...	...	...	...	...	...	...	...	200	199	...	...
Dumka Damin	...	44,422	22,275	22,147	3,672	3,882	9	2	4	1	1,868	2,060	16	...	1,795	1,820	126	1	753	686	28	...
	Bungalows.																					
	Shillinga ...	1,598	820	778	82	83	...	...	...	...	...	...	...	...	...	...	...	...	...	...	...	...
	Nurganj ...	5,309	2,657	2,652	597	647	...	...	...	...	...	...	...	...	...	...	...	...	10	2	...	...
	Katikund ...	7,341	3,650	3,691	1,007	1,022	...	...	...	...	...	...	...	...	...	...	...	...	204	201	...	...
	Jhillimilli ...	7,306	3,577	3,729	626	706	...	...	...	...	...	...	...	...	...	...	...	...	461	427	...	...
	Saldaha ...	3,419	1,770	1,640	263	264	...	...	...	...	...	...	...	...	...	...	...	...	8	5	...	...
	Mosnia ...	2,893	1,401	1,492	147	335	...	...	...	...	...	...	...	...	...	...	...	...	67	24	...	...
	Karudih ...	3,914	1,959	1,955	292	307	...	...	...	...	...	...	...	...	...	...	...	...	...	6	...	...
	Gopikandar ...	7,954	4,086	3,868	386	341	...	...	...	...	...	...	...	...	...	...	...	...	3	1	...	...
	Kuskira ...	4,688	2,375	2,313	272	276	...	...	...	...	...	...	...	...	...	...	...	...	...	...	...	...
Godda		298,217	146,979	151,238	91,801	95,658	5,105	4,890	1,731	33	18,768	22,003	127	7	67,928	68,765	3,501	108	21,685	21,871	1,312	24
	Godda ...	129,069	63,455	65,614	42,750	44,787	...	...	...	...	...	...	...	...	...	...	...	...	8,415	8,427	...	...
	Mahagama ...	101,530	50,377	51,153	31,425	31,928	...	...	...	...	...	...	...	...	...	...	...	...	11,883	12,144	...	...
	Pareya Hat ...	67,618	33,147	34,471	17,716	18,943	...	...	...	...	...	...	...	...	...	...	...	...	1,387	1,300	...	...
Godda Damin	...	89,584	44,727	44,857	7,770	7,914	114	79	30	...	1,358	1,388	14	...	6,298	6,447	184	14	2,139	2,042	38	2
	Bungalows.																					
	Simra I ...	14,173	7,055	7,118	2,407	2,538	...	...	...	...	...	...	...	...	...	...	...	...	615	597	...	...
	Simra II ...	7,802	3,867	3,935	954	998	...	...	...	...	...	...	...	...	...	...	...	...	102	80	...	...
	Telo ...	5,779	2,883	2,896	173	186	...	...	...	...	...	...	...	...	...	...	...	...	16	16	...	...
	Rajabhita ...	10,441	5,266	5,175	1,156	1,141	...	...	...	...	...	...	...	...	...	...	...	...	346	333	...	...
	Karmatanr I ...	2,820	1,368	1,452	244	265	...	...	...	...	...	...	...	...	...	...	...	...	102	120	...	...
	Karmatanr II	3,890	1,954	1,936	465	502	...	...	...	...	...	...	...	...	...	...	...	...	97	105	...	...

PROVINCIAL TABLE II—*continued.*

POPULATION OF REVENUE THANAS AND POLICE-STATIONS BY RELIGION AND LITERACY.

REVENUE THANA.	POLICE-STATION, SARDARI CIRCLE OR BUNGALOW.	CHRISTIANS. No. of persons. Males.	CHRISTIANS. No. of persons. Females.	CHRISTIANS. No. literate. Males.	CHRISTIANS. No. literate. Females.	TRIBAL. No. of persons. Males.	TRIBAL. No. of persons. Females.	TRIBAL. No. literate. Males.	TRIBAL. No. literate. Females.	OTHERS. No. of persons. Males.	OTHERS. No. of persons. Females.	OTHERS. No. literate. Males.	OTHERS. No. literate. Females.	NUMBER LITERATE (AGED 7 AND OVER). Persons.	Total. Males.	Total. Females.	Aged 7—13. Males.	Aged 7—13. Females.	Aged 14—23. Males.	Aged 14—23. Females.	Aged 24 and over. Males.	Aged 24 and over. Females.	Literate in English. Males.	Literate in English. Females.
1	2	24	25	26	27	28	29	30	31	32	33	34	35	36	37	38	39	40	41	42	43	44	45	46
SANTAL PARGANAS—continued.																								
	Kumirdaha ...	...	...	...	...	1,105	1,186	...	...	...	...	...	...	...	...	...	...	...	...	...	...	...	...	...
	Amjora	6	3	...	...	1,165	1,230	...	...	...	...	...	...	...	...	...	...	...	...	...	...	...	...	...
	Sukjora	11	10	...	...	411	396	...	...	3	2	...	...	...	...	...	...	...	...	...	...	...	...	...
	Patjore	...	...	...	...	1,449	1,567	...	...	...	...	...	...	...	...	...	...	...	...	...	...	...	...	...
	Dighi	32	34	...	...	2,444	2,448	...	...	...	...	...	...	...	...	...	...	...	...	...	...	...	...	...
	Gando	57	49	...	...	3,313	3,413	...	...	...	...	...	...	...	...	...	...	...	...	...	...	...	...	...
	Baromesia ...	24	24	...	...	3,377	3,438	...	...	...	...	...	...	...	...	...	...	...	...	...	...	...	...	...
	Dhaka	112	124	...	...	1,283	1,310	...	...	...	...	...	...	...	...	...	...	...	...	...	...	...	...	...
	Dhanbasa ...	32	25	...	...	2,949	3,063	...	...	...	...	...	...	...	...	...	...	...	...	...	...	...	...	...
	Jagatpur ...	4	5	...	...	1,624	1,740	...	...	...	...	...	...	...	...	...	...	...	...	...	...	...	...	...
	Banspahari	2	3	...	...	2,463	2,513	...	...	...	...	...	...	...	...	...	...	...	...	...	...	...	...	...
	Porgbodih	1	...	...	...	1,371	1,389	...	...	...	...	...	...	...	...	...	...	...	...	...	...	...	...	...
	Sapchala	4	7	...	...	2,006	2,058	...	...	...	...	...	...	...	...	...	...	...	...	...	...	...	...	...
	Gorasala	3	2	...	...	2,217	2,201	...	...	...	...	...	...	...	...	...	...	...	...	...	...	...	...	...
	Bangamosila	16	21	...	...	2,213	2,301	...	...	...	...	...	...	...	...	...	...	...	...	...	...	...	...	...
	Tesria ...	108	126	...	...	2,748	2,677	...	...	...	...	...	...	...	...	...	...	...	...	...	...	...	...	...
	Dudhua ...	17	16	...	...	2,891	2,961	...	...	...	...	...	...	...	...	...	...	...	...	...	...	...	...	...
	Dhanghara	53	50	...	...	1,662	1,756	...	...	...	...	...	...	...	...	...	...	...	...	...	...	...	...	...
	Kasba ...	...	...	...	...	956	1,018	...	...	...	...	...	...	...	...	...	...	...	...	...	...	...	...	...
	Haripur ...	72	65	...	...	1,622	1,756	...	...	...	...	...	...	...	...	...	...	...	...	...	...	...	...	...
	Benagaria ...	357	344	...	...	1,412	1,549	...	...	...	...	...	...	...	...	...	...	...	...	...	...	...	...	...
	Rajbandh ...	5	17	...	...	1,583	1,708	...	...	...	...	...	...	...	...	...	...	...	...	...	...	...	...	...
Dumka Damin ...	...	563	516	155	130	17,396	17,083	132	26	1	...	...	...	613	455	158	104	33	104	43	247	83	96	39
	Bungalows.																							
	Shillinga ...	11	10	...	...	727	686	...	...	...	...	...	...	...	...	...	...	...	...	...	...	...	...	...
	Nurganj	70	67	...	...	1,960	1,936	...	...	...	...	...	...	...	...	...	...	...	...	...	...	...	...	...
	Katikund ...	73	74	...	...	2,366	2,304	...	...	...	...	...	...	...	...	...	...	...	...	...	...	...	...	...
	Jhilimili	26	18	...	...	2,464	2,578	...	...	...	...	...	...	...	...	...	...	...	...	...	...	...	...	...
	Taldaha ...	134	145	...	...	1,314	1,236	...	...	1	...	...	...	...	...	...	...	...	...	...	...	...	...	...
	Masnia ...	11	8	...	...	1,176	1,225	...	...	...	...	...	...	...	...	...	...	...	...	...	...	...	...	...
	Karudih ...	60	61	...	...	1,607	1,481	...	...	...	...	...	...	...	...	...	...	...	...	...	...	...	...	...
	Gopikandar ...	105	120	...	...	3,572	3,536	...	...	...	...	...	...	...	...	...	...	...	...	...	...	...	...	...
	Kuskira ...	13	13	...	...	2,090	2,024	...	...	...	...	...	...	...	...	...	...	...	...	...	...	...	...	...
Godda ...	...	314	317	74	45	33,089	33,392	471	7	...	...	...	...	7,339	7,116	223	881	56	1,775	74	4,460	93	2,077	62
	Godda	168	167	...	...	12,122	12,233	...	...	...	...	...	...	...	...	...	...	...	...	...	...	...	...	...
	Mahagama ...	39	51	...	...	7,030	7,030	...	...	...	...	...	...	...	...	...	...	...	...	...	...	...	...	...
	Pareya Hat ...	107	99	...	...	13,937	14,129	...	...	...	...	...	...	...	...	...	...	...	...	...	...	...	...	...
Godda Damin ...	...	304	211	33	19	14,614	14,690	231	14	...	...	...	...	579	520	59	33	5	186	19	351	35	29	4
	Bungalows.																							
	Simra I ...	26	36	...	...	4,007	3,960	...	...	...	...	...	...	...	...	...	...	...	...	...	...	...	...	...
	Simra II ...	34	33	...	...	2,777	2,824	...	...	...	...	...	...	...	...	...	...	...	...	...	...	...	...	...
	Telo ...	...	...	...	...	2,693	2,694	...	...	...	...	...	...	...	...	...	...	...	...	...	...	...	...	...
	Rajabhita ...	39	40	...	...	3,736	3,661	...	...	...	...	...	...	...	...	...	...	...	...	...	...	...	...	...
	Karmatanr I	16	27	...	...	1,006	1,046	...	...	...	...	...	...	...	...	...	...	...	...	...	...	...	...	...
	Karmatanr II	1	3	...	...	1,391	1,327	...	...	...	...	...	...	...	...	...	...	...	...	...	...	...	...	...

PROVINCIAL TABLE II—*continued.*

POPULATION OF REVENUE THANAS AND POLICE-STATIONS BY RELIGION AND LITERACY.

REVENUE THANA.	POLICE-STATION, SARDARI CIRCLE OR BUNGALOW.	POPULATION.			HINDUS.														MUSLIMS.			
					TOTAL HINDUS.		BRAHMANS.				DEPRESSED CLASSES.				OTHER HINDUS.							
							Number of persons.		*Number literate.*		*Number of persons.*		*Number literate.*		*Number of persons.*		*Number literate.*		*Number of persons.*		*Number literate.*	
		Persons.	Males.	Females.	Males.	Females.	Males.	Females.	Males.	Females.	Males.	Females.	Males.	Females.	Males.	Females.	Males.	Females.	Males.	Females.	Males.	Females.
1	2	3	4	5	6	7	8	9	10	11	12	13	14	15	16	17	18	19	20	21	22	23
SANTAL PARGANAS—continued.	Karmataur Hill Tract.	1,661	851	810	...	...	...	...	...	...	...	...	...	...	...	...	...	...	...	...	...	...
	Sundar Pahari	5,020	2,529	2,491	160	136	...	...	...	...	...	...	...	...	...	...	...	...	26	16	...	...
	Sundar Pahari Hill Tract.	416	203	213	...	...	...	...	...	...	...	...	...	...	...	...	...	...	...	...	...	...
	Dhamni ...	3,018	1,491	1,522	478	455	...	...	...	...	...	...	...	...	...	...	...	...	10	18	...	...
	Dhamni Hill Tract.	490	252	238	...	...	...	...	...	...	...	...	...	...	...	...	...	...	...	...	...	...
	Chandna I ...	3,496	1,695	1,801	55	58	...	...	...	...	...	...	...	...	...	...	...	...	...	...	...	...
	Chandna II ...	4,406	2,222	2,184	102	106	...	...	...	...	...	...	...	...	...	...	...	...	1	...	...	...
	Chandna Hill Tract.	2,424	1,183	1,241	4	5	...	...	...	...	...	...	...	...	...	...	...	...	...	...	...	...
	Bokrabandh I	3,463	1,742	1,721	84	84	...	...	...	...	...	...	...	...	...	...	...	...	...	...	...	...
	Bokrabandh II	2,402	1,196	1,206	31	31	...	...	...	...	...	...	...	...	...	...	...	...	...	...	...	...
	Boarijore ...	17,889	8,071	8,918	1,372	1,310	...	...	...	...	...	...	...	...	...	...	...	...	815	757	...	...
Jamtara Thana ...	...	243,858	123,530	120,338	61,322	59,528	2,615	1,705	1,141	111	10,475	10,874	302	12	43,232	40,859	5,811	231	11,311	10,837	783	32
	Sardari Circles.																					
	Jamtara ...	7,870	4,218	3,652	2,781	2,358	...	...	...	...	...	...	...	...	...	...	...	...	285	244	...	...
	Mihijam ...	9,702	4,918	4,784	2,317	2,206	...	...	...	...	...	...	...	...	...	...	...	...	644	622	...	...
	Kandahit ...	9,382	4,725	4,657	2,631	2,575	...	...	...	...	...	...	...	...	...	...	...	...	116	97	...	...
	Bagdahori ...	9,383	4,702	4,681	3,301	3,390	...	...	...	...	...	...	...	...	...	...	...	...	316	310	...	...
	Ghati ...	10,867	5,387	5,480	2,308	2,342	...	...	...	...	...	...	...	...	...	...	...	...	1,067	1,000	...	...
	Dakhinbahal	11,736	5,970	5,766	2,668	3,666	...	...	...	...	...	...	...	...	...	...	...	...	1,401	1,293	...	...
	Morro ...	5,182	2,570	2,612	1,407	1,445	...	...	...	...	...	...	...	...	...	...	...	...	405	430	...	...
	Narainpur ...	12,537	6,299	6,238	2,745	2,761	...	...	...	...	...	...	...	...	...	...	...	...	1,240	1,266	...	...
	Pindari ...	9,253	4,795	4,458	2,784	2,433	...	...	...	...	...	...	...	...	...	...	...	...	701	640	...	...
	Kalajhoria ...	9,170	4,598	4,572	2,118	2,114	...	...	...	...	...	...	...	...	...	...	...	...	974	985	...	...
	Pabia ...	8,911	4,417	4,494	1,756	1,830	...	...	...	...	...	...	...	...	...	...	...	...	509	465	...	...
	Dhobona ...	12,838	6,506	6,332	1,542	1,573	...	...	...	...	...	...	...	...	...	...	...	...	708	670	...	...
	Bhorehand ...	6,800	3,418	3,382	1,426	1,455	...	...	...	...	...	...	...	...	...	...	...	...	135	136	...	...
	Galchhand ...	7,121	3,614	3,507	1,499	1,452	...	...	...	...	...	...	...	...	...	...	...	...	232	220	...	...
	Ladna ...	8,100	3,984	4,116	1,177	1,167	...	...	...	...	...	...	...	...	...	...	...	...	51	41	...	...
	Dhadkia ...	8,287	4,242	4,045	1,560	1,458	...	...	...	...	...	...	...	...	...	...	...	...	28	20	...	...
	Tilaki ...	5,546	2,833	2,713	1,391	1,303	...	...	...	...	...	...	...	...	...	...	...	...	20	28	...	...
	Geria ...	7,687	3,837	3,850	1,910	1,964	...	...	...	...	...	...	...	...	...	...	...	...	59	50	...	...
	Sagaria ...	6,695	3,355	3,340	2,167	2,199	...	...	...	...	...	...	...	...	...	...	...	...	18	...	...	...
	Sairketia ...	11,432	5,813	5,619	3,787	3,708	...	...	...	...	...	...	...	...	...	...	...	...	42	28	...	...
	Asna ...	10,014	5,234	4,780	1,935	1,783	...	...	...	...	...	...	...	...	...	...	...	...	96	68	...	...
	Jalain ...	7,246	3,566	3,680	2,061	2,029	...	...	...	...	...	...	...	...	...	...	...	...	69	69	...	...
	Sundarpur ...	9,130	4,638	4,492	1,930	1,849	...	...	...	...	...	...	...	...	...	...	...	...	524	508	...	...
	Karaya ...	5,538	2,789	2,749	1,585	1,580	...	...	...	...	...	...	...	...	...	...	...	...	71	55	...	...
	Khajuri ...	8,800	4,505	4,295	2,797	2,064	...	...	...	...	...	...	...	...	...	...	...	...	37	31	...	...
	Amba ...	10,761	5,405	5,356	3,378	3,319	...	...	...	...	...	...	...	...	...	...	...	...	395	406	...	...
	Kasta ...	8,744	4,573	4,171	2,687	2,414	...	...	...	...	...	...	...	...	...	...	...	...	103	69	...	...
	Afzalpur ...	5,126	2,609	2,517	1,659	1,651	...	...	...	...	...	...	...	...	...	...	...	...	156	108	...	...
Rajmahal	...	131,862	66,778	65,084	41,914	40,438	1,431	960	580	130	9,168	9,437	155	4	31,315	30,001	3,608	288	18,119	17,779	1,730	165
	Rajmahal ...	60,890	30,389	30,501	18,846	18,908	...	...	...	...	...	...	...	...	...	...	...	...	7,796	7,755	...	...
	Barharwa ...	38,440	19,106	19,334	10,141	10,184	...	...	...	...	...	...	...	...	...	...	...	...	6,217	6,375	...	...
	Sahibganj ...	32,532	17,283	15,249	12,927	11,346	...	...	...	...	...	...	...	...	...	...	...	...	4,106	3,649	...	...

PROVINCIAL TABLE II—*continued*.

POPULATION OF REVENUE THANAS AND POLICE-STATIONS BY RELIGION AND LITERACY.

REVENUE THANA.	POLICE-STATION, SARDARI CIRCLE OR BUNGALOW.	CHRISTIANS. *No. of persons.* Males.	CHRISTIANS. *No. of persons.* Females.	CHRISTIANS. *No. literate.* Males.	CHRISTIANS. *No. literate.* Females.	TRIBAL. *No. of persons.* Males.	TRIBAL. *No. of persons.* Females.	TRIBAL. *No. literate.* Males.	TRIBAL. *No. literate.* Females.	OTHERS. *No. of persons.* Males.	OTHERS. *No. of persons.* Females.	OTHERS. *No. literate.* Males.	OTHERS. *No. literate.* Females.	NUMBER LITERATE (AGED 7 AND OVER). TOTAL. Persons.	TOTAL. Males.	TOTAL. Females.	AGED 7—13. Males.	AGED 7—13. Females.	AGED 14—23. Males.	AGED 14—23. Females.	AGED 24 AND OVER. Males.	AGED 24 AND OVER. Females.	LITERATE IN ENGLISH. Males.	LITERATE IN ENGLISH. Females.
1	2	24	25	26	27	28	29	30	31	32	33	34	35	36	37	38	39	40	41	42	43	44	45	46
SANTAL PARGANAS—continued.																								
	Karmatanr Hill Tract.	...	...	...	...	861	810	...	...	...	...	...	...	...	...	...	...	...	...	...	...	...	...	...
	Sundar Pahari	10	12	...	...	2,383	2,327	...	...	...	...	...	...	...	...	...	...	...	...	...	...	...	...	...
	Sundar Pahari Hill Tract.	...	...	...	...	203	218	...	...	...	...	...	...	...	...	...	...	...	...	...	...	...	...	...
	Dhamni ...	34	31	...	...	965	1,018	...	...	...	...	...	...	...	...	...	...	...	...	...	...	...	...	...
	Dhamni Hill Tract.	...	...	...	...	252	238	...	...	...	...	...	...	...	...	...	...	...	...	...	...	...	...	...
	Chandna I	1	2	...	...	1,639	1,741	...	...	...	...	...	...	...	...	...	...	...	...	...	...	...	...	...
	Chandna II ...	7	5	...	...	2,022	1,983	...	...	...	...	...	...	...	...	...	...	...	...	...	...	...	...	...
	Chandna Hill Tract.	...	...	...	...	1,179	1,236	...	...	...	...	...	...	...	...	...	...	...	...	...	...	...	...	...
	Bokrabandh I	...	...	...	...	1,658	1,637	...	...	...	...	...	...	...	...	...	...	...	...	...	...	...	...	...
	Bokrabandh II	...	...	...	...	1,165	1,175	...	...	...	...	...	...	...	...	...	...	...	...	...	...	...	...	...
	Boarijore ...	46	42	...	...	6,738	6,800	...	...	...	...	...	...	...	...	...	...	...	...	...	...	...	...	...
Jamtara Thana ...	...	853	644	282	130	50,084	49,329	427	35	...	...	...	...	9,297	8,746	551	892	98	2,147	195	5,707	258	1,593	60
	Sardari Circles.																							
	Jamtara ...	8	9	...	...	1,144	1,041	...	...	...	...	...	...	...	...	...	...	...	...	...	...	...	...	...
	Mihijam ...	28	50	...	...	1,029	1,906	...	...	...	...	...	...	...	...	...	...	...	...	...	...	...	...	...
	Kandahit ...	5	4	...	...	1,973	1,981	...	...	...	...	...	...	...	...	...	...	...	...	...	...	...	...	...
	Bagdahari ...	...	...	...	...	1,026	981	...	...	...	...	...	...	...	...	...	...	...	...	...	...	...	...	...
	Ghati ...	...	...	...	...	1,117	1,139	...	...	...	...	...	...	...	...	...	...	...	...	...	...	...	...	...
	Dakhinbahal	14	20	...	...	1,887	1,788	...	...	...	...	...	...	...	...	...	...	...	...	...	...	...	...	...
	Morro ...	4	6	...	...	694	731	...	...	...	...	...	...	...	...	...	...	...	...	...	...	...	...	...
	Narainpur ...	4	3	...	...	2,310	2,208	...	...	...	...	...	...	...	...	...	...	...	...	...	...	...	...	...
	Pindari ...	123	133	...	...	1,187	1,353	...	...	...	...	...	...	...	...	...	...	...	...	...	...	...	...	...
	Kalajhoria ...	9	5	...	...	1,497	1,488	...	...	...	...	...	...	...	...	...	...	...	...	...	...	...	...	...
	Pabia ...	20	26	...	...	2,123	2,184	...	...	...	...	...	...	...	...	...	...	...	...	...	...	...	...	...
	Dhobona ...	1	8	...	...	4,265	4,086	...	...	...	...	...	...	...	...	...	...	...	...	...	...	...	...	...
	Bhorchand ...	43	47	...	...	1,815	1,744	...	...	...	...	...	...	...	...	...	...	...	...	...	...	...	...	...
	Gaichhand ...	38	34	...	...	1,845	1,801	...	...	...	...	...	...	...	...	...	...	...	...	...	...	...	...	...
	Ladna ...	112	96	...	...	2,044	2,813	...	...	...	...	...	...	...	...	...	...	...	...	...	...	...	...	...
	Dhadkia ...	...	...	...	...	2,654	2,567	...	...	...	...	...	...	...	...	...	...	...	...	...	...	...	...	...
	Tilaki ...	3	2	...	...	1,510	1,480	...	...	...	...	...	...	...	...	...	...	...	...	...	...	...	...	...
	Geria ...	2	4	...	...	1,866	1,832	...	...	...	...	...	...	...	...	...	...	...	...	...	...	...	...	...
	Sagaria ...	35	23	...	...	1,135	1,118	...	...	...	...	...	...	...	...	...	...	...	...	...	...	...	...	...
	Sairketia ...	...	...	...	...	1,984	1,885	...	...	...	...	...	...	...	...	...	...	...	...	...	...	...	...	...
	Asna ...	377	163	...	...	2,826	2,816	...	...	...	...	...	...	...	...	...	...	...	...	...	...	...	...	...
	Jalain ...	...	...	...	...	1,436	1,583	...	...	...	...	...	...	...	...	...	...	...	...	...	...	...	...	...
	Sundarpur ...	5	9	...	...	2,176	2,126	...	...	...	...	...	...	...	...	...	...	...	...	...	...	...	...	...
	Karaya ...	1	...	...	...	1,132	1,114	...	...	...	...	...	...	...	...	...	...	...	...	...	...	...	...	...
	Khajuri ...	...	...	...	...	1,671	1,600	...	...	...	...	...	...	...	...	...	...	...	...	...	...	...	...	...
	Amba ...	...	...	...	...	1,632	1,651	...	...	...	...	...	...	...	...	...	...	...	...	...	...	...	...	...
	Kasta ...	10	10	...	...	1,773	1,678	...	...	...	...	...	...	...	...	...	...	...	...	...	...	...	...	...
	Afzalpur ...	...	...	...	...	794	758	...	...	...	...	...	...	...	...	...	...	...	...	...	...	...	...	...
Rajmahal	...	240	261	115	77	6,495	6,602	35	1	10	4	6	...	6,889	6,224	665	673	155	1,271	228	4,280	282	736	22
	Rajmahal ...	59	48	...	...	3,686	3,789	...	...	2	1	...	...	...	...	...	...	...	...	...	...	...	...	...
	Barharwa ...	74	79	...	...	2,674	2,696	...	...	...	...	...	...	...	...	...	...	...	...	...	...	...	...	...
	Sahibganj ...	107	134	...	...	136	117	...	...	8	3	...	...	...	...	...	...	...	...	...	...	...	...	...

PROVINCIAL TABLE II—*continued.*

POPULATION OF REVENUE THANAS AND POLICE-STATIONS BY RELIGION AND LITERACY.

REVENUE THANA.	POLICE-STATION, SARDARI CIRCLE OR BUNGALOW.	POPULATION.			HINDUS.														MUSLIMS.			
					TOTAL HINDUS.		BRAHMANS.				DEPRESSED CLASSES.				OTHER HINDUS.							
							Number of persons.		*Number literate.*		*Number of persons.*		*Number literate.*		*Number of persons.*		*Number literate.*		*Number of persons.*		*Number literate.*	
		Persons.	Males.	Females.	Males.	Females.	Males.	Females.	Males.	Females.	Males.	Females.	Males.	Females.	Males.	Females.	Males.	Females.	Males.	Females.	Males.	Females.
1	2	3	4	5	6	7	8	9	10	11	12	13	14	15	16	17	18	19	20	21	22	23
SANTAL PARGANAS—concluded.																						
Rajmahal Damin ...	...	199,274	98,641	100,433	17,843	18,200	131	83	64	10	5,304	5,457	61	6	12,408	12,660	753	29	5,704	5,632	256	16
	Bungalows.																					
	Kusma	11,241	5,595	5,646	1,208	1,252	...	...	...	...	...	...	...	...	...	...	...	...	316	307	...	...
	Kusma Hill Tract.	1,327	667	660	3	5	...	...	...	...	...	...	...	...	...	...	...	...	...	...	...	...
	Raksi ...	16,491	8,087	8,404	1,797	1,855	...	...	...	...	...	...	...	...	...	...	...	...	386	292	...	...
	Barhit ...	25,076	12,415	12,661	3,812	2,822	...	...	...	...	...	...	...	...	...	...	...	...	1,900	1,918	...	...
	Barhit Hill Tract.	2,258	1,084	1,174	...	...	...	...	...	...	...	...	...	...	...	...	...	...	...	...	...	...
	Ranga ...	12,046	6,032	6,014	1,048	1,041	...	...	...	...	...	...	...	...	...	...	...	...	272	230	...	...
	Durgapur ...	6,655	3,294	3,361	391	378	...	...	...	...	...	...	...	...	...	...	...	...	137	124	...	...
	Maharajpur ...	8,592	4,254	4,338	1,848	1,873	...	...	...	...	...	...	...	...	...	...	...	...	130	116	...	...
	Maharajpur Hill Tract.	888	456	432	...	...	...	...	...	...	...	...	...	...	...	...	...	...	...	...	...	...
	Banjhi ...	16,255	8,046	8,209	1,079	1,126	...	...	...	...	...	...	...	...	...	...	...	...	48	52	...	...
	Banjhi Hill Tract.	952	469	483	...	...	...	...	...	...	...	...	...	...	...	...	...	...	...	...	...	...
	Bario ...	19,797	9,840	9,957	1,868	1,899	...	...	...	...	...	...	...	...	...	...	...	...	828	810	...	...
	Bario Hill Tract.	2,064	1,000	1,064	...	...	...	...	...	...	...	...	...	...	...	...	...	...	...	...	...	...
	Brindaban ...	14,151	7,130	7,021	949	934	...	...	...	...	...	...	...	...	...	...	...	...	147	135	...	...
	Brindaban Hill Tract.	3,862	1,955	1,907	...	...	...	...	...	...	...	...	...	...	...	...	...	...	...	...	...	...
	Pathna ...	12,604	6,157	6,447	1,543	1,557	...	...	...	...	...	...	...	...	...	...	...	...	391	358	...	...
	Pathna Hill Tract.	2,870	1,387	1,483	...	...	...	...	...	...	...	...	...	...	...	...	...	...	...	...	...	...
	Sukrogarh ...	9,636	4,780	4,856	1,743	1,783	...	...	...	...	...	...	...	...	...	...	...	...	485	454	...	...
	Sukrogarh Hill Tract.	3,565	1,874	1,691	5	3	...	...	...	...	...	...	...	...	...	...	...	...	1	...	...	...
	Taljhari ...	4,878	2,473	2,407	440	475	...	...	...	...	...	...	...	...	...	...	...	...	40	37	...	...
	Taljhari Hill Tract.	1,223	629	594	...	...	...	...	...	...	...	...	...	...	...	...	...	...	...	...	...	...
	Mandro I ..	9,382	4,594	4,788	426	436	...	...	...	...	...	...	...	...	...	...	...	...	280	306	...	...
	Mandro II ...	10,849	5,308	5,541	681	760	...	...	...	...	...	...	...	...	...	...	...	...	443	493	...	...
	Mandro Hill Tract.	2,611	1,316	1,295	2	1	...	...	...	...	...	...	...	...	...	...	...	...	...	...	...	...
Pakaur ...	...	197,177	97,873	99,304	24,935	24,960	736	578	378	62	5,171	5,405	62	2	19,038	18,887	2,173	114	21,705	22,174	1,800	106
	Pakaur ...	59,545	29,535	30,010	7,944	7,909	...	...	...	...	...	...	...	...	...	...	...	...	11,891	12,153	...	...
	Pakuria ...	37,628	18,760	18,868	3,700	3,606	...	...	...	...	...	...	...	...	...	...	...	...	1,700	1,721	...	...
	Maheshpur ...	68,679	33,918	34,761	8,203	8,310	...	...	...	...	...	...	...	...	...	...	...	...	5,363	5,630	...	...
	Hiranpur Bazar	(a)34,926	17,898	17,028	6,314	6,029	...	...	...	...	...	...	...	...	...	...	...	...	3,504	2,949	...	...
Pakaur Damin ...	...	(a)78,397	40,150	38,247	4,267	3,761	44	22	13	1	986	926	6	...	3,237	2,818	173	10	2,158	1,650	60	5
	Bungalows.																					
	Hiranpur ...	8,278	4,211	4,067	789	730	...	...	...	...	...	...	...	...	...	...	...	...	982	938	...	...
	Surma ...	6,248	3,144	3,106	104	101	...	...	...	...	...	...	...	...	...	...	...	...	2	...	...	...
	Dumria ...	5,728	2,892	2,836	618	588	...	...	...	...	...	...	...	...	...	...	...	...	230	247	...	...
	Litipara ...	5,562	2,830	2,732	116	130	...	...	...	...	...	...	...	...	...	...	...	...	...	...	...	...
	Parerkolha ...	5,773	2,970	2,803	187	169	...	...	...	...	...	...	...	...	...	...	...	...	46	40	...	...
	Dumarchir ...	5,745	2,924	2,821	83	70	...	...	...	...	...	...	...	...	...	...	...	...	8	6	...	...
	Alubera ...	5,408	2,712	2,696	142	131	...	...	...	...	...	...	...	...	...	...	...	...	2	...	...	...
	Amrapara ...	9,056	4,535	4,521	653	623	...	...	...	...	...	...	...	...	...	...	...	...	103	106	...	...
	Simlong ...	5,258	2,719	2,539	82	90	...	...	...	...	...	...	...	...	...	...	...	...	4	7	...	...
	Dharampur ..	8,573	4,292	4,281	140	127	...	...	...	...	...	...	...	...	...	...	...	...	30	28	...	...
	Kunjobona ...	5,342	2,758	2,584	51	39	...	...	...	...	...	...	...	...	...	...	...	...	...	...	...	...
	Surujbera ...	3,824	1,925	1,899	76	67	...	...	...	...	...	...	...	...	...	...	...	...	...	...	...	...

PROVINCIAL TABLE II—*continued*.

POPULATION OF REVENUE THANAS AND POLICE-STATIONS BY RELIGION AND LITERACY.

REVENUE THANA.	POLICE-STATION, SARDARI CIRCLE OR BUNGALOW.	CHRISTIANS. No. of persons. Males.	Females.	No. literate. Males.	Females.	TRIBAL. No. of persons. Males.	Females.	No. literate. Males.	Females.	OTHERS. No. of persons. Males.	Females.	No. literate. Males.	Females.
1	3	34	35	36	27	38	39	30	31	32	33	34	35
SANTAL PARGANAS—concluded.													
Rajmahal Damin ...	*Bungalows.*	1,426	1,513	376	191	73,865	75,088	291	48	3		1	...
	Kusma ...	66	70	...	...	4,005	4,017	...	...		...	...	
	Kusma Hill Tract.	...	...	...	...	664	655	...	...	...	...	...	...
	Raksi ...	62	92	...		5,922	6,165	...	...	...	...	...	...
	Barhit	130	140	...		7,573	7,781		...	...	...	...	...
	Barhit Hill Tract.		...		...	1,084	1,174		...		...	...	...
	Ranga ...	90	86	...		4,632	4,657	...		...	...	...	...
	Durgapur	210	165	...		2,556	3,674	...	...	...	...	...	
	Maharajpur ..	61	51			3,215	3,208	...		...	...		
	Maharajpur Hill Tract	33	44		...	423	388	...	...	...	...	...	...
	Banjhi	1	3	...	...	6,918	7,029	...	...	...	...	...	...
	Banjhi Hill Tract.		...	...	...	460	483	...	...		...	...	...
	Bario ...	21	26	...	...	7,123	7,222	...	...	...	...	...	...
	Bario Hill Tract.		...	...	...	1,000	1,064	...	...	...	...	...	...
	Brindaban ..	74	70	...	...	5,957	5,882	...	...	3	...	...	...
	Brindaban Hill Tract.		...	...	...	1,065	1,907	...	...	...	...	...	...
	Pathna ..	154	328	...	...	4,069	4,304	...	...	...	...	...	...
	Pathna Hill Tract.	49	63	...	...	1,338	1,430	...	...	...	...	...	...
	Sukrogarh ..	4	5	...	...	2,548	2,614		...	...	...	...	...
	Sukrogarh Hill Tract.	31	23	...	...	1,837	1,665	...	...	...	...	...	...
	Taljhari ...	324	251	...	...	1,608	1,644	...	...	...	...	...	...
	Taljhari Hill Tract.	14	16	...	...	616	579		...	...	...	...	...
	Mandro I ...	45	37	...	...	3,843	4,019	...	...	...	...	...	...
	Mandro II ...	37	35		...	4,147	4,253	...	...	...	...	...	...
	Mandro Hill Tract.	...		...	...	1,314	1,294	...	...	...	...	...	...
Pakaur ...	...	900	1,024	92	142	50,333	51,146	390	12	...		...	...
	Pakaur ...	277	388	...	...	9,423	9,561		...	...	...	...	...
	Pakuria	384	308		...	13,076	13,246		...	...	...	...	...
	Maheshpur ..	199	300	...	...	20,154	20,612	...	...	...	...	...	...
	Hiranpur Bazar	171	147	...	...	7,909	7,903	...	...	...	...	...	...
Pakaur Damin ...	*Bungalows.*	167	157	39	113	33,558	32,079	70	1			...	...
	Hiranpur	53	40	...	...	2,387	2,350	...	...	...	...	...	...
	Surma	36	38	...	...	3,002	2,906	...	...	...	...	...	...
	Dumria ...	5	8	...	...	2,039	1,993	...	...	...	...	...	...
	Litipara ...	...	...	...	...	2,714	2,602		...	...	...	...	...
	Parerkolha .	5	6	...	...	2,732	2,588			...	...	...	...
	Dumarchir	7	8	...	...	2,826	2,737	...	...	...	...	...	...
	Alubera	4	6	...	...	2,564	2,559	...	...	...	...	...	...
	Amrapara ...	17	17	...	...	3,763	3,775	...	...		...	...	...
	Simlong ..	...	...	...	...	2,033	2,442	...	...		...	...	...
	Dharampur ..	7	10	...	...	4,115	4,116	...	...	...	...	...	...
	Kunjobona ...	2	2	...	...	3,705	3,543	...	...	...	...	...	...
	Surujbera ...	...	...	...	...	1,840	1,832	...	...	...	...	...	...

REVENUE THANA.	POLICE-STATION, SARDARI CIRCLE OR BUNGALOW.	NUMBER LITERATE (AGED 7 AND OVER). TOTAL. Persons.	Males.	Females.	Aged 7—13. Males.	Females.	Aged 14—23. Males.	Females.	Aged 24 and over. Males.	Females.	Literate in English. Males.	Females.
1	3	36	37	38	39	40	41	42	43	44	45	46
Rajmahal Damin ...	*Bungalows.*	2,101	1,802	390	172	81	421	117	1,209	101	100	31
	Kusma ...	...	...	...	...	...	...	...	...	...	...	...
	Kusma Hill Tract.	...	...	...	...	...	...	...	...	...	...	...
	Raksi ...	...	...	...	...		...	...	...	...	...	...
	Barhit	...	...		...	...	...	...	...	...	...	...
	Barhit Hill Tract.	...	...	...	...	...	...	...	...	...	...	...
	Ranga ...	...	...		...	...	...	...	...	...	...	...
	Durgapur	...	...	...	...	...	...	...	...	...	...	...
	Maharajpur ..	...	...	...	...	...		...	...	...	...	...
	Maharajpur Hill Tract	...	...	...	...	...	...	...	...	...	...	...
	Banjhi	...	...	...	...	...	...	...	...	...	...	...
	Banjhi Hill Tract.	...	...	...	...	...	...	...	...	...	...	...
	Bario ...	...	...	...	...	...	...	...	...	...	...	...
	Bario Hill Tract.	...	...	...	...	...	...	...	...	...	...	...
	Brindaban ..	...	...	...	...	...	...	...	...	...	...	...
	Brindaban Hill Tract.	...	...	...	...	...	...	...	...	...	...	...
	Pathna ..	...	...	...	...	...	...	...	...	...	...	...
	Pathna Hill Tract.	...	...	...	...		...	...	...	...	...	...
	Sukrogarh ..	...	...	...	...	...	...	...	...	...	...	...
	Sukrogarh Hill Tract.	...	...	...	...	...	...	...	...	...	...	...
	Taljhari ...	...	...	...	...	...	...	...	...	...	...	...
	Taljhari Hill Tract.	...	...	...	...	...	...	...	...	...	...	...
	Mandro I ...	...	...	...	...	...	...	...	...	...	...	...
	Mandro II ...	...	...	...	...	...	...	...	...	...	...	...
	Mandro Hill Tract.	...	...	...	...	...	...	...	...	...	...	...
Pakaur ...	...	5,339	4,901	438	516	88	1,006	136	3,380	214	381	25
	Pakaur ...	...	...	...	...	...	...	...	...	...	...	...
	Pakuria	...	...	...	...	...	...	...	...	...	...	...
	Maheshpur ..		...	...	...	...	...	...	...	...	...	...
	Hiranpur Bazar	...	...	...	...	...	...	...	...	...	...	...
Pakaur Damin ...	*Bungalows.*	499	369	130	15	29	74	16	280	65	21	4
	Hiranpur		...	...	...	...	...	...	...	...	...	...
	Surma	...	...	...	...	...	...		...	...	...	...
	Dumria ...	...	...		...	...	...		...	...	...	...
	Litipara ...	...	...	...	...		...	...	...	...	...	...
	Parerkolha .	...	...	...			...	...	...	...	...	...
	Dumarchir	...	...	...	...	...	...	...	...	...	...	...
	Alubera	...	...	...	...	...	...	...	...	...	...	...
	Amrapara ...	...	...	...	...	...	...	...	...	...	...	...
	Simlong ..	...	...	...	...	...	...	...	...	...	...	...
	Dharampur ..	...	...	...	...	...	...	...	...	...	...	...
	Kunjobona ...	...	...	...	...	...	...	...	...	...	...	...
	Surujbera ...	...	...	...	...	...	...	...	...	...	...	...

(a) *Pakaur Damin* includes three mauzas (*Kamalghati*, *Jabardaha* and *Hiranpur Bazar*) which belong to police-station *Hiranpur Bazar*.

PROVINCIAL TABLE II—*continued.*

Population of Revenue Thanas and Police-stations by Religion and Literacy.

Revenue Thana.	Police-station.	Population. Persons.	Population. Males.	Population. Females.	Hindus. Total Hindus. Males.	Hindus. Total Hindus. Females.	Brahmans. Number of persons. Males.	Brahmans. Number of persons. Females.	Brahmans. Number literate. Males.	Brahmans. Number literate. Females.	Depressed Classes. Number of persons. Males.	Depressed Classes. Number of persons. Females.	Depressed Classes. Number literate. Males.	Depressed Classes. Number literate. Females.	Other Hindus. Number of persons. Males.	Other Hindus. Number of persons. Females.	Other Hindus. Number literate. Males.	Other Hindus. Number literate. Females.	Muslims. Number of persons. Males.	Muslims. Number of persons. Females.	Muslims. Number literate. Males.	Muslims. Number literate. Females.
1	2	3	4	5	6	7	8	9	10	11	12	13	14	15	16	17	18	19	20	21	22	23
CUTTACK	...	**2,176,707**	**1,028,134**	**1,148,573**	**996,424**	**1,110,406**	**89,859**	**96,162**	**36,595**	**1,919**	**185,941**	**206,106**	**3,012**	**79**	**720,624**	**808,138**	**105,858**	**7,718**	**29,965**	**36,139**	**5,307**	**528**
Cuttack	...	**237,148**	117,897	119,251	110,142	111,000	9,121	7,592	5,188	515	19,629	21,189	427	23	81,392	82,210	17,014	1,869	6,619	6,685	1,756	106
	Cuttack Town	**64,197**	35,489	28,708	29,437	22,476	...	...	...	...	...	...	...	...	...	...	...	...	5,075	4,786	...	...
	Cuttack Sadr	**112,525**	53,582	58,943	52,436	57,499	...	...	...	...	...	...	...	...	...	...	...	...	1,111	1,416	...	...
	Tangi ...	**60,426**	28,826	31,600	28,269	31,025	...	...	...	...	...	...	...	...	...	...	...	...	433	483	...	...
Banki	...	**84,406**	40,984	43,422	40,603	43,095	3,543	3,787	1,199	93	4,175	4,592	92	2	32,885	34,716	3,372	310	172	138	47	1
	Banki ...	**64,136**	31,303	32,833	30,959	32,534	...	...	...	...	...	...	...	...	...	...	...	...	135	110	...	...
	Baideswar ...	**20,270**	9,681	10,589	9,644	10,561	...	...	...	...	...	...	...	...	...	...	...	...	37	28	...	...
Salipur	...	**286,449**	134,106	142,343	118,155	134,410	11,528	12,740	5,118	341	23,061	28,086	387	12	82,666	93,584	12,356	1,013	6,946	7,927	1,019	157
	Salipur ...	**143,728**	67,784	75,944	63,843	70,690	...	...	...	...	...	...	...	...	...	...	...	...	3,936	5,239	...	...
	Mahanga ...	**82,304**	37,793	44,511	36,613	43,057	...	...	...	...	...	...	...	...	...	...	...	...	1,180	1,454	...	...
	Keshnagar ...	**40,417**	18,529	21,888	17,699	20,654	...	...	...	...	...	...	...	...	...	...	...	...	830	1,234	...	...
Tirtol	...	**193,491**	91,901	101,590	90,053	98,982	6,204	6,628	2,539	101	13,720	15,003	194	4	70,129	77,351	7,726	470	1,842	2,601	240	8
	Tirtol ...	**141,391**	66,330	75,061	64,607	72,576	...	...	...	...	...	...	...	...	...	...	...	...	1,717	2,478	...	...
	Ersama ...	**52,100**	25,571	26,529	25,446	26,406	...	...	...	...	...	...	...	...	...	...	...	...	125	123	...	...
Jagatsinghpur ...	...	**306,497**	143,783	162,714	140,465	158,304	14,030	15,488	5,179	210	28,643	31,832	305	10	97,784	110,984	11,465	788	3,316	4,409	487	21
	Jagatsinghpur	**154,648**	72,665	81,983	70,763	79,401	...	...	...	...	...	...	...	...	...	...	...	...	1,000	2,581	...	...
	Gobindpur ...	**82,379**	38,601	43,778	37,572	42,408	...	...	...	...	...	...	...	...	...	...	...	...	1,020	1,370	...	...
	Balikuda ...	**69,470**	32,517	36,953	32,130	36,405	...	...	...	...	...	...	...	...	...	...	...	...	387	458	...	...
Kendrapara	...	**248,069**	117,312	130,757	114,712	127,537	9,036	10,315	4,250	130	17,500	20,001	366	10	87,186	97,221	13,498	778	2,588	3,210	433	43
	Kendrapara	**134,909**	63,576	71,333	61,552	68,022	...	...	...	...	...	...	...	...	...	...	...	...	2,016	2,401	...	...
	Patkura ...	**113,160**	53,736	59,424	53,160	58,615	...	...	...	...	...	...	...	...	...	...	...	...	572	809	...	...
Patamundi	...	**127,112**	58,446	68,666	57,591	67,782	4,570	5,284	2,164	87	11,046	11,920	414	5	41,966	50,578	8,911	301	798	834	108	4
	Patamundi ...	**100,913**	45,572	55,341	44,839	54,561	...	...	...	...	...	...	...	...	...	...	...	...	724	776	...	...
	Mahakalpara	**26,199**	12,874	13,325	12,752	13,221	...	...	...	...	...	...	...	...	...	...	...	...	74	58	...	...
Aul or Rajabari ...	...	**121,317**	56,240	65,077	55,420	64,146	3,400	3,554	1,225	41	8,932	9,612	140	3	43,088	50,980	5,627	419	813	931	69	5
	Aul ...	**87,962**	40,008	47,954	39,256	47,075	...	...	...	...	...	...	...	...	...	...	...	...	752	879	...	...
	Rajnagar ...	**33,355**	16,232	17,123	16,164	17,071	...	...	...	...	...	...	...	...	...	...	...	...	61	52	...	...
Jajpur	...	**281,789**	129,596	152,193	125,798	147,588	14,687	17,166	4,624	168	29,722	33,863	361	5	81,389	97,539	13,911	965	3,796	4,601	616	71
	Jajpur ...	**156,781**	71,868	84,913	69,613	82,218	...	...	...	...	...	...	...	...	...	...	...	...	2,253	2,691	...	...
	Binjharpur ...	**125,008**	57,738	67,280	56,185	65,370	...	...	...	...	...	...	...	...	...	...	...	...	1,543	1,910	...	...
Dharamshala	...	**310,429**	147,869	162,560	143,485	157,562	12,822	13,608	5,100	234	28,524	30,988	326	6	102,139	112,966	11,078	715	4,075	4,803	542	22
	Dharamshala ..	**118,614**	56,156	62,458	54,531	60,553	...	...	...	...	...	...	...	...	...	...	...	...	1,581	1,864	...	...
	Sukinda ...	**44,584**	21,902	22,682	21,811	22,584	...	...	...	...	...	...	...	...	...	...	...	...	90	98	...	...
	Barehana ...	**85,518**	40,597	44,921	39,010	43,117	...	...	...	...	...	...	...	...	...	...	...	...	1,575	1,780	...	...
	Korai ...	**61,713**	29,214	32,499	28,133	31,308	...	...	...	...	...	...	...	...	...	...	...	...	829	1,052	...	...

PROVINCIAL TABLE II—*continued.*

Population of Revenue Thanas and Police-stations by Religion and Literacy.

Revenue Thana.	Police-station.	Christians. No. of persons. Males.	Christians. No. of persons. Females.	Christians. No. literate. Males.	Christians. No. literate. Females.	Tribal. No. of persons. Males.	Tribal. No. of persons. Females.	Tribal. No. literate. Males.	Tribal. No. literate. Females.	Others. No. of persons. Males.	Others. No. of persons. Females.	Others. No. literate. Males.	Others. No. literate. Females.	Number literate (aged 7 and over). Total. Persons.	Total. Males.	Total. Females.	Aged 7—13. Males.	Aged 7—13. Females.	Aged 14—23. Males.	Aged 14—23. Females.	Aged 24 and over. Males.	Aged 24 and over. Females.	Literate in English. Males.	Literate in English. Females.
1	2	24	25	26	27	28	29	30	31	32	33	34	35	36	37	38	39	40	41	42	43	44	45	46
CUTTACK	...	**1,222**	**1,651**	**786**	**1,033**	**272**	**166**	**9**	...	**251**	**211**	**92**	**9**	**162,945**	**151,659**	**11,286**	**12,476**	**2,084**	**34,679**	**3,805**	**104,504**	**5,397**	**12,259**	**609**
Cuttack	...	1,063	1,514	692	960	45	34	8	...	28	18	23	9	28,679	25,108	3,571	1,873	690	6,410	1,174	16,826	1,707	5,808	535
	Cuttack Town	946	1,427	...	...	9	1	...	...	22	18	...	...	...	...	...	...	...	...	...	...	...	...	...
	Cuttack Sadr	39	28	...	...	...	...	...	...	6	...	...	...	...	...	...	...	...	...	...	...	...	...	...
	Tangi ...	88	50	...	...	36	33	...	...	...	...	...	...	...	...	...	...	...	...	...	...	...	...	...
Banki	...	2	6	2	1	...	...	...	...	207	183	66	...	5,185	4,778	407	498	99	1,003	158	3,277	150	346	3
	Banki ...	2	6	...	...	...	...	...	...	207	183	...	...	...	...	...	...	...	...	...	...	...	...	...
	Baideswar ...	...	...	...	...	...	...	...	...	...	...	...	...	...	...	...	...	...	...	...	...	...	...	...
Salipur	...	5	6	4	3	...	...	...	...	...	...	...	...	20,410	18,884	1,526	1,452	200	4,194	500	13,238	826	1,388	10
	Salipur ...	5	6	...	...	...	...	...	...	...	...	...	...	...	...	...	...	...	...	...	...	...	...	...
	Mahanga ..	...	...	...	...	...	...	...	...	...	...	...	...	...	...	...	...	...	...	...	...	...	...	...
	Keshnagar ...	...	...	...	...	...	...	...	...	...	...	...	...	...	...	...	...	...	...	...	...	...	...	...
Tirtol	...	6	7	6	1	...	...	...	...	...	...	...	...	11,289	10,705	584	771	108	2,417	217	7,517	259	322	6
	Tirtol ...	6	7	...	...	...	...	...	...	...	...	...	...	...	...	...	...	...	...	...	...	...	...	...
	Ersama ...	...	...	...	...	...	...	...	...	...	...	...	...	...	...	...	...	...	...	...	...	...	...	...
Jagatsinghpur	...	2	1	1	...	...	...	...	...	...	...	...	...	18,466	17,437	1,029	1,484	176	3,887	350	12,066	508	812	10
	Jagatsinghpur	2	1	...	...	...	...	...	...	...	...	...	...	...	...	...	...	...	...	...	...	...	...	...
	Gobindpur ...	...	...	...	...	...	...	...	...	...	...	...	...	...	...	...	...	...	...	...	...	...	...	...
	Balikuda ...	...	...	...	...	...	...	...	...	...	...	...	...	...	...	...	...	...	...	...	...	...	...	...
Kendrapara	...	9	10	9	3	...	...	...	...	3	...	...	...	19,519	18,546	973	1,804	227	4,313	321	12,429	425	1,177	18
	Kendrapara ...	8	10	...	...	...	1	...	...	...	...	...	...	...	...	...	...	...	...	...	...	...	...	...
	Patkura ...	1	...	...	...	...	...	...	...	3	...	...	...	...	...	...	...	...	...	...	...	...	...	...
Patamundi	...	57	50	23	30	...	...	...	...	...	...	...	...	12,137	11,620	517	1,131	109	2,646	180	7,843	219	481	5
	Patamundi ...	9	4	...	...	...	...	...	...	...	...	...	...	...	...	...	...	...	...	...	...	...	...	...
	Mahakalpara	48	46	...	...	...	...	...	...	...	...	...	...	...	...	...	...	...	...	...	...	...	...	...
Aul or Rajabari ...	...	7	...	7	..	...	...	...	...	...	...	...	...	7,536	7,068	468	610	92	1,533	168	4,925	208	218	3
	Aul ...	...	...	...	...	...	...	...	...	...	...	...	...	...	...	...	...	...	...	...	...	...	...	...
	Rajnagar ...	7	...	...	...	...	...	...	...	...	...	...	...	...	...	...	...	...	...	...	...	...	...	...
Jajpur	...	1	3	...	2	...	...	...	...	1	1	...	...	20,713	19,512	1,201	1,458	205	4,411	385	13,649	611	983	10
	Jajpur ...	1	3	...	...	...	...	...	...	1	1	...	...	...	...	...	...	...	...	...	...	...	...	...
	Binjharpur ...	...	...	...	...	...	...	...	...	...	...	...	...	...	...	...	...	...	...	...	...	...	...	...
Dharamshala	...	70	54	42	33	227	132	1	...	12	9	3	...	19,011	18,001	1,010	1,401	178	3,865	348	12,735	489	724	9
	Dharamshala	44	41	...	...	...	...	...	...	...	...	...	...	...	...	...	...	...	...	...	...	...	...	...
	Sukinda ...	1	...	...	...	...	...	...	...	...	...	...	...	...	...	...	...	...	...	...	...	...	...	...
	Barohana ...	2	6	...	...	...	...	...	...	10	9	...	...	...	...	...	...	...	...	...	...	...	...	...
	Korai ...	23	7	...	...	227	132	...	...	2	...	...	...	...	...	...	...	...	...	...	...	...	...	...

BALASORE AND ANGUL.]

PROVINCIAL TABLE II—*continued.*

POPULATION OF REVENUE THANAS AND POLICE-STATIONS BY RELIGION AND LITERACY.

REVENUE THANA	POLICE-STATION	POPULATION			HINDUS														MUSLIMS			
					TOTAL HINDUS		BRAHMANS				DEPRESSED CLASSES				OTHER HINDUS				*Number of persons*		*Number literate.*	
							Number of persons		*Number literate*		*Number of persons*		*Number literate*		*Number of persons*		*Number literate*					
		Persons	Males	Females	Males	Females	Males	Females	Males	Females	Males	Females	Males	Females	Males	Females	Males	Females	Males	Females	Males	Females
1	2	3	4	5	6	7	8	9	10	11	12	13	14	15	16	17	18	19	20	21	72	23
BALASORE		**990,600**	**480,518**	**510,082**	**457,943**	**486,738**	**54,655**	**56,003**	**22,419**	**1,194**	**50,380**	**54,930**	**1,551**	**76**	**352,908**	**375,805**	**50,269**	**2,907**	**15,661**	**16,074**	**1,956**	**270**
Bhadrak		171,884	78,889	92 995	73,233	86,420	10,765	12 041	4 074	188	12,754	14 376	222	3	49 714	60,003	6,474	340	5 612	6,547	464	37
	Bhadrak	131,624	60,039	71 585	54 870	65,481													5 125	6 076	..	..
	Banta ..	40,260	18,850	21,410	18,363	20,939													487	471		..
Basudebpur	Basudebpur	78,757	36,549	42,208	35,945	41,573	5,269	5,751	2,210	101	3,858	3,618	148		27,818	32,204	4 127	226	604	635	69	5
Dhamnagar		133,711	61,758	71,953	60,381	70,507	9,421	10,321	3,636	150	9 095	10,398	239	2	41 865	49,788	6,637	456	1,376	1,446	267	15
	Dhamnagar	89,657	40 967	49,690	39,646	48,284													1 320	1 406		...
	Bhandaripukhuri	43,054	20,791	22,263	20,735	22,223													56	40		..
Chandbali	Chandbali	62,419	30,092	32 327	29,600	31,943	2,687	2,882	1,053	22	1,777	1,931	40	1	24,936	27,130	2,981	120	465	345	123	4
Soro		191,755	91 974	99,781	90,481	98,316	13,634	14,072	5,510	187	12 241	13 518	469	15	04 606	70,726	9 204	588	1 401	1 439	186	34
	Soro	93,582	45,845	47,737	45,005	46,887													840	850		
	Khaira ..	48,112	22 753	25 359	22,484	25,126								..					229	209		
	Simulia	50,061	23,376	26,685	22,992	26,303													332	380		
Balasore		111,759	58 230	53 529	53,993	49,401	6,486	5,344	2,881	176	4,174	4 067	172	20	43,333	39,990	6 707	663	3 192	3,053	647	130
	Balasore	84,988	44 558	40,430	40,812	36,871													2 706	2,485		
	Remna	26,771	13,672	13,099	13,181	12,530													486	568		
Jaleswar	Jaleswar	56,899	28 684	28,215	24,396	23,703	1,401	1,254	780	83	2,044	1,984	137	9	20 951	20,465	2,789	165	411	346	45	4
Baliapal		108,107	55,552	52,555	53,868	50,947	3,021	2,786	1,379	239	2,537	2,316	85	14	48,310	45 845	6,579	158	1 156	1,034	82	31
	Baliapal	35,702	18,384	17,318	17,656	16,621													263	104		
	Bhograi	72,405	37,168	35,237	36,212	34,326													893	840		
Basta		75,309	38,790	36,519	36,046	33,928	1,771	1,552	896	39	2,900	2,722	49	3	31 375	29,654	4,771	182	1 394	1,229	133	10
	Basta	46,608	24,043	22,565	22,237	20,857													867	744		
	Singla	28,701	14,747	13,954	13,809	13,071													527	485		
ANGUL ...		**222,736**	**108,925**	**113,811**	**80,344**	**83,319**	**2,359**	**2,186**	**1,205**	**71**	**15,516**	**16,202**	**548**	**16**	**62,469**	**64,931**	**4,728**	**437**	**176**	**117**	**92**	**7**
Angul		140,458	68,694	71,764	68 383	71,430	2,163	2,070	1,103	65	10 757	11,372	478	16	55,413	57,988	4,149	423	160	105	71	6
	Angul	62,004	30 242	31,762	30,034	31,582	1,451	1,440	739	45	5,171	5 395	284	12	23,412	24 747	1 471	256	122	83	47	3
	Bantala	19,880	9,635	10,245	9,619	10,231	316	315	178	15	1 710	1 874	88		7 593	8 042	600	53	16	14	7	1
	Jarpara	21,596	10,507	11,089	10,503	11,081	135	147	54	1	1,321	1 428	32	1	9,047	9,506	729	48	4	8	2	2
	Purunakot	8,464	4 264	4,200	4,208	4,156	41	1	33	1	476	484	8	1	3 691	3,601	295	7	14		13	
	Chhendipada	28,514	14,046	14,468	13 989	14,380	220	167	99	3	2 079	2 211	66	2	11 670	12,002	1,054	64	4		2	
Phulbani		82,278	40 231	42,047	12,011	11,889	196	116	102	6	4 759	4,830	70		7,056	6,943	579	14	16	12	11	1
	Phulbani	22,996	11,306	11,690	3 461	3,405	92	49	51	4	1 421	1,484	25		1,948	1,872	248	10	11	9	7	
	Khejuripara	21,846	10,649	11,197	4,212	4,147	56	38	25	2	2,550	2,544	25		1 606	1,565	102		2	3	2	1
	Phiringia	19,971	9 697	10,274	2,697	2,876	38	21	21		737	743	18		2 122	2,112	180		1		1	
	Gochhapara	17,465	8,579	8,886	1,441	1,461	10	8	5		51	59	2		1,380	1,394	49	4	2		1	

207

PROVINCIAL TABLE II—*continued.*

POPULATION OF REVENUE THANAS AND POLICE-STATIONS BY RELIGION AND LITERACY.

Revenue Thana.	Police-station.	Christians: No. of persons. Males.	Christians: No. of persons. Females.	Christians: No. literate. Males.	Christians: No. literate. Females.	Tribal: No. of persons. Males.	Tribal: No. of persons. Females.	Tribal: No. literate. Males.	Tribal: No. literate. Females.	Others: No. of persons. Males.	Others: No. of persons. Females.	Others: No. literate. Males.	Others: No. literate. Females.
1	2	34	35	36	37	28	29	30	31	32	33	34	35
BALASORE	...	**685**	**690**	**356**	**368**	**6,220**	**6,576**	**29**	**1**	**9**	**4**	**1**	...
Bhadrak	...	44	38	10	10	...	...	...	...	...	...	...	...
	Bhadrak ...	44	38	...	...	...	...	...	...	...	...	...	...
	Banta ...	...	...	...	...	...	...	...	...	...	...	...	...
Basudebpur	Basudebpur ...	...	...	...	...	...	...	...	...	...	...	...	...
Dhamnagar	...	1	...	1	...	...	...	...	...	...	...	...	...
	Dhamnagar ...	1	...	...	...	...	...	...	...	...	...	...	...
	Bhandaripukhuri.	...	...	...	...	...	...	...	...	...	...	...	...
Chandbali	Chandbali ...	27	30	9	10	...	...	...	...	...	...	...	...
Soro	...	3	2	1	1	40	24	...	...	...	...	...	...
	Soro ...	...	...	...	...	...	...	...	...	...	...	...	...
	Khaira ...	...	...	...	...	40	24	...	...	...	...	...	...
	Similia ...	3	2	...	...	...	...	...	...	...	...	...	...
Balasore	...	350	366	212	241	686	795	6	...	9	4	1	...
	Balasore ...	349	366	...	...	682	794	...	...	9	4	...	...
	Remna ...	1	...	...	...	4	1	...	...	...	...	...	...
Jaleswar	Jaleswar ...	172	173	91	83	3,705	3,993	21	1	...	...	...	...
Baliapal	...	1	...	1	...	527	574	2	...	...	...	...	...
	Baliapal ...	1	...	...	...	464	503	...	...	...	...	...	...
	Bhograi ...	...	...	...	...	63	71	...	...	...	...	...	...
Basta ...	...	88	83	22	23	1,262	1,380	...	...	...	...	...	...
	Basta ...	21	16	...	...	918	1,048	...	...	...	...	...	...
	Singla ...	67	66	...	...	344	332	...	...	...	...	...	...
ANGUL	...	**156**	**151**	**89**	**59**	**28,249**	**30,224**	**367**	**5**	...	...	...	...
Angul	...	104	117	52	38	97	112	...	...	...	...	...	...
	Angul ...	86	97	41	36	...	...	...	...	...	...	...	...
	Bantala ...	...	...	...	...	...	...	...	...	...	...	...	...
	Jarpara ...	...	...	...	...	...	...	...	...	...	...	...	...
	Purnakot ...	2	...	2	...	40	44	...	...	...	...	...	...
	Chhendipada	16	20	9	2	57	68	...	...	...	...	...	...
Phulbani	...	52	34	37	21	28,152	30,112	367	5	...	...	...	...
	Phulbani ...	42	30	31	19	7,792	8,246	124	1	...	...	...	...
	Khejuripara ...	7	3	3	2	6,428	7,044	166	...	...	...	...	...
	Phiringia ...	2	...	2	...	6,797	7,397	49	...	...	...	...	...
	Gochhapara ...	1	...	1	...	7,135	7,425	28	4	...	...	...	...

Revenue Thana.	Police-station.	Number literate (aged 7 and over): Total. Persons.	Total. Males.	Total. Females.	Aged 7—13. Males.	Aged 7—13. Females.	Aged 14—23. Males.	Aged 14—23. Females.	Aged 24 and over. Males.	Aged 24 and over. Females.	Literate in English. Males.	Literate in English. Females.
1	2	36	37	38	39	40	41	42	43	44	45	46
BALASORE	...	**81,397**	**76,581**	**4,816**	**6,126**	**777**	**16,277**	**1,614**	**54,178**	**2,425**	**4,505**	**86**
Bhadrak	...	11,831	11,253	578	756	106	2,392	108	8,105	272	752	14
	Bhadrak ...	...	...	...	...	...	...	...	...	...	...	...
	Banta ...	...	...	...	...	...	...	...	...	...	...	...
Basudebpur	Basudebpur ...	6,886	6,554	332	684	64	1,018	116	4,852	152	146	1
Dhamnagar	...	11,342	10,710	632	837	94	2,230	211	7,653	337	465	19
	Dhamnagar ...	...	...	...	...	...	...	...	...	...	...	...
	Bhandaripukhuri.	...	...	...	...	...	...	...	...	...	...	...
Chandbali	Chandbali ...	4,372	4,206	166	303	17	838	50	3,065	99	172	4
Soro	...	16,195	15,370	825	1,191	110	3,443	371	10,736	444	498	15
	Soro ...	...	...	...	...	...	...	...	...	...	...	...
	Khaira ...	...	...	...	...	...	...	...	...	...	...	...
	Similia ...	...	...	...	...	...	...	...	...	...	...	...
Balasore	...	11,865	10,626	1,239	879	208	2,433	403	7,324	628	1,717	31
	Balasore ...	...	...	...	...	...	...	...	...	...	...	...
	Remna ...	...	...	...	...	...	...	...	...	...	...	...
Jaleswar	Jaleswar ...	4,208	3,863	345	303	58	917	115	2,644	177	401	12
Baliapal	...	8,570	8,128	443	801	79	1,808	158	5,519	205	215	...
	Baliapal ...	...	...	...	...	...	...	...	...	...	...	...
	Bhograi ...	...	...	...	...	...	...	...	...	...	...	...
Basta ...	...	6,128	5,871	257	373	44	1,218	93	4,380	121	130	...
	Basta ...	...	...	...	...	...	...	...	...	...	...	...
	Singla ...	...	...	...	...	...	...	...	...	...	...	...
ANGUL	...	**7,614**	**7,019**	**595**	**1,226**	**175**	**1,935**	**177**	**3,858**	**243**	**457**	**26**
Angul	...	6,401	5,853	548	1,352	164	1,638	170	3,163	214	332	23
	Angul ...	3,934	3,582	352	300	106	871	107	1,111	139	222	23
	Bantala ...	942	873	69	83	15	200	18	591	36	30	...
	Jarpara ...	864	817	47	72	11	186	18	559	18	15	...
	Purnakot ...	360	351	9	25	1	62	6	264	2	35	...
	Chhendipada	1,301	1,230	71	273	31	319	21	638	19	30	1
Phulbani	...	1,213	1,166	47	174	11	297	7	695	39	135	3
	Phulbani ...	520	486	34	88	7	129	6	269	21	108	3
	Khejuripara ...	338	323	5	50	...	78	...	195	5	6	...
	Phiringia ...	271	271	...	31	...	68	...	172	...	6	...
	Gochhapara ...	94	86	8	5	4	22	1	59	3	5	...

PROVINCIAL TABLE II—*continued.*

POPULATION OF REVENUE THANAS AND POLICE-STATIONS BY RELIGION AND LITERACY.

REVENUE THANA	POLICE-STATION.	POPULATION.			HINDUS. Total Hindus.		Brahmans. Number of persons.		Brahmans. Number literate.		Depressed classes. Number of persons.		Depressed classes. Number literate.		Other Hindus. Number of persons.		Other Hindus. Number literate.		MUSLIMS. Number of persons.		MUSLIMS. Number literate.	
		Persons.	Males.	Females.	Males.	Females.	Males	Females.	Males	Females	Males	Females	Males.	Females	Males.	Females.	Males.	Females.	Males	Females.	Males.	Females.
1	2	3	4	5	6	7	8	9	10	11	12	13	14	15	16	17	18	19	20	21	22	23
PURI		**1,035,154**	**500,214**	**534,940**	**488,555**	**522,594**	**44,749**	**47,083**	**17,406**	**1,106**	**62,024**	**65,919**	**739**	**13**	**381,782**	**409,522**	**42,159**	**3,627**	**10,875**	**11,643**	**1,417**	**129**
Puri		255,921	127,152	128,669	126,098	127,907	15,473	15,604	6,234	494	13,852	14,028	137	3	96,773	98,275	9,656	892	932	679	195	10
	Puri town	37,568	20,703	16,865	20,239	16,652													344	131		
	Puri Sadr	69,545	34,484	35,061	34,429	35,009													54	52		
	Satyabadi	74,906	36,245	38,661	36,033	38,484													211	176		
	Bramhagiri	58,424	28,059	30,365	27,799	30,121													260	244		
	Krishnaprashad	15,378	7,661	7,717	7,598	7,641													68	76		
Gop		128,914	63,396	65,518	61,454	63,407	4,315	4,318	1,383	29	9,352	9,576	38	4	47,887	49,513	3,604	141	1,942	2,111	177	16
	Gop	59,350	29,240	30,110	28,708	29,506													532	604		
	Kakatpur	69,564	34,156	35,408	32,746	33,901													1,410	1,507		
Pipli		272,890	130,881	142,009	127,568	138,336	12,590	14,004	4,919	244	23,173	24,657	209		91,806	99,675	10,486	821	3,137	3,433	315	15
	Pipli	59,981	29,055	30,926	28,314	30,084													611	664		
	Balianta	39,759	18,801	20,958	18,675	20,796													126	163		
	Nimapara	74,434	35,817	38,617	34,886	37,655													931	962		
	Delang	46,818	22,394	24,424	22,108	24,116													284	299		
	Balipatna	51,898	24,814	27,084	23,585	25,685													1,185	1,345		
Khurda		262,560	124,790	137,770	120,317	132,795	8,874	9,264	3,702	303	12,223	13,668	202	6	90,220	109,863	13,433	1,346	3,996	4,536	654	85
	Khurda	82,087	38,681	43,406	36,926	41,327													1,695	2,016		
	Jatni	32,521	16,262	16,259	15,010	15,079													928	899		
	Bolgarh	35,114	16,341	18,773	15,819	18,046													522	727		
	Bhubaneswar	38,476	18,662	19,814	18,290	19,470													340	308		
	Begunia	51,880	23,906	27,974	23,464	27,461													442	512		
	Chandaka	22,482	10,938	11,544	10,808	11,413													69	74		
Banpur		114,969	53,995	60,974	53,118	60,079	3,597	3,893	1,269	36	3,424	3,090	63		46,097	52,196	4,981	427	868	885	76	3
	Banpur	63,854	29,965	33,889	29,638	33,567													321	314		
	Tangi	51,115	24,030	27,065	23,480	26,512													547	571		
SAMBALPUR		**880,945**	**431,460**	**449,485**	**426,029**	**444,149**	**17,489**	**18,004**	**8,823**	**826**	**18,856**	**19,630**	**473**	**13**	**389,684**	**406,515**	**26,873**	**1,397**	**2,008**	**1,805**	**614**	**66**
Sambalpur	Sambalpur	57,553	28,231	29,322	27,298	28,443	2,788	2,469	1,700	255	1,216	1,351	48	..	23,294	24,633	2,324	230	732	708	265	34
Jharsugra	Jharsugra	51,125	25,284	25,841	24,365	24,984	1,063	937	407	47	2,099	2,240	30	..	21,306	21,807	1,638	124	468	443	115	15
Laikera	Laikera	51,043	24,940	26,103	24,895	26,084	283	252	148	5	2,143	2,162	30		22,469	23,670	843	29	37	17	10	.
Mura	Mura	30,089	14,805	15,284	14,582	15,075	387	375	172	4	1,524	1,596	19		12,671	13,104	583	12	66	49	9	..
Rampella	Rampella	32,385	15,715	16,670	15,530	16,437	963	1,012	503	70	1,291	1,375	41	...	13,276	14,050	964	32	77	96	13	
Katarbagha	Katarbagha	39,711	19,272	20,439	18,128	19,238	857	976	402	46	1,093	1,131	18	.	16,179	17,131	1,099	54	60	49	31	2
Sason	Sason	32,388	15,502	16,886	15,287	16,672	686	891	311	18	658	696	5	.	13,943	15,145	561	14	36	18	11	1
Dhama	Dhama	30,934	14,711	16,223	14,587	16,135	1,335	1,391	581	48	394	383	19		12,958	14,361	676	24	11		8	.
Mundher	Mundher	18,311	9,018	9,293	8,938	9,196	138	100	68	7	742	764		1	8,563	8,823	170	2	26	14	8	..
Bargarh	Bargarh	60,956	29,831	31,125	29,646	30,936	1,773	1,808	902	133	734	786	50	3	27,139	28,342	4,374	304	82	68	31	4
Attabira	Attabira	53,985	26,253	27,732	26,161	27,635	1,527	1,062	738	48	1,014	1,064	13		23,620	24,909	1,325	46	40	43	12	2
Sohela	Sohela	44,660	21,954	22,706	21,718	22,449	410	374	245	18	684	764	32	2	20,624	21,311	2,074	117	82	86	19	5
Ambabhona	Ambabhona	31,041	15,200	15,841	15,179	15,822	230	234	115	4	898	906	16		14,051	14,682	846	25	5	8	2	...
Padampur	Padampur	41,974	20,814	21,160	20,547	20,918	527	482	217	11	646	624	12	4	19,374	19,812	870	29	109	96	31	
Bheran	Bheran	50,386	24,344	26,042	24,332	26,035	1,686	2,220	749	43	656	654	1	1	21,990	23,161	1,184	41	12	7	1	...
Bijepur	Bijepur	43,455	21,432	22,023	21,334	21,932	430	430	194	6	588	614	15	..	20,316	20,888	776	15	9	0	4	..
Melchhamunda	Melchhamunda	26,640	13,245	13,395	13,090	13,252	319	334	147	17	402	393	12	1	12,378	12,585	751	31	10	12	3	..
Gaisilat	Gaisilat	29,251	14,559	14,692	14,530	14,672	367	348	160	2	275	264	3		13,888	14,060	469	19	3	1	2	
Jagdalpur	Jagdalpur	34,705	17,303	17,402	17,226	17,327	154	143	55	1	609	547	9	..	16,463	16,637	489	10	21	7	8	
Barpali	Barpali	47,434	23,127	24,307	23,063	24,242	777	800	447	34	655	739	92		21,631	22,703	3,582	198	24	22	14	3
Bhatli	Bhatli	43,947	21,430	22,517	21,247	22,331	793	752	354	7	733	794	6	1	19,721	20,785	1,146	47	42	29	11	...
Paikmal	Paikmal	28,972	14,490	14,482	14,337	14,334	101	75	29		303	383	2		13,933	13,976	179	4	47	24	9	...

PROVINCIAL TABLE II—*continued.*

Population of Revenue Thanas and Police-stations by Religion and Literacy.

Revenue Thana.	Police-station.	Christians. No. of persons. Males.	Christians. No. of persons. Females.	Christians. No. literate. Males.	Christians. No. literate. Females.	Tribal. No. of persons. Males.	Tribal. No. of persons. Females.	Tribal. No. literate. Males.	Tribal. No. literate. Females.	Others. No. of persons. Males.	Others. No. of persons. Females.	Others. No. literate. Males.	Others. No. literate. Females.
1	2	24	25	26	27	28	29	30	31	32	33	34	35
PURI	...	**768**	**768**	**412**	**341**	...	...	...	...	**16**	**5**	**14**	**3**
Puri	...	130	83	68	42	...	...	...	...	2	...	2	...
	Puri Town ...	118	82	...	...	...	...	...	...	2	...	...	...
	Puri Sadr ...	1	...	...	...	...	...	...	...	...	...	...	...
	Satyabadi ...	1	1	...	...	...	...	...	...	...	...	...	...
	Bramhagiri ...	...	...	...	...	...	...	...	...	...	...	...	...
	Krishnaprashad	...	...	...	...	...	...	...	...	...	...	...	...
Gop	...	...	...	...	...	...	...	...	...	...	...	...	...
	Gop ...	...	...	...	...	...	...	...	...	...	...	...	...
	Kakatpur ...	...	...	...	...	...	...	...	...	...	...	...	...
Pipli	...	176	341	67	61	...	...	...	...	...	...	...	...
	Pipli ...	130	178	...	...	...	...	...	...	...	...	...	...
	Balianta ...	...	...	...	...	...	...	...	...	...	...	...	...
	Nimapara ...	...	...	...	...	...	...	...	...	...	...	...	...
	Delang ...	2	9	...	...	...	...	...	...	...	...	...	...
	Balipatna ...	44	54	...	...	...	...	...	...	...	...	...	...
Khurda	...	463	434	272	235	...	...	...	...	14	5	12	3
	Khurda ...	58	63	...	...	...	...	...	...	2	1	...	
	Jatni ...	316	278	...	...	...	...	...	...	8	3	...	...
	Bolgarh ...	...	...	...	...	...	...	...	...	...	...	...	...
	Bhubaneswar	29	35	...	...	...	...	...	...	3	1	...	...
	Begunia ...	...	1	...	...	...	...	...	...	...	...	...	...
	Chandaka ...	60	58	...	...	...	...	...	...	1	...	...	...
Banpur	...	9	10	5	3	...	...	...	...	...	...	...	...
	Banpur ...	6	8	...	...	...	...	...	...	...	...	...	...
	Tangi ...	3	2	...	...	...	...	...	...	...	...	...	...
SAMBALPUR	...	**1,780**	**1,838**	**335**	**99**	**1,554**	**1,630**	**11**	...	**89**	**63**	**39**	**6**
Sambalpur	Sambalpur ...	168	129	92	30	27	36	2	...	6	7	3	3
Jharsugra	Jharsugra ...	240	221	78	30	173	180	...	...	20	24	13	3
Laikera	Laikera ...	2	1	2	1	2	1	...	...	4	...	...	...
Mura	Mura ...	150	152	15	1	7	8	...	...	...	...	...	...
Rampella	Rampella ...	35	43	1	...	83	96	...	...	...	...	...	...
Katarbagha	Katarbagha ...	75	94	7	...	1,000	1,058	6	...	...	...	...	...
Sason	Sason ...	164	171	23	4	8	13	...	...	17	12	11	...
Dhama	Dhama ...	1	1	1	...	111	84	...	...	1	3	1	...
Mundher	Mundher ...	54	83	4	...	...	...	...	...	...	...	...	...
Bargarh	Bargarh ...	86	100	20	14	14	21	1	...	3	...	1	...
Attabira	Attabira ...	36	34	...	...	16	21	...	...	...	...	...	...
Sohela	Sohela ...	154	171	14	1	...	...	...	...	...	...	...	...
Ambabhona	Ambabhona ...	15	10	4	...	1	1	...	...	...	...	...	...
Padampur	Padampur ...	139	144	13	2	3	2	...	...	16	...	4	...
Bheran	Bheran ...	...	...	...	...	...	...	...	...	...	...	...	...
Bijepur	Bijepur ...	80	82	6	...	...	...	...	...	...	...	...	...
Melchhamunda	Melchhamunda	136	131	2	...	...	...	...	...	...	...	...	...
Gaisilat	Gaisilat ...	26	19	2	...	...	...	...	...	...	...	...	...
Jagdalpur	Jagdalpur ...	51	63	9	2	...	...	...	...	5	...	5	...
Barpali	Barpali ...	37	43	24	5	3	...	...	...	...	...	...	...
Bhatli	Bhatli ...	87	91	19	...	54	66	3	...	...	...	...	...
Paikmal	Paikmal ...	46	61	...	...	52	56	...	...	8	17	1	...

Revenue Thana.	Police-station.	Number literate (aged 7 and over). Total. Persons.	Total. Males.	Total. Females.	Aged 7—13. Males.	Aged 7—13. Females.	Aged 14—23. Males.	Aged 14—23. Females.	Aged 24 and over. Males.	Aged 24 and over. Females.	Literate in English. Males.	Literate in English. Females.
1	2	36	37	38	39	40	41	42	43	44	45	46
PURI	...	**67,366**	**62,147**	**5,219**	**4,887**	**916**	**12,973**	**1,607**	**44,287**	**2,696**	**4,474**	**261**
Puri	...	17,733	16,292	1,44[illegible]	1,173	213	3,390	431	11,729	797	1,889	93
	Puri Town ...	...	...	...	...	...	...	...	...	...	...	...
	Puri Sadr ...	...	...	...	...	...	...	...	...	...	...	...
	Satyabadi ...	...	...	...	...	...	...	...	...	...	...	...
	Bramhagiri ...	...	...	...	...	...	...	...	...	...	...	...
	Krishnaprashad	...	...	...	...	...	...	...	...	...	...	...
Gop	...	5,291	5,101	190	355	41	1,036	64	3,720	85	98	1
	Gop ...	...	...	...	...	...	...	...	...	...	...	...
	Kakatpur ...	...	...	...	...	...	...	...	...	...	...	...
Pipli	...	17,137	15,996	1,141	1,103	161	3,562	334	11,331	646	407	5
	Pipli ...	...	...	...	...	...	...	...	...	...	...	...
	Balianta ...	...	...	...	...	...	...	...	...	...	...	...
	Nimapara ...	...	...	...	...	...	...	...	...	...	...	...
	Delang ...	...	...	...	...	...	...	...	...	...	...	...
	Balipatna ...	...	...	...	...	...	...	...	...	...	...	...
Khurda	...	20,342	18,364	1 978	1,653	395	3,742	634	12,969	949	1,777	182
	Khurda ...	...	...	...	...	...	...	...	...	...	...	...
	Jatni ...	...	...	...	...	...		...	...	...	...	...
	Bolgarh ...	...	...	...	...	...	...	...	...	...	...	...
	Bhubaneswar	...	...	...	...	...	...	...	...	...	...	...
	Begunia ...	...	...	...	...	...	...	...	...	...	...	...
	Chandaka ...	...	...	...	...	...	...	...	...	...	...	...
Banpur	...	6,863	6,394	469	603	106	1,253	144	4,538	219	343	...
	Banpur ...	...	...	...	...	...	...	...	...	...	...	...
	Tangi ...	...	...	...	...	...	...	...	...	...	...	...
SAMBALPUR	...	**39,575**	**37,168**	**2,407**	**2,824**	**515**	**8,349**	**660**	**25,995**	**1,232**	**2,449**	**82**
Sambalpur	Sambalpur ...	4,982	4,431	551	468	119	1,251	134	2,692	298	1,139	36
Jharsugra	Jharsugra ...	2,590	2,371	219	133	26	480	62	1,740	131	346	36
Laikera	Laikera ...	1,068	1,033	35	29	8	219	7	785	20	23	1
Mura	Mura ...	765	748	17	22	3	132	3	594	11	25	...
Rampella	Rampella ...	1,623	1,521	102	123	22	324	30	1,074	50	115	...
Katarbagha	Katarbagha ...	1,666	1,562	104	31	25	312	32	1,160	47	49	1
Sason	Sason ...	959	922	37	40	6	189	15	683	16	44	2
Dhama	Dhama ...	1,358	1,286	72	80	15	275	19	922	38	47	...
Mundher	Mundher ...	260	250	10	1	3	43	1	206	6	11	...
Bargarh	Bargarh ...	5,927	5,469	458	544	105	1,273	117	3,652	236	262	4
Attabira	Attabira ...	2,184	3,088	96	176	17	413	30	1,490	49	47	...
Sohela	Sohela ...	2,527	2,384	143	133	35	667	41	1,584	67	35	1
Ambabhona	Ambabhona ...	1,012	983	29	40	4	185	7	758	18	14	1
Padampur	Padampur ...	1,192	1,146	46	68	6	248	15	830	25	80	...
Bheran	Bheran ...	2,020	1,935	85	112	20	367	32	1,456	33	24	...
Bijepur	Bijepur ...	1,016	995	21	36	...	193	2	766	19	28	...
Melchhamunda	Melchhamunda	964	915	49	76	12	233	11	616	26	11	...
Gaisilat	Gaisilat ...	657	636	21	28	...	150	9	458	12	17	...
Jagdalpur	Jagdalpur ...	588	575	13	40	...	138	8	397	5	17	...
Barpali	Barpali ...	4,399	4,159	240	448	78	883	62	2,828	100	78	...
Bhatli	Bhatli ...	1,594	1,539	55	115	10	338	23	1,086	22	28	...
Paikmal	Paikmal ...	224	220	4	2	1	37	...	181	3	10	...

PROVINCIAL TABLE II—*continued.*

POPULATION OF REVENUE THANAS AND POLICE-STATIONS BY RELIGION AND LITERACY.

REVENUE THANA	POLICE STATION	POPULATION			HINDUS														MUSLIMS			
					TOTAL HINDUS		BRAHMANS				DEPRESSED CLASSES				OTHER HINDUS							
							Number of persons		*Number literate*		*Number of persons*		*Number literate.*		*Number of persons*		*Number literate*		*Number of persons*		*Number literate.*	
		Persons	Males	Females	Males	Females	Males	Females	Males	Females	Males	Females	Males	Females	Males	Females	Males	Females	Males	Females	Males	Females.
1	2	3	4	5	6	7	8	9	10	11	12	13	14	15	16	17	18	19	20	21	22	23
HAZARIBAGH		**1,517,357**	**751,956**	**765,401**	**597,528**	**610,571**	**19,376**	**17,428**	**6,126**	**557**	**137,893**	**148,362**	**696**	**25**	**440,259**	**444,781**	**22,155**	**1,385**	**34,799**	**36,695**	**4,046**	**185**
Barhi		59,110	28 392	30,718	24,274	26 443	733	724	137	5	4,467	5,120	5		19,075	20,510	494	17	3,124	3 365	35	1
	Barhi	31,330	15,265	16,065	13,503	14 228													1,762	1,837		
	Barahkatha	27,780	13,127	14,653	10 771	12,214													1 362	1,528		..
Hazaribagh		110,873	53,459	57,414	43,742	47,335	2 009	1,643	961	167	11,208	14,425	113	8	30,435	31,268	3,142	344	8 428	8,906	926	93
	Hazaribagh ...	78,894	38 466	40 428	30,220	31,895													7 346	7,743		...
	Ichak	31,979	14 993	16,986	13,522	15,440													1 082	1,163		
Bagodar	Bagodar	84,049	41,261	42,788	34,128	35,533	1,067	935	230	1	4,675	5,394	2	2	28,366	29,204	460	1	4,860	5,086	104	.
Barkagaon		73,370	36,243	37,127	31,233	33,030	1 097	1,108	247	8	9,340	9,671	15	1	20,796	31,251	548	4	3 088	3,181	66	7
	Barkagaon	47,942	23,488	24,454	19,754	20,583													2,338	2,477		
	Tandwa	25,428	12,755	12,673	11,479	11,447													750	704	.	..
Ramgarh		110,441	55,522	54,919	45,370	45,006	870	760	345	21	4,453	4,443	40	1	40,047	39,783	1,624	29	5,284	5,006	423	15
	Ramgarh	70,427	35,461	34 966	30 381	30 043													4,015	3,828		
	Gola	40,014	20,061	19,953	14,989	14,963												..	1 260	1,178		.
Gumia	Gumia	44,580	22,728	21,852	14,935	14,640	221	178	80	6	2,590	2,530			12,114	11,932	594	35	1 841	1 584	58	1
Mandu	Mandu	47,078	23 668	23,410	16,736	16,755	273	214	100	1	3,341	3,549	9		13,122	12,992	365	5	1,726	1 580	57	
Petarbar	Petarbar	83,643	42,017	41 026	26 438	25 204	1,075	1,033	363	25	4,663	4,413	19		20,690	19 758	600	21	2 636	2 505	146	4
Kodarma		107,052	52,406	54,646	45 619	47 805	1,219	1,173	426	39	7,258	8,156	40		37,142	38,476	1,673	78	6 603	6 692	211	4
	Kodarma	74,089	36,726	37 363	32 265	33 109													4 282	4,115		
	Jainagar	32,963	15 680	17 283	13,354	14,696													2 320	2 577		
Chauparan		73,640	36,330	37,310	33,011	33,982	1 061	1,074	305	7	9,383	9,759	10		22,567	23,140	763	23	3 236	3 266	88	.
	Chauparan	45,366	22 514	22 852	20 234	20,546													2 197	2,244		
	Itkhori	28,274	13,816	14,458	12,777	13,436													1 039	1 022		
Hunterganj		70,958	35,479	35 479	32,382	34,175	576	632	141	5	17,811	17,766	39		14,195	13 787	604	2	3 037	3 256	175	1
	Hunterganj	45,300	22,468	22,832	21,062	21 260										...			1 346	1 515		
	Partabpur	25,658	13,011	12 647	11,320	10,906													1 691	1,741		...
Chatra		57,942	28 704	29,238	25,785	26 093	1 138	1,136	199	8	9,242	9,544	14	1	15,405	15,423	505	7	2 880	3 120	116	1
	Chatra	42,753	21 331	21,422	18 984	18 882													2 310	2,515		...
	Gidhaur	15,189	7,373	[illegible]816	6,801	7 211													570	605		..
Simaria		36,334	17,978	18 356	16,271	16,597	338	378	67	2	8,826	9,080	9		7,107	7,130	354	3	1 469	1 516	27	...
	Simaria	22,824	11 216	11 608	9,796	10 158													1 188	1,207		...
	Lowalong	13,510	6,762	6,748	6,475	6,439													281	300		
Gawan		72,561	35 919	36 642	28,863	29,830	723	679	183	7	6,682	7,133	33	6	21,458	22 097	1,101	51	3 640	3,805	326	1
	Gawan ...	52,762	26 522	26,240	20 273	20 453				..									2 843	2,797		..
	Satgawan	19,799	9,397	10,402	8,590	9,386									..	...			797	1 008		..
Kharagdiha		99,110	47,767	51,343	39 554	43,417	2,161	2,119	727	26	6,990	8,192	32	1	30,683	32,106	1,720	46	5 243	6 092	176	8
	Jamua	57,525	27,325	30 200	23 451	25 566													3 686	4 419		
	Deori	41,585	20,442	21,143	16 403	16,851													1 557	1,673		..
Dhanwar		87,165	41,208	45,957	33 543	37,269	1,231	1,098	331	4	5,738	6,037	51		26,583	29,234	1,422	54	7 220	8 234	70	
	Dhanwar	53,050	25 264	27,786	20 296	22,268													4 750	5 323		.
	Birni	34,115	15,944	18,171	13,246	15,001													2 470	2,911		..
Giridih		155,494	78 064	77,430	51,646	51,156	2,285	1 657	962	172	12,689	13,652	336	1	36,672	35,847	4 014	523	13 267	13,050	1,346	98
	Giridih ...	84,408	43,086	41,323	30,389	29 301								..					8 112	7,723		
	Bengabad .	32,883	16 102	16 781	11 071	11 628													1,011	2,013	..	..
	Gande ..	38,202	18,876	19,326	10 186	10 227													3,244	3,314	.	..
Dumri		143,957	74 211	69,746	53,719	50,203	1,170	888	422	51	8 747	8,519	38	4	43,802	40,886	2,202	136	7 180	6,651	396	21
	Dumri	41,118	20,482	20 636	14 315	14 578													3,223	3,213		..
	Nawadih	36,550	18,166	18,384	14,045	14 126													1,055	2,034		..
	Pirtanr .	27,051	13,656	13,395	6,917	6 870													572	592		..
	Bermo .	39,238	21,907	17,331	18,442	14,719													1,430	812	..	...

PROVINCIAL TABLE II—*continued*.

POPULATION OF REVENUE THANAS AND POLICE-STATIONS BY RELIGION AND LITERACY.

REVENUE THANA.	POLICE-STATION.	CHRISTIANS. No. of persons. Males	Females.	No. literate. Males.	Females.	TRIBAL. No. of persons. Males.	Females.	No. literate. Males.	Females.	OTHERS. No. of persons. Males.	Females.	No. literate. Males.	Females.	NUMBER LITERATE (AGED 7 AND OVER). TOTAL. Persons	Males.	Females.	Aged 7–13. Males.	Females	Aged 14–23. Males.	Females.	Aged 24 and over. Males.	Females.	Literate in English. Males.	Females.
1	2	24	25	26	27	28	29	30	31	32	33	34	35	36	37	38	39	40	41	42	43	44	45	46
HAZARIBAGH ...		**1,706**	**1,463**	**798**	**520**	**67,192**	**65,964**	**302**	**38**	**731**	**503**	**348**	**33**	**37,814**	**35,071**	**2,743**	**3,990**	**577**	**3,599**	**332**	**22,482**	**1,334**	**5,204**	**596**
Barhi ...	...	34	22	9	3	970	889	...	...	...	...		...	696	670	26	80	...	142	2	446	24	41	3
	Barhi ...	...	...	...	...	...	...	...	...	...	...	...	...		...	...	...	...	...	...	...	...	...	...
	Barabkatha ...	34	23	...	...	970	889	...	...	...	...	...		...	...	...	...	...	...	...	...	...	...	...
Hazaribagh ...	...	614	546	362	281	526	500	...	...	150	118	68	8	6,423	5,592	831	796	172	1,606	380	3,191	379	1,916	261
	Hazaribagh ...	603	539	...	...	161	143	...	...	136	108	...			...	...	...	...	...	...	...	...	...	...
	Ichak ...	11	7	...	...	364	366	...	...	14	10	...			...	...	...	...	...	...	...	...	...	...
Bagodar ...	Bagodar ...	5	15	5	15	2,213	2,130	...	...	35	15	18	...	836	817	19	43	4	274	4	500	11	437	...
Barkagaon ...	...	24	17	5	...	1,905	1,898	...	...	3	1	1	...	902	883	20	105	...	190	3	557	17	21	...
	Barkagaon ...	14	17	...	...	1,379	1,376	...	...	3	1	...	...		...	...	...	...	...	...	...	...	...	...
	Tandwa ...	...	...	...	...	526	522	...	...	...	...		...	...	...	...	...	...	...	...	...	...	...	...
Ramgarh ...	...	83	66	31	6	4,768	4,834	46	6	17	17	2		2,589	2,511	78	379	20	601	22	1,631	30	240	4
	Ramgarh ...	77	66	...	...	971	1,012		...	17	17		...		...		...	...	...	...	...	...	...	...
	Gola ...	6	...	...	...	3,797	3,812	...	...	...	...	...			...	...	...	...	...	...	...	...	...	...
Gumia ...	Gumia ...	99	66	32	16	5,711	5,465	2	...	162	97	24	2	852	790	62	75	11	189	21	526	30	82	6
Mandu ...	Mandu ...	145	104	21	5	5,061	4,971	1	...	...	...	...		464	453	11	31	1	106	3	316	7	85	2
Petarbar ...	Petarbar ...	6	23	2	7	13,541	13,290	28	1	6	4	5	1	1,312	1,253	59	127	17	338	18	788	24	54	3
Kodarma ...	...	76	47	51	28	39	58	...	...	70	44	50	1	2,496	2,351	145	148	37	544	37	1,659	71	265	19
	Kodarma ...	71	39	...	...	39	58	...	...	69	42	...	...		...	...	...	...	...	...	...	...	...	...
	Jainagar ...	5	8	...	...	...	...	...	...	1	2	...	...		...	...	...	...	...	...	...	...	...	...
Chauparan ...	...	7	2	7	...	55	46	...	...	21	14	12	2	1,116	1,085	31	105	2	253	4	727	25	67	2
	Chauparan ...	7	2	...	...	55	46	...	...	21	14	...	...		...	...	...	...	...	...	...	...	...	...
	Itkhori ...	...	...	...	...	...	...	...	...	...	...	...	...	...	...	...	...	...	...	...	...	...	...	...
Hunterganj ...	...	2	...	1	...	...	...	...	...	68	48	33	...	1,001	993	8	66	...	177	...	751	8	25	...
	Hunterganj ...	2	...	...	...	...	...	...	...	68	48	...	...	...	...	...	...	...	...	...	...	...	...	...
	Partabpur ...		...	...	...	...	...	...	...	...	...	...	...		...	...	...	...	...	...	...	...	...	...
Chatra ...	...	9	12	8	6	2	...	1	...	19	13	5	2	976	941	35	78	14	309	5	654	10	58	1
	Chatra ...	7	12	...	...	2	...	...	...	19	13	...	...		...	...	...	...	...	...	...		...	...
	Gidhaur ...	2	...	...	...	...	...	...	...	...	...	...	...	...		...	...	...	...	...		...	...	...
Simaria ...	...	...	...	...	...	238	243	2	...	...	...	...	...	466	459	7	43	1	116	2	300	4	10	...
	Simaria ...	...	...	...	...	232	243	...	...	...	...	...	...	...	...	...	...	...	...	...	...	...	...	...
	Lowalong ...	...	...	...	...	6	...	...	...	...	...	...	...	...	...	...	...	...	...	...	...	...	...	...
Gawan ...	...	39	40	38	13	3,377	2,958	72	31	...	...	...	...	1,761	1,652	109	131	24	338	26	1,123	59	75	12
	Gawan ...	39	40	...	...	3,367	2,950	...	...	...	...	...	...	...	...	...	...	...	...	...	...	...	...	...
	Satgawan ...	...	...	...	...	10	8	...	...	...	...	...	...		...	...	...	...	...	...	...	...	...	...
Kharagdiha	...	13	14	...	11	3,657	3,820	16	...	...	...	...	...	2,753	2,681	92	294	26	667	34	1,700	42	107	3
	Jamua ...	1	...	...	...	187	215	...	...	...	...	...	...	...	...	...	...	...	...	...	...	...	...	...
	Deori ...	12	14	...	...	3,470	3,605	...	...	...	...	...	...	...	...	...	...	...	...	...		...	...	...
Dhanwar ...	...	...	...	...	...	437	454	...	...	...	...	...	...	1,932	1,874	58	362	16	427	21	1,065	21	59	2
	Dhanwar ...	...	...	...	...	218	195	...	...	...	...	...	...	...	...	...	...	...	...	...	...	...	...	...
	Birni ...	...	...	...	...	219	259	...	...	...	...	...	...		...	...	...	...	...	...	...	...	...	...
Giridih ...	...	214	211	106	90	12,904	12,993	96	...	33	30	24		7,670	6,786	584	867	193	1,630	285	4,289	406	1,295	336
	Giridih ...	189	183	...	...	4,364	4,096	...	...	32	30	...	...	...	...	...	...	...	...	...	...	...	...	...
	Bengabad ...	15	19	...	...	3,104	3,121	...	...	1	...	...	...	...	...	...	...	...	...	...	...	...	...	...
	Gande ...	10	9	...	...	5,436	5,776	...	...	...	...	...	...	...	...	...	...	...	...	...	...	...	...	...
Dumri ...	...	356	278	120	39	12,789	12,407	38	...	167	117	85	17	3,569	3,301	268	301	39	793	75	2,207	154	367	42
	Dumri ...	1	...	...	...	2,943	2,845	...	...	...	...	...	...		...	...	...	...	...	...	...	...	...	...
	Nawadih ...	10	5	...	...	2,156	2,219	...	...	...	...	...	...		...	...	...	...	...	...	...	...	...	...
	Pirtanr ...	109	98	...	...	5,945	5,748	...	...	113	87	...	...	...	...	...	...	...	...	...	...	...	...	...
	Bermo ...	298	175	...	...	1,745	1,595	...	...	54	30	...	...	...	...	...	...	...	...	...	...	...	...	...

RANCHI.]

PROVINCIAL TABLE II—*continued.*

POPULATION OF REVENUE THANAS AND POLICE-STATIONS BY RELIGION AND LITERACY.

REVENUE THANA	POLICE-STATION	Population: Persons	Population: Males	Population: Females	Hindus: Total Hindus: Males	Hindus: Total Hindus: Females	Brahmans: Number of persons: Males	Brahmans: Number of persons: Females	Brahmans: Number literate: Males	Brahmans: Number literate: Females	Depressed Classes: Number of persons: Males	Depressed Classes: Number of persons: Females	Depressed Classes: Number literate: Males	Depressed Classes: Number literate: Females	Other Hindus: Number of persons: Males	Other Hindus: Number of persons: Females	Other Hindus: Number literate: Males	Other Hindus: Number literate: Females	Muslims: Number of persons: Males	Muslims: Number of persons: Females	Muslims: Number literate: Males	Muslims: Number literate: Females
1	2	3	4	5	6	7	8	9	10	11	12	13	14	15	16	17	18	19	20	21	22	23
RANCHI		**1,567,149**	**777,063**	**790,086**	**433,323**	**436,169**	**6,549**	**4,836**	**2,716**	**512**	**40,225**	**40,065**	**642**	**106**	**386,549**	**391,274**	**16,636**	**2,122**	**33,778**	**32,269**	**2,320**	**229**
Lohardaga	Lohardaga	**99,298**	48,305	50,903	35 431	37,616	534	417	106	16	1 461	1 502	24	44	33,426	35 697	1,513	207	4,590	4 510	422	52
Kuru	Kuru	**32,405**	15,523	16 882	6,393	6,400	105	92	27	2	830	876	6	2	5,457	5,492	143	6	2,136	2,121	67	5
Burmu	Burmu	**27,475**	13,818	13 657	9,602	9,460	90	95	40	3	1,881	1,828	8		7,631	7,537	201	50	843	832	69	4
Mandar	Mandar	**58,133**	27,166	30,967	13,945	15,770	270	266	70	28	496	485	17	6	13,179	15,019	348	552	3,207	3,146	185	35
Bero	Bero	**43,010**	10,943	23,067	12,746	14,667	158	166	26		247	372			12,341	14,129	215	20	1,799	1,765	38	2
Lapung	Lapung	**27,264**	13,165	14 099	5,472	5,575	54	63	15	6	526	574	8		4,892	4 938	152	8	53	44	3	
Ranchi		**194,007**	99 031	94 976	64,895	61,721	2,383	1 504	1,232	390	4,718	4,653	195	15	57,794	55,564	4,597	880	13,311	13,455	716	67
	Ranchi Sadr	**143,490**	72 113	71,377	49,760	49,139											...		7,072	6,498		
	Ranchi Kotwali	**50,517**	26,918	23,599	15,135	12,582													6,139	5,967		
Ormanjh	Ormanjhi	**22 261**	11,241	11 020	7,860	7,752	37	36	4	2	639	601	14	2	7,184	7,035	269	3	1,359	1,303	122	2
Silli	Silli	**43,349**	21,614	21,735	21,084	21,275	172	152	72	9	1,661	1,730	32		19,251	19,393	916	45	378	320	20	
Angara	Angara	**34,437**	17,358	17 079	11 574	11,449	28	23	7		1,409	1,576	6		10,137	9,850	97	16	350	347	45	10
Karra	Karra	**43,169**	21,087	22,082	5,974	5 965	120	140	55	2	1,003	978	14		4,851	4,847	195		347	371	66	3
Torpa	Torpa	**60,468**	29 500	30,959	7,930	8 091	71	58	20	...	1,297	1,317	5	1	6,571	6,716	106	18	144	186	5	
Khunti	Khunti	**86,940**	43,314	43 536	11,461	11 267	181	157	46	6	2 642	2,248	49	1	8 638	8,862	432	38	398	344	56	3
Bundu	Bundu	**32,882**	16,454	16 428	14 211	14 244	155	109	83	9	1 067	1,073	7	4	12,989	13,062	868	73	194	194	46	2
Sonahatu	Sonahatu	**43,417**	21,557	21,860	21,216	21,546	204	254	73	10	1,436	1,630	35	6	19,528	19,672	749	34	132	107	20	3
Tamar	Tamar	**107,024**	53 654	53 370	41,225	41,476	234	177	78	3	4,142	3,966	64	14	36,849	37,333	1 419	40	349	241	68	2
Bishunpur	Bishunpur	**18,370**	9 331	9,039	6,107	6,009	16	10	5	..	210	196	3		5,971	5,803	40	8	15	16	5	1
Chainpur	Chainpur	**56,272**	28,153	28,119	11 063	10,754	26	20	7		635	661	1		10,402	10,073	39	5	268	236	1	5
Ghaghra	Ghaghra	**38,637**	19,164	19,473	7,763	7,732	131	137	27	2	351	390	13		7,281	7,205	266	9	227	173	12	2
Sesai	Sesai	**70,192**	34 276	35,916	24,272	25,457	251	241	120	2	650	606	5	..	23,371	24,610	800	16	1,341	1,256	55	1
Gumla	Gumla	**56,891**	28,815	28,076	11,908	11,199	313	199	106	3	1,314	1,108	10		10,381	9 892	546	12	1,109	1,008	72	1
Baidih	Raidih	**31,519**	15,751	15,768	10 048	10,129	77	29	50	1	455	486	1		9,516	9,614	181	8	107	101	6	
Palkot	Palkot	**33,081**	16,419	16,662	8,860	8,043	181	104	84		1,510	1,457	12	1	7,178	7,381	417	31	85	62	29	7
Basia	Basia	**70,514**	34,306	36,208	13,654	14,228	192	156	103	3	1,706	1,698	35	5	11,956	12,375	699	5	180	200	14	2
Bano	Bano	**40,349**	19,970	20 379	8 695	8 685	20	16	13	2	870	850	7		7,799	7,819	133	2	159	171	15	2
Kolebira	Kolebira	**61,721**	30,808	30,913	12,236	11,867	197	125	82	3	2,390	2,325	28	2	9,740	9,417	356	4	185	143	30	1
Simdega		**87,689**	43,899	43,790	17,091	16,690	189	72	106		3,635	3,625	29		13,267	12,093	705	7	475	400	96	5
	Simdega	**51,637**	25,845	25,792	11 117	10 905													242	199		
	Thethaitangar	**36,052**	18,054	17,998	5,974	5 785													233	201		
Kurdeg		**46,475**	23 432	23 043	10,308	10,143	100	23	55	1	1,239	1,174	14	5	8,969	8,946	234	16	147	119	28	3
	Kurdeg	**35,230**	17,716	17 514	7,954	7,940													130	106		...
	Bolba	**11,245**	5,716	5,529	2,354	2,203													17	13		

PROVINCIAL TABLE II—*continued.*

POPULATION OF REVENUE THANAS AND POLICE-STATIONS BY RELIGION AND LITERACY.

REVENUE THANA.	POLICE-STATION.	CHRISTIANS. *No. of persons.*		*No. literate.*		TRIBAL. *No. of persons.*		*No. literate.*		OTHERS. *No. of persons.*		*No. literate.*		NUMBER LITERATE (AGED 7 AND OVER). TOTAL.			AGED 7–13.		AGED 14–23.		AGED 24 AND OVER.		LITERATE IN ENGLISH.	
		Males.	Females.	Males.	Females.	Males.	Females.	Males.	Females.	Males.	Females.	Males.	Females.	Persons.	Males.	Females.	Males.	Females.	Males.	Females.	Males.	Females.	Males.	Females.
1	2	24	25	26	27	28	29	30	31	32	33	34	35	36	37	38	39	40	41	42	43	44	45	46
RANCHI	...	**130,114**	**132,494**	**16,493**	**4,316**	**179,477**	**188,770**	**2,060**	**705**	**371**	**384**	**96**	**15**	**42,970**	**34,963**	**8,007**	**5,181**	**2,025**	**9,482**	**2,695**	**20,300**	**3,287**	**4,709**	**977**
Lohardaga	Lohardaga ...	1,560	1,607	194	104	6,735	7,251	71	1	...	...	...	...	2,754	2,330	434	413	100	618	128	1,300	167	172	10
Kuru...	Kuru ...	691	723	75	8	6,304	7,578	30	9	...	...	...	...	380	348	32	25	7	119	10	204	15	13	...
Burmu	Burmu ...	65	49	13	4	3,308	3,316	134	169	...	...	...	...	704	465	239	63	64	140	52	262	123	17	...
Mandar	Mandar ...	2,620	2,902	225	101	7,304	9,059	323	429	...	...	...	...	2,319	1,168	1,151	227	408	233	103	708	550	29	2
Bero	Bero ...	1,839	2,031	152	308	3,559	4,604	26	5	...	...	...	...	791	456	335	106	115	129	110	221	101	43	44
Lapung	Lapung ...	1,693	1,885	307	62	5,947	6,595	30	4	...	...	...	...	485	405	80	25	20	82	28	298	32	8	...
Ranchi	...	8,981	8,940	2,680	1,774	11,866	11,805	280	10	78	55	42	15	12,911	9,751	3,160	1,800	599	3,968	1,187	4,983	1,374	3,315	815
	Ranchi Sadr ...	4,970	5,385	...	...	10,288	10,337	...	...	23	18	...	..	...	...	...	...	...	...	...	...	...	...	...
	Ranchi Kotwali	4,011	3,555	...	...	1,578	1,468	...	...	55	37	...	...		...	...	...	...	...	...	...	...	...	...
Ormanjhi	Ormanjhi ...	45	44	7	4	1,977	1,921	24	...	...	...	...	...	453	440	13	33	3	90	5	317	5	9	2
Silli	Silli ...	49	45	13	2	108	95	2	...	...	...	...	...	1,111	1,055	56	123	12	268	16	664	28	67	2
Angara	Angara ...	443	488	35	8	4,991	4,715	124	31	...	...	...	...	388	314	74	47	10	38	28	220	36	5	...
Karra	Karra ...	3,473	3,473	303	154	11,293	12,273	66	5	...	...	...	...	862	698	164	120	66	173	49	309	40	11	...
Torpa	Torpa ...	8,608	8,936	507	105	13,813	13,740	76	1	5	6	2	...	846	721	125	44	15	182	45	495	62	56	...
Khunti	Khunti ...	7,046	7,260	876	338	24,389	24,633	290	14	20	22	4	...	2,153	1,753	400	261	101	435	135	1,037	164	90	36
Bundu	Bundu ...	218	228	7	...	1,723	1,625	6	...	108	117	10	...	1,114	1,026	88	113	28	248	33	660	27	48	1
Sonahatu...	Sonahatu ...	...	...	...	...	206	207	7	...	1	...	...	...	937	884	53	113	11	206	16	560	26	15	...
Tamar	Tamar ...	2,940	2,900	138	34	8,961	8,860	53	2	159	184	38	...	1,953	1,858	95	105	23	501	36	1,162	36	16	1
Bishunpur	Bishunpur ...	846	769	100	6	2,273	2,245	6	...	..	...	...	...	174	150	15	27	5	51	6	81	4	11	...
Chainpur...	Chainpur ...	16,015	16,347	384	25	807	782	1	...	...	...	...	...	468	433	35	58	4	141	7	234	24	26	9
Ghaghra	Ghaghra ..	612	622	63	19	10,562	10,346	119	10	...	...	...	...	541	490	43	68	5	118	10	313	27	53	2
Sesai	Sesai ...	1,345	1,400	90	20	7,418	7,796	83	2	...	...	...	...	1,199	1,158	41	35	7	209	14	704	20	19	1
Gumla	Gumla ...	1,385	1,352	123	36	14,413	14,427	105	5	...	...	...	...	1,019	962	57	33	10	227	23	643	24	98	1
Raidih	Raidih ...	5,582	5,533	299	81	14	6	3	...	...	...	...	...	630	540	90	66	17	141	30	333	34	28	...
Palkot	Palkot ...	2,563	2,507	115	24	4,902	5,161	46	1	...	...	...	...	766	702	64	68	12	164	23	480	20	34	1
Basia	Basia ...	10,606	11,373	1,192	410	9,576	10,407	69	2	...	...	...	...	2,539	2,112	427	449	143	538	194	1,125	90	232	39
Bano	Bano ...	5,020	5,064	363	80	6,096	6,439	28	1	...	...	...	...	646	559	87	41	19	144	37	374	31	72	4
Kolebira	Kolebira ...	10,487	10,686	623	122	7,900	8,218	42	2	...	...	...	...	1,304	1,170	134	100	37	321	65	740	32	64	1
Simdega	...	23,166	23,361	1,352	343	3,167	3,339	15	2	...	...	...	...	3,560	2,303	357	363	114	662	135	1,278	118	112	11
	Simdega ...	13,131	13,304	...	...	1,855	1,384	...	...	...	...	...	...	...	...	...	...	...	...	...	...	...	...	...
	Thethaitangar	10,035	10,057	...	...	1,312	1,955	...	...	...	...	...	...	...	...	...	...	...	...	...	...	...	...	...
Kurdeg	...	12,127	11,853	459	144	850	929	4	...	...	...	...	...	963	794	169	140	61	256	69	398	39	56	5
	Kurdeg ...	9,138	8,914	...	...	494	554	...	...	...	...	...	...	...	...	...	...	...	...	...	...	...	...	...
	Bolba ...	2,989	2,938	...	...	356	375	...	...	...	...	...	...	...	...	...	...	...	...	...	...	...	...	...

27

PROVINCIAL TABLE II—*continued*.

POPULATION OF REVENUE THANAS AND POLICE-STATIONS BY RELIGION AND LITERACY.

REVENUE THANA.	POLICE-STATION.	POPULATION.			HINDUS.														MUSLIMS.			
					TOTAL HINDUS.		BRAHMANS.				DEPRESSED CLASSES.				OTHER HINDUS.							
							Number of persons.		*Number literate.*		*Number of persons.*		*Number literate.*		*Number of persons.*		*Number literate.*		*Number of persons.*		*Number literate.*	
		Persons.	Males.	Females.	Males.	Females.	Males.	Females.	Males.	Females.	Males.	Females.	Males.	Females.	Males.	Females.	Males.	Females.	Males.	Females.	Males.	Females.
1	2	3	4	5	6	7	8	9	10	11	12	13	14	15	16	17	18	19	20	21	22	23
PALAMAU	...	**818,736**	**409,778**	**408,958**	**335,519**	**334,442**	**17,552**	**17,569**	**4,665**	**227**	**106,290**	**107,420**	**415**	**43**	**211,677**	**209,453**	**10,953**	**794**	**37,369**	**37,132**	**1,926**	**223**
Daltonganj	...	149,760	74,656	75,104	63,648	63,971	4,657	4,563	1,161	74	21,048	21,009	79	10	37,943	38,319	2,714	276	7,305	7,470	445	34
	Daltonganj ...	86,834	43,473	43,361	37,045	36,863	...	...	...	...	...	...	...	...	...	...	...	...	4,312	4,406	...	...
	Lesleganj ...	31,772	15,600	16,172	13,868	14,384	...	...	...	...	...	...	...	...	...	...	...	...	1,220	1,257	...	...
	Panki ...	31,154	15,583	15,671	12,735	12,724	...	...	...	...	...	...	...	...	...	...	...	...	1,773	1,807	...	...
Garhwa	...	130,286	64,541	65,745	52,162	53,310	3,500	3,631	903	14	15,347	15,874	47	2	33,255	33,815	1,814	74	8,902	9,061	303	14
	Garhwa ...	77,775	38,261	39,514	30,531	31,586	...	...	...	...	...	...	...	...	...	...	...	...	6,129	6,387	...	...
	Untari ...	52,511	26,280	26,231	21,631	21,724	...	...	...	...	...	...	...	...	...	...	...	...	2,773	2,674	...	...
Ranka	...	47,262	23,892	23,370	18,446	17,920	252	140	120	6	5,665	5,817	15	3	12,529	11,963	363	18	1,427	1,294	61	4
	Ranka ...	37,205	18,718	18,487	14,552	14,333	...	...	...	...	...	...	...	...	...	...	...	...	1,285	1,185	...	...
	Bhandaria ...	10,057	5,174	4,883	3,894	3,587	...	...	...	...	...	...	...	...	...	...	...	...	142	109	...	...
Chhatarpur	...	62,809	31,810	30,999	29,650	28,823	396	351	113	16	11,105	11,124	76	6	18,140	17,348	848	101	1,652	1,686	99	34
	Chhatarpur ...	41,792	21,246	20,546	19,592	18,961	...	...	...	...	...	...	...	...	...	...	...	...	1,182	1,128	...	...
	Hariharganj ...	21,017	10,564	10,453	10,058	9,862	...	...	...	...	...	...	...	...	...	...	...	...	470	558	...	...
Patan	...	107,528	53,446	54,082	47,085	47,758	3,965	4,252	881	51	15,867	15,984	32	2	27,233	27,522	1,295	107	5,453	5,411	169	10
	Patan ...	41,028	20,135	20,893	17,893	18,544	...	...	...	...	...	...	...	...	...	...	...	...	1,721	1,804	...	...
	Bisrampur ...	29,391	14,582	14,809	13,113	13,386	...	...	...	...	...	...	...	...	...	...	...	...	1,401	1,369	...	...
	Manatu ...	37,109	18,729	18,380	16,079	15,628	...	...	...	...	...	...	...	...	...	...	...	...	2,331	2,238	...	...
Husainabad	...	143,477	72,160	71,317	63,813	62,972	3,831	4,007	1,114	51	19,660	19,617	60	7	40,322	39,348	2,101	93	7,311	7,290	306	66
	Husainabad ...	78,088	39,437	38,651	34,119	33,263	...	...	...	...	...	...	...	...	...	...	...	...	5,174	5,275	...	...
	Bhaunathpur	65,389	32,723	32,666	29,694	29,709	...	...	...	...	...	...	...	...	...	...	...	...	2,137	2,015	...	...
Balumath	...	80,851	40,177	40,674	27,798	27,937	432	377	139	6	9,183	9,654	55	2	18,193	18,006	886	42	2,444	2,342	202	39
	Balumath ...	54,706	27,075	27,631	19,344	19,670	...	...	...	...	...	...	...	...	...	...	...	...	2,010	1,975	...	...
	Chandwa ...	26,145	13,102	13,043	8,454	8,267	...	...	...	...	...	...	...	...	...	...	...	...	434	367	...	...
Latehar	...	63,804	32,588	31,216	25,134	24,154	409	356	157	9	7,559	7,543	37	2	17,166	16,255	833	48	2,384	2,051	193	14
	Latehar ...	43,554	21,962	21,592	16,321	16,125	...	...	...	...	...	...	...	...	...	...	...	...	1,435	1,258	...	...
	Barwadih ...	20,250	10,626	9,624	8,813	8,029	...	...	...	...	...	...	...	...	...	...	...	...	949	793	...	...
Mahuadanr	...	32,959	16,508	16,451	7,783	7,597	40	12	17	...	856	808	14	9	6,887	6,777	119	35	491	527	58	8
	Mahuadanr ...	24,500	12,158	12,342	5,456	5,446	...	...	...	...	...	...	...	...	...	...	...	...	399	437	...	...
	Garu ...	8,459	4,350	4,109	2,327	2,151	...	...	...	...	...	...	...	...	...	...	...	...	92	90	...	...
SINGHBHUM	...	**929,802**	**469,421**	**460,381**	**237,465**	**222,610**	**9,204**	**6,696**	**4,762**	**1,017**	**47,930**	**44,887**	**1,479**	**93**	**180,331**	**171,027**	**18,672**	**1,853**	**16,543**	**10,211**	**2,953**	**289**
Chakradharpur... ...	Chakradharpur	133,335	65,397	67,938	22,959	23,154	1,121	983	211	7	4,717	4,728	85	2	17,121	17,443	855	59	1,810	1,557	247	6
Kolhan	Chaibasa ...	335,644	162,056	173,588	49,914	50,484	268	313	121	25	5,039	4,826	86	...	44,617	45,345	2,526	274	1,654	1,367	320	42
Manoharpur	Manoharpur...	66,228	33,259	32,969	20,978	20,875	562	517	65	4	3,222	3,131	34	1	17,204	17,227	560	21	316	240	4	4
Ghatsila	...	394,595	208,709	185,886	143,614	128,007	7,273	4,883	4,365	981	34,952	32,202	1,274	90	101,389	91,012	14,731	1,499	12,763	7,038	2,373	237
	Ghatsila ...	117,082	60,491	56,591	37,226	34,649	...	...	...	...	...	...	...	...	...	...	...	...	1,619	865	...	...
	Bistopur ...	30,876	18,733	12,143	12,741	8,594	...	...	...	...	...	...	...	...	...	...	...	...	3,797	2,035	...	...
	Jugsalai ...	29,072	16,078	12,994	9,641	7,166	...	...	...	...	...	...	...	...	...	...	...	...	1,739	1,198	...	...
	Sakchi ...	23,562	14,233	9,329	10,550	6,879	...	...	...	...	...	...	...	...	...	...	...	...	2,447	1,601	...	...
	Golmuri ...	26,596	16,101	10,495	10,251	6,880	...	...	...	...	...	...	...	...	...	...	...	...	2,384	749	...	...
	Baharagora ...	72,631	36,312	36,319	20,261	26,238	...	...	...	...	...	...	...	...	...	...	...	...	108	52	...	...
	Kalikapur ...	64,687	31,564	33,123	23,707	24,734	...	...	...	...	...	...	...	...	...	...	...	...	536	430	...	...
	Swaspur ...	30,089	15,197	14,892	13,235	12,957	...	...	...	...	...	...	...	...	...	...	...	...	133	108	...	...

PROVINCIAL TABLE II—*continued.*

Population of Revenue Thanas and Police-stations by Religion and Literacy.

Revenue Thana.	Police-station.	Christians. No. of persons. Males.	Christians. No. of persons. Females.	Christians. No. literate. Males.	Christians. No. literate. Females.	Tribal. No. of persons. Males.	Tribal. No. of persons. Females.	Tribal. No. literate. Males.	Tribal. No. literate. Females.	Others. No. of persons. Males.	Others. No. of persons. Females.	Others. No. literate. Males.	Others. No. literate. Females.
1	3	24	25	26	27	28	29	30	31	32	33	34	35
PALAMAU	...	**4,242**	**4,365**	**323**	**167**	**32,632**	**33,015**	**58**	**5**	**16**	**4**	**15**	...
Daltonganj	...	53	100	36	56	3,643	3,560	14	...	9	3	9	...
	Daltonganj ...	53	100	...	...	2,056	1,989	...	...	9	3	...	...
	Leslieganj ...	...	...	...	...	512	531	...	...	...	...	...	...
	Panki ...	...	...	...	...	1,075	1,040	...	...	...	...	...	...
Garhwa	...	3	...	3	...	3,474	3,374	...	...	...	...	...	...
	Garhwa ...	3	...	...	...	1,598	1,541	...	...	...	...	...	...
	Untari ...	...	...	...	...	1,876	1,833	...	...	...	...	...	...
Ranka	...	...	...	...	...	4,019	4,156	...	...	...	...	...	...
	Ranka ...	...	...	...	...	2,881	2,969	...	...	...	...	...	...
	Bhandaria ...	...	...	...	...	1,138	1,187	...	...	...	...	...	...
Chhatarpur	...	...	...	...	...	506	490	1	...	2	...	2	...
	Chhatarpur ...	...	...	...	...	470	457	...	...	2	...	...	...
	Hariharganj ...	...	...	...	...	36	33	...	...	...	...	...	...
Patan	...	1	...	...	...	907	913	2	...	...	...	...	...
	Patan ...	...	...	...	...	531	545	...	...	...	...	...	...
	Bisrampur ...	...	...	...	...	68	54	...	...	...	...	...	...
	Manatu ...	1	...	...	...	318	314	...	...	...	...	...	...
Husainabad	...	20	10	20	10	1,016	1,045	1	...	...	...	...	...
	Husainabad ...	20	10	...	...	124	103	...	...	...	...	...	...
	Bhaunathpur	...	...	...	...	892	942	...	...	...	...	...	...
Balumath	...	62	77	21	11	9,868	10,317	30	5	5	1	4	...
	Balumath ...	23	27	...	...	5,698	5,959	...	...	...	...	...	...
	Chandwa ...	39	50	...	...	4,170	4,358	...	...	5	1	...	...
Latehar	...	69	41	53	17	5,001	4,970	6	...	...	...	...	...
	Latehar ...	66	39	...	...	4,140	4,170	...	...	...	...	...	...
	Barwadih ...	3	2	...	...	861	800	...	...	...	...	...	...
Mahuadanr	...	4,035	4,137	190	73	4,199	4,190	3	...	...	...	...	...
	Mahuadanr ...	3,941	4,052	...	...	2,362	2,407	...	...	...	...	...	...
	Garu ...	94	85	...	...	1,837	1,783	...	...	...	...	...	...
SINGHBHUM	...	**10,056**	**9,496**	**3,051**	**1,247**	**202,616**	**216,722**	**4,132**	**114**	**2,741**	**1,342**	**1,063**	**155**
Chakradharpur	Chakradharpur	3,303	3,374	591	254	37,323	35,850	517	38	2	3	2	...
Kolhan	Chaibassa ...	1,062	1,106	330	216	109,413	129,626	3,179	54	13	3	4	...
Manoharpur	Manoharpur...	3,035	2,974	339	106	8,927	5,871	27	7	3	...	3	...
Ghatsila	...	2,656	2,044	1,801	673	46,953	47,375	409	35	2,723	1,336	994	155
	Ghatsila ...	370	302	...	...	21,067	20,785	...	...	207	84	...	...
	Bistopur ...	911	797	...	...	130	108	...	...	1,154	609	...	...
	Jugsalai ...	203	123	...	...	4,366	4,439	...	...	129	73	...	...
	Sakchi ...	269	198	...	...	441	355	...	...	523	296	...	...
	Golmuri ...	816	613	...	...	1,949	1,977	...	...	701	271	...	...
	Baharagora ...	4	5	...	...	9,939	10,024	...	...	...	...	...	...
	Kalikapur ...	70	80	...	...	7,261	7,879	...	...	...	...	...	...
	Swaspur ...	13	6	...	...	1,810	1,818	...	...	6	3	...	...

Revenue Thana.	Police-station.	Number literate (aged 7 and over). Total. Persons.	Total. Males.	Total. Females.	Aged 7–13. Males.	Aged 7–13. Females.	Aged 14–23. Males.	Aged 14–23. Females.	Aged 24 and over. Males.	Aged 24 and over. Females.	Literate in English. Males.	Literate in English. Females.
1	3	36	37	38	39	40	41	42	43	44	45	46
PALAMAU	...	**19,754**	**18,295**	**1,459**	**2,381**	**326**	**4,568**	**427**	**11,346**	**706**	**1,327**	**56**
Daltonganj	...	4,908	4,458	450	629	87	1,166	131	2,663	242	627	19
	Daltonganj ...	...	...	...	...	...	...	...	...	...	...	...
	Leslieganj ...	...	...	...	...	...	...	...	...	...	...	...
	Panki ...	...	...	...	...	...	...	...	...	...	...	...
Garhwa	...	3,174	3,070	104	383	20	803	35	1,886	49	132	2
	Garhwa ...	...	...	...	...	...	...	...	...	...	...	...
	Untari ...	...	...	...	...	...	...	...	...	...	...	...
Ranka	...	590	559	31	69	4	124	12	366	15	11	...
	Ranka ...	...	...	...	...	...	...	...	...	...	...	...
	Bhandaria ...	...	...	...	...	...	...	...	...	...	...	...
Chhatarpur	...	1,296	1,139	157	137	22	312	49	700	86	16	...
	Chhatarpur ...	...	...	...	...	...	...	...	...	...	...	...
	Hariharganj ...	...	...	...	...	...	...	...	...	...	...	...
Patan	...	2,549	2,379	170	339	37	596	41	1,443	92	18	3
	Patan ...	...	...	...	...	...	...	...	...	...	...	...
	Bisrampur ...	...	...	...	...	...	...	...	...	...	...	...
	Manatu ...	...	...	...	...	...	...	...	...	...	...	...
Husainabad	...	3,919	3,692	227	468	46	832	85	2,392	96	175	11
	Husainabad ...	...	...	...	...	...	...	...	...	...	...	...
	Bhaunathpur	...	...	...	...	...	...	...	...	...	...	...
Balumath	...	1,422	1,317	105	138	46	314	25	865	34	132	5
	Balumath ...	...	...	...	...	...	...	...	...	...	...	...
	Chandwa ...	...	...	...	...	...	...	...	...	...	...	...
Latehar	...	1,371	1,281	90	158	19	312	26	811	43	109	11
	Latehar ...	...	...	...	...	...	...	...	...	...	...	...
	Barwadih ...	...	...	...	...	...	...	...	...	...	...	...
Mahuadanr	...	525	400	125	70	45	108	31	222	40	37	5
	Mahuadanr ...	...	...	...	...	...	...	...	...	...	...	...
	Garu ...	...	...	...	...	...	...	...	...	...	...	...
SINGHBHUM	...	**40,820**	**36,052**	**4,768**	**3,962**	**833**	**9,513**	**1,745**	**22,577**	**2,190**	**9,793**	**1,189**
Chakradharpur	Chakradharpur	2,864	2,508	356	313	55	731	93	1,665	200	684	199
Kolhan	Chaibassa ...	7,176	6,565	611	838	121	1,864	218	3,765	272	1,238	64
Manoharpur	Manoharpur...	1,174	1,032	142	141	57	321	43	570	43	100	21
Ghatsila	...	29,606	25,947	3,659	2,671	600	6,597	1,393	16,679	1,666	7,931	905
	Ghatsila ...	...	...	...	...	...	...	...	...	...	...	...
	Bistopur ...	...	...	...	...	...	...	...	...	...	...	...
	Jugsalai ...	...	...	...	...	...	...	...	...	...	...	...
	Sakchi ...	...	...	...	...	...	...	...	...	...	...	...
	Golmuri ...	...	...	...	...	...	...	...	...	...	...	...
	Baharagora ...	...	...	...	...	...	...	...	...	...	...	...
	Kalikapur ...	...	...	...	...	...	...	...	...	...	...	...
	Swaspur ...	...	...	...	...	...	...	...	...	...	...	...

MANBHUM.]

PROVINCIAL TABLE II—*continued.*

Population of Revenue Thanas and Police-stations by Religion and Literacy.

Revenue Thana.	Police-station.	Population: Persons.	Population: Males.	Population: Females.	Hindus, Total Hindus: Males.	Hindus, Total Hindus: Females.	Brahmans, Number of persons: Males.	Brahmans, Number of persons: Females.	Brahmans, Number literate: Males.	Brahmans, Number literate: Females.	Depressed Classes, Number of persons: Males.	Depressed Classes, Number of persons: Females.	Depressed Classes, Number literate: Males.	Depressed Classes, Number literate: Females.	Other Hindus, Number of persons: Males.	Other Hindus, Number of persons: Females.	Other Hindus, Number literate: Males.	Other Hindus, Number literate: Females.	Muslims, Number of persons: Males.	Muslims, Number of persons: Females.	Muslims, Number literate: Males.	Muslims, Number literate: Females.
1	2	3	4	5	6	7	8	9	10	11	12	13	14	15	16	17	18	19	20	21	22	23
MANBHUM	...	**1,810,890**	**940,009**	**870,881**	**824,012**	**768,515**	**44,823**	**38,196**	**18,344**	**1,707**	**210,694**	**197,818**	**4,590**	**223**	**568,495**	**532,501**	**47,540**	**3,828**	**61,712**	**49,665**	**4,897**	**415**
Jhalda	...	130,369	65,443	64,026	62,063	61,798	1,771	1,530	712	41	9,370	9,775	230	16	50,921	50,493	3,069	217	3,214	2,982	155	35
	Jhalda ...	33,272	16,740	16,532	15,543	15,450	...	...	...	...	...	...	...	...	...	...	...	...	1,195	1,076	...	...
	Jaipur ...	97,097	48,703	48,394	46,520	46,348	...	...	...	...	...	...	...	...	...	...	...	...	2,019	1,906	...	...
Purulia	...	313,433	157,742	155,691	146,946	145,775	9,604	8,421	4,401	536	35,417	36,035	1,078	25	101,925	101,319	10,190	988	8,726	7,877	674	60
	Purulia ...	120,203	60,703	59,495	54,876	53,969	...	...	...	...	...	...	...	...	...	...	...	...	4,696	4,366	...	...
	Balarampur ...	49,706	25,161	24,545	23,858	23,492	...	...	...	...	...	...	...	...	...	...	...	...	1,167	932	...	...
	Hura ...	47,960	24,053	23,907	23,026	22,969	...	...	...	...	...	...	...	...	...	...	...	...	953	846	...	...
	Arsha ...	48,788	24,532	24,256	22,712	22,566	...	...	...	...	...	...	...	...	...	...	...	...	1,169	1,049	...	...
	Pancha ...	46,776	23,288	23,488	22,474	22,759	...	...	...	...	...	...	...	...	...	...	...	...	741	684	...	...
Baghmundi	Baghmundi ...	47,344	24,044	23,300	23,240	22,572	500	423	208	21	6,117	6,016	149	7	16,633	16,133	700	17	690	606	57	...
Chandil	...	123,115	61,904	61,211	54,145	53,497	647	470	281	9	18,179	17,397	632	13	35,819	35,630	2,248	18	1,115	966	141	1
	Chandil ...	78,610	39,526	39,084	32,553	32,142	...	...	...	...	...	...	...	...	...	...	...	...	454	330	...	...
	Ichagarh ...	44,505	22,378	22,127	21,592	21,355	...	...	...	...	...	...	...	...	...	...	...	...	661	636	...	...
Barabhum	...	162,502	81,546	80,956	79,028	78,001	2,172	1,891	895	20	16,336	16,616	503	10	60,520	60,094	3,678	368	2,118	1,944	223	1
	Barabhum	66,476	32,972	33,504	31,323	31,902	...	...	...	...	...	...	...	...	...	...	...	...	1,513	1,462	...	...
	Patamda ...	60,128	30,456	29,672	29,813	29,088	...	...	...	...	...	...	...	...	...	...	...	...	409	347	...	...
	Bandwan ...	35,898	18,118	17,780	17,892	17,611	...	...	...	...	...	...	...	...	...	...	...	...	106	135	...	...
Manbazar	Manbazar ...	109,590	54,782	54,808	53,587	53,769	2,220	1,870	770	19	11,605	12,128	184	51	39,762	39,761	3,248	33	1,188	1,039	89	...
Raghunathpur	...	152,080	77,579	74,501	65,794	63,393	6,280	5,999	2,619	219	20,674	19,777	393	12	38,840	37,616	5,435	455	4,171	3,410	564	36
	Raghunathpur	83,354	42,256	41,098	38,701	37,877	...	...	...	...	...	...	...	...	...	...	...	...	2,433	2,006	...	...
	Santuri ...	28,672	14,161	14,511	8,627	8,790	...	...	...	...	...	...	...	...	...	...	...	...	519	459	...	...
	Nituria ...	40,054	21,162	18,892	18,466	16,726	...	...	...	...	...	...	...	...	...	...	...	...	1,219	855	...	...
Gaurandi	Kashipur ...	63,441	31,612	31,829	24,373	24,499	1,814	1,687	869	44	7,396	7,484	187	15	15,162	15,328	1,690	26	734	752	56	1
Para	Para ...	53,446	26,512	26,934	23,815	24,303	2,022	2,167	731	39	8,183	8,286	86	5	13,610	13,849	1,284	43	2,599	2,569	248	21
Chas	...	134,478	67,906	66,572	62,285	61,480	6,509	5,927	2,043	90	15,315	15,482	208	34	40,461	40,071	3,247	130	5,080	4,554	379	64
	Chas ...	72,552	36,342	36,210	33,330	33,367	...	...	...	...	...	...	...	...	...	...	...	...	2,995	2,827	...	...
	Chandankiari	61,926	31,564	30,362	28,955	28,113	...	...	...	...	...	...	...	...	...	...	...	...	2,085	1,727	...	...
Gobindpur	Gobindpur ...	50,823	25,564	25,259	15,883	15,470	744	623	161	15	3,309	3,475	38	1	11,780	11,372	680	...	4,862	4,814	212	2
Jherria	...	211,966	127,429	84,537	110,036	74,240	5,779	3,230	2,576	512	31,254	31,240	250	13	73,003	49,770	6,305	706	14,462	8,296	1,064	71
	Jherria ...	116,406	70,339	46,067	60,628	40,448	...	...	...	...	...	...	...	...	...	...	...	...	8,131	4,581	...	...
	Kenduadih ...	55,314	35,105	20,209	30,659	17,793	...	...	...	...	...	...	...	...	...	...	...	...	3,662	1,987	...	...
	Dhanbad ...	40,246	21,985	18,261	18,749	15,999	...	...	...	...	...	...	...	...	...	...	...	...	2,669	1,728	...	...
Topchanchi	...	128,921	71,629	57,292	61,052	49,123	2,553	1,962	1,082	94	17,079	13,573	568	12	41,430	33,588	3,079	130	7,938	5,678	778	111
	Topchanchi ...	32,396	17,059	15,337	13,108	11,872	...	...	...	...	...	...	...	...	...	...	...	...	2,403	1,931	...	...
	Bagmara ...	41,307	22,841	18,466	20,327	16,592	...	...	...	...	...	...	...	...	...	...	...	...	2,008	1,445	...	...
	Katras ...	55,218	31,729	23,489	27,617	20,659	...	...	...	...	...	...	...	...	...	...	...	...	3,522	2,302	...	...
Nirsa	...	84,443	43,455	40,988	31,594	29,954	1,766	1,618	890	30	8,177	8,234	78	5	21,651	20,102	2,438	682	3,745	3,161	243	12
	Nirsa ...	60,403	30,469	29,934	22,145	21,943	...	...	...	...	...	...	...	...	...	...	...	...	2,313	2,093	...	...
	Chirkunda ...	24,040	12,986	11,054	9,440	8,011	...	...	...	...	...	...	...	...	...	...	...	...	1,432	1,069	...	...
Tundi	Tundi ...	44,939	22,862	22,077	10,223	10,058	443	378	97	9	2,283	2,300	16	4	7,498	7,375	250	15	1,075	1,017	45	...

PROVINCIAL TABLE II—*continued.*

POPULATION OF REVENUE THANAS AND POLICE-STATIONS BY RELIGION AND LITERACY.

REVENUE THANA.	POLICE-STATION.	CHRISTIANS. No. of persons. Males.	CHRISTIANS. No. of persons. Females.	CHRISTIANS. No. literate. Males.	CHRISTIANS. No. literate. Females.	TRIBAL. No. of persons. Males.	TRIBAL. No. of persons. Females.	TRIBAL. No. literate. Males.	TRIBAL. No. literate. Females.	OTHERS. No. of persons. Males.	OTHERS. No. of persons. Females.	OTHERS. No. literate. Males.	OTHERS. No. literate. Females.	NUMBER LITERATE (AGED 7 AND OVER). Total. Persons.	Total. Males.	Total. Females.	Aged 7—13. Males.	Aged 7—13. Females.	Aged 14—23. Males.	Aged 14—23. Females.	Aged 24 and over. Males.	Aged 24 and over. Females.	Literate in English. Males.	Literate in English. Females.
1	2	24	25	26	27	28	29	30	31	32	33	34	35	36	37	38	39	40	41	42	43	44	45	46
MANBHUM	...	**3,922**	**3,734**	**1,496**	**363**	**50,253**	**48,907**	**257**	**14**	**110**	**60**	**22**	**6**	**84,142**	**77,146**	**6,996**	**8,069**	**1,077**	**19,106**	**2,265**	**50,031**	**3,654**	**12,306**	**1,208**
Jhalda	...	160	137	33	44	7	9	...	...	...	...	...	...	4,572	4,219	353	562	81	1,035	110	2,622	162	190	29
	Jhalda ...	3	6	...	...	...	...	...	...	...	...	...	...	...	...	...	...	...	...	...	...	...	...	...
	Jaipur ...	157	131	...	...	7	9	...	...	...	...	...	...	...	...	...	...	...	...	...	...	...	...	...
Purulia ...	...	934	1,011	151	171	1,136	1,028	4	...	...	...	...	...	18,378	16,598	1,780	1,998	335	4,347	560	10,253	886	2,497	169
	Purulia ...	882	958	...	...	254	202	...	...	...	...	...	...	...	...	...	...	...	...	...	...	...	...	...
	Balarampur ...	7	13	...	...	129	108	...	...	...	...	...	...	...	...	...	...	...	...	...	...	...	...	...
	Hura ...	1	...	...	...	73	72	...	...	...	...	...	...	...	...	...	...	...	...	...	...	...	...	...
	Arsha ...	44	40	...	...	607	601	...	...	...	...	...	...	...	...	...	...	...	...	...	...	...	...	...
	Paneha ...	...	...	...	...	73	45	...	...	...	...	...	...	...	...	...	...	...	...	...	...	...	...	...
Baghmundi	Baghmundi ...	114	122	57	32	...	...	...	...	...	...	...	...	1,248	1,171	77	163	17	287	26	731	34	81	2
Chandil	...	84	100	13	12	6,525	6,621	33	...	35	27	...	...	3,401	3,348	53	248	10	871	7	2,229	36	105	13
	Chandil ...	22	17	...	...	6,497	6,595	...	...	...	...	...	...	...	...	...	...	...	...	...	...	...	...	...
	Ichagarh ...	62	83	...	...	28	26	...	...	35	27	...	...	...	...	...	...	...	...	...	...	...	...	...
Barahabhum	...	8	4	2	...	392	407	3	...	...	...	...	...	5,703	5,304	399	611	24	1,387	114	3,406	261	157	...
	Barahabhum	4	2	...	...	132	138	...	...	...	...	...	...	...	...	...	...	...	...	...	...	...	...	...
	Patamda ...	3	1	...	...	231	236	...	...	...	...	...	...	...	...	...	...	...	...	...	...	...	...	...
	Banduan ..	1	1	...	...	29	33	...	...	...	...	...	...	...	...	...	...	...	...	...	...	...	...	...
Manbazar	Manbazar ...	4	7	3	3	3	3	...	...	...	...	...	...	4,350	4,244	106	439	22	1,076	24	2,729	60	166	...
Raghunathpur	...	717	779	337	97	6,849	6,905	61	2	48	15	13	5	10,238	9,412	826	1,117	158	2,213	244	6,082	424	1,602	114
	Raghunathpur	635	701	...	...	487	434	...	...	...	...	...	...	...	...	...	...	...	...	...	...	...	...	...
	Santuri ...	21	21	...	...	4,994	5,241	...	...	...	...	...	...	...	...	...	...	...	...	...	...	...	...	...
	Nithuria ...	61	57	...	...	1,368	1,240	...	...	48	15	...	...	...	...	...	...	...	...	...	...	...	...	...
Gaurandi	Kashipur ...	24	17	14	7	6,482	6,561	73	12	...	...	...	...	2,994	2,889	105	238	17	718	42	1,933	46	157	9
Para	Para ...	98	63	35	16	...	...	...	...	...	...	...	...	2,498	2,374	124	240	17	590	35	1,544	72	84	19
Chas	...	137	100	96	79	404	438	2	...	...	...	...	...	6,372	5,975	397	649	58	1,384	118	3,942	221	1,430	141
	Chas ...	17	16	...	...	...	...	...	...	...	...	...	...	...	...	...	...	...	...	...	...	...	...	...
	Chandankiari	120	84	...	...	404	438	...	...	...	...	...	...	...	...	...	...	...	...	...	...	...	...	...
Gobindpur	Gobindpur ...	1	...	...	...	4,868	4,075	4	...	...	...	...	...	1,122	1,104	18	140	5	266	6	678	7	66	3
Jherria	...	797	634	257	168	2,118	1,350	9	...	16	17	9	1	11,961	10,490	1,471	839	220	2,437	640	7,224	711	3,147	398
	Jherria ...	234	184	...	...	1,339	861	...	...	7	3	...	...	...	...	...	...	...	...	...	...	...	...	...
	Kenduadih ...	170	110	...	...	608	314	...	...	6	5	...	...	...	...	...	...	...	...	...	...	...	...	...
	Dhanbad ...	393	340	...	...	171	175	...	...	8	9	...	...	...	...	...	...	...	...	...	...	...	...	...
Topchanchi	...	267	215	238	113	2,382	2,276	12	...	5	...	...	...	6,217	5,757	460	357	54	1,490	157	3,910	240	1,761	147
	Topchanchi ...	112	96	...	...	1,436	1,438	...	...	...	...	...	...	...	...	...	...	...	...	...	...	...	...	...
	Bagmara ...	44	45	...	...	457	394	...	...	5	...	...	...	...	...	...	...	...	...	...	...	...	...	...
	Katras ...	111	74	...	...	489	454	...	...	...	...	...	...	...	...	...	...	...	...	...	...	...	...	...
Nirsa	...	183	145	67	36	7,927	6,727	47	...	6	1	...	...	4,535	3,761	774	330	59	951	254	2,430	461	742	162
	Nirsa ...	8	4	...	...	6,003	5,395	...	...	...	...	...	...	...	...	...	...	...	...	...	...	...	...	...
	Chirkunda ...	175	141	...	...	1,924	1,332	...	...	6	1	...	...	...	...	...	...	...	...	...	...	...	...	...
Tundi	Tundi ...	404	400	83	25	11,160	10,807	9	...	...	...	...	...	553	500	53	48	10	134	19	318	24	31	2

PROVINCIAL TABLE II—*continued.*

FEUDATORY STATES.]

POPULATION OF REVENUE THANAS AND POLICE-STATIONS BY RELIGION AND LITERACY.

STATE GROUP.	NAME OF STATE.	POPULATION.			HINDUS.														MUSLIMS.			
					TOTAL HINDUS.		BRAHMANS.				DEPRESSED CLASSES.				OTHER HINDUS.							
							Number of persons.		*Number literate.*		*Number of persons.*		*Number literate.*		*Number of persons.*		*Number literate.*		*Number of persons.*		*Number literate.*	
		Persons.	Males.	Females.	Males.	Females.	Males.	Females.	Males.	Females.	Males.	Females.	Males	Females.	Males.	Females.	Males.	Females.	Males.	Females.	Males.	Females.
1	2	3	4	5	6	7	8	9	10	11	12	13	14	15	16	17	18	19	20	21	22	23
ORISSA STATES ...	...	**4,465,385**	**2,196,691**	**2,268,694**	**1,999,547**	**2,067,629**	**67,058**	**65,374**	**26,122**	**1,953**	**311,048**	**311,130**	**6,114**	**154**	**1,621,446**	**1,691,125**	**97,558**	**6,390**	**8,975**	**8,125**	**1,825**	**108**
	Athgarh ...	**50,148**	24,843	25,305	24,543	25,024	1,438	1,387	668	46	2,960	2,901	86	4	20,145	20,736	2,319	245	140	126	20	1
	Talcher ...	**69,702**	34,674	35,028	34,341	34,788	1,736	1,773	973	45	6,637	5,809	306	...	26,968	27,206	5,091	284	120	57	27	2
	Mayurbhanj ...	**889,603**	442,378	447,225	435,570	440,849	5,972	4,937	3,340	450	74,347	74,854	1,689	30	355,251	361,058	18,857	1,160	2,854	2,456	457	26
	Nilgiri ...	**68,594**	34,117	34,477	34,033	34,418	2,347	2,166	770	35	6,416	6,516	57	...	25,270	25,736	1,771	138	36	16	12	...
	Keonjhar ...	**460,609**	227,143	233,466	185,974	192,262	6,231	6,279	3,192	139	56,040	48,108	856	14	123,703	137,875	7,875	356	693	622	178	5
	Pal Lahara ...	**27,974**	13,835	14,139	13,820	14,127	183	141	109	3	6,301	4,621	122	9	7,336	9,365	1,303	70	15	11	8	...
	Dhenkanal ...	**284,326**	136,646	147,680	136,229	147,301	7,288	7,666	4,129	355	22,237	22,995	1,152	23	106,704	116,640	17,891	1,045	399	361	156	11
	Athmallik ...	**64,272**	32,287	31,985	31,968	31,672	625	544	267	16	4,253	4,310	62	3	27,090	26,918	1,422	97	51	33	9	...
	Hindol ...	**48,896**	23,419	25,477	23,208	25,329	1,040	2,164	785	49	3,390	3,404	75	...	17,968	19,651	1,530	108	45	59	10	1
	Narsinghpur	**40,878**	19,925	20,953	19,854	20,881	1,504	1,660	550	37	2,651	2,677	44	2	15,699	16,544	1,611	148	69	70	22	1
	Baramba ...	**46,688**	22,596	24,092	22,050	33,559	1,673	1,737	516	32	2,515	2,642	24	...	17,862	19,180	946	60	112	68	30	1
	Tigiria ...	**24,822**	12,141	12,681	11,644	12,153	983	1,006	200	4	907	992	...	1	9,755	10,155	537	35	256	232	9	...
	Khandpara ...	**77,929**	37,381	40,648	37,219	40,600	3,645	3,883	1,754	130	3,389	3,656	313	...	30,185	33,067	5,738	430	56	38	26	4
	Nayagarh ...	**142,406**	67,221	75,185	66,681	74,615	5,521	5,589	1,627	62	9,103	9,783	55	...	52,057	59,243	3,616	327	299	324	47	2
	Ranpur ...	**47,711**	22,412	25,299	22,217	25,000	1,480	1,637	524	13	1,884	2,191	12	...	18,853	21,262	1,345	78	195	200	25	5
	Daspalla ...	**43,402**	20,896	22,506	20,848	22,479	806	825	415	33	3,076	3,220	75	...	16,961	18,434	1,620	141	45	25	23	1
	Baud ...	**135,248**	67,070	68,178	66,956	68,052	1,667	1,610	623	42	2,537	2,682	48	4	62,752	63,860	2,374	206	106	113	20	2
	Bamra ...	**151,047**	73,285	77,762	71,834	76,264	1,340	1,234	656	100	12,516	13,247	322	9	57,978	61,783	3,296	194	137	135	34	1
	Rairakhol ...	**35,710**	17,727	17,983	16,519	16,743	295	276	85	6	1,836	1,885	10	...	14,388	14,582	512	14	16	20	5	...
	Sonpur ...	**237,920**	117,067	120,853	116,623	120,483	8,435	8,120	1,615	59	3,374	3,721	53	1	104,814	108,631	2,512	154	287	266	23	...
	Patna ...	**566,924**	280,305	286,619	263,861	269,324	5,581	5,070	1,821	99	6,431	6,566	52	5	251,849	257,588	6,332	444	562	457	146	14
	Kalahandi ...	**513,716**	252,438	261,278	217,134	224,316	3,545	3,434	1,264	46	49,518	51,807	250	20	164,071	169,075	3,868	262	322	355	71	4
	Gangpur ...	**356,674**	176,959	179,715	106,000	106,766	2,300	1,861	1,099	142	22,375	25,956	581	29	81,325	78,959	4,731	344	2,068	1,944	426	25
	Bonai ...	**80,186**	40,026	40,160	20,336	20,629	524	455	142	11	6,350	6,597	70	1	13,462	13,577	560	42	94	58	23	2
CHOTA NAGPUR STATES ...	...	**186,622**	**91,731**	**94,891**	**63,461**	**64,241**	**2,146**	**1,790**	**999**	**161**	**13,337**	**13,756**	**331**	**3**	**47,978**	**48,695**	**3,287**	**358**	**1,323**	**1,093**	**222**	**20**
	Saraikela ...	**143,525**	70,990	72,535	48,787	48,719	1,707	1,355	774	139	10,754	10,962	254	3	36,326	36,402	2,595	301	1,039	805	171	14
	Kharsawan ...	**43,097**	20,741	22,356	14,674	15,522	430	435	225	22	2,583	2,794	77	...	11,652	12,293	692	57	294	288	51	6

PROVINCIAL TABLE II—*concluded.*

POPULATION OF REVENUE THANAS AND POLICE-STATIONS BY RELIGION AND LITERACY.

STATE GROUP.	NAME OF STATE.	CHRISTIANS. *No. of persons.* Males.	CHRISTIANS. *No. of persons.* Females.	CHRISTIANS. *No literate.* Males.	CHRISTIANS. *No literate.* Females.	TRIBAL. *No. of persons.* Males.	TRIBAL. *No. of persons.* Females.	TRIBAL. *No. literate.* Males.	TRIBAL. *No. literate.* Females.	OTHERS. *No. of persons.* Males.	OTHERS. *No. of persons.* Females.	OTHERS. *No. literate.* Males.	OTHERS. *No. literate.* Females.
1	2	24	25	26	27	28	29	30	31	32	33	34	36
ORISSA STATES ...	...	**36,878**	**37,590**	**1,873**	**438**	**150,172**	**154,330**	**514**	**21**	**1,119**	**1,029**	**142**	**30**
	Athgarh ...	160	165	69	69	...	...	...	..	...	...	...	...
	Talcher ...	68	45	22	6	118	130	...	...	18	3	4	2
	Mayurbhanj...	478	412	88	33	3,463	3,501	33	1	18	7	10	5
	Nilgiri ...	49	43	22	20	...	...	...	..	...	...	...	...
	Keonjhar ..	71	69	43	18	40,102	40,319	98	3	3	4	3	...
	Pal Lahara ...	...	1	...	1	...	...	...	...	...	...	...	...
	Dhenkanal .	18	17	11	6	...	...	..	..	...	1	...	...
	Athmallik .	5	1	5	1	263	279	5	...	1	...	...	...
	Hindol ...	2	...	2	...	74	89	...	...	...	...	...	...
	Narsinghpur	2	3	1	1	..	...	...	...	...	...	...	...
	Baramba ...	5	3	4	3	.	...	..	...	429	443	13	...
	Tigiria ...	...	..	...	...	...	...	...	...	241	246	1	1
	Khandpara ...	6	4	5	3	...	...	...	...	...	...	...	...
	Nayagarh ...	9	4	5	3	333	242	1	.	...	...	...	...
	Ranpur ...	...	...	...	...	...	...	...	..	...	...	...	...
	Daspalla ...	8	3	6	1	...	...	...	...	...	...	...	...
	Band ...	8	13	4	8	...	...	..	...	...	..	...	...
	Bamra ...	644	720	24	8	604	625	2	1	20	18	18	6
	Bairakhol ...	2	3	...	3	1,190	1,217	3		...	..	...	...
	Sonpur ...	4	4	3	...	146	90	5	...	5	2	1	1
	Patna ...	3,491	3,618	223	73	12,093	13,072	94	7	309	248	71	7
	Kalahandi ...	57	64	1	..	34,874	36,518	32	...	51	40	17	6
	Gangpur ...	30,210	30,961	1,282	153	38,603	40,040	236	7	18	4	5	...
	Bonai ...	1,647	1,469	53	8	18,049	18,004	25	2	...	..	...	...
CHOTA NAGPUR STATES ...	...	**179**	**185**	**41**	**19**	**26,746**	**29,352**	**207**	**15**	**22**	**20**	**9**	**1**
	Saraikela ...	153	158	36	18	21,006	22,847	152	15	15	6	9	1
	Kharsawan ...	26	27	5	1	5,740	6,505	55	...	7	14	...	...

STATE GROUP.	NAME OF STATE.	NUMBER LITERATE (AGED 7 AND OVER). TOTAL. Persons.	TOTAL. Males.	TOTAL. Females.	AGED 7—13. Males.	AGED 7—13. Females.	AGED 14—23. Males.	AGED 14—23. Females.	AGED 24 AND OVER. Males.	AGED 24 AND OVER. Females.	LITERATE IN ENGLISH. Males.	LITERATE IN ENGLISH. Females.
1	2	36	37	38	39	40	41	42	43	44	45	46
ORISSA STATES ...	...	**143,237**	**134,148**	**9,089**	**16,994**	**2,252**	**32,068**	**2,807**	**85,086**	**4,030**	**7,847**	**248**
	Athgarh ...	3,556	3,171	385	365	81	798	114	2,008	190	168	6
	Talcher ...	6,662	6,323	339	895	63	1,344	96	4,084	181	285	10
	Mayurbhanj...	26,178	24,474	1,704	3,373	303	6,431	578	15,070	763	1,957	46
	Nilgiri ...	2,815	2,632	183	218	25	596	70	1,818	88	113	5
	Keonjhar ..	11,770	11,335	535	1,180	129	2,507	181	7,543	235	605	19
	Pal Lahara ...	1,524	1,441	83	351	41	291	10	899	26	118	...
	Dhenkanal .	24,778	23,339	1,439	4,708	396	5,314	435	13,317	608	699	14
	Athmallik .	1,887	1,770	117	276	56	474	37	1,020	24	101	...
	Hindol ...	2,560	2,402	158	198	30	490	44	1,705	94	120	3
	Narsinghpur	2,416	2,237	179	411	83	536	60	1,390	36	133	...
	Baramba ...	1,638	1,534	104	167	15	385	36	983	53	98	3
	Tigiria ...	788	747	41	61	2	194	19	492	20	79	1
	Khandpara ...	8,320	7,736	584	1,274	177	1,703	171	4,759	236	207	3
	Nayagarh ...	5,645	5,351	294	856	97	1,221	80	3,274	117	160	1
	Ranpur ...	2,002	1,906	96	110	6	385	83	1,411	57	98	2
	Daspalla ...	2,315	2,139	176	276	60	544	51	1,319	65	81	1
	Band ...	3,339	3,077	263	372	70	736	87	1,969	105	205	5
	Bamra ...	4,673	4,352	321	620	92	997	97	2,735	133	295	16
	Bairakhol ...	637	615	23	30	1	160	8	426	13	32	...
	Sonpur ...	4,427	4,212	215	234	31	832	57	3,146	127	223	4
	Patna ...	9,388	8,730	640	738	190	2,323	177	5,088	282	745	41
	Kalahandi ...	5,821	5,483	338	258	55	1,344	108	3,881	175	315	6
	Gangpur ...	9,159	8,360	799	1,026	184	2,247	234	5,087	381	886	57
	Bonai ...	939	873	66	92	16	217	18	564	33	126	5
CHOTA NAGPUR STATES ...	...	**5,673**	**5,096**	**577**	**585**	**84**	**1,260**	**133**	**3,251**	**360**	**646**	**26**
	Saraikela ...	4,482	3,991	491	448	69	1,011	113	2,532	310	521	18
	Kharsawan ...	1,191	1,105	86	137	15	249	21	719	50	125	5

Census of India, 1931

VOLUME VII

BIHAR AND ORISSA

PART III

ADMINISTRATIVE VOLUME

By W. G. LACEY, I.C.S.,

Superintendent of Census Operations, Bihar and Orissa.

SUPERINTENDENT, GOVERNMENT PRINTING,
BIHAR AND ORISSA, PATNA
1933

TABLE OF CONTENTS